AVID

READER

PRESS

Out on a Limb

Selected Writing
1989-2021

Andrew Sullivan

AVID READER PRESS

New York   London   Toronto   Sydney   New Delhi

AVID READER PRESS
An Imprint of Simon & Schuster, Inc.
1230 Avenue of the Americas
New York, NY 10020

First Avid Reader Press hardcover edition August 2021

AVID READER PRESS and colophon are trademarks of Simon & Schuster, Inc.

For information about special discounts for bulk purchases,
please contact Simon & Schuster Special Sales at 1-866-506-1949
or business@simonandschuster.com.

The Simon & Schuster Speakers Bureau can bring authors to
your live event. For more information or to book an event,
contact the Simon & Schuster Speakers Bureau at 1-866-248-3049
or visit our website at www.simonspeakers.com.

Interior design by Kyle Kabel

Manufactured in the United States of America

1   3   5   7   9   10   8   6   4   2

Library of Congress Cataloging-in-Publication Data has been applied for.

ISBN 978-1-5011-5589-5
ISBN 978-1-5011-5593-2 (ebook)

To my readers

Contents

Introduction   XV

Here Comes the Groom   I
August 27, 1989 | *THE NEW REPUBLIC*

The Two Faces of Bensonhurst   7
July 1, 1990 | *THE NEW REPUBLIC*

Gay Life, Gay Death: The Siege of a Subculture   I5
December 17, 1990 | *THE NEW REPUBLIC*

Taken Unseriously   3I
May 6, 1991 | *THE NEW REPUBLIC*

Quilt   35
November 9, 1992 | *THE NEW REPUBLIC*

The Politics of Homosexuality   39
May 10, 1993 | *THE NEW REPUBLIC*

Alone Again, Naturally   59
November 28, 1994 | *THE NEW REPUBLIC*

When Plagues End: Notes on the Twilight of an Epidemic   75
November 10, 1996 | *THE NEW YORK TIMES*

My America   97
November 24, 1996 | *THE SUNDAY TIMES*

The Princess Bride   101
September 21, 1997 | *THE NEW REPUBLIC*

Unsung Heroine   105
September 27, 1998 | *THE NEW YORK TIMES*

Going Down Screaming   109
October 11, 1998 | *THE NEW YORK TIMES*

What's So Bad about Hate?   127
September 26, 1999 | *THE NEW YORK TIMES*

The He Hormone   145
April 2, 2000 | *THE NEW YORK TIMES MAGAZINE*

The "Invisible Man"   163
January 12, 2003 | *TIME* magazine

I Am Bear; Hear Me Roar   165
August 3, 2003 | *SALON*

Integration Day   171
May 17, 2004 | *THE NEW YORK TIMES*

Log Cabin Republican   175
January 12, 2005 | *THE DISH*

Life Lesson   181
February 7, 2005 | *THE NEW REPUBLIC*

Superstar   185
April 17, 2005 | *THE NEW REPUBLIC*

Crisis of Faith   189
May 2, 2005 | *THE NEW REPUBLIC*

Still Here, So Sorry   205
June 21, 2005 | *THE ADVOCATE*

The End of Gay Culture   209
October 24, 2005 | *THE NEW REPUBLIC*

The Abolition of Torture   225

December 19, 2005 | *THE NEW REPUBLIC*

Islamo-Bullies Get a Free Ride from the West   237

February 12, 2006 | *THE SUNDAY TIMES*

Gay Cowboys Embraced by Redneck Country   241

February 26, 2006 | *THE SUNDAY TIMES*

When Not Seeing Is Believing   245

October 2, 2006 | *TIME* magazine

The Reagan of the Left?   253

May 24, 2007 | *THE DISH*

A Married Man   257

August 21, 2007 | *THE DISH*

Goodbye to All That: Why Obama Matters   261

December 2007 | *THE ATLANTIC*

How Did I Get Iraq Wrong?   275

March 21, 2008 | *SLATE*

Phobia at the Gates   279

May 14, 2008 | *THE WASHINGTON POST*

Why I Blog   283

November 2008 | *THE ATLANTIC*

Republican Taliban Declare Jihad on Obama   297

February 15, 2009 | *THE SUNDAY TIMES*

Mad, Maddening America, the Wisest of All   301

February 22, 2009 | *THE SUNDAY TIMES*

Obama's Race Dream Is Swiftly Shackled   305

July 26, 2009 | *THE SUNDAY TIMES*

Leaving the Right   309

December 1, 2009 | *THE DISH*

Obama, Trimmer   3¹3
December 2, 2009 | *THE DISH*

Dear Ta-Nehisi   3¹7
December 1, 2011 | *THE DISH*

Why Continue to Build the Settlements?   3²1
March 30, 2012 | *THE DISH*

Christianity in Crisis   3²7
April 2, 2012 | *NEWSWEEK*

The First Elite Conservative to Say Enough   335
July 2, 2012 | *THE DISH*

Thatcher, Liberator   339
April 8, 2013 | *THE DISH*

Surprised by Grief   343
August 6, 2013 | *THE DISH*

Rush Limbaugh Knows Nothing about Christianity   347
December 3, 2013 | *THE DISH*

What Is the Meaning of Pope Francis?   353
December 17, 2013 | *THE DISH*

Democracies End When They Are Too Democratic   379
May 1, 2016 | *NEW YORK* magazine

I Used to Be a Human Being   399
September 19, 2016 | *NEW YORK* magazine

America and the Abyss   4¹5
November 3, 2016 | *NEW YORK* magazine

America Wasn't Built for Humans   4²3
September 19, 2017 | *NEW YORK* magazine

Kaepernick's Message Is Getting Lost—
Along with the Facts on Race and Police Violence   44¹
September 29, 2017 | *NEW YORK* magazine

We All Live on Campus Now   445

February 9, 2018 | *NEW YORK* magazine

The Poison We Pick   451

February 20, 2018 | *NEW YORK* magazine

Just Say Yes to Drugs   469

May 25, 2018 | *NEW YORK* magazine

America's New Religions   473

December 7, 2018 | *NEW YORK* magazine

The Nature of Sex   479

February 1, 2019 | *NEW YORK* magazine

Why Joe Biden Might Be the Best Bet to Beat Trump   485

May 3, 2019 | *NEW YORK* magazine

A Plague Is an Apocalypse. But It Can Bring a New World.   491

July 21, 2020 | *NEW YORK* magazine

The Unbearable Whiteness of the Classics   509

February 5, 2021 | *THE WEEKLY DISH*

Two Sexes. Infinite Genders.   515

February 26, 2021 | *THE WEEKLY DISH*

Acknowledgments   521

Index   523

Introduction

My first day in journalism was my last day of college. My dad picked me up in Oxford on a Sunday morning and my summer internship at the *Daily Telegraph* began that afternoon. In 1984, still just twenty years old, I entered the dark and vast building on the original Fleet Street, the place Evelyn Waugh had made eternal in his satirical novel about journalism, *Scoop*. My boss was Bill Deedes, a man widely deemed to be the model for the character, William Boot, at the center of Waugh's work. But the acting editor that afternoon was a man called T. E. Utley, a renowned high Tory intellectual, who was completely blind, chain-smoked, and wore a patch over one eye, like a pirate.

I'd expected some sort of orientation, filling out some forms, settling into a desk, you know, first-day bureaucracy. Instead, I was instructed to write the third of three editorials, anonymously, which gave me some relief, but quickly, which didn't. It was midafternoon, I had until 7 p.m. to finish, and I had no subject matter. It happened to be the day of an annual festival commemorating the Tolpuddle Martyrs, a group of early union organizers in 1834, who had been convicted of organizing a fraternity to resist a wage cut (and subsequently pardoned). The paper needed around six hundred words on a subject I had absolutely no knowledge of.

"Good luck, dear boy," Utley declared. "You can research it in the cuttings." And so I rushed into a room full of filing cabinets in which every *Telegraph* story had been cut out and catalogued under various subjects. Sure enough, a few articles about the history of the Tolpuddle heroes were there, and, using all the skills my Oxford training in extemporaneous bullshitting had given me, I hacked out a piece, comparing the noble objectives of early unions with the excesses of the late-twentieth-century kind. I typed it out on three pages on an electric typewriter, with blue carbon paper between them. Around 6:30 p.m.,

I read the editorial to Utley, who was pacing in his office, a cigarette lingering in his hands. He walked slowly from one wall until he met the other side, and then turned around and did the same again. There was a gray line of ash about three feet above the floor, permanently marking where his cigarette had grazed the wall over the years.

"Fine, dear boy," he pronounced as I finished. "Let's have a drink!"

Over three decades later, I write for my own Substack newsletter, *The Weekly Dish*. I do it in silence at home on a laptop that can instantly convey my words to anyone with an internet connection in the entire world. I broadcast my own interviews; I have no editors; I can publish instantly within seconds of a news event, and have been pumping out digital journalism for two decades. Almost every aspect of my profession has been technologically revolutionized since that first day in a lost era; editors endure but with far less leverage to guide the discourse; readers respond instantly, and often venomously; countless papers have folded; a few behemoths remain; the web has become a place of riotous, ubiquitous, deafeningly democratic media. The entire world has shifted; politics and ideology have moved on; characters and personalities have died and arrived; and I, weeks after that first internship, left for America, where I have lived ever since.

The essays, reviews, columns, articles, and blog posts that appear in these pages reflect the technological, cultural, and political transformations that have taken place in the post–Cold War world—and, of course, chart my own evolution as a writer and thinker. They are arranged in chronological order because they form, in retrospect, a kind of political and social history, seen through the imperfect and provisional eyes of one writer. My criteria for inclusion were pieces that still might have something vivid and memorable to say, essays that captured a particular moment in time, a wide diversity of topics, and a record that helps explain the consistency of my own philosophical small-*c* conservatism that has guided me all this time.

I have been criticized for abandoning the right, and for criticizing the left. I have also been assailed as a defender of the right and a hater of the left. Among the political figures I have supported and voted for these past forty years: Thatcher, Major, Blair, Cameron, and Johnson in Britain; Reagan, Bush, Clinton, Dole, Bush, Kerry, Obama, Clinton, and Biden. Among the causes I have passionately supported: marriage equality, legalization of recreational drugs, the Persian Gulf War, the Iraq War, welfare reform, the candidacy and presidency of Barack Obama, and a very expansive concept of free speech. Among those causes I have furiously opposed: the US adoption of torture in the war on terror, the Iraq War, religious fundamentalism in politics, both the Republican and Democratic parties, mass immigration, deficit spending, tribalism, critical theory, and Trump.

They all reflect a singular form of conservatism that emerges from the thought of Michael Oakeshott responding to the contingent facts of unfolding history. My models for thought and writing run from Burke to Orwell. And my greatest failure of judgment, my shamefully excessive defense of the Iraq War, was, in retrospect, a moment when I abandoned that conservatism under the torrent of emotion and trauma in the wake of 9/11. I haven't included that excess, of which I remain ashamed, but I have included one of many essays in which I held myself to account for the misjudgment. The one substantive change I will readily concede in my thought was a distinctive move away from American military interventionism after the Iraq debacle.

There is also a kind of history here of the biggest civil-rights shift of the last three decades—gay equality. From my first essay in defense of marriage equality, through the terrors of the AIDS epidemic, toward a new conception of the politics of homosexuality, and the end of gay culture, I've included many of the pieces that helped shape the debate, and won the argument. There is, too, an autobiography of sorts of my Catholic faith, my attempt to reconcile it with my sexual orientation, and of an evolving and dying Christianity in the West, from the certainties of John Paul II to the mercy of Pope Francis. There is equally a story of what happened to conservatism and the right in these decades—a brutal tale of decline, decadence, and then implosion. There is a consistent and impassioned defense of liberalism and limited government against identity politics and illiberal government in all its forms.

Some of these essays caused a commotion. My early writing on gay rights inflamed conservatives, and my opposition to critical queer theory and outing incensed my fellow gays. My publishing a symposium on Charles Murray and Richard Herrnstein's book on IQ and society, *The Bell Curve*, in 1994 in *The New Republic* is still deployed to stigmatize my work—and so I include an essay defending the airing of sometimes-painful topics, as long as they are motivated by good faith and backed by evidence and data. My refusal to defend the state of Israel in its policy of settling occupied territory with many of its own fanatical citizens led to my being called an anti-Semite.

I have never tried to be popular. I defended Monica Lewinsky against Bill Clinton, and Bill Clinton against Kenneth Starr. An essay insisting on the biological roots of masculinity enraged some feminists; my opposition to "hate crime" legislation maddened my fellow gays; my account of the moment AIDS in America no longer qualified as a plague was denounced; my ferocious attack on the Bush administration's endorsement of torture caused me to be canceled on the right in 2003. Similarly, my refusal to bow to critical race and gender theory last year—and my horror at the riots in America in 2020—caused me to be fired by my own magazine, *New York*.

I hope it's not self-aggrandizing to say that some of these essays also helped change America. My construction of the central arguments for marriage equality and for openly gay service members in the 1990s played a real role in bringing about lasting reform. My early support for Barack Obama, especially my cover essay making the case for his candidacy in October 2007, played a part in rebooting Obama's fundraising and credibility in his long shot for the presidency.

My essays and blog posts on torture helped rip the veil off the euphemisms of "enhanced interrogation" and made the case for a thorough investigation. My early grasp of the unique threat Donald Trump posed to liberal democracy helped define the looming era of crisis and chaos. My innovation of online journalism, especially blogging, shifted how some writers engaged the internet—and helped forge what is now widely regarded as a golden era for online writing. Along the way, I've included some lesser topics: on the arrival of "bears" in the gay subculture; on the appeal of Princess Diana; the death of my first dog.

The forms vary: from reports on the ground to longer essays to blog posts and diaries. They come from *The New Republic*, *Newsweek*, *The Atlantic*, *Time*, *The New York Times*, *The Sunday Times* (of London), *Salon*, *New York* magazine, and also my own blog, and now newsletter, *The Weekly Dish*. But the goal has always been the same: to look at the world, to make sense of it as best I can, and to tell the truth. And my ideal reader has always been the same as well: happy to read arguments with which they strongly disagree, tolerant of my misfires, and open to any argument from anyone, regardless of identity or ideology. Writing online is much more a dialogue than writing on paper, and I'm proud to say my readers have alternately educated and engaged me, driven me nuts, and provided solace.

I used to call this the general reader. Online, those dedicated to my blog, *The Weekly Dish*, came to call themselves Dishheads. None of them agreed with me about everything; most disagreed vehemently from time to time, and let me know; still others changed my mind, or opened their hearts and souls to me, as they, too, tried to make sense of the world.

Those devoted, querulous readers, loyally disloyal, never dull, were always helping me to understand something better. These readers have made my life possible, and have been with me every step of the way. Which is why this book is devoted to them.

—ANDREW SULLIVAN
February 20, 2021

Out on a Limb

Here Comes the Groom

A (Conservative) Case for Gay Marriage

August 27, 1989 | *THE NEW REPUBLIC*

———————

L ast month in New York, a court ruled that a gay lover had the right to stay in his deceased partner's rent-controlled apartment because the lover qualified as a member of the deceased's family. The ruling deftly annoyed almost everybody. Conservatives saw judicial activism in favor of gay rent control: three reasons to be appalled. Chastened liberals (such as the *New York Times* editorial page), while endorsing the recognition of gay relationships, also worried about the abuse of already-stretched entitlements that the ruling threatened. What neither side quite contemplated is that they both might be right, and that the way to tackle the issue of unconventional relationships in conventional society is to try something both more radical and more conservative than putting courts in the business of deciding what is and is not a family. That alternative is the legalization of civil gay marriage.

The New York rent-control case did not go anywhere near that far, which is the problem. The rent-control regulations merely stipulated that a "family" member had the right to remain in the apartment. The judge ruled that to all intents and purposes a gay lover is part of his lover's family, inasmuch as a "family" merely means an interwoven social life, emotional commitment, and some level of financial interdependence.

It's a principle now well established around the country. Several cities have "domestic partnership" laws, which allow relationships that do not fit into the category of heterosexual marriage to be registered with the city and qualify for benefits that up till now have been reserved for straight married couples. San Francisco, Berkeley, Madison, and Los Angeles all have legislation, as does the politically correct Washington, D.C., suburb, Takoma Park. In these cities, a variety of interpersonal arrangements qualify for health insurance, bereavement leave, insurance, annuity and pension rights, housing rights (such as rent-controlled apartments), adoption and inheritance rights. Eventually, according to gay lobby groups, the aim is to include federal income tax and veterans' benefits as well. A recent case even involved the right to use a family member's accumulated frequent-flier points. Gays are not the only beneficiaries; heterosexual "live-togethers" also qualify.

There's an argument, of course, that the current legal advantages extended to married people unfairly discriminate against people who've shaped their lives in less conventional arrangements. But it doesn't take a genius to see that enshrining in the law a vague principle like "domestic partnership" is an invitation to qualify at little personal cost for a vast array of entitlements otherwise kept crudely under control.

To be sure, potential DPs have to prove financial interdependence, shared living arrangements, and a commitment to mutual caring. But they don't need to have a sexual relationship or even closely mirror old-style marriage. In principle, an elderly woman and her live-in nurse could qualify. A couple of uneuphemistically confirmed bachelors could be DPs. So could two close college students, a pair of seminarians, or a couple of frat buddies. Left as it is, the concept of domestic partnership could open a Pandora's box of litigation and subjective judicial decision-making about who qualifies. You either are or are not married; it's not a complex question. Whether you are in a "domestic partnership" is not so clear. More important, the concept of domestic partnership chips away at the prestige of traditional relationships and undermines the priority we give them. This priority is not necessarily a product of heterosexism.

Consider heterosexual couples. Society has good reason to extend legal advantages to heterosexuals who choose the formal sanction of marriage over simply living together. They make a deeper commitment to one another and to society; in exchange, society extends certain benefits to them. Marriage provides an anchor, if an arbitrary and weak one, in the chaos of sex and relationships to which we are all prone. It provides a mechanism for emotional stability, economic security, and the healthy rearing of the next generation. We rig the law in its favor not because we disparage all forms of relationship other than the nuclear family, but because we recognize that not to promote marriage would be to ask too much of human virtue. In the context of the weakened family's effect upon the poor, it might also invite social disintegration. One of the worst products of the New Right's "family values" campaign is that its extremism and hatred of diversity has disguised this more measured and more convincing case for the importance of the marital bond.

The concept of domestic partnership ignores these concerns, indeed directly attacks them; this is a pity, since one of its most important objectives— providing some civil recognition for gay relationships—is a noble cause and one completely compatible with the defense of the family. But the way to go about it is not to undermine straight marriage; it is to legalize old-style marriage for gays.

The gay movement has ducked this issue primarily out of fear of division. Much of the gay leadership clings to notions of gay life as essentially outsider, antibourgeois, radical. Marriage, for them, is co-optation into straight society. For the Stonewall generation, it is hard to see how this vision of conflict will ever fundamentally change. But for many other gays—my guess, a majority— while they don't deny the importance of rebellion twenty years ago and are grateful for what was done, there's now the sense of a new opportunity. A need to rebel has quietly ceded to a desire to belong. To be gay and to be bourgeois no longer seems such an absurd proposition. Certainly since AIDS, to be gay and to be responsible has become a necessity.

Gay marriage squares several circles at the heart of the domestic partnership debate. Unlike domestic partnership, it allows for recognition of gay relation-ships, while casting no aspersions on traditional marriage. It merely asks that gays be allowed to join in. Unlike domestic partnership, it doesn't open up avenues for heterosexuals to get benefits without the responsibilities of marriage, or a nightmare of definitional litigation. And unlike domestic partnership, it harnesses to an already-established social convention the yearnings for stability and acceptance among a fast-maturing gay community.

Gay marriage also places more responsibilities upon gays: it says for the first time that gay relationships are not better or worse than straight relationships, and that the same is expected of them. And it's clear and dignified. There's a legal benefit to a clear, common symbol of commitment. There's also a personal benefit. One of the ironies of domestic partnership is that it's not only more complicated than marriage; it's more demanding, requiring an elaborate statement of intent to qualify. It amounts to a substantial invasion of privacy. Why, after all, should gays be required to prove commitment before they get married in a way we would never dream of asking of straights?

Legalizing gay marriage would offer homosexuals the same deal society now offers heterosexuals: general social approval and specific legal advantages in exchange for a deeper and harder-to-extract-yourself-from commitment to another human being. Like straight marriage, it would foster social cohesion, emotional security, and economic prudence. Since there's no reason gays should not be allowed to adopt or be foster parents, it could also help nurture children. And its introduction would not be some sort of radical break with social custom. As it has become more acceptable for gay people to acknowledge their loves publicly, more and more have committed themselves to one another for life in full view of their families and their friends. A law institutionalizing gay marriage would merely reinforce a healthy social trend. It would also, in the wake of AIDS, qualify as a genuine public-health measure. Those conservatives who deplore promiscuity among some homosexuals should be among the first to support it. Burke could have written a powerful case for it.

The argument that gay marriage would subtly undermine the unique legitimacy of straight marriage is based upon a fallacy. For heterosexuals, straight marriage would remain the most significant—and only legal—social bond. Gay marriage could only delegitimize straight marriage if it were a real alternative to it, and this is clearly not true. To put it bluntly, there's precious little evidence that straights could be persuaded by any law to have sex with—let alone marry—someone of their own sex. The only possible effect of this sort would be to persuade gay men and women who force themselves into heterosexual marriage (often at appalling cost to themselves and their families) to find a focus for their family instincts in a more personally positive environment. But this is clearly a plus, not a minus: gay marriage could both avoid a lot of tortured families and create the possibility for many happier ones. It is not, in short, a denial of family values. It's an extension of them.

Of course, some would claim that any legal recognition of homosexuality is a de facto attack upon heterosexuality. But even the most hardened conservatives recognize that gays are a permanent minority and aren't likely to go away. Since persecution is not an option in a civilized society, why not coax gays into traditional values rather than rail incoherently against them?

There's a less elaborate argument for gay marriage: It's good for gays. It provides role models for young gay people who, after the exhilaration of coming out, can easily lapse into short-term relationships and insecurity with no tangible goal in sight. My own guess is that most gays would embrace such a goal with as much (if not more) commitment as straights.

Even in our society as it is, many lesbian relationships are virtual textbook cases of monogamous commitment. Legal gay marriage could also help bridge the gulf often found between gays and their parents. It could bring the essence of gay life—a gay couple—into the heart of the traditional straight family in a way the family can most understand and the gay offspring can most easily acknowledge. It could do as much to heal the gay-straight rift as any amount of gay-rights legislation.

If these arguments sound socially conservative, that's no accident. It's one of the richest ironies of our society's blind spot toward gays that essentially conservative social goals should have the appearance of being so radical. But gay marriage is not a radical step. It avoids the mess of domestic partnership; it is humane; it is conservative in the best sense of the word. It's also practical. Given the fact that we already allow legal gay relationships, what possible social goal is advanced by framing the law to encourage these relationships to be unfaithful, undeveloped, and insecure?

The Two Faces of Bensonhurst

July 1, 1990 | *THE NEW REPUBLIC*

A REPORT FROM THE NEIGHBORHOOD

Twentieth Avenue in Bensonhurst starts in the Hudson River, where it's called Gravesend Bay, only a couple of miles from the Atlantic Ocean. You can see the ocean across the Belt Parkway, but Bensonhurst rarely looks. The neighborhood focuses inland, toward the hub of Eighty-Sixth Street, with its railway track suspended some sixty feet above the road, and beyond all the way down to Fiftieth.

On a summer afternoon on Eighty-Sixth, youngsters hang out on the street corners, near clothing stores called Male Ego and Women's Dreams. There are wedding dress stores in between the pizzerias, and photograph studios with pictures of Italian newlyweds grinning at each other under white-fenced porticos. There are also Korean groceries, Chinese takeouts, and dozens of Off-Track Betting offices. Blacks mingle with whites and Hispanics in Asian-run stores. Italian and Chinese, Yiddish and Korean are spoken here, under the traffic on the streets.

As you walk down Twentieth and farther into Bensonhurst, the place gets a little seedier: there are a few vacant lots and more discount stores. But on either side of the avenue stretch tree-lined streets, small redbrick houses, porches, and lawns. Two black women chat on the corner. Four kids in yarmulkes stand around a car. A Korean family sits out on the porch, next to a plaster donkey and a statue of Our Lady of Guadalupe on the lawn, covered in cellophane to protect her from the rain. A little farther down, the brown brick 1970s building

7

of St. Dominic's Church, with bingo at 11:30 on Tuesdays and Fridays, and farther down still, P.S. 205, cardboard butterfly cutouts pasted to the windows.

Once you've walked this far, it comes as something of a surprise to realize you've already passed the spot where Joseph Fama killed Yusuf Hawkins on August 23, 1989. The killing took place at Sixty-Ninth and Twentieth Avenue, near Yang's Deli and Joe Klein's Dental Supplies, within shooting distance of the cellophaned Lady of Guadalupe. The central, recurrent question of Bensonhurst is how these two things came together: how a seemingly model neighborhood of inner-city calm and easy coexistence became a watchword for racial hate.

As far as the residents of Bensonhurst are concerned, the answer to this question is simple. What connects their neighborhood to racism was a random act, made infamous by a hysterical media and by a few black activists. It could have happened anywhere else, they argue; it just happened to happen here. I could find only one individual in six days in the neighborhood who didn't share this belief. Along Eighteenth Avenue stores carried blue ribbons in their windows (next to World Cup soccer posters) as a sign of a desired reconciliation. "It's the people who did this," explained an Italian deli owner. "We want peace. Unity. Sharpton's only happy when people are killing people."

It turned out, however, that the blue ribbons were not some spontaneous outburst of generosity: a couple of store owners admitted that a local group of citizens had brought them around. And there's considerable evidence to support the Bensonhurst of media legend. The whites who greeted the Sharpton marches by holding up "Joey Fama for President" placards, brandishing watermelons, and twirling basketballs were not all outsiders. And even those keen to tell you prejudice does not exist end by relating a couple of incidents that prove it does.

A young Italian claimed there was no fundamental problem. He then told me he'd given up a job in real estate after finding that landlords never rented to perfectly qualified non-Italians. A black woman, who said she'd never had any trouble, also admitted that white teenagers called her "Brillo pad" and "nigger" while she was standing at a bus stop. One black family who had been bequeathed a row house on an Italian street lasted only a few months before they felt they had to leave. Many complained about being followed around in stores by managers who assume that any black is a shoplifter. One woman said her change had been thrown at her in the supermarket. The integrated high schools are, according to several graduates, hardly immune from racial abuse.

Still, there is something about the earnestness with which so many residents of Bensonhurst insist on their good intentions that is difficult to dismiss. The people of the neighborhood were almost desperately concerned that their efforts at racial harmony not be slighted and adamant that real progress had been made. And what was interesting even about the anecdotes of racism was not so much the stories themselves as the tone in which they were conveyed. It was not one of desperation, or even of resentment. The tales were invariably part of a larger story about how racism was not that big a problem in their lives, and how, if anything, things had gotten better in the past few years. Perhaps the most surprising exponents of this view are the neighborhood's seven thousand or so blacks. Of the score or so blacks I spoke with, who either worked or lived in Bensonhurst, only one sided unequivocally with Sharpton. And only he had actually marched. Most blamed Sharpton for much of the trouble: "As far as I can see, one person started all this, and that's Al Sharpton," a black woman told me. "I've never experienced any prejudice. I felt a little tension in the grocery store just after it happened. But once they get to know your face, it's OK. It's not your color. It's whether they know you or not." "I blame Al Sharpton," said another black woman. "He's making life worse for all the black people who work here. He shouldn't blame everybody. I don't." A few blacks reported that it was the marches, rather than the original incident, that had intensified racial hatred in the neighborhood.

This other, more banal, Bensonhurst creeps up on you slowly. It strikes you first in the easy racial mixing on the streets. But it's perhaps best illustrated in a few of the residents themselves. Take Kenny, a twenty-eight-year-old Italian American, who like many his age in Bensonhurst still lives with his family. He took me around the neighborhood one day in the pouring rain, pointing out, with what came close to pride, the black, Jewish, Hispanic, and Italian enclaves of his home. In the course of the conversation, he let it slip that one sister had married a divorced Puerto Rican (the family calls him Poncho to his face), another was dating a man a decade or so younger than herself, and a brother was dating a Chinese girl. His Italian-Catholic immigrant family seemed to be taking all this in stride. According to Kenny, even black-white dating is acceptable if the man is white and the woman black. The reverse is more problematic, a fact that has as much to do with prevailing sexism as with racism.

A host of other stories corroborates this kind of picture. A local truck driver said that his fellow drivers were all black. "One of them is really black. I call him the gorilla. But, you know, we're like this." He put his arm around my shoulder. "And if I get into trouble out on the road, who am I going to rely on?" A local Hispanic man said he was so sick of the media hype of local racism he wouldn't turn on the television when the Fama verdict was announced. He said it brought out racist feelings he didn't want to feel. Another Italian said he recently took his pregnant wife to predominantly black Coney Island at 1 a.m., something he'd never have done a few years ago: "Where else am I going to get sausage and peppers at one o'clock in the morning?"

Or take Father Barozzi, a priest at St. Dominic's. He's a genial Italian, with a heavy accent, and effortlessly Catholic. At 4 p.m. he asked me whether I wanted scotch in my coffee or a glass of wine. His church, a few blocks from the site of the Hawkins murder, is making a genuine effort to counter bigotry. (Both David Dinkins and Al Sharpton visited it recently to announce an agreement to suspend temporarily the protest marches through the neighborhood.) This spring Barozzi held what he calls a "black month" for children in church education. Pictures of Martin Luther King Jr. and other prominent black Americans were put up in the sanctuary; a black priest was invited to give sermons at all Masses one weekend; prayer vigils were held at the murder site. Yet Barozzi also recounts the number of Italians he knows who have been mugged by blacks; speaks of what he sees as the disagreeable way of life of blacks—loud music late at night, the lack of strong family values, and so on—and reminds you that he is a northern Italian, with Anglo-Saxon blood in his veins. He is obviously a good man, but one whose effectiveness in this immigrant community means sharing some of the unconscious racism he is at other times trying to break down.

Or take Gerard. Born and brought up in Bensonhurst, he's a wiry, almost nerdy Italian in early middle age who made it to Columbia College and Law School. He went to Wall Street as a corporate tax lawyer, but in his twenties decided to do something for his old neighborhood and started a basketball team for local youth. This was in 1974. His first team practice was with three Italians, a Puerto Rican, and two blacks, in Most Precious Blood parish's converted bingo hall. It didn't get off to an auspicious start. "We hadn't been there fifteen minutes when a vanload of white kids pulled up and started pounding the windows, with bricks in their hands."

Gerard didn't give up the scheme despite mounting abuse. Each practice was a war of nerves as he shipped black kids from the nearby Marlboro Projects into a white neighborhood. There followed a white boycott of the team and some rough years in which his safety was threatened. Gerard gave up his job in Manhattan, set up a local law practice, and focused on what was becoming for him something of a religious vocation. He called the team Flames Neighborhood Youth Association, referring to the Holy Spirit. In 1977, as if in a movie plot, the team won the entire Catholic Youth Organization championship for Queens and Brooklyn. Suddenly all the neighborhood kids, black and white, wanted to be on the team. These days Gerard runs several teams, some in the CYO tournament and some in in-house competitions.

According to Gerard, the last decade has seen real progress in race relations in Bensonhurst: "Gradually, a really profound change has taken place. These kids from the projects have no fear at all anymore of walking down the block to the gym." Even this year, with the Hawkins killing occurring just before the season, no major trouble has taken place. In an early incident, a white from Bensonhurst maced a black from Coney Island outside practice one evening, but it turned out to be a typical teenage fight. Gerard sums up his tactics for dealing with it like this: "First you isolate the guy who did it, rather than force other people to side with him. . . . I told the black kid we'd deal with it, and we did. That was it. No police. No report. No press. No Al Sharpton."

I spent an afternoon with Gerard in the Marlboro Projects. Six thousand people live in these buildings, vast, square, redbrick monoliths, divided in the center by a road: a bleak, modernist contrast to the cozy row houses only blocks away. The projects are situated on the outskirts of Bensonhurst, cut off on three sides by railway tracks, and on the other by the vast elevated line. The symbolism of this massive barrier is clear. What unites the center of Bensonhurst is the very thing pushing these people out. Since the mid-1970s the projects have been predominantly black. The rest of Bensonhurst, though racially diverse and a workplace for many blacks, has virtually no black residents at all.

Everyone seemed genuinely glad to see Gerard, and vice versa. When pressed, they talked with disarming honesty about the racism they confront.

None say it's getting worse. "They used to come here with sticks, stakes, and bricks," a twenty-nine-year-old remembers. "But all that came to a cease-stop." Others said racism was the least of their problems. "What they should think about doing is putting lights in the park here," said Charlie. "If you go anywhere else they have lights in the park. You could play basketball at night then. If you give them something to do you wouldn't get so much stuff going on." The stuff going on is a sharp rise in black-on-black killings and drug use in Marlboro. Gerard can rattle off the names of eight kids he knew who have been killed, and reckons the majority of the kids he knows have sold crack at one time or another. This year he was hoping to round off the season without a death on his teams, but two weeks ago another young black basketball player was shot. Joseph, a smart fifteen-year-old who plans to be an electrical engineer in Queens, says coolly of the interracial hype: "We don't have a history of killing them. We have a history of killing us."

To these people, Sharpton has a kind of cruel irrelevance. Sharpton hasn't come to the projects, and few here have gone to his marches. "We don't exist for him," one young black told me. "He's a mystery to me. At least he could have held a meeting here in the park. There ain't nobody coming to talk to us." The frustration is palpable: of all the problems facing the residents of Marlboro Projects—drugs, guns, poor housing, family breakdown, constant violence— none is at the center of the Bensonhurst furor. "If I was a publicity guy, I'd say, 'Racism, racism, racism,' because it's a great way to get media and grants," says Gerard. "But that's not the reality. For the most part, if a black person wants to get ahead, he can get ahead. A black guy from the Marlboro Projects can't get ahead, not because he's black, but because he's in the projects."

On Thursday, May 31, the Coalition for Harmony, an interfaith community group, held its first neighborhood open forum since the Hawkins killing. It took place in the Cotillion Terrace on Eighteenth Avenue, a few blocks from the murder site. It's a ballroom of sorts, with glass chandeliers and mirrors in the shape of peacock feathers on the wall. On the stage there were backlit pictures of waterfalls, next to a banner proclaiming: "Peace! Love! Harmony!" A bevy of clergy were due to speak, chaired by former assemblyman Arnaldo Ferraro. Around fifteen hundred locals showed up: very few youngsters, and no blacks except one cleric from Bedford-Stuyvesant and someone to lead hymn singing at the end.

The meeting began with an invocation in Italian, after which the entire audience made the sign of the cross. Then the assembled clergy spoke in platitudes for nearly an hour. Finally the current assemblyman, Peter Abbate, was invited to speak. As he got up, there were murmurings in the crowd. He announced that there was going to be another Sharpton march on Saturday. He asked them all to stay at home to avoid hostile media coverage. The last weekend's boycott of the march had been very successful: "We're asking you again, ignore it, go about your daily business. Don't give him the forum that he wants." The reaction began slowly at first, as people started standing up behind me, shouting random abuse at Abbate. Ferraro turned on him: "Why do we have to lock ourselves behind closed doors when they invade our territory?" A hysterical woman started yelling near the front: "Yusuf Hawkins's murder was not a racial incident. People don't know the truth. No one knows the truth."

Throughout this noise, some residents patiently waited by microphones at the front of the hall. A sort of hush intermittently let them be heard. Halting speeches in broken English were made in a flood of wounded pride and anger: "We are not racial," sobbed one woman. "I never have trouble with anybody." Another shouted: "We've lost control of our house and our street. My children are chased out of the schoolyard by the police when the marchers come. Why do they keep on coming here?"

About half the crowd was now standing and yelling. The assemblyman urged peace and harmony. A woman shrieked: "My peace and harmony went out of the window on August 24 when they arrested eight Italian boys and told all the black and Hispanic boys that they had nothing to do with it." It was Mrs. Mondello, the mother of Keith Mondello, one of the convicted boys. Abbate responded, "I know how you feel, Mrs. Mondello." "You can't know how I feel," she yelled back. "No one knows how I feel." "Let them march without the cops!" shouted a man at the back of the room. "Don't take away the rights of the people!"

A few residents went up to the microphones to appeal for calm. An older man said, "We're all minorities. We should stick together. They're just going to pick us off one by one." A young, nervous girl ventured, "There is racism in Bensonhurst," and the place erupted once again. The grievances went on and on. How much was this costing us? How come you can't get a permit for a block party with a month's notice and Sharpton gives the police two days' notice and the main high street shuts down? "Tell me," yelled one man. "Why are we afraid to walk the streets on Saturday? We should not be held hostage in our own houses." The only hush was for Mrs. Mondello, whose main point was that Gina Feliciano "is now and has only ever been a low-life, drug-using prostitute whore." At this, the meeting exploded into menacing cheers.

It's not clear whether this is the Bensonhurst that will emerge from the agony of the last few months. Certainly the maximum sentences handed down last week to Fama and Mondello will likely take the sting out of Sharpton's marches. But whatever happens, another Bensonhurst clearly exists. It's difficult to spend much time in the neighborhood without being more impressed by the honesty with which people discuss their problems and their awkward attempts to deal with them than with the fear and suspicion lurking beneath the surface. It may, of course, all explode into the rage of that Thursday night. But if it does, not all of Bensonhurst will be behind it. Some even seem to grasp the larger symbolism of what is at stake. They ended the meeting, in a desperate bid to avoid complete chaos, with a clumsy invocation to sing "God Bless America." I thought it would be a fiasco. As it was, everyone stood and awkwardly held hands. And when they sang, "My home, sweet home," they raised up their arms.

Gay Life, Gay Death:
The Siege of a Subculture

December 17, 1990 | *THE NEW REPUBLIC*

I n the living room of a friend of mine, there's a coffee table crammed with photographs. One stands out: four young men in tuxes taken three years ago. They're all grinning, in classic college-buddy group-shot mode. Of the four, two are now dead. One died two years ago, the second in early November, when Kaposi's Sarcoma (KS), the cancerous lesions common to people with AIDS, entered his lungs. Tom, the third of the tuxes, was diagnosed with the AIDS virus (HIV) five years ago. He found out his status soon after burying his lover of four years, who also died of AIDS.

Three years ago, despite treatment with the antiviral drug AZT, Tom came down with his first major AIDS-related infection. His skin is now covered with KS. Because of an intestinal infection that doesn't enable him to digest food, an intravenous drip feeds him fourteen hours a day. His immune system is so weak that the plastic line keeps getting infected, so he has to go into the hospital from time to time to have it replaced. His lover of the past five years, Steve, the fourth tux, is HIV-negative, and is preparing for a new life on his own. Five in their close circle of friends have died in the past month alone.

This kind of familiarity with death is unique in modern times. With the advent of effective hygiene and medicine, death has long since ceased to be common among young people. If anything, death has grown more distant for the majority, a tragedy occurring either very occasionally in the otherwise healthy or among the old and frail, who are safely hospitalized beyond our immediate awareness and responsibility.

But for gay men in America in 1990, none of this applies anymore. Death is less an event than an environment. One hundred thousand people have now died of AIDS. This year almost as many have died as died in all the previous years put together. Ten times as many will die as have died. More young men have lost their lives to AIDS than died in the entire Vietnam War. Forty percent of these deaths have been among IV drug users and others of both sexes. (Nothing here is designed to diminish their predicament.) But 60 percent have been among gay men. While the outside world thinks the worst is over, eight hundred thousand people, on the lowest estimates, now face the hard task of actually dying.

This fact is transforming life for an entire section of America. Largely invisible and almost incomprehensible to outsiders, gay men and their families now live lives alien to modernity's rhythms. Death is ubiquitous. Friends and lovers die with random, rapid consistency. Time horizons shorten. Death is mentionable again. Indeed, it is unavoidable. Gay men now live essentially as medievals among moderns: habituated to mortality in a world of health, besieged by death in the midst of oblivious life.

The gay cities within cities in America are in this sense medieval communities. The dying coexist with the living, and the dead clutter the address books of the dying as bones once festooned the charnel houses of medieval city dwellers.

There is a further twist. Gay men must not only live as medievals among moderns, but also live as moderns, still wedded to the contemporary alienation from mortality, yet forced into encounters with extinction that the broader culture finds strange, distasteful. This dichotomy—modern and medieval, living and dying—is creating divisions among and within gay men, too, divisions as hard to acknowledge publicly as they are privately unavoidable.

It is a commonplace that AIDS has united the gay "community" in newfound fraternity. But this is at best a half-truth. There are, of course, countless stories of reconciliation and courage in the face of the virus. Nothing here is meant to slight the truth of those experiences. But AIDS has also unmistakably widened the rifts among gay men. There are those with the virus, and those who are free of it. There are those who know many who have died, and those who do not. There are those who are dying and those who are not. In this crucible of solidarity, the divisions already in gay society are being cruelly exposed.

I

Phil Zwickler is a fiery, stocky, fast-talking former filmmaker who has AIDS. He now runs a newsletter for people with AIDS and recently made a gripping short film called *Fear of Disclosure*, about relationships between people who test positive for HIV and people who test negative. I met him in his small, ramshackle office in downtown Manhattan. His lover, Jimmy, died a few years ago. Zwickler was barred from the funeral by Jimmy's family, and lived with the fear that he would die, too, and the guilt that he may actually have infected a man he loved. All this I learned within minutes, a function of the candor many people with AIDS display. After a few minutes of questioning, Zwickler's candor grew. "I'm angry at you," he said. "I know you won't have sex with me, not because of what I look like, not because of who I am, but because of a virus in my blood."

Perhaps the commonest misconception about the impact of AIDS among gay men is that it is restricted to the sick and the dying. In fact, its impact may be just as powerful among the well and the living. The vast majority of HIV-positive men are healthy and asymptomatic. And no HIV-negative gay man has lived without the risk and fear of HIV infection. Gay life and gay death are not separate issues, meeting occasionally at the bedside or the grave. They are wedded to each other.

The points of contact generate friction, of which Zwickler's passion is a sign. The divide between healthy HIV-positive men and healthy HIV-negative men has not yet been broached in the mainstream gay press. But it's evident in the personal columns: "HIV+ seeks same"; "Fun bright, passionate GWM, 41, 5' 8", 148, HIV-, wants to meet similar quality men"; "GWM, 40, 6' 200lbs, looking to meet younger GWM 20-29 for a lasting monogamous relationship. Disease-free as I am." This subtle, pervasive segregation among gay men is a growing feature of gay life. It has its roots in fear, although, paradoxically, not so much the fear of actually contracting HIV anymore. It's quite clear now that the virus is extremely hard to catch. Most gay men assume that kissing, oral sex, and anal sex with a condom are permissibly safe activities. So the phobia

of sex with someone who is HIV-positive has an element of the irrational
about it, as far as medical risk is concerned. "Fear" merges with stigmatization
of the sick. "They're the biggest hypocrites in the world," a positive man told
me of wary negatives. "They hide behind this knowledge of safe sex and go
to bed with anybody. But as soon as they find out you're positive, they drop
you like a stone."

There is also simply the gulf of experience between those with the virus
and those free of it. Coming to terms with being HIV-positive is, for many, a
transforming experience, and it becomes difficult to form relationships with
people whose lives are untouched. "Ultimately," an HIV-negative who'd had
a failed relationship with an HIV-positive told me, "that person is having an
experience you're not having, and you'll never know him, however hard you
try." Another HIV-positive with an HIV-negative lover spoke of the broader difference in attitudes the virus generated. Daily, petty squabbles, which obsessed
his lover, seemed irrelevant to him: "I once screamed at my boyfriend, 'There
are times when I wish you were positive, because none of these things would
mean anything to you at all.'"

This dynamic of mistrust, fear, and stigmatization has further complications.
One man whose lover became ill with AIDS told me he found it hard to take
the HIV test, not just because of his own fear of death, but because of the
barriers it might have erected between them. He waited until his lover died,
and discovered that he was negative. With that, he also saw the real reason
for his earlier avoidance: "At the back of my mind, I guess I was afraid that I
might have given it to him. That I might have killed him."

The danger of mutual transmission is a constant source of friction, and
there is no escape from it. Even an HIV-positive man can be made sicker by
reinfection with the virus, whether from his own lover or from someone else.
The result is a curious turn of fate. Far from bringing couples closer together or
encouraging monogamy, AIDS has actually pushed people apart. It has made
intimacy harder, trust less tangible, selfishness more acceptable. It may not be
what some have called sexual apartheid, but it does amount to a kind of sexual
and emotional zoning, an invisible wall between men who are themselves
walled off from an outside world.

The effects of this can be seen everywhere in gay life, from the cult of the
healthy body in bodybuilding to the nervous inquiries on the second date about

health. The divisions between HIV-positives and negatives are also reflected in politics. Queer Nation, a radical offshoot of ACT UP, the AIDS Coalition To Unleash Power, concentrates on countering homophobia with a range of actions from kiss-ins to marches urging gays to bash back against antigay violence. To outsiders they seem just one more gang of gay activists. Among some AIDS activists, however, they're known as "ACT UP for Negatives," people for whom the fight against AIDS is not so personal and therefore not so desperate. San Francisco's ACT UP recently split between a faction focused entirely on AIDS and another more concerned with other gay issues. Behind the split lay positive-negative tensions. Alongside the usual rifts in any activist group between radicals and moderates, assimilationists and separatists, in today's gay politics there's the added factor of who has HIV and who doesn't.

These tensions inevitably lead to a raising up of the drawbridge of emotional commitment, to a retreat in the face of fear. In some ways safe sex is the apotheosis of this self-isolation. Safe sex can be the outcome of a life in which certain risks — of love, commitment, selflessness — are less likely to be taken. It's revealing that, according to safe sex counselors at Gay Men's Health Crisis (GMHC), the premier AIDS-care organization in New York, the most common "relapsers" from safe sex are not promiscuous, anonymous experimenters, but couples in long-standing, healthy, monogamous relationships. By protecting themselves against the virus, gay men also find themselves protected against intimacy.

This has led not to an abandonment of sex, but to a revival of it. As sex has become not merely physically but emotionally safer, it's become more popular. The back rooms, bathhouses, and compulsive anonymous sex of a decade or so ago may have gone. But so, too, has the terrified celibacy of the first stage of the epidemic. "Sex is completely glorified and accepted. A seventies culture has come back," a young gay journalist told me.

The club scene has also experienced a revival. Two of the more popular New York bars these days are The Men's Room and Sod-O-Mee. The former is a pounding cavern, with sixty-foot ceilings, slides of nude men on the walls, and go-go boys, steroid-pumped to bursting, gyrating on boxes amid hundreds of mainly shirtless men. The latter looks like any small dance club, with one difference. Above the dance floor there's a giant video screen showing pornography as the somewhat conventional crowd below bops to Madonna. All along the bar, video screens show the same genital images. Go-go boys in cellophane jockstraps sway in front of them. It's a symbol of a new sexuality: sensual, garish, safe, for the first time a full reflection of the phrase "mutual masturbation," in which emotions, as well as bodily fluids, are kept carefully apart.

The new sexuality, however, offers only the chimera of relief. In willful nostalgia, the old Saint club, a legendary gay bar in the East Village that has long since ceased regular business, has been revived. In its heyday it was the focus of 1970s erotica. The old building is now defunct, but the glamorous crowd rents out other clubs to re-create the experience. And, indeed, it feels almost the same: throbbing disco music, near-perfect torsos, omnipresent drugs, and anonymous groping in the dark corners. But the fragility of the forgetting is apparent. The Halloween costume party was held this year at Studio 54, a sacred relic of an era gone by. An HIV-positive man showed up, scantily clad, erotically beckoning, his skin revealing the telltale signs of Kaposi's Sarcoma. He came as a court jester.

II

Salem United Methodist Church is in the heart of Harlem on 129th Street and Seventh Avenue. One evening last October it was the site of a "Service of Love, Remembrance, and Hope" for people with AIDS. The high point of the "Harlem Week of Prayer for AIDS," it involved several local pastors. Perhaps because of the rain outside, it was a small congregation, with almost as many people up front as in the pews. The music was from the Addicts Rehabilitation Center Choir, the first hymn: "On Christ, the solid rock, I stand; / All other ground is sinking sand, all other ground is sinking sand."

We were called to prayer. The readings were read. A few people paid tribute to those who had died of AIDS. A young man in African garb recited a poem, calling upon all those black men who had died of AIDS to return to the fold of black history: "Jesus is calling, for you and for me. Death is coming for you and for me. Come home, all you who are weary. Come home." A large woman shuffled forward, dressed in a checked cardigan and a flattened black felt hat: "In my little corner of the world," she said, "I saw my son slip away. But I looked to the hills whence cometh my strength. And we kept the faith." Tentative amens echoed through the building.

The service was faintly unreal: a scattering of embarrassed people focusing on death as if it were still an occasional, tragic intervention in normal life. The point of the evening, it turned out, was to force the assembled pastors, who had done very little to acknowledge the scope of AIDS in their congregations, to listen to the Rev. James Forbes Jr., the pastor of Riverside Church.

His text was the parable of the Good Samaritan. His aim was to confront the pharisaism of today's Christians toward those with AIDS. He spoke of a gay parishioner. "He asked me, as he lay there dying of AIDS, he said, 'What's God's attitude toward me? . . . Don't tell me something just to cheer me up. Just tell me the truth.'" The church went silent. For the first time that evening, the subject of homosexuality—not AIDS, not IV drug use, not poverty—was addressed. "What he wanted to know was not whether God would forgive him, not even whether God would love him, but whether God would affirm him." Forbes turned to look at the pastors: "I wonder very much what you would have told him." After an awkward pause, he continued: "There is a part of the Church that can only deal with respectable problematics. But grace is able to deal with any problematic." People shifted in their seats. "We have to deal with sexuality. Why do we have to allow Oprah Winfrey to tell the truth before we do?" A handful of people walked out.

AIDS is now affecting black and Hispanic New Yorkers more than it is affecting whites. In 1986, according to New York's Health Systems Agency, 30 percent of AIDS cases were black and 23 percent Hispanic. Now that's 31 and 26 percent, respectively. By 1993 the percentages are forecast at 35 percent and 30 percent. Thirty-seven percent of black and Hispanic AIDS cases are due to gay transmission; and experts believe this is an underestimate, since many black and Hispanic men would sooner admit to being a junkie than to being gay.

This, perhaps, is the most alarming feature of black gay life. In addition to the familiar problems of urban minorities, poor black gay men also have to deal with extraordinary homophobia. In talking to minority men with AIDS, it was hard to avoid the impression that the level of denial is measurably greater, the pain more intense, the isolation more complete than among whites. Stories of hushed burials, of families collecting sons' bodies from hospitals and not allowing friends or lovers to pay tribute, of bashings and neglect are commonplace, and usually told by people who request anonymity. Even among elites—perhaps especially among elites—homophobia is intense. Of the fifty-nine board members of the Black Leadership Commission on AIDS, the core minority group in New York confronting the problem, only one, project director Gregory Broyles, is openly gay. He's had to fight hard to get the fact of homosexuality acknowledged at its meetings.

"By being black, I'm separated from the white gay community, and being gay, I'm separated from the African American community," is how Broyles puts the black gay predicament. The black press rarely deals with gay men with AIDS: recent issues of *Emerge* and *Spin*, guest-edited by Spike Lee, for example, focused on the threat to women and children. According to gay black men I interviewed, there is even a belief among many young blacks that only whites are gay, and therefore AIDS is irrelevant to blacks. Lies about the cause of early deaths merely perpetuate this myth. The truth is, a generation of young black men is disappearing in a silence broken only by the occasional, sparsely attended church service.

Take Kevin, for example, although that's not his real name. He lives on a run-down street in the middle of Spanish Harlem, the only black man on the block. He hasn't seen any family members for nineteen years, and most of his friends are white. Few neighbors know he has the disease, although some know he's gay. He has heard women whispering "faggot" on the street as he walks by. It's a term that can be more than psychologically wounding. A man with AIDS on Kevin's block got badly beaten up recently when his neighbors found out he had the disease.

The walls of Kevin's dilapidated apartment are lined with classical music tapes, the floors cluttered with dumbbells, a reminder of the days when he was a bodybuilder. Twirls of flypaper hang from the ceiling like garlands. Kevin got really sick two years ago. He found he couldn't make his second shift as a security guard because of acute chills. He ended up in the hospital with tuberculosis. Since then he's had pneumonia, herpes, and KS. As we talked he scratched the KS lesions repeatedly, and had recently taken to picking at them with needles to relieve the itching. Halfway through our conversation, he suddenly said, quite calmly: "I can't see your face. I can't see you. I've got these spots in front of my eyes. Strange little horizontal lines." He was probably in the early stages of going blind.

His isolation is triple: race, sexuality, disease. In his first stay in the hospital, for TB, the three had come together: "A doctor came in and said would I like to go to the tenth floor? I said no, and he said wouldn't you like to be with your own kind? And I never knew what that was. . . . So two doctors came in and they said to me like I was getting a Christmas present, they said, yes, you've got it. And I said, got what? And they said, you've got AIDS. I said how much longer have I got? And they said three years at the most." That was two years ago.

When black gay men are visible, and the real cause of their deaths acknowledged, the reaction is often vicious. "All we've ever had is the power of the dick, the power over women," one young black gay man told me. "So if one dick likes another dick, that's a problem. They think: This faggot is in my community. I can't have that." The younger generation seems to be getting more—not less—bigoted. Black role models, like Eddie Murphy, crack jokes about people with AIDS. Rap spews antigay venom across the airwaves. As the black family has disintegrated, the pressure on middle-class gay men to get married gets stronger. One man told me the worst comments he had ever had were from women, resentful of a "good man" refusing to have a family.

It's no surprise, then, that the AIDS activist groups are overwhelmingly white. What's odd is their silence about the homophobia affecting minorities. ACT UP, while protesting the white Catholic Church's stance against safe sex education, has failed to attack black churches that follow the same policy. The Minority Task Force on AIDS (MTFA), the only black group fighting AIDS on the streets of Harlem, holds safe sex workshops in black churches, which are required by pastors not to mention anal sex, condoms, or homosexuality, unless specifically asked about them. According to activists I spoke with, many pastors in Harlem are themselves closeted gay men, who mask their own homosexuality by refusing to acknowledge it in their congregations. Yet ACT UP has not "outed" these men or even protested their negligence. Such an act, activists explain off the record, would be racist.

A large part of the minority gay predicament is the result of whites' reluctance to face a problem that does not affect them. But just as problematic as white neglect is homophobia among healthy, heterosexual blacks. One black AIDS activist I spoke with lamented that if the minority groups fighting AIDS were to disappear tomorrow, nobody but a few white people would care: "Our white allies drive us crazy, but they're still our allies, and our racial compatriots don't give two shits about us." Broyles of the Black Leadership Commission on AIDS complains that elected officials never see blacks lobbying on AIDS, and so it is hard to attract funding. Ronald Johnson, who runs MTFA, blames minority officials as well: "There's not one black or Hispanic legislator who has done a goddamned thing about AIDS in this city, state, or country. And that's disgusting."

MTFA's offices are a few connected rooms in a dilapidated apartment building on 115th Street. MTFA has a handful of staff, and doesn't even have the word "AIDS" written on its door, for fear of reprisal. The contrast with the gleaming, five-story office block of GMHC—with its designer logo and color-coded office suites—could not be more acute. According to Johnson, the plight of black gay men with AIDS is dire not simply because of all the other problems affecting the sick—crime, poverty, drugs—but because AIDS has not even begun to enter the collective consciousness. Changing behavior is virtually impossible when the very people at risk don't acknowledge that they are at risk. A bathhouse still operates in Harlem. Denial by gay men of their own homosexuality is the norm. Drug use is commonly related to sex: "For black gay men who are still struggling with guilt over their homosexuality, drugs help them get over that guilt hump in order to be able to have sex at all," Johnson explains.

The group most able to help—the educated black middle class—is made up of the very people, according to Johnson, least willing to confront the taboo of homosexuality. The Dinkins administration, he claims, is more comfortable dealing with Tim Sweeney, the white head of GMHC, than with Johnson, who is black: "I broke one of the unspoken rules of the black community: if you're a homosexual, keep it to yourself."

Among Hispanics, the situation is more acute. The rate of infection is growing fastest in this population, yet if anything, the denial is greater than among blacks. Homophobia is arguably more profound among Hispanics than other ethnic groups, but gay sex may be more common. According to gay Hispanic men I interviewed, anal sex is very prevalent among "straight" Hispanic men. One now openly gay man said he'd had far more sex with his straight male friends when he was in the closet than he's had since. The deep taboo, he argued, is not against sex between men as such, but against admitting it and forming relationships. This is exactly the toughest scenario for AIDS education: those most vulnerable to the disease are those least likely to admit they're vulnerable.

The gay Hispanic population in New York is concentrated in Queens and isolated from white gays. There are Hispanic clubs—Studio 88, La Escuelita, The Love Boat—and a Hispanic gay culture, which, according to the few Hispanic men prepared to talk about it, is more close-knit and monogamous than white gay life. This isolation makes access to help difficult, as does the immigrant experience: "Their families don't know; they don't have legal papers; they don't have good access to treatment," explained Luis, an HIV-positive Hispanic man in his twenties. "A lot don't speak English. And they're afraid that if they go to the hospital, they will get deported." He plans to tell his mother about his condition when she visits from the Dominican Republic this month: "It's kind of sad," he points out. "She said one day that if I ever got sick, she would die. The pain will be something like that. So you see how scary it is for me to tell her. Of course, she will not die. She will live."

Among the varieties of gay death, the minority experience is the least accessible. Often the first thing the broader society sees of it is an emaciated black or Hispanic man in a hospital, adamantly claiming he's an IV drug user. And it's no accident that as the disease has shifted to these populations, it has become less visible. In the pew in front of me at the Salem service, a thin young black man stood on his own. From time to time he left to go to the rest room. Throughout, he mopped his face and neck with small pieces of brown paper, and clutched his body with his arms, cradling himself into temporary comfort. I didn't know whether to talk to him. Those around looked through him, caught in that awkward gap between patronizing and addressing his pain.

After the final hymn, we talked. When his illness became intense, he was forced to live with his mother and give up work. He lived in the South Bronx but was still here at 11:30 p.m. because he wanted "to do something." And besides, he couldn't stand being trapped in bed any longer. He was in touch with GMHC and was supposed to go to a clinical trial for a new experimental drug that day in New Jersey. He had felt too sick to go.

III

So much has been written about ACT UP that it's easy to overlook its most compelling characteristic. Perhaps a majority of its youthful members will be dead in a few years' time. They are, of course, not alone in this. About 30 percent of GMHC's staff, for example, is thought to be HIV-positive. But the combination of nearing death and political activism makes for a unique phenomenon. ACT UP is not merely a brigade of gay-rights activists. It is not even a countercultural crusade for the rights of others. It is a movement primarily designed to prevent the demise of its own.

Most are candid about this: "For me, it's therapy," a wiry, HIV-positive former Wall Streeter told me. "I've always admitted that. But it's not the therapy of comfort. It's the therapy of seeing that change can happen. It's self-empowerment in its true form. It's a sense of power." He said this last word with the curious intensity of many ACT UP members. They are high on power, a high intensified by the liberation of coming to terms with one's own mortality.

The high has a drawback. It generates what can only be called fanaticism. Artfully crafted slogans baldly state the message: "Silence = Death," "We Die. They Do Nothing." One poster shows a picture of New York's commissioner of health, Stephen Joseph. The slogan: "Deadlier than the virus." Designed by graphic artists and advertising executives, they have a sharpness that echoes the look of mass advertising and throws it back in the face of its complacent consumers. Stretched across the chests of men who would look at home in Soloflex ads, the logos come close to morbid camp. The result is a kind of designer revolt, an AIDS aesthetic. Halfway through an ACT UP meeting, the shout goes up: "The merchandising has arrived!" and there's a rush to the T-shirt counter.

This aesthetic is allied to intelligence. The Treatment & Data Committee—a subgroup of ACT UP—has helped revolutionize federal procedures for the testing of experimental drugs through scrutiny of the bureaucracy and science of AIDS. It has engendered respect and admiration—as well as frustration—among scientists and bureaucrats. Its latest campaign is to make five major opportunistic infections treatable within eighteen months, by speeding up the drug-trials process. In stark contrast to the sometimes-hair-raising antics of the rest of ACT UP, T&D is coldly rational—and effective. T&D pressured Burroughs Wellcome to halve the price of AZT, the only effective (but flawed) treatment for HIV.

Still, there's something unsettling about ACT UP that is not easily allayed by understanding its context or its success. The intelligence is sometimes distorted by the Manichaean vision of those confronting death. It's a matter of dogma to ACT UP members, for example, that there's no moral difference between negligent complicity in the AIDS crisis and the act of murder. Yet there are clearly complex arguments about levels of AIDS funding that won't fit into this framework. Cogent arguments also exist for "outing" powerful closeted gay men who are actively homophobic, but in the hands of *Outweek*, a new magazine closely allied to ACT UP, outing has become a way of enforcing ideological conformity on illiberal lines. Articles in *Outweek* have backed taking away free speech from anyone alleged to be homophobic and have urged the use of violence against straight "oppressors." A recent cover featured a lesbian pointing a gun at the reader, with the headline: "Taking aim at bashers." Another proclaimed: "We Hate Straights." That some of this material is presented as camp merely heightens the ugliness of the message.

The ACT UP meeting I attended in New York was held in a theater, the drama taking place as much in the auditorium as on stage. Unlike other radical groups, ACT UP is, internally at least, democratic—sometimes painfully so. The meeting went on for hours, accommodating loquacious bores who were each allowed their say. There seemed no moral pressure on dissent, or even on tedium; merely ecstatic cheering to greet the elect.

The meeting's main agenda was a forthcoming day of action that would shut down the major traffic arteries in New York on December 10. Activists were going to raid the subways, lie down on bridges, clog the freeways, descend into tunnels—all to press the case for socialized medicine. The objections from the floor were ones any sane activist would make: The demo would backfire; it would enrage commuters, alienate potential supporters. It might affect sick people, caught in traffic jams, even cause deaths. And the date clashed with another planned demonstration for national health care.

Little of this carried any weight. At the worry about the sick came a shout from the back:

"We're sick." At the chance of deaths: "We're dying every day." A young woman spoke from the balcony: "This is a great action. This is my fantasy action." Someone yelled from the stage: "Desperate situations require desperate means. It's not going to get better. It's going to get worse. If Larry Kramer's sermons haven't moved you, move yourselves!"

Kramer, an HIV-positive playwright in his fifties, founded ACT UP. Sitting on the stage in a large smock, he smiled quietly throughout, like an old, wise child. His presence among the largely young men and women was a little like that of a guru, except, unlike most gurus, his influence was not to moderate the passion around him, or to direct it to more contemplative ends. It was to intensify it. He began the meeting with a soft-spoken announcement that he wanted to set up a group to do target practice, to learn how to use guns against the police and gay bashers. His point in the demo debate was to back the radicals. He mentioned last year's demo that broke up a Mass at St. Patrick's Cathedral, and provoked a storm of hostility: "We couldn't have gotten worse publicity than the church action, and that put us on the map. . . . Don't use the backlash argument as an excuse. They're not going to like us. They hate us anyway."

ACT UP, as Kramer's brainchild, is not about rational persuasion. As the meeting overwhelmingly approved the action, it was clear it was not supported despite its possible drawbacks, but because of them. "Oh, of course it's a nightmare. That's what I like about it," remarked the man sitting next to me. ACT UP members wish as much to express a contradiction, to give vent to desperation, as to achieve any particular end. Their politics wills the rejection it courts. "They hate us anyway," as Kramer succinctly put it. In any other group of people, this would be called a death wish. But among the dying, a death wish is also a curious way of staying alive.

It's no exaggeration to say that this wish, the experience of it, the feel of it, has changed a segment of gay life permanently. It has replaced strategies of pleading with those of demanding. It has substituted candor for apology. It has absorbed the momentum of the post-Stonewall gay sensibility and gone on the desperate offensive. But at the same time, ACT UP has inevitably alienated a whole group of gay men—those whose own view of their sexuality is more opaque, whose politics is more complex, whose lives are not so transformed.

"Outing" is the most obvious feature of this rift, a declaration of war by some gay men upon others who are less committed in the struggle against death. Not so long ago the closet was sacred territory. No fellow gay would invade its sanctuary. Now every closeted gay man has to fear the animosity of his fellow gays as much as straights. This is a conscious strategy of intimidation, one that most ACT UP members willingly celebrate. And when it isn't manifested in hate, it finds expression in scorn. "They're just being left behind," one angry ACT UP member told me of closeted and apolitical gay men. "They're just not relevant anymore."

By breaking the taboo against aggressively candid homosexuality and the greater taboo against aggressively candid death, ACT UP has not only strained understanding between gays and straights. It has also torn apart the code of security among gays. In the long run this may turn out for the best, as more gay men acknowledge their sexuality and refuse to be patronized by society as a whole. But in the short run another threat has emerged to the rhythm and unity of gay life. And this one comes from within, and in the rhetoric of transfiguration.

IV

There is a metaphor in Tolstoy's *The Death of Ivan Ilych* that sticks in the mind. At the very end of his life, Ivan struggles against death until finally becoming reconciled: suddenly some force struck him in the chest and side, making it still harder to breathe, and he fell through the hole and there at the bottom was a light. What had happened to him was like the sensation one sometimes experiences in a railway carriage when one thinks one is going backward while one is really going forward and suddenly becomes aware of the real direction.

Since almost the beginning of the AIDS crisis, gay men have had an acute sense of going backward. At first it seemed as if the worst would happen, but there was no massive public backlash, no branding, no quarantine. Then came the more difficult challenge of mass death, often unnoticed and almost always misunderstood. Gay lives quietly and increasingly attained a brutalizing concentration as the number of deaths mounted. As the crisis deepens, it's hard not to concur with one man with AIDS I met in New York: "How strong can we be? How much 'empowerment' does it take? How many support groups do I have to attend to talk about my 'feelings'? Sometimes I feel weak and afraid, and no one can help do anything about it. I hate it when that happens, but it does."

Denial is still there: denial of death, of the racial and viral barriers that exist among gay men, of the costs of cathartic political activity. And with this, an avoidance of the intimacy the crisis demands. At this point, perhaps, it is only fair to say that going backward is an understatement. There is no light beneath us in this hole. The hopeful idea that a community is being forged in the face of death is untrue, not because it is beyond the capacity of gay people, but because there is nothing as isolating as one's own extinction. There is, ultimately, no community of the dying. There are only the dying.

If there is an occasional sense that the railway carriage is actually going forward, it is perhaps in the strengthening of gay identity that has begun to be felt, the knowledge that a new, less ravaged generation of gay men will replace the one that is soon going to be missing, and that it will surely gain something from knowledge of the current horror. There is also the awareness that we have gained subtle, private strength from meeting death in this way. And there is the consolation that at least one myth about gay life, held by gays and straights alike, has finally been put to rest. It is an irony of the isolating nature of death that it is also curiously universalizing. Gay men die like straight men die. Loneliness, it turns out, is not the condition of being homosexual. It is the condition of being human.

Taken Unseriously

May 6, 1991 | *THE NEW REPUBLIC*

The death of Michael Oakeshott was greeted in America the same way it was greeted in the English village in which he lived for the last three decades of his life. Almost no one noticed. Those among the villagers who read the obituaries in the London papers were surprised to learn that their neighbor, the sprightly, reclusive octogenarian, who drove a blue MG sports car and lived in a rustic cottage on the edge of a quarry, had been regarded as one of the most original political philosophers of the century. Josiah Lee Auspitz, in a forthcoming article in *The American Scholar*, tells how the pastor at the sparse Anglican funeral even got Oakeshott's first name wrong, as the coffin tipped into the earth. The villagers knew who he was, of course. The shopkeepers recognized his face; others knew that his wife was a painter; his neighbors had seen a variety of odd characters troop in and out of the old man's cottage over the years. They just didn't know what he did. And they had no idea what he meant.

Michael Oakeshott wrote only two books in his life. The first, published in 1933, was an ambitious, intense attempt to describe all of experience—no less—in the philosophical idiom of Hegel and F. H. Bradley. He called it *Experience and Its Modes*, finding in experience different "modes" of seeing the world: science, history, practical life, and, in a later afterthought, poetry. All of experience, he argued, could be found somewhere in these worlds, if you looked hard and carefully enough. His second book, *On Human Conduct*, published in 1975, was an account of one mode: practical life, the world in which most of us spend most of our days. In it, he fleshed out a philosophy of law and of politics. Between these two tomes, Oakeshott taught—he ran the politics department at the London School of Economics for many years—and wrote a batch of essays and reviews. His only other work, *A Guide to the Classics*, was not a disquisition on Romans and Greeks, but a guide to horse racing. Of his intellectual achievements, the most unchallenged is his theory of history, which ranks perhaps with Vico's in its originality and scope.

Sounds dry enough, and some of it, frankly, is dry. To me, however, Oakeshott meant something a little different. I first came across him in an essay I found while doing some reading on Hobbes. It's not one of his most accessible, and, to tell the truth, I didn't understand a good deal of it. But there was something in the assurance of its prose that stuck somewhere in my mind. The essay was in a collection of his, *Rationalism in Politics*. A couple of months later I came across it again in a secondhand bookstore and took it home. I started reading. Within four years of that discovery, I'd tracked down and read everything Oakeshott had published, and spent a year doing little else but trying to puzzle him out. It was about as painless a way of writing a doctorate as I could have imagined.

Toward the end of my labors, I got to meet the man himself. I wrote to ask him whether he would be willing to discuss his work (mine was only the third dissertation ever written on him), and he wrote back, in his elegant calligraphy, that he'd be glad to. I found my way to his village, Langton Matravers, by train from London, and arrived in midmorning, in the cloying November mist of southern England. He was waiting at the garden gate, with a mischievous grin on his face, and hustled me inside. The cottage was made entirely of slate and had no central heating. I discovered only three rooms: a cramped kitchen to one side, a poky guest room, and a living room, turned into a makeshift duplex, with a ladder leading to the second story, which this eighty-nine-year-old clambered up each day to get to bed. The walls were lined with books, in various languages, from Victorian potboiler novels to Hegel's *Phenomenology*. He made me coffee, and a meticulous four-course lunch, and, in front of a coal fire, we talked.

My trouble with Oakeshott had always been with his restraint. He started his intellectual life with a grand attempt to perceive the truth about the world, and over the decades had slowly shifted into an elegant digression about the world's texture. His last essay was actually a work of allegorical fiction, as if the struggle to perceive the truth had proved too demanding to continue, even pointless. I raised the issue: Did he share the philosophical lassitude of so many of his contemporaries? He replied by saying that giving up the search for "the truth" was not equivalent to believing that it did not exist. His restraint came from modesty, not nihilism. Everything is true, he averred, so long as it is not taken for anything more than it is. The nuances were everything, perhaps more thoroughly within our reach, perhaps the only way ultimately to understand the whole.

As in philosophy, religion. Oakeshott's first essays concerned religious truth, but since the 1930s there had been an utter silence. Faith, one could glean from between the lines of his writing, was too acute, even too crushing, an obligation to sustain; or too important, too mysterious, to write about. He seemed even to enjoy the ambiguity of half belief, seeing sin as the occasion of a fascinating conversation with oneself and with God, rather than as an oppressive encumbrance to happiness. "After all," he quipped, half seriously, "who would want to be saved?" God might even prefer us as we are: we're more interesting flawed, and, without flaws, no real love is possible anyway, either between us, or between us and God. Love, Oakeshott explained, has its origins in mutual amusement, and ends in "total acceptance" of the other person. Or as he put it in one of his essays, "Friends are not concerned with what can be made of one another, but only with the enjoyment of one another; and the condition of enjoyment is a ready acceptance of what is and the absence of any desire to change or improve."

This radical acceptance of what is he put at the heart of his idea of the conservative temperament, and it is why many modern conservatives find him so awkward a figure. This disposition is alien to them: it is fickle, aloof, humane, where they are consistent, engaged, and rationalist. Oakeshott couldn't care less about politics as such, who wins and loses, what is now vulgarly called the battle of ideas. He cared about understanding the relations between human beings, and he saw the vagaries of human beings as occasions for celebration, rather than correction. His paradigm was dramatic, not programmatic. His life was poetic, not prosaic. His conservative politics were not a means to repress man's exuberance, but a way to allow it to flourish when politics ends. In this, he was out of his time, but also curiously at home in it: a wildflower planted among our wheat.

Quilt

November 9, 1992 | *THE NEW REPUBLIC*

I first saw the AIDS quilt three years ago, on its last trip to Washington, when it was only a few thousand panels in size and fit comfortably in the Ellipse in front of the White House. Last weekend, at twenty-six thousand panels (one-sixth of the number of deaths in the United States so far), it filled most of the vast space between the Washington Monument and the Reflecting Pool. Neither experience was forgettable, and neither still even faintly morbid. Like the Vietnam Memorial, a few minutes' walk away, the quilt has to be entered in order to be understood, a piece of interactive architecture of both public and private space.

But unlike the Vietnam Memorial, the quilt is a buoyantly colorful, even witty, monument. It doesn't immortalize its commemorated in regimented calligraphy; its geography is not the remarkable, black snowdrift of casualties, but a kind of chaotic living room, in which the unkempt detritus of human beings—their jeans, photographs, glasses, sneakers, letters—is strewn on the ground, as if expecting the people to whom they belonged to return. People walk over this cluttered landscape, looking like tourists, caught between grief and curiosity, saying little, peering intently down at the ground. As you approach the quilt from the rest of the Mall, toward a place where tens of thousands of people are congregated, noise actually subsides.

The panels themselves are tacky and vital, and therefore more chilling: you are invited to grieve over faded Streisand albums, college pennants, grubby bathrobes, cheesy Hallmark verses, and an endless battery of silk-screen seventies kitsch. Unlike the formulas of official memorials, each panel manages to speak its own language in its own idiom; you have to stop at each one and rethink.

Camus suggested in *La Peste* that the most effective way to conceive of large numbers of deaths was to think in terms of movie theaters, but the quilt dispenses with such mind games by simply reproducing shards of the lives of the fallen, like overheard, private conversations.

Some panels are made by lovers, others by parents, friends, even children of the dead; and some are made by those whose names appear on them and speak with uncanny candor. "Life's A Bitch And Then You Die," quips one. Even the names themselves rebel against any attempt to regiment them. In the program, some people are identified with full names, others with first names, others with nicknames. There are sixteen Keiths; and one Uncle Keith; twenty-eight Eds; one Ed & Robert; eighty-two Davids; one David Who Loved The Minnesota Prairie; one mysterious David — Library of Congress; and one David — Happy Birthday. Some go only by two initials — T.J.; others spell it out in full — Dr. Robert P. Smith, Arthur James Stark Jr., HM1 James T. Carter, USN; others are reduced to symbols — five stars (unnamed) "commemorating five theater people who have died"; still others are summoned up by nothing but a baseball cap and an epitaph. Celebrities, of course, creep in — I counted four Sylvesters and twenty-nine Ryan Whites — but they are scattered randomly among their peers. The most piercing: Roy Cohn's. A simple inscription: "Bully. Coward. Victim."

The democracy of the plague is enhanced by the unending recital of names over the loudspeaker, as friends and relatives and strangers read out the death roll. The names resonate with metronomic specificity, adding an aural dimension to the visual litany. "Patrick J. Grace, Dan Hartland, Ron Lopez, Edwina Murphy, Mark Jon Starr, Billy, Kim John Orofino, Frank, Bob Flowers, Sergeant Rick Fenstermaker, US Marine Corps . . . " Many of the two-minute recitations end in "and my brother and best friend" or "my sweet little sister" or some such personal touch. From time to time, a mother's voice cracks over "my precious son and best friend," and the visitors to the quilt visibly stiffen at once, their throats caught in another, numb moment of unexpected empathy. I bumped into an acquaintance. "What's going on?" I asked, lamely. "Oh, just looking for friends."

Just when you're ready to sink into moroseness, however, the panels turn on you. Since this act of remembrance is one our public authorities have not sanctioned (neither President Reagan nor Bush walked the couple of hundred yards to visit the quilt), it is mercifully free of decorum. Drag-queen creations—taffeta, pumps, and pearls embroidered across silk—jostle next to the overalls of manual workers and the teddy bears of show-tune queens. There's plenty of bawdiness, even eroticism, and a particularly humanizing touch you don't find in cemeteries: a lot of the spelling is wrong. Many of the epitaphs have a lightly ironic edge to them, coming close to a kind of death camp: "The Fabulous Scott Tobin"; "Dennis. We Didn't Get To Know Each Other Very Well, And Now We Never Will." My favorite panel ornament was a Lemon Pledge–scent furniture polish can.

Others simply shock you into reality: "Hopefully the family now understands" inscribed beneath a pair of someone's jeans; "For the friend who still cannot be named—and for all of us who live in a world where secrets must be kept." And another: "You still owe me two years, but I forgive you and will always love you. I never located your parents. Maybe someone will see this and tell them."

The point of it all, of course, is not merely to release grief, but to affirm the dignity of those who have died so young and in the face of unique public disdain. For many of the families who came to D.C. last weekend, the event was the end of an extraordinary journey to grapple not simply with their loved ones' deaths, but with their lives. A few short years ago virtually everyone I saw at the quilt was gay. This time the presence of families—predominantly heterosexual—was overwhelming. These were ordinary people who through their loved ones' deaths were asserting, beyond their own sorrow, the overcoming of their own shame. Being there was a catharsis not simply of the horrors of the disease, but of the bigotry that stalked so many of those on the ground and, by association, those who reared them.

This is one way in which AIDS has surely changed America. With the collapse of the closet, a collapse accelerated by HIV, attacks on gay people are now attacks on our families and friends as well. They will no longer go unanswered. "I have done nothing wrong. I am not worthless. I do mean something," as one panel put it. "This is my beloved son," echoed another, "in whom I am well pleased."

The Politics of Homosexuality

A Case for a New Beginning

May 10, 1993 | *THE NEW REPUBLIC*

Over the last four years I have been sent letters from strangers caught in doomed, desperate marriages because of repressed homosexuality and witnessed several thousand virtually naked, muscle-bound men dance for hours in the middle of New York City, in the middle of the day. I have lain down on top of a dying friend to restrain his hundred-pound body as it violently shook with the death throes of AIDS and listened to soldiers equate the existence of homosexuals in the military with the dissolution of the meaning of the United States. I have openly discussed my sexuality on a TV talk show and sat on the porch of an apartment building in downtown D.C. with an arm around a male friend and watched as a dozen cars in a half hour slowed to hurl abuse. I have seen mass advertising explicitly cater to an openly gay audience and watched my own father break down and weep at the declaration of his son's sexuality.

These different experiences of homosexuality are not new, of course. But that they can now be experienced within one life (and that you are now reading about them) is new. The cultural categories and social departments into which we once successfully consigned sexuality—departments that helped us avoid the anger and honesty with which we are now confronted—have begun to collapse. Where once there were patterns of discreet and discrete behavior to follow, there is now only an unnerving confusion of roles and identities. Where once there was only the unmentionable, there are now only the unavoidable: gays, "queers," homosexuals, closet cases, bisexuals, the "out" and the "in," paraded for every heterosexual to see. As the straight world has been confronted with this, it has found itself reaching for a response: embarrassment, tolerance, fear, violence, oversensitivity, recognition. When Sam Nunn conducts hearings, he knows there is no common discourse in which he can now speak, that even the words he uses will betray worlds of conflicting experience and anxieties. Yet speak he must. In place of the silence that once encased the lives of homosexuals, there is now a loud argument. And there is no easy going back.

This fracturing of discourse is more than a cultural problem; it is a political problem. Without at least some common ground, no effective compromise to the homosexual question will be possible. Matters may be resolved, as they have been in the case of abortion, by a standoff in the forces of cultural war. But unless we begin to discuss this subject with a degree of restraint and reason, the visceral unpleasantness that exploded earlier this year will dog the question of homosexuality for a long time to come, intensifying the anxieties that politics is supposed to relieve.

There are as many politics of homosexuality as there are words for it, and not all of them contain reason. And it is harder perhaps in this passionate area than in any other to separate a wish from an argument, a desire from a denial. Nevertheless, without such an effort, no true politics of sexuality can emerge. And besides, there are some discernible patterns, some sketches of political theory that have begun to emerge with clarity. I will discuss here only four, but four that encompass a reasonable span of possible arguments. Each has a separate analysis of sexuality and a distinct solution to the problem of gay-straight relations. Perhaps no person belongs in any single category; and they are by no means exclusive of one another. What follows is a brief description of each: why each is riven by internal and external conflict; and why none, finally, works.

I

The first I'll call, for the sake of argument, the conservative politics of sexuality. Its view of homosexuality is as dark as it is popular as it is unfashionable. It informs much of the opposition to allowing openly gay men and women to serve in the military and can be heard in living rooms, churches, bars, and computer bulletin boards across America. It is found in most of the families in which homosexuals grow up and critically frames many homosexuals' view of their own identity. Its fundamental assertion is that homosexuality as such does not properly exist. Homosexual behavior is aberrant activity, either on the part of heterosexuals intent on subverting traditional society or by people who are prey to psychological, emotional, or sexual dysfunction.

For adherents to the conservative politics of sexuality, therefore, the homosexual question concerns everyone. It cannot be dismissed merely as an affliction of the individual but is rather one that afflicts society at large. Since society depends on the rearing of a healthy future generation, the existence of homosexuals is a grave problem. People who would otherwise be living productive and socially beneficial lives are diverted by homosexuality into unhappiness and sterility, and they may seek, in their bleak attempts at solace, to persuade others to join them. Two gerundives cling to this view of homosexuals: "practicing" and "proselytizing." And both are habitually uttered with a mixture of pity and disgust.

The politics that springs out of this view of homosexuality has two essential parts: with the depraved, it must punish; with the sick, it must cure. There are, of course, degrees to which these two activities can be promoted. The recent practice in modern liberal democracies of imprisoning homosexuals or subjecting them to psychological or physiological "cures" is a good deal less repressive than the camps for homosexuals in Castro's Cuba, the spasmodic attempt at annihilation in Nazi Germany, or the brutality of modern Islamic states. And the sporadic entrapment of gay men in public restrooms or parks is a good deal less repressive than the systematic hunting down and discharging of homosexuals that we require of our armed forces. But the differences are matters of degree rather than of kind, and the essential characteristic of the conservative politics of homosexuality is that it pursues the logic of repression. Not for conservatives the hypocrisy of those who tolerate homosexuality in private and abhor it in public. They seek rather to grapple with the issue directly and to sustain the carapace of public condemnation and legal sanction that can keep the dark presence of homosexuality at bay.

This is not a distant politics. In twenty-four states sodomy is still illegal, and the constitutionality of these statutes was recently upheld by the Supreme

Court. Much of the Republican Party supports this politics with varying degrees of sympathy for the victims of the affliction. The Houston convention was replete with jokes by speaker Patrick Buchanan that implicitly affirmed this view. Banners held aloft by delegates asserted "Family Rights For Ever, Gay Rights Never," implying a direct trade-off between tolerating homosexuals and maintaining the traditional family.

In its crudest and most politically dismissible forms, this politics invokes biblical revelation to make its civic claims. But in its subtler form, it draws strength from the natural law tradition, which, for all its failings, is a resilient pillar of Western thought. Following a Thomist argument, conservatives argue that the natural function of sexuality is clearly procreative, and that all expressions of it outside procreation destroy human beings' potential for full and healthy development. Homosexuality—far from being natural—is clearly a perversion of, or turning away from, the legitimate and healthy growth of the human person.

Perhaps the least helpful element in the current debate is the assertion that this politics is simply bigotry. It isn't. Many bigots may, of course, support it, and by "bigots" I mean those whose "visceral recoil" from homosexuals (to quote Buchanan) expresses itself in thuggery and name-calling. But there are some who don't support antigay violence and who sincerely believe discouragement of homosexuality by law and "curing" homosexuals is in the best interest of everybody.

Nevertheless, this politics suffers from an increasingly acute internal contradiction and an irresistible external development. It is damaged, first, by the growing evidence that homosexuality does in fact exist as an identifiable and involuntary characteristic of some people, and that these people do not as a matter of course suffer from moral or psychological dysfunction; that it is, in other words, as close to "natural" as any human condition can be. New data about the possible genetic origins of homosexuality are only one part of this development. By far the most important element is the testimony of countless homosexuals. The number who say their orientation is a choice make up only a tiny minority, and the candor of those who say it isn't is overwhelming. To be sure, it is in the interests of gay people to affirm their lack of choice over the matter; but the consensus among homosexuals, the resilience of lesbian and gay minorities in the face of deep social disapproval and even a plague, suggests that homosexuality, whatever one would like to think, simply is not often chosen. A fundamental claim of natural law is that its truths are self-evident: across continents and centuries, homosexuality is a self-evident fact of life.

How large this population is does not matter. One percent or 10 percent: as long as a small but persistent part of the population is involuntarily gay, then the entire conservative politics of homosexuality rests on an unstable footing. It becomes simply a politics of denial or repression. Faced with a sizable and inextinguishable part of society, it can only pretend that it does not exist, or needn't be addressed, or can somehow be dismissed. This politics is less coherent than even the politics that opposed civil rights for blacks thirty years ago, because at least that had some answer to the question of the role of blacks in society, however subordinate. Today's conservatives have no role for homosexuals; they want them somehow to disappear, an option that was once illusory and is now impossible.

Some conservatives and conservative institutions have recognized this. They've even begun to use the term "homosexual," implicitly accepting the existence of a constitutive characteristic. Some have avoided it by the innovative term "homosexualist," but most cannot do so without a wry grin on their faces. The more serious opponents of equality for homosexuals finesse the problem by restricting their objections to "radical homosexuals," but the distinction doesn't help. They are still forced to confront the problem of unradical homosexuals, people whose sexuality is, presumably, constitutive. To make matters worse, the Roman Catholic Church—the firmest religious proponent of the conservative politics of homosexuality—has explicitly conceded the point. It declared in 1975 that homosexuality is indeed involuntary for many. In the recent Universal Catechism, the Church goes even further. Homosexuality is described as a "condition" of a "not negligible" number of people who "do not choose" their sexuality and deserve to be treated with "respect, compassion and sensitivity." More critically, because of homosexuality's involuntary nature, it cannot of itself be morally culpable (although homosexual acts still are). The doctrine is thus no longer "hate the sin but love the sinner"; it's "hate the sin but accept the condition," a position unique in Catholic theology, and one that has already begun to creak under the strain of its own tortuousness.

But the loss of intellectual solidity isn't the only problem for the conservative politics of homosexuality. In a liberal polity, it has lost a good deal of its political coherence as well. When many people in a liberal society insist upon their validity as citizens and human beings, repression becomes a harder and harder task. It offends against fundamental notions of decency and civility to treat them as simple criminals or patients. To hunt them down, imprison them for private acts, subject government workers to surveillance and dismissal for reasons related to their deepest sense of personal identity becomes a policy not simply cruel but politically impossible in a civil order. For American society to return to the social norms around the question of homosexuality of a generation ago would require a renewed act of repression that not even many zealots could contemplate. What generations of inherited shame could not do, what AIDS could not accomplish, what the most decisive swing toward conservatism in the 1980s could not muster, must somehow be accomplished in the next few years. It simply cannot be done.

So even Patrick Buchanan is reduced to joke telling, senators to professions of ignorance, military leaders to rationalizations of sheer discomfort. For those whose politics are a mere extension of religious faith, such impossibilism is part of the attraction (and spiritually, if not politically, defensible). But for conservatives who seek to act as citizens in a secular, civil order, the dilemma is terminal. An unremittingly hostile stance toward homosexuals runs the risk of sectarianism. At some point, not reached yet but fast approaching, their politics could become so estranged from the society in which it operates that it could cease to operate as a politics altogether.

II

The second politics of homosexuality shares with the first a conviction that homosexuality as an inherent and natural condition does not exist. Homosexuality, in this politics, is a cultural construction, a binary social conceit (along with heterosexuality) forced upon the sexually amorphous (all of us). This politics attempts to resist this oppressive construct, subverting it and subverting the society that allows it to fester. Where the first politics takes as its starting point the Thomist faith in nature, the second springs from the Nietzschean desire to surpass all natural necessities, to attack the construct of "nature" itself. Thus the pursuit of a homosexual existence is but one strategy of many to enlarge the possibility for human liberation.

Call this the radical politics of homosexuality. For the radicals, like the conservatives, homosexuality is definitely a choice: the choice to be a "queer," the choice to subvert oppressive institutions, the choice to be an activist. And it is a politics that, insofar as it finds its way from academic discourse into gay activism (and it does so fitfully), exercises a peculiar fascination for the adherents of the first politics. At times, indeed, both seem to exist in a bond of mutual contempt and admiration. That both prefer to use the word "queer," the one in private, the other in irony, is only one of many resemblances. They both react with disdain to those studies that seem to reflect a genetic source for homosexuality; and they both favor, to some extent or other, the process of outing, because for both it is the flushing out of deviant behavior: for conservatives, of the morally impure, for radicals, of the politically incorrect. For conservatives, radical "queers" provide a frisson of cultural apocalypse and a steady stream of funding dollars. For radicals, the religious right can be tapped as an unreflective and easy justification for virtually any political impulse whatsoever.

Insofar as this radical politics is synonymous with a subcultural experience, it has stretched the limits of homosexual identity and expanded the cultural space in which some homosexuals can live. In the late 1980s the tactics of groups like ACT UP and Queer Nation did not merely shock and anger, but took the logic of shame abandonment to a thrilling conclusion. To exist within their sudden energy was to be caught in a liberating rite of passage, which, when it did not transgress into political puritanism, exploded many of the cozy assumptions of closeted homosexual and liberal heterosexual alike.

This politics is as open-ended as the conservative politics is closed-minded. It seeks an end to all restrictions on homosexuality, but also the subversion of heterosexual norms, as taught in schools or the media. By virtue of its intellectual origins, it affirms a close connection with every other minority group, whose cultural subversion of white, heterosexual, male norms is just as vital. It sees its crusades—now for an AIDS czar, now against the Catholic Church's abortion stance, now for the Rainbow Curriculum, now against the military ban—as a unified whole of protest, glorifying in its indiscriminateness as in its universality.

But like the conservative politics of homosexuality, which also provides a protective ghetto of liberation for its disciples, the radical politics of homosexuality now finds itself in an acute state of crisis. Its problem is twofold: its conception of homosexuality is so amorphous and indistinguishable from other minority concerns that it is doomed to be ultimately unfocused; and its relationship with the views of most homosexuals—let alone heterosexuals—is so tenuous that at moments of truth (like the military ban) it strains to have a viable politics at all.

The trouble with gay radicalism, in short, is the problem with subversive politics as a whole. It tends to subvert itself. ACT UP, for example, an AIDS group that began in the late 1980s as an activist group dedicated to finding a cure and better treatment for people with AIDS, soon found itself awash in a cacophony of internal division. Its belief that sexuality was only one of many oppressive constructions meant that it was constantly tempted to broaden its reach, to solve a whole range of gender and ethnic grievances. Similarly, each organizing committee in each state of this weekend's march on Washington was required to have a 50 percent "minority" composition. Even Utah. Although this universalist temptation was not always given in to, it exercised an enervating and dissipating effect on gay radicalism's political punch.

More important, the notion of sexuality as cultural subversion distanced it from the vast majority of gay people who not only accept the natural origin of their sexual orientation, but wish to be integrated into society as it is. For most gay people—the closet cases and barflies, the construction workers and investment bankers, the computer programmers and parents—a "queer" identity is precisely what they want to avoid. In this way, the radical politics of homosexuality, like the conservative politics of homosexuality, is caught in a political trap. The more it purifies its own belief about sexuality, the less able it is to engage the broader world as a whole. The more it acts upon its convictions, the less able it is to engage in politics at all.

For the "queer" fundamentalists, like the religious fundamentalists, this is no problem. Politics for both groups is essentially an exercise in theater and rhetoric, in which dialogue with one's opponent is an admission of defeat. It is no accident that ACT UP was founded by a playwright, since its politics was essentially theatrical: a fantastic display of rhetorical pique and visual brilliance. It became a national media hit, but eventually its lines became familiar and the audience's attention wavered. New shows have taken its place and will continue to do so: but they will always be constrained by their essential nature, which is performance, not persuasion.

The limits of this strategy can be seen in the politics of the military ban. Logically, there is no reason for radicals to support the ending of the ban: it means acceptance of presumably one of the most repressive institutions in American society. And, to be sure, no radical arguments have been made to end the ban. But in the last few months, "queers" have been appearing on television proclaiming that gay people are just like anybody else and defending the right of gay Midwestern Republicans to serve their country. In the pinch, "queer" politics was forced to abandon its theoretical essence if it was to advance its purported aims: the advancement of gay equality. The military ban illustrated the dilemma perfectly. As soon as radicalism was required actually to engage America, its politics disintegrated. Similarly, "queer" radicalism's doctrine of cultural subversion and separatism has the effect of alienating those very gay Americans most in need of support and help: the young and teenagers. Separatism is even less of an option for gays than for any other minority, since each generation is literally umbilically connected to the majority. The young are permanently in the hands of the other. By erecting a politics on a doctrine of separation and difference from the majority, "queer" politics ironically broke off dialogue with the heterosexual families whose cooperation is needed in every generation, if gay children are to be accorded a modicum of dignity and hope.

There's an argument, of course, that radicalism's politics is essentially instrumental; that by stretching the limits of what is acceptable it opens up space for more moderate types to negotiate; that without ACT UP and Queer Nation no progress would have been made at all. But this both insults the theoretical integrity of the radical position (they surely do not see themselves as mere adjuncts to liberals) and underestimates the scope of the gay revolution that has been quietly taking place in America. Far more subversive than media-grabbing demonstrations on the evening news has been the slow effect of individual, private Americans becoming more open about their sexuality. The emergence of role models, the development of professional organizations and student groups, the growing influence of openly gay people in the media, and the extraordinary impact of AIDS on families and friends have dwarfed radicalism's impact on the national consciousness. Likewise, the greatest public debate about homosexuality yet—the military debate—took place not because radicals besieged the Pentagon, but because of the ordinary and once-anonymous Americans within the military who simply refused to acquiesce in their own humiliation any longer. Their courage was illustrated not in taking to the streets in rage but in facing their families and colleagues with integrity.

And this presents the deepest problem for radicalism. As the closet slowly collapses, as gay people enter the mainstream, as suburban homosexuals and Republican homosexuals emerge blinking into the daylight, as the gay ghettos of the inner cities are diluted by the gay enclaves of the suburbs, the whole notion of a separate and homogeneous "queer" identity will become harder to defend. Far from redefining gay identity, "queer" radicalism may actually have to define itself in opposition to it. This is implicit in the punitive practice of "outing" and in the increasingly antigay politics of some "queer" radicals. But if "queer" politics is to survive, it will have to either be proved right about America's inherent hostility to gay people or become more insistent in its separatism. It will have to intensify its hatred of straights or its contempt for gays. Either path is likely to be as culturally creative as it is politically sterile.

III

Between these two cultural poles, an appealing alternative presents itself. You can hear it in the tone if not the substance of civilized columnists and embarrassed legislators, who are united most strongly by the desire that this awkward subject simply go away. It is the moderate politics of homosexuality. Unlike the conservatives and radicals, the moderates do believe that a small number of people are inherently homosexual, but they also believe that another group is susceptible to persuasion in that direction and should be dissuaded. These people do not want persecution of homosexuals, but they do not want overt approval either. They are most antsy when it comes to questions of the education of children but feel acute discomfort in supporting the likes of Patrick Buchanan and Pat Robertson.

Thus their politics has all the nuance and all the disingenuousness of classically conservative politics. They are not intolerant, but they oppose the presence of openly gay teachers in school; they have gay friends but hope their child isn't homosexual; they are in favor of ending the military ban but would seek to do so either by reimposing the closet (ending discrimination in return for gay people never mentioning their sexuality) or by finding some other kind of solution, such as simply ending the witch-hunts. If they support sodomy laws (*pour decourager les autres*), they prefer to see them unenforced. In either case, they do not regard the matter as very important. They are ambivalent about domestic partnership legislation but are offended by gay marriage. Above all, they prefer that the subject of homosexuality be discussed with delicacy and restraint, and are only likely to complain to their gay friends if they insist upon "bringing the subject up" too often.

This position, too, has a certain coherence. It insists that politics is a matter of custom as well as principle and that, in the words of Nunn, caution on the matter of sexuality is not so much a matter of prejudice as of prudence. It places a premium on discouraging the sexually ambivalent from resolving their ambiguity freely in the direction of homosexuality, because, society being as it is, such a life is more onerous than a heterosexual one. It sometimes exchanges this argument for the more honest one: that it wishes to promote procreation and the healthy rearing of the next generation and so wishes to create a cultural climate that promotes heterosexuality.

But this politics, too, has become somewhat unstable, if not as unstable as the first two. And this instability stems from an internal problem and a related external one. Being privately tolerant and publicly disapproving exacts something of a psychological cost on those who maintain it. In theory, it is not the same as hypocrisy; in practice, it comes perilously close. As the question of homosexuality refuses to disappear from public debate, explicit positions have to be taken. What once could be shrouded in discretion now has to be argued in public. For those who privately do not believe that homosexuality is inherently evil or always chosen, it has become increasingly difficult to pretend otherwise in public. Silence is an option—and numberless politicians are now availing themselves of it—but increasingly a decision will have to be made. Are you in favor of or against allowing openly gay women and men to continue serving their country? Do you favor or oppose gay marriage? Do you support the idea of gay civil-rights laws? Once these questions are asked, the gentle ambiguity of the moderates must be flushed out; they have to be forced either into the conservative camp or into formulating a new politics that does not depend on a code of discourse that is fast becoming defunct.

They cannot even rely upon their gay friends anymore. What ultimately sustained this politics was the complicity of the gay elites in it: their willingness to stay silent when a gay joke was made in their presence, their deference to the euphemisms—"roommate," "friend," "companion"—that denoted their lovers, husbands, and wives, their support of the heterosexual assumptions of polite society. Now that complicity, if not vanished, has come under strain. There are fewer and fewer J. Edgar Hoovers and Roy Cohns, and the thousands of discreet gay executives and journalists, businessmen and politicians who long deferred to their sexual betters in matters of etiquette. AIDS rendered their balancing act finally absurd. Many people—gay and straight—were forced to have the public courage of their private convictions. They had to confront the fact that their delicacy was a way of disguising shame, that their silence was a means of hiding from themselves their intolerance. This is not an easy process; indeed, it can be a terrifying one for both gay and straight people alike. But there comes a point after which omissions become commissions; and that point, if not here yet, is coming. When it arrives, the moderate politics of homosexuality will be essentially over.

IV

The politics that is the most durable in our current attempt to deal with the homosexual question is the contemporary liberal politics of homosexuality. Like the moderates, the liberals accept that homosexuality exists, that it is involuntary for a proportion of society, that for a few more it is an option, and that it need not be discouraged. Viewing the issue primarily through the prism of the civil-rights movement, the liberals seek to extend to homosexuals the same protections they have granted to other minorities. The prime instrument for this is the regulation of private activities by heterosexuals, primarily in employment and housing, to guarantee nondiscrimination against homosexuals.

Sometimes this strategy is echoed in the rhetoric of Edward Kennedy, who, in the hearings on the military gay ban, linked the gay-rights agenda with the work of such disparate characters as John Kennedy, Cesar Chavez, and Martin Luther King Jr. In other places, it is reflected in the fact that sexual orientation is simply added to the end of a list of minority conditions, in formulaic civil-rights legislation. And this strategy makes a certain sense. Homosexuals are clearly subject to private discrimination in the same way as many other minorities, and linking the causes helps defuse some of the trauma that the subject of homosexuality raises. Liberalism properly restricts itself to law—not culture—in addressing social problems; and by describing all homosexuals as a monolithic minority, it is able to avoid the complexities of the gay world as a whole, just as blanket civil-rights legislation draws a veil over the varieties of black America by casting the question entirely in terms of nonblack attitudes.

But this strategy is based on two assumptions: that sexuality is equivalent to race in terms of discrimination and that the full equality of homosexuals can be accomplished by designating gay people as victims. Both are extremely dubious. And the consequence of these errors is to mistarget the good that liberals are trying to do.

Consider the first. Two truths (at least) profoundly alter the way the process of discrimination takes place against homosexuals and against racial minorities and distinguish the history of racial discrimination in this country from the history of homophobia. Race is always visible; sexuality can be hidden. Race is in no way behavioral; sexuality, though distinct from sexual activity, is profoundly linked to a settled pattern of behavior.

For lesbians and gay men, the option of self-concealment has always existed and still exists, an option that means that in a profound way, discrimination against them is linked to their own involvement, even acquiescence. Unlike blacks three decades ago, gay men and lesbians suffer no discernible communal economic deprivation and already operate at the highest levels of society: in boardrooms, governments, the media, the military, the law, and industry. They may have advanced so far because they have not disclosed their sexuality, but their sexuality as such has not been an immediate cause for their disadvantage. In many cases, their sexuality is known, but it is disclosed at such a carefully calibrated level that it never actually works against them. At lower levels of society, the same pattern continues. As in the military, gay people are not uniformly discriminated against; openly gay people are.

Moreover, unlike blacks or other racial minorities, gay people are not subject to inherited patterns of discrimination. When generation after generation is discriminated against, a cumulative effect of deprivation may take place, where the gradual immiseration of a particular ethnic group may intensify with the years. A child born into a family subject to decades of accumulated poverty is clearly affected by a past history of discrimination in terms of his or her race. But homosexuality occurs randomly anew with every generation. No sociological pattern can be deduced from it. Each generation gets a completely fresh start in terms of the socioeconomic conditions inherited from the family unit.

This is not to say that the psychological toll of homosexuality is less problematic than that of race, but that it is different: in some ways better; in others, worse. Because the stigma is geared toward behavior, the level of shame and collapse of self-esteem may be more intractable. To reach puberty and find oneself falling in love with members of one's own sex is to experience a mixture of self-discovery and self-disgust that never leaves a human consciousness. If the stigma is attached not simply to an obviously random characteristic, such as skin pigmentation, but to the deepest desires of the human heart, then it can eat away at a person's sense of his own dignity with peculiar ferocity. When a young person confronts her sexuality, she is also completely alone. A young heterosexual black or Latino girl invariably has an existing network of people like her to interpret, support, and explain the emotions she feels when confronting racial prejudice for the first time. But a gay child generally has no one. The very people she would most naturally turn to—the family—may be the very people she is most ashamed in front of.

The stigma attached to sexuality is also different from that attached to race because it attacks the very heart of what makes a human being human: her ability to love and be loved. Even the most vicious persecution of racial minorities allowed, in many cases, for the integrity of the marital bond or the emotional core of a human being. When it did not, when Nazism split husbands from wives, children from parents, when apartheid or slavery broke up familial bonds, it was clear that a particularly noxious form of repression was taking place. But the stigma attached to homosexuality begins with such a repression. It forbids, at a child's earliest stage of development, the possibility of the highest form of human happiness. It starts with emotional terror and ends with mild social disapproval. It's no accident that, later in life, when many gay people learn to reconnect the bonds of love and sex, they seek to do so in private, even protected from the knowledge of their family.

This unique combination of superficial privilege, acquiescence in repression, and psychological pain is a human mix no politics can easily tackle. But it is the mix liberalism must address if it is to reach its goal of using politics to ease human suffering. The internal inconsistency of this politics is that by relying on the regulation of private activity, it misses this, its essential target—and may even make matters worse. In theory, a human rights statute sounds like an ideal solution, a way for straights to express their concern and homosexuals to legitimate their identity. But in practice, it misses the point. It might grant workers a greater sense of security were they to come out in the office; and it might, by the publicity it generates, allow for greater tolerance and approval of homosexuality generally. But the real terror of coming out is deeper than economic security, and is not resolved by it; it is related to emotional and interpersonal dignity. However effective or comprehensive antidiscrimination laws are, they cannot reach far enough to tackle this issue; it is one that can only be addressed person by person, life by life, heart by heart.

For these reasons, such legislation rarely touches the people most in need of it: those who live in communities where disapproval of homosexuality is so intense that the real obstacles to advancement remain impervious to legal remedy. And even in major urban areas, it can be largely irrelevant. (On average, some 1 to 2 percent of antidiscrimination cases have to do with sexual orientation; in Wisconsin, which has had such a law in force for more than a decade and is the largest case study, the figure is 1.1 percent.) As with other civil-rights legislation, those least in need of it may take fullest advantage: the most litigious and articulate homosexuals, who would likely brave the harsh winds of homophobia in any case.

Antidiscrimination laws scratch the privileged surface, while avoiding the problematic depths. Like too many drugs for AIDS, they treat the symptoms of the homosexual problem without being anything like a cure; they may buy some time, and it is a cruel doctor who, in the face of human need, would refuse them. But they have about as much chance of tackling the deep roots of the gay-straight relationship as AZT has of curing AIDS. They want to substitute for the traumatic and difficult act of coming out the more formal and procedural act of legislation. But law cannot do the work of life. Even culture cannot do the work of life. Only life can do the work of life.

As the experience in Colorado and elsewhere shows, this strategy of using law to change private behavior also gives a fatal opening to the conservative politics of homosexuality. Civil-rights laws essentially dictate the behavior of heterosexuals, in curtailing their ability to discriminate. They can, with justification, be portrayed as being an infringement of individual liberties. If the purpose of the liberal politics is to ensure the equality of homosexuals and their integration into society, it has thus achieved something quite peculiar. It has provided fuel for those who want to argue that homosexuals are actually seeking the infringement of heterosexuals' rights and the imposition of their values onto others. Much of this is propaganda, of course, and is fueled by fear and bigotry. But it works because it contains a germ of truth. Before most homosexuals have even come out of the closet, they are demanding concessions from the majority, including a clear curtailment of economic and social liberties, in order to ensure protections few of them will even avail themselves of. It is no wonder there is opposition, or that it seems to be growing. Nine states now have propositions to respond to what they see as the "special rights" onslaught.

In the process, the liberal politics of homosexuality has also reframed the position of gays in relation to straights. It has defined them in a permanent supplicant status, seeing gay freedom as dependent on straight enlightenment, achievable only by changing the behavior of heterosexuals. The valuable political insight of radicalism is that this is a fatal step. It could enshrine forever the notion that gay people are a vulnerable group in need of protection. By legislating homosexuals as victims, it sets up a psychological dynamic of supplication that too often only perpetuates cycles of inadequacy and self-doubt. Like blacks before them, gay people may grasp at what seems to be an escape from the prison of self-hatred, only to find it is another prison of patronized victimology. By seeking salvation in the hands of others, they may actually entrench in law and in their minds the notion that their equality is dependent on the goodwill of their betters. It isn't. This may have made a good deal of sense in the case of American blacks, with a clear and overwhelming history of accumulated discrimination and a social ghetto that seemed impossible to breach. But for gay people—already prosperous, independent, and on the brink of real integration—that lesson should surely now be learned. To place our self-esteem in the benevolent hands of contemporary liberalism is more than a mistake. It is a historic error.

v

If there were no alternative to today's liberal politics of homosexuality, it should perhaps be embraced by default. But there is an alternative politics that is imaginable, which once, too, was called liberal. It begins with the view that for a small minority of people, homosexuality is an involuntary condition that can be neither denied nor permanently repressed. It adheres to an understanding that there is a limit to what politics can achieve in such an area, and trains its focus not on the behavior of private heterosexual citizens but on the actions of the public and allegedly neutral state. While it eschews the use of law to legislate culture, it strongly believes that law can affect culture indirectly. Its goal would be full civil equality for those who, through no fault of their own, happen to be homosexual; and would not deny homosexuals, as the other four politics do, their existence, integrity, dignity, or distinctness. It would attempt neither to patronize nor to exclude.

This liberal politics affirms a simple and limited criterion: that all public (as opposed to private) discrimination against homosexuals be ended and that every right and responsibility that heterosexuals enjoy by virtue of the state be extended to those who grow up different. And that is all. No cures or reeducations; no wrenching civil litigation; no political imposition of tolerance; merely a political attempt to enshrine formal civil equality, in the hope that eventually the private sphere will reflect this public civility. For these reasons, it is the only politics that actually tackles the core political problem of homosexuality and perhaps the only one that fully respects liberalism's public–private distinction. For these reasons, it has also the least chance of being adopted by gays and straights alike.

But is it impossible? By sheer circumstance, this politics has just been given its biggest boost since the beginning of the debate over the homosexual question. The military ban is by far the most egregious example of proactive government discrimination in this country. By conceding, as the military has done, the excellent service that many gay and lesbian soldiers have given to their country, the military has helped shatter a thousand stereotypes about their nature and competence. By focusing on the mere admission of homosexuality, the ban has purified the debate into a matter of the public enforcement of homophobia. Unlike antidiscrimination law, the campaign against the ban does not ask any private citizens to hire or fire anyone of whom they do not approve; it merely asks public servants to behave the same way with avowed homosexuals as with closeted ones.

Because of its timing, because of the way in which it has intersected with the coming of age of gay politics, the military debate has a chance of transforming the issue for good. Its real political power—and the real source of the resistance to it—comes from its symbolism. The acceptance of gay people at the heart of the state, at the core of the notion of patriotism, is anathema to those who wish to consign homosexuals to the margins of society. It offends conservatives by the simplicity of its demands, and radicals by the traditional-ism of the gay people involved; it dismays moderates, who are forced publicly to discuss this issue for the first time; and it disorients liberals, who find it hard to fit the cause simply into the rubric of minority politics. For instead of seeking access, as other minorities have done, gays in the military are simply demanding recognition. They start not from the premise of suppliance, but of success, of proven ability and prowess in battle, of exemplary conduct and ability. This is a new kind of minority politics. It is less a matter of complaint than of pride; less about subversion than about the desire to contribute equally.

The military ban also forces our society to deal with the real issues at stake in dealing with homosexuals. The country has been forced to discuss sleeping arrangements, fears of sexual intimidation, the fraught emotional relations between gays and straights, the violent reaction to homosexuality among many young males, the hypocrisy involved in much condemnation of gays, and the possible psychological and emotional syndromes that make homosexu-als allegedly unfit for service. Like a family engaged in the first, angry steps toward dealing with a gay member, the country has been forced to debate a subject honestly—even calmly—in a way it never has before. This is a clear and enormous gain. Whatever the result of this process, it cannot be undone.

But the critical measure necessary for full gay equality is something deeper and more emotional perhaps than even the military. It is equal access to marriage. As with the military, this is a question of formal public discrimina-tion. If the military ban deals with the heart of what it is to be a citizen, the marriage ban deals with the core of what it is to be a member of civil society. Marriage is not simply a private contract; it is a social and public recognition of a private commitment. As such it is the highest public recognition of our personal integrity. Denying it to gay people is the most public affront possible to their civil equality.

This issue may be the hardest for many heterosexuals to accept. Even those tolerant of homosexuals may find this institution so wedded to the notion of heterosexual commitment that to extend it would be to undo its very essence. And there may be religious reasons for resisting this that require far greater discussion than I can give them here. But civilly and emotionally, the case is compelling. The heterosexuality of marriage is civilly intrinsic only if it is understood to be inherently procreative, and that definition has long been abandoned in civil society. In contemporary America, marriage has become a way in which the state recognizes an emotional and economic commitment of two people to each other for life. No law requires children to consummate it. And within that definition, there is no civil way it can logically be denied to homosexuals, except as a pure gesture of public disapproval. (I leave aside here the thorny issue of adoption rights, which I support in full. They are not the same as the right to marriage and can be legislated, or not, separately.)

In the same way, emotionally, marriage is characterized by a kind of commitment that is rare even among heterosexuals. Extending it to homosexuals need not dilute the special nature of that commitment, unless it is understood that gay people, by their very nature, are incapable of it. History and experience suggest the opposite. It is not necessary to prove that gay people are more or less able to form long-term relationships than straights for it to be clear that, at least, some are. Giving these people a right to affirm their commitment doesn't reduce the incentive for heterosexuals to do the same, and even provides a social incentive for lesbians and gay men to adopt socially beneficial relationships.

But for gay people, it would mean far more than simple civil equality. The vast majority of us — gay and straight — are brought up to understand that the apex of emotional life is found in the marital bond. It may not be something we achieve, or even ultimately desire, but its very existence premises the core of our emotional development. It is the architectonic institution that frames our emotional life. The marriages of others are a moment for celebration and self-affirmation; they are the way in which our families and friends reinforce us as human beings. Our parents consider our emotional lives to be more important than our professional ones, because they care about us at our core, not at our periphery. And it is not hard to see why the marriage of an offspring is often regarded as the high point of any parent's life.

Gay people always know this essential affirmation will be denied them. Thus their relationships are given no anchor, no endpoint, no way of integrating them fully into the network of family and friends that makes someone a full member of civil society. Even when those relationships become essentially the same as — or even stronger than — straight relationships, they are never accorded the dignity of actual equality. Husbands remain "friends"; wives remain "partners." The very language sends a powerful signal of fault, a silent assumption of internal disorder or insufficiency. The euphemisms—and the brave attempt to pretend that gay people don't need marriage—do not successfully conceal the true emotional cost and psychological damage that this signal exacts. No true progress in the potential happiness of gay teenagers or in the stability of gay adults or in the full integration of gay and straight life is possible, or even imaginable, without it.

These two measures—simple, direct, requiring no change in heterosexual behavior and no sacrifice from heterosexuals—represent a politics that tackles the heart of homophobia while leaving homophobes their freedom. It allows homosexuals to define their own future and their own identity and does not place it in the hands of the other. It makes a clear, public statement of equality, while leaving all the inequalities of emotion and passion to the private sphere, where they belong. It does not legislate private tolerance; it declares public equality. It banishes the paradigm of victimology and replaces it with one of integrity. It requires one further step, of course, which is to say the continuing effort for honesty on the part of homosexuals themselves. This is not easily summed up in the crude phrase "coming out," but it finds expression in the myriad ways in which gay men and lesbians talk, engage, explain, confront, and seek out the other. Politics cannot substitute for this; heterosexuals cannot provide it. And, while it is not in some sense fair that homosexuals have to initiate the dialogue, it is a fact of life. Silence, if it does not equal death, equals the living equivalent.

It is not the least of the ironies of this politics that its objectives are in some sense not political at all. The family is prior to the liberal state; the military is coincident with it. Heterosexuals would not conceive of such rights as things to be won, but as things that predate modern political discussion. But it says something about the unique status of homosexuals in our society that we now have to be political in order to be prepolitical. Our battle is not for political victory but for personal integrity. Just as many of us had to leave our families in order to join them again, so now as citizens we have to embrace politics, if only ultimately to be free of it. Our lives may have begun in simplicity, but they have not ended there. Our dream, perhaps, is that they might.

Alone Again, Naturally

November 28, 1994 | *THE NEW REPUBLIC*

In everyone there sleeps
A sense of life lived according to love.
To some it means the difference they could make
By loving others, but across most it sweeps
As all they might have done had they been loved.
That nothing cures.

—Philip Larkin, "Faith Healing"

I can remember the first time what, for the sake of argument, I will call my sexuality came into conflict with what, for the sake of argument, I will call my faith. It was time for Communion in my local parish church, Our Lady and St. Peter's, a small but dignified building crammed between an Indian restaurant and a stationery shop, opposite a public restroom, on the main street of a smallish town south of London called East Grinstead. I must have been around fifteen or so. Every time I received Communion, I attempted, following my mother's instructions, to offer up the sacrament for some current problem or need: my mother's health, an upcoming exam, the starving in Bangladesh, or whatever. Most of these requests had to do with either something abstract and distant, like a cure for cancer, or something extremely tangible, like a better part in the school play. Like much else in my faith life, they were routine and yet not completely drained of sincerity. But rarely did they address something that could unsettle the comfort of my precocious adolescence. This time, however, as I filed up to the Communion rail to face mild-mannered Father Simmons for the umpteenth time, something else intervened. Please, I remember asking almost offhandedly of God, after a quick recital of my other failings, help me with that.

I didn't have a name for it, since it was, to all intents and purposes, nameless. I don't think I'd ever heard it mentioned at home, except once when my mother referred to someone who had behaved inappropriately on my father's town rugby team. (He had been dealt with, she reported darkly.) At high school, the subject was everywhere and nowhere: at the root of countless jokes but never actualized as something that could affect anyone we knew. But this ubiquity and abstraction brought home the most important point: uniquely among failings, homosexuality was so abominable it could not even be mentioned. The occasions when it was actually discussed were so rare that they stand out even now in my mind: our Latin teacher's stating that homosexuality was obviously wrong since it meant "sticking your dick in the wrong hole"; the graffiti in the public restroom in Reigate High Street: "My mother made me a homosexual," followed closely by, "If I gave her the wool, would she make me one too?" Although my friends and family never stinted in pointing out other faults on my part, this, I knew, would never be confronted. So when it emerged as an irresistible fact of my existence, and when it first seeped into my life of dutiful prayer and worship, it could be referred to only in the inarticulate void of that Sunday evening before Communion.

From the beginning, however—and this is something many outside the Church can find hard to understand—my sexuality was part of my faith life, not a revolt against it. Looking back, I realize that that moment at the Communion rail was the first time I had actually addressed the subject of homosexuality explicitly in front of anyone; and I had brought it to God in the moments before the most intimate act of sacramental Communion. Because it was something I was deeply ashamed of, I felt obliged to confront it; but because it was also something inextricable—even then—from the core of my existence, it felt natural to enlist God's help rather than his judgment in grappling with it. There was, of course, considerable tension in this balance of alliance and rejection; but there was also something quite natural about it, an accurate reflection of anyone's compromised relationship with what he or she hazards to be the divine.

To the outsider, faith often seems a kind of cataclysmic intervention, a Damascene moment of revelation and transformation, and no doubt, for a graced few, this is indeed the experience. But this view of faith is often, it seems to me, a way to salve the unease of a faithless life by constructing the alternative as something so alien to actual experience that it is safely beyond reach. Faith for me has never been like that. The moments of genuine intervention and spiritual clarity have been minuscule in number and, when they have occurred, hard to discern and harder still to understand. In the midst of this uncertainty, the sacraments, especially that of Communion, have always been for me the only truly reliable elements of direction, concrete instantiations of another order. Which is why, perhaps, it was at Communion that the subject reared its confusing, shaming presence.

The two experiences came together in other ways too. Like faith, one's sexuality is not simply a choice; it informs a whole way of being. But like faith, it involves choices—the choice to affirm or deny a central part of one's being, the choice to live a life that does not deny but confronts reality. It is, like faith, mysterious, emerging clearly one day, only to disappear the next, taking different forms—of passion, of lust, of intimacy, of fear. And like faith, it points toward something other and more powerful than the self. The physical communion with the other in sexual life hints at the same kind of transcendence as the physical Communion with the Other that lies at the heart of the sacramental Catholic vision.

So when I came to be asked, later in life, how I could be gay and Catholic, I could answer only that I simply was. What to others appeared a simple contradiction was, in reality, the existence of these two connected, yet sometimes parallel, experiences of the world. It was not that my sexuality was involuntary and my faith chosen and that therefore my sexuality posed a problem for my faith; nor was it that my faith was involuntary and my sexuality chosen so that my faith posed a problem for my sexuality. It was that both were chosen and unchosen continuously throughout my life, as parts of the same search for something larger. As I grew older, they became part of me, inseparable from my understanding of myself. My faith existed at the foundation of how I saw the world; my sexuality grew to be inseparable from how I felt the world.

I am aware that this formulation of the problem is theologically flawed. Faith, after all, is not a sensibility; in the Catholic sense, it is a statement about reality that cannot be negated by experience. And there is little doubt about what the authority of the Church teaches about the sexual expression of a homosexual orientation. But this was not how the problem first presented itself. The immediate difficulty was not how to make what I did conform with what the Church taught me (until my early twenties, I did very little that could be deemed objectively sinful with regard to sex), but how to make who I was conform with what the Church taught me. This was a much more difficult proposition. It did not conform to a simple contradiction between self and God, as that afternoon in the Communion line attested. It entailed trying to understand how my adolescent crushes and passions, my longings for human contact, my stumbling attempts to relate love to life, could be so inimical to the Gospel of Christ and His Church, how they could be so unmentionable among people I loved and trusted.

So I resorted to what many young homosexuals and lesbians resort to. I found a way to expunge love from life, to construct a trajectory that could somehow explain this absence, and to hope that what seemed so natural and overwhelming could somehow be dealt with. I studied hard to explain away my refusal to socialize; I developed intense intellectual friendships that bordered on the emotional, but I kept them restrained in a carapace of artificiality to prevent passion from breaking out. I adhered to a hopelessly pessimistic view of the world, which could explain my refusal to take part in life's pleasures, and to rationalize the dark and deep depressions that periodically overwhelmed me.

No doubt some of this behavior was part of any teenager's panic at the prospect of adulthood. But looking back, it seems unlikely that this pattern had nothing whatsoever to do with my being gay. It had another twist: it sparked an intense religiosity that could provide me with the spiritual resources I needed to fortify my barren emotional life. So my sexuality and my faith entered into a dialectic: my faith propelled me away from my emotional and sexual longing, and the deprivation that this created required me to resort even more dogmatically to my faith. And as my faith had to find increasing power to restrain the hormonal and emotional turbulence of adolescence, it had to take on a caricatured shape, aloof and dogmatic, ritualistic and awesome. As time passed, a theological austerity became the essential complement to an emotional emptiness. And as the emptiness deepened, the austerity sharpened.

In a remarkable document titled "Declaration on Certain Questions Concerning Sexual Ethics," issued by the Vatican in 1975, the Sacred Congregation for the Doctrine of the Faith made the following statement regarding the vexed issue of homosexuality: "A distinction is drawn, and it seems with some reason, between homosexuals whose tendency comes from a false education, from a lack of normal sexual development, from habit, from bad example, or from other similar causes, and is transitory or at least not incurable; and homosexuals who are definitively such because of some kind of innate instinct or a pathological constitution judged to be incurable."

The Church was responding, it seems, to the growing sociological and psychological evidence that, for a small minority of people, homosexuality is unchosen and unalterable. In the context of a broad declaration on a whole range of sexual ethics, this statement was something of a minor digression (twice as much space was devoted to the "grave moral disorder" of masturbation); and it certainly didn't mean a liberalization of doctrine about the morality of homosexual acts, which were "intrinsically disordered and can in no case be approved of."

Still, the concession complicated things. Before 1975 the modern Church, when it didn't ignore the matter, had held a coherent view of the morality of homosexual acts. It maintained that homosexuals, as the modern world had come to define them, didn't really exist; rather, everyone was essentially a heterosexual and homosexual acts were acts chosen by heterosexuals, out of depravity, curiosity, impulse, predisposition, or bad moral guidance. Such acts were an abuse of the essential heterosexual orientation of all humanity; they were condemned because they failed to link sexual activity with a binding commitment between a man and a woman in a marriage, a marriage that was permanently open to the possibility of begetting children. Homosexual sex was condemned in exactly the same way and for exactly the same reasons as premarital heterosexual sex, adultery, or contracepted sex: it failed to provide the essential conjugal and procreative context for sexual relations. The reasoning behind this argument rested on natural law. Natural-law teaching, drawing on Aristotelian and Thomist tradition, argued that the sexual nature of man was naturally linked to both emotional fidelity and procreation so that, outside of this context, sex was essentially destructive of the potential for human flourishing: "the full sense of mutual self-giving and human procreation in the context of true love," as the encyclical *Gaudium et Spes* put it. But suddenly a new twist had been made to this argument. There was, it seems, in nature, a group of people who were "definitively" predisposed to violation of this natural law; their condition was "innate" and "incurable." Insofar as it was innate—literally *innatus* or "inborn"—this condition was morally neutral, since anything involuntary could not be moral or immoral; it simply was. But always and everywhere, the activity to which this condition led was "intrinsically disordered and [could] in no case be approved of." In other words, something fundamentally in nature always and everywhere violated a vital part of the nature of human beings; something essentially blameless was always and everywhere blameworthy if acted upon.

The paradox of this doctrine was evident even within its first, brief articulation. Immediately before stating the intrinsic disorder of homosexuality, the text averred that in "the pastoral field, these homosexuals must certainly be treated with understanding and sustained in the hope of overcoming their personal difficulties. . . . Their culpability will be judged with prudence." This compassion for the peculiar plight of the homosexual was then elaborated: "This judgment of Scripture does not of course permit us to conclude that all those who suffer from this anomaly are personally responsible for it. . . ." Throughout, there are alternating moments of alarm and quiescence; tolerance and panic; categorical statement and prudential doubt.

It was therefore perhaps unsurprising that, within a decade, the Church felt it necessary to take up the matter again. The problem could have been resolved by a simple reversion to the old position, the position maintained by fundamentalist Protestant churches: that homosexuality was a hideous, yet curable, affliction of heterosexuals. But the Church doggedly refused to budge from its assertion of the natural occurrence of constitutive homosexuals—or from its compassion for and sensitivity to their plight. In Cardinal Joseph Ratzinger's 1986 letter, "On the Pastoral Care of Homosexual Persons," this theme is actually deepened, beginning with the title.

To non-Catholics, the use of the term "homosexual person" might seem a banality. But the term "person" constitutes in Catholic moral teaching a profound statement about the individual's humanity, dignity, and worth; it invokes a whole range of rights and needs; it reflects the recognition by the Church that a homosexual person deserves exactly the same concern and compassion as a heterosexual person, having all the rights of a human being, and all the value, in the eyes of God. This idea was implicit in the 1975 declaration, but was never advocated. Then there it was, eleven years later, embedded in Ratzinger's very title. Throughout his text, homosexuality, far from being something unmentionable or disgusting, is discussed with candor and subtlety. It is worthy of close attention: "[T]he phenomenon of homosexuality, complex as it is and with its many consequences for society and ecclesial life, is a proper focus for the Church's pastoral care. It thus requires of her ministers attentive study, active concern and honest, theologically well-balanced counsel." And here is Ratzinger on the moral dimensions of the unchosen nature of homosexuality: "[T]he particular inclination of the homosexual person is not a sin." Moreover, homosexual persons, he asserts, are "often generous and giving of themselves." Then, in a stunning passage of concession, he marshals the Church's usual arguments in defense of human dignity in order to defend homosexual dignity:

> It is deplorable that homosexual persons have been and are the object of violent malice in speech or in action. Such treatment deserves condemnation from the Church's pastors wherever it occurs. It reveals a kind of disregard for others which endangers the most fundamental principles of a healthy society. The intrinsic dignity of each person must always be respected in word, in action and in law.

Elsewhere, Ratzinger refers to the homosexual's "God-given dignity and worth," condemns the view that homosexuals are totally compulsive as a "demeaning assumption," and argues that "the human person, made in the image and likeness of God, can hardly be adequately described by a reductionist reference to his or her sexual orientation."

Why are these statements stunning? Because they reveal how far the Church had, by the mid-1980s, absorbed the common sense of the earlier document's teaching on the involuntariness of homosexuality, and had had the courage to reach its logical conclusion. In Ratzinger's letter, the Church stood foursquare against bigotry, against demeaning homosexuals either by antigay slander or violence or by pro-gay attempts to reduce human beings to one aspect of their personhood. By denying that homosexual activity was totally compulsive, the Church could open the door to an entire world of moral discussion about ethical and unethical homosexual behavior, rather than simply dismissing it all as pathological. What in 1975 had been "a pathological constitution judged to be incurable" was, eleven years later, a "homosexual person," "made in the image and likeness of God."

But this defense of the homosexual person was only half the story. The other half was that, at the same time, the Church strengthened its condemnation of any and all homosexual activity. By 1986 the teachings condemning homosexual acts were far more categorical than they had been before. Ratzinger had guided the Church into two simultaneous and opposite directions: a deeper respect for homosexuals and a sterner rejection of almost anything they might do.

At the beginning of the 1986 document, Ratzinger bravely confronted the central paradox: "In the discussion which followed the publication of the [1975] declaration . . . an overly benign interpretation was given to the homosexual condition itself, some going so far as to call it neutral or even good. Although the particular inclination of the homosexual person is not a sin, it is a more or less strong tendency ordered toward an intrinsic moral evil and thus the inclination itself must be seen as an objective disorder." Elsewhere, he reiterated the biblical and natural-law arguments against homosexual relations. Avoiding the problematic nature of the Old Testament's disavowal of homosexual acts (since these are treated in the context of such "abominations" as eating pork and having intercourse during menstruation, which the Church today regards with equanimity), Ratzinger focused on Saint Paul's admonitions against homosexuality: "Instead of the original harmony between Creator and creatures, the acute distortion of idolatry has led to all kinds of moral excess. Paul is at a loss to find a clearer example of this disharmony than homosexual relations." There was also the simple natural-law argument: "It is only in the marital relationship that the use of the sexual faculty can be morally good. A person engaging in homosexual behavior therefore acts immorally." The point about procreation was strengthened by an argument about the natural, "complementary union able to transmit life," which is heterosexual marriage. The fact that homosexual sex cannot be a part of this union means that it "thwarts the call to a life of that form of self-giving which the Gospel says is the essence of Christian living." Thus "homosexual activity" is inherently "self-indulgent." "Homosexual activity," Ratzinger's document claimed in a veiled and ugly reference to HIV, is a "form of life which constantly threatens to destroy" homosexual persons.

This is some armory of argument. The barrage of statements directed against "homosexual activity," which Ratzinger associates in this document exclusively with genital sex, is all the more remarkable because it occurs in a document that has otherwise gone further than might have been thought imaginable in accepting homosexuals into the heart of the Church and of humanity. Ratzinger's letter was asking us, it seems, to love the sinner more deeply than ever before, but to hate the sin even more passionately. This is a demand with which most Catholic homosexuals have at some time or other engaged in anguished combat.

It is also a demand that raises the central question of the two documents and, indeed, of any Catholic homosexual life: How intelligible is the Church's theological and moral position on the blamelessness of homosexuality and the moral depravity of homosexual acts? This question is the one I wrestled with in my early twenties, as the increasing aridity of my emotional life began to conflict with the possibility of my living a moral life. The distinction made some kind of sense in theory; but in practice, the command to love oneself as a person of human dignity yet hate the core longings that could make one emotionally whole demanded a sense of detachment or a sense of cynicism that seemed inimical to the Christian life. To deny lust was one thing; to deny love was another. And to deny love in the context of Christian doctrine seemed particularly perverse. Which begged a prior question: Could the paradoxes of the Church's position reflect a deeper incoherence at their core?

One way of tackling the question is to look for useful analogies to the moral paradox of the homosexual. Greed, for example, might be said to be an innate characteristic of human beings, which, in practice, is always bad. But the analogy falls apart immediately. Greed is itself evil; it is prideful, a part of original sin. It is not, like homosexuality, a blameless natural condition that inevitably leads to what are understood as immoral acts. Moreover, there is no subgroup of innately greedy people, nor a majority of people in which greed never occurs. Nor are the greedy to be treated with respect. There is no paradox here, and no particular moral conundrum.

Aquinas suggests a way around this problem. He posits that some things that occur in nature may be in accordance with an individual's nature, but somehow against human nature in general: "for it sometimes happens that one

of the principles which is natural to the species as a whole has broken down
in one of its individual members; the result can be that something which runs
counter to the nature of the species as a whole, happens to be in harmony with
nature for a particular individual: as it becomes natural for a vessel of water
which has been heated to give out heat." Forget, for a moment, the odd view
that somehow it is more "natural" for a vessel to exist at one temperature than
another. The fundamental point here is that there are natural urges in a particular person that may run counter to the nature of the species as a whole. The
context of this argument is a discussion of pleasure: How is it, if we are to trust
nature (as Aquinas and the Church say we must), that some natural pleasures
in some people are still counter to human nature as a whole? Aquinas's only
response is to call such events functions of sickness, what the modern Church
calls "objective disorder." But here, too, the analogies he provides are revealing:
they are bestiality and cannibalism. Aquinas understands each of these activities
as an emanation of a predilection that seems to occur more naturally in some
than in others. But this only reveals some of the special problems of lumping
homosexuality in with other "disorders." Even Aquinas's modern disciples (and,
as we've seen, the Church) concede that involuntary orientation to the same
gender does not spring from the same impulses as cannibalism or bestiality.
Or indeed that cannibalism is ever a "natural" pleasure in the first place, in
the way that, for some bizarre reason, homosexuality is.

What, though, of Aquinas's better argument—that a predisposition to homosexual acts is a mental or physical illness that is itself morally neutral, but always
predisposes people to inherently culpable acts? Here, again, it is hard to think
of a precise analogy. Down syndrome, for example, occurs in a minority and
is itself morally neutral; but when it leads to an immoral act, such as, say, a
temper tantrum directed at a loving parent, the Church is loath to judge that
person as guilty of choosing to break a commandment. The condition excuses
the action. Or take epilepsy: if an epileptic person has a seizure that injures
another human being, she is not regarded as morally responsible for her actions,
insofar as they were caused by epilepsy. There is no paradox here either, but
for a different reason: with greed, the condition itself is blameworthy; with
epilepsy, the injurious act is blameless.

Another analogy can be drawn. What of something like alcoholism? This
is a blameless condition, as science and psychology have shown. Some people

have a predisposition to it; others do not. Moreover, this predisposition is linked, as homosexuality is, to a particular act. For those with a predisposition to alcoholism, having a drink might be morally disordered, destructive to the human body and spirit. So, alcoholics, like homosexuals, should be welcomed into the Church, but only if they renounce the activity their condition implies.

Unfortunately, even this analogy will not hold. For one thing, drinking is immoral only for alcoholics. Moderate drinking is perfectly acceptable, according to the Church, for nonalcoholics. On the issue of homosexuality, to follow the analogy, the Church would have to say that sex between people of the same gender would be—in moderation—fine for heterosexuals but not for homosexuals. In fact, of course, the Church teaches the opposite, arguing that the culpability of homosexuals engaged in sexual acts should be judged with prudence and less harshly than the culpability of heterosexuals who engage in "perversion."

But the analogy to alcoholism points to a deeper problem. Alcoholism does not ultimately work as an analogy because it does not reach to the core of the human condition in the way that homosexuality, following the logic of the Church's arguments, does. If alcoholism is overcome by a renunciation of alcoholic acts, then recovery allows the human being to realize his or her full potential, a part of which, according to the Church, is the supreme act of self-giving in a life of matrimonial love. But if homosexuality is overcome by a renunciation of homosexual emotional and sexual union, the opposite is achieved: the human being is liberated into sacrifice and pain, barred from the matrimonial love that the Church holds to be intrinsic, for most people, to the state of human flourishing. Homosexuality is a structural condition that restricts the human being, even if homosexual acts are renounced, to a less than fully realized life. In other words, the gay or lesbian person is deemed disordered at a far deeper level than the alcoholic: at the level of the human capacity to love and be loved by another human being, in a union based on fidelity and self-giving. Their renunciation of such love also is not guided toward some ulterior or greater goal—as the celibacy of the religious orders is designed to intensify their devotion to God. Rather, the loveless homosexual's destiny is precisely toward nothing, a negation of human fulfillment, which is why the Church understands that such persons, even in the act of obedient self-renunciation, are called "to enact the will of God in their life by joining whatever sufferings and difficulties they experience in virtue of their condition to the sacrifice of the Lord's cross."

This suggests another analogy: the sterile person. Here, too, the person is structurally barred by an innate or incurable condition from the full realization of procreative union with another person. One might expect that such people would be regarded in exactly the same light as homosexuals. They would be asked to commit themselves to a life of complete celibacy and to offer up their pain toward a realization of Christ's sufferings on the cross. But that, of course, is not the Church's position. Marriage is available to sterile couples or to those past child-bearing age; these couples are not prohibited from having sexual relations.

One is forced to ask: What rational distinction can be made, on the Church's own terms, between the position of sterile people and that of homosexual people with regard to sexual relations and sacred union? If there is nothing morally wrong, per se, with the homosexual condition or with homosexual love and self-giving, then homosexuals are indeed analogous to those who, by blameless fate, cannot reproduce. With the sterile couple, it could be argued, miracles might happen. But miracles, by definition, can happen to anyone. What the analogy to sterility suggests, of course, is that the injunction against homosexual union does not rest, at heart, on the arguments about openness to procreation, but on the Church's failure to fully absorb its own teachings about the dignity and worth of homosexual persons. It cannot yet see them as it sees sterile heterosexuals: people who, with respect to procreation, suffer from a clear, limiting condition, but who nevertheless have a potential for real emotional and spiritual self-realization, in the heart of the Church, through the transfiguring power of the matrimonial sacrament. It cannot yet see them as truly made in the image of God.

But this, maybe, is to be blind in the face of the obvious. Even with sterile people, there is a symbolism in the union of male and female that speaks to the core nature of sexual congress and its ideal instantiation. There is no such symbolism in the union of male with male or female with female. For some Catholics, this "symbology" goes so far as to bar even heterosexual intercourse from positions apart from the missionary—face-to-face, male to female—in a symbolic act of love devoid of all nonprocreative temptation. For others, the symbology is simply about the notion of "complementarity," the way in which each sex is invited in the act of sexual congress—even when they are sterile—to perceive the mystery of the other; when the two sexes are the same, in contrast, the act becomes one of mere narcissism and self-indulgence, a higher form of masturbation. For others still, the symbolism is simply about Genesis, the story of Adam and Eve, and the essentially dual, male-female center of the natural world. Denying this is to offend the complementary dualism of the universe.

But all these arguments are arguments for the centrality of heterosexual sexual acts in nature, not their exclusiveness. It is surely possible to concur with these sentiments, even to laud their beauty and truth, while also conceding that it is nevertheless also true that nature seems to have provided a spontaneous and mysterious contrast that could conceivably be understood to complement— even dramatize—the central male-female order. In many species and almost all human cultures, there are some who seem to find their destiny in a similar but different sexual and emotional union. They do this not by subverting their own nature, or indeed human nature, but by fulfilling it in a way that doesn't deny heterosexual primacy, but rather honors it by its rare and distinct otherness. As albinos remind us of the brilliance of color, as redheads offer a startling contrast to the blandness of their peers, as genius teaches us, by contrast, the virtue of moderation, as the disabled person reveals to us in negative form the beauty of the fully functioning human body, so the homosexual person might be seen as a natural foil to the heterosexual norm, a variation that does not eclipse the theme, but resonates with it. Extinguishing—or prohibiting—homosexuality is, from this point of view, not a virtuous necessity, but the real crime against nature, a refusal to accept the pied beauty of God's creation, a denial of the way in which the other need not threaten but may actually give depth and contrast to the self.

This is the alternative argument embedded in the Church's recent grappling with natural law, that is just as consonant with the spirit of natural law as the Church's current position. It is more consonant with what actually occurs in nature, seeks an end to every form of natural life, and upholds the dignity of each human person. It is so obvious an alternative to the Church's current stance that it is hard to imagine the forces of avoidance that have kept it so firmly at bay for so long.

For many homosexual Catholics, life within the Church is a difficult endeavor. In my twenties, as I attempted to unite the possibilities of sexual longing and emotional commitment, I discovered what many heterosexuals and homosexuals had discovered before me: that it is a troubling and troublesome mission. There's a disingenuous tendency, when discussing both homosexual and heterosexual emotional life, to glamorize and idealize the entire venture. To posit the possibility of a loving union, after all, is not to guarantee its achievement. There is also a lamentable inclination to believe that all conflicts can finally be resolved; that the homosexual Catholic's struggle can be removed by a simple theological coup de main; that the conflict is somehow deeper than many other struggles in the Church—of women, say, or of the divorced. The truth is that pain, as Christ taught, is not a reason to question truth; it may indeed be a reason to embrace it.

But it must also be true that to dismiss the possibility of a loving union for homosexuals at all—to banish from the minds and hearts of countless gay men and women the idea that they, too, can find solace and love in one another—is to create the conditions for a human etiolation that no Christian community can contemplate without remorse. What finally convinced me of the wrongness of the Church's teachings was not that they were intellectually so confused, but that in the circumstances of my own life—and of the lives I discovered around me—they seemed so destructive of the possibilities of human love and self-realization. By crippling the potential for connection and growth, the Church's teachings created a dynamic that in practice led not to virtue but to pathology; by requiring the first lie in a human life, which would lead to an entire battery of others, they contorted human beings into caricatures of solitary eccentricity, frustrated bitterness, incapacitating anxiety—and helped perpetuate all the human wickedness and cruelty and insensitivity that such lives inevitably carry in their wake. These doctrines could not in practice do what they wanted to do: they could not both affirm human dignity and deny human love.

This truth is not an argument; it is merely an observation. But observations are at the heart not simply of the Church's traditional Thomist philosophy, but also of the phenomenological vision of the current pope. To observe these things, to affirm their truth, is not to oppose the Church, but to hope in it, to believe in it as a human institution that is yet the eternal vessel of God's love. It is to say that such lives as those of countless gay men and lesbians must ultimately affect the Church not because our lives are perfect, or without contradiction, or without sin, but because our lives are in some sense also the life of the Church.

I remember, in my own life, the sense of lung-filling exhilaration I felt as my sexuality began to be incorporated into my life, a sense that was not synonymous with recklessness or self-indulgence—although I was not immune from those things either—but a sense of being suffused at last with the possibility of being fully myself before those I loved and before God. I remember the hopefulness of parents regained and friendships restored in a life that, for all its vanities, was at least no longer premised on a lie covered over by a career. I remember the sense a few months ago in a pew in a cathedral, as I reiterated the same pre-Communion litany of prayers that I had spoken some twenty years earlier, that, for the first time, the love the Church had always taught that God held for me was tangible and redemptive. I had never felt it fully before; and, of course, like so many spiritual glimpses, I have rarely felt it since. But I do know that it was conditioned not on the possibility of purity, but on the possibility of honesty. That honesty is not something that can be bought or won in a moment. It is a process peculiarly prone to self-delusion and self-doubt. But it is one that, if it is to remain true to itself, the Church cannot resist forever.

When Plagues End: Notes on the Twilight of an Epidemic

November 10, 1996 | *THE NEW YORK TIMES*

I

First, the things I resist remembering, the things that make the good news almost as unbearable as the bad.

I arrived late at the hospital, fresh off the plane. It was around 8:30 in the evening and there had been no light on in my friend Patrick's apartment, so I went straight to the intensive-care unit. When I arrived, my friend Chris's eyes were a reddened blear of fright, the hospital mask slipped down under his chin. I went into the room. Pat was lying on his back, his body contorted so his neck twisted away and his arms splayed out, his hands palms upward, showing the intravenous tubes in his wrists. Blood mingled with sweat in the creases of his neck; his chest heaved up and down grotesquely with the pumping of the respirator that was feeding him oxygen through a huge plastic tube forced down his throat. His greenish-blue feet poked out from under the bedspread, as if separate from the rest of his body. For the first time in all of his illnesses, his dignity had been completely removed from him. He was an instrument of the instruments keeping him alive.

The week before, celebrating his thirty-first birthday in his hometown on the Gulf Coast of Florida, we swam together in the dark, warm waters that he had already decided would one day contain his ashes. It was clear that he knew something was about to happen. One afternoon on the beach, he got up to take

75

a walk with his newly acquired beagle and glanced back at me a second before he left. All I can say is that, somehow, the glance conveyed a complete sense of finality, the subtlest but clearest sign that it was, as far as he was concerned, over. Within the space of three days, a massive fungal infection overtook his lungs, and at midnight on the fourth day his vital signs began to plummet.

I was in the hall outside the intensive-care room when a sudden rush of people moved backward out of it. Pat's brother motioned to me and others to run, and we sped toward him. Pat's heart had stopped beating, and after one attempt was made to restart it, we intuitively acquiesced, surrounded him and prayed: his mother and father and three brothers, his boyfriend, ex-boyfriend, and a handful of close friends. When the priest arrived, each of us received Communion.

I remember that I slumped back against the wall at the moment of his dying, reaching out for all the consolation I had been used to reaching for—the knowledge that the final agony was yet to come, the memory of pain that had been overcome in the past—but since it was happening now, and now had never felt so unavoidable, no relief was possible. Perhaps this is why so many of us find it hard to accept that this ordeal as a whole may be over. Because it means that we may now be required to relent from our clenching against the future and remember—and give meaning to—the past.

II

Most official statements about AIDS—the statements by responsible scientists, by advocate organizations, by doctors—do not, of course, concede that this plague is over. And, in one sense, obviously, it is not. Someone today will be infected with HIV. The vast majority of HIV-positive people in the world, and a significant minority in America, will not have access to the expensive and effective new drug treatments now available. And many Americans—especially blacks and Latinos—will still die. Nothing I am saying here is meant to deny that fact, or to mitigate its awfulness. But it is also true—and in a way that most people in the middle of this plague privately recognize—that something profound has occurred these last few months. The power of the newest drugs, called protease inhibitors, and the even greater power of those now in the pipeline, is such that a diagnosis of HIV infection is not just different in degree today than, say, five years ago. It is different in kind. It no longer signifies death. It merely signifies illness.

The reality finally sank in for me at a meeting in Manhattan this summer of the Treatment Action Group, an AIDS advocacy organization. TAG lives and breathes skepticism; a few of its members had lambasted me only nine months before for so much as voicing optimism about the plague. But as soon as I arrived at the meeting—held to discuss the data presented at the just-completed AIDS conference in Vancouver, British Columbia—I could sense something had changed. Even at 8 p.m., there was a big crowd—much larger, one of the organizers told me, than at the regular meetings. In the middle sat Dr. David Ho, a pioneering AIDS researcher, and Dr. Martin Markowitz, who presided over recent clinical trials of the new treatments. The meeting began with Ho and Markowitz revisiting the data. They detailed how, in some trials of patients taking the new protease inhibitors used in combination with AZT and another drug called 3TC, the amount of virus in the bloodstream was reduced on average a hundred- to a thousandfold. To put it another way: most people with HIV can have anywhere between five thousand and a few million viral particles per milliliter of their blood. After being treated for a few weeks with the new drugs, and being subjected to the most sensitive tests available, many patients had undetectable levels of the virus in their bloodstreams. That is, no virus could be found. And, so far, the results were holding up.

When Ho finished speaking, the questions followed like firecrackers. How long did it take for the virus to clear from the bloodstream? Was it possible that the virus might still be hiding in the brain or the testes? What could be done for the people who weren't responding to the new drugs? Was there resistance to the new therapy? Could a new, even more lethal viral strain be leaking into the population? The answers that came from Ho and Markowitz were just as insistent. No, this was not a "cure." But the disappearance of the virus from the bloodstream went beyond the expectations of even the most optimistic of researchers. There was likely to be some effect on the virus, although less profound, in the brain or testes, and new drugs were able to reach those areas better. The good news was that HIV seemed primarily to infect cells that have a short half-life, which means that if the virus is suppressed completely for two years or so, the body might have time to regenerate tissue that was "aviremic." And since the impact of the drugs was so powerful, it was hard for resistance to develop because resistance is what happens when the virus mutates in the presence of the drugs—and there was no virus detectable in the presence of the drugs.

The crowd palpably adjusted itself, and a few chairs squeaked. These are the hard-core skeptics, I remember thinking to myself, and even they can't disguise what is going through their minds. There were caveats, of course. The latest drugs were very new, and large studies had yet to be done. There was already clinical evidence that a small minority of patients, especially those in late-stage disease, were not responding as well to the new drugs and were experiencing a "breakout" of the virus after a few weeks or months. Although some people's immune systems seemed to improve, others' seemed damaged for good. The long-term toxicity of the drugs themselves—their impact on the liver, for example—could mean that patients might undergo a miraculous recovery at the start, only to die from the effects of treatment in later life. And the drugs were often debilitating. I tested positive in 1993, and I have been on combination therapy ever since. When I added the protease inhibitors in March, the nausea, diarrhea, and constant fatigue had, at first, been overwhelming.

Still, after the meeting, a slightly heady feeling wafted unmistakably over the crowd. As we spilled out into the street, a few groups headed off for a late dinner, others to take their protease drugs quickly on empty stomachs, others still to bed. It was after ten, and I found myself wandering aimlessly into a bar, where late-evening men in suits gazed up at muscle-boy videos, their tired faces and occasional cruising glances a weirdly comforting return to normalcy. But as I checked my notebook at the door, and returned to the bar to order a drink, something a longtime AIDS advocate said to me earlier that day began to reverberate in my mind. He had been talking about the sense of purpose and destiny he had once felt upon learning he was positive. "It must be hard to find out you're positive now," he had said darkly. "It's like you really missed the party."

III

Second, the resistance to memory.

At six o'clock in the morning in the Roseland Ballroom in Manhattan on a Sunday last spring the crowds were still thick. I had arrived four hours earlier, after a failed attempt to sleep. A chaotic throng of men crammed the downstairs lobby, trying to check coats. There were no lines as such, merely a subterranean, almost stationary mosh pit, stiflingly hot, full of lean, muscular bodies glacially drifting toward the coat-check windows. This was, for some, the high point of the year's gay male social calendar. It's called the Black Party, one of a number of theme parties held year-round by a large, informal group of affluent, mainly white, gay men and several thousand admirers. It's part of what's been dubbed the "circuit," a series of vast dance parties held in various cities across the country and now a central feature of an emergent post-AIDS gay "lifestyle."

When people feared that the ebbing of AIDS would lead to a new burst of promiscuity, to a return to the 1970s in some joyous celebration of old times, they were, it turns out, only half-right. Although some bathhouses have revived, their centrality to gay life has all but disappeared. What has replaced sex is the idea of sex; what has replaced promiscuity is the idea of promiscuity, masked, in the increasing numbers of circuit parties around the country, by the ecstatic drug-enhanced high of dance music. These are not mass celebrations at the dawn of a new era; they are raves built upon the need for amnesia.

Almost nothing has been written in the mainstream media about these parties, except when they have jutted their way into controversy. A new circuit party, called Cherry Jubilee in Washington, incurred the wrath of Representative Robert Dornan because drugs had been used in a federal building leased for the event. The annual Morning Party in August on Fire Island, held to raise money for Gay Men's Health Crisis in New York, was criticized on similar grounds by many homosexuals themselves. But in general, these parties have grown in number with a remarkable secrecy, reminiscent of the old, closeted era when completely bifurcated gay lives were the norm. But their explosion on the scene—there are now at least two a month, involving tens of thousands of gay men in cities as diverse as Pittsburgh and Atlanta—is interesting for more than their insight into party culture.

The events are made possible by a variety of chemicals: steroids, which began as therapy for men wasting from AIDS and recently spawned yet another growing sub-subculture of huge bodybuilders; and psychotherapeutic designer drugs, primarily Ecstasy, which creates feelings of euphoria and emotional bonding, and ketamine, an animal anesthetic that disconnects the conscious thought process from the sensory body. On the surface the parties could be taken for a mass of men in superb shape merely enjoying an opportunity to let off steam. But underneath, masked by the drugs, there is an air of strain, of sexual danger translated into sexual objectification, the unspoken withering of the human body transformed into a reassuring inflation of muscular body mass.

As the morning stretched on, my friends and I stood in the recess of a bar as the parade of bodies passed relentlessly by. Beyond, a sea of men danced the early morning through, strobe lights occasionally glinting off the assorted deltoids, traps, lats, and other muscles gay men have come to fetishize. At the party's peak—around 5 a.m.—there must have been about six thousand men in the room, some parading on a distant stage, others locked in a cluster of rotating pecs, embracing one another in a drug-induced emotional high.

For a group of men who have witnessed a scale of loss historically visited only upon war generations, it was a curious spectacle. For some, I'm sure, the drugs helped release emotions they could hardly address alone or sober; for others, perhaps, the ritual was a way of defying their own infections, their sense of fragility, or their guilt at survival. For others still, including myself, it was a puzzle of impulses. The need to find some solidarity among the loss, to assert some crazed physicality against the threat of sickness, to release some of the toxins built up over a decade of constant anxiety. Beyond everything, the desire to banish the memories that will not be banished, to shuck off—if only till the morning—the maturity that plague had brutally imposed.

IV

I talk about this as a quintessentially homosexual experience, not because AIDS is a quintessentially homosexual experience. Across the world, it has affected far, far more heterosexuals than homosexuals; in America, it has killed half as many intravenous drug users as gay men. And its impact has probably been as profound on many heterosexual family members and friends as it has been on the gay men at ground zero of the epidemic. But at the same time, AIDS was and is inextricable from the question of homosexuality in the psyche of America because it struck homosexuals first and from then on became unalterably woven into the deeper and older question of homosexual integration.

In so many ways it was a bizarre turn of events. In the past, plagues were often marked by their lack of discrimination, by the way in which they laid low vast swaths of the population with little regard for station or wealth or sex or religion. But AIDS was different from the beginning. It immediately presented a political as much as a public-health problem. Before homosexuals had even been acknowledged as a central presence in American life, they were suddenly at the heart of a health crisis as profound as any in modern American history. It was always possible, of course, that, with such a lack of societal preparation, America might have responded the way many Latin American and Asian countries responded—with almost complete silence and denial—or that the gay world itself might have collapsed under the strain of its own immolation. But over the long run something somewhat different happened. AIDS and its onslaught imposed a form of social integration that may never have taken place otherwise. Forced to choose between complete abandonment of the gay subculture and an awkward first encounter, America, for the most part, chose the latter. A small step, perhaps, but an enormous catalyst in the renegotiation of the gay-straight social contract.

And an enormous shift in our understanding of homosexuality itself. Too much has been made of the analogy between AIDS and the Jewish Holocaust, and they are, indeed, deeply distinct phenomena. One was an act of calculated human evil, designed to obliterate an entire people from the center of Europe. The other is a natural calamity, singling out a group of despised outsiders by virtue of a freak of nature, and a disease that remained asymptomatic long enough to wipe out thousands before anyone knew what was happening. But insofar as each catastrophe changed forever the way a minority group was viewed by the world, the two have eerie parallels.

The hostility to homosexuals, after all, has far more in common with anti-Semitism than it does with racism. Homosexuals, like Jews, are not, in the psychology of group hatred, despised because they are deemed to be weak or inferior, but precisely because they are neither. Jews and homosexuals appear in the hater's mind as small, cliquish, and very powerful groups, antipathetic to majority values, harboring secret contempt for the rest of society, and sustaining a ghetto code of furtiveness and disguise. Even the details resonate. The old libel against Jews—that they would drink the blood of Christian children—has an echo today in the bigot's insistence that he has nothing against homosexuals per se, but doesn't want them allowed near his kids. The loathing for each group is closely linked to fear—and the fear is fanned, in many ways, by the distortion of a particular strain in Christian theology.

But that fear was abated, in both cases, by extraordinary contingent historic events. The Holocaust did many things to the structure of anti-Semitism, but in one hideous swoop it helped destroy the myth that Jews were somehow all-powerful. The mounds of bodies, the piles of artifacts, and the grotesque physical torture that the Jews of Europe suffered did not exactly indicate power. Out of that powerlessness, of course, came a new form of power, in the shape of achieved Zionism. But the idea of Jewish victimhood seared by mass murder into the Western consciousness was seared indelibly—and it remains one of the strongest weapons against the canards of anti-Semitism today.

Similarly, if on a far smaller scale, AIDS has dramatically altered the psychological structure of homophobia. By visiting death upon so many, so young, AIDS ripped apart the notion of subterranean inviolability that forms such a potent part of the fear of homosexuals. As tens of thousands of sons and uncles and brothers and fathers wasted away in the heart of America, the idea that homosexuals maintained a covert power melted into a surprised form of shock and empathy. For some, the old hatreds endured, of course, but for others an unsought and subtle transformation began to take shape. What had once been a strong fear of homosexual difference, disguising a mostly silent awareness of homosexual humanity, became the opposite. The humanity slowly trumped the difference. Death, it turned out, was a powerfully universalizing experience. Suddenly acquiescence in gay baiting and gay bashing became, even in its strongholds, inappropriate at a moment of tragedy. The victimization of gay men by a disease paradoxically undercut their victimization by a culture. There was no longer a need to kick them, when they were already down.

I think this helps explain the change in the American psyche these last ten years from one of fearful stigmatization of homosexuals to one of awkward acceptance. And it's revealing that the same thing did not really happen to the many other victims of the plague. With inner-city blacks and Latinos, with intravenous drug users, there was no similar cultural transformation, no acceleration of social change. And that was because with these groups, there had never been a myth of power. They had always been, in the majority psyche, a series of unknowable victims. AIDS merely perpetuated what was already understood and, in some ways, intensified it. With gay men, in contrast, a social revolution had been initiated. Once invisible, they were now unavoidable; once powerful subversives, they were now dying sons.

AIDS, then, was an integrator. If the virus separated, death united. But there was a twist to this tale. As the straight world found itself at a moment of awkward reconciliation, the gay world discovered something else entirely. At a time when the integration of homosexuals into heterosexual life had never been so necessary or so profound, the experience of AIDS as a homosexual experience created bonds and loyalties and solidarities that homosexuals had never experienced before. As it forced gay men out into the world, it also intensified the bonds among them; as it accelerated an integration, it forged an even deeper separation. The old question of assimilation versus separatism became strangely moot. Now, both were happening at once—and feeding off the same psychological roots.

I remember the first time I used the word "we" in print in reference to gay men. It was in an article I was writing as I witnessed my first AIDS death—of a stranger I had volunteered to help out in his final months. He was thirty-two years old when I got to know him, back in 1990. Without AIDS, we would never have met, and the experience changed my sense of gay identity for good. Before then, although I had carefully denied it, I had quietly distanced myself from much of what I thought of as "gay culture." Tom helped to change this.

He was the stereotype in so many ways—the seventies mustache, the Alcoholics Anonymous theology, the Miss America Pageant fan, the college swim coach. But he was also dying. His skin was clammy and pale. His apartment smelled of Maxwell House coffee and disinfectant and the gray liquid that was his constant diarrhea. I remember one day lying down on top of him to restrain him as his brittle, burning body shook uncontrollably with the convulsions of fever. I had never done such a thing to a grown man before, and as I did, the defenses I had put up between us, the categories that until then had helped me make sense of my life and his, these defenses began to crumble into something more like solidarity.

For others, the shift was more dramatic. Their own incipient deaths unleashed the unfiltered rage of the late 1980s, as decades of euphemism and self-loathing exploded into one dark, memorable flash of activism. The fire behind ACT UP was by its very nature so combustible that it soon burned out. But its articulation of a common identity—the unsustainable starkness of its definition of homosexuality—left a residue behind.

And I began to understand the pull of this identity more instinctively. Suddenly it seemed, as my twenties merged into my thirties, everyone was infected. Faces you had gotten used to seeing in the gym kept turning up on the obit pages. New friends took you aside to tell you they had just tested positive. Old flames suddenly were absent from the bars. I remember thinking that a new term was needed for something that was happening to me with increasing frequency: I would be walking along a street and see an old man coming toward me whom I vaguely recognized. And then I would realize that it wasn't an old man; it was someone I knew who had just gone through some bout with pneumonia or some intestinal parasite. Like Scott, a soldier I had gotten to know as a 220-pound, 6-foot-3-inch, blue-eyed, blond-haired bundle of energy. During the gays-in-the-military affair early in the Clinton administration, I had urged him to come out to his commanders and troops, sure that the new president would protect him. He told me I had to be out of my mind, and, of course, as it turned out, I was. And then, a few weeks later, he bumped into me on the street and confided the real reason he didn't want to confront anyone. He was HIV-positive and needed the Army's support. He told me with genuine anguish, as if the knowledge of his disease demanded a courage his disease would also have punished.

Then, a mere year later, I saw him with a cane (literally), his spirit completely broken, his body shrunk to 140 pounds, his breath gone after the shortest walk, his eyes welling with the bitterness of physical pain and isolation. His lover of several years somehow endured the ordeal, nursing him every inch of the way, until Scott became a ninety-pound skeletal wreck, unable to walk, his hair weak and gray and glassy, his eyes sunken miserably into a scaly face. Scott never fully reconciled with his family. And after Scott died, his lover told me that his last words had been, "Tell my mother I hate her."

When I would tell my straight friends, or my work colleagues or my family, about these things, it wasn't that they didn't sympathize. They tried hard enough. It was just that they sensed that the experience was slowly and profoundly alienating me from them. And they sensed that it was more than just a cultural difference. The awareness of the deaths of one's peers and the sadness evoked and the pain you are forced to witness—not just the physical pain, but all the psychological fear and shame that AIDS unleashed—all this was slowly building a kind of solidarity that eventually eliminated my straight friends from the most meaningful part of my life. There comes a point at which the experience goes so deep that it becomes almost futile to communicate it. And as you communicate less and less and experience more and more, you find yourself gravitating to the people who have undergone the same experiences, the ones who know instinctively, the people to whom you do not have to explain.

I remember the moment when my friend Patrick told me he had AIDS. We had been friends for a long time, yet the meaning of that friendship had never been fully clear to us. But at that moment we were able to look each other in the eye and tell each other we would be there for each other, whatever it took and however hard it became. I don't think I had ever made such a commitment before—to anyone. It survived watching him waste away, seeing him buckled over on the floor, thumping the ground from the pain of his infections; it survived him messing himself in panic as he fumbled with his IV; it survived his bloody-minded resistance to risky treatments that might have helped him; it survived the horrifying last hours in the intensive-care unit and the awkward silences with his family a year after he passed away. It survives still, as does the need to find a way to give it meaning in his absence.

For a long time I never broke down or cried about any of this—the dozens of acquaintances who have died, the handful of friends I have mourned or resisted mourning, the sudden flashes of panic at the thought of my own mortality. But late one night I caught sight of Senator Bob Kerrey on *Nightline*. He was speaking haltingly of his relationship with Lewis Puller, the paralyzed Vietnam veteran who had survived the war, only to ultimately succumb to depression, alcoholism, and, finally, suicide. There was in Kerrey's bitter, poignant farewell a sense that only he and a few others would fully understand Puller's anguish. Kerrey grasped, because he had experienced, what it was to face extreme danger and witness in the most graphic way possible the deaths of his closest friends and colleagues, only to come home and find those experiences denied or ignored or simply not understood. And as he spoke, I felt something break inside me. Kerrey knew, as Mark Helprin expressed so beautifully in his novel *A Soldier of the Great War*, what almost every gay man, in a subtler, quieter way, has also learned: "The war was still in him, and it would be in him for a long time to come, for soldiers who have been blooded are soldiers forever. They never fit in. . . . That they cannot forget, that they do not forget, that they will never allow themselves to heal completely, is their way of expressing their love for friends who have perished. And they will not change because they have become what they have become to keep the fallen alive."

At the time of this writing, almost three times as many young Americans have died of AIDS as died in the entire Vietnam War.

v

In Camus's novel *The Plague*, the description of how plagues end is particularly masterful. We expect a catharsis, but we find merely a transition; we long for euphoria, but we discover only relief tinged with, in some cases, regret and depression. For some, there is a zeal that comes with the awareness of unsought liberation, and the need to turn such arbitrary freedom into meaningful creation. For many more, there is even—with good reason—a resistance to the good news itself because "the terrible months they had lived through had taught them prudence." The reactions to the news, Camus notes, are "diverse to the point of incoherence." Many refuse to believe that there is any hope at all, burned by dashed expectations one time too many, "imbued with a skepticism so thorough that it was now a second nature." Others found the possibility of an end too nerve-racking to bear and almost dared the plague to kill them before it was too late.

And even now, among friends, there are those who refuse to be tested for a virus that, thanks to the new treatments, might be eliminated from the bloodstream. And there are those who are HIV-positive who are still waiting to take the drugs and are somehow unable to relinquish the notion that being positive is a death sentence that they can endure only alone. And there are those many who, having taken all the drugs they can, have found that for some reason the drugs will not work for them and watch as their friends recover while they still sink into the morass of sickness made all the more bitter by the good news around them. And those more who, sensing an abatement of the pressure, have returned, almost manically, to unsafe sexual behavior, as if terrified by the thought that they might actually survive, that the plague might end and with it the solidarity that made it endurable.

You can already feel, beneath the surface, the fraying of the bonds. A friend in New York, HIV-positive for ten years, contemplates breaking up with his boyfriend because he suddenly realizes he is going to live. "I felt safe where I was," he tells me. "But now I feel like an attractive person again. It's more what you're radiating inside—the feeling that, finally, you're not a potential burden. I mean, maybe I'm not a potential burden." Another positive friend, this one an AIDS advocate of hardened credentials, feels the meaning of his life slipping away. "At some point, you just have to go on," he says. "You say that was a great period in your life, but it's a big world and at some point you have to find a way to slip back into it and try and be a happy citizen. What I want is a boyfriend I love, a job that doesn't make me crazy, and good friends."

But normalcy, of course, is problematic for gay America. The "normalcy" of gay life before AIDS is something few can contemplate and fewer remember. There are ways (the circuit parties) in which that history is repeated as farce, and ways (like the small revival of sex clubs) in which it is repeated as tragedy. But the solidarity of the plague years is becoming harder and harder to sustain. For the first time, serious resentment is brewing among HIV-positive men about the way in which AIDS has slowly retreated from the forefront of gay politics. And among the longest-term survivors, there is a depressing sense that a whole new generation of post-AIDS gay men have no understanding of the profundity with which their own lives have become suffused.

Take John Dugdale, a thirty-six-year-old photographer living in New York, tall and chiseled, with dark hair and even darker eyes. But when Dugdale looks at you these days, he merely looks toward you. Some time ago, he became almost blind from an AIDS-related virus. He took the new drugs, experienced euphoria as they obliterated the virus from his blood, crashed again a few months later as the virus returned, then experienced yet another high as his health improved once more. He knows his own survival is tenuous and is depressed by the shallowness of a culture that is clearly beginning to move on. As we chatted recently, he recalled with not a little edge a particular moment at the Black Party in New York earlier this year. It concerned a friend of his with AIDS, a bodybuilder who still prized himself on being able to consort with the best of the competition. There was one problem: he had lesions on his body, lesions he refused to have treated. And when he took his shirt off that night to dance with the throng, the lesions were all too visible. Not so long ago, they might have been viewed as war medals. Now, they're something different. "This guy came up to him," Dugdale recalled, "and said: 'Would you please put your shirt on? You're ruining it for everybody else.'"

For some, of course, the ebbing of AIDS could mean that the old divisions between HIV-positive and HIV-negative men could heal. With a less catastrophic diagnosis, the difference in life span—and self-definition—between negative and positive men might narrow. But there is also another possibility: that with a smaller and smaller percentage of gay men having HIV, the isolation of those infected will actually increase, and that those with full-blown AIDS could feel more intensely alone than before.

Even at the showing of the AIDS Memorial Quilt in Washington this year, the divides were subtly present. There were those who went to see the quilt itself or went to the candlelight vigil and those who went only to the many parties that filled the weekend. (In truth, many went to all.) And the internal tensions were palpable. It is as if many HIV-positive men have emerged from transformingly deep spiritual experiences only to reenter a culture that seems, at least in part, to be returning to the superficial. And the lifting of the veil of terror has served, paradoxically, only to isolate them still further in a subculture that has less time and less energy to sympathize or understand. The good news from the laboratory has robbed them not simply of the drama and intensity of their existence but also of the recognition of that drama and intensity. And even among their own kind.

VI

A difference between the end of AIDS and the end of many other plagues: for the first time in history, a large proportion of the survivors will not simply be those who escaped infection, or were immune to the virus, but those who contracted the illness, contemplated their own deaths, and still survived. If for some this leads to bitterness, for others it suggests something else entirely. It is not so much survivor guilt as survivor responsibility. It is the view of the world that comes from having confronted and defeated the most terrifying prospect imaginable and having survived. It is a view of the world that has encompassed the darkest possibilities for homosexual—and heterosexual—existence and now envisions the opposite: the chance that such categories could be set aside, that the humanity of each could inform the humanity of the other.

Greg Scott is a Washingtonian I've known for years. We're both in our early thirties, and as the plague has unfolded over the last decade it has affected us in different ways. Greg is from a traditional southern family, and when he was thrown out of the Navy for being a homosexual, he threw himself into years of furious activism. When I first came to know him, he was renowned in D.C. for hanging around bars and staring wildly at passersby as a prelude to either lecturing or seducing them. For a short period of time, he would follow me around D.C. screaming, "Collaborator!" to punish me for the sin of writing or voicing politically incorrect views. But we both knew, at some level, that we were in the epidemic together, and so when I saw him slowly declining over the last two years, I felt a part of myself declining as well. My friend Pat once described Greg as "hanging by the same length of rope" as he was, so for some time I half expected to see Greg's face in the crowded obituary columns of the local gay paper along with the dozens of other faces I had known or seen over the years. When I wrote an op-ed piece a year ago hailing the latest breakthroughs in AIDS research, Greg came up to me in a bar and regaled me. "This is not a survivable disease!" he yelled over the music. "What do you know about it, anyway?"

So I learned to avoid Greg as far as I could. I never relished our meetings. Since he didn't know I was positive, too, our conversations had this false air about them. The solidarity I felt was one I could not fully express, and it ate away at me. I occasionally spotted him walking his dog in the neighborhood, his body, always thin, now skeletal, his large, staring eyes disfigured by lesions, his gait that of a sixty-year-old. When my parents visited, I pointed him out from a distance on the street, in some doomed attempt to help them understand: "See. That's my friend Greg." Read: "See. That's my friend Greg. Do you see what this is doing to us?" Last fall, Greg was taking morphine twice a day. He was on a regimen of sixty pills a day and was virtually bedridden. So when I caught sight of him five months ago, I literally jumped.

I had grown used to the shock of seeing someone I knew suddenly age twenty or thirty years in a few months; now I had to adjust to the reverse. People I had seen hobbling along, their cheekbones poking out of their skin, their eyes deadened and looking down, were suddenly restored into some strange spectacle of health, gazing around as amazed as I was to see them alive. Or you'd see them in the gym, skin infections still lingering, but their muscles slowly growing back, their skull-faces beginning to put on some newly acquired flesh. This is what Greg now looked like, his round blue eyes almost tiny in his wide, pudgy face, his frame larger than I remembered it: bulky, lumbering, heavy.

In one of those bizarre coincidences, I bumped into him the day I quit my job as editor of *The New Republic*. He was one of the first people I was able to tell, and from the minute I spoke to him, I could tell he was changed. The anger was somehow gone; a calm had replaced it. He seemed to understand intuitively why I might want to take time to rethink my life. As we parted, we hugged awkwardly. This was a new kind of solidarity—not one of painful necessity, but of something far more elusive. Hope, perhaps? Or merely the shared memory of hopelessness?

Since then, I've become used to Greg's describing the contours of what he calls his "second life." And he describes its emergence in a way that is shared by more people than just him. The successive physical and material losses of his illness stripped him, he recalls, of everything he once had, and allowed him, in a way that's unique to the terminally ill, to rebuild himself from scratch. "There were times I was willing to accept that it was over," he says. "But things were never fully tied up. There were too many things I had done wrong, things I wanted to amend, things I still wanted to do. I was hanging on tenaciously out of some moral judgment of myself because I knew I hadn't got it right the first time."

In his progressive illness, Greg had lost first his energy, then his ability to digest food, then his job, then his best friend, and then most of his possessions, as he sold them off to pay for medications. But he hung on. "In the early days," he remembers, "I couldn't imagine going through all that to stay alive. My friend Dennis would say that I'd never go that far. But then he died. Looking back, it's absurd the lengths I went to. I'd never realized I cared so much about myself." (Greg's story brings to mind that of another friend: his illness finally threatened his sight, and he had to decide whether to pursue a treatment that involved an injection of a liquid directly into the eyeball. In other words, he had to watch as the needle came closer and closer and finally penetrated his eye. I remember asking him how on Earth he could go through with it. "But I want to see," he told me.)

"When you're in bed all day, you're forced to consider what really matters to you," Greg elaborates. "When the most important thing you do in a day is your bowel movement, you learn to value every single source of energy. You go into yourself and you feel different from other people, permanently different." Some gains are subtle. "It sparked a new relationship with my grandmother. Like me, she was suddenly finding she couldn't drive her car anymore, so we bonded in a way we'd never bonded before. You suddenly see how people are valuable. I mean, if you're healthy, who has time for this old lady? And suddenly this old lady and I have so much in common. And I still have that. That's a gain. I have an appreciation and love for her that I never fully had before." Some gains are even more profound. "My grandfather would say, 'You don't squeak under the bottom wire unless you're meant to.' And I feel that there's this enormous responsibility on me that I've never felt before. And it's a pleasant responsibility. I mean, lay it on me."

"Responsibility" is, perhaps, an unusual word for Greg to be using, and until AIDS it was not one usually associated with homosexuality. Before AIDS, gay life—rightly or wrongly—was identified with freedom from responsibility, rather than with its opposite. Gay liberation was most commonly understood as liberation from the constraints of traditional norms, almost a dispensation that permitted homosexuals the absence of responsibility in return for an acquiescence in second-class citizenship. This was the Faustian bargain of the pre-AIDS closet: straights gave homosexuals a certain amount of freedom; in return, homosexuals gave away their self-respect. But with AIDS, responsibility became a central, imposing feature of gay life. Without it, lovers would die alone or without proper care. Without it, friends would contract a fatal disease because of lack of education. Without it, nothing would be done to stem the epidemic's wrath. In some ways, even the seemingly irresponsible outrages of ACT UP were the ultimate act of responsibility. They came from a conviction that someone had to lead, to connect the ghetto to the center of the country, because it was only by such a connection that the ghetto could be saved.

And in the experience of plague, what Greg felt on a personal level was repeated thousands of times. People who thought they didn't care for one another found that they could. Relationships that had no social support were found to be as strong as any heterosexual marriage. Men who had long since gotten used to throwing their own lives away were confronted with the possibility that they actually did care about themselves and wanted to survive and failed to see themselves as somehow inferior to their heterosexual peers. A culture that had been based in some measure on desire became a culture rooted in strength. Of course, not everyone experienced such epiphanies. Some cracked; others died bitter or alone. Many failed to confront the families and workplaces and churches in ways that would have helped provide the capacity to survive. But many others did. And what didn't destroy them made them only more resistant to condescension.

And as gay culture shifted in this way, so did gay politics. The radicalism of ACT UP segued into the radicalism of homosexuals in the military and same-sex marriage. From chipping away at the edges of heterosexual acceptance, suddenly the central ramparts were breached. Once gay men had experienced beyond any doubt the fiber of real responsibility—the responsibility for life and death, for themselves and others—more and more found it impossible to acquiesce in second-class lives. They demanded full recognition of their service to their country, and equal treatment under the law for the relationships they had cherished and sustained in the teeth of such terror. AIDS wasn't the only thing that created this transformation of gay demands, but it was surely linked to them at a deep psychological level.

Plagues and wars do this to people. They force them to ask more funda-mental questions of who they are and what they want. Out of the First World War came women's equality. Out of the second came the welfare state. Out of the Holocaust came the state of Israel. Out of cathartic necessity and loss and endurance comes, at least for a while, a desire to turn these things into some-thing constructive, to appease the trauma by some tangible residue that can give meaning and dignity to what has happened. Hovering behind the politics of homosexuality in the midst of AIDS and after AIDS is the question of what will actually be purchased from the horror. What exactly, after all, did a third of a million Americans die for? If not their fundamental equality, then what?

VII

Last, the things I want to remember.

In the past six months, I have begun to believe I will live a normal life. By "normal," of course, I don't mean without complications. I take twenty-three pills a day—large cold pills I keep in the refrigerator, pills that, until very recently, made me sick and tired in the late afternoon. But normal in the sense that mortality, or at least the insistence of mortality, doesn't hold my face to the wall every day. I mean I live with the expectation that life is not immediately fragile; that if I push it, it will not break.

It is a strange feeling, this, and a little hard to communicate. When you have spent several years girding yourself for the possibility of death, it is not so easy to gird yourself instead for the possibility of life. What you expect to greet with the euphoria of victory comes instead like the slow withdrawal of an excuse. And you resist it. The intensity with which you had learned to approach each day turns into a banality, a banality that refuses to understand or even appreciate the experience you have just gone through.

Of course, I remember feeling this banality before and I remember the day it ended. I remember the doctor offering me a couple of pieces of candy, before we walked back into his office and he fumbled a way of telling me I was HIV-positive. I've thought about that moment a lot in the past few months. When my doctor called recently to tell me that my viral load was now unde-tectable, part of me wanted to feel as if that first moment of mortality had been erased. But, of course, that moment can never be erased. And not simply because I cannot dare hope that one day the virus might be wiped completely from my system, but because some experiences can never be erased. Blurred, perhaps, and distanced, but never gone for good. And, in fact, beneath the sudden exhilaration, part of me also wants to keep the moment alive, since it allowed me to see things that I had never been able to see before.

I saw, to begin with, that I was still ashamed. Even then—even in me, someone who had thought and worked and struggled to banish the stigma and the guilt and the fear of my homosexuality—I instinctively interpreted this illness as something that I deserved. Its arrival obliterated all the carefully constructed confidence in my own self-worth. It showed me in a flash how so much of that achievement had been illusory—how, in a pinch, I still loathed and feared an inextricable part of who I was.

The diagnosis was so easily analogized to my sexuality not simply because of how I got it but also because it was so confoundingly elusive. I felt no sickness. I had no symptoms. There was nothing tangible against which I could fight—no perceptible, physical ailment that medicine could treat. So it seemed less like an illness than like some amorphous, if devastating, condition of life. Suddenly it existed as my homosexuality had always existed, as something no one from the outside could glean, something I alone could know and something that always promised a future calamity.

For days after my diagnosis, I went through periodic, involuntary shaking spasms. My head literally sank onto my chest; I found it hard to look up or see where I was going. The fear of death and sense of failure—and the knowledge that there was nothing I could do to escape this awareness—kept me staring at the sidewalk. At night, asleep, exhaustion gave way to anxiety as panic woke me up. And then, one morning, a couple of weeks later, after walking with a friend to get some coffee and muffins for breakfast, I realized in the first few sips of coffee that for a few short seconds of physical pleasure I had actually forgotten what had just happened to me. I realized then that it was going to be possible to forget, that the human mind could find a way to absorb the knowledge that we are going to die and yet continue to live as if we are not. I experienced in some awful, concentrated fashion what I used to take for granted.

From then on, I suppose, I began the journey back. I realized that my diagnosis was no different in kind from the diagnosis every mortal being lives with—only different in degree. By larger and larger measures, I began to see the condition not as something constricting, but as something liberating— liberating because it forced me to confront more profoundly than ever before whether or not my sexuality was something shameful (I became convinced that it was not), and liberating because an awareness of the inevitability of death is always the surest way to an awareness of the tangibility of life.

And unlike so many others who are told they are going to die, and so many people who had been told they were HIV-positive before me, I had time and health and life ahead. In one way, as I still lost friend after friend, and as others lived with griefs that would never be expunged, I experienced this with a certain amount of guilt. But also, as someone graced by the awareness of a fatal disease but not of its fatality, a heightened sense of the possibilities of living. I realized I could do what I wanted to do, write what I wanted to write, be with the people I wanted to be with. So I wrote a book with a calm I had never felt before about a truth I had only belatedly come to believe. The date I inscribed in its preface was two years to the day since my diagnosis: a first weapon against the virus and a homage to its powers of persuasion.

And for a precious short time, like so many other positive people, I also sensed that the key to living was not a concentration on fighting the mechanics of the disease (although that was essential) or fighting the mechanics of life (although that is inevitable), but an indifference to both of their imponderables. In order to survive mentally, I had to find a place within myself where plague couldn't get me, where success and failure in such a battle were of equal consequence. This was not an easy task. It required resisting the emotional satisfaction of being cured and the emotional closure of death itself. But in that, of course, it resembled merely what we all go through every day. Living, I discovered for the second, but really the first, time, is not about resolution; it is about the place where plague can't get you.

Only once or twice did I find that place, but now I live in the knowledge of its existence.

So will an entire generation.

My America

November 24, 1996 | *THE SUNDAY TIMES*

———————

My old colleague, the legendary British journalist and drunk Henry Fairlie, had a favorite story about his long, lascivious love affair with America. He was walking down a suburban street one afternoon in a suit and tie, passing familiar rows of detached middle-American dwellings and lush, green Washington lawns. In the distance a small boy—aged perhaps six or seven—was riding his bicycle toward him.

And in a few minutes, as their paths crossed on the pavement, the small boy looked up at Henry and said, with no hesitation or particular affectation: "Hi." As Henry told it, he was so taken aback by this unexpected outburst of familiarity that he found it hard to say anything particularly coherent in return. And by the time he did, the boy was already trundling past him into the distance.

In that exchange, Henry used to reminisce, so much of America was summed up. That distinctive form of American manners, for one thing: a strong blend of careful politeness and easy informality. But beneath that, something far more impressive. It never occurred to that little American boy that he should be silent, or know his place, or defer to his elder. In America, a six-year-old cyclist and a fifty-five-year-old journalist were equals. The democratic essence of America was present there on a quiet street on a lazy summer afternoon.

Henry couldn't have imagined that exchange happening in England—or Europe, for that matter. Perhaps now, as European—and especially British—society has shed some of its more rigid hierarchies, it could. But what thrilled him about that exchange is still a critical part of what makes America an enduringly liberating place. And why so many of us who have come to live

97

here find, perhaps more than most native Americans, a reason to give thanks this Thanksgiving.

When I tuck into the turkey on Thursday, I'll have three things in particular in mind. First, the country's pathological obsession with the present. America is still a country where the past is anathema. Even when Americans are nostalgic, they are nostalgic for a myth of the future. What matters for Americans, in small ways and large, is never where you have come from—but where you are going, what you are doing now, or what you are about to become. In all the years I have lived in America—almost a decade and a half now—it never ceases to amaze me that almost nobody has ever demanded to know by what right I belong here. Almost nobody has asked what school I went to, what my family is like, or what my past contains. (In Britain I was asked those questions on a daily, almost hourly, basis.) Even when I took it on myself to be part of the American debate, nobody ever questioned my credentials for doing so. I don't think that could ever happen in a European context (when there's a gay American editor of *The Spectator*, let me know). If Europeans ever need to know why Ronald Reagan captured such a deep part of the American imagination, this is surely part of the answer. It was his reckless futurism (remember Star Wars and supply-side economics?) and his instinctive, personal generosity.

Second, I'm thankful for the American talent for contradiction. The country that sustained slavery for longer than any other civilized country is also the country that has perhaps struggled more honestly for the notion of racial equality than any other. The country that has a genuine public ethic of classlessness also has the most extreme economic inequality in the developed world. The country that is most obsessed with pressing the edge of modernity also has the oldest intact Constitution in the world. The country that still contains a powerful religious right has also pushed the equality of homosexuals further than ever before in history. A country that cannot officially celebrate Christmas (it would erase the boundary between church and state) is also one of the most deeply religious nations on the planet. Americans have learned how to reconcile the necessary contradictions not simply because their country is physically big enough to contain them, but because it is spiritually big enough to contain them. Americans have learned how to reconcile the necessary contradictions of modern life with a verve and a serenity few others can muster. It is a deeply reassuring achievement.

Third, I'm thankful because America is, above all, a country of primary colors. Sometimes the pictures Americans paint are therefore not as subtle, or as elegant, or even as brilliant as masterpieces elsewhere. But they have a vigor and a simplicity that is often more viscerally alive. Other nations may have become bored with the Enlightenment, or comfortable in postmodern ennui. Americans find such postures irrelevant. Here the advertisements are cruel, the battles are stark, and the sermons are terrifying. And here, more than anywhere else, the most vital of arguments still go on. Does God exist? Are the races equal? Can the genders get along? Americans believe that these debates can never get tired, and that their resolution still matters, because what happens in America still matters in the broader world. At its worst, this can bespeak a kind of arrogance and crudeness. But at its best, it reflects a resilient belief that the great questions can always be reinvented and that the answers are always relevant. In the end, I have come to appreciate this kind of naïvete as a deeper form of sophistication. Even the subtlest of hues, after all, are merely primary colors mixed.

At the end of November each year this restless, contradictory, and simple country finds a way to celebrate itself. The British, as befits a people at ease with themselves, do not have a national day. When the French do, their insecurity shows. Even America, on the Fourth of July, displays a slightly neurotic excess of patriotism. But on Thanksgiving, the Americans resolve the nationalist dilemma. They don't celebrate themselves; they celebrate their good fortune. And every November, as I reflect on a country that can make even an opinionated Englishman feel at home, I know exactly how they feel.

The Princess Bride

September 21, 1997 | *THE NEW REPUBLIC*

F rom the moment she danced with John Travolta, she became an honorary American. It wasn't the kind of thing royalty does, but the kind of thing every young American woman fantasizes about.

In that early act alone, and in countless other gestures in the subsequent years, Diana tapped into those suburban American dreams, and more than fulfilled them. Her appeal was to the masses—women especially. Perhaps that helps explain the extraordinary crowds and impromptu shrines at the British embassy and consulates in America last week. There is nobody except perhaps Ronald Reagan whose death could have prompted such a spontaneous and shocking expression of American grief.

Diana, one now realizes, was a princess in a country where aristocracy remains the object of forbidden fascination, a rebel in a nation dedicated to subversion, a mega-celebrity in a culture that prizes celebrity above all, and a philanthropist in a society where charity is the paramount social virtue. She was an American phenomenon just as surely as she was a British institution.

The wedding began it all—parading every cliché Americans attach to royal tradition. For Americans, whose country began in modernity, the need for such ancient connections, for a history that recedes seamlessly into myth, is overwhelming. So they were glued to the television in the early hours all those sixteen years ago, as they were yesterday, watching the gut-wrenching conclusion. Some would attribute this fascination to traditional American Anglophilia, but something far more interesting was also at work. You can feel it in the way Americans spoke of Diana. They referred to her in a way they never applied to other members of the royal family.

From the beginning, Americans saw her as a clearly modern figure, someone who they not only respected, but envied. The monarchy she represented did not seem some archaic remnant of a lost empire, but a vibrant innovation in the global media age.

When the American networks attempted to bring on commentators on the tragedy, they immediately resorted to Hollywood. Tom Selleck and George Clooney expostulated on the trials of celebrity. Tom Cruise told of being stalked by the same paparazzi in that same Paris tunnel. And, yes, Travolta remembered his moment in history. The stars of Los Angeles saw in Diana a peer, and the tabloids and TV talk shows treated her like a studio star of another era. She appeared on the cover of *People* magazine forty-three times in a mere decade—more than any Hollywood persona. But she was beyond Hollywood's grasp, as surely as she was beyond the palace's.

And this surely was her innovation. Max Weber first distinguished between two types of power—the traditional and the charismatic. The one depended on the trappings of state, of nation, and of history. The other rested purely on the aura of the person in question. In general, these two elements are separate, but occasionally—and memorably—they coincide. They collided with Kennedy, who fashioned a new presidency out of a form of celebrity power. And with Reagan, who learned the art of charisma in the Hollywood that perfected it.

Diana, as an international figure, was also in their league. She needed the traditional monarchy as the august setting for her acting out, and its majesty and tradition provided the essential contrast for her modernity. But she brought to it her own sexual energy and iconic poise.

The result was a new level of cultural power, and helps explain the psychic shock Americans as well as Britons are now experiencing. When the fusion of the traditional and charismatic occurs, and when it is transmitted with unprecedented ferocity by the global media, it shapes the mass consciousness almost subliminally. Many of us saw images of Diana more frequently than our own parents or siblings. She penetrated our lives more fully than many of our friends—and this is as true of Americans, for whom she was a media staple, as of Britons. It is no surprise, then, that her sudden death, multiplied in millions and millions of lives, could generate a response that has verged on mass hysteria. At the British embassy in Washington, the mounds of flowers and votive candles, of almost idolatrous tributes and lugubrious verses, suggested that for Americans, she was their princess too.

When I asked people why they felt the way they did, the responses were typically eclectic. They ranged from the HIV-infected gay man who remembered that first handshake to the black woman who recalled Diana's visits to the American inner city. Others, in her generation particularly, felt numbed. "She was a good person; you could tell that," was one simple explanation. And the effect of the princess reaching across class and nationality and birth to engage the lives of the unfortunate burned itself into the American consciousness.

Americans in particular mourn the felling of a rebel. From the beginning, they saw in Diana a human being trapped in a traditional setting, and egged her on in her journey of self-discovery. The loveless marriage, the rigid protocol, the demands of appearance—all these Americans instinctively suspected. A nation of immigrants, of people who have escaped at some point in their family history from the stifling demands of the Old World, they needed no tutor in the appeal of Diana. They identified effortlessly with her, and longed to set her free.

Her association with Dodi Fayed brought no raised eyebrows on this side of the Atlantic, no snippy disdain for his ethnicity or origins. *People* magazine summed up the sentiment exactly in its headline: "A Guy for Di." She needed a date or, better still, a lover. Americans, after all, wrote the "pursuit of happiness" into their very Declaration of Independence. So they did not fail for a minute to understand the last few years of Diana's life.

And they bonded with her lifestyle. This was a woman, one recalls, who employed a personal trainer and a therapist—and didn't conceal the fact. She took her sons to McDonald's in baseball caps and hugged them in amusement parks. She was a breath of fresh evolved air in an institution that reeked of stale dysfunction. Even her public appearances seemed more in tune with American photo ops than British royal audiences. Her ability to sit down with children, to perch on hospital beds, to shake hands with AIDS patients, to wear her emotions on her sleeve, struck a deep, American chord. Indeed, as the years went by, the unassuming English rosebud increasingly resembled an Oprahfied, American bloom. She spoke of the need for "space and time "; she confessed her feelings on national television; she turned her own illnesses into a crusade for self-help. In all this, she was following an American script, and a highly contemporary one.

Her final role—as international charity doyenne—was also shaped on an American model. Charity has long been a function of the English aristocracy, and, indeed, monarchy. But Diana's fusion of glamour and fashion and charity seemed far closer to the model of American society hostesses than English country wives. And Diana's thinly veiled social liberalism—her comfort among people with AIDS, minorities, gay men, and the disabled—echoed, and indeed surpassed, theirs. That Katharine Graham, the last great Washington hostess and proprietor of *The Washington Post*, was a close friend says a great deal about Diana's membership in a peculiarly American club. And she was a member, not merely a guest.

This is not to say that Diana did not retain her essential British identity. Indeed, what was inspiring about her to many Americanized Brits was how she was able to lend to Britishness a new, and distinctly American, quality. She was, in this sense, a New Brit Princess, not so much hostile to the old order as impatient with it, and prepared to go to war with it if necessary.

In this, Americans were her friends and allies; but the British had the most at stake. For those of us who believe in our native country, and who see what she represented and tried to bring about, her death is particularly heart-wrenching. "I am not a political person," she said in a recent, charitable speech. But, of course, she was. She represented the forces of change against the serried ranks of crusty resistance, and the possibility of personal happiness and integrity in a country that has sacrificed too many people on the fake altars of propriety and duty.

Her funeral, in its majesty and scale and aura, will inevitably be contrasted with Churchill's. But with Churchill, the funeral was a burial of something already gone. Diana's young death points in exactly the opposite direction and is therefore more poignant. In burying Churchill, we buried the past. In burying Diana, in some deep and gnawing way, we have buried a future.

Unsung Heroine

September 27, 1998 | *THE NEW YORK TIMES*

Forget the pro-Clinton backlash. Isn't it past time for a pro-Monica backlash? Throughout the hideous Clinton soap opera, no one has had to endure so much for so long as the twenty-five-year-old from Beverly Hills. Ms. Lewinsky has been let down by her lover, her best friend, her lawyers, her advisers, and by the public.

She has seen the most intimate details of her private life published by virtually every newspaper in the world, has had her mental fitness questioned by the president and every half-baked pop psychologist who can make it onto cable television; she has had her clothing turned into Jay Leno jokes and her weight inspected with all the delicacy one normally expects from the supermarket tabloids. And all the while, she has been essentially under house arrest, her life suspended indefinitely in midair. For all this, she has been rewarded with a public approval rating barely distinguishable from Mike Tyson's.

Sexism, it seems, rules. In the public's mind, Mr. Clinton is a foolish man who cannot control his libido. But Ms. Lewinsky is a tramp, for whom no empathy is possible. Mr. Clinton may be an adulterer, but adulterers can be forgiven. Not so the foul temptress, even when she's less than half the man's age. Mr. Clinton, thanks to the release of his videotaped testimony, has been awarded with a back eddy of sympathy for having his sex life turned into a news event. But Ms. Lewinsky, it seems, asked for it.

Yet whose private life, one wonders, has been more brutally exposed in all this? Who was forced to spend days and days in front of grand-jury interrogators and who voluntarily spent four hours? And who chose public life in the first place? Mr. Clinton or Ms. Lewinsky?

In all this, Ms. Lewinsky has few allies. Unlike Paula Jones, she receives no support from the right. For enjoying and owning her sexuality, Ms. Lewinsky is a pariah among conservatives. And she can expect no support from liberal feminists. Suddenly, in the third wave of victimless feminism, the intern has to stand up for herself. This was not, these feminists now argue, a case of sexual exploitation. It was an example of a young woman deploying her sexual skills to advance her career. Postfeminist Katie Roiphe derided any notion that Ms. Lewinsky was ever "an innocent used for sexual purposes."

Excuse me? If this wasn't a case of exploitation, then what is? Is there any greater power differential than that between a twenty-two-year-old intern and the most powerful man on Earth? If this was not sexual exploitation, then sexual exploitation simply does not exist. Sometimes, even in the brave new world of postfeminism, victimization still happens. And, at the hands of Bill Clinton, Monica Lewinsky was a sexual and emotional victim.

It also seems to me that Ms. Lewinsky, alone among the major characters, has behaved for the most part decently through this saga. Apart from a few understandable tantrums, she was relatively understanding. Yes, she told several friends, but she was having an affair with the president, for goodness' sake!

Yes, she asked for a good job in New York. But that was after she had been fired for her love affair, exiled to a job she hated, and left with her phone calls unreturned. And even then, she never explicitly threatened to blackmail the president or go to the press. Her direst threat was to tell her own mother! Even now, she has kept an honorable silence, when the temptation to defend herself must be enormous.

For a very long time, she did all she could to avoid betraying her lover, even to the point of signing an affidavit that denied the affair. Once cornered, she resolved to tell the whole truth. The most stunning aspect of the Starr report is how far this young woman was prepared to go to abide by the law, even to the extent of opening herself up to grotesque public scrutiny. What a contrast with the president. If this morality tale is essentially about honesty, then Ms. Lewinsky is clearly its heroine.

It says something about the president's seductive narcissism that, even now, he has made this affair about himself, and somehow become the victim. But Monica Lewinsky uniquely deserves that honor. Exploited by a lover, betrayed by a friend, hounded by inquisitors, and violated by the media, she has paid far more than a reasonable price for the sin of misplaced, youthful love. She surely deserves much better. From all of us.

Going Down Screaming

October 11, 1998 | *THE NEW YORK TIMES*

I can't remember now at which point during the Starr report I stopped reading. Maybe it was the sudden prim reminder that "the President's wife" was out of the country during one of President Clinton's hallway trysts. Or the superfluously wounding inference that the president was considering leaving his wife after his second term. Or the inclusion of the date for one of the president's liaisons: Easter Sunday. Or any one of the points when it simply became obvious that the narrative, compelling and lucid as it was, seemed to be building a case not so much for the president's public, legal impropriety but for a private, moral iniquity. And I stopped reading not because I sympathize with President Clinton's repeated public lies, or his abuse of power and of his office. (I still think he should resign.) Nor because I am instinctively a liberal. I stopped reading at some point because it became depressingly clear that the Starr report and its aftermath represents not simply a case study in what has gone wrong with an American presidency, but also a case study in what has gone wrong with American conservatism.

To be sure, Bill Clinton goaded the independent counsel into some of this detail by the hairsplitting of his legal defense. But not all of it. And to be sure, Bill Clinton, by his failure to settle, and then to apologize, and then to tell the truth, was responsible in the first place for the nine months of trauma. But again, not entirely. For Bill Clinton was responsible for none of the prurient, lip-pursing moralism of the report, nor for the subsequent, egregious outspilling of grand-jury testimony. Proof of perjury or obstruction of justice required none of this, as most Americans immediately understood. This moral obsessiveness was the creation of Kenneth Starr and something far larger than Kenneth Starr. It was the creation of a conservatism become puritanism, a conservatism that has long lost sight of the principles of privacy and restraint, modesty and constitutionalism, which used to be its hallmarks.

This scolding, moralizing conservatism is one with a lineage; it is the construction of a cadre of influential intellectuals who bear as much responsibility as anybody for the constitutional and cultural damage this moment may have already wrought. And they will bear an even greater responsibility if the ultimate victim of this spectacle is the reputation and future of conservatism itself.

The Lewinsky Kulturkampf, after all, did not come out of nowhere. Since the implosion of Reaganism during the administration of George H. W. Bush, and the evaporation of anticommunism with the collapse of the Soviet Union, American conservatism has been in a period of radical intellectual reconstruction. Much of this reconstruction has occurred in journals and magazines and seminars largely unnoticed by the general public, but quite openly and candidly discussed among the conservative intellectual elites. And the dominant ideas that have emerged in the last few years bear only the faintest resemblance to the major themes of the 1980s: economic freedom, smaller government, and personal choice. Although libertarians are certainly numbered among the intellectuals of the right of the late 1990s, they are clearly on the defensive. What is galvanizing the right-wing intelligentsia at century's end is a different kind of conservatism altogether: much less liberal, far less economic, and only nominally skeptical of government power. It is inherently pessimistic—a return to older, conservative themes of cultural decline, moralism, and the need for greater social control. As much European as American in its forebears, this conservatism is not afraid of the state or its power to set a moral tone or coerce a moral order. A mix of big-government conservatism and old-fashioned puritanism, this new orthodoxy was waiting to explode on the political scene when Monica Lewinsky lighted the fuse.

You can see it in the current congressional races. The issues that are driving the Republican base this fall have little to do with economics or politics or national security. They are issues of morals: infidelity and honesty, abortion, family cohesion, and homosexual legitimacy. Much of this, as has been widely reported, is because of the evangelical Protestants who now make up the Republican activist base. Some of it is also because of Bill Clinton, who has done more to give credibility to the far right's conviction about moral collapse than anyone. But this is only half the story. If the remoralization of conservative politics has been fueled by events and by Republican activists, it has also been diligently refueled by conservative thinkers. The new moralism has been enforced with a rigidity that puts old-style leftists to shame. It is an orthodoxy, to put it bluntly, of cultural and moral revolution: a wholesale assault on the beliefs and practices of an entire post-1960s settlement. And, if recent polls hold out, it could be on the verge of coming to power in November.

The centrality of this moralism to the Lewinsky saga was perhaps best put by David Frum, one of the brightest of the young conservative thinkers now writing. "What's at stake in the Lewinsky scandal," Frum wrote candidly in the February 16, 1998, issue of *The Weekly Standard*, a conservative magazine, "is not the right to privacy, but the central dogma of the baby boomers: the belief that sex, so long as it's consensual, ought never to be subject to moral scrutiny at all."

It would be hard to put better what was so surprising, and so dismaying, about the Starr report and the Republican Congress's subsequent behavior. The report was driven, as the Republican leadership seems to be, not merely to prove perjury but to expose immorality. In this universe, privacy is immaterial, hence the gratuitous release of private telephone conversations, private correspondence, and even details of the most private of human feelings. For these conservatives, there is only a right, as Starr revealingly wrote, to a "private family life." A private, nonfamily life is fair game for prosecution and exposure.

No conservative thinker has done more to advance this new moralism than William Kristol, best known for his urbane appearances on *This Week with Sam Donaldson and Cokie Roberts*, and about as close as Washington has to a dean of intellectual conservatism. And no journal has done more to propagate, defend, and advance this version of conservatism than the magazine Kristol edits, *The Weekly Standard*, founded in 1995 by Rupert Murdoch. Most of this year, Kristol and *The Standard* have gleefully egged on Republicans in their moral crusade. As early as May—at a time when it seemed the Clinton-Lewinsky scandal might dissipate—Kristol urged Republican congressional candidates to forget other issues in the fall and campaign solely on the issue of the president's morals. "If [Republicans] do that," he argued, "they will win big in November. And their victory will be more than a rejection of Clinton. It will be a rejection of Clintonism—a rejection of defining the presidency, and our public morality, down."

His magazine has been relentless in presenting the scandal as a moral crisis for the nation. Thanks to the president's affair with Lewinsky, *The Standard*'s writers were finally able to see unreservedly in Clinton what they had desperately tried to see in him from the start, but which Clinton's own conservatism had blurred: the apotheosis of the 1960s. The Clinton White House, in the liberated words of Peter Collier in *The Standard*, is "a place where denatured New Left politics meets denatured New Age therapeutics." In February, *The Standard* put on its cover a cartoon of Clinton-as-satyr on the White House lawn grappling with a nude Paula Jones and a nude Monica Lewinsky, surrounded by other naked women in bushes and on a swing, with the one-word headline "Yow!" Almost one out of two subsequent covers in 1998 have focused on the Lewinsky affair. One of the few breaks from Lewinsky coverage was a September cover article on Clinton's alleged genesis. "1968: A Revolting Generation Thirty Years On," the headline blared. The connection with Clinton was not exactly underplayed.

But perhaps no edition of *The Standard* captured the current state of American conservatism better than the one that came out immediately after the Starr report was made public. Its cover portrayed Starr as Mark McGwire, with the headline: "Starr's Home Run." Inside, page after page of anti-Clinton coverage, anchored by an essay by Kristol advocating a full House vote for impeachment of the president within a month, was followed by a long, surreal article by a reporter attending a four-day World Pornography Conference. Six pages of explicit sex, interspersed with coy condescension, followed. (The cover teased with the headline: "Among the Pornographers.") One of many graphic scenes in the article occurs in a ladies' restroom: "Unprompted, [Dr. Susan Block] removes a rubber phallus from her purse and hikes up [her assistant] LaVonne's dress, baring her derriere. Block paddles it and kisses it while LaVonne coos." The article was so lurid that *The Standard*'s editors prefaced it with a note: "Because of the subject matter, some material in this article is sexually explicit and may offend some readers." The weird porno-puritanism of the Starr report does not exist, it seems, in a vacuum. It comes out of a degenerated conservative political and literary culture.

The only issue to rival Lewinsky for prominence among conservative intel-lectuals in 1998 was homosexuality. But in some ways, this was only apposite. For the new conservatives, the counterattack on homosexual legitimacy is of a piece with the battle against presidential adultery. They see no distinction between an argument for same-sex marriage, for example, and a presidential defense of adultery, because in their eyes, there is no context in which a homosexual relationship can be moral. Homosexuality, for the puritanical conservatives, is not a condition or even a way of life; it is a disease. And again, the intelligentsia led the way—with Kristol at the heart of it.

If most Americans were a little surprised by the religious right's advertising campaign last July in defense of "curing" homosexuals, then they had not been following closely the drift on the intellectual right. As usual, Bill Kristol was at the heart of it. In June 1997, he gave the concluding address at a Washington conservative conference dedicated, as its brochure put it, to exposing homo-sexuality as "the disease that it is." Kristol shared the podium with a variety of clergy members and therapists who advocated a spiritual and psychoanalytic "cure" for homosexuals. One speaker, a priest, described homosexuality as "a way of life that is marked by compulsion, loneliness, depression and disease," comprising a "history-limiting horizon of a sterile worldview divorced from the promise and peril of successor generations." Another speaker decried legal contraception and abortion as the "homosexualization of heterosexual sex," and bemoaned that nonprocreative trends among white Europeans was leading to "race death."

In the broad advertising campaign last summer, sponsored by groups allied with those who organized the D.C. conference, homosexuals were portrayed as sick and in need of therapy. The notion that homosexuality was involun-tary was dismissed, with Starr-like certainty, as a violation of "the truth." The Senate majority leader, Trent Lott, said that homosexuals were guilty not of a public crime, but of a private "sin." Again, *The Standard* had pioneered this politics, routinely decrying any public destigmatization of homosexuals, and calling, in one article in late 1996, for the "reaffirmation by states of a sodomy law" that would imprison gay men for private sex as a counterstrike against the threat of same-sex marriage.

The Weekly Standard's obsession with the Lewinsky scandal and homo-sexuality may seem an odd conjunction of issues, but the joint crusades have uncanny echoes in the halls of Congress. So Representative Bob Barr was the pioneer of the Defense of Marriage Act, and the author of the first resolution to impeach the president. And Trent Lott, while leading the charge against the president's immorality in recent weeks, also ensured that the nomination of James Hormel as US Ambassador to Luxembourg was held up purely because of Hormel's homosexuality. And among the most aggressive supporters of impeachment—the House Judiciary Committee members Charles T. Canady and Bob Inglis, for example—have been the most virulently hostile to gay rights in the current Congress.

But there is one issue above all others at the center of this new conservatism. That issue is not adultery or even homosexuality, although both have come to play a significant part in it. It is abortion. Its importance to the new generation of conservative intellectuals is easily underestimated, and far too easily ascribed simply to the influence of religious activists. In fact, abortion is at the center of current Republican orthodoxy as much because of conservative intellectuals as evangelical activists. Since this may not be self-evident, I'll let one of those intellectuals stress it himself. Here is a writer in *The Standard*, taking a rare break earlier this year from the Lewinsky obsession:

> Republicans talk a lot about being a majority party, about becoming a governing party, about shaping a conservative future. *Roe* and abortion are the test. For if Republicans are incapable of grappling with this moral and political challenge; if they cannot earn a mandate to overturn *Roe* and move toward a postabortion America, then in truth, there will be no conservative future. Other issues are important, to be sure, and a governing party will have to show leadership on those issues as well. But *Roe* is central. . . .

Who wrote this paragraph? Pat Robertson? Patrick Buchanan? Randy Tate? The answer, again, is William Kristol. His seamless merging of the Lewinsky scandal with the right's other social concerns is perhaps what makes him so integral to the new conservatism. Always, however, the key social issue is abortion. He put the argument most revealingly in the February 1997 issue of the neoconservative political monthly *Commentary*. "The truth is," Kristol wrote, "that abortion is today the bloody crossroads of American politics. It is where judicial liberation (from the Constitution), sexual liberation (from traditional mores) and women's liberation (from natural distinctions) come together. It is the focal point for liberalism's simultaneous assault on self-government, morals and nature. So, challenging the judicially imposed regime of abortion-on-demand is key to a conservative reformation in politics, in morals, and in beliefs."

The choice of words is revealing here. Not just politics, a realm conservatives were once comfortable restricting themselves to, but "morals" and "beliefs." And not revolution or reform but "reformation." Kristol's conservatism is happy with the vocabulary of religious war. Earlier this year, Kristol argued that "abortion is likely to emerge as the central issue in the Presidential campaign of 2000."

In the 1980s, the outlawing of abortion was framed in the somewhat liberal terms of saving human life and protecting human rights. And that is why a smattering of left-leaning intellectuals also signed on as antiabortion advocates. But in the 1990s, the conservative emphasis has changed. Now the banning of abortion is linked primarily to an attack on the Supreme Court's judicial activism in other areas as well (prayer in schools, women's equality, and gay rights foremost among them) and to the more general sexual liberty of the society as a whole. Abortion is central to a reassertion of what Kristol called "traditional mores" and of "natural distinctions" between the sexes. It is not unrelated to the Lewinsky obsession and the antigay crusade. In fact, it is the anchor of both.

Bizarrely enough, abortion has even come to play a role in the reformulation of Republican foreign policy. After all, the main obstacle to Republican financing of the United Nations has not been that body's wasteful bureaucracy, or even the United Nations' infringement of American sovereignty, but rather its support of birth-control initiatives in the developing world. And the critical issue that seems to have tilted the right toward rampant hostility to China has not so much been Beijing's Communist regime or its militarism but Beijing's specifically anti-Christian bent.

In a long article two years ago in *Foreign Affairs* that Kristol cowrote with another *Standard* regular, Robert Kagan, the connection between domestic puritanism and foreign-policy interventionism was made explicit: "The remoralization of America at home," Kristol and Kagan wrote, "ultimately requires the remoralization of American foreign policy."

China has been the case study, becoming the overwhelming foreign-policy obsession of the fin-de-siècle right. Kristol and *The Standard* have long advocated a policy of containment and economic sanctions against China almost identical to the one fashioned for the Soviet Union for several decades. Kristol has also argued for a large increase in defense spending and a policy of international isolation of the Chinese. The posture against China is not related to Beijing's puny military power as such, but to its moral indecency. Gone is the realism that was once the hallmark of conservative foreign policy.

Kristol's "remoralization" model here might seem, on first glance, to be Ronald Reagan. But it is interesting to see the differences between the Reaganism of the 1980s and Kristolism of the late 1990s. The historical context is the most striking contrast. Reagan tackled a monolithic, militarized Soviet state with global ambitions, military occupation of half of Europe and Central Asia, and an arsenal immensely larger than China's is today. Although Reagan didn't hesitate to talk about Soviet communism in moral terms, he was also a foreign-policy realist who deftly changed tack when he saw that real change had occurred within the Soviet bloc. Reagan's foreign-policy moralism was also, with regard to China, far less strident than with regard to the Soviet Union, precisely because Beijing had never entertained the global ambitions of Moscow, and also because he recognized the economic and social freedoms that were even then making China a vastly different country—and a far more complex diplomatic problem—than the Soviet Union.

In the same way, it's worth remembering that Reagan's domestic moralism was also of a very different variety from that of today's conservatives. Rather than sternly criticizing liberal mores, Reagan tended to ignore them, preferring to praise conservative ones, finding in small human examples object lessons of traditional virtue. It was occasionally a goofy moralism, but also a sunny one. Rather than pinpoint moral demons, Reagan would point out moral heroes in the gallery of the Congress during his State of the Union addresses. Whereas conservatives in the 1990s obsessed about Clinton's draft dodging, Reagan went to Normandy to eulogize a different kind of ethic. It is a telling contrast.

Reagan's view of America was never bleak, and he was careful to stay away from the front lines of the cultural wars. Although he was nominally antiabortion, for example, he never attended an antiabortion rally. Moralism, for him, was always a vague but essentially positive construct. As he was a divorced man who rarely went to church, this was a fittingly modest—and conservative—approach to the world. And it was far more in touch with the center of American culture.

Kristol's version of Reaganism, in other words, is an oddly displaced one. It transfers concepts—like containment—to a historical context in which they no longer make sense, and a sensibility—moralism—in a way that inverts its original spirit. Reagan's heirs of the 1990s have turned the man into an ism, his sense of right into orthodoxy, his smile into a scowl.

And they have done so with a vehemence and activism that can only be called characterologically leftist. Of course, because so many of the neoconservatives once hailed from the left, this imprint is unsurprising. It manifests itself in the structures of old-left activity: the magazines and journals dedicated to the correct line; the messianic faith in the capacity of politics to transform the world; the infighting, and the incessant definition and redefinition of ideology. One of the best descriptions of this evolution actually occurred in *The Standard*, expressed by a conservative writer with a bent for subtlety, David Brooks. It is from an article on "Rich Republicans," a group despised by the troops of the far right and treated with thinly veiled disdain by the magazine. But Brooks put his finger on a critical shift in conservatism in a rare moment of *Standard* self-awareness:

> It used to be liberals who railed against the complacency of the American electorate, but now it's conservatives who long to see a little more mass outrage. It used to be liberals who based their politics on abstract notions more than concrete realities, but now it's conservatives who like to emphasize that ideas have consequences. It used to be liberal intellectuals who longed for the drama and turmoil that put them center stage, but now the habits of the New Class, both good and bad, have migrated rightward.

That is putting it mildly.

But if you want to go to the spiritual nerve center of the new conservatism, you have to dig deeper than the weekly journalism of *The Standard*, and examine the other major new conservative journal of the 1990s, *First Things*. Few people outside the conservative new class will have heard of the monthly, which is devoted to matters of politics, culture, and religion, and edited by a former left-wing activist turned Catholic neoconservative priest, Rev. Richard John Neuhaus. But like *The Standard*, it is very much of its time, and like *The Standard*, too, it is deeply influential. Its editorial board includes respected scholars of the communitarian right, like George Weigel, Mary Ann Glendon, and Michael Novak; the neoconservative doyenne, Midge Decter, is also on the board.

Reading through the pages of *First Things*, one begins to understand why conservatism as a political movement has become, in many ways, a somewhat strained version of a neoreligious revival. A key phalanx of its intellectual gurus has, in fact, abandoned the secular underpinnings of the American constitutional experiment as a whole. These writers have been dubbed "theo-conservatives," because of their religious bent. And, indeed, the intellectual basis on which their politics is built is a radically theocratic reinterpretation of the Constitution itself.

"The great majority of those who signed the Declaration [of Independence]," Neuhaus wrote in the November 1997 edition of *First Things*, "and of those who wrote and ratified the Constitution thought themselves to be orthodox Christians, typically of Calvinist leanings. It never entered their heads that in supporting this new order they were signing on to a minimalist creed incompatible with their Christian profession."

So the distinction between church and state, in Neuhaus's mind, has been vastly overplayed. All that the Constitution instituted, he would argue, was that no single religious group would become the official religion of the government. The Constitution certainly did not imply that Christianity would be forbidden to dominate the public ethos and institutions of American government.

That same order should, according to Neuhaus, apply today. For the theo-conservatives, the secular neutrality of modern American law and government is, in fact, no neutrality at all, but the willful imposition by liberal elites of what Neuhaus has dubbed "secular monism." Neuhaus has no compunction in arguing that government itself—and its constitutional instrument, the Supreme Court—should uphold as public policy and law the articles of faith of orthodox Christians. The current secular order, he maintains, amounts to "the exclusion of the deepest convictions of most Americans from our politics and law"—what Neuhaus calls "perverse pluralism."

What of non-Christian minorities in this divinely sanctioned order? What of those who do not, for example, adhere to Kenneth Starr's view of "private family life," or who do not even adhere to Christianity? Neuhaus insists that he doesn't want "a sacred public square, but a civil public square." Nevertheless, his main guarantee that non-Christian minorities would not be excluded from power is that Christians themselves would be urged to exercise "renewed opposition to every form of invidious prejudice or discrimination." The guarantee of minority freedom, in other words, would be majority benevolence. It is perhaps unsurprising that when Neuhaus gathered a group of public thinkers and ministers to endorse a statement reflecting this orthodoxy, in October 1997, there were no Jews among the signers.

It is also unsurprising that the object of this group of thinkers' deepest animosity is the current Supreme Court, the critical enforcer of what the magazine has dubbed "thinly disguised totalitarianism." The Court's deference to cultural pluralism and its defense of individual conscience and a right to privacy against communal and religious authority is anathema to the theo-conservatives. But even the most dogged critics of the theo-conservatives failed to anticipate the lengths to which they would go in pressing their case. In what became an infamous ideological fracas two years ago, *First Things* actually argued for seditious activities on the part of conservative Christians "ranging from noncompliance to civil disobedience to morally justified revolution" against what it called, with echoes of the New Left, the "morally illegitimate" American "regime."

The critical backdrop to this, of course, is the intellectual right's conception of the continued ascendancy of sixties liberalism. The pages of *The Standard* and *First Things* are crammed with horror at the decline of American politics and culture into nihilism, self-indulgence, and rampant liberal individualism. In this picture of moral chaos, there is little space for nuance. So Bill Clinton, arguably the most conservative Democratic president since Truman, becomes, for these conservatives, the apex of 1960s liberalism. The fact that he balanced the budget, signed welfare-reform legislation, has shredded many civil liberties in the war against terrorism, is in favor of the death penalty, and signed the Defense of Marriage Act is immaterial to his conservative enemies. For the model of cultural collapse to work, Clinton must represent its nadir.

In the same way, the decade of the 1990s, which has seen cultural and social conservatism spread throughout the middle classes, and Republican control of House and Senate, is, to these intellectuals, a decade of unabashed liberal hegemony. The country may seem quiescent, even conservative, but a radical liberal takeover is still in full swing. Here is the novelist Mark Helprin, former speech writer for Bob Dole and darling of the *Wall Street Journal* op-ed page, on the necessity for full-scale cultural war at the end of the century. Writing in *Commentary* last winter, he called the Democrats "proponents of a revolution in American life in which the tough talk came in the 60's and the sweet talk comes now."

But though the left revolution may be swathed in positiveness and pleasantries, it is a revolution nonetheless. It is a revolution in which individual rights have become group rights, in which responsibility has become entitlement, marriage has become divorce, birth has become abortion, medicine has become euthanasia, homosexuality is a norm, murder is neither a surprise nor necessarily punishable, pornography is piped into almost every home, gambling is legal, drugs are rife, students think Alaska is an island south of Los Angeles, and mothers of small children are sent off to war with great fanfare and pride.

By any measure, this is an extraordinary outpouring of anxiety. It is also, in almost all of its particulars, false. To take a few examples: Helprin claims that murder is neither a surprise nor necessarily punishable at the end of the century. Yet in the 1990s murder rates have been dropping precipitously and the prison population and execution rate are at record highs. Helprin claims drugs are rife. Yet drug use is far below the levels of two decades ago. He says that responsibility has become entitlement. Yet a Democratic president recently ended the federal welfare entitlement and welfare rolls have been free-falling nationwide. He argues that marriage has become divorce. Yet again, divorce rates have been steadily dropping for a decade. He says that birth has become abortion. And yet abortion rates are now at their lowest since 1975. One begins to wonder what country Helprin is living in.

Indeed, it seems at times as if conservatives in the last few years have been unable to take yes for an answer. As the country becomes more conservative, the right sees liberalism everywhere. It is almost as if the habits of beleaguerment have completely blinded conservative intellectuals to their own success. They need the adrenaline rush of persecution and the thrill of ideological battle. So if the enemy doesn't exist, they need to invent one, by concocting ever more fanciful conspiracies of the left, by fatally misreading the character and politics of Bill Clinton, by constructing a Manichaean cultural universe where good and bad are always inseparable from right and left and where politics is always a war and never a conversation. And so an era of peace and prosperity and conservative cultural values has been transformed in their eyes into a liberal hell. These conservatives have become like Japanese soldiers on a distant island who don't realize the war is over. And even when they're told, they disbelieve it, because they need the war, even if the war itself has no reality except in the prose of Mark Helprin.

If one man alone could personify this hysterical pessimism about America, it would have to be Robert Bork. There are perhaps few more tragic examples of the degeneration of conservatism into puritanism than this once-piercing intellectual. Not so long ago, Bork was a pillar of conservative intellectual rigor and elegance. To be sure, his constitutional views placed him well outside the mainstream of liberal legal discourse, but even his enemies credited him with philosophical consistency, a sometimes tart and witty pen, and a brilliant legal mind. He was famously subjected to one of the most scurrilous attempts to smear a Supreme Court nominee in recent history. (For the record, I supported Bork's nomination and wrote one of the first articles attacking his opponents for extremism and inaccuracy.)

But even in the wake of that inevitably embittering experience, Bork kept his cool. His memoir-cum-essay after the event, *The Tempting of America*, was a restrained, sometimes-funny, always-compelling defense of extreme judicial passivity in constitutional law. In that book, he was firm even with the ideologues of his own side, warning conservatives not to respond to liberals in kind, nor to appoint an ideologically conservative judiciary, which would be just as activist as the alternative. "Conservatives," he wrote, "who now, by and large, want neutral judges, may decide to join the game and seek activist judges with conservative views. Should that come to pass, those who have tempted the courts to political judging will have gained nothing for themselves but will have destroyed a great and essential institution."

Not many people outside conservative activist circles seem to have read Bork's latest book, published in 1996, but it became a *New York Times* best seller on the strength of its sales to conservative book clubs alone. It was called *Slouching towards Gomorrah*. In it, Bork describes contemporary America as a hellish "moral chaos," "punctuated by spasms of violence and eroticism." He predicts "the coming of a new Dark Ages." Much of this, he argues, is the product of modern liberalism, which has destroyed constitutional democracy by fomenting radical individualism and egalitarianism. Far from being in a conservative era, today's America, according to Bork, is dominated by the left, which has no viable opposition: "There is no group of comparable size and influence to balance the extremists of modern liberalism, no 'right' that has a similarly destructive program in mind."

The only hope, Bork posits, is "the rise of an energetic, optimistic and politically sophisticated religious conservatism." Thus the prophet of judicial restraint puts his weight behind the untrammeled religious right, just as surely as Kristol and Neuhaus.

The extremity of Bork's oratory is matched only by the simplicity of his argument. He makes almost no distinctions between the Clintonian liberalism of the 1990s and the radicalism of the 1960s. It is, for Bork, all of a piece. A president whose economic policy is designed to please bond traders, who bombs Sudan and Afghanistan without warning, and who declares that the era of big government is over is simply a cover for liberal radicalism. And the agenda is terrifying: "Modern liberalism," Bork avers, "the descendant and spiritual heir of the New Left, is what fascism looks like when it has captured significant institutions, most notably the universities, but has no possibility of becoming a mass movement or of gaining power over government or the broader society through force or the threat of force." The Clintons, it seems, are Nazis manqués.

One pillar of Bork's case is that liberalism cannot win democratically, so it uses the courts and the executive to flout the popular will. And yet, at the same time, the people, in Bork's view, are depraved as well, spawning a popular culture that is in "a free fall, with the bottom not yet in sight." Indeed, Bork's book was an early indicator of a new theme among conservatives: not simply a hatred of liberal elites, but a contempt for the mass of Americans. Such disdain, of course, has come to a head during the Lewinsky affair. As public indifference to the scandal has continued, and as Clinton's approval ratings have remained buoyant despite a pitiless series of embarrassments, the new conservatives have had little alternative but to blame Americans for their lack of judgment.

Hence the title of William Bennett's latest book, *The Death of Outrage*. Hence the religious-right icon James Dobson's recent statement of disappointment in the American people in a letter to his group, Focus on the Family. "What has alarmed me throughout this episode," Dobson wrote, "has been the willingness of my fellow citizens to rationalize the President's behavior even as they suspected, and later knew, he was lying. I am left to conclude that our greatest problem is not in the Oval Office. It is with the people of this land."

Once upon a time, this kind of distaste for America was the preserve of liberals and leftists who made up what was called the Blame America First crowd. Today's conservatives have added a new twist to this. They are in danger of becoming the Blame Americans First crowd. Bork is particularly caustic in this regard. Here is his assessment of popular culture at the end of the century: "What America increasingly produces and distributes is now propaganda for every perversion and obscenity imaginable. If many of us accept the assumptions on which that is based, and apparently many do, then we are well on our way to an obscene culture."

The only possible hope in all this, according to Bork, is either a fundamentalist religious revival or a sobering great depression. (Bork seems to welcome both possibilities.) Or, if all else fails, a restitution of government censorship. In an interview last year with the magazine *Christianity Today*, Bork was refreshingly candid about this. He would gladly use government power to restrict the dissemination of objectionable speech and images. When asked by the magazine what an American Civil Liberties Union lawyer would say about this, Bork replied that the lawyer would say, "'You are inhibiting my liberty and my right to express myself.' And the answer to that is, Yes, that is precisely what we are after."

Thus modern conservatism, which began as a movement of personal liberation from the state and intellectual skepticism in response to ideological certainty, has become its precise opposite. Convinced that society is in mortal moral and cultural peril, the most influential conservative intellectuals have made their peace with big government, censorship, and the presence of sectarian dogma in politics. The supremacy of this way of thinking among conservatives is perhaps best illustrated by David Frum, a young writer who has long supported a more economically based conservatism, one that would return the movement to its 1980s emphasis on tax cuts and smaller government. But his rationale for such a move in his recent book, *Dead Right*, is revealing. He wants to limit government not to expand personal freedom, but to so rob the middle class of financial security that they would have little choice but to return to the social mores of the 1950s. In order not to fall through the widening cracks of the vanishing welfare state, Americans would have no option, Frum argues, but to strengthen family ties, avoid divorce, and cling more carefully to children, spouses, and parents.

In other words, even those conservative thinkers who still argue for a low-tax, small-government philosophy have been unable to make headway with their peers without cloaking their case in the austerity of moral revival. The blithe optimism of Reagan, the joy that conservatives once took in the sheer unpredictability of a free people in a free society, has been replaced by a dark dread of how people could misuse such freedom, and the desperate need to coerce them back into line.

In the 1990s, as America has experienced a phenomenal burst of new wealth, as conservative values have enjoyed a revival among the young, as divorce and abortion have dropped, as welfare has been transformed and fiscal prudence restored, intellectual conservatives have responded by launching a bitter crusade to save the country from hell. No wonder that during the Lewinsky matter Republicans consistently misread the public mood and the popular culture. No wonder they managed to let one of the most duplicitous presidents in history seem an object of unjust persecution. No wonder they have yet no clue how to engage or inspire the vibrant, new America that their predecessors did so much to bring about.

This is not to say, of course, that morality is not an important, or an importantly conservative, issue. Conservatives have always been concerned with morality—and rightly so. They have long understood that political order rests upon a vibrant civil society, and on the morality that such a society sustains. But conservatives have also always been aware of the dangers of excessively policing that morality, and of the evils that can occur when the morally certain gain power. Hence the apparent conservative paradox. Conservatives want morality, but they don't want the big government that could effectively enforce it. For true conservatives, the evils of moral chaos are usually outweighed by the evils of a moralizing big brother.

And so conservatives have learned over the years to live with a little paradox. They have resisted the temptation either to become morally indifferent libertarians or to become morally repugnant ideologues. Although they have worried about moral and social trends, they have resisted easy pessimism and the jeremiad. And they have left the impositions of morals to the churches and preachers and mothers and fathers and teachers and friends of America to sort out. When it comes to preaching, true conservatives would much prefer to praise the examples of Mark McGwire and Sammy Sosa than to demonize the likes of Dennis Rodman or Marv Albert.

Above all, true conservatives have not been depressed by freedom. This, after all, is where the modern conservative movement in America started in the 1950s — in a revolt against the creeping power of the postwar welfare state. When American conservatives lose sight of that central strain in their philosophy, when their love of freedom becomes an afterthought to their concern for morality, then they lose sight of what makes them both conservative and quintessentially American. They lose sight of what distinguishes them from the darker history of European conservatism, and what sets them apart even from the government-friendly Toryism of their English cousins.

Truly American conservatives would not recoil at the greater liberty enjoyed by women, racial minorities, and homosexuals, as the truly American conservative Barry Goldwater showed. In the last decade, true American conservatives would have been heartened by the declines in divorce, crime, and teenage births, and encouraged by the move among gay people for more stable, responsible relationships. They would have been elated by the collapse of collectivism and totalitarianism abroad, and encouraged by the return of fiscal prudence and social responsibility at home. They would have seen in Bill Clinton a dangerous proclivity for dishonesty and abuse of power, but they would not have seen him as the degenerate apotheosis of an entire generation — let alone an entire nation. And they would have seen the emergence of religious dogmatists on the far right as a threat to constitutional order and political civility, not as a boon for votes.

Above all, true conservatives would not have fatally overplayed their hand and tried to impeach a president not for illegality but for immorality, and they wouldn't have shredded the virtues of privacy and decency and common sense for the emotional release of a cultural jihad. Today's conservatives — the intellectuals in particular — have begun to replace skepticism with certainty, faith in ordinary people with contempt for the masses, religion with theocracy. These are fools' bargains. And unworthy of conservatism itself.

Moreover, this shift has also undoubtedly weakened, rather than strengthened, the ability of conservatives to address moral issues in a limited but compelling way. When conservative extremists accuse Bill Clinton of murder, when Republicans make a divisive, difficult issue like abortion a litmus test for moral purity, then most Americans will be reluctant to listen to them when they worry about illegitimacy, juvenile crime, or presidential law breaking. Conservative moralizing, in other words, requires a certain temperance to be truly effective.

Of course, conservatives have now achieved a political ascendancy regardless of these mistakes. Thanks in part to the collapse of the liberal alternative, and to the self-destruction of Bill Clinton, the flaws of religious zeal and moral authoritarianism have not prevented conservatives' rise to cultural and political power. That makes the danger of hubris all the greater and the need for self-restraint all the more pressing. In the past, conservatives have rightly been praised as much for what they haven't done as for what they have. Maybe today's conservative generation, poised on the brink of unprecedented power, will heed that lesson. But maybe, God help us, they won't.

What's So Bad about Hate?

Schoolyard Shootings, Matthew Shepard, Genocide

September 26, 1999 | *THE NEW YORK TIMES*

I

I wonder what was going on in John William King's head two years ago when he tied James Byrd Jr.'s feet to the back of a pickup truck and dragged him three miles down a road in rural Texas. King and two friends had picked up Byrd, who was black, when he was walking home, half-drunk, from a party. As part of a bonding ritual in their fledgling white supremacist group, the three men took Byrd to a remote part of town, beat him, and chained his legs together before attaching them to the truck. Pathologists at King's trial testified that Byrd was probably alive and conscious until his body finally hit a culvert and split in two. When King was offered a chance to say something to Byrd's family at the trial, he smirked and uttered an obscenity.

We know all these details now, many months later. We know quite a large amount about what happened before and after. But I am still drawn, again and again, to the flash of ignition, the moment when fear and loathing became hate, the instant of transformation when King became hunter and Byrd became prey.

What was that? And what was it when Buford Furrow Jr., longtime member of Aryan Nations, calmly walked up to a Filipino American mailman he happened to spot, asked him to mail a letter, and then shot him at point-blank range? Or when Russell Henderson beat Matthew Shepard, a young gay man, to a pulp, removed his shoes, and then, with the help of a friend, tied him to a post, like a dead coyote, to warn off others?

For all our documentation of these crimes and others, our political and moral disgust at them, our morbid fascination with them, our sensitivity to their social meaning, we seem at times to have no better idea now than we ever had of what exactly they were about. About what that moment means when, for some reason or other, one human being asserts absolute, immutable superiority over another. About not the violence, but what the violence expresses. About what—exactly—hate is. And what our own part in it may be.

I find myself wondering what hate actually is in part because we have created an entirely new offense in American criminal law—a "hate crime"—to combat it. And barely a day goes by without someone somewhere declaring war against it. Last month President Clinton called for an expansion of hate-crime laws as "what America needs in our battle against hate." A couple of weeks later, Senator John McCain used a campaign speech to denounce the "hate" he said poisoned the land. New York's mayor, Rudolph Giuliani, recently tried to stop the Million Youth March in Harlem on the grounds that the event was organized by people "involved in hate marches and hate rhetoric."

The media concurs in its emphasis. In 1985, there were eleven mentions of "hate crimes" in the national media database Nexis. By 1990, there were more than a thousand. In the first six months of 1999, there were seven thousand. "Sexy fun is one thing," wrote a *New York Times* reporter about sexual assaults in Woodstock '99's mosh pit. "But this was an orgy of lewdness tinged with hate." And when Benjamin Smith marked the Fourth of July this year by targeting blacks, Asians, and Jews for murder in Indiana and Illinois, the story wasn't merely about a twisted young man who had emerged on the scene. As *The Times* put it, "Hate arrived in the neighborhoods of Indiana University, in Bloomington, in the early-morning darkness."

But what exactly was this thing that arrived in the early-morning darkness? For all our zeal to attack hate, we still have a remarkably vague idea of what it actually is. A single word, after all, tells us less, not more. For all its emotional punch, "hate" is far less nuanced an idea than prejudice, or bigotry, or bias, or anger, or even mere aversion to others. Is it to stand in for all these varieties of human experience—and everything in between? If so, then the war against it will be so vast as to be quixotic. Or is "hate" to stand for a very specific idea or belief, or set of beliefs, with a very specific object or group of objects? Then waging war against it is almost certainly unconstitutional. Perhaps these kinds of questions are of no concern to those waging war on hate. Perhaps it is enough for them that they share a sentiment that there is too much hate and never enough vigilance in combating it. But sentiment is a poor basis for law, and a dangerous tool in politics. It is better to leave some unwinnable wars unfought.

II

Hate is everywhere. Human beings generalize all the time, ahead of time, about everyone and everything. A large part of it may even be hardwired. At some point in our evolution, being able to know beforehand who was friend or foe was not merely a matter of philosophical reflection. It was a matter of survival. And even today it seems impossible to feel a loyalty without also feeling a disloyalty, a sense of belonging without an equal sense of unbelonging. We're social beings. We associate. Therefore we disassociate. And although it would be comforting to think that the one could happen without the other, we know in reality that it doesn't. How many patriots are there who have never felt a twinge of xenophobia?

Of course by "hate," we mean something graver and darker than this kind of lazy prejudice. But the closer you look at this distinction, the fuzzier it gets. Much of the time, we harbor little or no malice toward people of other backgrounds or places or ethnicities or ways of life. But then a car cuts you off at an intersection and you find yourself noticing immediately that the driver is a woman, or black, or old, or fat, or white, or male. Or you are walking down a city street at night and hear footsteps quickening behind you. You look around and see that it is a white woman and not a black man, and you are instantly relieved. These impulses are so spontaneous they are almost involuntary. But where did they come from? The mindless need to be mad at someone—anyone—or the unconscious eruption of a darker prejudice festering within?

In 1993, in San Jose, California, two neighbors—one heterosexual, one homosexual—were engaged in a protracted squabble over grass clippings. (The full case is recounted in *Hate Crimes*, by James B. Jacobs and Kimberly Potter.) The gay man regularly mowed his lawn without a grass catcher, which prompted his neighbor to complain on many occasions that grass clippings spilled over onto his driveway. Tensions grew until one day the gay man mowed his front yard, spilling clippings onto his neighbor's driveway, prompting the straight man to yell an obscene and common antigay insult. The wrangling escalated. At one point, the gay man agreed to collect the clippings from his neighbor's driveway but then later found them dumped on his own porch. A fracas ensued with the gay man spraying the straight man's son with a garden hose, and the son hitting and kicking the gay man several times, yelling anti-gay slurs. The police were called, and the son was eventually convicted of a hate-motivated assault, a felony. But what was the nature of the hate: antigay bias or suburban property-owner madness?

Or take the Labor Day parade last year in Broad Channel, a small island in Jamaica Bay, Queens. Almost everyone there is white, and in recent years a group of local volunteer firefighters has taken to decorating a pickup truck for the parade in order to win the prize for "funniest float." Their themes have tended toward the outrageously provocative. Beginning in 1995, they won prizes for floats depicting "Hasidic Park," "Gooks of Hazzard," and "Happy Gays." Last year, they called their float "Black to the Future, Broad Channel 2098." They imagined their community a century hence as a largely black enclave, with every stereotype imaginable: watermelons, basketballs, and so on. At one point during the parade, one of them mimicked the dragging death of James Byrd. It was caught on videotape, and before long the entire community was depicted as a caldron of hate.

It's an interesting case, because the float was indisputably in bad taste and the improvisation on the Byrd killing was grotesque. But was it hate? The men on the float were local heroes for their volunteer work; they had no record of bigoted activity, and were not members of any racist organizations. In previous years, they had made fun of many other groups and saw themselves more as provocateurs than bigots. When they were described as racists, it came as a shock to them. They apologized for poor taste but refused to confess to bigotry. "The people involved aren't horrible people," protested a local woman. "Was it a racist act? I don't know. Are they racists? I don't think so."

If hate is a self-conscious activity, she has a point. The men were primarily motivated by the desire to shock and to reflect what they thought was their community's culture. Their display was not aimed at any particular black people, or at any blacks who lived in Broad Channel—almost none do. But if hate is primarily an unconscious activity, then the matter is obviously murkier. And by taking the horrific lynching of a black man as a spontaneous object of humor, the men were clearly advocating indifference to it. Was this an aberrant excess? Or the real truth about the men's feelings toward African Americans? Hate or tastelessness? And how on Earth is anyone, even perhaps the firefighters themselves, going to know for sure?

Or recall H. L. Mencken. He shared in the anti-Semitism of his time with more alacrity than most and was an indefatigable racist. "It is impossible," he wrote in his diary, "to talk anything resembling discretion or judgment into a colored woman. They are all essentially childlike, and even hard experience does not teach them anything." He wrote at another time of the "psychological stigmata" of the "Afro-American race." But it is also true that, during much of his life, day to day, Mencken conducted himself with no regard to race, and supported a politics that was clearly integrationist. As the editor of his diary has pointed out, Mencken published many black authors in his magazine, *The American Mercury*, and lobbied on their behalf with his publisher, Alfred A. Knopf. The last thing Mencken ever wrote was a diatribe against racial segregation in Baltimore's public parks. He was good friends with leading black writers and journalists, including James Weldon Johnson, Walter White, and George S. Schuyler, and played an underappreciated role in promoting the Harlem Renaissance.

What would our modern view of hate do with Mencken? Probably ignore him, or change the subject. But, with regard to hate, I know lots of people like Mencken. He reminds me of conservative friends who oppose almost every measure for homosexual equality yet genuinely delight in the company of their gay friends. It would be easier for me to think of them as haters, and on paper, perhaps, there is a good case that they are. But in real life, I know they are not. Some of them clearly harbor no real malice toward me or other homosexuals whatsoever.

They are as hard to figure out as those liberal friends who support every gay-rights measure they have ever heard of but do anything to avoid going into a gay bar with me. I have to ask myself in the same, frustrating kind of way: Are they liberal bigots or bigoted liberals? Or are they neither bigots nor liberals, but merely people?

III

Hate used to be easier to understand. When Sartre described anti-Semitism in his 1946 essay "Anti-Semite and Jew," he meant a very specific array of firmly held prejudices, with a history, an ideology, and even a pseudoscience to back them up. He meant a systematic attempt to demonize and eradicate an entire race. If you go to the website of the World Church of the Creator, the organization that inspired young Benjamin Smith to murder in Illinois earlier this year, you will find a similarly bizarre, pseudorational ideology. The kind of literature read by Buford Furrow before he rained terror on a Jewish kindergarten last month and then killed a mailman because of his color is full of the same paranoid loopiness. And when we talk about hate, we often mean this kind of phenomenon.

But this brand of hatred is mercifully rare in the United States. These professional maniacs are to hate what serial killers are to murder. They should certainly not be ignored; but they represent what Harold Meyerson, writing in *Salon*, called "niche haters": cold-blooded, somewhat deranged, often poorly socialized psychopaths. In a free society with relatively easy access to guns, they will always pose a menace.

But their menace is a limited one, and their hatred is hardly typical of anything very widespread. Take Buford Furrow. He famously issued a "wake-up call" to "kill Jews" in Los Angeles, before he peppered a Jewish community center with gunfire. He did this in a state with two Jewish female senators, in a city with a large, prosperous Jewish population, in a country where out of several million Jewish Americans, a total of sixty-six were reported by the FBI as the targets of hate-crime assaults in 1997. However despicable Furrow's actions were, it would require a very large stretch to describe them as representative of anything but the deranged fringe of an American subculture.

Most hate is more common and more complicated, with as many varieties as there are varieties of love. Just as there is possessive love and needy love, family love and friendship, romantic love and unrequited love, passion and respect; affection and obsession, so hatred has its shadings. There is hate that fears, and hate that merely feels contempt; there is hate that expresses power, and hate that comes from powerlessness; there is revenge, and there is hate that comes from envy. There is hate that was love, and hate that is a curious expression of love. There is hate of the other, and hate of something that reminds us too much of ourselves. There is the oppressor's hate, and the victim's hate. There is hate that burns slowly, and hate that fades. And there is hate that explodes, and hate that never catches fire.

The modern words that we have created to describe the varieties of hate—"sexism," "racism," "anti-Semitism, "homophobia"—tell us very little about any of this. They tell us merely the identities of the victims; they don't reveal the identities of the perpetrators, or what they think, or how they feel. They don't even tell us how the victims feel. And this simplicity is no accident. Coming from the theories of Marxist and post-Marxist academics, these "isms" are far better at alleging structures of power than at delineating the workings of the individual heart or mind. In fact, these "isms" can exist without mentioning individuals at all.

We speak of institutional racism, for example, as if an institution can feel anything. We talk of "hate" as an impersonal noun, with no hater specified. But when these abstractions are actually incarnated, when someone feels something as a result of them, when a hater actually interacts with a victim, the picture changes. We find that hates are often very different phenomena one from another, that they have very different psychological dynamics, that they might even be better understood by not seeing them as varieties of the same thing at all.

There is, for example, the now-unfashionable distinction between reasonable hate and unreasonable hate. In recent years, we have become accustomed to talking about hates as if they were all equally indefensible, as if it could never be the case that some hates might be legitimate, even necessary. But when some eight hundred thousand Tutsis are murdered under the auspices of a Hutu regime in Rwanda, and when a few thousand Hutus are killed in revenge, the hates are not commensurate. Genocide is not an event like a hurricane, in which damage is random and universal; it is a planned and often-merciless attack of one group upon another. The hate of the perpetrators is a monstrosity. The hate of the victims, and their survivors, is justified. What else, one wonders, were surviving Jews supposed to feel toward Germans after the Holocaust? Or, to a different degree, South African blacks after apartheid? If the victims overcome this hate, it is a supreme moral achievement. But if they don't, the victims are not as culpable as the perpetrators. So the hatred of Serbs for Kosovars today can never be equated with the hatred of Kosovars for Serbs.

Hate, like much of human feeling, is not rational, but it usually has its reasons. And it cannot be understood, let alone condemned, without knowing them. Similarly, the hate that comes from knowledge is always different from the hate that comes from ignorance. It is one of the most foolish clichés of our time that prejudice is always rooted in ignorance, and can usually be overcome by familiarity with the objects of our loathing. The racism of many southern whites under segregation was not appeased by familiarity with southern blacks; the virulent loathing of Tutsis by many Hutus was not undermined by living next door to them for centuries. Theirs was a hatred that sprang, for whatever reasons, from experience. It cannot easily be compared with, for example, the resilience of anti-Semitism in Japan, or hostility to immigration in areas where immigrants are unknown, or fear of homosexuals by people who have never knowingly met one.

The same familiarity is an integral part of what has become known as "sexism." Sexism isn't, properly speaking, a prejudice at all. Few men live without knowledge or constant awareness of women. Every single sexist man was born of a woman, and is likely to be sexually attracted to women. His hostility is going to be very different from that of, say, a reclusive member of Aryan Nations toward Jews he has never met.

In her book *The Anatomy of Prejudices*, the psychotherapist Elisabeth Young-Bruehl proposes a typology of three distinct kinds of hate: obsessive, hysterical, and narcissistic. It's not an exhaustive analysis, but it's a beginning in any serious attempt to understand hate rather than merely declaring war on it. The obsessives, for Young-Bruehl, are those, like the Nazis or Hutus, who fantasize a threat from a minority, and obsessively try to rid themselves of it. For them, the very existence of the hated group is threatening. They often describe their loathing in almost physical terms: they experience what Patrick Buchanan, in reference to homosexuals, once described as a "visceral recoil" from the objects of their detestation. They often describe those they hate as diseased or sick, in need of a cure. Or they talk of "cleansing" them, as the Hutus talked of the Tutsis, or call them "cockroaches," as Yitzhak Shamir called the Palestinians. If you read material from the Family Research Council, it is clear that the group regards homosexuals as similar contaminants. A recent posting on its web site about syphilis among gay men was headlined "Unclean."

Hysterical haters have a more complicated relationship with the objects of their aversion. In Young-Bruehl's words, hysterical prejudice is a prejudice that "a person uses unconsciously to appoint a group to act out in the world forbidden sexual and sexually aggressive desires that the person has repressed." Certain kinds of racists fit this pattern. White loathing of blacks is, for some people, at least partly about sexual and physical envy. A certain kind of white racist sees in black America all those impulses he wishes most to express himself but cannot. He idealizes in "blackness" a sexual freedom, a physical power, a Dionysian release that he detests but also longs for. His fantasy may not have any basis in reality, but it is powerful nonetheless. It is a form of love-hate, and it is impossible to understand the nuances of racism in, say, the American South, or in British Imperial India, without it.

Unlike the obsessives, the hysterical haters do not want to eradicate the objects of their loathing; rather, they want to keep them in some kind of permanent and safe subjugation in order to indulge the attraction of their repulsion. A recent study, for example, found that the men most likely to be opposed to equal rights for homosexuals were those most likely to be aroused by homoerotic imagery. This makes little rational sense, but it has a certain psychological plausibility. If homosexuals were granted equality, then the hysterical gay hater might panic that his repressed passions would run out of control, overwhelming him and the world he inhabits.

A narcissistic hate, according to Young-Bruehl's definition, is sexism. In its most common form, it is rooted in many men's inability even to imagine what it is to be a woman, a failing rarely challenged by men's control of our most powerful public social institutions. Women are not so much hated by most men as simply ignored in nonsexual contexts, or never conceived of as true equals. The implicit condescension is mixed, in many cases, with repressed and sublimated erotic desire. So the unawareness of women is sometimes commingled with a deep longing or contempt for them.

Each hate, of course, is more complicated than this, and in any one person hate can assume a uniquely configured combination of these types. So there are hysterical sexists who hate women because they need them so much, and narcissistic sexists who hardly notice that women exist, and sexists who oscillate between one of these positions and another. And there are gay bashers who are threatened by masculine gay men and gay haters who feel repulsed by effeminate ones. The soldier who beat his fellow soldier Barry Winchell to death with a baseball bat in July had earlier lost a fight to him. It was the image of a macho gay man—and the shame of being bested by him—that the vengeful soldier had to obliterate, even if he needed a gang of accomplices and a weapon to do so. But the murderers of Matthew Shepard seem to have had a different impulse: a visceral disgust at the thought of any sexual contact with an effeminate homosexual. Their anger was mixed with mockery, as the cruel spectacle at the side of the road suggested.

In the same way, the pathological anti-Semitism of Nazi Germany was obsessive, inasmuch as it tried to cleanse the world of Jews; but also, as Daniel Jonah Goldhagen shows in his book *Hitler's Willing Executioners*, hysterical. The Germans were mysteriously compelled as well as repelled by Jews, devising elaborate ways, like death camps and death marches, to keep them alive even as they killed them. And the early Nazi phobia of interracial sex suggests as well a lingering erotic quality to the relationship, partaking of exactly the kind of sexual panic that persists among some homosexual haters and antimiscegenation racists. So the concept of "homophobia," like those of "sexism" and "racism," is often a crude one. All three are essentially cookie-cutter formulas that try to understand human impulses merely through the one-dimensional identity of the victims, rather than through the thoughts and feelings of the haters and hated.

This is deliberate. The theorists behind these "isms" want to ascribe all blame to one group in society—the "oppressors"—and render specific others—the "victims"—completely blameless. And they want to do this in order in part to side unequivocally with the underdog. But it doesn't take a genius to see how this approach, too, can generate its own form of bias. It can justify blanket condemnations of whole groups of people—white straight males, for example—purely because of the color of their skin or the nature of their sexual orientation. And it can condescendingly ascribe innocence to whole groups of others. It does exactly what hate does: it hammers the uniqueness of each individual into the anvil of group identity. And it postures morally over the result.

In reality, human beings and human acts are far more complex, which is why these isms and the laws they have fomented are continually coming under strain and challenge. Once again, hate wriggles free of its definers. It knows no monolithic groups of haters and hated. Like a river, it has many eddies, backwaters, and rapids. So there are anti-Semites who actually admire what they think of as Jewish power, and there are gay haters who look up to homosexuals and some who want to sleep with them. And there are black racists, racist Jews, sexist women, and anti-Semitic homosexuals. Of course there are.

IV

Once you start thinking of these phenomena less as the "isms" of sexism, racism, and "homophobia," once you think of them as independent psycho-logical responses, it's also possible to see how they can work in a bewildering variety of ways in a bewildering number of people. To take one obvious and sad oddity: people who are demeaned and objectified in society may develop an aversion to their tormentors that is more hateful in its expression than the prejudice they have been subjected to. The FBI statistics on hate crimes throw up an interesting point. In America in the 1990s, blacks were up to three times as likely as whites to commit a hate crime, to express their hate by physically attacking their targets or their property. Just as sexual abusers have often been victims of sexual abuse, and wife-beaters often grew up in violent households, so hate criminals may often be members of hated groups.

Even the Columbine murderers were in some sense victims of hate before they were purveyors of it. Their classmates later admitted that Dylan Klebold and Eric Harris were regularly called "faggots" in the corridors and class-rooms of Columbine High and that nothing was done to prevent or stop the harassment. This climate of hostility doesn't excuse the actions of Klebold and Harris, but it does provide a more plausible context. If they had been black, had routinely been called "n*gg*r" in the school, and had then exploded into a shooting spree against white students, the response to the matter might well have been different. But the hate would have been the same. In other words, hate victims are often hate victimizers as well. This doesn't mean that all hates are equivalent, or that some are not more justified than others. It means merely that hate goes both ways; and if you try to regulate it among some, you will find yourself forced to regulate it among others.

It is no secret, for example, that some of the most vicious anti-Semites in America are black, and that some of the most virulent anti-Catholic bigots in America are gay. At what point, we are increasingly forced to ask, do these phenomena become as indefensible as white racism or religious toleration of antigay bigotry? That question becomes all the more difficult when we notice that it is often minorities who commit some of the most hate-filled offenses against what they see as their oppressors. It was the mainly gay AIDS activist group ACT UP that perpetrated the hateful act of desecrating Communion hosts at a Mass at St. Patrick's Cathedral in New York. And here is the playwright Tony Kushner, who is gay, responding to the Matthew Shepard beating in *The Nation* magazine: "Pope John Paul II endorses murder. He, too, knows the price of discrimination, having declared anti-Semitism a sin. . . . He knows that discrimination kills. But when the Pope heard the news about Matthew Shepard, he, too, worried about spin. And so, on the subject of gay-bashing, the Pope and his cardinals and his bishops and priests maintain their cynical political silence. . . . To remain silent is to endorse murder." Kushner went on to describe the pope as a "homicidal liar."

Maybe the passion behind these words is justified. But it seems clear enough to me that Kushner is expressing hate toward the institution of the Catholic Church, and all those who perpetuate its doctrines. How else to interpret the way in which he accuses the pope of cynicism, lying, and murder? And how else either to understand the brutal parody of religious vocations expressed by the Sisters of Perpetual Indulgence, a group of gay men who dress in drag as nuns and engage in sexually explicit performances in public? Or T-shirts with the words "Recovering Catholic" on them, hot items among some gay and lesbian activists? The implication that someone's religious faith is a mental illness is clearly an expression of contempt. If that isn't covered under the definition of hate speech, what is?

Or take the following sentence: "The act male homosexuals commit is ugly and repugnant and afterwards they are disgusted with themselves. They drink and take drugs to palliate this, but they are disgusted with the act and they are always changing partners and cannot be really happy." The thoughts of Pat Robertson or Patrick Buchanan? Actually, that sentence was written by Gertrude Stein, one of the century's most notable lesbians. Or take the following, about how beating up "black boys like that made us feel good inside. . . . Every time I drove my foot into his [expletive], I felt better." It was written to describe the brutal assault of an innocent bystander for the sole reason of his race. By the end of the attack, the victim had blood gushing from his mouth as his attackers stomped on his genitals. Are we less appalled when we learn that the actual sentence was how beating up "white boys like that made us feel good inside. . . . Every time I drove my foot into his [expletive], I felt better?" It was written by Nathan McCall, an African American who later in life became a successful journalist at *The Washington Post* and published his memoir of this "hate crime" to much acclaim.

In fact, one of the stranger aspects of hate is that the prejudice expressed by a group in power may often be milder in expression than the prejudice felt by the marginalized. After all, if you already enjoy privilege, you may not feel the anger that turns bias into hate. You may not need to. For this reason, most white racism may be more influential in society than most black racism — but also more calmly expressed.

So may other forms of minority loathing — especially hatred within minorities. I'm sure that black conservatives like Clarence Thomas or Thomas Sowell have experienced their fair share of white racism. But I wonder whether it has ever reached the level of intensity of the hatred directed toward them by other blacks? In several years of being an openly gay writer and editor, I have experienced the gamut of responses to my sexual orientation. But I have only directly experienced articulated, passionate hate from other homosexuals. I have been accused over the years by other homosexuals of being a sellout, a hypocrite, a traitor, a sexist, a racist, a narcissist, a snob. I've been called selfish, callous, hateful, self-hating, and malevolent. At a reading, a group of lesbian activists portrayed my face on a poster within the crosshairs of a gun. Nothing from the religious right has come close to such vehemence.

I am not complaining. No harm has ever come to me or my property, and much of the criticism is rooted in the legitimate expression of political differences. But the visceral tone and style of the gay criticism can only be described as hateful. It is designed to wound personally, and it often does. But its intensity comes in part, one senses, from the pain of being excluded for so long, of anger long restrained bubbling up and directing itself more aggressively toward an alleged traitor than an alleged enemy. It is the hate of the hated. And it can be the most hateful hate of all. For this reason, hate-crime laws may themselves be an oddly biased category—biased against the victims of hate. Racism is everywhere, but the already-victimized might be more desperate, more willing to express it violently. And so more prone to come under the suspicious eye of the law.

v

And why is hate for a group worse than hate for a person? In Laramie, Wyoming, the now-famous epicenter of "homophobia," where Matthew Shepard was brutally beaten to death, vicious murders are not unknown. In the previous twelve months, a fifteen-year-old pregnant girl was found east of the town with seventeen stab wounds. Her thirty-eight-year-old boyfriend was apparently angry that she had refused an abortion and left her in the Wyoming foothills to bleed to death. In the summer of 1998, an eight-year-old Laramie girl was abducted, raped, and murdered by a pedophile, who disposed of her young body in a garbage dump. Neither of these killings was deemed a hate crime, and neither would be designated as such under any existing hate-crime law. Perhaps because of this, one crime is an international legend; the other two are virtually unheard of.

But which crime was more filled with hate? Once you ask the question, you realize how difficult it is to answer. Is it more hateful to kill a stranger or a lover? Is it more hateful to kill a child than an adult? Is it more hateful to kill your own child than another's? Under the law before the invention of hate crimes, these decisions didn't have to be taken. But under the law after hate crimes, a decision is essential. A decade ago, a murder was a murder. Now, in the era when group hate has emerged as our cardinal social sin, it all depends.

The supporters of laws against hate crimes argue that such crimes should be disproportionately punished because they victimize more than the victim. Such crimes, these advocates argue, spread fear, hatred, and panic among whole populations, and therefore merit more concern. But, of course, all crimes victimize more than the victim, and spread alarm in the society at large. Just think of the terrifying church shooting in Texas only two weeks ago. In fact, a purely random murder may be even more terrifying than a targeted one, since the entire community, and not just a part of it, feels threatened. High rates of murder, robbery, assault, and burglary victimize everyone, by spreading fear, suspicion, and distress everywhere. Which crime was more frightening to more people this summer: the mentally ill Buford Furrow's crazed attacks in Los Angeles, killing one, or Mark Barton's murder of his own family and several random day traders in Atlanta, killing twelve? Almost certainly the latter. But only Furrow was guilty of "hate."

One response to this objection is that certain groups feel fear more intensely than others because of a history of persecution or intimidation. But doesn't this smack of a certain condescension toward minorities? Why, after all, should it be assumed that gay men or black women or Jews, for example, are as a group more easily intimidated than others? Surely in any of these communities there will be a vast range of responses, from panic to concern to complete indifference. The assumption otherwise is the kind of crude generalization the law is supposed to uproot in the first place. And among these groups, there are also likely to be vast differences. To equate a population once subjected to slavery with a population of Mexican immigrants or third-generation Holocaust survivors is to equate the unequatable. In fact, it is to set up a contest of vulnerability in which one group vies with another to establish its particular variety of suffering, a contest that can have no dignified solution.

Rape, for example, is not classified as a "hate crime" under most existing laws, pitting feminists against ethnic groups in a battle for recognition. If, as a solution to this problem, everyone, except the white straight able-bodied male, is regarded as a possible victim of a hate crime, then we have simply created a two-tier system of justice in which racial profiling is reversed, and white straight men are presumed guilty before being proved innocent, and members of minorities are free to hate them as gleefully as they like. But if we include the white straight male in the litany of potential victims, then we have effectively abolished the notion of a hate crime altogether. For if every crime is possibly a hate crime, then it is simply another name for crime. All we will have done is widened the search for possible bigotry, ratcheted up the sentences for everyone, and filled the jails up even further.

Hate-crime-law advocates counter that extra penalties should be imposed on hate crimes because our society is experiencing an "epidemic" of such crimes. Mercifully, there is no hard evidence to support this notion. The federal government has only been recording the incidence of hate crimes in this decade, and the statistics tell a simple story. In 1992, there were 6,623 hate-crime incidents reported to the FBI by a total of 6,181 agencies, covering 51 percent of the population. In 1996, there were 8,734 incidents reported by 11,355 agencies, covering 84 percent of the population. That number dropped to 8,049 in 1997. These numbers are, of course, hazardous. They probably underreport the incidence of such crimes, but they are the only reliable figures we have. Yet even if they are faulty as an absolute number, they do not show an epidemic of "hate crimes" in the 1990s.

Is there evidence that the crimes themselves are becoming more vicious? None. More than 60 percent of recorded hate crimes in America involve no violent, physical assault against another human being at all, and, again, according to the FBI, that proportion has not budged much in the 1990s. These impersonal attacks are crimes against property or crimes of "intimidation." Murder, which dominates media coverage of hate crimes, is a tiny proportion of the total. Of the 8,049 hate crimes reported to the FBI in 1997, a total of eight were murders. Eight. The number of hate crimes that were aggravated assaults (generally involving a weapon) in 1997 is less than 15 percent of the total. That's 1,207 assaults too many, of course, but to put it in perspective, compare it with a reported 1,022,492 "equal opportunity" aggravated assaults in America in the same year. The number of hate crimes that were physical assaults is half the total. That's 4,000 assaults too many, of course, but to put it in perspective, it compares with around 3.8 million "equal opportunity" assaults in America annually.

The truth is, the distinction between a crime filled with personal hate and a crime filled with group hate is an essentially arbitrary one. It tells us nothing interesting about the psychological contours of the specific actor or his specific victim. It is a function primarily of politics, of special-interest groups carving out particular protections for themselves, rather than a serious response to a serious criminal concern. In such an endeavor, hate-crime-law advocates cram an entire world of human motivations into an immutable, tiny box called hate, and hope to have solved a problem. But nothing has been solved, and some harm may even have been done.

In an attempt to repudiate a past that treated people differently because of the color of their skin, or their sex, or religion or sexual orientation, we may merely create a future that permanently treats people differently because of the color of their skin, or their sex, religion, or sexual orientation. This notion of a hate crime, and the concept of hate that lies behind it, takes a psychological mystery and turns it into a facile political artifact. Rather than compounding this error and extending even further, we should seriously consider repealing the concept altogether.

To put it another way: violence can and should be stopped by the government. In a free society, hate can't and shouldn't be. The boundaries between hate and prejudice and between prejudice and opinion and between opinion and truth are so complicated and blurred that any attempt to construct legal and political fire walls is a doomed and illiberal venture. We know by now that hate will never disappear from human consciousness; in fact, it is probably, at some level, definitive of it. We know after decades of education measures that hate is not caused merely by ignorance, and after decades of legislation, that it isn't caused entirely by law.

To be sure, we have made much progress. Anyone who argues that America is as inhospitable to minorities and to women today as it has been in the past has not read much history. And we should, of course, be vigilant that our most powerful institutions, most notably the government, do not actively or formally propagate hatred; and ensure that the violent expression of hate is curtailed by the same rules that punish all violent expression.

But after that, in an increasingly diverse culture, it is crazy to expect that hate, in all its variety, can be eradicated. A free country will always mean a hateful country. This may not be fair, or perfect, or admirable, but it is reality, and while we need not endorse it, we should not delude ourselves into thinking we can prevent it. That is surely the distinction between toleration and tolerance. Tolerance is the eradication of hate; toleration is coexistence despite it. We might do better as a culture and as a polity if we concentrated more on achieving the latter rather than the former. We would certainly be less frustrated.

And by aiming lower, we might actually reach higher. In some ways, some expression of prejudice serves a useful social purpose. It lets off steam; it allows natural tensions to express themselves incrementally; it can siphon off conflict through words, rather than actions. Anyone who has lived in the ethnic shouting match that is New York City knows exactly what I mean. If New Yorkers disliked one another less, they wouldn't be able to get on so well. We may not all be able to pull off a Mencken—bigoted in words, egalitarian in action—but we might achieve a lesser form of virtue: a human acceptance of our need for differentiation, without a total capitulation to it.

Do we not owe something more to the victims of hate? Perhaps we do. But it is also true that there is nothing that government can do for the hated that the hated cannot better do for themselves. After all, most bigots are not foiled when they are punished specifically for their beliefs. In fact, many of the worst haters crave such attention and find vindication in such rebukes. Indeed, our media's obsession with "hate," our elevation of it above other social misdemeanors and crimes, may even play into the hands of the pathetic and the evil, may breathe air into the smoldering embers of their paranoid loathing. Sure, we can help create a climate in which such hate is disapproved of—and we should. But there is a danger that if we go too far, if we punish it too much, if we try to abolish it altogether, we may merely increase its mystique, and entrench the very categories of human difference that we are trying to erase.

For hate is only foiled not when the haters are punished but when the hated are immune to the bigot's power. A hater cannot psychologically wound if a victim cannot psychologically be wounded. And that immunity to hurt can never be given; it can merely be achieved. The racial epithet only strikes at someone's core if he lets it, if he allows the bigot's definition of him to be the final description of his life and his person—if somewhere in his heart of hearts, he believes the hateful slur to be true. The only final answer to this form of racism, then, is not majority persecution of it, but minority indifference to it. The only permanent rebuke to homophobia is not the enforcement of toler-ance, but gay equanimity in the face of prejudice. The only effective answer to sexism is not a morass of legal proscriptions, but the simple fact of female success. In this, as in so many other things, there is no solution to the problem. There is only a transcendence of it. For all our rhetoric, hate will never be destroyed. Hate, as our predecessors knew better, can merely be overcome.

The He Hormone

April 2, 2000 | *THE NEW YORK TIMES MAGAZINE*

I t has a slightly golden hue, suspended in an oily substance and injected in a needle about half as thick as a telephone wire. I have never been able to jab it suddenly in my hip muscle, as the doctor told me to. Instead, after swabbing a small patch of my rump down with rubbing alcohol, I push the needle in slowly until all three inches of it are submerged. Then I squeeze the liquid in carefully, as the muscle often spasms to absorb it. My skin sticks a little to the syringe as I pull it out, and then an odd mix of oil and blackish blood usually trickles down my hip.

I am so used to it now that the novelty has worn off. But every now and again the weirdness returns. The chemical I am putting in myself is synthetic testosterone: a substance that has become such a metaphor for manhood that it is almost possible to forget that it has a physical reality. Twenty years ago, as it surged through my pubescent body, it deepened my voice, grew hair on my face and chest, strengthened my limbs, made me a man. So what, I wonder, is it doing to me now?

There are few things more challenging to the question of what the difference between men and women really is than to see the difference injected into your hip. Men and women differ biologically mainly because men produce ten to twenty times as much testosterone as most women do and this chemical, no one seriously disputes, profoundly affects physique, behavior, mood, and self-understanding. To be sure, because human beings are also deeply socialized, the impact of this difference is refracted through the prism of our own history and culture. But biology, it is all too easy to forget, is at the root of this process. As more people use testosterone medically, as more use testosterone-based steroids in sports and recreation, and as more research explores the behavioral effects of this chemical, the clearer the power of that biology is. It affects every aspect of our society, from high divorce rates and adolescent male violence to the exploding cults of bodybuilding and professional wrestling. It helps explain, perhaps better than any other single factor, why inequalities between men and women remain so frustratingly resilient in public and private life. This summer, when an easy-to-apply testosterone gel hits the market, and when more people experience the power of this chemical in their own bodies, its social importance, once merely implicit, may get even harder to ignore.

My own encounter with testosterone came about for a simple medical reason. I am HIV-positive, and two years ago, after a period of extreme fatigue and weight loss, I had my testosterone levels checked. It turned out that my body was producing far less testosterone than it should have been at my age. No one quite knows why, but this is common among men with long-term HIV. The usual treatment is regular injections of artificial testosterone, which is when I experienced my first manhood supplement.

At that point I weighed around 165 pounds. I now weigh 185 pounds. My collar size went from a 15 to a 17½ in a few months; my chest went from 40 to 44. My appetite in every sense of that word expanded beyond measure. Going from napping two hours a day, I now rarely sleep in the daytime and have enough energy for daily workouts and a hefty work schedule. I can squat more than 400 pounds. Depression, once a regular feature of my life, is now a distant memory. I feel better able to recover from life's curveballs, more persistent, more alive. These are the long-term effects. They are almost as striking as the short-term ones.

Because the testosterone is injected every two weeks and it quickly leaves the bloodstream, I can actually feel its power on almost a daily basis. Within hours, and at most a day, I feel a deep surge of energy. It is less edgy than a double espresso, but just as powerful. My attention span shortens. In the two or three days after my shot, I find it harder to concentrate on writing and feel the need to exercise more. My wit is quicker, my mind faster, but my judgment is more impulsive. It is not unlike the kind of rush I get before talking in front of a large audience, or going on a first date, or getting on an airplane, but it suffuses me in a less abrupt and more consistent way. In a word, I feel braced. For what? It scarcely seems to matter.

And then after a few days, as the testosterone peaks and starts to decline, the feeling alters a little. I find myself less reserved than usual, and more garrulous. The same energy is there, but it seems less directed toward action than toward interaction, less toward pride than toward lust. The odd thing is that, however much experience I have with it, this lust peak still takes me unawares. It is not like feeling hungry, a feeling you recognize and satiate. It creeps up on you. It is only a few days later that I look back and realize that I spent hours of the recent past socializing in a bar or checking out every potential date who came vaguely over my horizon. You realize more acutely than before that lust is a chemical. It comes; it goes. It waxes; it wanes. You are not helpless in front of it, but you are certainly not fully in control.

Then there's anger. I have always tended to bury or redirect my rage. I once thought this an inescapable part of my personality. It turns out I was wrong. Late last year, mere hours after a T shot, my dog ran off the leash to forage for a chicken bone left in my local park. The more I chased her, the more she ran. By the time I retrieved her, the bone had been consumed, and I gave her a sharp tap on her rear end. "Don't smack your dog!" yelled a burly guy a few yards away. What I found myself yelling back at him is not printable in this magazine, but I have never used that language in public before, let alone bellowed it at the top of my voice. He shouted back, and within seconds I was actually close to hitting him. He backed down and slunk off. I strutted home, chest puffed up, contrite beagle dragged sheepishly behind me. It wasn't until half an hour later that I realized I had been a complete jerk and had nearly gotten into the first public brawl of my life. I vowed to inject my testosterone at night in the future.

That was an extreme example, but other, milder ones come to mind: losing my temper in a petty argument; innumerable traffic confrontations; even the occasional slightly too prickly column or e-mail flameout. No doubt my previous awareness of the mythology of testosterone had subtly primed me for these feelings of irritation and impatience. But when I place them in the larger context of my new testosterone-associated energy, and of what we know about what testosterone tends to do to people, then it seems plausible enough to ascribe some of this increased edginess and self-confidence to that biweekly encounter with a syringe full of manhood.

Testosterone, oddly enough, is a chemical closely related to cholesterol. It was first isolated by a Dutch scientist in 1935 from mice testicles and successfully synthesized by the German biologist Adolf Butenandt. Although testosterone is often thought of as the definition of maleness, both men and women produce it. Men produce it in their testicles; women produce it in their ovaries and adrenal glands. The male body converts some testosterone to estradiol, a female hormone, and the female body has receptors for testosterone, just as the male body does. That's why women who want to change their sex are injected with testosterone and develop male characteristics, like deeper voices, facial hair, and even baldness. The central biological difference between adult men and women, then, is not that men have testosterone and women don't. It's that men produce much, much more of it than women do. An average woman has forty to sixty nanograms of testosterone in a deciliter of blood plasma. An average man has three hundred to one thousand nanograms per deciliter.

Testosterone's effects start early—really early. At conception, every embryo is female and unless hormonally altered will remain so. You need testosterone to turn a fetus with a Y chromosome into a real boy, to masculinize his brain and body. Men experience a flood of testosterone twice in their lives: in the womb about six weeks after conception and at puberty. The first fetal burst primes the brain and the body, endowing male fetuses with the instinctual knowledge of how to respond to later testosterone surges. The second, more familiar adolescent rush—squeaky voices, facial hair, and all—completes the process. Without testosterone, humans would always revert to the default sex, which is female. The Book of Genesis is therefore exactly wrong. It isn't women who are made out of men. It is men who are made out of women. Testosterone, to stretch the metaphor, is Eve's rib.

The effect of testosterone is systemic. It engenders both the brain and the body. Apart from the obvious genital distinction, other differences between men's and women's bodies reflect this: body hair, the ratio of muscle to fat, upper-body strength, and so on. But testosterone leads to behavioral differences as well. Since it is unethical to experiment with human embryos by altering hormonal balances, much of the evidence for this idea is based on research conducted on animals. A Stanford research group, for example, as reported in Deborah Blum's book *Sex on the Brain*, injected newborn female rats with testosterone. Not only did the female rats develop penises from their clitorises, but they also appeared fully aware of how to use them, trying to have sex with other females with merry abandon. Male rats who had their testosterone blocked after birth, on the other hand, saw their penises wither or disappear entirely and presented themselves to the female rats in a passive, receptive way. Other scientists, theorizing that it was testosterone that enabled male zebra finches to sing, injected mute female finches with testosterone. Sure enough, the females sang. Species in which the female is typically more aggressive, like hyenas in female-run clans, show higher levels of testosterone among the females than among the males. Female sea snipes, which impregnate the males and leave them to stay home and rear the young, have higher testosterone levels than their mates. Typical "male" behavior, in other words, corresponds to testosterone levels, whether exhibited by chromosomal males or females.

Does this apply to humans? The evidence certainly suggests that it does, though much of the "proof" is inferred from accidents. Pregnant women who were injected with progesterone (chemically similar to testosterone) in the 1950s to avoid miscarriage had daughters who later reported markedly tomboyish childhoods. Ditto girls born with a disorder that causes their adrenal glands to produce a hormone like testosterone rather than the more common cortisol. The moving story, chronicled in John Colapinto's book *As Nature Made Him*, of David Reimer, who as an infant was surgically altered after a botched circumcision to become a girl, suggests how long-lasting the effect of fetal testosterone can be. Despite a ruthless attempt to socialize David as a girl, and to give him the correct hormonal treatment to develop as one, his behavioral and psychological makeup was still ineradicably male. Eventually, with the help of more testosterone, he became a full man again. Female-to-male transsexuals report a similar transformation when injected with testosterone. One, Susan/Drew Seidman, described his experience in *The Village Voice* last November. "My sex-drive went through the roof," Seidman recalled. "I felt like I had to have sex once a day or I would die. . . . I was into porn as a girl, but now I'm really into porn." For Seidman, becoming a man was not merely physical. Thanks to testosterone, it was also psychological. "I'm not sure I can tell you what makes a man a man," Seidman averred. "But I know it's not a penis."

The behavioral traits associated with testosterone are largely the cliché-ridden ones you might expect. The Big T correlates with energy, self-confidence, competitiveness, tenacity, strength, and sexual drive. When you talk to men in testosterone therapy, several themes recur. "People talk about extremes," one man in his late thirties told me. "But that's not what testosterone does for me. It makes me think more clearly. It makes me think more positively. It's my Saint John's wort." A man in his twenties said: "Usually, I cycle up the hill to my apartment in twelfth gear. In the days after my shot, I ride it easily in sixteenth." A forty-year-old executive who took testosterone for body-building purposes told me: "I walk into a business meeting now and I just exude self-confidence. I know there are lots of other reasons for this, but my company has just exploded since my treatment. I'm on a roll. I feel capable of almost anything."

When you hear comments like these, it's no big surprise that strutting peacocks with their extravagant tails and bright colors are supercharged with testosterone and that mousy little male sparrows aren't. "It turned my life around," another man said. "I felt stronger—and not just in a physical sense. It was a deep sense of being strong, almost spiritually strong." Testosterone's antidepressive power is only marginally understood. It doesn't act in the precise way other antidepressants do, and it probably helps alleviate gloominess primarily by propelling people into greater activity and restlessness, giving them less time to think and reflect. (This may be one reason women tend to suffer more from depression than men.) Like other drugs, T can also lose potency if overused. Men who inject excessive amounts may see their own production collapse and experience shrinkage of their testicles and liver damage.

Individual effects obviously vary, and a person's internal makeup is affected by countless other factors—physical, psychological, and external. But in this complex human engine, testosterone is gasoline. It revs you up. A 1997 study took testosterone samples from 125 men and 128 women and selected the 12 with the lowest levels of testosterone and the 15 with the highest. They gave them beepers, asked them to keep diaries and paged them twenty times over a four-day period to check on their actions, feelings, thoughts, and whereabouts. The differences were striking. High-testosterone people "experienced more arousal and tension than those low in testosterone," according to the study. "They spent more time thinking, especially about concrete problems in the immediate present. They wanted to get things done and felt frustrated when they could not. They mentioned friends more than family or lovers."

Unlike Popeye's spinach, however, testosterone is also, in humans at least, a relatively subtle agent. It is not some kind of on-off switch by which men are constantly turned on and women off. For one thing, we all start out with different baseline levels. Some women may have remarkably high genetic T levels, some men remarkably low, although the male-female differential is so great that no single woman's T level can exceed any single man's, unless she, or he, has some kind of significant hormonal imbalance. For another, and this is where the social and political ramifications get complicated, testosterone is highly susceptible to environment. T levels can rise and fall depending on external circumstances — short term and long term. Testosterone is usually elevated in response to confrontational situations — a street fight, a marital spat, a presidential debate — or in highly charged sexual environments, like a strip bar or a pornographic web site. It can also be raised permanently in continuously combative environments, like war, although it can also be suddenly lowered by stress.

Because testosterone levels can be measured in saliva as well as in blood, researchers like Alan Booth, Allan Mazur, J. Richard Udry, and particularly James M. Dabbs, whose book *Heroes, Rogues and Lovers* will be out this fall, have compiled quite a database on these variations. A certain amount of caution is advisable in interpreting the results of these studies. There is some doubt about the validity of onetime samples to gauge underlying testosterone levels. And most of the studies of the psychological effects of testosterone take place in culturally saturated environments, so that the difference between cause and effect is often extremely hard to disentangle. Nevertheless, the sheer number and scale of the studies, especially in the last decade or so, and the strong behavioral correlations with high testosterone, suggest some conclusions about the social importance of testosterone that are increasingly hard to gainsay.

Testosterone is clearly correlated in both men and women with psychological dominance, confident physicality, and high self-esteem. In most combative, competitive environments, especially physical ones, the person with the most T wins. Put any two men in a room together and the one with more testosterone will tend to dominate the interaction. Working women have higher levels of testosterone than women who stay at home, and the daughters of working women have higher levels of testosterone than the daughters of housewives. A 1996 study found that in lesbian couples in which one partner assumes the male, or "butch," role and another assumes the female, or "femme," role, the "butch" woman has higher levels of testosterone than the "femme" woman. In naval medical tests, midshipmen have been shown to have higher average

levels of testosterone than plebes. Actors tend to have more testosterone than
ministers, according to a 1990 study. Among seven hundred male prison inmates
in a 1995 study, those with the highest T levels tended to be those most likely to
be in trouble with the prison authorities and to engage in unprovoked violence.
This is true among women as well as among men, according to a 1997 study of
eighty-seven female inmates in a maximum-security prison. Although high testosterone levels often correlate with dominance in interpersonal relationships,
it does not guarantee more social power. Testosterone levels are higher among
blue-collar workers, for example, than among white-collar workers, according
to a study of more than four thousand former military personnel conducted in
1992. A 1998 study found that trial lawyers—with their habituation to combat,
conflict, and swagger—have higher levels of T than other lawyers.

The salient question, of course, is, How much of this difference in aggression and dominance is related to environment? Are trial lawyers naturally
more testosteroned, and does that lead them into their profession? Or does
the experience of the courtroom raise their levels? Do working women have
naturally higher T levels, or does the prestige of work and power elevate their
testosterone? Because of the limits of researching such a question, it is hard to
tell beyond a reasonable doubt. But the social context clearly matters. It is even
possible to tell who has won a tennis match not by watching the game, but by
monitoring testosterone-filled saliva samples throughout. Testosterone levels
rise for both players before the match. The winner of any single game sees
his T production rise; the loser sees it fall. The ultimate winner experiences a
postgame testosterone surge, while the loser sees a collapse. This is true even
for people watching sports matches. A 1998 study found that fans backing the
winning side in a college basketball game and a World Cup soccer match saw
their testosterone levels rise; fans rooting for the losing teams in both games saw
their own T levels fall. There is, it seems, such a thing as vicarious testosterone.

One theory to explain this sensitivity to environment is that testosterone
was originally favored in human evolution to enable successful hunting and
combat. It kicks in, like adrenaline, in anticipation of combat, mental or
physical, and helps you prevail. But a testosterone crash can be a killer too.
Toward the end of my two-week cycle, I can almost feel my spirits dragging.
In the event of a just-lost battle, as Matt Ridley points out in his book *The
Red Queen*, there's a good reason for this to occur. If you lose a contest with

prey or a rival, it makes sense not to pick another fight immediately. So your body wisely prompts you to withdraw, filling your brain with depression and self-doubt. But if you have made a successful kill or defeated a treacherous enemy, your hormones goad you into further conquest. And people wonder why professional football players get into postgame sexual escapades and violence. Or why successful businessmen and politicians often push their sexual luck.

Similarly, testosterone levels may respond to more long-term stimuli. Studies have shown that inner-city youths, often exposed to danger in high-crime neighborhoods, may generate higher testosterone levels than unthreatened, secluded suburbanites. And so high T levels may not merely be responses to a violent environment; they may subsequently add to it in what becomes an increasingly violent, sexualized cycle. (It may be no accident that testosterone-soaked ghettos foster both high levels of crime and high levels of illegitimacy.) In the same way, declines in violence and crime may allow T levels to drop among young inner-city males, generating a virtuous trend of further reductions in crime and birth rates. This may help to explain why crime can decline precipitously, rather than drift down slowly, over time. Studies have also shown that men in long-term marriages see their testosterone levels progressively fall and their sex drives subsequently decline. It is as if their wives successfully tame them, reducing their sexual energy to a level where it is more unlikely to seek extramarital outlets. A 1993 study showed that single men tended to have higher levels of testosterone than married men and that men with high levels of testosterone turned out to be more likely to have had a failed marriage. Of course, if you start out with higher T levels, you may be more likely to fail at marriage, stay in the sexual marketplace, see your testosterone increase in response to this, and so on.

None of this means, as the scientists always caution, that testosterone is directly linked to romantic failure or violence. No study has found a simple correlation, for example, between testosterone levels and crime. But there may be a complex correlation. The male-prisoner study, for example, found no general above-normal testosterone levels among inmates. But murderers and armed robbers had higher testosterone levels than mere car thieves and burglars. Why is this not surprising? One of the most remarkable, but least commented on, social statistics available is the sex differential in crime. For decades, arrest rates have shown that an overwhelmingly disproportionate number of arrestees are male. Although the sex differential has narrowed since the chivalrous 1930s, when the male-female arrest ratio was twelve to one, it remains almost four to one, a close echo of the testosterone differential between men and women. In violent crime, men make up an even bigger proportion. In 1998, 89 percent of murders in the United States, for example, were committed by men. Of course, there's a nature-nurture issue here as well, and the fact that the sex differential in crime has decreased over this century suggests that environment has played a part. Yet despite the enormous social changes of the last century, the differential is still four to one, which suggests that underlying attributes may also have a great deal to do with it.

This, then, is what it comes down to: testosterone is a facilitator of risk—physical, criminal, personal. Without the influence of testosterone, the cost of these risks might seem to far outweigh the benefits. But with testosterone charging through the brain, caution is thrown to the wind. The influence of testosterone may not always lead to raw physical confrontation. In men with many options it may influence the decision to invest money in a dubious enterprise, jump into an ill-advised sexual affair, or tell an egregiously big whopper. At the time, all these decisions may make some sort of testosteroned sense. The White House, anyone?

The effects of testosterone are not secret; neither is the fact that men have far more of it than women. But why? As we have seen, testosterone is not synonymous with gender; in some species, it is the female who has most of it. The relatively new science of evolutionary psychology offers perhaps the best explanation for why that's not the case in humans. For neo-Darwinians, the aggressive and sexual aspects of testosterone are related to the division of labor among hunter-gatherers in our ancient but formative evolutionary past. This division—men in general hunted; women in general gathered—favored differing levels of testosterone. Women need some testosterone—for self-defense, occasional risk-taking, strength—but not as much as men. Men use it to increase their potential to defeat rivals, respond to physical threats in strange environments, maximize their physical attractiveness, prompt them to spread their genes as widely as possible, and defend their home if necessary.

But the picture, as most good evolutionary psychologists point out, is more complex than this. Men who are excessively testosteroned are not that attractive to most women. Although they have the genes that turn women on—strong jaws and pronounced cheekbones, for example, are correlated with high testosterone—they can also be precisely the unstable, highly sexed creatures that childbearing, stability-seeking women want to avoid. There are two ways, evolutionary psychologists hazard, that women have successfully squared this particular circle. One is to marry the sweet class nerd and have an affair with the college quarterback: that way you get the good genes, the good sex, and the stable home. The other is to find a man with variable T levels, who can be both stable and nurturing when you want him to be and yet become a muscle-bound, bristly gladiator when the need arises. The latter strategy, as Emma Bovary realized, is sadly more easily said than done.

So over millennia, men with high but variable levels of testosterone were the ones most favored by women and therefore most likely to produce offspring, and eventually us. Most men today are highly testosteroned, but not rigidly so. We don't have to live at all times with the T levels required to face down a woolly mammoth or bed half the village's young women. We can adjust so that our testosterone levels make us more suitable for co-parenting or for simply sticking around our mates when the sexual spark has dimmed. Indeed, one researcher, John Wingfield, has found a suggestive correlation in bird species between adjustable testosterone levels and males that have an active role to play in rearing their young. Male birds with consistently high testosterone levels tend to be worse fathers; males with variable levels are better dads. So there's hope for the new man yet.

From the point of view of men, after all, constantly high testosterone is a real problem, as any fifteen-year-old boy trying to concentrate on his homework will tell you. I missed one deadline on this article because it came three days after a testosterone shot and I couldn't bring myself to sit still long enough. And from a purely genetic point of view, men don't merely have an interest in impregnating as many women as possible; they also have an interest in seeing that their offspring are brought up successfully and their genes perpetuated. So for the male, the conflict between sex and love is resolved, as it is for the female, by a compromise between the short-term thrill of promiscuity and the long-term rewards of nurturing children. Just as the female does, he optimizes his genetic outcome by a stable marriage and occasional extramarital affairs. He is just more likely to have these affairs than a woman. Testosterone is both cause and effect of this difference.

And the difference is a real one. This is so obvious a point that we sometimes miss it. But without that difference, it would be hard to justify separate sports leagues for men and women, just as it would be hard not to suspect judicial bias behind the fact that of the ninety-eight people executed last year in the United States, 100 percent came from a group that composes a little less than 50 percent of the population; that is, men. When the discrepancy is racial, we wring our hands. That it is sexual raises no red flags. Similarly, it is not surprising that 55 percent of everyone arrested in 1998 was under the age of twenty-five—the years when male testosterone levels are at their natural peak.

It is also controversial yet undeniable that elevating testosterone levels can be extremely beneficial for physical and mental performance. It depends, of course, on what you're performing in. If your job is to whack home runs, capture criminals, or play the market, then testosterone is a huge advantage. If you're a professional conciliator, office manager, or teacher, it is probably a handicap. Major League Baseball was embarrassed that Mark McGwire's 1998 season home-run record might have been influenced by his use of androstene-dione, a legal supplement that helps increase the body's own production of testosterone. But its own study into andro's effects concluded that regular use of it clearly raises T levels and so improves muscle mass and physical strength, without serious side effects. Testosterone also accelerates the rate of recovery from physical injury. Does this help make sense of McGwire's achievement? More testosterone obviously didn't give him the skill to hit seventy home runs, but it almost certainly contributed to the physical and mental endurance that helped him do so.

Since most men have at least ten times as much T as most women, it therefore makes sense not to have coed baseball leagues. Equally, it makes sense that women will be underrepresented in a high-testosterone environ-ment like military combat or construction. When the skills required are more cerebral or more endurance related, the male-female gap may shrink, or even reverse itself. But otherwise, gender inequality in these fields is primarily not a function of sexism, merely of common sense. This is a highly controversial position, but it really shouldn't be. Even more unsettling is the racial gap in testosterone. Several solid studies, published in publications like *Journal of the National Cancer Institute*, show that black men have on average 3 to 19 percent more testosterone than white men. This is something to consider when we're told that black men dominate certain sports because of white racism or economic class rather than black skill. This reality may, of course, feed stereotypes about blacks being physical but not intellectual. But there's no evidence of any trade-off between the two. To say that someone is physically gifted is to say nothing about his mental abilities, as even NFL die-hards have come to realize. Indeed, as Jon Entine points out in his new book, *Taboo*, even the position of quarterback, which requires a deft mix of mental and physical strength and was once predominantly white, has slowly become less white as talent has been rewarded. The percentage of blacks among NFL quarterbacks is now twice the percentage of blacks in the population as a whole.

But fears of natural difference still haunt the debate about gender equality. Many feminists have made tenacious arguments about the lack of any substantive physical or mental differences between men and women as if the political equality of the sexes depended on it. But to rest the equality of women on the physical and psychological equivalence of the sexes is to rest it on sand. In the end, testosterone bites. This year, for example, Toys "R" Us announced it was planning to redesign its toy stores to group products most likely to be bought by the same types of consumers: in marketing jargon, "logical adjacencies." The results? Almost total gender separation. "Girl's World" would feature Easy-Bake Ovens and Barbies; "Boy's World," trucks and action figures. Though Toys "R" Us denied that there was any agenda behind this—its market research showed that gender differences start as young as two years old—such a public outcry ensued that the store canceled its plans. Meanwhile, Fox Family Channels is about to introduce two new, separate cable channels for boys and girls, Boyz Channel and Girlz Channel, to attract advertisers and consumers more efficiently. Fox executives told *The Wall Street Journal* that their move is simply a reflection of what Nielsen-related research tells them about the viewing habits of boys and girls: that, "in general terms, girls are more interested in entertainment that is relationship-oriented," while boys are "more action-oriented." T, anyone? After more than two decades of relentless legal, cultural, and ideological attempts to negate sexual difference between boys and girls, the market has turned around and shown that very little, after all, has changed.

Advocates of a purely environmental origin for this difference between the sexes counter that gender socialization begins very early and is picked up by subtle inferences from parental interaction and peer pressure, before being reinforced by the collective culture at large. Most parents observing toddlers choosing their own toys and play patterns can best judge for themselves how true this is. But as Matt Ridley has pointed out, there is also physiological evidence of very early mental differences between the sexes, most of it to the advantage of girls. Ninety-five percent of all hyperactive kids are boys; four times as many boys are dyslexic and learning disabled as girls. There is a greater distinction between the right and left brain among boys than girls, and worse linguistic skills. In general, boys are better at spatial and abstract tasks, girls at communication. These are generalizations, of course. There are many, many boys who are great linguists and model students, and vice versa. Some boys even prefer, when left to their own devices, to play with dolls as well as trucks. But we are talking of generalities here, and the influence of womb-given testosterone on those generalities is undeniable.

Some of that influence is a handicap. We are so used to associating testosterone with strength, masculinity, and patriarchal violence that it is easy to ignore that it also makes men weaker in some respects than women. It doesn't correlate with economic power: in fact, as we have seen, blue-collar workers have more of it than white-collar workers. It gets men into trouble. For reasons no one seems to understand, testosterone may also be an immune suppressant. High levels of it can correspond, as recent studies have shown, not only with baldness but also with heart disease and a greater susceptibility to infectious diseases. Higher levels of prostate cancer among blacks, some researchers believe, may well be related to blacks' higher testosterone levels. The aggression it can foster and the risks it encourages lead men into situations that often wound or kill them. And higher levels of testosterone-driven promiscuity make men more prone to sexually transmitted diseases. This is one reason that men live shorter lives on average than women. There is something, in other words, tragic about testosterone. It can lead to a certain kind of male glory; it may lead to valor or boldness or impulsive romanticism. But it also presages a uniquely male kind of doom. The cockerel with the brightest comb is often the most attractive and the most testosteroned, but it is also the most vulnerable to parasites. It is as if it has sacrificed quantity of life for intensity of experience, and this trade-off is a deeply male one.

So it is perhaps unsurprising that those professions in which this trade-off is most pronounced—the military, contact sports, hazardous exploration, venture capitalism, politics, gambling—tend to be disproportionately male. Politics is undoubtedly the most controversial because it is such a critical arena for the dispersal of power. But consider for a moment how politics is conducted in our society. It is saturated with combat, ego, conflict, and risk. An entire career can be lost in a single gaffe or an unexpected shift in the national mood. This ego-driven roulette is almost as highly biased toward the testosteroned as wrestling. So it makes some sense that after almost a century of electorates made up by as many women as men, the number of female politicians remains pathetically small in most Western democracies. This may not be endemic to politics; it may have more to do with the way our culture constructs politics. And it is not to say that women are not good at government. Those qualities associated with low testosterone—patience, risk aversion, empathy—can all lead to excellent governance. They are just lousy qualities in the crapshoot of electoral politics.

If you care about sexual equality, this is obviously a challenge, but it need not be as depressing as it sounds. The sports world offers one way out. Men and women do not compete directly against one another; they have separate tournaments and leagues. Their different styles of physical excellence can be appreciated in different ways. At some basic level, of course, men will always be better than women in many of these contests. Men run faster and throw harder. Women could compensate for this by injecting testosterone, but if they took enough to be truly competitive, they would become men, which would somewhat defeat the purpose.

The harder cases are in those areas in which physical strength is important but not always crucial, like military combat or manual labor. And here the compromise is more likely to be access but inequality in numbers. Finance? Business? Here, where the testosterone-driven differences may well be more subtly psychological, and where men may dominate by discrimination rather than merit, is the trickiest arena. Testosterone-induced impatience may lead to poor decision-making, but low-testosterone risk aversion may lead to an inability to seize business opportunities. Perhaps it is safest to say that unequal numbers of men and women in these spheres are not prima facie evidence of sexism. We should do everything we can to ensure equal access, but it is foolish to insist that numerical inequality is always a function of bias rather than biology. This doesn't mean we shouldn't worry about individual cases of injustice, just that we shouldn't be shocked if gender inequality endures. And we should recognize that affirmative action for women (and men) in all arenas is an inherently utopian project.

Then there is the medical option. A modest solution might be to give more women access to testosterone to improve their sex drives, aggression, and risk affinity and to help redress their disadvantages in those areas as compared with men. This is already done for severely depressed women, or women with hormonal imbalances, or those lacking an adequate sex drive, especially after menopause. Why not for women who simply want to rev up their will to power? Its use needs to be carefully monitored because it can also lead to side effects, like greater susceptibility to cancer, but that's what doctors are there for. And since older men also suffer a slow drop-off in T levels, there's no reason they should be cold-shouldered either. If the natural disadvantages of gender should be countered, why not the natural disadvantages of age? In some ways, this is already happening. Among the most common drugs now available through internet doctors and pharmacies, along with Viagra and Prozac, is testosterone. This summer, with the arrival of AndroGel, the testosterone gel created as a medical treatment for those 4 to 5 million men who suffer from low levels of testosterone, recreational demand may soar.

Or try this thought experiment: What if parents committed to gender equity opted to counteract the effect of testosterone on boys in the womb by complementing it with injections of artificial female hormones? That way, structural gender difference could be eradicated from the beginning. Such a policy would lead to "men and women with normal bodies but identical feminine brains," Matt Ridley posits. "War, rape, boxing, car racing, pornography and hamburgers and beer would soon be distant memories. A feminist paradise would have arrived." Today's conservative cultural critics might also be enraptured. Promiscuity would doubtless decline, fatherhood improve, crime drop, virtue spread. Even gay men might start behaving like lesbians, fleeing the gym and marrying for life. This is a fantasy, of course, but our increasing control and understanding of the scientific origins of our behavior, even of our culture, is fast making those fantasies things we will have to actively choose to forgo.

But fantasies also tell us something. After a feminist century, we may be in need of a new understanding of masculinity. The concepts of manliness, of gentlemanly behavior, of chivalry have been debunked. The New Age bonding of the men's movement has been outlived. What our increasing knowledge of testosterone suggests is a core understanding of what it is to be a man, for better and worse. It is about the ability to risk for good and bad; to act, to strut, to dare, to seize. It is about a kind of energy we often rue but would surely miss. It is about the foolishness that can lead to courage or destruction, the beauty that can be strength or vanity. To imagine a world without it is to see more clearly how our world is inseparable from it and how our current political pieties are too easily threatened by its reality.

And as our economy becomes less physical and more cerebral, as women slowly supplant men in many industries, as income inequalities grow and more highly testosteroned blue-collar men find themselves shunted to one side, we will have to find new ways of channeling what nature has bequeathed us. I don't think it's an accident that in the last decade there has been a growing focus on a muscular male physique in our popular culture, a boom in crass men's magazines, an explosion in violent computer games, or a professional wrestler who has become governor. These are indications of a cultural displacement, of a world in which the power of testosterone is ignored or attacked, with the result that it reemerges in cruder and less social forms. Our main task in the gender wars of the new century may not be bringing women fully into our society, but keeping men from seceding from it, rerouting testosterone for constructive ends, rather than ignoring it for political point making.

For my part, I'll keep injecting the Big T. Apart from how great it makes me feel, I consider it no insult to anyone else's gender to celebrate the uniqueness of one's own. Diversity need not mean the equalization of difference. In fact, true diversity requires the acceptance of difference. A world without the unruly, vulnerable, pioneering force of testosterone would be a fairer and calmer, but far grayer and duller, place. It is certainly somewhere I would never want to live. Perhaps the fact that I write this two days after the injection of another two hundred milligrams of testosterone into my bloodstream makes me more likely to settle for this colorful trade-off than others. But it seems to me no disrespect to womanhood to say that I am perfectly happy to be a man, to feel things no woman will ever feel to the degree that I feel them, to experience the world in a way no woman ever has. And to do so without apology or shame.

The "Invisible Man"

January 12, 2003 | *TIME* magazine

He was, to purloin Ralph Ellison's phrase, the "invisible man" of the civil-rights movement. In the struggle for African American dignity, he was perhaps the most critical figure that many people have never heard of. Which is why, as we prepare to observe Martin Luther King Jr. Day on January 20, it's worth taking a look at the life and lessons of one Bayard Rustin.

Born in 1912 into a Quaker family in West Chester, Pennsylvania, Rustin from an early age dedicated his life to social causes. Trained as an activist by the Quakers, Rustin went to New York City and dabbled in Communist Party activity before quitting in disgust in 1941. Mentored by black labor organizer A. Philip Randolph, Rustin worked in the trade-union movement before becoming a conscientious objector in World War II. He took his pacifism to an extreme, going to a federal penitentiary rather than in any way aiding the war effort.

It was in the late 1940s that Rustin found his real calling—initiating one of the first Freedom Rides through the South to protest and confront legal segregation and becoming a key background figure in encouraging the desegregation of the armed forces. As an advocate of pacifism and nonviolence, Rustin was critical in advising a young and still-uncertain Martin Luther King Jr. on how to conduct an effective civil-rights protest in Montgomery, Alabama. But Rustin's greatest achievement was organizing the 1963 March on Washington, immortalized by King's "I Have a Dream" speech. Thereafter, Rustin never gave up his advocacy for a variety of causes at home and abroad, and was a brave and eloquent voice resisting the Black Power movement that raged in the wake of King's assassination.

Reading about and watching the poignant new PBS documentary about his life (coproduced and codirected by Bennett Singer) and reading his prose, one is struck by a central, inspiring fact. Rustin never wavered in his belief in true racial integration. He saw the civil-rights movement not as a protest against America or an indictment of it but as a way for America to live up to its own principles. In stark contrast to Malcolm X, with whom he civilly debated, Rustin emphasized not what white Americans owed blacks or what blacks could do in a separatist ghetto but what blacks could contribute in a truly equal and integrated America. "I believe the great majority of the Negro people, black people, are not seeking anything from anyone," Rustin told Malcolm X in 1960. "They are seeking to become full-fledged citizens." The simplicity of that statement is as impressive as its moral clarity.

So why his invisibility? Rustin, you see, was a proud and exuberant gay man. From adolescence on, he displayed an ease with his sexual orientation that was extremely rare at that time. He seemed to feel neither guilt nor shame. He had two very public relationships in his life (both with white men), and he came to see his struggle as a homosexual as inextricable from his struggle as a black man in America. But neither mainstream society nor even the civil-rights leadership could cope with his honesty. In 1953, he was arrested for sexual activity in a car—a "morals charge" that embarrassed his allies, humiliated him, and was brutally exploited by, among others, Strom Thurmond. So, like many public gay men, Rustin was forced into a defensive crouch because of his sex life. Having struggled for his dignity as an African American, he was still subject to the dehumanization implicit in homophobia.

But, amazingly, Rustin never showed bitterness. He had every right to be inflamed against the white Establishment, which at one point sentenced him to hard labor on a chain gang as punishment for his early civil-rights protests. And he had every reason to be embittered by his black allies, for their acquiescence in the gay baiting. Yet somehow he rose above both. In one telling incident, he completed his sentence on the chain gang by writing a conciliatory letter to the sadistic white officer who ran the prison. Somehow, Rustin never succumbed to the anger that was his right; his spirit remained as light and as positive as his beautiful tenor voice. And all these years later, that's what endures: the memory of a man unbeaten by the hate around him, dreaming of a future in which the work of integration, black and white, gay and straight, is the moral—and joyful—duty of all of us.

I Am Bear; Hear Me Roar

August 3, 2003 | *SALON*

I was flattered at first. A burly, stubbled, broad-shouldered man, who could barely keep tufts of hair from sprouting from under his T-shirt corners, leered at me across the bar. He was drunk, alas. But it was five minutes to closing and this was Provincetown in July. "You know what I think is so fucking hot about you?" he ventured. I batted my eyelashes. "Your potbelly, man," he went on. "It's so fucking hot." Then he reached over and rubbed.

It was Bear Week in Ptown. Bear Week? Well, where do I begin? Every time I try and write a semiserious sociological assessment of the phenomenon, I find myself erasing large amounts of text. Part of being a bear is not taking being a bear too seriously. And almost every bear and bear admirer I asked during the festivities came up with different analyses of what it is or might be to be a "bear." But no one can deny that bears are one of the fastest-growing new subcultures in gay America—and that their emergence from the forests into the sunlight is culturally fascinating. Quite what it means for the future of gay America is another thing entirely. But my, er, gut tells me it's, er, a big deal. So here's my own idiosyncratic, CIA-unapproved take on what this new and obviously growing phenomenon in the gay sub-subculture amounts to.

Bearism grew up in San Francisco at places like the revived Lone Star bar in the early 1990s and has metastasized since. From a bunch of heavy, hairy fellas getting together casually, it's now a full-scale phenom, with *American Bear* magazine, a "bear flag," bear conferences, a *Bear Book*, "Bearotica," and on and on. Perhaps the most obvious place to start is physical appearance. "Bears" almost all have facial hair—the more the better. Of all the various characteristics of Beardom, this seems to be one of the most essential. The Ur-bears have bushy beards that meander down their necks and merge with a large forest of chest and back hair to provide a sort of all-hair body environment. Bears are also big guys. Yes, I know that might come off as a bit of a euphemism. A townie friend of mine suggested making T-shirts for the week, with the slogan "Fat Is the New Black." But obesity, while not unknown, is not that widespread. Bears at their most typical look like regular, beer-drinking, unkempt men in their thirties, forties, and fifties. They have guts. They have furry backs. They don't know what cologne is and they tend not to wear deodorant. One mode of interaction is the occasional sniff of each other's armpits. Nature's narcotic.

Bears are known secondly for their attitude. They're friendly—more Yogi than "Bears Gone Wild." They're mellow. They're flirtatious in a nonimposing kind of way. If a bear sees another hot-looking bear, his most likely expression will be the one word: "Woof." (Yes, I know that sounds like a dog. But somehow it makes sense.) The sexual tension isn't that tense, because the sexual imperative is less present than in other gay subcultures. This came home to me this year in Provincetown, because in a gay resort town in the summer you get to see the various sub-subcultures intermingle or follow one another. The contrasts can be quite severe.

To give one example: we have what the locals call Circuit Week over July 4 when all the party boys show up to take drugs, dance, and drink bottled water for days on end. I have no problem with that. But the perfect torsos, testoster-oned rivalry, crystal nerves, and endless egg whites all make for a somewhat overwrought time. When the bears arrive, all that unease evaporates. They're cheerful; they don't give a shit what others think of them; they're more overtly social than sexual; they drink rather than do drugs; they seem, on the whole, older and far more grown-up than their party-boy cousins. They eat and drink and joke and cuddle and stroke and generally have a great time. And their mellowness is wonderfully infectious.

Whence the name? Well, it's obvious in a way. They kinda look like bears. Big and burly and friendly, they are legions of Yogis, followed by quite a few Boo-Boos. The smaller, younger ones tend to be known as "cubs." The more muscular ones go by the name of "muscle bears." Some leaner types who aren't that hairy but enjoy the atmosphere that follows the bears are known as "otters." There are other nuances. Bears like to enjoy the outdoors and organize joint camping trips and festivals in the forests. They tend not to have kids, and they avoid politics. To the outside world, they are largely invisible, because they don't fit the obvious stereotype of gay men, the kind that is featured prominently, and somewhat offensively, on *Queer Eye for the Straight Guy* and *Boy Meets Boy*. These bears look more like the straight guys than the queer eyes.

But their masculinity is of a casual, unstrained type. One of the least reported but significant cultural shifts among gay men in recent years has been a greater ease with the notion of being men and a refusal to acquiesce in the notion that gayness is somehow in conflict with masculinity. In the past, gay manifestations of masculinity have taken a somewhat extreme or caricatured form—from the leathermen to the huge bodybuilders. Bears, to my mind, represent a welcome calming down of this trend. They are unabashedly masculine but undemonstrative about it. They are attractive precisely because they don't try so hard. And they add to their outdoorsy gruffness an appealing interior softness. They have eschewed the rock-hard muscle torso for the round and soft and hairy belly.

As always, Camille Paglia gets it just about right, when she writes: "In their defiant hirsutism, gay bears are more virile than the generic bubble-butt junior stud, since body hair is stimulated by testosterone. But the bears' fatness resembles not the warlike Viking mass of a Hells Angel but the capacious bosom of the earth mother. The gay bear is simultaneously animalistic and nurturing, a romp in the wild followed by nap time on a comfy cushion."

That captures something of their unforced maleness. But Paglia underestimates, I think, a rebellion among many gay men both against the feminizing impulses of the broader culture on the right and left and against prevailing norms in gay culture as a whole. In recent years, after all, men have come under withering attack—not just from the PC post-modernist left, which tends to view all forms of unabashed maleness as oppressive, but also from the nannying right, which views men as socially irresponsible sexual miscreants.

Bears are simply saying that they're men first and unashamed of it. More, in fact. What they're saying is that central to the gay male experience is an actual love of men. And men are not "boys"; they're not feminized, hairless, fatless icons on a dance floor. They're grumpy and kind and responsible, and also happy to be themselves. There is no contradiction between being a gay man and being a man as traditionally understood. And if that includes cracking open a six-pack and watching the game, or developing a beer-and-nachos belly, or working in a blue-collar job, or having the clothes sense of the average checkout guy, or preferring the company of men to women, then so be it.

But what bears also do, of course, is take this frumpy, ordinary image of undemonstrative masculinity and eroticize it. Instead of sexualizing the perfect abs or the biggest bicep, bears look at a mature man's belly and see in it the essence of maleness and the mother lode of their sexual attraction. What women (and, now, the gay men on *Queer Eye*) often do to their men—clean them up, domesticate them, clothe them properly, groom them, tame them—is exactly what bears resist. Go to the Dug-Out at the edge of the West Side Highway in New York on a Sunday afternoon, and you'll find a den of cheerful, frisky, thick, and hairy guys, all enjoying a few beers and their own gender. Or check out the club XL in London and find hundreds of big, fat, hairy blokes dancing to their hearts' content until the early hours of the morning, without the slightest sense of self-awareness or embarrassment. In London, even the "potbelly" is becoming formally eroticized.

Bears also resist the squeaky-clean and feminized version of manhood that appears in most gay magazines and even pornography. Take a look at *The Advocate* and *Out* and you will barely find a man over thirty with a gut or a hairy chest anywhere. But that's what most men—including gay men—end up like! Bears in this sense represent the maturation of gay male culture. For the first time, we have a critical mass of older generations of gay men who have always been out but who don't identify with the boyishness and effeminacy of the old-school gay subculture. And they're not looking to replicate or mimic the male-female relationship in any way. Yes, there are "bears" and "cubs." But you are just as likely to find two mature, big guys who are simply into each other. As equals. As men.

Some of this aesthetic, of course, is rooted in class. Upper-middle-class and middle-class bears tend to idealize the working-class stiff; and working-class bears, for the first time perhaps, find their natural state of physical being publicly celebrated rather than ignored. I made a point of asking multiple bears during Bear Week what they did for a living. Yes, there were architects and designers and writers. But there were also computer technicians, delivery truck drivers, construction workers, salesmen, and so on. Again, what we're seeing, I think, is another manifestation of the growth and breadth of gay culture in the new millennium. As the gay world recovers from AIDS, and as the closet continues to collapse, the numbers of gay men keep growing and the diversity of what was once called the gay experience is exploding.

At some point, in fact, it might be asked if bears are a subset of gay culture or simply a culture to themselves. From Ptown, it's pretty clear to me that the "circuit" set, for example, has next to nothing in common with bears and vice versa. Even the leather bars recognize bears as a discrete subculture. The impression of gayness that you get from, say, *The New York Times'* "Sunday Styles" section is light-years away from what the bear subculture represents. In this sense, bears might be "post-gay" inasmuch as their fundamental identity is far more complex than any simple expression of their same-sex attraction.

And, as with most developments in gay culture, they could well influence straight culture as well. Bears, after all, are the straight guys in gay culture. Their very ordinariness makes them more at ease with regular straight guys; but their very ordinariness in some ways is also extremely culturally subversive. Drag queens, after all, are hardly the cutting edge anymore. Straight people love their gay people flaming, or easily cordoned off from the straight experience. Bears reveal how increasingly difficult this is. Their masculinity is indistinguishable in many ways from straight male masculinity—which accounts, in some ways, for their broader invisibility in the culture. They are both more integrated and yet, by their very equation of regular masculinity with gayness, one of the more radical and transformative gay phenomena out there right now.

But perhaps I'm getting ahead of myself. There's a lovely exchange in the invaluable book *Bears on Bears* that captures some of the weirdness of trying to explain such a natural and cheerful development too abstractly. Rex Wockner, furry gay journalist, is talking to Wayne Hoffman, another bear follower:

REX WOCKNER: A few intellectual eastern bears may think it's about subverting the dominant paradigm. Here on the West Coast, it's about sex.

WAYNE HOFFMAN: It's more about ignoring the dominant paradigm than rejecting it actively, in my humble opinion.

REX WOCKNER: It's more about not using words like "dominant paradigm."

I take Rex's point. In some ways, bears represent gay men's long-delayed embrace of their own masculinity in its simplest and sexiest form. In other ways, they represent gay men's desire for normalcy, for a world in which their natural state of being men is neither constrained nor tortured nor contrived. In a strange and undemonstrative way, it's therefore a sign of the extraordinary fluidity of a gay male culture that is changing out of all recognition before, perhaps, with accelerating integration, it disappears for good.

Integration Day

May 17, 2004 | *THE NEW YORK TIMES*

Today is the day that gay citizens in this country cross a milestone of equality. Gay couples will be married in Massachusetts—their love and commitment and responsibility fully cherished for the first time by the society they belong to. It is also, amazingly enough, the day of the fiftieth anniversary of *Brown v. Board of Education*, the Supreme Court ruling that ended racial segregation in schools across America. We should be wary of facile comparisons. The long march of African Americans to civil equality was and is deeply different from the experience and legacy of gay Americans. But in one respect, the date is fitting, for both *Brown* and this new day revolve around a single, simple, and yet deeply elusive idea: integration.

It is, first, a human integration. Marriage, after all, is perhaps the chief mechanism for integrating new families into old ones. The ceremony is a unifying ritual, one in which peers and grandparents meet, best friends and distant relatives chatter. It's hard for heterosexuals to imagine being denied this moment. It is, after all, regarded in our civil religion as the "happiest day of your life." And that is why the denial of such a moment to gay family members is so jarring and cruel. It rends people from their own families; it builds an invisible but unscalable wall between them and the people they love and need.

You might think from some of the discussion of marriage rights for same-sex couples that homosexuals emerge fully grown from under a gooseberry bush in San Francisco. But we don't. We are born into families across the country in every shape and form imaginable. Allowing gay people to marry is therefore less like admitting a group of citizens into an institution from which they have been banned than it is simply allowing them to stay in the very families in which they grew up.

I remember the moment I figured out I was gay. Right then, I realized starkly what it meant: there would never be a time when my own family would get together to celebrate a new, future family. I would never have a relationship as valid as my parents' or my brother's or my sister's. It's hard to describe what this realization does to a young psyche, but it is profound. At that moment, the emotional segregation starts, and all that goes with it: the low self-esteem, the notion of sex as always alien to a stable relationship, the pain of having to choose between the family you were born into and the love you feel.

You recover, of course, and move on. But even when your family and friends embrace you, there is still the sense of being "separate but equal." And this is why the images from Massachusetts today will strike such a chord. For by insisting on nothing more nor less than marriage, the Massachusetts Supreme Judicial Court has abolished that invisible wall that divides families within themselves. This is an integration of the deepest kind.

It is, second, a civil integration. That is why the term "gay marriage" is a misnomer. Today is not the day "gay marriage" arrives in America. Today is the first time that civil marriage has stopped excluding homosexual members of our own families. These are not "gay marriages." They are marriages. What these couples are affirming is not something new; it is as old as humanity itself. What has ended—in one state, at least—is separatism. We have taken a step toward making homosexuality a nonissue, toward making gay citizens merely and supremely citizens.

This is why I am so surprised by the resistance of many conservatives to this reform. It is the most pro-family measure imaginable—keeping families together, building new ones, strengthening the ties between generations. And it is a profound rebuke to identity politics of a reductionist kind, to the separatism that divides our society into categories of gender and color and faith. This is why some elements of the old left once opposed such a measure, after all. How much more striking, then, that the left has been able to shed its prejudices more successfully than the right.

I cannot think of another minority whom conservatives would seek to exclude from family life and personal responsibility. But here is a minority actually begging for a chance to contribute on equal terms, to live up to exactly the same responsibilities as everyone else, to refuse to accept what President Bush calls the "soft bigotry of low expectations." And, so far, with some exceptions, gay citizens have been told no. Conservatives, with the president chief among them, have said to these people that they are beneath the dignity of equality and the promises of American life. They alone are beneath the fold of family.

But this time, these couples have said yes—and all the president can do (today, at least) is watch. It is a private moment and a public one. And it represents, just as *Brown* did in a different way, the hope of a humanity that doesn't separate one soul from another and a polity that doesn't divide one citizen from another. It is integration made real, a love finally come home: after centuries of pain and stigma, the "happiest day of our lives."

Log Cabin Republican

How Gay Was Lincoln?

January 12, 2005 | ANDREWSULLIVAN.COM

How gay was Abraham Lincoln? By asking the question that way, it's perhaps possible to avoid the historically futile, binary question of "gay" versus "straight." Futile, because we are talking about a man who lived well over a century ago, at a time when the very concepts of gay and straight did not exist. And C. A. Tripp, author of *The Intimate World of Abraham Lincoln*, was, despite the crude assertions of some reviewers, a Kinseyite who believed in a continuum between gay and straight. If completely heterosexual is a Kinsey 1 and completely homosexual is a Kinsey 6, Tripp puts Lincoln as a 5. Reading his engrossing, if uneven, book, I'd say you could make a case that Lincoln was, in fact, a 4. It's going to be a subjective judgment, and I'm no Lincoln scholar. In any particular piece of evidence that Tripp discovers, I'd say it's easy to dismiss his theory. But when you review all the many pieces of the Lincoln emotional-sexual puzzle, the homosexual dimension gets harder and harder to ignore. As conservative writer Richard Brookhiser has noted, all we can say with complete confidence is that "on the evidence before us, Lincoln loved men, at least some of whom loved him back." That's a pretty good definition of the core truth of homosexuality.

That Tripp has an "ax to grind" is to my mind unfair. Yes, he sought to understand the homosexual experience better. But he was a Kinseyite social scientist, not a New Left propagandist. His database of Lincoln material is regarded as superb and invaluable to Lincoln scholars everywhere. He had a PhD in clinical psychology, and a mastery of the facts of Darwin's life as well. Yes, he was gay. But being gay can also be an advantage in this respect. The contours of a closeted gay life—the subtle effects of concealed homosexuality on behavior, public and private—are most easily recognized by other gay men, for the simple reason that many have experienced the same things. And the very nature of a closeted life is that it is hard to discern from the surface. I don't doubt that my own view that Lincoln was obviously homosexual is affected by my personal recognition of some aspects of the story, especially in his early years. The danger, of course, is overidentification and projection. But the danger of underidentification is also there—and it may well have impeded real research into what made Lincoln tick. Certainly if you're looking for clear evidence of sexual relationships between men in Lincoln's time in the official historical record, you'll come to the conclusion that no one was gay in the nineteenth century. But of course, many were.

But was Lincoln? Here's what I'd say are the most persuasive facts. Lincoln never developed deep emotional relations with any women, including his wife. Even the few snippets we have of early romances, or his deeply strained courtship of Mary Todd, suggest a painful attempt to live up to social norms, not a regular heterosexual life. His marriage was a disaster, by all accounts. Why? Well, ask Brookhiser in *The New York Times*, who tries to exonerate Todd from charges of being cruel and psychopathic as well as corrupt: "Explosive, imperious, profligate, she may well have been mad. But in fairness to her, Lincoln was maddening—remote and unavailable, when he was not physically absent." Hmmm. Remote, emotionally unavailable, running away to hang with men whenever he could. Ring a bell? Not in Brookhiser's mind.

Or take this wonderful passage about one of Lincoln's early crushes, Billy Greene, who subsequently remarked that Lincoln's "thighs were as perfect as a human being could be." Brookhiser remarks: "Everyone saw that Lincoln was tall and strong, but this seems rather gushing." Gushing? I'd say. When you also realize that the primary form of gay sex back then was "inter-femoral," i.e., ejaculating by humping between the thighs, you might get a slightly different idea of what Lincoln's intimate was talking about. And, yes, they slept together—in a cot-bed. Remember that Lincoln was well over six feet tall. It was a tight fit. As Greene said himself, "when one turned over the other had to do likewise." So just picture the actual scene: two young men inseparable and spooning each night in bed. Gay? Whatever would give you that idea?

For me, the memoir of Lincoln's stepmother was also enlightening. Not that she thought her stepson was gay. Nor even that he "was not very fond of girls, as he seemed to me." Merely his reclusiveness, emotional distance, resorting to learning and bookishness, as well as a bawdy, sexually frank side when with peers. Yes, not definitive—many straight kids have similar experiences. But Lincoln was also the classic "best little boy in the world" type in childhood—one of the largest categories of gay male childhood there is.

He slept with his first major love, Joshua Speed, for four years. Yes, this was not as odd as it might seem today. But sleeping with him the very day they met? And doing so for four more years—when an aspiring young lawyer could easily have found lodgings of his own? No one denies that their friendship was intense, that they were often inseparable, and that when Speed finally left town Lincoln had a complete nervous breakdown. (This last, vital fact is omitted from Brookhiser's review.) Speed's and Lincoln's letters detailing their approach to marriage are redolent of white-knuckled panic. Any gay man who has experienced the agony of a lover's being propelled by social pressure to marry a woman will recognize the emotional power of this moment in Lincoln's life. (Speed couldn't actually consummate his own marriage.)

Yes, Lincoln's fitful, reluctant engagement to Mary Todd had also fallen through. But he had never shown that much interest in her, had been distant and ambivalent in the courtship. But Speed? Inseparable. "Yours forever" as Abe's letters to Speed always ended. And when Speed left him: "I am now the most miserable man living. . . whether I shall ever be better I can not tell; I awfully forbode I shall not. To remain as I am is impossible; I must die or be better, it appears to me." In fact, of course, Lincoln suffered from acute bouts of depression for his entire life. It seems loopy to ignore the possibility that this was related to his being denied a real or meaningful love life. But then if you're heterosexual and have never experienced such emotional desolation, why would you look in the first place?

What else? Lincoln slept with another man in the White House when his wife was away. To those who say this was normal for nineteenth-century men, I wonder if they could find another example of a president asking a young captain to sleep with him in his bed when his wife was away. They even shared a night shirt, according to a contemporary source. "What stuff" indeed! Lincoln befriended the younger man instantly, kept him in his close confidence, and refused for a while to let his company be reassigned away from the White House. Tripp finds evidence for several other crushes and possible affairs. Previous historians have noticed a "lavender" streak in Lincoln's life and loves. Tripp's own readings of the literary evidence do sometimes stretch things, but only because he's working from the assumption that if Lincoln had been gay, would these actions, events, and relationships make more sense? The reader can make up her own mind. It seems to me that Lincoln's emotional life makes more sense if one assumes his homosexuality than his heterosexuality. But he was not exclusively either.

As for sex, Tripp is very clear at many points that he has no solid evidence. But what evidence of sex was there at the time, except for children? It would scarcely have been reported. But equally, the standard for men in the past must surely not be that they were always celibate. The absence of acknowledgment of sex doesn't mean it didn't happen. Lincoln's extreme comfort with sexual bawdiness does not strike one as coming from someone who practiced extreme self-denial. Masturbation was far more stigmatized than it is today. So in those four years sleeping in the same bed as Speed, when and how did Lincoln ejaculate? It seems highly unlikely to me that in over a thousand nights in the same bed nothing sexual occurred. Lincoln is an icon, but he was also a human being.

The usual suspects have weighed in aggressively to counter these facts. *The Weekly Standard*, from its sophomoric cover image of a simpering gay caricature of Lincoln to its hiring of a crank to denounce the book as a "hoax" and "fraud," is a useful exhibit in the degeneration of conservative discourse. But what's interesting to me is that even if you gloss all Lincoln's male relationships as homosocial or homoerotic rather than homosexual, they still paint a picture that would offend today's Republican Establishment. Whatever Lincoln was, he was very at ease expressing love, intimacy, and affection for other men. The last thing he was, was sexually prudish. His early doggerel poem about the progeny that results from anal sex with another man—he has the two men married, no less!—would be regarded by today's conservatives as worthy of protest to the FCC.

But today's right-wingers are right about one thing. The truth about Lincoln—his unusual sexuality, his comfort with male-male love and sex—is not a truth today's Republican leaders want to hear. They are well-advised to attack and suppress it. They are more closely related to the forces Lincoln defeated than those he championed, and his candor, honesty, and brave forging of a homosocial and homoerotic life in plain sight would appall them. The real Lincoln is their greatest rebuke, which is why they will do all they can to obscure the complicated, fascinating truth about the man whose legacy they are intent on betraying.

Life Lesson

February 7, 2005 | *THE NEW REPUBLIC*

H illary Rodham Clinton is absolutely right. I've waited many years to write that sentence, but, hey, if you live long enough . . . I'm referring to her superb speech earlier this week on the politics and morality of abortion. There were two very simple premises to Clinton's argument: a) the right to legal abortion should remain, and b) abortion is always and everywhere a moral tragedy. It seems to me that if we are to reduce abortions to an absolute minimum (and who, exactly, opposes that objective?), then Clinton's formula is the most practical. Her key sentences: "We can all recognize that abortion in many ways represents a sad, even tragic choice to many, many women. . . . The fact is that the best way to reduce the number of abortions is to reduce the number of unwanted pregnancies in the first place."

Echoing her husband's inspired notion that abortion should be "safe, legal, and rare," the senator from New York seemed to give new emphasis to that last word: "rare." Hers is, in that respect, a broadly pro-life position. Not in an absolutist, logically impeccable fashion — which would require abolishing all forms of legal abortion immediately — but in a pragmatic, moral sense. In a free society, the ability of a woman to control what happens to her own body will always and should always be weighed in the balance against the right of an unborn child to life itself. And if she and the Democrats can move the debate away from the question of abortion's legality toward abortion's immorality, then they stand a chance of winning that debate in the coming years.

For too long, supporters of abortion rights have foolishly and callously trivi-alized the moral dimensions of the act of ending human life in the womb. They have insisted that no profound moral cost is involved. They remain seemingly impassive in the face of the horrors of partial-birth abortion. They talk in the abstract language of "reproductive rights" and of a "war against women." To acknowledge that human life is valuable from conception to death has been, at times, beyond their capacity. They have seemed blind to the fact that, as Naomi Wolf once alluded in this magazine, mothers and children have souls and that, in every abortion, one soul is destroyed and another wounded. And they seem far too dismissive of the fact that the concerns of many pro-life Americans are not rooted in intolerance but in the oldest liberal traditions of the protection of the weak.

All this has undermined the pro-choice movement. Its members seem godless in a faithful culture. They have come to seem indifferent to pain, almost glib in the face of human tragedy. Of course, this may not be true in the hearts and minds of many pro-choice activists. But, in the arena of public debate, it is the cold corner into which their rhetoric has condemned them.

How to change? Clinton's approach is the right one. Acknowledge up front the pain of abortion and its moral gravity. Defend its legality only as a terrible compromise necessary for the reduction of abortions in general, for the rights of women to control their own wombs, and for the avoidance of unsafe, amateur abortions. And then move to arenas where liberals need have no qualms: aggressive use of contraception and family planning, expansion and encouragement of adoption, and a rhetorical embrace of the "culture of life." One reason that John Kerry had such a hard time reaching people who have moral qualms about abortion was his record and rhetoric: a relentless defense of abortion rights—even for third-trimester unborn children—with no emphasis on the moral costs of such a callous disregard of human dignity. You cannot have such a record and then hope to convince others that you care about the sanctity of life.

Clinton did one other thing as well. She paid respect to her opponents. She acknowledged the genuine religious convictions of those who oppose all abortion. She recognized how communities of faith have often been the most successful in persuading young women to refrain from teenage sex. She challenged her pro-choice audience by pointing out that "seven percent of American women who do not use contraception account for fifty-three percent of all unintended pregnancies." She also cited research estimating that fifteen thousand abortions per year are by women who have been sexually assaulted—one of several reasons, she said, that morning-after emergency contraception should be made available over the counter. By focusing on contraception, she appeals to all those who oppose abortion but who do not follow the abstinence-only movement's rigid restrictions on the surest way to prevent them.

But even this is not enough for the Democrats to move the issue out of its current impasse. The party needs to end its near fatwa on pro-life politicians and spokespeople. Harry Reid and Tim Roemer are a start. The Democrats should learn from President Bush's canny use of the issue. He is firmly pro-life. And yet he gave several pro-choice politicians key slots at the Republican convention. The new number two at the Republican National Committee, Jo Ann Davidson, is pro-choice. When the Republicans are more obviously tolerant of dissent than Democrats, something has gone awry. One obvious option: find every way to back Pennsylvania's Robert Casey Jr. in his campaign to wrest a Senate seat from the most extreme and intolerant pro-life absolutist, Rick Santorum. Or take a leaf from Tony Blair's book. In his cabinet, the thirty-six-year-old education secretary, Ruth Kelly, is adamantly pro-life as a matter of conscience and is even a member of the ultraconservative Catholic group Opus Dei. Her personal views on this do not impact her political position—or Blair's own support for abortion rights. But her inclusion in the Labour Party shows a recognition that, on such profound moral issues, party lines are inappropriate—and often self-defeating.

In some ways, this does not mean a change of principle. Democrats can still be, and almost certainly should be, for the right to legal abortion. But, instead of beginning their conversation with that right, they should start by acknowledging a wrong. Abortion is always wrong. How can we keep it legal while doing all we can to reduce its damage? Call it a pro-life pro-choice position. And argue for it with moral passion. If you want to win a "values" debate, it helps to advance what Democrats value. And one of those obvious values is the fewer abortions the better. Beyond the polarizing rhetoric, a simple message: saving one precious life at a time.

Superstar

April 17, 2005 | *THE NEW REPUBLIC*

H e was an actor. And his greatest and most innovative skill as pontiff was the creation of drama and symbolism. You only had to observe one of his peripatetic papal visits to see that, as I was lucky enough to do in San Antonio. The modern-looking stage, the vast crowds that this pope knew he could summon anywhere in the world, the carefully planned photo ops—they all created a series of mirrors focusing back on the man himself. He communicated as much by stirring addresses in dozens of languages as by a deeply creased brow, a smile, or a tear. This dramatization of self continued until his death. We have been told that his last gesture was an attempt to bless the huge crowd assembled outside St. Peter's. He was on stage until the end.

Before him, none of this was imaginable. Karol Wojtyła took the painstakingly acquired, centuries-long mystique of the secluded, sacred papacy and cashed it in across the globe. His superstar presence alone was the overwhelming message—whether to those in Africa who felt excluded from the global church, or to the Poles chafing under Soviet tyranny, or to those Catholics in Central and South America battling poverty, inequality, and the growing force of evangelical Protestantism. Even English Catholics felt something profound when the pope visited Great Britain for the first time since the Reformation. The Church had always understood the importance of pageantry and drama and personality. But Wojtyła actually reinvented the form for a world of mass media.

It took a while to realize that this personalization of the Church—and its identification with one man before all others—was more than drama. Wojtyła leveraged this new stardom to reassert a far older idea of the papacy—as the central, unaccountable force in the Church. The Second Vatican Council had opened authority up, placing the hierarchy on a more equal footing with the lay faithful in understanding the tenets of faith. It had also led to all sorts of chaotic improvisation and confusion. Wojtyła shut this process down—the good alongside the bad. He didn't reverse the council (it was beyond his will or power). But he ignored and suppressed it in critical areas. National churches were given little leeway. Dissent within the Church was forbidden. The pope silenced even debate of issues that were not of fundamental doctrinal importance, such as the prudential, managerial questions of whether priests could marry or whether women could become priests. These, he asserted, were eternal arrangements that were beyond discussion, even if maintaining them had led to a crisis in the Church's very existence in some countries.

This man so hostile to intellectual debate was, paradoxically, an intellectual, although an idiosyncratic one. His faith was a strange mixture of esoteric phenomenological reflections and medieval attachments to various saints, miracles, and practices. He made few fundamental changes. But he resolutely appointed loyalists to every position he could, and he elevated the secretive and ultraconservative order of Opus Dei to unheard-of influence. On matters of human sexuality and the "culture of life," he moved Catholic teaching away from prudential balance to eternal absolutes—that life is equally sacred, whether it is a nanosecond after conception or decades into a persistent vegetative state. The distinctions made by Catholics in the past—between, say, a naturally aborted embryo and a third-trimester baby, or between "ordinary" and "extraordinary" means for maintaining life—were downplayed. Why? Perhaps because the pope believed the danger of new technologies required as radical an opposition as possible.

Did he succeed? If, by "success," we mean the maintenance of the truth in the face of error, then only God knows. If, by "success," we mean asserting the truths of Christianity against the lies of communism, then the answer is an unequivocal yes. But if, by "success," we mean winning the argument against secular democracy in the West, the answer must be no. This European pope oversaw an unprecedented collapse of the Church in its European heartland. Under his papacy, vocations for the priesthood barely kept up with population in the developing world and simply collapsed in the West. Protestantism boomed in South America. Mass attendance in North America fell, along with donations. And the quality of the priesthood went from mediocre to terrible. If you judge a successful leader by the caliber of men he inspires to follow him, then the judgment on John Paul II is damning.

Under his papacy, the Church was also guilty of allowing the rape and molestation of vast numbers of children and teenagers, and of systematically covering the crimes up. It is hard to understand how the leader of any lay organization would have stayed in office after allowing such criminality. But how the leader of the Catholic Church survived without even an attempt at papal accountability is still astonishing. A pope who devoted enormous energy to explicating why the only moral expression of human sexuality is marital heterosexual intercourse presided over the rape of thousands of children by his own priests. What was his response? He protected the chief enabler of the abuse in the United States, Cardinal Bernard Law, and used the occasion of his own Church's failing to blame homosexuals in general. Attempting to grapple with the real question would have meant a debate about priestly celibacy, homosexuality, pedophilia, and the Church's disproportionately gay priesthood. But this pope was far more interested in closing debates than in opening them.

I have a personal stake in this as well, of course. I'm a Catholic now withdrawn from Communion whose entire adult life has been in Wojtyła's shadow. And, as a homosexual, I watched as the Church refused to grapple with even basic questions and ran, terrified, from its own deep psychosexual dysfunction. "Be not afraid," this pope counseled us. But he was deeply afraid of the complicated truth about human sexuality and the dark truth about his own Church's crimes. This was a pope who, above all, knew how to look away. But people—faithful people—noticed where he couldn't look. And they grieved, even as, in the aftermath of this brittle, showboating papacy, they now hope.

Crisis of Faith

How Fundamentalism Is Splitting the GOP

May 2, 2005 | *THE NEW REPUBLIC*

———————

In this present crisis, government is not the solution to our problem. Government is the problem.

—Ronald Reagan, January 20, 1981

We have a responsibility that, when somebody hurts, government has got to move.

—George W. Bush, September 1, 2003

Conservatism isn't over. But it has rarely been as confused. Today's conservatives support limited government. But they believe the federal government can intervene in a state court's decisions in a single family's struggle over life and death. They believe in restraining government spending. But they have increased such spending by a mind-boggling 33 percent in a mere four years. They believe in self-reliance. But they have just passed the most expensive new entitlement since the heyday of Great Society liberalism: the Medicare prescription-drug benefit. They believe that foreign policy is about the pursuit of national interest and that the military should be used only to fight and win wars. Yet they have embarked on an extraordinarily ambitious program of military-led nation building in the Middle East. They believe in states' rights, but they want to amend the Constitution to forbid any state from allowing civil marriage or equivalent civil unions for gay couples. They believe in free trade. But they have imposed tariffs on a number of industries, most famously steel. They believe in balanced budgets. But they have abandoned fiscal discipline and added a cool trillion dollars to the national debt in one presidential term.

One reason for conservatism's endurance in the face of such contradiction, of course, is the extreme weakness—intellectual and organizational—of the opposition. Liberalism ceased being a vibrant force in the American public weal two decades ago. The left never recovered from the collapse of communism, the dismal failure of social democracy across Western Europe, and the demise of Japan's command economy in the 1980s. Domestically, a liberal claim on the presidency never recovered from Jimmy Carter and the first two years of Bill Clinton. Conservatism, broadly understood, has occupied the White House for twenty-three of the past twenty-five years. No unreconstructed liberal stands a chance of winning it in the near future—hence Hillary Clinton's moderate makeover.

Conservatism has endured also because it slowly absorbed much of the old liberal spirit. Who, after all, are the most vocal moral crusaders of today? Christian conservatives, who deploy government power against all sorts of perceived wrongs—sexual trafficking, AIDS in Africa, gay unions, poor parenting, teen sex, indecent television, and euthanasia, among many. Almost no Democrat speaks with the moral conviction of religious Republicans. And, when liberalism has been outrun on moral fervor, precious little oxygen remains to revive it—especially with austere, patrician leaders like John Kerry and Al Gore or angry pop-culture ranters like Michael Moore.

But conservatism's very incoherence may be one reason for its endurance. In its long road to victory, the Republican Party has regularly preferred the promise of power to the satisfaction of schism. It has long been pro-government and antigovernment. It has contained Rockefeller and Goldwater, Nixon and Reagan, Bush I and Bush II. As a governing philosophy, it has been able to tack for decades from statism to laissez-faire, from big government to individual freedom, with only occasional discomfort. Conservatism's resilience has been a function of its internal ideological diversity and balance. The more closely you look, however, the deeper the division has become in the last few years, intensifying dramatically since last fall's election. Which is why, this time, the balancing act may finally be coming undone.

Let me be rash and describe the fundamental divide within conservatism as a battle between two rival forms. The two forms I'm referring to are ideal types. I know very few conservatives who fit completely into one camp or the other, and these camps do not easily comport with the categories we have become used to deploying—categories like "libertarian," "social conservative," "paleoconservative," "fiscal conservative and social liberal," and so on. There is, I think, a deeper rift, and a more fundamental one.

Call one the conservatism of faith and the other the conservatism of doubt. They have coexisted in the past but are becoming less and less compatible as the conservative ascendancy matures. Start with the type now dominant in Republican discourse: the conservatism of faith. This conservatism states conservative principles—and, indeed, eternal insights into the human condition—as a matter of truth. Because these conservatives believe that the individual is inseparable from her political community and civilization, there can be no government neutrality in promoting such truths. Either a government's laws affirm virtue or they affirm vice. And the meaning of virtue and vice can be understood either by reflecting on the Judeo-Christian moral tradition or by inferring from philosophical understandings what human nature in its finest form should be. These truths are not culturally relative; they are universally valid.

The state, therefore, has a duty to protect, at a minimum, all human life, meaning it must regulate abortion and end-of-life decisions. The conservatism of faith sees nothing wrong with channeling $2 billion of public money to religious charities, as the Bush administration boasts; or with spending government money to promote sexual abstinence as a moral good; or with telling parents in government literature that a gay child may need therapy. Science must be hedged by faith, as the teaching of evolution is questioned and pharmacists are allowed to refuse prescriptions for contraception on religious grounds. And public education must have a moral component. As President Bush said in his first State of the Union, "Values are important, so we have tripled funding for character education to teach our children not only reading and writing, but right from wrong." The "we" referred to here is the federal government. The alternative, in the eyes of faith conservatives, would be to allow those with a different morality to promote a rival agenda. Since neutrality is impossible, conservative truths trump secular values.

What matters to conservatives of faith is therefore less the size of government than its meaning and structure. If it is harnessed to uphold their definition of the good life — protecting a stable family structure, upholding biblical morality, protecting the vulnerable — then its size is irrelevant, as long as it doesn't overwhelm civil society. Indeed, using government to promote certain activities (the proper care of children, support for the poor, legal privileges for heterosexual relationships) and to deter others (recreational drug use, divorce, gay unions, abortion, indecent television) is integral to the conservative project. Bush has added another twist to this philosophy, seeking to expand government programs not only from the top down, but from the bottom up, by incorporating new mechanisms that give citizens more choice. Hence Health Savings Accounts in Medicare and personal accounts within Social Security. If that actually means more government borrowing and spending, so be it. If government must be expanded to give more people a sense of "ownership" within government programs, fine. This is what remains of conservatism's old belief in individual freedom. The new conservatism of faith has substituted real choice in a free market for regulated choice within an ever-expanding welfare state.

There is nothing especially new about this kind of conservatism. Bismarck and Disraeli pioneered it in Europe in the nineteenth century, using imperial foreign policy, domestic paternalism, and religious piety to cement new majorities. In the United States, it has less of a pedigree, because the power of the federal government was historically far more restrained than in Europe. But the use of government to impose morality is obviously an old American theme — whether in the abolitionist or temperance campaigns or even, to some extent, in Jim Crow laws and the civil-rights movement. A country that has amended its Constitution to forbid drinking alcohol is no stranger to big-government conservatism.

Of course, it is equally true that, since Franklin Roosevelt vastly expanded the federal government, conservatism has been associated with resistance to its power rather than encouragement of its deployment. The conservative wing of the GOP backed states' rights against civil rights. Conservatives opposed the New Deal. Ronald Reagan equated Medicare with the end of American freedom. The difference today is that acceptance of big government has not meant mere acquiescence in the liberal orthodoxy, but a conscious attempt to use government for moral ends. As Republicans found that it was hard to reduce the size of government, they decided to stop worrying and deploy it for their own goals.

As a result, Republicans now support institutions they previously vilified: whereas they once wanted to abolish the federal Department of Education, now they want to wield it to advance their own agenda on educational standards and morals (no wonder that, in four years, Bush has doubled—yes, doubled—its budget). They are willing to concern themselves with aspects of human life that conservatives once believed should be free of all government interference. In his 2003 State of the Union speech, Bush said, "I propose a four-hundred-and-fifty-million-dollar initiative to bring mentors to more than a million disadvantaged junior high students and children of prisoners. . . . I propose a new six-hundred-million-dollar program to help an additional three hundred thousand Americans receive [drug] treatment over the next three years." And the conservative movement, begun partially in resistance to federal intervention in what was regarded as the states' spheres of influence, today has endorsed dramatic federal supremacy over state prerogatives. The No Child Left Behind Act entailed a massive transfer of power from states to the federal government—not just a difference from Reagan-era conservatism, but its opposite.

No wonder the size of government has exploded. The federal government now spends around $22,000 per household per year—up from a little under $19,000 in 2000. Total government spending has increased by an astonishing 33 percent since 2000. This isn't all about post–September 11 defense and homeland security. According to the Heritage Foundation, a conservative think tank, since 2001, federal spending on housing and commerce has jumped 86 percent, community and regional development 71 percent, and Medicaid some 46 percent. One of Bush's closest confidants and longtime chief of staff, Andy Card, described the president's own vision of his role as president: "It struck me as I was speaking to people in Bangor, Maine, that this president sees America as we think about a ten-year-old child. . . . I know, as a parent, I would sacrifice all for my children." In Bush's case, paternalism isn't a metaphor. It's a commitment worth trillions of dollars of other people's money.

The single most influential architect of this conservatism, Karl Rove, sees this as a virtue, not a problem. In a recent speech to conservative activists, according to John Heilemann of *New York* magazine, "Rove rejected the party's 'reactionary' and 'pessimistic' past, in which it stood idly by while 'liberals were setting the pace of change and had the visionary goals.' Now, he went on, the GOP has seized the 'mantle of idealism,' dedicating itself to 'putting government on the side of progress and reform, modernization and greater freedom.'" The model for Rove's conservatism, in other words, is liberalism. The difference is merely how government directs its vast power, and for whom. In some cases, where the conservatism of faith seeks to use government power to protect the weak, it is indistinguishable from liberalism. It is no accident, I think, that left-liberals like Jesse Jackson and Ralph Nader embraced the cause of Bush's federal intervention in the Terri Schiavo case. And it is equally no accident that sincere internationalist liberals see much to admire in Bush's hyperliberal foreign policy, or that long-standing campaigners for action against HIV/AIDS in the developing world have been pleasantly surprised by his activism and generosity. The fact that the president almost never publicly worries about levels of public spending and debt is also music to traditionally liberal ears. Only bitterness has prevented many on the left from seeing that this administration is on their side on many issues. Or, perhaps, that this president has brilliantly co-opted liberal rhetoric for big-government conservatism.

What other kind of conservatism is there? The alternative philosophical tradition begins in precise opposition to the new conservatives' confidence in faith and reason as direct, accessible routes to universal truth. The conservatism of doubt asks how anyone can be sure that his view of what is moral or good is actually true. Conservatives of doubt note that even the most dogmatic of institutions, such as the Catholic or Mormon churches, have changed their views over many centuries, and that, even within such institutions, there is considerable debate about difficult moral issues. They understand that significant critiques of human reason—Nietzsche, anyone?—have rendered the philosophical quest for self-evident truth even more precarious in the modern world. Such conservatives are not nihilists or devotees of what Pope Benedict XVI has called "the dictatorship of relativism." They merely believe that the purported choice between moral absolutism and complete relativism, between God and moral anarchy, is a phony one. Their alternative is a skeptical, careful, prudential approach to all moral questions—and suspicion of anyone claiming to hold the absolute truth. Since such an approach rarely provides a simple answer persuasive to everyone within a democratic society, we live with moral and cultural pluralism.

For conservatives of faith, such pluralism can allow error to flourish—and immorality to become government policy—and therefore must be limited. A conservative of doubt, however, does not regard the existence of such pluralism as a problem. He sees it as an unavoidable fact of modernity, an invitation to lives that are more challenging and autonomous than in more traditional societies. Even when conservatives of doubt disagree with others' moral convictions, they recognize that, in a free, pluralist society, those other views deserve a hearing. So a conservative who believes abortion is always immoral can reconcile herself to a polity in which abortion is still legal, if regulated. Putting government power unequivocally on the side of one view of morality—especially in extremely controversial areas—must always be balanced against the rights and views of citizens who dissent. And, precisely because complete government neutrality may be impossible on these issues, government should tread as lightly as possible. The key in areas of doubt is to do as little harm as possible. Which often means, with respect to government power, doing as little as possible.

Doubt, in other words, means restraint. And restraint of government is the indispensable foundation of human freedom. The modern liberal European state was founded on such doubt. In the seventeenth century, men like Thomas Hobbes and John Locke looked at the consequences of various faiths battling for control of the moralizing state—and they balked. They saw civil war, religious extremism, torture, burnings at the stake, police states, and the Inquisition. They saw polities like Great Britain's ravaged by sectarian squabbles over what the truth is, how it is discovered, and how to impose it on a society as a whole. And they made a fundamental break with ancient and medieval political thought by insisting that government retreat from such areas—that it leave the definition of the good life to private citizens, to churches uncontaminated by government, or to universities that would seek and discuss competing views of the truth.

In the modern world, where disagreement among citizens is even deeper and more diverse than three centuries ago, conservatives of doubt see their tradition as more necessary than ever. As the fusion of religious fundamentalism with politics has destroyed Muslim society and politics, so, these conservatives fear, it threatens Western freedom as well—in subtler, milder, Christian forms. Conservatives of doubt are not necessarily atheists or amoralists. Many are devout Christians who embrace a strong separation of church and state—for the sake of religion as much as politics. Others may be Oakeshottian skeptics, or Randian individualists, or Burkean pragmatists, or libertarian idealists. But they all agree that the only solution to deep social disagreement is not a forced supremacy of a majority or minority, but an attempt to keep government as neutral as possible, power as close to people as possible, and as much economic power in the hands of the private sector as possible.

For such conservatives, divided government is therefore critical. Judicial checks on democratic majorities are as vital as legislative checks on executive abuse. (They are just as queasy removing such parliamentary checks as the filibuster.) The same goes for keeping policymaking as close as possible to states and localities. Why? Because human knowledge is fallible, and those closest to the issues are more likely to get solutions right than people a long way away. The notion that the federal government should actively endorse one religion's perspective on social policy would appall such conservatives. So would the idea that individual states cannot legitimately experiment with policies on which there is no national consensus—such as stem-cell research or marriage rights.

Such conservatives are delighted at Bush's tax cuts in principle. But they also doubt whether financing them entirely by borrowing is a real tax cut. If you do not cut spending by the same amount (or almost the same amount) as you have cut taxes, you are merely postponing a fiscal reckoning. Conservatives of doubt question the faith of supply-side economics, where all economic trade-offs are banished. They suspect that either the government will have to raise taxes at some point to pay off its debts or it will have to devalue its currency, or allow inflation. The chances of an administration tackling government spending after endorsing it enthusiastically for four years strikes these conservatives as unlikely. Hence their disillusion with Bush. They worry that this president has effectively granted legitimacy to vast areas of government power that the left will soon seize on to consolidate the welfare state and raise taxes under the banner of debt reduction.

This ever-expanding entitlement state offends conservatives of doubt as deeply as the theo-conservative religious state. Their reasoning? At any given moment, wealth that is absorbed by the government is not available to individuals. The more of a country's wealth the government controls, the less freedom for that country's citizens. For a conservative of doubt, the market is a much more reliable indicator of how individuals actually want to live their lives than a government directive or program. Why? Again, the argument rests on an understanding of human wisdom. Since error is inevitable in human choice, better to lessen the chances for those errors to be magnified and compounded by one predominant actor—the government. The more dispersed power is, the less chance for catastrophe.

Is this conservatism philosophically strong enough to endure? Rich Lowry of *National Review* recently argued that it is not: "The secularist view misses that freedom is grounded in truths, in the God-given dignity of man as a rational creature and in our fundamental equality. This is why the pope could say, 'God created us to be free.' If the idea of freedom is detached from these truths, it has no secure ground, because the strong will inevitably attempt to dominate the weak unless checked by moral truths (see slavery or segregation or communism)." Without Christianity, Lowry argues, the rights of the individual will be trampled. But what if Lowry's fellow citizen is an atheist? How can the atheist be persuaded to consent to truths that are only solidly grounded in a faith he doesn't share? And what happens when even those who share the same faith disagree profoundly on its moral and political consequences? Lowry seems to forget that men of Christian faith strongly opposed and backed slavery and segregation—and used biblical texts to do so.

The defense of human freedom offered by conservatives of doubt, on the other hand, is founded on more accessible and less contentious arguments. Such conservatives can point to the Constitution itself as the basis of US political life, and its Enlightenment concept of freedom as sturdy enough without extra-constitutional theology. (The purpose of the Constitution was to preserve the Declaration of Independence's right to "life, liberty and the pursuit of happiness." The word "virtue" is not included in that phrase. Its omission is the single greatest innovation of the US founding.) They can point to the astonishing success and durability of the US experiment to buttress the notion that the Constitution is a much more stable defense of human equality than that inherent in any religion. The Constitution itself has far wider support among citizens than any theological argument. To put it another way: you don't need an actual religion when you already have a workable civil version in place.

What, though, happens to moral appeals in politics? They do not disappear, especially in a place as deeply religious as the United States. But they express themselves in crusades for personal salvation, evangelism, or social work, rather than in legislative change. Compare President George H. W. Bush's praise for "a thousand points of light" as a critical voluntary complement to the welfare state with George W. Bush's channeling of public money into religious social programs. The one is premised on a conservatism of doubt; the second, on a conservatism of faith. In that sense, the new conservatism seems to believe that faith communities cannot do their work adequately without government help. It has less faith in faith than conservatives of doubt do.

For the last few decades, enough has united conservatives of doubt and conservatives of faith to keep the coalition in one rickety piece. Both groups were passionately anticommunist, even if there were some disagreements on strategy and tactics. Today both groups are just as hostile to Islamist terrorism and fundamentalism. Both groups have historically backed lower taxes. Both oppose affirmative action and gun control. And there have been conservative personalities who have managed to appeal to both sides—Ronald Reagan is the exemplar.

Conservatism is stronger for containing both traditions. The contribution of Christianity to Western notions of human freedom is indisputable, and conservatives of doubt have no desire to minimize that fact. Similarly, conservative Christians have historically been aware of the need for limited government in order to protect the very freedoms that allow their faith to flourish. Besides, the West has long alternated between periods that emphasized the need for collective moral action and those that demanded smaller government and greater individual freedom. Conservatism's diverse philosophical pedigree has allowed it to adapt and endure as a political philosophy.

In the last part of the twentieth century, conservatism in Great Britain and the United States threaded both needles, dramatically increasing individual economic freedom through lower taxes, while retaining respect for moral tradition and stability for family structure and individual responsibility. You might describe Reagan and Margaret Thatcher as people who, in a collectivist age, had faith in the conservatism of doubt. But, as this wave of conservatism ratcheted back government power, and as left-of-center parties—Bill Clinton's Democrats and Tony Blair's New Labour—all but acquiesced to the new order, the right's intellectual energy sought new projects. Conservatism had won much in the 1990s, even as liberal parties ruled: taxes were not raised to anything like the levels of the past; fiscal discipline became entrenched; issues like tackling welfare and crime found their way to the liberal wing of the Anglo-American political spectrum.

What, then, was the right to do? In Great Britain, it has hewed to the center-right and failed to unseat an essentially center-right government under Blair. It has endorsed marginally lower taxes, but essentially reconciled itself to Blair's incremental increase in government and the social liberalization of the past thirty years. (Compared with Bush's spending habits, Blair is a Thatcherite.) In the United States, however, conservatives of faith saw their opportunity and reversed many years of limited-government philosophy in order to install a bigger, more morally attuned, more powerful government.

At the same time, the nature and content of the faith of these postmillennial conservatives changed. It was no longer that of mainstream Protestantism or even of most American Catholics. It was a version of faith that was resurgent around the world as the new millennium passed: a fundamentalist and author-itarian revival that took hold in all the major religions. And it was this funda-mentalism that made the new faith conservatism more radical and far-reaching than in the past. It kept the radical edge of conservatism razor-sharp.

Fundamentalism, by its very nature, eschews compromise. It is not an infer-ential philosophy, drawing on experience or history to come to a conclusion about the appropriate way to act or legislate on any given issue. It derives its purpose from fixed texts: the Bible or the Koran. In its Catholic form, it vests unalterable authority in the pope rather than in the more heterodox laity or even broader clergy, and it brooks no internal dissent or debate. Because the tenets of fundamentalism are inviolable and its standards are mandatory, fundamentalists are inevitably uneasy in the modern West. The culture affronts them in every way—and the affront demands a response. Women in combat? Against God's will. Same-sex marriage? An oxymoron. Abortion? Always and everywhere to be forbidden by law. Stem-cell research on embryos? Dr. Mengele reborn.

The idea that there can be prudential compromises on issues like the right to die, or same-sex marriage, or stem-cell research is a difficult one for fundamentalists. Since there is no higher authority than God, and since there can be no higher priority than obeying him, the entire notion of separating politics and religion is inherently troublesome to the fundamentalist mind. Whereas for older types of conservatives, religion informed their view of the world and shaped the way they entered civil discourse, the new conservatives of faith bring their religious tenets, unmediated, into the public square.

Two recent controversies highlight this new stridency. The Schiavo case revealed something profound about the new conservatism. Old conservatives would have been reluctant to intervene politically in a horrifying family dispute. They would have been comfortable letting local courts or state law govern the case. And they would have acquiesced to due process, whatever qualms they might have had about the details. Today's fundamentalists, by contrast, could see little nuance in the Schiavo case: scant concern for family prerogatives, state law, judicial review, and all other painstaking proceduralism. The fundamental truth for them was that Schiavo was being murdered. A woman who had been in a persistent vegetative state for fifteen years was, for some, indistinguishable from a healthy adult. Some thought her husband's legal rights were rendered less germane by his allegedly sinful private life. The state legislature, governor, and then the federal Congress were cajoled to intervene. The president flew back to Washington to sign legislation designed for one specific case. If there was once a balance between conservatives of doubt and conservatives of faith, that balance was abandoned. It was abandoned as conservatives of faith morphed into conservatives of fundamentalism.

The fundamentalist conservatives were able to corral the most powerful people in the Republican Party to do their will. The major organs of conservative opinion—*The Weekly Standard, National Review*—both backed the fundamentalist position. *The Standard* published a long essay arguing that even if Schiavo had signed a living will citing her desire to be allowed to die if she succumbed to a permanent vegetative state, she should have been kept alive indefinitely. Morality trumped autonomy. Indeed, the whole notion of individual autonomy was deemed a threat to what conservatism was seeking to defend. The judge in the Schiavo case was vilified, along with the rest of the judiciary. House majority leader Tom DeLay promised retribution against the judges who ruled in the case. Senator John Cornyn made a speech, which he subsequently retracted in part, saying that decisions like the Schiavo ruling made violence against judges more understandable. Conservatives at a conference in Washington, D.C., called Justice Anthony Kennedy's jurisprudence "satanic." James Dobson, arguably the most powerful evangelical leader in the United States, compared the Supreme Court to the Ku Klux Klan. A religious-right conference baldly declared that the Democratic Party was fighting a war against all "people of faith." It was blessed by the Senate majority leader, Bill Frist.

On same-sex marriage, conservatives of faith have been equally uncompromising. In response to several court cases across the country that edged closer and closer to giving legal equality to gays and lesbians, conservatives in Washington responded by proposing—as a first resort—a constitutional amendment prohibiting marriage and any of its benefits from being granted to same-sex couples. Again, what's interesting is just how far-reaching the initial position was. Several other conservative positions were ruled out in advance: that marriage is a conservative institution that should include gays; that states should be allowed to figure out their own marriage policies as they have done for decades; that no action need be taken as long as the Defense of Marriage Act remained on the books, preventing one state's marriages from being foisted on another; or that conservatives could support civil unions or halfway measures that could grant gays some, but not all, of the rights of heterosexual marriage.

In various state constitutional amendments, again actively promoted by the Republican Party, gay couples were also denied benefits or protections. Judges—some liberal, many conservative—were described as "activists" or "extremists" if they applied their state constitution's guarantees of equal protection to gay couples. The rhetoric was extraordinary. Letting gays marry was equated with the "abolition" of marriage, even though no one was proposing to change heterosexual marriage rights one iota. "Homosexuals . . . want to destroy the institution of marriage," James Dobson said. "It will destroy the Earth."

How were conservatives of doubt supposed to respond to these fundamentalist incursions into the conservative discourse? A few dissented. The Schiavo case seemed finally to embolden traditional conservatives into defending due process and limited government. (Some are even defending the filibuster as an essential tool for limited and divided government.) But they failed to blunt the fundamentalist position within the Republican Party or to dilute the venomous attacks on the judiciary that followed. On the marriage issue, even those with openly gay offspring, such as Vice President Dick Cheney, were forced to toe the party line. The religious right's insistence that homosexuality is a psychological disease requiring treatment forced the president to avoid ever using the words "gay" or "lesbian" or "homosexual" in his speeches; even recognizing the existence of gay citizens was too much for the social right. No surprise, then, that the 2004 Republican Party platform called for constitutional amendments banning all legal benefits and protections for gay couples everywhere in the United States. In a society with a big openly gay population, this was not a politics of moderation. It was and is a crusade.

Crusades, however, are not means of persuasion. They are means of coercion. And so it is no accident that the crusading Republicans are impatient with institutional obstacles in their way. The judiciary, which is designed to check executive and legislative decisions, is now the first object of attack. Bare-knuckled character assassination of opponents is part of the repertoire: just look at the Swift Boat smears of John Kerry. The filibuster is attacked. The mass media is targeted, not simply to correct bad or biased reporting, but to promote points of view that are openly sectarian, even if, as in the case of Armstrong Williams, you have to pay for people to endorse your views. Religious-right dominance of the party machinery, in an electoral landscape remade by gerrymandering, means that few opponents of fundamentalist politics have a future in the Republican Party. It's telling that none of the biggest talents in the Republican Party will ever be its nominee for president. John McCain, Arnold Schwarzenegger, George Pataki, and Rudy Giuliani could never survive the fundamentalist-dominated primaries.

Indeed, by their very nature, conservatives of doubt are not particularly aggressive politicians. Fiscal conservatives have been coy in expressing their outrage at Bush's massive spending and borrowing, easily silenced by the thought that Democrats would be even worse. Defenders of an independent judiciary are drowned out by the talk radio/Fox News/ blog-driven megaphone of loathing for unaccountable judges. Many moderate conservatives voted for the law to protect Schiavo. Republican defenders of gay marriage are few and far between. Those few voices of dissent are increasingly portrayed as mavericks or has-beens. You will find precious little time for people like Christie Todd Whitman on talk radio or in the conservative blogosphere.

But that doesn't mean that the arguments of doubt conservatism are flimsy or unnecessary. In fact, they may be increasingly critical to conservatism's survival. An ideologically polarized country, in which one party uses big government for its own moral purposes and the other wields it for its own, is not one that can long maintain a civil discourse. Politics becomes war, letting a key Republican leader like DeLay genially boast that his supporters are armed. What conservatism has long offered is a messy defense of procedure and moderation, doubt and limits, attributes that make civilized politics possible and are often appreciated only when they are lost. But, by then, it is sometimes too late.

I'm not saying that Republicanism is headed for an institutional crack-up. What I am saying is that, unless the religious presence within Republicanism becomes less dogmatic and fundamentalist, the conservative coalition as we have known it cannot long endure. Advocates for government restraint cannot, in good conscience, keep supporting a party that believes in its own God-given mission to change people's souls. Believers in fiscal discipline cannot keep backing an administration that boasts of its huge spending increases and has no intention of changing. Those inclined to prudence cannot join forces with fanatics (at least not in times when national security doesn't hang in the balance). Retreating to the Democrats is not an option. Small-government conservatives are even less powerful within the opposition's base than in the GOP's. Bill Clinton's small-*c* conservatism was made possible only by what now looks like a blessed interaction with a Republican Congress. The only pragmatic option is to persuade those who run the Republican Party that religious zeal is a highly unstable base for conservative politics: it is divisive, inflammatory, and intolerant of the very mechanisms that keep freedom alive.

This doesn't mean purging Christians from the GOP. It means filtering religious faith through the skeptical and moderate strands of conservative thought. It means replacing zeal with religious humility; it means accepting that trading compromise of religious principles for political compromise is an ineluctable and vital democratic task. It means a lower temperature within conservative circles on issues like abortion, stem-cell research, and gay rights. And it means a renewed commitment to restraining government from its democratic instinct to act too often, too quickly, and too expensively.

But that is not the prime reason for standing up for the conservatism of doubt in a time of religious certainty. Imagine if the Rove formula is actually a successful one. Imagine a dominant political party devoted to expanding government as a means of moral revival, using national security to achieve a tiny democratic majority. The long connection between Republicanism and the expansion of individual freedom could be severely compromised. The attractiveness of a conservatism of doubt rests ultimately not on its ability to corral majorities. It rests on its central insight: that politics is not religion; that the US guarantee of freedom is for all, not merely the majority; that political freedom must mean economic freedom, and that freedom is imperiled by fiscal recklessness; that there are worse things than doing nothing, especially if that "something" is the imposition of a divisive moral agenda.

There may come a reckoning for this political moment—and it may soon peak or deflate or be undone by its own hubris. Or it may not. What has to endure is not merely a reformed liberalism that can one day take government away from its current masters, but rather a conservatism that does not assent to its own corruption at the hands of zealots. This doesn't mean hostility to religion. It means keeping religion in its safest place—away from the trappings of power. And it means keeping politics in its safest place—as the proper arrangement of our common obligations, and not as a means to save or transform our lives and souls. If we are fighting such a conservatism of faith abroad—and that is the core of the war on Islamist terrorism—then why should it be so hard to confront it in much milder forms at home? This was, once upon a time, the central conservative calling. Why not again?

Still Here, So Sorry

June 21, 2005 | *THE ADVOCATE*

People are in such denial about how serious HIV is. Unfortunately, the best prevention is seeing people die.

—Michael Weinstein,
president of the AIDS Healthcare Foundation

I'm sorry. It has taken me a long time to say this, but it's time: I'm sorry. It's been almost twelve years since I became infected with HIV, and I haven't died yet. I haven't even had the decency to get sick. I am a walking, talking advertisement for why HIV seems not such a big deal to the younger generation—and indeed, many in my own age bracket. I know this is a terrible thing, and I promise in the future to do better. As gay activist Michelangelo Signorile recently told *The New York Times*, "If everyone in your group is beautiful, taking steroids, barebacking, and HIV-positive, having the virus doesn't seem like such a bad thing."

I'm sorry. At the tender age of forty-one—a year longer than I once thought I would live—I have never felt better. HIV transformed my life, made me a better and braver writer, prompted me to write the first big book pushing marriage rights, got me to take better care of my health, improved my sex life, and deepened my spirituality. I'm sorry. I'll try to do better. Yes, I take testosterone and human growth hormone, and I now weigh 190 pounds. I discovered a couple of abs in my midsection the other day. I'll try to disguise them. Do they sell burkas online? I've even enjoyed sex more since I became positive—more depth, more intimacy, more appreciation of life itself. Sorry.

I look physically and mentally healthier than ever. Sorry again. I know that by just going daily to the gym, walking on the beach, or dancing at the occasional circuit party I am the cause of more people getting infected with HIV. I have helped persuade them by my very existence that HIV isn't such a curse, that it can be survived, that it can be treated effectively, that you can live well and long with HIV if you look after yourself and stay alert and informed. I'm sorry. I'm almost as bad as those damn drug ads showing people with HIV triumphing over adversity. In the future I'll try to look sicker. Or I'll stay home more. Promise. I'll try to get depressed. I won't work out. I'll stay off television. I will never tell anyone that treatments are far less onerous than they used to be (and I went through medication hell for several years in the 1990s). I'll even repeat the lie that HIV transmission rates are exploding because of people like me, even though the latest solid data show HIV rates to be stabilizing or even declining in many cities. (A decline in infection rates in New York City last year! Sorry again. I shouldn't have told you that. It will make you less scared.) If all else fails, I'll tell people I may have got "super-AIDS," an old, extremely rare, now-debunked viral strain that is being successfully treated in one gay man in New York City. Promise.

I'd even be prepared to stop taking my meds if that would help. The trouble is, like many other people with HIV, I did that three years ago. My CD4 count remained virtually unchanged, and only recently have I had to go back on meds. Five pills once a day. No side effects to speak of. I know that others go through far worse, and I don't mean to minimize their trials. But the bottom line is that HIV is fast becoming another diabetes.

You can see the symptoms. Far fewer gay men are dying of AIDS anymore. Sometimes local gay papers have no AIDS obits for weeks on end. C'mon, pozzies. You can do better than that! Do you have no sense of social responsibility? Young negative men need to see more of us keeling over in the streets, or they won't be scared enough to avoid a disease that may, in the very distant future, kill them off. You know, like any number of other diseases might. They may even stop believing that this is a huge, escalating crisis, threatening to wipe out homosexual life on this planet.

What are those happy HIV-positive men thinking of? Die, damn it.

Of course, we could always be thrilled that so many people are living longer and better lives with HIV. We could celebrate our reclaiming of sexuality
after years of terror. We could even try new strategies for risk reduction among
gay men—strategies that emphasize positive ways to care for our health rather
than negative ways to scare the bejeezus out of everyone. But then we'd have
no more people to scapegoat and blame, would we?

The End of Gay Culture

Assimilation and Its Meaning

October 24, 2005 | *THE NEW REPUBLIC*

For the better part of two decades, I have spent much of every summer in the small resort of Provincetown, at the tip of Cape Cod. It has long attracted artists, writers, the offbeat, and the bohemian; and, for many years now, it has been to gay America what Oak Bluffs in Martha's Vineyard is to black America: a place where a separate identity essentially defines a separate place. No one bats an eye if two men walk down the street holding hands, or if a lesbian couple peck each other on the cheek, or if a drag queen dressed as Cher careens down the main strip on a motor scooter. It's a place, in that respect, that is sui generis. Except that it isn't anymore. As gay America has changed, so, too, has Provincetown. In a microcosm of what is happening across this country, its culture is changing.

Some of these changes are obvious. A real-estate boom has made Province-town far more expensive than it ever was, slowly excluding poorer and younger visitors and residents. Where, once, gayness trumped class, now the reverse is true. Beautiful, renovated houses are slowly outnumbering beach shacks, once crammed with twentysomething, hand-to-mouth misfits or artists. The role of lesbians in the town's civic and cultural life has grown dramatically, as it has in the broader gay world. The faces of people dying from or struggling with AIDS have dwindled to an unlucky few. The number of children of gay couples has soared, and, some weeks, strollers clog the sidewalks. Bar life is not nearly as central to socializing as it once was. Men and women gather on the beach, drink coffee on the front porch of a store, or meet at the film festival or Spiritus Pizza.

And, of course, week after week this summer, couple after couple got married—well over a thousand in the year and a half since gay marriage has been legal in Massachusetts. Outside my window on a patch of beach that somehow became impromptu hallowed ground, I watched dozens get hitched—under a chuppah or with a priest, in formalwear or beach clothes, some with New Age drums and horns, even one associated with a full-bore Mass. Two friends lighted the town monument in purple to celebrate; a tuxedoed male couple slipping onto the beach was suddenly greeted with a huge cheer from the crowd; an elderly lesbian couple attached cans to the back of their Volkswagen and honked their horn as they drove up the high street. The heterosexuals in the crowd knew exactly what to do. They waved and cheered and smiled. Then, suddenly, as if learning the habits of a new era, gay bystanders joined in. In an instant, the difference between gay and straight receded again a little.

But here's the strange thing: these changes did not feel like a revolution. They felt merely like small, if critical, steps in an inexorable evolution toward the end of a distinctive gay culture. For what has happened to Provincetown this past decade, as with gay America as a whole, has been less like a political revolution from above than a social transformation from below. There is no single gay identity anymore, let alone a single look or style or culture. Memorial Day sees the younger generation of lesbians, looking like lost members of a boy band, with their baseball caps, preppy shirts, short hair, and earrings. Independence Day brings the partiers: the "circuit boys," with perfect torsos, a thirst for nightlife, designer drugs, and countless bottles of water. For a week in mid-July, the town is dominated by "bears"—chubby, hairy, unkempt men with an affinity for beer and pizza. Family Week heralds an influx of children and harried gay parents. Film Festival Week brings in the artsy crowd. Women's Week brings the more familiar images of older lesbians: a landlocked flotilla of windbreakers and sensible shoes. East Village bohemians drift in throughout the summer; quiet male couples spend more time browsing gourmet groceries and Realtors than cruising night spots; the predictable population of artists and writers—Michael Cunningham and John Waters are fixtures—mix with openly gay lawyers and cops and teachers and shrinks.

Slowly but unmistakably, gay culture is ending. You see it beyond the poignant transformation of Ptown: on the streets of the big cities, on university campuses, in the suburbs where gay couples have settled, and in the entrails of the internet. In fact, it is beginning to dawn on many that the very concept of gay culture may one day disappear altogether. By that, I do not mean that homosexual men and lesbians will not exist—or that they won't create a community of sorts and a culture that sets them in some ways apart. I mean simply that what encompasses gay culture itself will expand into such a diverse set of subcultures that "gayness" alone will cease to tell you very much about any individual. The distinction between gay and straight culture will become so blurred, so fractured, and so intermingled that it may become more helpful not to examine them separately at all.

For many in the gay world, this is both a triumph and a threat. It is a triumph because it is what we always dreamed of: a world in which being gay is a nonissue among our families, friends, and neighbors. But it is a threat in the way that all loss is a threat. For many of us who grew up fighting a world of now-inconceivable silence and shame, distinctive gayness became an integral part of who we are. It helped define us not only to the world but also to ourselves. Letting that go is as hard as it is liberating, as saddening as it is invigorating. And, while social advance allows many of us to contemplate this gift of a problem, we are also aware that in other parts of the country and the world the reverse may be happening. With the growth of fundamentalism across the religious world—from Pope Benedict XVI's Vatican to Islamic fatwas and American evangelicalism—gayness is under attack in many places, even as it wrests free from repression in others. In fact, the two phenomena are related. The new antigay fervor is a response to the growing probability that the world will one day treat gay and straight as interchangeable humans and citizens rather than as estranged others. It is the end of gay culture—not its endurance—that threatens the old order. It is a simple fact that, across the state of Massachusetts, "gay marriage" has just been abolished. The marriage licenses gay couples receive are indistinguishable from those given to straight couples. On paper, the difference is now history. In the real world, the consequences of that are still unfolding.

Quite how this has happened (and why) are questions that historians will fight over someday, but certain influences seem clear even now—chief among them the HIV epidemic. Before AIDS hit, a fragile but nascent gay world had formed in a handful of major US cities. The gay culture that exploded from it in the 1970s had the force of something long suppressed, and it coincided with a more general relaxation of social norms. This was the era of the post-Stonewall New Left, of the Castro and the West Village, an era where sexuality forged a new meaning for gayness: of sexual adventure, political radicalism, and cultural revolution.

The fact that openly gay communities were still relatively small and geographically concentrated in a handful of urban areas created a distinctive gay culture. The central institutions for gay men were baths and bars, places where men met each other in highly sexualized contexts and where sex provided the commonality. Gay resorts had their heyday—from Provincetown to Key West. The gay press grew quickly and was centered around classified personal ads or bar and bath advertising. Popular culture was suffused with stunning displays of homosexual burlesque: the music of Queen, the costumes of the Village People, the flamboyance of Elton John's debut; the advertising of Calvin Klein; and the intoxication of disco itself, a gay creation that became emblematic of an entire heterosexual era. When this cultural explosion was acknowledged, when it explicitly penetrated the mainstream, the results, however, were highly unstable: Harvey Milk was assassinated in San Francisco and Anita Bryant led an antigay crusade. But the emergence of an openly gay culture, however vulnerable, was still real.

And then, of course, catastrophe. The history of gay America as an openly gay culture is not only extremely short—a mere thirty years or so—but also engulfed and defined by a plague that struck almost poignantly at the headiest moment of liberation. The entire structure of emergent gay culture—sexual, radical, subversive—met a virus that killed almost everyone it touched. Virtually the entire generation that pioneered gay culture was wiped out—quickly. Even now, it is hard to find a solid phalanx of gay men in their fifties, sixties, or seventies—men who fought from Stonewall or before for public recognition and cultural change. And those who survived the nightmare of the 1980s to mid-'90s were often overwhelmed merely with coping with plague, or fearing it themselves, or fighting for research or awareness or more effective prevention.

This astonishing story might not be believed in fiction. And, in fiction, it might have led to the collapse of such a new, fragile subculture. AIDS could have been widely perceived as a salutary retribution for the gay revolution;

it could have led to quarantining or the collapse of nascent gay institutions. Instead, it had the opposite effect. The tens of thousands of deaths of men from every part of the country established homosexuality as a legitimate topic more swiftly than any political manifesto could possibly have done. The images of gay male lives were recorded on quilts and in countless obituaries; men whose homosexuality might have been euphemized into nonexistence were immediately identifiable and gone. And those gay men and lesbians who witnessed this entire event became altered forever, not only emotionally, but also politically—whether through the theatrical activism of ACT UP or the furious organization of political gays among the Democrats and some Republicans. More crucially, gay men and lesbians built civil institutions to counter the disease; they forged new ties to scientists and politicians; they found themselves forced into more intense relations with their own natural families and the families of loved ones. Where bathhouses once brought gay men together, now it was memorial services. The emotional and psychic bonding became the core of a new identity. The plague provided a unifying social and cultural focus.

But it also presaged a new direction. That direction was unmistakably outward and integrative. To borrow a useful distinction deployed by the writer Bruce Bawer, integration did not necessarily mean assimilation. It was not a wholesale rejection of the gay past, as some feared and others hoped. Gay men wanted to be fully part of the world, but not at the expense of their own sexual freedom (and safer sex became a means not to renounce that freedom but to save it). What the epidemic revealed was how gay men—and, by inference, lesbians—could not seal themselves off from the rest of society. They needed scientific research, civic support, and political lobbying to survive, in this case literally. The lesson was not that sexual liberation was mistaken, but rather that it wasn't enough. Unless the gay population was tied into the broader society, unless it had roots in the wider world, unless it brought into its fold the heterosexual families and friends of gay men and women, the gay population would remain at the mercy of others and of misfortune. A ghetto was no longer an option.

When the plague receded in the face of far more effective HIV treatments in the mid-nineties and gay men and women were able to catch their breath and reflect, the question of what a more integrated gay culture might actually mean reemerged. For a while, it arrived in a vacuum. Most of the older male generation was dead or exhausted, and so it was only natural, perhaps, that the next generation of leaders tended to be lesbian—running the major gay political groups and magazines. Lesbians also pioneered a new baby boom, with more lesbian couples adopting or having children. HIV-positive gay men developed different strategies for living suddenly posthumous lives. Some retreated into quiet relationships; others quit jobs or changed their careers completely; others chose the escapism of what became known as "the circuit," a series of rave parties around the country and the world where fears could be lost on the drug-enhanced dance floor; others still became lost in a suicidal vortex of crystal meth, internet hookups, and sex addiction. HIV-negative men, many of whom had lost husbands and friends, were not so different. In some ways, the toll was greater. They had survived disaster with their health intact. But, unlike their HIV-positive friends, the threat of contracting the disease still existed while they battled survivors' guilt. The plague was over but not over; and, as they saw men with HIV celebrate survival, some even felt shut out of a new sub-subculture, suspended between fear and triumph but unable to experience either fully.

Then something predictable and yet unexpected happened. While the older generation struggled with plague and post-plague adjustment, the next generation was growing up. For the first time, a cohort of gay children and teens grew up in a world where homosexuality was no longer a taboo subject and where gay figures were regularly featured in the press. If the image of gay men for my generation was one gleaned from the movie *Cruising* or, subsequently, *Torch Song Trilogy*, the image for the next one was MTV's *Real World*, Bravo's *Queer Eye*, and Richard Hatch winning the first *Survivor*. The new emphasis was on the interaction between gays and straights and on the diversity of gay life and lives. Movies featured and integrated gayness. Even more dramatically, gays went from having to find hidden meaning in mainstream films—somehow identifying with the aging, campy female lead in a way the rest of the culture missed—to everyone, gay and straight, recognizing and being in on the joke of a character like Big Gay Al from *South Park* or Jack from *Will & Grace*.

There are now openly gay legislators. Ditto Olympic swimmers and gymnasts and Wimbledon champions. Mainstream entertainment figures—from George Michael, Ellen DeGeneres, and Rosie O'Donnell to edgy musicians, such as the Scissor Sisters, Rufus Wainwright, or Bob Mould—now have their sexual orientation as a central, but not defining, part of their identity. The National Lesbian and Gay Journalists Association didn't exist when I became a journalist. Now it has thirteen hundred dues-paying members in twenty-four chapters around the country. Among Fortune 500 companies, twenty-one provided domestic partner benefits for gay spouses in 1995. Today, 216 do. Of the top Fortune 50 companies, forty-nine provide nondiscrimination protections for gay employees. Since 2002, the number of corporations providing full protections for openly gay employees has increased sevenfold, according to the Human Rights Campaign (HRC). Among the leaders: the defense giant Raytheon and the energy company Chevron. These are not traditionally gay-friendly work environments. Nor is the Republican Party. But the offspring of such leading Republican lights as Dick Cheney, Alan Keyes, and Phyllis Schlafly are all openly gay. So is the spokesman for the most antigay senator in Congress, Rick Santorum.

This new tolerance and integration—combined, of course, with the increased ability to connect with other gay people that the internet provides— has undoubtedly encouraged more and more gay people to come out. The hard data for this are difficult to come by (since only recently have we had studies that identified large numbers of gays) and should be treated with caution. Nevertheless, the trend is clear. If you compare data from, say, the 1994 National Health and Social Life Survey with the 2002 National Survey of Family Growth, you will find that women are nearly three times more likely to report being gay, lesbian, or bisexual today than they were eight years ago, and men are about 1.5 times more likely. There are no reliable statistics on openly gay teens, but no one doubts that there has been an explosion in visibility in the last decade—around three thousand high schools have "gay-straight" alliances. The census, for its part, recorded a threefold increase in the number of same-sex unmarried partners from 1990 to 2000. In 2000, there were close to six hundred thousand households headed by a same-sex couple, and a quarter of them had children. If you want to know where the push for civil marriage rights came from, you need look no further. This was not an agenda invented by activists; it was a movement propelled by ordinary people.

So, as one generation literally disappeared and one generation found itself shocked to still be alive, a far larger and more empowered one emerged on the scene. This new generation knew very little about the gay culture of the

seventies, and its members were oblivious to the psychically formative experience of plague that had shaped their elders. Most came from the heart of
straight America and were more in tune with its new, mellower attitude toward
gayness than the embattled, defensive urban gay culture of the pre-AIDS
era. Even in evangelical circles, gay kids willing to acknowledge and struggle
publicly with their own homosexuality represented a new form of openness.
The speed of the change is still shocking. I'm only forty-two, and I grew up
in a world where I literally never heard the word "homosexual" until I went
to college. It is now not uncommon to meet gay men in their early twenties
who took a boy as their date to the high-school prom. When I figured out I
was gay, there were no role models to speak of and, in the popular culture,
homosexuality was either a punch line or an embarrassed silence. Today's
cultural climate could not be more different. And the psychological impact
on the younger generation cannot be overstated.

After all, what separates homosexuals and lesbians from every other minority
group is that they are born and raised within the bosom of the majority. Unlike
Latino or Jewish or black communities, where parents and grandparents and
siblings pass on cultural norms to children in their most formative stages, each
generation of gay men and lesbians grows up being taught the heterosexual
norms and culture of their home environments or absorbing what passes for
their gay identity from the broader culture as a whole. Each shift in mainstream
culture is therefore magnified exponentially in the next generation of gay children. To give the most powerful example: A gay child born today will grow up
knowing that, in many parts of the world and in parts of the United States, gay
couples can get married just as their parents did. From the very beginning of
their gay lives, in other words, they will have internalized a sense of normality,
of human potential, of self-worth—something that my generation never had
and that previous generations would have found unimaginable. That shift in
consciousness is as profound as it is irreversible.

To give another example: Black children come into society both uplifted
and burdened by the weight of their communal past—a weight that is transferred within families or communities or cultural institutions, such as the
Church, that provide a context for self-understanding, even in rebellion. Gay
children have no such support or burden. And so, in their most formative
years, their self-consciousness is utterly different from that of their gay elders.

That's why it has become increasingly difficult to distinguish between gay and straight teens today—or even young gay and straight adults. Less psychologically wounded, more self-confident, less isolated, young gay kids look and sound increasingly like young straight kids. On the dozens of college campuses I have visited over the past decade, the shift in just a few years has been astounding. At a Catholic institution like Boston College, for example, a generation ago there would have been no discussion of homosexuality. When I visited recently to talk about that very subject, the preppy, conservative student president was openly gay.

When you combine this generational plasticity with swift demographic growth, you have our current explosion of gay civil society, with a dispropor-tionately young age distribution. I use the term "civil society" in its classic Tocquevillian and Burkean sense: the little platoons of social organization that undergird liberal democratic life. The gay organizations that erupted into being as AIDS killed thousands in the eighties—from the Gay Men's Health Crisis to the AIDS Project Los Angeles to the Whitman-Walker Clinic in Washington—struggled to adapt to the swift change in the epidemic in the mid-nineties. But the general principle of communal organization endured. If conservatives had been open-minded enough to see it, they would have witnessed a classic tale of self-help and self-empowerment.

Take, for example, religious life, an area not historically associated with gay culture. One of the largest single gay organizations in the country today is the Metropolitan Community Church, with over forty thousand active members. Go to, yes, Dallas, and you'll find the Cathedral of Hope, one of the largest religious structures in the country, with close to four thousand congregants—predominantly gay. Almost every faith now has an explicitly gay denomination associated with it—Dignity for gay Catholics, Bet Mishpachah for gay Jews, and so on. But, in many mainstream Protestant churches and among Reform Jews, such groups don't even exist because the integration of gay believers is now mundane. These groups bring gays together in a context where sexuality is less a feature of identity than faith, where the interaction of bodies is less central than the community of souls.

In contrast, look at bar life. For a very long time, the fundamental social institution for gay men was the gay bar. It was often secluded—a refuge, a safe zone, and a clearing house for sexual pickups. Most bars still perform some of those functions. But the internet dealt them a body blow. If you are merely looking for sex or a date, the web is now the first stop for most gay men. The result has been striking. Only a decade ago, you could wander up the West Side Highway in New York City and drop by several leather bars. Now, only one is left standing, and it is less a bar dedicated to the ornate codes of seventies leather culture than a place for men who adopt a more masculine self-presentation. My favorite old leather bar, the Spike, is now the "Spike Gallery." The newer gay bars are more social than sexual, often with restaurants, open windows onto the street, and a welcoming attitude toward others, especially the many urban straight women who find gay bars more congenial than heterosexual pickup joints.

Even gay political organizations often function more as social groups than as angry activist groups. HRC, for example, raises funds and lobbies Congress. Around 350,000 members have contributed in the last two years. It organizes itself chiefly through a series of formal fundraising dinners in cities across the country—from Salt Lake City to Nashville. These dinners are a social venue for the openly gay bourgeoisie: in tuxedos and ball gowns, they contribute large sums and give awards to local businesses and politicians and community leaders. There are silent auctions, hired entertainers, even the occasional bake sale. The closest heterosexual equivalent would be the Rotary Club. These dinners in themselves are evidence of the change: from outsider rebellion to bourgeois organization.

Take a look at the gay press. In its shallower forms—glossy lifestyle magazines—you are as likely to find a straight Hollywood star on the cover as any gay icon. In its more serious manifestations, such as regional papers like the *Washington Blade* or *Southern Voice*, the past emphasis on sex has been replaced with an emphasis on domesticity. A recent issue of *The Blade* had an eight-page insert for escort ads, personals, and the kind of material that, two decades ago, would have been the advertising mainstay of the main paper. But in the paper itself are twenty-three pages of real-estate ads and four pages of home-improvement classifieds. There are columns on cars, sports, DVDs, and local plays. The core ad base, according to its editor, Chris Crain, now comprises heterosexual-owned-and-operated companies seeking to reach the gay market. The editorial tone has shifted as well. Whereas *The Blade* was once ideologically rigid—with endless reports on small activist cells and a strident left-wing slant—now it's much more like a community paper that might be published for any well-heeled ethnic group. Genuine ideological differences are now aired, rather than bitterly decried as betrayal or agitprop. Editorials regularly take Democrats to task as well as Republicans. The maturation has been as swift as it now seems inevitable. After all, in 2004 one-quarter of self-identified gay voters backed a president who supported a constitutional ban on gay marriage. If the gay world is that politically diverse under the current polarized circumstances, it has obviously moved well beyond the time it was synonymous with radical left politics.

How gay men and lesbians express their identity has also changed. When openly gay identity first emerged, it tended toward extremes of gender expression. When society tells you that gay men and lesbians are not fully male or female, the response can be to overcompensate with caricatures of each gender or to rebel by blurring gender lines altogether. Effeminate "queens" were balanced by hypermasculine bikers and musclemen; lipstick lesbians were offset by classically gruff "bull dykes." All these sub-subcultures still exist. Many feel comfortable with them; and, thankfully, we see fewer attempts to marginalize them. But the polarities in the larger gay population are far less pronounced than they once were; the edges have softened. As gay men have become less defensive about their masculinity, their expression of it has become subtler. There is still a pronounced muscle and gym culture, but there are also now openly gay swimmers and artists and slobs and every body type in between. Go watch a gay rugby team compete in a regional tournament with straight teams and you will see how vast but subtle the revolution has been. And, in fact, this is the trend: gay civil associations in various ways are interacting with parallel straight associations in a way that leaves their gay identity more and more behind. They're rugby players first, gay rugby players second.

One of the newest reflections of this is what is known as "bear" culture: heavy, hirsute, unkempt guys who revel in their slovenliness. Their concept of what it means to be gay is very different from that of the obsessive gym rats with torsos shaved of every stray hair. Among many younger gay men, the grungy look of their straight peers has been adopted and tweaked to individual tastes. Even among bears, there are slimmer "otters" or younger "cubs" or "muscle bears," who combine gym culture with a bear sensibility. The

varieties keep proliferating; and, at the rate of current change, they will soon
dissipate into the range of identities that straight men have to choose from.
In fact, these variations of masculinity may even have diversified heterosexual male culture as well. While some gay men have proudly adopted some
classically straight signifiers—beer bellies and back hair—many straight men
have become "metrosexuals." Trying to define "gay culture" in this mix is an
increasingly elusive task.

Among lesbians, Ellen DeGeneres's transition from closeted sitcom star
to out-lesbian activist and back to appealingly middle-brow daytime talk-show
host is almost a microcosm of diversifying lesbian identity in the past decade.
There are still classic butch-femme lesbian partnerships, but more complex
forms of self-expression are more common now. With the abatement in many
places of prejudice, lesbian identity is formed less by reaction to hostility than
by simple self-expression. And this, after all, is and was the point of gay liberation: the freedom not merely to be gay according to some preordained type,
but to be yourself, whatever that is.

You see this even in drag, which once defined gayness in some respects
but now is only one of many expressions. Old-school drag, the kind that dominated the fifties, sixties, and seventies, often consisted of female impersonators
performing torch songs from various divas. The more miserable the life of
the diva, the better able the performer was to channel his own anguish and
drama into the show. After all, gayness was synonymous with tragedy and
showmanship. Judy Garland, Marilyn Monroe, Bette Davis: these were the
models. But today's drag looks and feels very different. The drag impresario of
Provincetown, a twisted genius called Ryan Landry, hosts a weekly talent show
for local drag performers called *Showgirls*. Attending it each Monday night
is Ptown's equivalent of weekly Mass. A few old-school drag queens perform,
but Landry sets the tone. He makes no attempt to look like a woman, puts on
hideous wigs (including a horse mask and a pair of fake boobs perched on his
head), throws on ill-fitting dresses, and performs scatological song parodies.
Irony pervades the show. Comedy defines it. Gay drag is inching slowly toward
a version of British pantomime, where dada humor and absurd, misogynist
parodies of womanhood are central. This is post-drag; straight men could do it
as well. This year, the longest-running old-school drag show—*Legends*—finally
closed down. Its audience had become mainly heterosexual and old.

This new post-gay cultural synthesis has its political counterpart. There was once a ferocious debate among gays between what might be caricatured as "separatists" and "assimilationists." That argument has fizzled. As the gay population has grown, it has become increasingly clear that the choice is not either-or but both-and. The issue of civil marriage reveals this most graphically. When I first argued for equal marriage rights, I found myself assailed by the gay left for social conservatism. I remember one signing for my 1995 book, *Virtually Normal*, the crux of which was an argument for the right to marry. I was picketed by a group called Lesbian Avengers, who depicted my argument as patriarchal and reactionary. They crafted posters with my face portrayed within the crosshairs of a gun. Ten years later, lesbian couples make up a majority of civil marriages in Massachusetts and civil unions in Vermont; and some of the strongest voices for marriage equality have been lesbians, from the pioneering lawyer Mary Bonauto to writer E. J. Graff. To its credit, the left—gay male and lesbian—recognized that what was at stake was not so much the corralling of all gay individuals into a conformist social institution as a widening of choice for all. It is still possible to be a gay radical or rigid leftist. The difference now is that it is also possible to be a gay conservative, or traditionalist, or anything else in between.

Who can rescue a uniform gay culture? No one, it would seem. The generation most psychologically wedded to the separatist past is either dead from HIV or sidelined. But there are still enclaves of gay distinctiveness out there. Paradoxically, gay culture in its old form may have its most fertile ground in those states where homosexuality is still unmentionable and where openly gay men and women are more beleaguered: the red states. Earlier this year, I spoke at an HRC dinner in Nashville, Tennessee, where state politicians are trying to bar gay couples from marrying or receiving even basic legal protections. The younger gay generation is as psychologically evolved there as anyplace else. They see the same television and the same internet as gay kids in New York. But their social space is smaller. And so I found a vibrant gay world, but one far more cohesive, homogeneous, and defensive than in Massachusetts. The strip of gay bars—crammed into one place rather than diffuse, as in many blue-state cities—was packed on a Saturday night. The mix of old and young, gay and lesbian, black, white, and everything in between reminded me of Boston in the eighties. The tired emblems of the past—the rainbow flags and leather outfits—retained their relevance there.

The same goes for black and Latino culture, where homophobia, propped up by black churches and the Catholic hierarchy respectively, is more intense than in much of white society. It's no surprise that these are the populations also most at risk for HIV. The underground "down-low" culture common in black gay life means less acknowledgment of sexual identity, let alone awareness or disclosure of HIV status. The same repression that facilitated the spread of HIV among gay white men in the seventies now devastates black gay America, where the latest data suggest a 50 percent HIV infection rate. (Compare that with largely white and more integrated San Francisco, where recent HIV infection rates are now half what they were four years ago.) The extremes of gender expression are also more pronounced among minorities, with many gay black or Latino men either adopting completely female personalities or refusing to identify as gay at all. Here the past lives on. The direction toward integration is clear, but the pace is far slower.

And, when you see the internalized defensiveness of gays still living in the shadow of social hostility, any nostalgia one might feel for the loss of gay culture dissipates. Some still echo critic Philip Larkin's jest that he worried about the American civil-rights movement because it was ruining jazz. But the flipness of that remark is the point, and the mood today is less genuine regret—let alone a desire to return to those days—than a kind of wistfulness for a past that was probably less glamorous or unified than it now appears. It is indeed hard not to feel some sadness at the end of a rich, distinct culture built by pioneers who braved greater ostracism than today's generation will ever fully understand. But if there is a real choice between a culture built on oppression and a culture built on freedom, the decision is an easy one. Gay culture was once primarily about pain and tragedy, because that is what heterosexuals imposed on gay people and that was, in part, what gay people experienced. Gay culture was once primarily about sex, because that was how heterosexuals defined gay lives. But gay life, like straight life, is now and always has been about happiness as well as pain; it is about triumph as well as tragedy; it is about love and family as well as sex. It took generations to find the self-worth to move toward achieving this reality in all its forms—and an epidemiological catastrophe to accelerate it. If the end of gay culture means that we have a new complexity to grapple with and a new, less cramped humanity to embrace, then regret seems almost a rebuke to those countless generations who could only dream of the liberty so many now enjoy.

The tiny, rich space that gay men and women once created for themselves was, after all, the best they could do. In a metaphor coined by the philosopher Michael Walzer, they gilded a cage of exclusion with magnificent ornaments; they spoke to its isolation and pain; they described and maintained it with dignity and considerable beauty. But it was still a cage. And the thing that kept gay people together, that unified them into one homogeneous unit, and that defined the parameters of their culture and the limits of their dreams, was the bars on that cage. Past the ashes of thousands and through the courage of those who came before the plague and those who survived it, those bars are now slowly but inexorably being pried apart. The next generation may well be as free of that cage as any minority ever can be, and they will redefine gayness on its own terms and not on the terms of hostile outsiders. Nothing will stop this, since it is occurring in the psyches and souls of a new generation: a new consciousness that is immune to any law and propelled by the momentum of human freedom itself. While we should treasure the past, there is no recovering it. The futures—and they will be multiple—are just beginning.

The Abolition of Torture

Saving the United States from a Totalitarian Future

December 19, 2005 | *THE NEW REPUBLIC*

W hy is torture wrong? It may seem like an obvious question, or even one beneath discussion. But it is now inescapably before us, with the introduction of the McCain Amendment banning all "cruel, inhuman, and degrading treatment" of detainees by American soldiers and CIA operatives anywhere in the world. The amendment lies in legislative limbo. It passed the Senate in October by a vote of ninety to nine, but President Bush has vowed to veto any such blanket ban on torture or abuse, Vice President Cheney has prevailed upon enough senators and congressmen to prevent the amendment—and the defense appropriations bill to which it is attached—from moving out of conference, and my friend Charles Krauthammer, one of the most respected conservative intellectuals in Washington (and a *New Republic* contributing editor), has written a widely praised cover essay for *The Weekly Standard* endorsing the legalization of full-fledged torture by the United States under strictly curtailed conditions. We stand on the brink of an enormously important choice—one that is critical, morally as well as strategically, to get right.

This debate takes place after three years in which the Bush administration has defined "torture" in the narrowest terms and has permitted coercive, physical abuse of enemy combatants if "military necessity" demands it. It comes also after several internal Pentagon reports found widespread and severe abuse of detainees in Afghanistan, Iraq, and elsewhere that has led to at least two dozen deaths during interrogation. Journalistic accounts and reports by the International Committee of the Red Cross paint an even darker picture of secret torture sites in Eastern Europe and innocent detainees being murdered. Behind all this, the grim images of Abu Ghraib—the worst of which have yet to be released—linger in the public consciousness.

In this inevitably emotional debate, perhaps the greatest failing of those of us who have been arguing against all torture and "cruel, inhuman, and degrading treatment" of detainees is that we have assumed the reasons why torture is always a moral evil, rather than explicating them. But, when you fully ponder them, I think it becomes clearer why, contrary to Krauthammer's argument, torture, in any form and under any circumstances, is both anti-thetical to the most basic principles for which the United States stands and a profound impediment to winning a wider war that we cannot afford to lose.

Torture is the polar opposite of freedom. It is the banishment of all freedom from a human body and soul, insofar as that is possible. As human beings, we all inhabit bodies and have minds, souls, and reflexes that are designed in part to protect those bodies: to resist or flinch from pain, to protect the psyche from disintegration, and to maintain a sense of selfhood that is the basis for the concept of personal liberty. What torture does is use these involuntary, self-protective, self-defining resources of human beings against the integrity of the human being himself. It takes what is most involuntary in a person and uses it to break that person's will. It takes what is animal in us and deploys it against what makes us human. As an American commander wrote in an August 2003 e-mail about his instructions to torture prisoners at Abu Ghraib, "The gloves are coming off gentlemen regarding these detainees, Col. Boltz has made it clear that we want these individuals broken."

What does it mean to "break" an individual? As the French essayist Michel de Montaigne once commented, and Shakespeare echoed, even the greatest philosophers have difficulty thinking clearly when they have a toothache. These wise men were describing the inescapable frailty of the human experience, mocking the claims of some seers to be above basic human feelings and bodily needs. If that frailty is exposed by a toothache, it is beyond dispute in the case of torture. The infliction of physical pain on a person with no means of defending himself is designed to render that person completely subservient to his torturers. It is designed to extirpate his autonomy as a human being, to render his control as an individual beyond his own reach. That is why the term "break" is instructive. Something broken can be put back together, but it will never regain the status of being unbroken—of having integrity. When you break a human being, you turn him into something subhuman. You enslave him. This is why the Romans reserved torture for slaves, not citizens, and why slavery and torture were inextricably linked in the antebellum South.

What you see in the relationship between torturer and tortured is the absolute darkness of totalitarianism. You see one individual granted the most complete power he can ever hold over another. Not just confinement of his mobility—the abolition of his very agency. Torture uses a person's body to remove from his own control his conscience, his thoughts, his faith, his selfhood. The CIA's definition of "waterboarding"—recently leaked to ABC News—describes that process in plain English: "The prisoner is bound to an inclined board, feet raised and head slightly below the feet. Cellophane is wrapped over the prisoner's face and water is poured over him. Unavoidably, the gag reflex kicks in and a terrifying fear of drowning leads to almost instant pleas to bring the treatment to a halt." The ABC report then noted, "According to the sources, CIA officers who subjected themselves to the waterboarding technique lasted an average of 14 seconds before caving in. They said Al Qaeda's toughest prisoner, Khalid Sheikh Mohammed, won the admiration of interrogators when he was able to last between two and two and a half minutes before begging to confess."

Before the Bush administration, two documented cases of the US Armed Forces using "waterboarding" resulted in courts-martial for the soldiers implicated. In Donald Rumsfeld's post–September 11 Pentagon, the technique is approved and, we recently learned, has been used on at least eleven detainees, possibly many more. What you see here is the deployment of a very basic and inescapable human reflex—the desire not to drown and suffocate—in order to destroy a person's autonomy. Even the most hardened fanatic can only endure two and a half minutes. After that, he is indeed "broken."

The entire structure of Western freedom grew in part out of the searing experience of state-sanctioned torture. The use of torture in Europe's religious wars of the sixteenth and seventeenth centuries is still etched in our communal consciousness, as it should be. Then, governments deployed torture not only to uncover perceived threats to their faith-based autocracies, but also to "save" the victim's soul. Torturers understood that religious conversion was a difficult thing, because it necessitated a shift in the deepest recesses of the human soul. The only way to reach those depths was to deploy physical terror in the hopes of completely destroying the heretic's autonomy. They would, in other words, destroy a human being's soul in order to save it. That is what burning at the stake was—an indescribably agonizing act of torture that could be ended at a moment's notice if the victim recanted. In a state where theological doctrine always trumped individual liberty, this was a natural tactic.

Indeed, the very concept of Western liberty sprang in part from an understanding that if the state has the power to reach that deep into a person's soul and can do that much damage to a human being's person, then the state has extinguished all oxygen necessary for freedom to survive. That is why, in George Orwell's totalitarian nightmare, the final ordeal is, of course, torture. Any polity that endorses torture has incorporated into its own DNA a totalitarian mutation. If the point of the US Constitution is the preservation of liberty, the formal incorporation into US law of the state's right to torture—by legally codifying physical coercion, abuse, and even, in Krauthammer's case, full-fledged torture of detainees by the CIA—would effectively end the American experiment of a political society based on inalienable human freedom protected not by the good graces of the executive, but by the rule of law.

The Founders understood this argument. Its preeminent proponent was George Washington himself. As historian David Hackett Fischer memorably recounts in his 2004 book, *Washington's Crossing*: "Always some dark spirits wished to visit the same cruelties on the British and Hessians that had been inflicted on American captives. But Washington's example carried growing weight, more so than his written orders and prohibitions. He often reminded his men that they were an army of liberty and freedom, and that the rights of humanity for which they were fighting should extend even to their enemies. . . . Even in the most urgent moments of the war, these men were concerned about ethical questions in the Revolution."

Krauthammer has described Washington's convictions concerning torture as "pieties" that can be dispensed with today. He doesn't argue that torture is not evil. Indeed, he denounces it in unequivocal moral terms: "[T]orture is a terrible and monstrous thing, as degrading and morally corrupting to those who practice it as any conceivable human activity including its moral twin, capital punishment." But he maintains that the nature of the Islamofascist enemy after September 11 radically altered our interrogative options and that we are now not only permitted, but actually "morally compelled," to torture.

This is a radical and daring idea: that we must extinguish human freedom in a few cases in order to maintain it for everyone else. It goes beyond even the Bush administration's own formal position, which states that the United States will not endorse torture but merely "coercive interrogation techniques." (Such techniques, in the administration's elaborate definition, are those that employ physical force short of threatening immediate death or major organ failure.) And it is based on a premise that deserves further examination: that our enemies actually deserve torture; that some human beings are so depraved that, in Krauthammer's words, they "are entitled to no humane treatment."

Let me state for the record that I am second to none in decrying, loathing, and desiring to defeat those who wish to replace freedom with religious tyranny of the most brutal kind—and who have murdered countless innocent civilians in cold blood. Their acts are monstrous and barbaric. But I differ from Krauthammer by believing that monsters remain human beings. In fact, to reduce them to a subhuman level is to exonerate them of their acts of terrorism and mass murder—just as animals are not deemed morally responsible for killing. Insisting on the humanity of terrorists is, in fact, critical to maintaining their profound responsibility for the evil they commit.

And if they are human, then they must necessarily not be treated in an inhuman fashion. You cannot lower the moral baseline of a terrorist to the subhuman without betraying a fundamental value. That is why the Geneva Conventions have a very basic ban on "cruel treatment and torture," and "outrages upon personal dignity, in particular humiliating and degrading treatment"—even when dealing with illegal combatants like terrorists. That is why the Declaration of Independence did not restrict its endorsement of freedom merely to those lucky enough to find themselves on US soil—but extended it to all human beings, wherever they are in the world, simply because they are human.

Nevertheless, it is important to address Krauthammer's practical points. He is asking us to steel ourselves and accept that, whether we like it or not, torture and abuse may be essential in a war where our very survival may be at stake. He presents two scenarios in which he believes torture is permissible.

The first is the "ticking bomb" scenario, a hypothetical rarity in which the following conditions apply: a) a terrorist cell has planted a nuclear weapon or something nearly as devastating in a major city; b) we have captured someone in this cell; c) we know for a fact that he knows where the bomb is. In practice, of course, the likelihood of such a scenario is extraordinarily remote. Uncovering a terrorist plot is hard enough, capturing a conspirator involved in that plot is even harder, and realizing in advance that the person knows the whereabouts of the bomb is nearly impossible. (Remember, in the war on terrorism, we have already detained — and even killed — many innocents. Pentagon reports have acknowledged that up to 90 percent of the prisoners at Abu Ghraib, many of whom were abused and tortured, were not guilty of anything.) But let us assume, for the sake of argument, that all of Krauthammer's conditions apply. Do we have a right to torture our hypothetical detainee?

According to Krauthammer, of course we do. No responsible public official put in that position would refuse to sanction torture if he believed it could save thousands of lives. And, if it's necessary, Krauthammer argues, it should be made legal. If you have conceded that torture may be justified in one case, Krauthammer believes, you have conceded that it may be justified in many more. In his words, "Once you've established the principle, to paraphrase George Bernard Shaw, all that's left to haggle about is the price."

But this is too easy and too glib a formulation. It is possible to concede that, in an extremely rare circumstance, torture may be used without conceding that it should be legalized. One imperfect but instructive analogy is civil disobedience. In that case, laws are indeed broken, but that does not establish that the laws should be broken. In fact, civil disobedience implies precisely that laws should not be broken, and protesters who engage in it present themselves promptly for imprisonment and legal sanction on exactly those grounds. They do so for demonstrative reasons. They are not saying that laws don't matter. They are saying that laws do matter, that they should be enforced, but that their conscience in this instance demands that they disobey them.

In extremis, a rough parallel can be drawn for a president faced with the kind of horrendous decision on which Krauthammer rests his entire case. What should a president do? The answer is simple: he may have to break the law. In the Krauthammer scenario, a president might well decide that if the survival of the nation is at stake, he must make an exception. At the same time, he must subject himself—and so must those assigned to conduct the torture—to the consequences of an illegal act. Those guilty of torturing another human being must be punished—or pardoned *ex post facto*. If the torture is revealed to be useless, if the tortured man is shown to have been innocent or ignorant of the information he was tortured to reveal, then those responsible must face the full brunt of the law for, in Krauthammer's words, such a "terrible and monstrous thing." In Michael Walzer's formulation, if we are to have dirty hands, it is essential that we show them to be dirty.

What Krauthammer is proposing, however, is not this compromise, which allows us to retain our soul as a free republic while protecting us from catastrophe in an extremely rare case. He is proposing something very different: that our "dirty hands" be wiped legally clean before and after the fact. That is a Rubicon we should not cross, because it marks the boundary between a free country and an unfree one.

Krauthammer, moreover, misses a key lesson learned these past few years. What the hundreds of abuse and torture incidents have shown is that once you permit torture for someone somewhere, it has a habit of spreading. Remember that torture was originally sanctioned in administration memos only for use against illegal combatants in rare cases. Within months of that decision, abuse and torture had become endemic throughout Iraq, a theater of war in which, even Bush officials agree, the Geneva Conventions apply. The extremely coercive interrogation tactics used at Guantánamo Bay "migrated" to Abu Ghraib. In fact, General Geoffrey Miller was sent to Abu Ghraib specifically to replicate Guantánamo's techniques. According to former brigadier general Janis Karpinski, who had original responsibility for the prison, Miller ordered her to treat all detainees "like dogs." When Captain Ian Fishback, a West Point graduate and member of the Eighty-Second Airborne, witnessed routine beatings and abuse of detainees at detention facilities in Iraq and Afghanistan, often for sport, he tried to stop it. It took him a year and a half to get any response from the military command, and he had to go to Senator John McCain to make his case.

In short, what was originally supposed to be safe, sanctioned, and rare became endemic, disorganized, and brutal. The lesson is that it is impossible to quarantine torture in a hermetic box; it will inevitably contaminate the military as a whole. Once you have declared that some enemies are subhuman, you have told every soldier that every potential detainee he comes across might be exactly that kind of prisoner—and that anything can therefore be done to him. That is what the disgrace at Abu Ghraib proved. And Abu Ghraib produced a tiny fraction of the number of abuse, torture, and murder cases that have been subsequently revealed. The only way to control torture is to ban it outright. Everywhere. Even then, in wartime, some "bad apples" will always commit abuse. But at least we will have done all we can to constrain it.

Krauthammer's second case for torture is equally unpersuasive. For "slow-fuse" detainees—high-level prisoners like Khalid Sheikh Mohammed with potentially, if not immediately, useful intelligence—Krauthammer again takes the most extreme case and uses it to establish a general rule. He concedes that torture, according to almost every careful student and expert, yields highly unreliable information. Anyone can see that. If you are screaming for relief after a few seconds of waterboarding, you're likely to tell your captors anything, true or untrue, to stop the agony and terror. But Krauthammer then argues that unless you can prove that torture never works, it should always be retained as an option. "It may indeed be true that torture is not a reliable tool," he argues. "But that is very different from saying that it is never useful." And if it cannot be deemed always useless, it must be permitted—even when an imminent threat is not in the picture.

The problem here is an obvious one. You have made the extreme exception the basis for a new rule. You have said that if you cannot absolutely rule out torture as effective in every single case, it should be ruled in as an option for many. Moreover, if allowing torture even in the "ticking bomb" scenario makes the migration of torture throughout the military likely, this loophole blows the doors wide open. And how do we tell good intelligence from bad intelligence in such torture-infested interrogation? The short answer is: we cannot. By allowing torture for "slow-fuse" detainees, you sacrifice a vital principle for intelligence that is uniformly corrupted at best and useless at worst.

In fact, the use of torture and coercive interrogation by US forces in this war may have contributed to a profound worsening of our actionable intelligence. The key to intelligence in Iraq and, indeed, in Muslim enclaves in the West is gaining the support and trust of those who give terrorists cover but who are not terrorists themselves. We need human intelligence from Muslims and Arabs prepared to spy on and inform on their neighbors and friends and even family and tribe members. The only way they will do that is if they perceive the gains of America's intervention as greater than the costs, if they see clearly that cooperating with the West will lead to a better life and a freer world rather than more of the same.

What our practical endorsement of torture has done is removed that clear boundary between the Islamists and the West and made the two equivalent in the Muslim mind. Saddam Hussein used Abu Ghraib to torture innocents; so did the Americans. Yes, what Saddam did was exponentially worse. But, in doing what we did, we blurred the critical, bright line between the Arab past and what we are proposing as the Arab future. We gave Al Qaeda an enormous propaganda coup, as we have done with Guantánamo and Bagram, the "Salt Pit" torture chambers in Afghanistan, and the secret torture sites in Eastern Europe. In World War II, American soldiers were often tortured by the Japanese when captured. But FDR refused to reciprocate. Why? Because he knew that the goal of the war was not just Japan's defeat but Japan's transformation into a democracy. He knew that if the beacon of democracy—the United States of America—had succumbed to the hallmark of totalitarianism, then the chance for democratization would be deeply compromised in the wake of victory.

No one should ever underestimate the profound impact that the conduct of American troops in World War II had on the citizens of the eventually defeated Axis powers. Germans saw the difference between being liberated by the Anglo-Americans and being liberated by the Red Army. If you saw an American or British uniform, you were safe. If you didn't, the terror would continue in different ways. Ask any German or Japanese of the generation that built democracy in those countries and they will remind you of American values—not trumpeted by presidents in front of handpicked audiences, but demonstrated by the conduct of the US military during occupation. I grew up in Great Britain, a country with similar memories. In the dark days of the Cold War, I was taught that America, for all its faults, was still America. And that America did not, and constitutively could not, torture anyone.

If American conduct was important in Japan and Germany, how much more important is it in Iraq and Afghanistan? The entire point of the war on terrorism, according to the president, is to advance freedom and democracy in the Arab world. In Iraq, we had a chance not just to tell but to show the Iraqi people how a democracy acts. And, tragically, in one critical respect, we failed. That failure undoubtedly contributed to the increased legitimacy of the insurgency and illegitimacy of the occupation, and it made collaboration between informed Sunnis and US forces far less likely. What minuscule intelligence we might have plausibly gained from torturing and abusing detainees is vastly outweighed by the intelligence we have forfeited by alienating many otherwise sympathetic Iraqis and Afghans, by deepening the divide between the democracies, and by sullying the West's reputation in the Middle East. Ask yourself: Why does Al Qaeda tell its detainees to claim torture regardless of what happens to them in US custody? Because Al Qaeda knows that one of America's greatest weapons in this war is its reputation as a repository of freedom and decency. Our policy of permissible torture has handed Al Qaeda this weapon—to use against us. It is not just a moral tragedy. It is a pragmatic disaster. Why compound these crimes and errors by subsequently legalizing them, as Krauthammer (explicitly) and the president (implicitly) are proposing?

Will a ban on all "cruel, inhuman, and degrading treatment" render interrogations useless? By no means. There are many techniques for gaining intelligence from detainees other than using their bodies against their souls. You can start with the seventeen that appear in the Army Field Manual, tested by decades of armed conflict only to be discarded by this administration with barely the blink of an eye. Isolation, psychological disorientation, intense questioning, and any number of other creative techniques are possible. Some of the most productive may well be those in which interrogators are so versed in Islamic theology and Islamist subcultures that they win the confidence of prisoners and pry information out of them—something the United States, with its dearth of Arabic speakers, is unfortunately ill equipped to do.

Enemy combatants need not be accorded every privilege granted legitimate prisoners of war, but they must be treated as human beings. This means that, in addition to physical torture, wanton abuse of their religious faith is out-of-bounds. No human freedom is meaningful without religious freedom. The fact that Koran abuse has been documented at Guantánamo, that one prisoner at Abu Ghraib was forced to eat pork and drink liquor, that fake menstrual blood was used to disorient a strict Muslim prisoner at Guantánamo—these make winning the hearts and minds of moderate Muslims far harder. Such tactics have resulted in hunger strikes at Guantánamo—perhaps the ultimate sign that the coercive and abusive attempts to gain the cooperation of detainees has completely failed to achieve the desired results.

The war on terrorism is, after all, a religious war in many senses. It is a war to defend the separation of church and state as critical to the existence of freedom, including religious freedom. It is a war to persuade the silent majority of Muslims that the West offers a better way—more decency, freedom, and humanity than the autocracies they live under and the totalitarian theocracies waiting in the wings. By endorsing torture—on anyone, anywhere, for any reason—we help obliterate the very values we are trying to promote. You can see this contradiction in Krauthammer's own words: we are "morally compelled" to commit "a terrible and monstrous thing." We are obliged to destroy the village in order to save it. We have to extinguish the most basic principle that defines America in order to save America.

No, we don't. In order to retain fundamental American values, we have to banish from the United States the totalitarian impulse that is integral to every act of torture. We have to ensure that the virus of tyranny is never given an opening to infect the Constitution and replicate into something that corrupts as deeply as it wounds. We should mark the words of Ian Fishback, one of the heroes of this war: "Will we confront danger and adversity in order to preserve our ideals, or will our courage and commitment to individual rights wither at the prospect of sacrifice? My response is simple. If we abandon our ideals in the face of adversity and aggression, then those ideals were never really in our possession. I would rather die fighting than give up even the smallest part of the idea that is 'America.'" If we legalize torture, even under constrained conditions, we will have given up a large part of the idea that is America. We will have lost the war before we have given ourselves the chance to win it.

Islamo-Bullies Get a
Free Ride from the West

February 12, 2006 | *THE SUNDAY TIMES*

To see or not to see: that is now our question. For the past week and a half, the biggest global story has been the rioting, violence, and murder that has exploded over a dozen cartoons in a Danish newspaper.

Former president Bill Clinton has called the cartoons "totally outrageous." Many mainstream Muslims have claimed that they are indeed offended by them. The Archbishop of Canterbury has opined that they have hurt many feelings and cast a shadow over Christian-Muslim relations.

Others have claimed, in contrast, that the cartoons are tame and cannot even faintly be described as offensive—certainly no more offensive than any number of other cartoons that are published all the time.

That's my position, by the way. I think that much of the "offense" is contrived, that it has been manipulated by Islamists and the Syrian and Egyptian governments to advance their own agendas, and that *Jyllands-Posten*, the Danish newspaper that first published them, deserves high praise for facing down Islamist bullies.

But enough about me. What are you to think? You'd think, wouldn't you, it might be helpful to view the actual cartoons so you can see what on Earth this entire fuss is about. But the British and American media have decided that it is not their job to help you understand this story. In fact, it is their job to prevent you from fully understanding this story. As of this writing, no major newspaper in Britain has published the cartoons; the BBC has shown them only fleetingly and other networks have shied away. All have decided not to give you this critical information, without which no intelligent person can construct an informed and intelligent position on the matter. You're on your own.

The reasons given are conventional enough: the press doesn't want to inflame matters further; the cartoons are indeed offensive, and no editor has to publish images that would appall readers; reprinting would merely play into the hands of extremists; and so on.

The one argument you haven't heard is the one you hear off-camera. Many editors simply don't want to put their staffs at risk of physical danger. They have "offended" Muslims in the past and learned to regret it. In New York the editors of a free alternative paper, the *New York Press*, decided they wanted to run the cartoons so their readers could have a grasp of what this huge story is about.

The owner refused. The staff quit en masse. The editor claims the owner gave him a simple explanation: "I'm not putting lives in danger. We're not getting things blown up."

None of these arguments is risible. An editor has no responsibility to publish anything he doesn't want to. A publisher has every right to protect his own staff from physical danger. But what all the arguments amount to is simple: the press is refusing to do its job.

The fundamental job of journalists is to give you as much information as possible to make sense of the world around you. And in this story, where the entire controversy revolves around drawings, the press is suddenly coy. You can see Saddam Hussein in his underwear and members of the royal family in compromising positions. You can see Andres Serrano's famously blasphemous photograph of a crucifix in urine, called *Piss Christ*. But a political cartoon that deals with Islam? Not our job, sir. Move right along. Nothing to see here.

The withholding of truth has, of course, been one of the recurring themes of this war. We were not allowed to see the video deaths of those who jumped out of the World Trade Center. We were not allowed to see the coffins of soldiers arriving back in the United States. We are still not allowed to see the most revealing photographs of what really happened at Abu Ghraib (the legal case is still tied up in appeals).

We were not allowed to see the beheading of Nick Berg. And now we are not allowed to see . . . cartoons. Cartoons! The very things newspapers are designed in part to publish.

But then, of course, there is what makes this war different. This war is the first to take place in the online era. The web has made it possible to see almost all of it, if you look hard enough. Only the government-withheld Abu Ghraib pictures are seriously out of view for most people.

And so we have two media now in the world. We have the mainstream media whose job is increasingly not actually to disseminate information but to act as a moral steward for what is fit to print, to become an arbiter of sensitivity, good taste, and political correctness. And we have web pages like Wikipedia or the blogosphere to disseminate actual facts, data, images, and opinions that readers can judge with the benefit of all the facts, not just some of them.

If you want to see why newspapers are struggling, surely this is part of the reason. They have forgotten their fundamental task: to provide information.

Yes, the internet has its own censorship problems. Google just caved in to China. Yahoo! may even have helped identify a dissident to the Communist authorities.

Many oppressive governments have found ways to shut down websites, police access to the online world, and censor what readers can find. Your privacy may be at risk.

On the web there are no editors filtering fact from fiction. But in a case like this it's an easy decision. If you want the full story, including indispensable information to make sense of it, you have to go online. The good news, of course, is that the truth is still out there. Maybe we have the perfect solution: newspapers can sustain public propriety, while readers can find out the raw facts for themselves on the web. But the bad news is that the Islamists have just scored a huge victory.

Their hope has always been what can only be called creeping sharia. Bit by bit, free societies abandon small freedoms to accommodate the sensitivities of Muslims or Christian fundamentalists or the PC police or other touchy fanatics. Bit by bit, we cede our freedoms to fear and phony civility—all in the name of getting along.

Yes, in this new war of freedom versus fundamentalism I always anticipated appeasement. I just didn't expect the press to be among the first to wave the white flag.

Gay Cowboys Embraced
by Redneck Country

February 26, 2006 | *THE SUNDAY TIMES*

L ast December, when the movie *Brokeback Mountain* nudged nervously onto the cultural radar screen in the United States, the consensus was broad and wide. This movie was one step too far. It was yet another example of Hollywood's liberal bias. It wouldn't sell in the heartland.

"They're not going to go see the gay cowboys in Montana. I'm sorry. They're not going to do it," opined cable television's chief windbag Bill O'Reilly on December 20.

The liberal blogger Mickey Kaus wrote around the same time: "I'm highly skeptical that a movie about gay cowhands, however good, will find a large mainstream audience. I'll go see it, but I don't *want* to go see it. . . . When the film's national box office fails to live up to its hype and to the record attendance at a few early screenings, prepare to be subjected to a tedious round of guilt-tripping and chin-scratching."

The *Washington Post* columnist Charles Krauthammer made a new year's prediction about Oscar night: "*Brokeback Mountain* will have been seen in the theaters by 18 people — but the right 18 — and will win the Academy Award."

Something odd happened between the elite's assessment of the heartland and the heartland's assessment of *Brokeback Mountain*. No, it's no *The Lion, the Witch and the Wardrobe*. But of all the Oscar nominees it has racked up by far the biggest domestic grosses so far: more than $70 million at the last count (compared with, say, $22 million for the superb *Capote*). And that's before the potential Oscar boost. More interestingly, it's done remarkably well in the middle of the red states.

O'Reilly's Montana? In the eighty-five-year-old cinema in Missoula, Montana, the owner told the media: "It's been super every night since we started showing it." The movie did even better in Billings, a more conservative city in the state.

According to *Variety* magazine, some of the strongest audiences have been in Tulsa, Oklahoma; El Paso, Texas; Des Moines, Iowa; and Lubbock, Texas. Lubbock is the place George W. Bush calls his spiritual home and may well be the site for his presidential library. Greenwich Village it ain't.

What happened? There are various theories. Brilliant marketing pitched the movie as a love story and a Western, two genres well ingrained in middle-American tastes. Women dragged nervous husbands and boyfriends to see a film where the women could enjoy long, languorous views of Heath Ledger and Jake Gyllenhaal and the men could admire the scenery.

Blue-state liberals felt it some kind of social duty to see the film. Gays and lesbians flocked. The media hyped the "gay cowboy" movie and it generated more and more publicity, and thereby curiosity and thereby tickets.

The iconic phrase uttered by Gyllenhaal—"I wish I knew how to quit you"—has become part of the popular culture. The cover of last week's *New Yorker* had a parody of the now-famous poster, with Bush and Dick Cheney as the cowboys and Cheney blowing some steam off the top of his rifle.

Everyone seems to have an opinion about the film, especially those who haven't seen it. My own view is that *Brokeback* has done well primarily because it's an excellent film. It has a compelling story, two astonishing performances from Ledger and Michelle Williams, and an elegant screenplay from the great Western writer Larry McMurtry.

I still don't think the movie is in the same class as the brilliantly compressed short story by Annie Proulx on which it's based. But it's still way better than most films now offered by Hollywood, and it's a little depressing that we have to ask why a decent number of people would not want to see a rare example of Hollywood excellence.

As for the gay sex, it's barely in the movie, and the least convincing part of it.

Compared with the sex and violence usually served up by Hollywood films, *Brokeback* is *Mister Rogers' Neighborhood*. But there is something, perhaps, that explains the interest beyond mere artistic skill.

The past two decades have seen a huge shift in how homosexual people are viewed in the West. Where once they were identified entirely by sex, now more and more recognize that the central homosexual experience is the central heterosexual experience: love—maddening, humiliating, sustaining love.

That's what the marriage debate has meant and why the marriage movement, even where it has failed to achieve its immediate goals, has already achieved its long-term ambition: to humanize gay people, to tell the full, human truth about them.

And that truth includes the red states. The one thing you can say about the homosexual minority is that, unlike any other, it is not geographically limited and never has been. Red states produce as many gay kids as blue ones, and yet the heartland gay experience has rarely been portrayed and explored.

In America this is particularly odd, since the greatest gay writer in its history, Walt Whitman, was a man of the heartland. And you only have to read about the early years of Abraham Lincoln's life to see that same-sex love and friendship was integral to the making of America, especially in its wildernesses and frontiers.

You see that today even in the American gay vote, a third of which routinely backs Republicans. *Brokeback*, in other words, is not just a good movie, but a genuinely new one that tells a genuinely old story. It shows how gay men in America have families and have always had families. It shows them among themselves and among women. It shows them, above all, as men.

For the first time it reveals that homosexuality and masculinity are not necessarily in conflict, and that masculinity, even the suppressed, inarticulate masculinity of the American frontier, is not incompatible with love.

It provides a story to help people better understand the turbulent social change around them and the history they never previously recorded. That is what great art always does: it reveals the truth we are too scared to see and the future we already, beneath all our denial, understand.

When Not Seeing Is Believing

October 2, 2006 | *TIME* magazine

———————

Something about the visit to the United Nations by Iranian president Mahmoud Ahmadinejad refuses to leave my mind. It wasn't his obvious intention to pursue nuclear technology and weaponry. It wasn't his denial of the Holocaust or even his eager anticipation of Armageddon. It was something else entirely. It was his smile. In every interview, confronting every loaded question, his eyes seemed calm, his expression at ease, his face at peace. He seemed utterly serene.

What is the source of his extraordinary calm? Yes, he's in a relatively good place right now, with his Hezbollah proxies basking in a military draw with Israel. Yes, the United States is bogged down in a brutal war in Iraq. But Ahmadinejad is still unpopular at home, the Iranian economy is battered, and his major foes, Israel and the United States, far outgun him—for now.

So let me submit that he is smiling and serene not because he is crazy. He is smiling gently because for him, the most perplexing and troubling questions we all face every day have already been answered. He has placed his trust in the arms of God. Just because it isn't the God that many of us believe in does not detract from the sincerity or power of his faith. It is a faith that is real, all too real—gripping billions across the Muslim world in a new wave of fervor and fanaticism. All worries are past him, all anxiety, all stress. "Peoples, driven by their divine nature, intrinsically seek good, virtue, perfection, and beauty," Ahmadinejad said at the United Nations. "Relying on our peoples, we can take giant steps towards reform and pave the road for human perfection. Whether we like it or not, justice, peace, and virtue will sooner or later prevail in the world with the will of Almighty God."

Human perfection. Whether we like it or not. Justice, peace, and virtue. That concept of the beneficent, omnipotent will of God and the need to always submit to it, whether we like it or not, is not new. It has been present in varying degrees throughout history in all three great monotheisms—Judaism, Christianity, and Islam—from their very origins. And with it has come the utter certainty of those who say they have seen the face of God or have surrendered themselves to his power or have achieved the complete spiritual repose promised by the books of all three faiths: the Torah, the Gospels, the Koran. That is where the smile comes from.

Complete calm comes from complete certainty. In today's unnerving, globalizing, sometimes-terrifying world, such religious certainty is a balm more in demand than ever. In the new millennium, Muslims are not alone in grasping the relief of submission to authority. The new pope, despite his criticism of extremist religion and religious violence, represents a return to a more authoritarian form of Catholicism. In the Catholic triad of how we know truth—an eternal dialogue between papal authority, scriptural guidance, and the experience of the faithful—Benedict XVI has tilted the balance decisively back toward his own unanswerable truth.

What was remarkable about his recent address on Islam is what most critics missed. The bulk of his message was directed at the West, at its disavowal of religious authority and its embrace of what Benedict called "the subjective 'conscience.'" For Benedict, if your conscience tells you something that differs from his teaching, it is a false conscience, a sign not of personal integrity but of sin. And so he has silenced conscientious dissent within the Church and insisted on absolutism in matters like abortion, end-of-life decisions, priestly celibacy, the role of women, homosexuality, and interfaith dialogue.

In Protestant Christianity, especially in the United States, the loudest voices are the most certain and uncompromising. Many megachurches, which preach absolute adherence to inerrant Scripture, are thriving, while more moderate denominations are on the decline. That sense of certainty has even entered democratic politics in the United States. We have, after all, a proudly born-again president. And religious certainty surely cannot be disentangled from George W. Bush's utter conviction that he has made no mistakes in Iraq. "My faith frees me," the president once wrote. "Frees me to make the decisions that others might not like. Frees me to do the right thing, even though it may not poll well. Frees me to enjoy life and not worry about what comes next." In every messy context, the president seeks succor in a simple certainty—good versus evil, terror versus freedom—without sensing that wars are also won in the folds of uncertainty and guile, of doubt and tactical adjustment that are alien to the fundamentalist psyche.

I remember in my own faith journey that in those moments when I felt most lost in the world, I moved toward the absolutist part of my faith and gripped it with the white knuckles of fear. I brooked no dissent and patrolled my own soul for any hint of doubt. I required a faith not of sandstone but of granite.

Many Western liberals and secular types look at the zealotry closing in on them and draw an obvious conclusion: religion is the problem. As our global politics become more enamored of religious certainty, the stakes have increased, they argue, and they have a point. The evil terrorists of Al Qaeda invoke God as the sanction for their mass murder. And many beleaguered Americans respond by invoking God's certainty. And the cycle intensifies into something close to a religious war. When the presidents of the United States and Iran speak as much about God as about diplomacy, we have entered a newly dangerous era. The Islamist resurgence portends the worst. Imagine the fanaticism of sixteenth-century Christians, waging religious war and burning heretics at the stake. Now give them nukes. See the problem? Domestically, the resurgence of religious certainty has deepened our cultural divisions. And so our political discourse gets more polarized, and our global discourse gets close to impossible.

How, after all, can you engage in a rational dialogue with a man like Ahmadinejad, who believes that Armageddon is near and that it is his duty to accelerate it? How can Israel negotiate with people who are certain their instructions come from heaven and so decree that Israel must not exist in Muslim lands? Equally, of course, how can one negotiate with fundamentalist Jews who claim that the West Bank is theirs forever by biblical mandate? Or with fundamentalist Christians who believe that Israel's expansion is a biblical necessity rather than a strategic judgment?

There is, however, a way out. And it will come from the only place it can come from—the minds and souls of people of faith. It will come from the much-derided moderate Muslims, tolerant Jews, and humble Christians. The alternative to the secular-fundamentalist death spiral is something called spiritual humility and sincere religious doubt. Fundamentalism is not the only valid form of faith, and to say it is, is the great lie of our time.

There is also the faith that is once born and never experiences a catharsis or "born-again" conversion. There is the faith that treats the Bible as a moral fable as well as history and tries to live its truths in the light of contemporary knowledge, history, science, and insight. There is a faith that draws important distinctions between core beliefs and less vital ones—that picks and chooses between doctrines under the guidance of individual conscience.

There is the faith that sees the message of Jesus or Muhammad as a broad indicator of how we should treat others, of what profound holiness requires, and not as an account literally true in all respects that includes an elaborate theology that explains everything. There is the dry Deism of many of America's Founding Fathers. There is the cafeteria Christianity of, say, Thomas Jefferson, who composed a new, shortened gospel that contained only the sayings of Jesus that Jefferson inferred were the real words of the real rabbi. There is the open-minded treatment of Scripture of today's Episcopalianism and the socially liberal but doctrinally wayward faith of most lay Catholics. There is the sacramental faith that regards God as present but ultimately unknowable, that looks into the abyss and hopes rather than sees. And there are many, many more varieties.

But all those alternative forms come back to the same root. Those kinds of faith recognize one thing, first of all, about the nature of God and humankind, and it is this: if God really is God, then God must, by definition, surpass our human understanding. Not entirely. We have Scripture; we have reason; we have religious authority; we have our own spiritual experiences of the divine. But there is still something we will never grasp, something we can never know—because God is beyond our human categories. And if God is beyond our categories, then God cannot be captured for certain. We cannot know with the kind of surety that allows us to proclaim truth with a capital *T*. There will always be something that eludes us. If there weren't, it would not be God.

That kind of faith begins with the assumption that the human soul is fallible, that it can delude itself, make mistakes, and see only so far ahead. That, after all, is what it means to be human. No person has had the gift of omniscience. Yes, Christians may want to say that of Jesus. But even the Gospels tell us that Jesus doubted on the cross, asking why his own father seemed to have abandoned him. The mystery that Christians are asked to embrace is not that Jesus was God but that he was God-made-man, which is to say, prone to the feelings and doubts and joys and agonies of being human. Jesus himself seemed to make a point of that. He taught in parables rather than in abstract theories. He told stories. He had friends. He got to places late, he misread the actions of others, he wept, he felt disappointment, he asked as many questions as he gave answers, and he was often silent in self-doubt or elusive or afraid.

God-as-Omniscience, by definition, could do and be none of those things. Hence, the sacrifice entailed in God becoming man. So, at the core of the very Gospels on which fundamentalists rely for their passionate certainty is a definition of humanness that is marked by imperfection and uncertainty. Even in Jesus. Perhaps especially in Jesus.

As humans, we can merely sense the existence of a higher truth, a greater coherence than ourselves, but we cannot see it face-to-face. That is either funny or sad, and humans stagger from one option to the other. Neither beasts nor angels, we live in twilight, and we are unsure whether it is a prelude to morning or a prelude to night.

The sixteenth-century writer Michel de Montaigne lived in a world of religious war, just as we do. And he understood, as we must, that complete religious certainty is, in fact, the real blasphemy. As he put it, "We cannot worthily conceive the grandeur of those sublime and divine promises, if we can conceive them at all; to imagine them worthily, we must imagine them unimaginable, ineffable and incomprehensible, and completely different from those of our miserable experience. 'Eye cannot see,' says St. Paul, 'neither can it have entered into the heart of man, the happiness which God hath prepared for them that love him.'"

In that type of faith, doubt is not a threat. If we have never doubted, how can we say we have really believed? True belief is not about blind submission. It is about open-eyed acceptance, and acceptance requires persistent distance from the truth, and that distance is doubt. Doubt, in other words, can feed faith, rather than destroy it. And it forces us, even while believing, to recognize our fundamental duty with respect to God's truth: humility. We do not know. Which is why we believe.

In this sense, our religion, our moral life, is simply what we do. A Christian is not a Christian simply because she agrees to conform her life to some set of external principles or dogmas, or because at a particular moment in her life she experienced a rupture and changed herself entirely. She is a Christian primarily because she acts like one. She loves and forgives; she listens and prays; she contemplates and befriends; her faith and her life fuse into an unselfconscious unity that affirms a tradition of moral life and yet also makes it her own. In that nonfundamentalist understanding of faith, practice is more important than theory, love is more important than law, and mystery is seen as an insight into truth rather than an obstacle.

And that is how that kind of faith interacts with politics. If we cannot know for sure at all times how to govern our own lives, what right or business do we have telling others how to live theirs? From a humble faith comes toleration of other faiths. And from that toleration comes the oxygen that liberal democracy desperately needs to survive. That applies to all faiths, from Islam to Christianity. In global politics, it translates into a willingness to recognize empirical reality, even when it disturbs our ideology and interests. From moderate religion comes pragmatic politics. From a deep understanding of human fallibility comes the political tradition we used to call conservatism.

I remember my grandmother's faith. She was an Irish immigrant who worked as a servant for priests. In her later years she lived with us and we would go to Mass together. She was barely literate, the seventh of thirteen children. And she could rattle off the Hail Mary with the speed and subtlety of a NASCAR lap. There were times when she embarrassed me—with her broad Irish brogue and reflexive deference to clerical authority. Couldn't she genuflect a little less deeply and pray a little less loudly? And then, as I winced at her volume in my quiet church, I saw that she was utterly oblivious to those around her. She was someplace else. And there were times when I caught her in the middle of saying the Rosary when she seemed to reach another level altogether—a higher, deeper place than I, with all my education and privilege, had yet reached.

Was that the certainty of fundamentalism? Or was it the initiation into a mystery none of us can ever fully understand? I'd argue the latter. The eighteenth-century German playwright Gotthold Lessing said it best. He prayed a simple prayer: "If God were to hold all Truth concealed in his right hand, and in his left hand only the steady and diligent drive for Truth, albeit with the proviso that I would always and forever err in the process, and to offer me the choice, I would with all humility take the left hand, and say, Father, I will take this—the pure Truth is for You alone."

That sentiment is as true now as it was more than two centuries ago when Lessing wrote it. Except now the very survival of our civilization may depend on it.

The Reagan of the Left?

May 24, 2007 | *THE DISH*

I went to see Obama last night. He had a fundraiser at H20, a yuppie disco/restaurant in Southwest D.C. I was curious about how he is in person. I'm still absorbing the many impressions I got. But one thing stays in my head. This guy is a liberal. Make no mistake about that. He may, in fact, be the most effective liberal advocate I've heard in my lifetime. As a conservative, I think he could be absolutely lethal to what's left of the tradition of individualism, self-reliance, and small government that I find myself quixotically attached to.

And as a simple observer, I really don't see what's stopping him from becoming the next president. The overwhelming first impression that you get—from the exhausted but vibrant stump speech, the diverse nature of the crowd, the swell of the various applause lines—is that this is the candidate for real change. He has what Reagan had in 1980 and Clinton had in 1992: the wind at his back. Sometimes, elections really do come down to a simple choice: Change or more of the same? Look at the polls and forget ideology for a moment. What do Americans really want right now? Change. Who best offers them a chance to turn the page cleanly on an era most want to forget? It isn't Clinton, God help us. Edwards is so 2004. McCain is a throwback. Romney makes plastic look real. Rudy does offer something new for Republicans—the abortion-friendly, cross-dressing Jack Bauer. But no one captures the sheer, pent-up desire for a new start more effectively than Obama. From the content and structure of Obama's pitch to the base, it's also clear to me that whatever illusions I had about his small-*c* conservatism, he's a big-government liberal with—for a liberal—the most attractive persona and best-developed arguments since JFK.

I fear he could do to conservatism what Reagan did to liberalism. And just as liberals deserved a shellacking in 1980, so do "conservatives" today. In the Bush era, they have shown their own contempt for their own tradition. Who can blame Obama for exploiting the big-government arguments Bush has already conceded?

And just as Carter branded liberalism in a bad way for a generation, so Bush and his acolytes have poisoned the brand of conservatism for the foreseeable future. When you take a few steps back and look closely, you realize that Bush has managed to both betray conservatism and stigmatize it all at once. That's some achievement.

Obama's speech began and continued with domestic policy. War? What war? There was one tiny, fleeting mention of the terror threat. Yes, this is the base. Yes, the base's fixation is ending the war in Iraq. Yes, you can make an argument that withdrawal there now is a boon to the terror war. But Obama didn't make that argument. And it seems to me that the two biggest obstacles Obama will have next year are residual racism and concern that he doesn't fully grasp the seriousness of the Islamist terror threat. He's been proved right on Iraq—I'm sorry to say. And that good call—and the reasons he gave for it in 2003—will surely undermine the case against his "inexperience." *Inexperienced?* he'll rightly scoff. *If "experience" means backing the Iraq War, I'm glad I don't have as much of it as Clinton and McCain and Giuliani.* But he must tell us how we are to stay on offense in this war if he is to win over worriers like me. To listen to a stump speech five or so years after 9/11 and wait for almost half a speech until he mentions it is disconcerting. And yet, it is also bound up, surely, with his appeal. That appeal is partly to take us past the 9/11 moment, and describe a journey forward that isn't obviously into darkness.

Two further impressions. At a couple of points in his speech, he used the phrase: "This is not who we are." I was struck by the power of those words. He was reasserting that America is much more than George W. Bush and Dick Cheney and Gitmo and Abu Ghraib and Katrina and fear and obstinacy and isolation. And so he makes an argument for change in the language of restoration. The temperamental conservatives in America hear a form of patriotism, and the ideological liberals hear a note of radicalism. It's a powerful, unifying theme. He'd be smart to deepen and broaden it.

My favorite moment was a very simple one. He referred to the anniversary of the March on Selma, how he went and how he came back and someone (I don't remember who now) said to him:

"That was a great celebration of African American history."

To which Obama said he replied:

"No, no, no, no, no. That was not a great celebration of African American history. That was a celebration of American history."

Yes.

There's a reason for his wide appeal. The overwhelming question for me at this point in this historic campaign is a simple one: Who will stop him?

A Married Man

August 21, 2007 | *THE DISH*

So this is what it feels like? In a week's time, I'll be walking down the aisle with my soon-to-be husband. Our families are both coming for the big day. We're getting hitched in Massachusetts, where I've lived every summer for the past decade or so, and which is the only state in the United States where civil marriage is legal for everyone. Every now and again, I have to pinch myself. This is real? For me? It is hardly possible that it could be real for anyone. But me? After so long?

A brief personal history. In 1989, as a jejune junior editor at *The New Republic*, I got involved in an editorial argument about proposed domestic or civil partnerships for gay couples. The idea had emerged in the 1980s, in several major cities, partly because of the trauma of couples torn asunder by hostile relatives in the AIDS crisis. Some social conservatives were understandably worried that by setting up an institution like "domestic partnership," we were creating "marriage-lite," an institution that would spread to heterosexual couples and weaken the responsibilities and prestige of marriage itself. As a gay conservative, I found both arguments compelling. I saw the pressing need to give gay couples legal protection, but I could also see the danger that an easy-come-easy-go pseudomarriage could pose for the society as a whole. The solution, however, seemed blindingly obvious to me. "Well, why not let gays get married as well?" I asked. "Isn't that the true conservative position?"

My liberal bosses loved the idea of irritating conservatives with a conservative argument. So I obliged. The cover illustration was the first time a major magazine had put two guys on a wedding cake on the cover. And the piece created a mini-sensation. I enjoyed the buzz, but the more I thought about it, the more convinced I became that this was not just a necessary change, but a long-overdue one. With straight marriage no longer legally linked to children, and with gays desperately needing integration into their own families and society, it seemed like a no-brainer to me. It was a philosophical decision, not a personal one. I was in my twenties and had no intention of marrying myself. In fact, I was a pretty swinging bachelor. But it was the principle that mattered.

Almost two decades later, after years of intense political debate, after years of personal activism, court cases, congressional testimony, threatened constitutional amendments, civil disobedience, and a global revolution in marriage rights, the political has now become personal for me. It's a week away. And I officially have the jitters.

We decided on the most minimalist wedding possible — basically close family only. We're getting married in the same place — a beach house — that we're having the tiny reception. It's a block down the beach from where we live. We have the license, the judge, the clothes, the menu, the photographer (although he hasn't been in touch lately — gulp), and the rings. I've written out the civil liturgy. We've settled on the vows. I should relax now, right?

But the other night it hit me for the first time that this is really about to happen. I guess I just put it out of my head until it's only a matter of a week or so away. My fiancé, Aaron, and I have lived together for three years. I have no qualms about our actual relationship. For me, this is for life. But standing up in front of my family and my spouse's and saying the vows out loud has me in a state of butterflies. I can go on television and barely break a sweat, but I'm terrified of performing in front of my own family. I'm scared I'll lose it. I bawled through the last same-sex wedding I went to. When I was diagnosed with HIV fourteen years ago, I assumed this day would never come. And now it has, the emotional impact is a little hard to measure.

You fight for something, never expecting it to happen, let alone to you, and then it does, and it can overwhelm. Taking yes for an answer can be harder than no. Maybe it's a function of having overthought this issue for so long; maybe it's just handling a big family occasion of any sort (Christmas is bad enough). Maybe it's a lifetime in which my actual relationships have always been private, or so targeted by political enemies I've become very defensive. Maybe I'm scared that two decades of passionate advocacy in theory is easier than a simple act in practice. But whatever the reason, going public with my husband—even in front of our supportive families—is suddenly much tougher than I expected. My throat is a little dry. My stomach is a little unsettled.

My sister e-mailed support:

Don't worry, it is natural to stress, I practically had a baby the day before mine! 75 guests to the church, another 75 in the evening, the food, the flowers, the photos, all those people watching me! On the day it just felt like a dream, I felt like I was letting out a huge breath all day, like that waiting to exhale, I exhaled all day and it was wonderful.

Our wedding is much smaller. My old friend and marriage advocate Evan Wolfson reassured me as well:

You're supposed to be in a zombie-state till the beauty of it breaks through.

Are zombies nervous? They never seem to be. They just stagger forward. Oh, well. Here goes. . . .

> "I, Andrew, take you, Aaron,
> to be no other than yourself.
> Loving what I know of you,
> trusting what I don't yet know,
> with respect for your integrity,
> and faith in your abiding love for me,
> through all our years,
> and in all that life may bring us,
> for better or worse,
> for richer or poorer,
> in sickness and in health,
> till death do us part,
> I accept you as my husband
> and pledge my love to you."

So revolutionary for some, so simple for me. For the first time in my adult life, I will have a home.

Goodbye to All That: Why Obama Matters

December 2007 | *THE ATLANTIC*

The logic behind the candidacy of Barack Obama is not, in the end, about Barack Obama. It has little to do with his policy proposals, which are very close to his Democratic rivals' and which, with a few exceptions, exist firmly within the conventions of our politics. It has little to do with Obama's considerable skills as a conciliator, legislator, or even thinker. It has even less to do with his ideological pedigree or legal background or rhetorical skills. Yes, as the many profiles prove, he has considerable intelligence and not a little guile. But so do others, not least his formidably polished and practiced opponent Senator Hillary Clinton.

Obama, moreover, is no saint. He has flaws and tics: often tired, sometimes crabby, intermittently solipsistic, he's a surprisingly uneven campaigner.

A soaring rhetorical flourish one day is undercut by a lackluster debate performance the next. He is certainly not without self-regard. He has more experience in public life than his opponents want to acknowledge, but he has not spent much time in Washington and has never run a business. His lean physique, close-cropped hair, and stick-out ears can give the impression of a slightly pushy undergraduate. You can see why many of his friends and admirers have urged him to wait his turn. He could be president in five or nine years' time—why the rush?

But he knows, and privately acknowledges, that the fundamental point of his candidacy is that it is happening now. In politics, timing matters. And the most persuasive case for Obama has less to do with him than with the moment he is meeting. The moment has been a long time coming, and it is the result of a confluence of events, from one traumatizing war in Southeast Asia to another in the most fractious country in the Middle East. The legacy is a cultural climate that stultifies our politics and corrupts our discourse.

Obama's candidacy in this sense is a potentially transformational one. Unlike any of the other candidates, he could take America—finally—past the debilitating, self-perpetuating family quarrel of the Baby Boom generation that has long engulfed all of us. So much has happened in America in the past seven years, let alone the past forty, that we can be forgiven for focusing on the present and the immediate future. But it is only when you take several large steps back into the long past that the full logic of an Obama presidency stares directly—and uncomfortably—at you.

At its best, the Obama candidacy is about ending a war—not so much the war in Iraq, which now has a momentum that will propel the occupation into the next decade—but the war within America that has prevailed since Vietnam and that shows dangerous signs of intensifying, a nonviolent civil war that has crippled America at the very time the world needs it most. It is a war about war—and about culture and about religion and about race. And in that war, Obama—and Obama alone—offers the possibility of a truce.

The traces of our long journey to this juncture can be found all around us. Its most obvious manifestation is political rhetoric. The high temperature—Bill O'Reilly's nightly screeds against anti-Americans on one channel, Keith Olbermann's *Worst Person in the World* on the other; MoveOn.org's "General Betray Us" on the one side, Ann Coulter's *Treason* on the other; Michael Moore's accusation of treason at the core of the Iraq War, Sean Hannity's assertion of treason in the opposition to it—is particularly striking when you examine the generally minor policy choices on the table. Something deeper and more powerful than the actual decisions we face is driving the tone of the debate.

Even on issues that are seen as integral to the polarization, the practical stakes in this election are minor. A large consensus in America favors legal abortions during the first trimester and varying restrictions thereafter. Even in solidly red states, such as South Dakota, the support for total criminalization is weak. If *Roe* were to fall, the primary impact would be the end of a system more liberal than any in Europe in favor of one more in sync with the varied views that exist across this country. On marriage, the battles in the states are subsiding, as a bevy of blue states adopt either civil marriage or civil unions for gay couples and the rest stand pat. Most states that want no recognition for same-sex couples have already made that decision, usually through state constitutional amendments that allow change only with extreme difficulty. And the one state where marriage equality exists, Massachusetts, has decided to maintain the reform indefinitely.

Given this quiet, evolving consensus on policy, how do we account for the bitter, brutal tone of American politics? The answer lies mainly with the biggest and most influential generation in America: the Baby Boomers. The divide is still—amazingly—between those who fought in Vietnam and those who didn't, and between those who fought and dissented and those who fought but never dissented at all. By defining the contours of the Boomer generation, it lasted decades. And with time came a strange intensity.

The professionalization of the battle, and the emergence of an array of well-funded interest groups dedicated to continuing it, can be traced most proximately to the bitter confirmation fights over Robert Bork and Clarence Thomas, in 1987 and 1991 respectively. The presidency of Bill Clinton, who was elected with only 43 percent of the vote in 1992, crystallized the new reality. As soon as the Baby Boomers hit the commanding heights, the Vietnam power struggle rebooted. The facts mattered little in the face of such a divide. While Clinton was substantively a moderate conservative in policy, his countercultural origins led to the drama, ultimately, of religious warfare and even impeachment. Clinton clearly tried to bridge the Boomer split. But he was trapped on one side of it—and his personal foibles only reignited his generation's agonies over sex and love and marriage. Even the failed impeachment didn't bring the two sides to their senses, and the election of 2000 only made matters worse: Gore and Bush were almost designed to reflect the Boomers' and the country's divide, which deepened further.

The trauma of 9/11 has tended to obscure the memory of that unprecedentedly bitter election, and its nail-biting aftermath, which verged on a constitutional crisis. But its legacy is very much still with us, made far worse by President Bush's approach to dealing with it. Despite losing the popular vote, Bush governed as if he had won Reagan's forty-nine states. Instead of cementing a coalition of the center-right, Bush and Rove set out to ensure that the new evangelical base of the Republicans would turn out more reliably in 2004. Instead of seeing the post-sixties divide as a wound to be healed, they poured acid on it.

With 9/11, Bush had a reset moment—a chance to reunite the country in a way that would marginalize the extreme haters on both sides and forge a national consensus. He chose not to do so. It wasn't entirely his fault. On the left, the truest believers were unprepared to give the president the benefit of any doubt in the wake of the 2000 election, and they even judged the 9/11 attacks to be a legitimate response to decades of US foreign policy. Some could not support the war in Afghanistan, let alone the adventure in Iraq. As the Iraq War faltered, the polarization intensified. In 2004, the Vietnam argument returned with a new energy, with the Swift Boat attacks on John Kerry's Vietnam War record and CBS's misbegotten report on Bush's record in the Texas Air National Guard. These were the stories that touched the collective nerve of the political classes—because they parsed once again along the fault lines of the Boomer divide that had come to define all of us.

The result was an even deeper schism. Kerry was arguably the worst candidate on Earth to put to rest the post-1960s culture war—and his decision to embrace his Vietnam identity at the convention made things worse. Bush, for his part, was unable to do nuance. And so the campaign became a matter of symbolism—pitting those who took the terror threat "seriously" against those who didn't. Supporters of the Iraq War became more invested in asserting the morality of their cause than in examining the effectiveness of their tactics. Opponents of the war found themselves dispirited. Some were left to hope privately for American failure; others lashed out, as distrust turned to paranoia. It was and is a toxic cycle, in which the interests of the United States are supplanted by domestic agendas born of pride and ruthlessness on the one hand and bitterness and alienation on the other.

This is the critical context for the election of 2008. It is an election that holds the potential not merely to intensify this cycle of division but to bequeath it to a new generation, one marked by a new war that need not be—that should not be—seen as another Vietnam. A Giuliani-Clinton matchup, favored by the media elite, is a classic intragenerational struggle—with two deeply divisive and ruthless personalities ready to go to the brink. Giuliani represents that Nixonian disgust with anyone asking questions about, let alone actively protesting, a war. Clinton will always be, in the minds of so many, the young woman who gave the commencement address at Wellesley, who sat in on the Nixon implosion, and who once disdained baking cookies. For some, her husband will always be the draft dodger who smoked pot and wouldn't admit it. And however hard she tries, there is nothing Hillary Clinton can do about it. She and Giuliani are conscripts in their generation's war. To their respective sides, they are war heroes.

In normal times, such division is not fatal, and can even be healthy. It's great copy for journalists. But we are not talking about routine rancor. And we are not talking about normal times. We are talking about a world in which Islamist terror, combined with increasingly available destructive technology, has already murdered thousands of Americans, and tens of thousands of Muslims, and could pose an existential danger to the West. The terrible failures of the Iraq occupation, the resurgence of Al Qaeda in Pakistan, the progress of Iran toward nuclear capability, and the collapse of America's prestige and moral reputation, especially among those millions of Muslims too young to have known any American president but Bush, heighten the stakes dramatically.

Perhaps the underlying risk is best illustrated by our asking what the popular response would be to another 9/11–style attack. It is hard to imagine a reprise of the sudden unity and solidarity in the days after 9/11, or an outpouring of support from allies and neighbors. It is far easier to imagine an even more bitter fight over who was responsible (apart from the perpetrators) and a profound suspicion of a government forced to impose more restrictions on travel, communications, and civil liberties. The current president would be unable to command the trust, let alone the support, of half the country in such a time. He could even be blamed for provoking any attack that came.

Of the viable national candidates, only Obama and possibly McCain have the potential to bridge this widening partisan gulf. Polling reveals Obama to be the favored Democrat among Republicans. McCain's bipartisan appeal has receded in recent years, especially with his enthusiastic embrace of the latest phase of the Iraq War. And his personal history can only reinforce the Vietnam divide. But Obama's reach outside his own ranks remains striking. Why? It's a good question: How has a black, urban liberal gained far stronger support among Republicans than the made-over moderate Clinton or the southern charmer Edwards? Perhaps because the Republicans and independents who are open to an Obama candidacy see his primary advantage in prosecuting the war on Islamist terrorism. It isn't about his policies as such; it is about his person. They are prepared to set their own ideological preferences to one side in favor of what Obama offers America in a critical moment in our dealings with the rest of the world. The war today matters enormously. The war of the last generation? Not so much. If you are an American who yearns to finally get beyond the symbolic battles of the Boomer generation and face today's actual problems, Obama may be your man.

What does he offer? First and foremost: his face. Think of it as the most effective potential re-branding of the United States since Reagan. Such a re-branding is not trivial—it's central to an effective war strategy. The war on Islamist terror, after all, is two-pronged: a function of both hard power and soft power. We have seen the potential of hard power in removing the Taliban and Saddam Hussein. We have also seen its inherent weaknesses in Iraq, and its profound limitations in winning a long war against radical Islam. The next president has to create a sophisticated and supple blend of soft and hard power to isolate the enemy, to fight where necessary, but also to create an ideological template that works to the West's advantage over the long haul. There is simply no other candidate with the potential of Obama to do this. Which is where his face comes in.

Consider this hypothetical. It's November 2008. A young Pakistani Muslim is watching television and sees that this man—Barack Hussein Obama— is the new face of America. In one simple image, America's soft power has been ratcheted up not a notch, but a logarithm. A brown-skinned man whose father was an African, who grew up in Indonesia and Hawaii, who attended a majority-Muslim school as a boy, is now the alleged enemy. If you wanted the crudest but most effective weapon against the demonization of America that fuels Islamist ideology, Obama's face gets close. It proves them wrong about what America is in ways no words can.

The other obvious advantage that Obama has in facing the world and our enemies is his record on the Iraq War. He is the only major candidate to have clearly opposed it from the start. Whoever is in office in January 2009 will be tasked with redeploying forces in and out of Iraq, negotiating with neighboring states, engaging America's estranged allies, tamping down regional violence. Obama's interlocutors in Iraq and the Middle East would know that he never had suspicious motives toward Iraq, has no interest in occupying it indefinitely, and foresaw more clearly than most Americans the baleful consequences of long-term occupation.

This latter point is the most salient. The act of picking the next president will be in some ways a statement of America's view of Iraq. Clinton is running as a centrist Democrat—voting for war, accepting the need for an occupation at least through her first term, while attempting to do triage as practically as possible. Obama is running as the clearer antiwar candidate. At the same time, Obama's candidacy cannot fairly be cast as a McGovernite revival in tone or substance. He is not opposed to war as such. He is not opposed to the use of unilateral force either—as demonstrated by his willingness to target Al Qaeda in Pakistan over the objections of the Pakistani government. He does not oppose the idea of democratization in the Muslim world as a general principle or the concept of nation building as such. He is not an isolationist, as his support for the campaign in Afghanistan proves. It is worth recalling the key passages of the speech Obama gave in Chicago on October 2, 2002, five months before the war:

> I don't oppose all wars. And I know that in this crowd today, there is no shortage of patriots, or of patriotism. What I am opposed to is a dumb war. What I am opposed to is a rash war. . . . I know that even a successful war against Iraq will require a US occupation of undetermined length, at undetermined cost, with undetermined consequences. I know that an invasion of Iraq without a clear rationale and without strong international support will only fan the flames of the Middle East, and encourage the worst, rather than best, impulses of the Arab world, and strengthen the recruitment arm of Al Qaeda. I am not opposed to all wars. I'm opposed to dumb wars.

The man who opposed the war for the right reasons is for that reason the potential president with the most flexibility in dealing with it. Clinton is hemmed in by her past and her generation. If she pulls out too quickly, she will fall prey to the usual browbeating from the right—the same theme that has played relentlessly since 1968. If she stays in too long, the antiwar base of her own party, already suspicious of her, will pounce. The Boomer legacy imprisons her—and so it may continue to imprison us. The debate about the war in the next four years needs to be about the practical and difficult choices ahead of us—not about the symbolism or whether it's a second Vietnam.

A generational divide also separates Clinton and Obama with respect to domestic politics. Clinton grew up saturated in the conflict that still defines

American politics. As a liberal, she has spent years in a defensive crouch against triumphant post-Reagan conservatism. The mau-mauing that greeted her health-care plan and the endless nightmares of her husband's scandals drove her deeper into her political bunker. Her liberalism is warped by what you might call a Political Post-Traumatic Stress Syndrome. Reagan spooked people on the left, especially those, like Clinton, who were interested primarily in winning power. She has internalized what most Democrats of her generation have internalized: they suspect that the majority is not with them, and so some quotient of discretion, fear, or plain deception is required if they are to advance their objectives. And so the less adept ones seem deceptive, and the more practiced ones, like Clinton, exhibit the plastic-ness and inauthenticity that still plague her candidacy. She's hiding her true feelings. We know it, she knows we know it, and there is no way out of it.

Obama, simply by virtue of when he was born, is free of this defensiveness. Strictly speaking, he is at the tail end of the Boomer generation. But he is not of it.

"Partly because my mother, you know, was smack-dab in the middle of the Baby Boom generation," he told me. "She was only eighteen when she had me. So when I think of Baby Boomers, I think of my mother's generation. And you know, I was too young for the formative period of the sixties—civil rights, sexual revolution, Vietnam War. Those all sort of passed me by."

Obama's mother was, in fact, born only five years earlier than Hillary Clinton. He did not politically come of age during the Vietnam era, and he is simply less afraid of the right wing than Clinton is, because he has emerged on the national stage during a period of conservative decadence and decline. And so, for example, he felt much freer than Clinton to say he was prepared to meet and hold talks with hostile world leaders in his first year in office. He has proposed sweeping middle-class tax cuts and opposed drastic reforms of Social Security, without being tarred as a fiscally reckless liberal. (Of course, such accusations are hard to make after the fiscal performance of today's "conservatives.") Even his more conservative positions—like his openness to bombing Pakistan, or his support for merit pay for public-school teachers—do not appear to emerge from a desire or need to credentialize himself with the right. He is among the first Democrats in a generation not to be afraid or ashamed of what they actually believe, which also gives them more freedom to move pragmatically to the right, if necessary. He does not smell, as Clinton does, of political fear.

There are few areas where this Democratic fear is more intense than religion. The crude exploitation of sectarian loyalty and religious zeal by Bush and Rove succeeded in deepening the culture war, to Republican advantage. Again, this played into the divide of the Boomer years—between God-fearing Americans and the peacenik atheist hippies of lore. The Democrats have responded by pretending to a public religiosity that still seems strained. Listening to Hillary Clinton detail her prayer life in public, as she did last spring to a packed house at George Washington University, was at once poignant and repellent. Poignant because her faith may well be genuine, repellent because its Methodist genuineness demands that she not profess it so tackily. But she did. The polls told her to.

Obama, in contrast, opened his soul up in public long before any focus group demanded it. His first book, *Dreams from My Father*, is a candid, haunting, and supple piece of writing. It was not concocted to solve a political problem (his second, hackneyed book, *The Audacity of Hope*, filled that niche). It was a genuine display of internal doubt and conflict and sadness. And it reveals Obama as someone whose "complex fate," to use Ralph Ellison's term, is to be both believer and doubter, in a world where such complexity is as beleaguered as it is necessary.

This struggle to embrace modernity without abandoning faith falls on one of the fault lines in the modern world. It is arguably the critical fault line, the tectonic rift that is advancing the bloody borders of Islam and the increasingly sectarian boundaries of American politics. As humankind abandons the secular totalitarianisms of the last century and grapples with breakneck technological and scientific discoveries, the appeal of absolutist faith is powerful in both developing and developed countries. It is the latest in a long line of rebukes to liberal modernity—but this rebuke has the deepest roots, the widest appeal, and the attraction that all total solutions to the human predicament proffer. From the doctrinal absolutism of Pope Benedict's Vatican to the revival of fundamentalist Protestantism in the United States and Asia to the attraction for many Muslims of the most extreme and antimodern forms of Islam, the same phenomenon has spread to every culture and place.

You cannot confront the complex challenges of domestic or foreign policy today unless you understand this gulf and its seriousness. You cannot lead the United States without having a foot in both the religious and secular camps.

This, surely, is where Bush has failed most profoundly. By aligning himself with the most extreme and basic of religious orientations, he has lost many moderate believers and alienated the secular and agnostic in the West. If you cannot bring the agnostics along in a campaign against religious terrorism, you have a problem.

Here again, Obama, by virtue of generation and accident, bridges this deepening divide. He was brought up in a nonreligious home and converted to Christianity as an adult. But—critically—he is not born-again. His faith—at once real and measured, hot and cool—lives at the center of the American religious experience. It is a modern, intellectual Christianity. "I didn't have an epiphany," he explained to me. "What I really did was to take a set of values and ideals that were first instilled in me from my mother, who was, as I have called her in my book, the last of the secular humanists—you know, belief in kindness and empathy and discipline, responsibility—those kinds of values. And I found in the Church a vessel or a repository for those values and a way to connect those values to a larger community and a belief in God and a belief in redemption and mercy and justice. . . . I guess the point is, it continues to be both a spiritual, but also intellectual, journey for me, this issue of faith."

The best speech Obama has ever given was not his famous 2004 convention address, but a June 2007 speech in Connecticut. In it, he described his religious conversion:

> One Sunday, I put on one of the few clean jackets I had, and went over to Trinity United Church of Christ on Ninety-Fifth Street on the South Side of Chicago. And I heard Reverend Jeremiah A. Wright deliver a sermon called "The Audacity of Hope." And during the course of that sermon, he introduced me to someone named Jesus Christ. I learned that my sins could be redeemed. I learned that those things I was too weak to accomplish myself, he would accomplish with me if I placed my trust in him. And in time, I came to see faith as more than just a comfort to the weary or a hedge against death, but rather as an active, palpable agent in the world and in my own life.
>
> It was because of these newfound understandings that I was finally able to walk down the aisle of Trinity one day and affirm my Christian faith. It came about as a choice and not an epiphany. I didn't fall out in church, as folks sometimes do. The questions I had didn't magically disappear. The skeptical

bent of my mind didn't suddenly vanish. But kneeling beneath that cross on the South Side, I felt I heard God's spirit beckoning me. I submitted myself to his will, and dedicated myself to discovering his truth and carrying out his works.

To be able to express this kind of religious conviction without disturbing or alienating the growing phalanx of secular voters, especially on the left, is quite an achievement. As he said in 2006, "Faith doesn't mean that you don't have doubts." To deploy the rhetoric of evangelicalism while eschewing its occasional anti-intellectualism and hubristic certainty is as rare as it is exhilarating. It is both an intellectual achievement, because Obama has clearly attempted to wrestle a modern Christianity from the encumbrances and anachronisms of its past, and an American achievement, because it was forged in the only American institution where conservative theology and the Democratic Party still communicate: the black church.

And this, of course, is the other element that makes Obama a potentially transformative candidate: race. Here Obama again finds himself in the center of a complex fate, unwilling to pick sides in a divide that reaches back centuries and appears at times unbridgeable. His appeal to whites is palpable. I have felt it myself. Earlier this fall, I attended an Obama speech in Washington on tax policy that underwhelmed on delivery; his address was wooden, stilted, even tedious. It was only after I left the hotel that it occurred to me that I'd just been bored on tax policy by a national black leader. That I should have been struck by this was born in my own racial stereotypes, of course. But it won me over.

Obama is deeply aware of how he comes across to whites. In a revealing passage in his first book, he recounts how, in adolescence, he defused his white mother's fears that he was drifting into delinquency. She had marched into his room and demanded to know what was going on. He flashed her "a reassuring smile and patted her hand and told her not to worry." This, he tells us, was "usually an effective tactic," because people were satisfied as long as you were courteous and smiled and made no sudden moves. They were more than satisfied; they were relieved—such a pleasant surprise to find a well-mannered young black man who didn't seem angry all the time.

And so you have Obama's campaign for white America: courteous and smiling and with no sudden moves. This may, of course, be one reason for his still-lukewarm support among many African Americans, a large number of whom back a white woman for the presidency. It may also be because African Americans (more than many whites) simply don't believe that a black man can win the presidency, and so are leery of wasting their vote. And the persistence of race as a divisive, even explosive factor in American life was unmissable the week of Obama's tax speech. While he was detailing middle-class tax breaks, thousands of activists were preparing to march in Jena, Louisiana, after a series of crude racial incidents had blown up into a polarizing conflict.

Jesse Jackson voiced puzzlement that Obama was not at the forefront of the march. "If I were a candidate, I'd be all over Jena," he remarked. The South Carolina newspaper *The State* reported that Jackson said Obama was "acting like he's white." Obama didn't jump into the fray (no sudden moves), but instead issued measured statements on Jena, waiting till a late-September address at Howard University to find his voice. It was simultaneously an endorsement of black identity politics and a distancing from it:

> When I'm president, we will no longer accept the false choice between being tough on crime and vigilant in our pursuit of justice. Dr. King said: "It's not either/or; it's both/and." We can have a crime policy that's both tough and smart. If you're convicted of a crime involving drugs, of course you should be punished. But let's not make the punishment for crack cocaine that much more severe than the punishment for powder cocaine when the real difference between the two is the skin color of the people using them. Judges think that's wrong. Republicans think that's wrong, Democrats think that's wrong, and yet it's been approved by Republican and Democratic presidents because no one has been willing to brave the politics and make it right. That will end when I am president.

Obama's racial journey makes this kind of both/and politics something more than a matter of political compromise. The paradox of his candidacy is that, as potentially the first African American president in a country founded on slavery, he has taken pains to downplay the racial catharsis his candidacy implies. He knows race is important, and yet he knows that it turns destructive if it becomes the only important thing. In this he again subverts a Boomer paradigm, of black victimology or black conservatism. He is neither Al Sharpton nor Clarence Thomas, neither Julian Bond nor Colin Powell. Nor is he a post-racial figure like Tiger Woods, insofar as he has spent his life trying to reconnect with a black identity his childhood never gave him. Equally, he cannot be a Jesse Jackson. His white mother brought him up to be someone else.

In *Dreams from My Father*, Obama tells the story of a man with an almost eerily nonracial childhood, who has to learn what racism is, what his own racial identity is, and even what being black in America is. And so Obama's relationship to the black American experience is as much learned as intuitive. He broke up with a serious early girlfriend in part because she was white. He decided to abandon a post-racial career among the upper-middle classes of the East Coast in order to reengage with the black experience of Chicago's South Side. It was an act of integration—personal as well as communal—that called him to the work of community organizing.

This restlessness with where he was, this attempt at personal integration, represents both an affirmation of identity politics and a commitment to carving a unique personal identity out of the race, geography, and class he inherited. It yields an identity born of displacement, not rootedness. And there are times, I confess, when Obama's account of understanding his own racial experience seemed more like that of a gay teen discovering that he lives in two worlds simultaneously than that of a young African American confronting racism for the first time.

And there are also times when Obama's experience feels more like an immigrant story than a black memoir. His autobiography navigates a new and strange world of an American racial legacy that never quite defined him at his core. He therefore speaks to a complicated and mixed identity—not a simple and alienated one. This may hurt him among some African Americans, who may fail to identify with this fellow with an odd name. Black conservatives, like Shelby Steele, fear he is too deferential to the black Establishment. Black leftists worry that he is not beholden at all. But there is no reason why African Americans cannot see the logic of Americanism that Obama also represents, a legacy that is ultimately theirs as well. To be black and white, to have belonged to a nonreligious home and a Christian church, to have attended a majority-Muslim school in Indonesia and a black church in urban Chicago, to be more than one thing and sometimes not fully anything—this is an increasingly common experience for Americans, including many racial minorities. Obama expresses such a conflicted but resilient identity before he even utters a word.

And this complexity, with its internal tensions, contradictions, and moods, may increasingly be the main thing all Americans have in common.

None of this, of course, means that Obama will be the president some are dreaming of. His record in high office is sparse; his performances on the campaign trail have been patchy; his chief rival for the nomination, Senator Clinton, has bested him often with her relentless pursuit of the middle ground, her dogged attention to her own failings, and her much-improved speaking skills. At times, she has even managed to appear more inherently likable than the skinny, crabby, and sometimes-morose newcomer from Chicago. Clinton's most surprising asset has been the sense of security she instills. Her husband—and the good feelings that nostalgics retain for his presidency—has buttressed her case. In dangerous times, popular majorities often seek the conservative option, broadly understood.

The paradox is that Hillary makes far more sense if you believe that times are actually pretty good. If you believe that America's current crisis is not a deep one, if you think that pragmatism alone will be enough to navigate a world on the verge of even more religious warfare, if you believe that today's ideological polarization is not dangerous, and that what appears dark today is an illusion fostered by the lingering trauma of the Bush presidency, then the argument for Obama is not that strong. Clinton will do. And a Clinton-Giuliani race could be as invigorating as it is utterly predictable.

But if you sense, as I do, that greater danger lies ahead, and that our divisions and recent history have combined to make the American polity and constitutional order increasingly vulnerable, then the calculus of risk changes. Sometimes, when the world is changing rapidly, the greater risk is caution. Close-up in this election campaign, Obama is unlikely. From a distance, he is necessary. At a time when America's estrangement from the world risks tipping into dangerous imbalance, when a country at war with lethal enemies is also increasingly at war with itself, when humankind's spiritual yearnings veer between an excess of certainty and an inability to believe anything at all, and when sectarian and racial divides seem as intractable as ever, a man who is a bridge between these worlds may be indispensable.

We may in fact have finally found that bridge to the twenty-first century that Bill Clinton told us about. Its name is Obama.

How Did I Get Iraq Wrong?

March 21, 2008 | *SLATE*

I think I committed four cardinal sins.

HISTORICAL NARCISSISM

I was distracted by the internal American debate to the occlusion of the reality of Iraq. For most of my adult lifetime, I had heard those on the left decry American military power, constantly warn of quagmires, excuse what I regarded as inexcusable tyrannies, and fail to grasp that the nature of certain regimes makes their removal a moral objective. As a child of the Cold War and a proud Reaganite and Thatcherite, I regarded 1989 as almost eternal proof of the notion that the walls of tyranny could fall if we had the will to bring them down and the gumption to use military power when we could. I had also been marinated in neoconservative thought for much of the 1990s and seen the moral power of Western intervention in Bosnia and Kosovo. All this primed me for an ideological battle that was, in retrospect, largely irrelevant to the much more complex post–Cold War realities we were about to confront.

When I heard the usual complaints from the left about how we had no right to intervene, how Bush was the real terrorist, how war was always wrong, my trained ears heard the same cries that I had heard in the 1980s. So, I saw the opposition to the war as another example of a faulty Vietnam Syndrome, associated it entirely with the far left — or Boomer nostalgia — and was revolted by the antiwar marches I saw in Washington. I wasn't wrong about some of this. Some of those reflexes were at work (which is why I find Obama's far more pragmatic opposition so striking in retrospect). I became much too concerned with fighting that old internal ideological battle and failed to think freshly or realistically about what the consequences of intervention could be. I allowed myself to be distracted by an ideological battle when what was required was clear-eyed prudence.

NARROW MORALISM

I recall very clearly one night before the war began. I made myself write down the reasons for and against the war and realized that if there were question marks on both sides (the one point in favor I did not put a question mark over was the existence of stockpiles of WMD!), the deciding factor for me in the end was that I could never be ashamed of removing someone as evil as Saddam from power. I became enamored of my own morality and the righteousness of this single moral act. And he was a monster, as we discovered. But what I failed to grasp is that war is also a monster, and unless one weighs all the possibly evil consequences of an abstractly moral act, one hasn't really engaged in a truly serious moral argument. I saw war's unknowable consequences far too glibly.

UNCONSERVATISM

I heard and read about ancient Sunni and Shiite divisions, knew of the awful time the British had in running Iraq, but I had never properly absorbed the lesson. I bought the argument put forward by many neoconservatives that Iraq was one of the more secular and modern of Arab societies; that these divisions were not so deep; that all those pictures of men in suits and mustaches and women in Western clothing were the deeper truth about this rare, modern Arab society. I believed that it could, if we worked at it and threw enough money at it, be a model for the rest of the Arab Muslim world. I should add that I don't believe these ancient divides were necessarily as deep as they subsequently became in the unnecessary chaos that the Rumsfeld invasion unleashed. But I greatly underestimated them—and as someone who liked to think of myself as a conservative, I pathetically failed to appreciate how those divides never truly go away and certainly cannot be abolished by a Western magic wand. In that sense, I was not conservative enough. I let my hope—the hope that had been vindicated by the fall of the Soviet Union—get the better of my skepticism. There are times when that is a good thing. The Iraq War wasn't one of them.

MISREADING BUSH

Yes, the incompetence and arrogance were beyond anything I imagined. In 2000, my support for Bush was not deep. I thought he was an OK, unifying, moderate Republican who would be fine for a time of peace and prosperity. I was concerned—ha!—that Gore would spend too much. I was reassured by the experience and intelligence and pedigree of Cheney and Rumsfeld and Powell. Two of them had already fought and won a war in the Gulf. The bitter election battle hardened my loyalty. And once 9/11 happened, my support intensified as I hoped for the best. Bush's early speeches were magnificent. The Afghanistan invasion was defter than I expected. I got lulled. I wanted him to succeed—too much, in retrospect.

But my biggest misreading was not about competence. Wars are often marked by incompetence. It was a fatal misjudgment of Bush's sense of morality. I had no idea he was so complacent—even glib—about the evil that good intentions can enable. I truly did not believe that Bush would use 9/11 to tear up the Geneva Conventions. When I first heard of abuses at Gitmo, I dismissed them as enemy propaganda. I certainly never believed that a conservative would embrace torture as the central thrust of an anti-terror strategy and lie about it, and scapegoat underlings for it, and give us the indelible stain of Bagram and Camp Cropper and Abu Ghraib and all the other secret torture and interrogation sites that Bush and Cheney created and oversaw. I certainly never believed that a war I supported for the sake of freedom would actually use as its central weapon the deepest antithesis of freedom—the destruction of human autonomy and dignity and will that is torture. To distort this by shredding the English language, by engaging in newspeak that I had long associated with totalitarian regimes, was a further insult. And for me, it was yet another epiphany about what American conservatism had come to mean.

I know our enemy is much worse. I have never doubted that. I still have no qualms whatever in waging war to defeat it. But I never believed that America would do what America has done. Never. My misjudgment at the deepest moral level of what Bush and Cheney and Rumsfeld were capable of—a misjudgment that violated the moral core of the enterprise—was my worst mistake. What the war has done to what is left of Iraq—the lives lost, the families destroyed, the bodies tortured, the civilization trashed—was bad enough. But what was done to America—and the meaning of America—was unforgivable. And for that I will not and should not forgive myself.

Phobia at the Gates

May 14, 2008 | *THE WASHINGTON POST*

Twelve countries ban HIV-positive visitors, nonimmigrants and immigrants, from their territory: Armenia, Brunei, Iraq, Libya, Moldova, Oman, Qatar, the Russian Federation, Saudi Arabia, South Korea, Sudan, and . . . the United States. China recently acted to remove its ban on HIV-positive visitors because it feared embarrassment ahead of the Olympics. But America's ban remains.

It seems unthinkable that the country that has been the most generous in helping people with HIV should legally ban all non-Americans who are HIV-positive. But it's true: the leading center of public and private HIV research discriminates against those with HIV.

HIV is the only medical condition permanently designated in law—in the Immigration and Nationality Act—as grounds for inadmissibility to the United States. Even leprosy and tuberculosis are left to the discretion of the secretary of health and human services.

The ban can be traced to the panic that dominated discussion of the human immunodeficiency virus two decades ago. The ban was the brainchild of Senator Jesse Helms (who came to regret his initial hostility toward people with HIV and AIDS). President George H. W. Bush sought to drop the ban, but in 1993, after a scare about Haitian refugees, Congress wrote it into law.

I remember that year particularly because it was when I, a legal immigrant, became infected. With great lawyers, a rare O visa (granted to individuals in the arts and sciences), a government-granted HIV waiver, and thousands of dollars in legal fees, I have managed to stay in the United States. Nonetheless, because I am HIV-positive, I am not eligible to become a permanent resident.

Each year I have to leave the country and reapply for an HIV waiver to reenter. I have lived in the United States for almost a quarter century, have paid taxes, got married, and built a life here—but because of HIV, I am always vulnerable to being forced to leave for good. After a while, the stress of such insecurity gnaws away at your family and health.

I am among the most privileged non-Americans with HIV. Others live in fear of being exposed; many have to hide their medications when entering the country for fear of being discovered by Customs or Immigration. Couples have been split up and torn apart. International conferences on HIV and AIDS have long avoided meeting in the United States because of the ban, which violates UN standards for member states.

This law has lasted so long because no domestic constituency lobbies for its repeal. Immigrants or visitors with HIV are often too afraid to speak up. The ban itself is also largely unenforceable—it's impossible to take blood from all those coming to America, hold them until the results come through, and then deport those who test positive. Enforcement occurs primarily when immigrants volunteer their HIV status—as I have—or apply for permanent residence. The result is not any actual prevention of HIV coming into the United States but discrimination against otherwise legal immigrants who are HIV-positive.

Would treating HIV like any other medical condition cost the United States if such visitors or immigrants at some point became public dependents? It's possible—but all legal immigrants and their sponsors are required to prove that they can provide their own health insurance for at least ten years after being admitted. Making private health insurance a condition of visiting or immigrating with HIV prevents any serious government costs, and the tax dollars that would be contributed by many of the otherwise qualified immigrants would be a net gain for the government—by some estimates, in the tens of millions of dollars.

In the end, though, removing the ban is not about money. It's a statement that the United States does not discriminate against people with HIV and does not retain the phobias of the past. That's why repeal has been supported by a bipartisan group of senators, including Republicans Gordon Smith and Richard Lugar and Democrats John Kerry and Barack Obama, in an amendment to the reauthorization of the President's Emergency Plan for AIDS Relief. They know that immigration and public-health policy should not rest on stigma or fear. For the Bush administration, removing the Helms ban would be a final, fitting part of its admirable HIV and AIDS legacy.

It's also worth remembering that we are talking about legal immigrants and visitors, people who go through the process and seek to participate and contribute to this country. Making HIV the only medical condition that legally prevents someone from immigrating or even visiting is a signal to people with HIV that they have something to be ashamed of. That stigma is one of the greatest obstacles to tackling HIV across the world. The United States has done much to reduce this stigma; it makes no sense to perpetuate it in its own immigration policy.

People with HIV are no less worthy of being citizens of the United States than anyone else. All we ask is to be able to visit, live, and work in America and, for some of us, to realize our dream of becoming Americans—whether we are HIV-positive or not.

Why I Blog

November 2008 | *THE ATLANTIC*

The word "blog" is a conflation of two words: "web" and "log." It contains in its four letters a concise and accurate self-description: it is a log of thoughts and writing posted publicly on the World Wide Web. In the monosyllabic vernacular of the internet, "web log" soon became the word "blog."

This form of instant and global self-publishing, made possible by technology widely available only for the past decade or so, allows for no retroactive editing (apart from fixing minor typos or small glitches) and removes from the act of writing any considered or lengthy review. It is the spontaneous expression of instant thought—impermanent beyond even the ephemera of daily journalism. It is accountable in immediate and unavoidable ways to readers and other bloggers, and linked via hypertext to continuously multiplying references and sources. Unlike any single piece of print journalism, its borders are extremely porous and its truth inherently transitory. The consequences of this for the act of writing are still sinking in.

A ship's log owes its name to a small wooden board, often weighted with lead, that was for centuries attached to a line and thrown over the stern. The weight of the log would keep it in the same place in the water, like a provisional anchor, while the ship moved away. By measuring the length of line used up in a set period of time, mariners could calculate the speed of their journey (the rope itself was marked by equidistant "knots" for easy measurement). As a ship's voyage progressed, the course came to be marked down in a book that was called a log.

In journeys at sea that took place before radio or radar or satellites or sonar, these logs were an indispensable source for recording what actually happened. They helped navigators surmise where they were and how far they had traveled and how much longer they had to stay at sea. They provided accountability to a ship's owners and traders. They were designed to be as immune to faking as possible. Away from land, there was usually no reliable corroboration of events apart from the crew's own account in the middle of an expanse of blue and gray and green; and in long journeys, memories always blur and facts disperse. A log provided as accurate an account as could be gleaned in real time.

As you read a log, you have the curious sense of moving backward in time as you move forward in pages—the opposite of a book. As you piece together a narrative that was never intended as one, it seems—and is—more truthful. Logs, in this sense, were a form of human self-correction. They amended for hindsight, for the ways in which human beings order and tidy and construct the story of their lives as they look back on them. Logs require a letting go of narrative because they do not allow for a knowledge of the ending. So they have plot as well as dramatic irony—the reader will know the ending before the writer did.

Anyone who has blogged his thoughts for an extended time will recognize this world. We bloggers have scant opportunity to collect our thoughts, to wait until events have settled and a clear pattern emerges. We blog now—as news reaches us, as facts emerge. This is partly true for all journalism, which is, as its etymology suggests, daily writing, always subject to subsequent revision. And a good columnist will adjust position and judgment and even political loyalty over time, depending on events. But a blog is not so much daily writing as hourly writing. And with that level of timeliness, the provisionality of every word is even more pressing—and the risk of error or the thrill of prescience that much greater.

No columnist or reporter or novelist will have his minute shifts or constant small contradictions exposed as mercilessly as a blogger's are. A columnist can ignore or duck a subject less noticeably than a blogger committing thoughts to pixels several times a day. A reporter can wait—must wait—until every source has confirmed. A novelist can spend months or years before committing words to the world. For bloggers, the deadline is always now. Blogging is therefore to writing what extreme sports are to athletics: more free-form, more accident-prone, less formal, more alive. It is, in many ways, writing out loud.

You end up writing about yourself, since you are a relatively fixed point in this constant interaction with the ideas and facts of the exterior world. And in this sense, the historic form closest to blogs is the diary. But with this difference: a diary is almost always a private matter. Its raw honesty, its dedication to marking life as it happens and remembering life as it was, makes it a terrestrial log. A few diaries are meant to be read by others, of course, just as correspondence could be—but usually posthumously, or as a way to compile facts for a more considered autobiographical rendering. But a blog, unlike a diary, is instantly public. It transforms this most personal and retrospective of forms into a painfully public and immediate one. It combines the confessional genre with the log form and exposes the author in a manner no author has ever been exposed before.

I remember first grappling with what to put on my blog. It was the spring of 2000 and, like many a freelance writer at the time, I had some vague notion that I needed to have a presence "online." I had no clear idea of what to do, but a friend who ran a web-design company offered to create a site for me, and, since I was technologically clueless, he also agreed to post various essays and columns as I wrote them. Before too long, this became a chore for him, and he called me one day to say he'd found an online platform that was so simple I could henceforth post all my writing myself. The platform was called Blogger.

As I used it to post columns or links to books or old essays, it occurred to me that I could also post new writing—writing that could even be exclusive to the blog. But what? Like any new form, blogging did not start from nothing. It evolved from various journalistic traditions. In my case, I drew on my mainstream-media experience to navigate the virgin sea. I had a few early inspirations: the old "Notebook" section of *The New Republic*, a magazine that, under the editorial guidance of Michael Kinsley, had introduced a more English style of crisp, short commentary into what had been a more high-minded genre of American opinion writing. *The New Republic* had also pioneered a Diarist feature on the last page, which was designed to be a more personal, essayistic, first-person form of journalism. Mixing the two genres, I did what I had been trained to do—and improvised.

I'd previously written online as well, contributing to a LIST·SERV for gay writers and helping Kinsley initiate a more discursive form of online writing for *Slate*, the first magazine published exclusively on the web. As soon as I began writing this way, I realized that the online form rewarded a colloquial, unfinished tone. In one of my early Kinsley-guided experiments, he urged me not to think too hard before writing. So I wrote as I'd write an e-mail—with only a mite more circumspection. This is hazardous, of course, as anyone who has ever clicked Send in a fit of anger or hurt will testify. But blogging requires an embrace of such hazards, a willingness to fall off the trapeze rather than fail to make the leap.

From the first few days of using the form, I was hooked. The simple experience of being able to directly broadcast my own words to readers was an exhilarating literary liberation. Unlike the current generation of writers, who have only ever blogged, I knew firsthand what the alternative meant. I'd edited a weekly print magazine, *The New Republic*, for five years, and written countless columns and essays for a variety of traditional outlets. And in all this, I'd often chafed, as most writers do, at the endless delays, revisions, office politics, editorial fights, and last-minute cuts for space that dead-tree publishing entails. Blogging—even to an audience of a few hundred in the early days—was intoxicatingly free in comparison. Like taking a narcotic.

It was obvious from the start that it was revolutionary. Every writer since the printing press has longed for a means to publish himself and reach— instantly—any reader on Earth. Every professional writer has paid some dues waiting for an editor's nod, or enduring a publisher's incompetence, or being ground to literary dust by a legion of fact-checkers and copy editors. If you added up the time a writer once had to spend finding an outlet, impressing editors, sucking up to proprietors, and proofreading edits, you'd find another lifetime buried in the interstices. But with one click of the Publish Now button, all these troubles evaporated.

Alas, as I soon discovered, this sudden freedom from above was immediately replaced by insurrection from below. Within minutes of my posting something, even in the earliest days, readers responded. E-mail seemed to unleash their inner beast. They were more brutal than any editor, more persnickety than any copy editor, and more emotionally unstable than any colleague.

Again, it's hard to overrate how different this is. Writers can be sensitive, vain souls, requiring gentle nurturing from editors, and oddly susceptible to the blows delivered by reviewers. They survive, for the most part, but the thinness of their skins is legendary. Moreover, before the blogosphere, reporters and columnists were largely shielded from this kind of direct hazing. Yes, letters to the editor would arrive in due course and subscriptions would be canceled. But reporters and columnists tended to operate in a relative sanctuary, answerable mainly to their editors, not readers. For a long time, columns were essentially monologues published to applause, muffled murmurs, silence, or a distant heckle. I'd gotten blowback from pieces before—but in an amorphous, time-delayed, distant way. Now the feedback was instant, personal, and brutal.

And so blogging found its own answer to the defensive counterblast from the journalistic Establishment. To the charges of inaccuracy and unprofessionalism, bloggers could point to the fierce, immediate scrutiny of their readers. Unlike newspapers, which would eventually publish corrections in a box of printed spinach far from the original error, bloggers had to walk the walk of self-correction in the same space and in the same format as the original screw-up. The form was more accountable, not less, because there is nothing more conducive to professionalism than being publicly humiliated for sloppiness. Of course, a blogger could ignore an error or simply refuse to acknowledge mistakes. But if he persisted, he would be razzed by competitors and assailed by commenters and abandoned by readers. In an era when the traditional media found itself beset by scandals as disparate as Stephen Glass, Jayson Blair, and Dan Rather, bloggers survived the first assault on their worth. In time, in fact, the high standards expected of well-trafficked bloggers spilled over into greater accountability, transparency, and punctiliousness among the media powers that were. Even *New York Times* columnists were forced to admit when they had been wrong.

The blog remained a *superficial* medium, of course. By "superficial," I mean simply that blogging rewards brevity and immediacy. No one wants to read a nine-thousand-word treatise online. On the web, one-sentence links are as legitimate as thousand-word diatribes—in fact, they are often valued more. And, as Matt Drudge told me when I sought advice from the master in 2001, the key to understanding a blog is to realize that it's a broadcast, not a publication. If it stops moving, it dies. If it stops paddling, it sinks.

But the superficiality masked considerable depth—greater depth, from one perspective, than the traditional media could offer. The reason was a single technological innovation: the hyperlink. An old-school columnist can write eight hundred brilliant words analyzing or commenting on, say, a new think-tank report or scientific survey. But in reading it on paper, you have to take the columnist's presentation of the material on faith, or be convinced by a brief quotation (which can always be misleading out of context). Online, a hyperlink to the original source transforms the experience. Yes, a few sentences of bloggy spin may not be as satisfying as a full column, but the ability to read the primary material instantly—in as careful or shallow a fashion as you choose—can add much greater context than anything on paper. Even a blogger's chosen pull quote, unlike a columnist's, can be effortlessly checked against the original. Now this innovation, pre-dating blogs but popularized by them, is increasingly central to mainstream journalism.

A blog, therefore, bobs on the surface of the ocean but has its anchorage in waters deeper than those print media is technologically able to exploit. It disempowers the writer to that extent, of course. The blogger can get away with less and afford fewer pretensions of authority. He is—more than any writer of the past—a node among other nodes, connected but unfinished without the links and the comments and the track-backs that make the blogosphere, at its best, a conversation, rather than a production.

A writer fully aware of and at ease with the provisionality of his own work is nothing new. For centuries, writers have experimented with forms that suggest the imperfection of human thought, the inconstancy of human affairs, and the humbling, chastening passage of time. If you compare the meandering, questioning, unresolved dialogues of Plato with the definitive, logical treatises of Aristotle, you see the difference between a skeptic's spirit translated into writing and a spirit that seeks to bring some finality to the argument. Perhaps the greatest single piece of Christian apologetics, Pascal's *Pensées*, is a series of meandering, short, and incomplete stabs at arguments, observations, insights. Their lack of finish is what makes them so compelling—arguably more compelling than a polished treatise by Aquinas.

Or take the brilliant polemics of Karl Kraus, the publisher of and main writer for *Die Fackel*, who delighted in constantly twitting authority with slashing aphorisms and rapid-fire bursts of invective. Kraus had something rare in his day: the financial wherewithal to self-publish. It gave him a fearlessness that is now available to anyone who can afford a computer and an internet connection.

But perhaps the quintessential blogger *avant la lettre* was Montaigne. His essays were published in three major editions, each one longer and more complex than the previous. A passionate skeptic, Montaigne amended, added to, and amplified the essays for each edition, making them three-dimensional through time. In the best modern translations, each essay is annotated, sentence by sentence, paragraph by paragraph, by small letters (A, B, and C) for each major edition, helping the reader see how each rewrite added to or subverted, emphasized or ironized, the version before. Montaigne was living his skepticism, daring to show how a writer evolves, changes his mind, learns new things, shifts perspectives, grows older—and that this, far from being something that needs to be hidden behind a veneer of unchanging authority, can become a virtue, a new way of looking at the pretensions of authorship and text and truth. Montaigne, for good measure, also peppered his essays with myriads of what bloggers would call external links. His own thoughts are strewn with and complicated by the aphorisms and anecdotes of others. Scholars of the sources note that many of these "money quotes" were deliberately taken out of context, adding layers of irony to writing that was already saturated in empirical doubt.

To blog is therefore to let go of your writing in a way, to hold it at arm's length, open it to scrutiny, allow it to float in the ether for a while, and to let others, as Montaigne did, pivot you toward relative truth. A blogger will notice this almost immediately upon starting. Some e-mailers, unsurprisingly, know more about a subject than the blogger does. They will send links, stories, and facts, challenging the blogger's view of the world, sometimes outright refuting it, but more frequently adding context and nuance and complexity to an idea. The role of a blogger is not to defend against this but to embrace it. He is similar in this way to the host of a dinner party. He can provoke discussion or take a position, even passionately, but he also must create an atmosphere in which others want to participate.

That atmosphere will inevitably be formed by the blogger's personality. The blogosphere may, in fact, be the least veiled of any forum in which a writer dares to express himself. Even the most careful and self-aware blogger will reveal more about himself than he wants to in a few unguarded sentences and publish them before he has the sense to hit Delete. The wise panic that can paralyze a writer—the fear that he will be exposed, undone, humiliated—is not available to a blogger. You can't have blogger's block. You have to express yourself now, while your emotions roil, while your temper flares, while your humor lasts. You can try to hide yourself from real scrutiny, and the exposure it demands, but it's hard. And that's what makes blogging as a form stand out: it is rich in personality. The faux intimacy of the web experience, the closeness of the e-mail and the instant message, seeps through. You feel as if you know bloggers as they go through their lives, experience the same things you are experiencing, and share the moment. When readers of my blog bump into me in person, they invariably address me as Andrew. Print readers don't do that. It's Mr. Sullivan to them.

On my blog, my readers and I experienced 9/11 together, in real time. I can look back and see not just how I responded to the event, but how I responded to it at 3:47 that afternoon. And at 9:46 that night. There is a vividness to this immediacy that cannot be rivaled by print. The same goes for the 2000 recount, the Iraq War, the revelations of Abu Ghraib, the death of John Paul II, or any of the other history-making events of the past decade. There is simply no way to write about them in real time without revealing a huge amount about yourself. And the intimate bond this creates with readers is unlike the bond that *The Times*, say, develops with its readers through the same events. Alone in front of a computer, at any moment, are two people: a blogger and a reader. The proximity is palpable, the moment human — whatever authority a blogger has is derived not from the institution he works for but from the humanness he conveys. This is writing with emotion not just under but always breaking through the surface. It renders a writer and a reader not just connected but linked in a visceral, personal way. The only term that really describes this is "friendship." And it is a relatively new thing to write for thousands and thousands of friends.

These friends, moreover, are an integral part of the blog itself — sources of solace, company, provocation, hurt, and correction. If I were to do an inventory of the material that appears on my blog, I'd estimate that a good third of it is reader generated, and a good third of my time is spent absorbing readers' views, comments, and tips. Readers tell me of breaking stories, new perspectives, and counterarguments to prevailing assumptions. And this is what blogging, in turn, does to reporting. The traditional method involves a journalist searching for key sources, nurturing them, and sequestering them from his rivals. A blogger splashes gamely into a subject and dares the sources to come to him.

Some of this material — e-mails from soldiers on the front lines, from scientists explaining new research, from dissident Washington writers too scared to say what they think in their own partisan redoubts — might never have seen the light of day before the blogosphere. And some of it, of course, is dubious stuff. Bloggers can be spun and misled as easily as traditional writers—and the rigorous source assessment that good reporters do can't be done by e-mail. But you'd be surprised by what comes unsolicited into the in-box, and how helpful it often is.

Not all of it is mere information. Much of it is also opinion and scholarship, a knowledge base that exceeds the research department of any newspaper. A good blog is your own private Wikipedia. Indeed, the most pleasant surprise of blogging has been the number of people working in law or government or academia or rearing kids at home who have real literary talent and real knowledge, and who had no outlet—until now. There is a distinction here, of course, between the edited use of e-mailed sources by a careful blogger and the often-mercurial cacophony on an unmediated comments section. But the truth is out there—and the miracle of e-mail allows it to come to you.

Fellow bloggers are always expanding this knowledge base. Eight years ago, the blogosphere felt like a handful of individual cranks fighting with one another. Today, it feels like a universe of cranks, with vast, pulsating reader-ships, fighting with one another. To the neophyte reader, or blogger, it can seem overwhelming. But there is a connection between the intimacy of the early years and the industry it has become today. And the connection is human individuality.

The pioneers of online journalism—*Slate* and *Salon*—are still very popular, and successful. But the more memorable stars of the internet—even within those two sites—are all personally branded. *Daily Kos*, for example, is written by hundreds of bloggers, and amended by thousands of commenters. But it is named after Markos Moulitsas, who started it, and his own prose still provides a backbone to the front-page blog. The biggest news-aggregator site in the world, the Drudge Report, is named after its founder, Matt Drudge, who somehow conveys a unified sensibility through his selection of links, images, and stories. The vast, expanding universe of *The Huffington Post* still finds some semblance of coherence in the Cambridge-Greek twang of Arianna; the entire world of online celebrity gossip circles the drain of Perez Hilton; and the investigative journalism, reviewing, and commentary of *Talking Points Memo* is still tied together by the tone of Josh Marshall. Even *Slate* is unimaginable without Mickey Kaus's voice.

What endures is a human brand. Readers have encountered this phenom-enon before—*I. F. Stone's Weekly* comes to mind—but not to this extent. It stems, I think, from the conversational style that blogging rewards. What you want in a conversationalist is as much character as authority. And if you think of blogging as more like talk radio or cable news than opinion magazines or daily newspapers, then this personalized emphasis is less surprising. People have a voice for radio and a face for television. For blogging, they have a sensibility.

But writing in this new form is a collective enterprise as much as it is an individual one—and the connections between bloggers are as important as the content on the blogs. The links not only drive conversation; they drive readers. The more you link, the more others will link to you, and the more traffic and readers you will get. The zero-sum game of old media—in which *Time* benefits from *Newsweek*'s decline and vice versa—becomes win-win. It's great for *Time* to be linked to by *Newsweek* and the other way around. One of the most prized statistics in the blogosphere is therefore not the total number of readers or page views, but the "authority" you get by being linked to by other blogs. It's an indication of how central you are to the online conversation of humankind.

The reason this open-source market of thinking and writing has such poten-tial is that the always adjusting and evolving collective mind can rapidly filter out bad arguments and bad ideas. The flip side, of course, is that bloggers are also human beings. Reason is not the only fuel in the tank. In a world where no distinction is made between good traffic and bad traffic, and where emotion often rules, some will always raise their voice to dominate the conversation; others will pander shamelessly to their readers' prejudices; others will start online brawls for the fun of it. Sensationalism, dirt, and the ease of formulaic talking points always beckon. You can disappear into the partisan blogosphere and never stumble onto a site you disagree with.

But linkage mitigates this. A Democratic blog will, for example, be forced to link to Republican ones, if only to attack and mock. And it's in the interests of both camps to generate shared traffic. This encourages polarized slugfests. But online, at least you see both sides. Reading *The Nation* or *National Review* before the internet existed allowed for more cocooning than the wide-open online sluice gates do now. If there's more incivility, there's also more fluidity. Rudeness, in any case, isn't the worst thing that can happen to a blogger. Being ignored is. Perhaps the nastiest thing one can do to a fellow blogger is rip him apart and fail to provide a link.

A successful blog therefore has to balance itself between a writer's own take on the world and others. Some bloggers collect, or "aggregate," other bloggers' posts with dozens of quick links and minimalist opinion top spin: Glenn Reynolds at *Instapundit* does this for the right-of-center; Duncan Black at *Eschaton* does it for the left. Others are more eclectic, or aggregate links in a particular niche, or cater to a settled and knowledgeable reader base. A "blogroll" is an indicator of whom you respect enough to keep in your galaxy. For many years, I kept my reading and linking habits to a relatively small coterie of fellow political bloggers. In today's blogosphere, to do this is to embrace marginality. I've since added links to religious blogs and literary ones and scientific ones and just plain weird ones. As the blogosphere has expanded beyond anyone's capacity to absorb it, I've needed an assistant and interns to scour the web for links and stories and photographs to respond to and think about. It's a difficult balance, between your own interests and obsessions and the knowledge, insight, and wit of others—but an immensely rich one. There are times, in fact, when a blogger feels less like a writer than an online disc jockey, mixing samples of tunes and generating new melodies through mash-ups while also making his own music. He is both artist and producer—and the beat always goes on.

If all this sounds postmodern, that's because it is. And blogging suffers from the same flaws as postmodernism: a failure to provide stable truth or a permanent perspective. A traditional writer is valued by readers precisely because they trust him to have thought long and hard about a subject, given it time to evolve in his head, and composed a piece of writing that is worth their time to read at length and to ponder. Bloggers don't do this and cannot do this—and that limits them far more than it does traditional long-form writing.

A blogger will air a variety of thoughts or facts on any subject in no particular order other than that dictated by the passing of time. A writer will instead use time, synthesizing these thoughts, ordering them, weighing which points count more than others, seeing how his views evolved in the writing process itself, and responding to an editor's perusal of a draft or two. The result is almost always more measured, more satisfying, and more enduring than a blizzard of posts. The triumphalist notion that blogging should somehow replace traditional writing is as foolish as it is pernicious. In some ways, blogging's gifts to our discourse make the skills of a good traditional writer much more valuable, not less. The torrent of blogospheric insights, ideas, and arguments places a greater premium on the person who can finally make sense of it all, turning it into something more solid, and lasting, and rewarding.

The points of this essay, for example, have appeared in shards and fragments on my blog for years. But being forced to order them in my head and think about them for a longer stretch has helped me understand them better, and perhaps express them more clearly. Each week, after a few hundred posts, I also write an actual newspaper column. It invariably turns out to be more considered, balanced, and evenhanded than the blog. But the blog will always inform and enrich the column, and often serve as a kind of free-form, free-associative research. And an essay like this will spawn discussion best handled on a blog. The conversation, in other words, is the point, and the different idioms used by the conversationalists all contribute something of value to it. And so, if the defenders of the old media once viscerally regarded blogging as some kind of threat, they are starting to see it more as a portal, and a spur.

There is, after all, something simply irreplaceable about reading a piece of writing at length on paper, in a chair, or on a couch or in bed. To use an obvious analogy, jazz entered our civilization much later than composed, formal music. But it hasn't replaced it, and no jazz musician would ever claim that it could. Jazz merely demands a different way of playing and listening, just as blogging requires a different mode of writing and reading. Jazz and blogging are intimate, improvisational, and individual—but also inherently collective. And the audience talks over both.

The reason they talk while listening, and comment or link while reading, is that they understand that this is a kind of music that needs to be engaged rather than merely absorbed. To listen to jazz as one would listen to an aria is to miss the point. Reading at a monitor, at a desk, or on an iPhone provokes a querulous, impatient, distracted attitude, a demand for instant, usable information, that is simply not conducive to opening a novel or a favorite magazine on the couch. Reading on paper evokes a more relaxed and meditative response. The message dictates the medium. And each medium has its place—as long as one is not mistaken for the other.

In fact, for all the intense gloom surrounding the newspaper and magazine business, this is actually a golden era for journalism. The blogosphere has added a whole new idiom to the act of writing and has introduced an entirely new generation to nonfiction. It has enabled writers to write out loud in ways never seen or understood before. And yet it has exposed a hunger and need for traditional writing that, in the age of television's dominance, had seemed on the wane.

Words, of all sorts, have never seemed so now.

Republican Taliban Declare Jihad on Obama

February 15, 2009 | THE SUNDAY TIMES

G oodbye to all that? Washington, it appears, has other ideas. Barack Obama campaigned on a platform of pragmatic liberalism and an end to frothy ideological warfare in Washington. From the beginning of the campaign he went out of his way not to engage in Republican bashing or even Clinton bashing. He was intent on bringing reason and open-mindedness to America's often-fraught ideological debates. He was incandescently clear that he rejected the toxic partisan atmosphere that had dominated the Bill Clinton and George W. Bush years.

Since November he has largely walked the walk. Yes, there is a down payment on future government spending in the stimulus bill—on health care, the environment, and education. But given the urgency of the economic downturn and the few tools left to counter it, a little overshooting is not the worst option in the next eighteen months. And he did his best to accommodate Republican concerns—adding deeper and wider tax cuts than his own party was comfortable with.

He went to Capitol Hill to talk directly with members of the other party in the more ideological House of Representatives—spending more time with them than even Bush did. He asked three Republicans to be a part of his cabinet, including Robert Gates, Bush's defense secretary. He went to dinner with key Republican columnists before reaching out to those who had supported him in the election.

And this open hand was met with a punch in the face.

From the outset, the Republicans in Washington pored over the bill to find trivial issues to make hay with. They found some small funding for HIV and sexually transmitted diseases prevention; they jumped up and down about renovating the National Mall; they went nuts over a proposal — wait for it — to make some government buildings more energy efficient; they acted as if green research and federal funds for new school buildings were the equivalent of funding terrorism. And this after eight years in which they managed to turn a surplus into a trillion-dollar deficit and added a cool $32 trillion to the debt the next generation will have to pay for. Every now and again their chutzpah and narcissism take one's breath away. But it's all they seem to know.

John McCain gives you the flavor.

Fresh from a dinner in his honor hosted by Obama, he abruptly dismissed the stimulus package as the "same old" spending of the distant Democratic past. His closest Republican ally, Senator Lindsey Graham, declared: "This bill stinks." Pete Sessions, chairman of the National Republican Congressional Committee, explained that the Republican strategy was going to be modeled on jihadist insurgency. "I'm not joking," he added. "Insurgency we understand perhaps a little bit more because of the Taliban." Rush Limbaugh, the dominant figure among the Republican base, fresh from broadcasting a ditty called "Barack, the Magic Negro," declared in the first week of the new Congress that he hoped the new president would fail. The stimulus bill got no Republican votes in the House, and only three Republicans — all from the Obama-voting states of Pennsylvania and Maine — backed him in the Senate. McCain went to the floor of the Senate to growl that three votes did not make the bill bipartisan.

Bitter? At the end of last week we saw just how bitter. One of the Republicans who had agreed to serve in Obama's cabinet, Senator Judd Gregg of New Hampshire, abruptly pulled out, after what he described as "fair warning" to the president.

Gregg had been under intense pressure from the Republican base, especially in his home state, for cooperating with the devil.

He claimed the reason for his sudden withdrawal was that he couldn't stomach the stimulus. Yet only a week earlier he had said:

We need a robust [stimulus package].

I think the one that's pending is in the range we need. I do believe it's a good idea to do it at two levels, which this bill basically does, which is immediate stimulus and long-term initiatives which actually improve our competitiveness and our productivity.

He then tried to argue that his authority over the 2010 census as commerce secretary had been compromised.

But that turned out not to be true either: it was just that a census that could well add millions of Hispanic voters to the rolls had the Republicans eager to prevent a Republican imprimatur on it.

Gregg was a victim of fast-shifting Republican politics. Reeling from the election, watching a new president co-opt some of their numbers and get alarmingly high approval ratings from the public, members of the opposition party made a decision to become an insurgency.

From the disciplined House vote against any stimulus bill to the Gregg withdrawal, they are busy trying to revive the clear ideological warfare of the 1990s. As they did with Clinton sixteen years ago, they are going to war. The context—the worst global downturn in decades—is irrelevant. If you have safe Republican seats in a party dominated intellectually by rigid ideologues, then your path of least resistance is total political warfare. It is certainly easier than forging difficult and messy legislative compromises that might even redound to the president's advantage if the economy recovers.

It's not clear, however, that total war on the president is going to be a better way forward. Before the latest twist, a Gallup poll found that Obama's handling of the stimulus package had almost twice the public support as the Republicans'. In a period of acute economic anxiety, Americans outside the Republican base may not be so thrilled to find a replay of the 1990s.

Obama won in part because he seemed not part of that drama.

The Democrats and the liberal base have responded to all this with a mixture of cynicism and their own partisanship. They rolled their eyes at Obama's outreach to Republicans; they hated the inclusion of the other party in the cabinet and had to swallow hard not to complain about the post-partisan rhetoric. Their cynicism is well earned. But my bet is that Obama also understands that this is, in the end, the sweet spot for him. He has successfully branded himself by a series of conciliatory gestures as the man eager to reach out. If this is spurned, he can repeat the gesture until the public finds his opponents seriously off-key.

Ask yourself this question: Who, in the end, won the partisan warfare of the 1990s—Clinton or the Republicans? In 1993, the Republicans thought they had dispatched Clinton for good; he won reelection hands down three years later and left office, even after Monica Lewinsky, with high ratings. Obama may not believe that history repeats itself. But he's surely aware that it often rhymes.

Mad, Maddening America, the Wisest of All

February 22, 2009 | *THE SUNDAY TIMES*

A merica can drive you up the wall. To Europeans and world-weary Brits, it can sometimes seem almost barmy in its backwardness. It is a country where one state, Arkansas, has just refused to repeal a statute barring atheists from holding public office but managed in the same session to pass a law allowing guns in churches. It incarcerates a higher percentage of its population than even Russia and aborts more babies per capita than secular Europe.

Darwin remains a controversial figure, but Sarah Palin was a serious candidate to be vice president. Last week the California legislature took five days to prevent the entire state from going bankrupt; and more than three months after the election, and five months since the financial system went kablooey, the Treasury secretary had not mustered the staff sufficient to craft the details of a rescue package for the banks.

There are times in the quarter of a century since I arrived in America that I have been tempted to throw my hands up in frustration. To give a brutal, personal example, I've lived in the United States since 1984. I've made a home and a life here. But I still cannot even begin the process of becoming a citizen because the United States makes it illegal for anyone with HIV to get a green card. The ban was passed in the 1980s in a moment of total, ignorant panic. It took two decades to repeal it last summer, and the government bureaucracy still hasn't changed the regulation. Another small insanity: the residents of the city I live in, Washington, D.C., America's capital, do not have any representation in Congress. Since the founding of the country, the district has never been formally a part of a state, and so cannot, according to the Constitution, have representatives in the House or the Senate. Imagine the residents of Westminster not having any MPs in the Commons. The residents of Baghdad, in fact, have more democracy than the residents of Washington, but no one in government cares enough about this to actually amend the Constitution to make that change.

And yet I stay and love it and defend it, even as it can push me to bang my head against the wall at times and may eventually throw me out altogether. Why? Because I've learned over the years that the constitutional system that seems designed to prevent change has more wisdom in it than some more centralized parliamentary systems, and because the very chaotic, decentralized and often-irrational mess of American state and federal politics also allows for real innovation and debate in ways that simply do not occur as vibrantly elsewhere. The frustration and innovation are part of the same system. You cannot remove one without also stymieing the other.

Take gay rights, a cause dear to my heart. Many Europeans feel quite smug about their enlightenment, and the transformation of the debate in Britain in the past decade has been as profound as it has been welcome. But few doubt that America pioneered the gay-rights movement, as the movie *Milk*, up for eight Oscars tonight, underlines. New York, Los Angeles, and San Francisco in the 1970s forged a liberation movement that changed gay lives throughout the world.

Yet even now, though I have a marriage license, something no gay couple in Britain has, my five-year relationship is not recognized by the federal government. In Massachusetts, a state where gay marriage is legal and where I married my partner Aaron in August 2007, the license is no different in any respect from that given to heterosexual couples. Civil partnership may provide rights at a national level, but it is still indelibly a separate and lesser institution than marriage itself, and offers a lesser measure of the social, psychological, and cultural acceptance that civil marriage provides.

In California, gays just suffered a horrible setback as a majority narrowly voted to take away marriage rights. But at least they had a chance to get them in the first place. And the debate was a real and raw one—which made victory more meaningful and defeat more profound.

In America, the bigotry you face is real, unvarnished, and in the open. In Britain, it can come masked or euphemized or deflected into humor. It hurts much more to punch a brick wall than to punch a deep velvet cushion. But if you punch hard enough, the wall will one day crumble, while the pillow will constantly absorb the blows.

There is plenty of religious bigotry and fundamentalist rigidity and crude sectarianism in America. But there is also a clear and invigorating religious energy that takes the question of God seriously and does not recoil from it in apathy or world-weariness. Give me a fundamentalist to argue with any day over someone who has lost the will to care that much at all.

On race, of course, this is especially true. No civilized country sustained slavery as recently as America or defended segregation as tenaciously as the American South until just a generation ago. In my lifetime, mixed-race couples were legally barred from marrying in many states. But equally in my lifetime, a miscegenated man who grew up in Hawaii won a majority of the votes in the old slave state of Virginia to become the first minority president of any advanced Western nation.

That is the paradox of America, and after a while you find it hard to appreciate anything more coherent. What keeps America behind is also what keeps pushing it relentlessly, fitfully forward.

That Canadian genius Leonard Cohen put it best, perhaps. In his anthem "Democracy" he called the United States "the cradle of the best and of the worst."

You live with the worst because you yearn for the best, because the worst in its turn seems somehow to evoke the best. From the Civil War came Abraham Lincoln, from the Great Depression came Franklin D. Roosevelt, from segregation came Martin Luther King, and from George Bush came Barack Obama. America may indeed drive us up the wall, but it also retains a wondrous capacity to evoke the mountaintop and what lies beyond.

Obama's Race Dream
Is Swiftly Shackled

July 26, 2009 | *THE SUNDAY TIMES*

What do you call a black man with a PhD? The answer begins with an *n*. Yes, it's an old and bitter joke about the resilience of racial bias in America, but it got a new twist last week. The black man with a PhD was Henry Louis Gates Jr., one of the most distinguished scholars of African American history and culture at Harvard. His unexpected tormentor was a local policeman called James Crowley, a white, well-trained officer called to investigate a possible break-in.

The facts we know for sure are as follows. Ten days ago Gates got home from China in the afternoon to find his front door jammed. He forced it open with the help of his cabdriver, another black man. A white woman in the area called the police to report a possible burglary. Crowley showed up and saw a black man in the hallway of the house through the glass door. He asked Gates to step out onto the porch and talk to him. Gates refused.

The police report—written by Crowley—says he told Gates he was investigating a break-in in progress and Gates responded furiously: "Why? Because I'm a black man in America?" Gates tried to place a call to the local police chief, while telling Crowley he had no idea who he was "messing" with. The interaction quickly degenerated. After Gates had shown his Harvard identification, Crowley said he would leave. Gates then followed him to his front door, allegedly yelling that Crowley was racist. On his own porch, at his own

305

property, Gates was arrested for "disorderly conduct," handcuffed, and booked in at a local station.

The incident clearly struck a nerve. Boston has a fraught racial history. Gates, of course, is no underclass black man but among the country's elite, friends with the president, chums with Oprah Winfrey, a man given a small fortune by Harvard to build one of the best departments of African American studies in the world.

The affair got another lease of tabloid life when President Barack Obama was asked for his reaction to the incident and said that while Gates was a friend and he did not know the full facts, the police acted "stupidly" by arresting someone when there was proof he was in his own home.

So was this an example of excessive racial grievance on the part of Gates or excessive racial insensitivity on the part of Crowley—or a little bit of both? Such moments are fully understood only by the individuals involved—and even then the truth is murky in such emotional circumstances. But it is indeed unusual to arrest someone for "disorderly conduct" when he is on his own property.

Massachusetts law defines the perpetrators of "disorderly conduct" thus: "common night walkers, common street walkers, both male and female, common railers and brawlers, persons who with offensive and disorderly acts or language accost or annoy persons of the opposite sex, lewd, wanton and lascivious persons in speech or behavior, idle and disorderly persons, disturbers of the peace, keepers of noisy and disorderly houses and persons guilty of indecent exposure." Apparently, Gates's loud accusations of racism on a street in Cambridge at one o'clock in the afternoon in front of at most seven passersby and neighbors was a qualification for the charge. It's no big surprise that it was swiftly dropped.

Crowley gave an interview on Thursday after Obama's remarks, refusing to apologize. When asked what he thought of the president's comments, he smiled, paused, and said: "I didn't vote for him." The way he said it, the contempt in his voice and pride in his actions, helped to illuminate for me why Gates might have perceived racism. But the second police report—from an officer called Carlos Figueroa—testified that Gates initially refused to provide Crowley with any identification, yelling, "No, I will not!" and "This is what happens to black men in America!" and "You don't know who you're messing with."

Gates is not a merchant of racial grievance. He is a scholar who has won wealth and fame and respect for his work and who tends to eschew the kind of bald racial accusations he made that day. Maybe he was exhausted after a long trip and irritated by being unable to get into his home; to be confronted by an officer of the law asking if he was a burglar may well have been the last straw. He lost his cool. A black man should never lose his cool with a white policeman in America. Obama explained in his autobiography the unwritten code for black men in such situations: no sudden moves.

Would this have happened to a white man? That requires some unpacking. A white man seen breaking through the front door into a house in an affluent section of Cambridge, Massachusetts, might not have prompted a police call. Any suspect break-in, though, could justify a call to the local police station.

More important, a white man seeing a policeman call him onto his porch for identification would probably not have exploded the way Gates allegedly did. Nor, one might add, would a poor black man arrested on the streets of the largely African American neighborhood of Roxbury in Boston raise such a ruckus about "racism." Gates's response was a classic example of how successful black men in America feel when treated by the police in a manner used in the ghetto. That was also perhaps the reason for Obama's solidarity. What do you call a black man with a PhD again? Equally, I'd wager that if the policeman had seen an older white man wielding a cane through the glass door of a posh house, he would not have demanded that the man come out onto his porch and identify himself. He would have knocked, explained the reason for his visit, and instantly accepted a white man's explanation. Is this racism? If it has never happened to you, no. If it has, yes.

On the web, the comments sections on various blogs and stories were the most honest. Here is one view: "Butt the hell out Obama. You don't know the facts of the case, you weren't there, you're friends with the douchebag, you're black. Taking Obama's word is the same as judging a criminal by a jury of his fellow gangster peers."

Here is another: "Professor Gates might not have been arrested if he'd been more submissive—let the cop win the masculinity contest. Every brotha has played that game as well: you don't look the popo in the eye, you do say 'sir' a lot and maybe you won't get locked up. Then you go home and stew in the stuff that gives African American men low life expectancy." Yes, America has a black president. But some things haven't changed that much, have they?

Leaving the Right

December 1, 2009 | *THE DISH*

———

I t's an odd formulation in some ways as "the right" is not really a single entity. But there has to come a point at which a movement or party so abandons core principles or degenerates into such a rhetorical septic system that you have to take a stand. It seems to me that now is a critical time for more people whose principles lie broadly on the center-right to do so—against the conservative degeneracy in front of us. Those who have taken such a stand—to one degree or other—demand respect. And this blog, while maintaining its resistance to cliquishness, has been glad to link to writers as varied as Bruce Bartlett or David Frum or David Brooks or Steve Chapman or Kathleen Parker or Conor Friedersdorf or Jim Manzi or Jeffrey Hart or Daniel Larison, who have broken ranks in some way or other.

I can't claim the same courage as these folks because I've always been fickle in partisan terms. To have supported Reagan and Bush and Clinton and Dole and Bush and Kerry and Obama suggests I never had a party to quit. I think that may be because I wasn't born here. I have no deep loyalty to either American party in my bones or family or background, and admire presidents from both parties. My partisanship remains solely British—I'm a loyal Tory. But my attachment to the Anglo-American conservative political tradition, as I understand it, is real and deep and the result of sincere reflection on the world as I see it. And I want that tradition to survive because I believe it is a vital complement to liberalism in sustaining the genius and wonder of the modern West.

For these reasons, I found it intolerable after 2003 to support the movement
that goes by the name "conservative" in America. I still do, even though I am
much more of a limited-government type than almost any Democrat and
cannot bring myself to call myself a liberal (because I'm *not*). My reasons
were not dissimilar to Charles Johnson, who, like me, was horrified by 9/11,
loathes Jihadism, and wants to defeat it as effectively as possible. And his little
manifesto prompts me to write my own (the full version is in *The Conservative
Soul*). Here goes:

> I cannot support a movement that claims to believe in limited government but
> backed an unlimited domestic- and foreign-policy presidency that assumed
> illegal, extra-constitutional dictatorial powers until forced by the system to
> return to the rule of law.
>
> I cannot support a movement that exploded spending and borrowing and
> blames its successor for the debt.
>
> I cannot support a movement that so abandoned government's minimal and
> vital role to police markets and address natural disasters that it gave us
> Katrina and the financial meltdown of 2008.
>
> I cannot support a movement that holds torture as a core value.
>
> I cannot support a movement that holds that purely religious doctrine should
> govern civil political decisions and that uses the sacredness of religious
> faith for the pursuit of worldly power.
>
> I cannot support a movement that is deeply homophobic, cynically deploys
> fear of homosexuals to win votes, and gives off such a racist vibe that its
> share of the minority vote remains pitiful.
>
> I cannot support a movement which has no real respect for the institutions
> of government and is prepared to use any tactic and any means to fight
> political warfare rather than conduct a political conversation.
>
> I cannot support a movement that sees permanent war as compatible with
> liberal democratic norms and limited government.
>
> I cannot support a movement that criminalizes private behavior in the war
> on drugs.
>
> I cannot support a movement that would back a vice-presidential candidate
> manifestly unqualified and duplicitous because of identity politics and
> electoral cynicism.

I cannot support a movement that regards gay people as threats to their own families.

I cannot support a movement that does not accept evolution as a fact.

I cannot support a movement that sees climate change as a hoax and offers domestic oil exploration as the core plank of an energy policy.

I cannot support a movement that refuses ever to raise taxes, while proposing no meaningful reductions in government spending.

I cannot support a movement that refuses to distance itself from a demagogue like Rush Limbaugh or a nutjob like Glenn Beck.

I cannot support a movement that believes that the United States should be the sole global power, should sustain a permanent war machine to police the entire planet, and sees violence as the core tool for international relations.

Does this make me a "radical leftist," as Michelle Malkin would say? Emphatically not. But it sure disqualifies me from the current American right. To paraphrase Reagan, I didn't leave the conservative movement. It left me. And increasingly, I'm not alone.

Obama, Trimmer

December 2, 2009 | *THE DISH*

———————

Alex Massie flags this passage from E. D. Kain:

> *Conservatism is not only about limited government, and where it seeks to*
> *limit government it does so because it sees government as a force of instability. But*
> *what about those times when government is instead a force for stability? Defense*
> *leaps to mind. Conservatism, I would argue, is first and foremost about preserving*
> *or regaining a stable society. Liberty and prosperity are two of the most profound*
> *ways we can achieve a stable civilization. Limiting government often leads to*
> *both these things, and thus it is a means to an end, not an end in and of itself.*
>
> *And when limiting government actually brings about social chaos rather*
> *than social stability, then it's outworn its use. Perhaps this is why anarchy is*
> *such an impossible goal. At some point the benefit of removing the state from*
> *the equation no longer outweighs the cost.*

The underlying principle here is an Oakeshottian one: the *coherence* of
a polity matters more than any single ideological approach to politics. This
was Oakeshott's critique of Hayek after a fashion. If the market becomes an
ideology in itself, it ceases to be conservative. The real conservative tilts from
intervention to laissez-faire *depending on the circumstances*. He may lean
in the long run toward less government as a more stable principle in a free,
self-reliant, and increasingly diverse country than more government. But he
is always seeking the right prudential balance from exigency to exigency, from

era to era, from year to year. And government is never the enemy *tout court*. It is a necessary means to an end.

Oakeshott saw the politics of faith and the politics of skepticism as the two core principles guiding modern Western politics. He favored in his own day of government planning, rationalism, and left-liberal triumphalism the unfashionable tradition of freedom, mystery, markets, and personality. But he was always aware that government needed to act strongly sometimes and swiftly too. He was skeptical of excessive skepticism. A conservatism of doubt might be too sluggish in emergencies, as Oakeshott scholar Paul Franco notes, or deemed too frivolous at times. It could be incapable of summoning the necessary love or gratitude or patriotism from its subjects. So it can embrace government at times, to save civil society; and vice versa.

What the conservative is about, in other words, is *balance*. And that's why Oakeshott's famous metaphor for the kind of politician he admired was a "trimmer." And one of his treasured works of political writing was Halifax's sadly neglected *The Character of a Trimmer*. Today we regard a trimmer as a flip-flopper. But a trimmer in the nautical sense was a man simply tasked with trimming the sails and balancing the weight of a ship to ensure, as different winds prevailed, that the ship stayed upright and on an even keel. The role of the conservative statesman is, in Oakeshott's sense, to do the same thing—sometimes expanding government in discrete ways to ameliorate or adjust to new circumstances; sometimes restricting it for the same reasons. Here's his own description:

> The "trimmer" is one who disposes his weight so as to keep the ship upon an even keel. And our inspection of his conduct reveals certain general ideas at work. . . . Being concerned to prevent politics from running to extremes, he believes that there is a time for everything and that everything has its time—not providentially, but empirically. He will be found facing in whatever direction the occasion seems to require if the boat is to go even.

I think you can see the critique of left-liberalism in the 1970s as a classic conservative trimming of the excessive delusions of a liberalism become too powerful, too smug, and too ideological. That's why the original neoconservatives—Kristol, Bell, Glazer, et al.—were heroes to me.

But I also think you can see Clinton and Obama as necessary attempts to balance the excesses of this movement which inevitably succumbed to hubris, calcification, and ideological purism over time. What Bush and Cheney then did to the system in panicked response to the emergency of 9/11—a massive and radical attack on constitutional norms, a conflation of religious certainty and government, and a huge expansion of government power and spending—requires now a very intense period of Halifax-style balancing. Obama's moderation may, in fact, not be radical enough on Oakeshottian grounds. For trimming is not about always finding the middle option. It is about restoring balance, which may sometimes mean radicalism if it is preceded by serious imbalance.

This is a prudential task, not a theoretical one (the other core conservative insight). And we should judge this president and his opponents on the wisdom of their prudential decisions and positions. So far, it seems to me, Obama is the only game in town. Whether his judgment is right will only be determined by history. But his instincts, it seems to me, are genuinely that of a trimmer.

In the best possible sense of that term.

Dear Ta-Nehisi

December 1, 2011 | *THE DISH*

———

What infuriates many about me on the question of race is my refusal to assume that research into racial differences in IQ is inherently racist. Sorry, but I don't. I regard it as an empirical question, as I do for many human differences. But my colleague Ta-Nehisi Coates points to a deeper question and it is one I have wrestled with. How do I live with the knowledge that writing about such things as merely empirical matters, when they are freighted with profound historical evil, will deeply hurt many, and could help legitimize hateful abusers of information? What responsibility does a writer have for the consequences, good and bad, of good-faith pieces he writes? Is merely citing the massive amount of data showing clearly different racial distribution for IQ an offensive, cruel, and racist provocation? Is raising this subject worth anything anyway?

This is not the only time I have encountered this moral problem as a writer. Was I wrong to take gay reparative therapy seriously as an argument and accord some respect to its claims as to the origin of homosexuality, as I did in *Love Undetectable*? Was I aggravating sexism by writing my essay on testosterone for *The New York Times Magazine*? Am I encouraging anti-Semitism by writing what I think is the truth about the influence of the pro-Israel lobby in hobbling US interests in the Middle East? Did I encourage unsafe sex by writing "When Plagues End," in 1996, or undercut funding for AIDS research by revealing the breakthrough in treatment? Have I exacerbated the polarization I decry by calling those who approved or imposed "enhanced interrogation techniques" war criminals? Is "Christianist" too offensive a term even if it can be defended as a legitimate way to contrast it with live-and-let-live Christianity?

My core position is that a writer's core loyalty must be to the truth as best as he can discern it.

That's especially true in considered essays or books. On blogs, where sudden real-time judgment can lead you to occasional overstatements or errors, it is important to ensure that corrections, adjustments, or clarifications follow, and that dissent is open. (In publishing an extract from *The Bell Curve* in *The New Republic*, I also insisted in the same issue on publishing thirteen separate dissents.) The point is the truth. I believe that part of the role of the public writer is not to self-censor for fear of social or cultural stigma. And that's one reason I took to the blogosphere before many others: because it was a place where I felt the limits on total freedom of speech were the least powerful. It was a place where taboos were weakest.

In my mind, I regard my work as a writer as existing in a different mode from my everyday living. I am writing not with respect to any individual but for the general public—which I envision stripped of its particular racial, gender, religious, or whatever identities. If the truth hurts, so be it. In my role as a truth seeker—and it is a role, not my being—compassion and empathy are irrelevant.

Except they aren't.

The abstraction of the disinterested writer in pursuit of truth is an abstraction. And as a human being, I do not live in an abstract world. That I have wounded someone—like Ta-Nehisi—whom I revere as a writer and care about as a human being distresses me greatly. The friends I've lost from my recent Israel posts also grieve me. The friends I lost during the AIDS crisis—when I wrote things that violated the gay consensus—hurt me even more deeply. And to tell you the truth, I wonder whether my Christian faith is, in fact, compatible with the work I do. My compulsion to get to the bottom of highly contentious issues and my fixation on subjects where others smartly conclude the costs outweigh the gains ensure that I will continue to hurt people's feelings.

At one level, I wonder if this gift of freedom is not poisoned by my attraction to controversy rather than truth. I mean: Questioning a woman's own pregnancy is an act of profound hurt. My defense in that case is that the person in question was a potential president and therefore merits more scrutiny than others. Nonetheless, it must have been deeply hurtful to Palin's family and herself even to raise the subject if there was nothing to it. In my conscience, I concluded that what drove me was my simple inability to believe the story on the surface, and that a possible president of the United States who might have done such a thing was inconceivable. Similarly, I never believed that gender is entirely a social construction. Or that homosexual orientation is entirely genetic. My curiosity gets the better of me often.

I just know that it is hard for me to be a writer any other way. It seems to be in my nature—a querulous, insistent curiosity that sometimes relishes the hostility it often provokes. What I remain committed to is a constant reevaluation of these arguments and complete openness to new data. But the hurt remains.

One justification is that the truth counts, and that even if we are able to ignore it for a while, it won't become less true. What I fear about liberal democracy is that if it rests itself on untrue notions of substantive human equality—both individually and in groups—it will one day fail. Covering up resilient inequality merely kicks this can down the road. And at the rate neuroscience is going, the empirical research—using far more powerful techniques than IQ testing—could upend a lot of assumptions. Liberal democracy is better defended if it rests on formal civic moral equality, and not substantive, skills-based human equality. So, for example, it's a great argument for gay equality that homosexuality is 100 percent genetic. But I have never used that argument because the evidence isn't there for it. I think one should be careful about resting arguments on wobbly truth claims.

One resolution to this conflict is to quit the public arena for areas of life where general truths are not so central; to find another way to make a living, and live it without the danger of hurting so many feelings. Throughout my life, I have considered doing this, for spiritual, moral, and religious reasons. I fear there are too many times when I hurt more than heal, even though I don't intend to hurt. I fear that insisting on finding out reality at the expense of charity and empathy is not something a Christian should do lightly, if at all.

And so I ask Ta-Nehisi for forgiveness; not as a writer, where good faith and honesty alone matter, but as a friend and human being, where empathy counts.

Why Continue to
Build the Settlements?

March 30, 2012 | *THE DISH*

O ne of the more striking aspects of the preemptive strikes on Peter Beinart's tightly argued polemic *The Crisis of Zionism* is not just their viciousness, but their avoidance of the core issue of the book:

Why continue to build the settlements?

Is it not clear by now that the settlements' existence and relentless expansion are turning liberal Zionism into "something much darker"? What justification is there for continuing to build them, to add to them, to keep increasing the Jewish population in an area that under any two-state solution, Israel would presumably have to give up? Only today we read in *Haaretz* the following:

> *Civil Administration's maps and figures, disclosed here for the first time, suggest the barrier route was planned in accordance with the available land in the West Bank, intended to increase the area and population of the settlements.*
>
> *A total of 569 parcels of land were marked out, encompassing around 620,000 dunams (around 155,000 acres) — about 10 percent of the total area of the West Bank. Since the late 1990s, 23 of the unauthorized outposts were built on land included in the map. The Civil Administration is endeavoring to legalize some of these outposts, including Shvut Rahel, Rehelim and Hayovel.*
>
> *Etkes believes this indicates the settlers who built the outposts had access to the administration's research on available land — more proof of the government's*

deep involvement in the systematic violation of the law in order to expand settlements, he says.

Let us be clear. The Israeli government is systematically taking and holding the land that could be the Palestinians' future state. They have been doing so for decades. The deliberate population of occupied land violates the Geneva Conventions. The occupation itself enrages the Arab and Muslim world and creates a huge drag on the United States' strategic need to build up allies among emerging Arab democracies, and defuse Jihadism across the globe.

And Peter's book is explicitly about this problem. It lies at the center of his argument. And yet it is all but ignored by his critics. The trope responses are varied in their weary familiarity. Let us examine them.

The Palestinians have for a long time been their own worst enemies, and in the past have not sought peace. It's more complicated than that, but sure, for much of the past sixty years, the Palestinians bear a huge responsibility for their own situation.

Why continue to build the settlements?

Iran's nuclear development is the most urgent issue.

Let's concede that for the sake of argument, *but why continue to build the settlements?*

China occupies Tibet and you don't fixate on that.

Well, I *do* oppose the occupation of Tibet and if my own taxpayer's dollars were going directly to sustain that occupation, or to facilitate transfers of the Chinese population to Tibet to shift the demographic balance, I'd have an issue with that as well.

But why continue to build the settlements?

Obama made freezing the settlements a precondition for talks, so it's his fault, the Greater Israel lobby insists, that the two-state solution is going nowhere. But when the issue at hand is a division of land, and when one side, which holds almost all the raw power, wants to keep taking parts of that land while it is simultaneously negotiating its division, it's an impossible negotiation. You don't negotiate while simultaneously adding facts on the ground to tilt the talks your way. You freeze the situation; you talk to the other side. That's all Obama asked for—just a freeze of construction for a year. Netanyahu refused.

Even the ten-month alleged suspension made no measurable difference in the number of new homes built in the relevant year.

So again: *Why continue to build the settlements?*

And the reason for urgency is obvious: the faster the settlements grow in property, scale, and population, the harder it will be to remove them. The longer a democracy occupies a foreign country and people, the more it risks the moral corruption of imperial control of another people's destiny, of dehumanizing those you fear, of fueling the hatred you then use to justify further violence and coercion. Peter Beinart's book is a simple restatement of this truth.

It cannot be restated enough.

And the evasions of this central point of Beinart's book by its vitriolic critics are as legion as they are predictable. And they matter. Because the evaders do not want to answer the question: *Why continue to build the settlements?* They do not want to answer that question and dodge it relentlessly because the answer is obvious and devastating to their position.

The answer is that the settlements are there because the current Israeli government has no intention of ever dividing the land between Arabs and Jews in a way that would give the Palestinians anything like their own state, and have every intention of holding Judea and Samaria for ever. Netanyahu is, as Beinart rightly calls him, a monist. He is the son of his father, Ben-Zion, as Jeffrey Goldberg has also insisted on. But what Peter does is spell out one side of the Netanyahu vision that Goldberg elides.

Vladimir Jabotinsky was a huge influence on Netanyahu's father and Netanyahu himself. He's a complicated figure, as Beinart readily concedes. For Jabotinsky, what it all came down to in the end was "the single ideal: a Jewish minority *on both sides of the Jordan* as a first step towards the establishment of the State. That is what we call 'monism.'" My italics. The Revisionist Zionists (whence eventually Likud) envisaged a Jewish state that would not only include the West Bank but the East Bank as well, i.e., Jordan.

Ben-Zion Netanyahu followed Jabotinsky's vision, and his willingness, even eagerness, to use violence to achieve it: "We should conquer any disputed territory in the land of Israel. Conquer and hold it, even if it brings us years of war. . . . You don't return land." Ben-Zion Netanyahu even favored the "transfer" of Arabs living in Palestine to other Arab countries. In 2009, Netanyahu Sr. put his position this way to *Maariv*:

"The Jews and the Arabs are like two goats facing each other on a narrow bridge.
One must jump into the river." "What does the Arab's jump mean?" asked the
interviewer, trying to decipher the metaphor. Netanyahu explained: "That they
won't be able to face the war with us, which will include withholding food from
Arab cities, preventing education, terminating electrical power and more. They
won't be able to exist and they will run away from here."

Suddenly the situation in Gaza and much of the West Bank makes more
sense, doesn't it? It's a conscious relentless assault on the lives of Palestinians
to immiserate them to such an extent that they flee. And if you do not think
that Bibi Netanyahu's father isn't easily the biggest influence on his life and
worldview, read Jeffrey Goldberg. Money quote:

"Always in the back of Bibi's mind is Ben-Zion," one of the prime minister's
friends told me. "He worries that his father will think he is weak."

Ben-Zion is a radical and a fanatic and an illiberal Zionist, who sees the
world as forever 1938, the Arabs as a monolithic group of barbarians, and
foreswears any interaction with them except through force. You cannot understand the current Israeli government without grasping that it is led by the son
of the man who said this, and who shares his worldview. "The Arabs know
only force," Bibi has said. And here is the message from Ben-Zion on Iran, as
reported by Goldberg:

From the Iranian side, we hear pledges that soon—in a matter of days, even—the
Zionist movement will be put to an end and there will be no more Zionists in the
world. One is supposed to conclude from this that the Jews of the Land of Israel
will be annihilated, while the Jews of America, whose leaders refuse to pressure
Iran, are being told in a hinted fashion that the annihilation of the Jews will
not include them. . . . The Jewish people are making their position clear and
putting faith in their military power. The nation of Israel is showing the world
today how a state should behave when it stands before an existential threat:
by looking danger in the eye and calmly considering what should be done and
what can be done. And to be ready to enter the fray at the moment there is a
reasonable chance of success.

The key phrases are "faith in military power" and "enter the fray." Diplomacy with enemies is not in this mindset. Nor is any consideration but the defense and expansion of Greater Israel — "conquer and hold it" — even at the expense of what Ben-Zion has called "years of war." Am I attaching the view of this fascistic vision from father to son? Not according to Goldberg:

> *Many people in Likud Party circles have told me that those who discount Ben-Zion's influence on his son do so at their peril. "This was the father giving his son history's marching orders," one of the attendees told me. "I watched Bibi while his father spoke. He was completely absorbed."*

The mindset that believes that Israel should in principle include all of Jerusalem, all of the West Bank, and all of Jordan, that it must never, ever return lands it "conquered," that all Arabs are barbarians, incapable of being negotiated with, is exactly the same mindset that sees an existential threat from Iran — "in a matter of days even" — even though Iran has not yet got the capacity to make a single nuclear bomb, and if it did, would be facing over one hundred nuclear warheads coming back from Israel and the annihilation of most of its population. There's paranoia. And then there's irrationality.

And this irrationality is intrinsic to the current Israeli government's intent to hold on to the West Bank forever, restrict Palestinians (whose very nationhood is dismissed) into vast gated communities, where the gates exist to keep the inhabitants inside, and between which Israel effectively rules. The inhabitants of these "reservations" would have no vote in Israel itself. And they would occupy only a fraction of the West Bank. This is the best we can expect from a Netanyahu future. It is not the likeliest, which is the continued settlement and de facto annexation of the entire area (i.e., the last three years).

If I am wrong, and those remaining liberal Israelis who still believe in a democratic, pluralist Israel can find a way to remove the settlements and come to a 1967-based land-swap compromise, we may be able to view this Netanyahu-Lieberman era as a horrible period in a gradual path forward. But the one emotion I felt closing Peter's book was sadness. I don't think the data suggest that either a majority of Israelis or a majority of American Jews are prepared to challenge a policy of conquering and subjugating another people in this way. And Beinart's book is very persuasive in showing how the mere act of occupation—the way it sets up inherent distance between Jew and Arab, and constantly humiliates the Arab—is profoundly shifting Israeli culture in such a way as to make the younger generations even less likely to compromise with "the other" than the older ones.

Beinart's book has been attacked so mercilessly, in my view, because it clearly, methodically, even-handedly exposes the radical Zionism that threatens to eclipse Israeli democracy, corrupt Jewish ethics, and weaken American interests across the globe. And the key proof of his case is the continued, relentless expansion of West Bank settlements, and the ethnic social engineering in East Jerusalem. And so I ask again of Beinart's criticism to answer the core question of the book:

Why continue to build the settlements?

Christianity in Crisis

April 2, 2012 | NEWSWEEK

I f you go to the second floor of the National Museum of American History in Washington, D.C., you'll find a small room containing an eighteenth-century Bible whose pages are full of holes. They are carefully razor-cut empty spaces, so this was not an act of vandalism. It was, rather, a project begun by Thomas Jefferson when he was seventy-seven years old. Painstakingly removing those passages he thought reflected the actual teachings of Jesus of Nazareth, Jefferson literally cut and pasted them into a slimmer, different New Testament, and left behind the remnants (all on display until July 15). What did he edit out? He told us: "We must reduce our volume to the simple evangelists, select, even from them, the very words only of Jesus." He removed what he felt were the "misconceptions" of Jesus's followers, "expressing unintelligibly for others what they had not understood themselves." And it wasn't hard for him. He described the difference between the real Jesus and the evangelists' embellishments as "diamonds" in a "dunghill," glittering as "the most sublime and benevolent code of morals which has ever been offered to man." Yes, he was calling vast parts of the Bible religious manure.

When we think of Jefferson as the great architect of the separation of church and state, this, perhaps, was what he meant by "church": the purest, simplest, apolitical Christianity, purged of the agendas of those who had sought to use Jesus to advance their own power decades and centuries after Jesus's death. If Jefferson's greatest political legacy was the Declaration of Independence, this pure, precious moral teaching was his religious legacy. "I am a real Christian,"

Jefferson insisted against the fundamentalists and clerics of his time. "That is to say, a disciple of the doctrines of Jesus."

What were those doctrines? Not the supernatural claims that, fused with politics and power, gave successive generations wars, inquisitions, pogroms, reformations, and counterreformations. Jesus's doctrines were the practical commandments, the truly radical ideas that immediately leap out in the simple stories he told and which he exemplified in everything he did. Not simply love one another, but love your enemy and forgive those who harm you; give up all material wealth; love the ineffable Being behind all things, and know that this Being is actually your truest Father, in whose image you were made. Above all: give up power over others, because power, if it is to be effective, ultimately requires the threat of violence, and violence is incompatible with the total acceptance and love of all other human beings that is at the sacred heart of Jesus's teaching. That's why, in his final apolitical act, Jesus never defended his innocence at trial, never resisted his crucifixion, and even turned to those nailing his hands to the wood on the cross and forgave them, and loved them.

Whether or not you believe, as I do, in Jesus's divinity and resurrection—and in the importance of celebrating both on Easter Sunday—Jefferson's point is crucially important. Because it was Jesus's point. What does it matter how strictly you proclaim your belief in various doctrines if you do not live as these doctrines demand? What is politics if not a dangerous temptation toward controlling others rather than reforming oneself? If we return to what Jesus actually asked us to do and to be—rather than the unknowable intricacies of what we believe he was—he actually emerges more powerfully and more purely.

And more intensely relevant to our times. Jefferson's vision of a simpler, purer, apolitical Christianity couldn't be further from the twenty-first-century American reality. We inhabit a polity now saturated with religion. On one side, the Republican base is made up of evangelical Protestants who believe that religion must consume and influence every aspect of public life. On the other side, the last Democratic primary had candidates profess their faith in public forums, and more recently President Obama appeared at the National Prayer Breakfast, invoking Jesus to defend his plan for universal health care. The crisis of Christianity is perhaps best captured in the new meaning of the word "secular." It once meant belief in separating the spheres of faith and politics; it now means, for many, simply atheism. The ability to be faithful in a religious space and reasonable in a political one has atrophied before our eyes.

Meanwhile, organized religion itself is in trouble. The Catholic Church's hierarchy lost much of its authority over the American flock with the unilateral prohibition of the pill in 1968 by Pope Paul VI. But in the last decade, whatever shred of moral authority that remained has evaporated. The hierarchy was exposed as enabling, and then covering up, an international conspiracy to abuse and rape countless youths and children. I don't know what greater indictment of a church's authority there can be — except the refusal, even now, of the entire leadership to face their responsibility and resign. Instead, they obsess about others' sex lives, about who is entitled to civil marriage, and about who pays for birth control in health insurance. Inequality, poverty, even the torture institutionalized by the government after 9/11: these issues attract far less of their public attention.

For their part, the mainline Protestant churches, which long promoted religious moderation, have rapidly declined in the past fifty years. Evangelical Protestantism has stepped into the vacuum, but it has serious defects of its own. As *New York Times* columnist Ross Douthat explores in his unsparing new book, *Bad Religion: How We Became a Nation of Heretics*, many suburban evangelicals embrace a gospel of prosperity, which teaches that living a Christian life will make you successful and rich. Others defend a rigid biblical literalism, adamantly wishing away a century and a half of scholarship that has clearly shown that the canonized Gospels were written decades after Jesus's ministry, and are copies of copies of stories told by those with fallible memory. Still others insist that the Earth is merely six thousand years old — something we now know by the light of reason and science is simply untrue. And what group of Americans have pollsters found to be most supportive of torturing terror suspects? Evangelical Christians. Something has gone very wrong. These are impulses born of panic in the face of modernity, and fear before an amorphous "other." This version of Christianity could not contrast more strongly with Jesus's constant refrain: "Be not afraid." It would make Jefferson shudder.

It would also, one imagines, baffle Jesus of Nazareth. The issues that Christianity obsesses over today simply do not appear in either Jefferson's or the original New Testament. Jesus never spoke of homosexuality or abortion, and his only remarks on marriage were a condemnation of divorce (now common-place among American Christians) and forgiveness for adultery. The family? He disowned his parents in public as a teen, and told his followers to abandon theirs if they wanted to follow him. Sex? He was a celibate who, along with his followers, anticipated an imminent End of the World where reproduction was completely irrelevant.

All of which is to say something so obvious it is almost taboo: Christianity itself is in crisis. It seems no accident to me that so many Christians now embrace materialist self-help rather than ascetic self-denial—or that most Catholics, even regular churchgoers, have tuned out the hierarchy in embar-rassment or disgust. Given this crisis, it is no surprise that the fastest-growing segment of belief among the young is atheism, which has leapt in popularity in the new millennium. Nor is it a shock that so many have turned away from organized Christianity and toward "spirituality," co-opting or adapting the practices of meditation or yoga, or wandering as lapsed Catholics in an inquisitive spiritual desert. The thirst for God is still there. How could it not be, when the profoundest human questions—*Why does the universe exist rather than nothing? How did humanity come to be on this remote blue speck of a planet? What happens to us after death?*—remain as pressing and mysterious as they've always been?

That's why polls show a huge majority of Americans still believing in a Higher Power. But the need for new questioning—of Christian institutions as well as ideas and priorities—is as real as the crisis is deep.

Where to start? Jefferson's act of cutting out those parts of the Bible that offended his moral and scientific imagination is one approach. But another can be found in the life of a well-to-do son of a fabric trader in twelfth-century Italy who went off to fight a war with a neighboring city, saw his friends killed in battle in front of him, lived a year as a prisoner of war, and then experienced a clarifying vision that changed the world. In *Francis of Assisi: A New Biography*, Augustine Thompson cuts through the legends and apocryphal prayers to describe Saint Francis as he truly lived. Gone are the fashionable stories of an erstwhile hippie, communing with flowers and animals. Instead we have this typical young secular figure who suddenly found peace in service to those he previously shrank from: lepers, whose sores and lesions he tended to and whose company he sought—as much as for himself as for them.

The religious order that goes by his name began quite simply with a couple of friends who were captured by the sheer spiritual intensity of how Francis lived. His inspiration was even purer than Jefferson's. He did not cut out passages of the Gospels to render them more reasonable than they appear to the modern mind. He simply opened the Gospels at random—as was often the custom at the time—and found three passages. They told him to "sell what you have and give to the poor," to "take nothing for your journey," not even a second tunic, and to "deny himself" and follow the path of Jesus. That was it. So Francis renounced his inheritance, becoming homeless and earning food by manual labor. When that wouldn't feed him, he begged, just for food—with the indignity of begging part of his spiritual humbling.

Francis insisted on living utterly without power over others. As stories of his strangeness and holiness spread, more joined him and he faced a real dilemma: how to lead a group of men, and also some women, in an organization. Suddenly faith met politics. And it tormented, wracked, and almost killed him. He had to be last, not first. He wanted to be always the "lesser brother," not the founder of an order. And so he would often go on pilgrimages and ask others to run things. Or he would sit at the feet of his brothers at communal meetings and if an issue could not be resolved without his say-so, he would whisper in the leader's ear.

As Jesus was without politics, so was Francis. As Jesus fled from crowds, so did Francis—often to bare shacks in woodlands, to pray and be with God and nature. It's critical to recall that he did not do this in rebellion against orthodoxy or even church authority. He obeyed orders from bishops and even the pope himself. His main obsession wasn't nature, which came to sublime fruition in his final "Canticle of the Sun," but the cleanliness of the cloths, chalices, and ornaments surrounding the holy Eucharist.

His revulsion at even the hint of comfort or wealth could be extreme. As he lay dying and was offered a pillow to rest on, he slept through the night only to wake the next day in a rage, hitting the monk who had given him the pillow and recoiling in disgust at his own weakness in accepting its balm. One of his few commands was that his brothers never ride a horse; they had to walk or ride a donkey. What inspired his fellow Christians to rebuild and reform the Church in his day was simply his own example of humility, service, and sanctity.

A modern person would see such a man as crazy, and there were many at the time who thought so too. He sang sermons in the streets, sometimes just miming them. He suffered intense bouts of doubt, self-loathing, and depression. He had visions. You could have diagnosed his postwar conversion as an outgrowth of post-traumatic stress disorder. Or you can simply observe what those around him testified to: something special, unique, mysterious, holy. To reduce one's life to essentials, to ask merely for daily bread, forgiveness of others, and denial of self is, in many ways, a form of madness. It is also a form of liberation. It lets go of complexity and focuses on simplicity. Francis did not found an order designed to think or control. He insisted on the simplicity of manual labor, prayer, and the sacraments. That was enough for him.

It wouldn't be enough for most of us. And yet, there can be wisdom in the acceptance of mystery. I've pondered the incarnation my whole life. I've read theology and history. I think I grasp what it means to be both God and human—but I don't think my understanding is any richer than my Irish grandmother's. Barely literate, she would lose herself in the Rosary at Mass. In her simplicity, beneath her veil in front of a cascade of flickering candles, she seemed to know God more deeply than I, with all my education and privilege, ever will.

This doesn't imply, as some claim, the privatization of faith, or its relegation to a subordinate sphere. There are times when great injustices—slavery, imperialism, totalitarianism, segregation—require spiritual mobilization and public witness. But from Gandhi to King, the greatest examples of these movements renounce power as well. They embrace nonviolence as a moral example, and that paradox changes the world more than politics or violence ever can or will. When politics is necessary, as it is, the kind of Christianity I am describing seeks always to translate religious truths into reasoned, secular arguments that can appeal to those of other faiths and none at all. But it also means, at times, renouncing Caesar in favor of the Christ to whom Jefferson, Francis, my grandmother, and countless generations of believers have selflessly devoted themselves.

The saints, after all, became known as saints not because of their success in fighting political battles, or winning a few news cycles, or funding an anti-abortion super PAC. They were saints purely and simply because of the way they lived. And this, of course, was Jefferson's deeply American insight: "No man can conform his faith to the dictates of another. The life and essence of religion consists in the internal persuasion or belief of the mind."

Jefferson feared that the alternative to a Christianity founded on "internal persuasion" was a revival of the brutal, bloody wars of religion that America was founded to escape. And what he grasped in his sacrilegious mutilation of a sacred text was the core simplicity of Jesus's message of renunciation. He believed that stripped of the doctrines of the incarnation, resurrection, and the various miracles, the message of Jesus was the deepest miracle. And that it was radically simple. It was explained in stories, parables, and metaphors—not theological doctrines of immense complexity. It was proved by his willingness to submit himself to an unjustified execution. The cross itself was not the point; nor was the intense physical suffering he endured. The point was how he conducted himself through it all—calm, loving, accepting, radically surrendering even the basic control of his own body and telling us that this was what it means to truly transcend our world and be with God. Jesus, like Francis, was a homeless person, as were his closest followers. He possessed nothing—and thereby everything.

I have no concrete idea how Christianity will wrestle free of its current crisis, of its distractions and temptations, and above all its enmeshment with the things of this world. But I do know it won't happen by even more furious denunciations of others, by focusing on politics rather than prayer, by concerning ourselves with the sex lives and heretical thoughts of others rather than with the constant struggle to liberate ourselves from what keeps us from God. What Jefferson saw in Jesus of Nazareth was utterly compatible with reason and with the future; what Saint Francis trusted in was the simple, terrifying love of God for creation itself. That never ends.

This Christianity comes not from the head or the gut, but from the soul. It is as meek as it is quietly liberating. It does not seize the moment; it lets it be. It doesn't seek worldly recognition, or success, and it flees from power and wealth. It is the religion of unachievement. And it is not afraid. In the anxious, crammed lives of our modern twittering souls, in the materialist obsessions we cling to for security in recession, in a world where sectarian extremism threatens to unleash mass destruction, this sheer Christianity, seeking truth without the expectation of resolution, simply living each day doing what we can to fulfill God's will, is more vital than ever. It may, in fact, be the only spiritual transformation that can in the end transcend the nagging emptiness of our late-capitalist lives, or the cult of distracting contemporaneity, or the threat of apocalyptic war where Jesus once walked. You see attempts to find this everywhere—from experimental spirituality to resurgent fundamentalism. Something inside is telling us we need radical spiritual change.

But the essence of this change has been with us, and defining our own civilization, for two millennia. And one day soon, when politics and doctrine and pride recede, it will rise again.

The First Elite Conservative
to Say Enough

July 2, 2012 | *THE DISH*

M ulling over the Supreme Court ruling in favor of Obamacare this weekend, it occurred to me why this remains a BFD. It's not that we now have a reprieve for the idea of universal health care in the United States. Or even that we have an interpretation of the Commerce Clause that could eventually mean some nontrivial ratcheting back of the federal government's powers vis-à-vis the states. It is that a creature of the conservative movement, one of its youngest and most intelligent stars, saw the radicalism of the four dissenters . . . and balked.

He balked, it appears, because of his attachment to the court as an institution, because he was unwilling to trash its reputation by embroiling it in a deep and bitter partisan grudge match in the middle of a presidential campaign—when there was a plausible way out. He was also applying the logic of judicial restraint with respect to legislative wishes, interpreting the law to be as constitutional as it could possibly be deemed (i.e., in this case, viewing the mandate as part of the Congress's tax power). In these two ways, Roberts upheld a form of conservatism that is not synonymous with the interests of the Republican Party at any given moment. Which is so unusual these days one wants (pathetically) to stand up and cheer.

One of the most strikingly anticonservative aspects of today's allegedly conservative movement, after all, is its contempt for institutions, especially elite institutions that in any way limit the scope of fundamentalist ideology.

And so Newt Gingrich's crucial innovation was throwing out the politeness and manners and decorum and rules and traditions of the House of Representatives in order to gain power by populist demagoguery. You can see his legacy in Tom DeLay's implementation of the Medicare D entitlement under Bush, an essentially lawless and rule-free process that made a mockery of parliamentary procedure. You saw this contempt for the rule of law, if it got in the way of desired policy, in the torture policy under Bush, cynically making the patently illegal "legal" through cynicism and doublespeak.

Similarly, McConnell's use of the filibuster is essentially a display of contempt for the American constitutional system, rigging the system to nullify legislative majorities and to conduct politics as a zero-sum war for power, rather than as a means to debate, discuss, and implement necessary changes in an evolving society. The give-and-take of American constitutionalism has been essentially reduced by the GOP in the last two decades to take-and-take-some-more. They impeached one successful president, in an act so disproportionate to the offense (and the offense was real; Clinton was a shameless perjurer) that it helped gut any bipartisan functioning of an institution designed for deal-making across the aisles or within them. They treated the 2000 election, when Bush lost the popular vote, as a landslide mandate election—again with no deference to the other side or sense of governing as one nation.

After *Bush v. Gore* and then *Citizens United*, I think Roberts saw the full political and constitutional consequences of a radical Court vote to gut the key legislative achievement of a duly elected president and Congress. In other words, he put the institutions of American government before the demands of partisan power mongering. And he deftly nudged the issue back into the democratic process, where it more comfortably belongs.

I cannot say this is the moment the fever broke. The "movement right" is still furious at Roberts, pushing Romney as the principle-free instrument of their next round of institution smashing (Medicare). But that a conservative placed the country's institutional stability before ideological fervor is so rare at this point it deserves some kind of praise. It's a start. If the GOP is beaten this fall, it may even be seen as the moment the tide began to turn, and conservatism began to reach back toward its less feral traditions and ideas. Yes, I know I'm getting way ahead of myself here.

But at some point, conservatism must reemerge, if only because we so desperately need it. Conservatism is, after all, a philosophy that tends to argue that less equals more, that restraint is sometimes more powerful than action, that delay is often wiser than headlong revolution. It reveres traditional rules and existing institutions, especially endangered elite institutions that the Founders designed to check and cool the popular will. Roberts took a small step toward resuscitating that tradition last week.

It's the first seagull spotted after a decade or two on the open seas.

Thatcher, Liberator

April 8, 2013 | *THE DISH*

I remember reading an article in *Washington Monthly* back in the late 1980s by one of the smugger liberal British columnists, Polly Toynbee. It captured part of the true derangement that Margaret Thatcher brought out in her political foes. It was called simply: "Is Margaret Thatcher a Woman?" It's still online. It was a vicious attack on her having any feminist credentials. It included this magnificent lie:

> She has experienced nothing but advantage from her gender.

Toynbee's case is worth hearing out, but it's an instant classic of the worst British trait: resentment of others' success. No culture I know of is more brutally unkind to its public figures, hateful toward anyone with a degree of success or money, or more willing to ascribe an individual's achievements to something other than their own ability. The Britain I grew up with was, in this specific sense, profoundly leftist in the worst sense. It was cheap and greedy and yet hostile to anyone with initiative, self-esteem, and the ability to make money.

Yes: the British left would prefer to keep everyone poorer if it meant preventing a few getting richer. And the massively powerful trade-union movement worked every day to ensure that mediocrity was protected, individual achievement erased, and that all decisions were made collectively, i.e., with their veto. And so—to take the archetypal example—Britain's coal workers fought to make sure they could work unprofitable mines for years of literally lung-destroying existence and to pass it on to their sons for yet another generation of black lung. This "right to work" was actually paid for by anyone able to make a living in a country where socialism had effectively choked off all viable avenues for prosperity. And if you suggested that the coal industry needed to be shut down in large part or reshaped into something commercial, you were called, of course, a class warrior, a snob, a Tory fascist, etc. So hardworking Brits trying to make a middle-class living were taxed dry to keep the life spans of powerful mine workers short.

To put it bluntly: the Britain I grew up in was insane. The government owned almost all major manufacturing, from coal to steel to automobiles. *Owned.* It employed almost every doctor and owned almost every hospital. Almost every university and elementary and high school was government run. And in the 1970s, you could not help but realize as a young Brit that you were living in a decaying museum—some horrifying mixture of Eastern European grimness surrounded by the sculptured bric-a-brac of statues and buildings and edifices that spoke of an empire on which the sun had once never set. Now, in contrast, we lived on the dark side of the moon and it was made up of damp, slowly degrading concrete.

I owe my entire political obsession to the one person in British politics who refused to accept this state of affairs. You can read elsewhere the weighing of her legacy—but she definitively ended a truly poisonous, envious, inert period in Britain's history. She divided the country deeply—and still does. She divided her opponents even more deeply, which was how she kept winning elections. She made some serious mistakes—the poll tax, opposition to German unification, insisting that Nelson Mandela was a terrorist—but few doubt she altered her country permanently, reestablishing the core basics of a free society and a free economy that Britain had intellectually bequeathed to the world and yet somehow lost in its own class-ridden, envy-choked socialist detour to immiseration.

I was a teenage Thatcherite, an über-politics nerd who loved her for her utter lack of apology for who she was. I sensed in her, as others did, a final rebuke to the collectivist, egalitarian oppression of the individual produced by socialism and the stultifying privileges and caste identities of the class system. And part of that identity—the part no one ever truly gave her credit for—was her gender. She came from a small grocer's shop in a northern town and went on to educate herself in chemistry at Oxford, and then law. To put it mildly, those were not traditional decisions for a young woman with few means in the 1950s. She married a smart businessman, reared two children, and forged a political career from scratch in the most male-dominated institution imaginable: the Tory party.

She relished this individualist feminism and wielded it—coining a new and very transitive verb, "handbagging," to describe her evisceration of ill-prepared ministers or clueless interviewers. Perhaps in Toynbee's defense, Thatcher was not a feminist in the left-liberal sense: she never truly reflected on her pioneering role as a female leader, she never appointed a single other woman to her cabinet over eleven years, she was contemptuous toward identity politics, and the only tears she ever deployed (unlike Hillary Clinton) were as she departed from office, ousted by an internal coup, undefeated in any election she had ever run in as party leader.

Indira Gandhi and Golda Meir preceded her, but Thatcher's three election victories, the longest prime ministership since the 1820s, her alliance with the United States in defeating the Soviet Union, and her liberation of the British economy place her above their achievements. What inspires me still is the thought of a young woman in a chemistry lab at Oxford daring to believe that she could one day be prime minister—and not just any prime minister, but the defining public figure in British postwar political history.

That took vision and self-confidence of a quite extraordinary degree. It was infectious. And it made Thatcher and Thatcherism a much more complicated thing than many analyses contain.

Thatcher's economic liberalization came to culturally transform Britain. Women were empowered by new opportunities; immigrants, especially from South Asia, became engineers of growth; millions owned homes for the first time; the media broke free from union chains and fractured and multiplied in subversive and dynamic ways. Her very draconian posture provoked a punk radicalism in the popular culture that changed a generation. The seeds of today's multicultural, global London—epitomized by that Olympic ceremony—were sown by Thatcher's willpower.

And that was why she ultimately failed, as every politician always does. She wanted to return Britain to the tradition of her thrifty, traditional father; instead she turned it into a country for the likes of her son, a wayward, money-making opportunist. The ripple effect of new money, a new middle class, a new individualism meant that Blair's rebranded Britain — cool Britannia, with its rave subculture, its fashionistas, its new cuisine, its gay explosion, its street art, its pop music — was in fact something Blair inherited from Thatcher.

She was, in that sense, a liberator. She didn't constantly (or even ever) argue for women's equality; she just lived it. She didn't just usher in greater economic freedom; she unwittingly brought with it cultural transformation — because there is nothing more culturally disruptive than individualism and capitalism. Her 1940s values never retook: the Brits engaged in spending and borrowing binges long after she had left the scene, and what last vestiges of prudery remained were left in the dust.

Perhaps in future years, her legacy might be better seen as a last, sane defense of the nation-state as the least worst political unit in human civilization. Her deep suspicion of the European project was rooted in memories of the Blitz, but it was also prescient and wise. Without her, it is doubtful the British would have kept their currency and their independence. They would have German financiers going over the budget in Whitehall by now, as they are in Greece and Portugal and Cyprus. She did not therefore only resuscitate economic freedom in Britain; she kept Britain itself free as an independent nation. Neither achievement was inevitable; in fact, each was a function of a single woman's willpower. To have achieved both makes her easily the greatest twentieth-century prime minister after Churchill.

He saved Britain from darkness; she finally saw the lights come back on. And like Churchill, it's hard to imagine any other figure quite having the character, the willpower, and the grit to have pulled it off.

Surprised by Grief

August 6, 2013 | *THE DISH*

It's not as if I have any excuse (you warned me plenty of times), but I'm shocked by how wrecked I am right now. Patrick, Chris, and Jessie, thank God, have been holding down the fort on *The Dish*, because otherwise I'm not sure I could think about much else right now. How can the emotions be this strong? She was a dog, after all, not a spouse or a parent.

And yet, today, as I found myself coming undone again and again, I realized that living with another being in the same room for fifteen and a half years—even if she was just a mischievous, noisy, disobedient, charming, food-obsessed beagle—adds up to a lot of life together. I will never have a child, and she was the closest I'll likely get. And she was well into her teens when she died.

She was with me before *The Dish*; before my last boyfriend, Andy; before I met Aaron. She came from the same breeder as the beagle my friend Patrick got as he faced down AIDS at the end of his life. I guess she was one way to keep him in my life, so it was fitting that his ex-boyfriend drove me to the farm in Maryland to get her. I was going to get a boy and call him Orwell (poseur alert), but there were only girls left by the time we got there. I didn't know what I was doing, but this tiny little brown-faced creature ambled over to me and licked the bottom of my pants. She chose me. On the ride home, I realized I hadn't thought for a second what to call a girl dog, and then Dusty Springfield came on the radio.

My friends couldn't believe I'd get a dog or, frankly, be able to look after one. I was such a bachelor, a loner, a workaholic writer, and gay-marriage activist with relationships that ended almost as quickly as they had begun. I thought

343

getting a dog would help me become less self-centered. And of course it did. It *has* to. Suddenly you are responsible for another being that needs feeding and medicine and walking twice a day. That had to budge even me out of my narcissism and work mania.

But I also got her as the first positive step in my life after the depression I sank into after my viral load went to zero in 1997. I know it sounds completely strange, but the knowledge of my likely survival sent me into the pit of despair. I understand now it was some kind of survivor guilt, and, after so much loss, I had to go through it. I wrote my way out of the bleakness in the end—as usual. But this irrepressible little dog also pulled me feistily out.

She was entirely herself—and gleefully untrainable. I spent a large part of our first years together chasing her around bushes and trees and under wharfs, trying to grab something out of her mouth. She'd find a disgusting rotten fish way underneath a rotting pier, wedge herself in there, eat as much as she felt like, and then roll around in ecstasy as I, red-faced, bellowed from the closest vantage point I could get. There was the year that giant tuna carcass washed up on the sand and I lost her for a split second and nearly lost my mind looking for her until I realized she was *inside* the carcass, rendering herself so stinky it was worse than when she got skunked. But the smile on her face as she trotted right out was unforgettable. It was the same proud, beaming face that appeared from under a bush in Meridian Hill Park covered in human diarrhea, left by a homeless person. Score!

Good times: the countless occasions she peed in the apartment, always under my blogging chair, driving me to distraction; her one giant chocolate orgasm, when she devoured two boxes of Godiva chocolates left on the floor by a visiting friend, ate every one while we were out at dinner, and then forced me to chase her around the apartment when I got home, as she puked viscous chocolate goo over everything, until I slipped in it too. Yes, she survived. The rug? Not so much.

She was also, it has to be said, always emitting noise. She had a classic howl, and when the two of us lived in a tiny box at the end of a wharf she would bay instinctively at every person and every dog she saw come near. It's cute at first. But after a while, she drove most of my neighbors completely potty. I tried the citronella collar, but she found a way to howl that stayed just below the volume that triggered the spray. Howling was what she did. There was no way on Earth I was going to stop it.

But there was one exception to this rule. In my bachelor days, I'd stay out late in Ptown, trying to get laid, and often getting to sleep only in the early hours. I installed some floor-to-ceiling window blinds to block out the blinding sun over the water—so I could sleep late (this was before the blog). Dusty—usually so loud and restless—would wait patiently for me to wake up, and wedge herself between the bottom of the fabric of the blind and the glass in the window. That way, she kept an eye on all the various threats, while basking in the heat and light of the morning. And until the minute I stirred, despite all the coming and going around her, she uttered not a peep. In her entire life, she never woke me up. This is the deal, she seemed to tell me. You feed and walk me and house me on a beach all summer long, and I'll let you sleep in.

It was a deal. She never broke her part of it, and I just finished mine.

Rush Limbaugh Knows Nothing about Christianity

December 3, 2013 | *THE DISH*

———

Well, after Sarah Palin, another scholar of Catholicism has weighed in on Pope Francis. Rush Limbaugh has a truly gold-star hathos alert in a recent diatribe, brilliantly titled:

> *It's Sad How Wrong Pope Francis Is*
> *(Unless It's a Deliberate Mistranslation by Leftists)*

Does it get more awesomely hathetic than that?

In some ways, of course, Limbaugh is on to something. The pope of the Catholic Church really is offering a rebuttal to the pope of the Republican Party, which is what Limbaugh has largely become. In daily encyclicals, Rush is infallible in doctrine and not to be questioned in public. When he speaks on the airwaves, it is always ex cathedra. Callers can get an audience from him, but rarely a hearing. Dissent from his eternal doctrines means excommunication from the GOP and the designation of heretic. His is always the last word.

And in the Church of Limbaugh, market capitalism is an unqualified, eternal good. It is the everlasting truth about human beings. It is inextricable from any concept of human freedom. The fewer restrictions on it, the better. In that cocooned, infallible context, of course, Pope Francis is indeed a commie:

Listen to this. This is an actual quote from what he wrote. "The culture of prosperity deadens us. We are thrilled if the market offers us something new to purchase. In the meantime, all those lives stunted for lack of opportunity seem a mere spectacle. They fail to move us." I mean, that's pretty profound. That's going way beyond matters that are ethical. This is almost a statement about who should control financial markets. He says that the global economy needs government control. I'm telling you, I'm not Catholic, but I know enough to know that this would have been unthinkable for a pope to believe or say just a few years ago.

Really? Limbaugh specifically invokes the great anticommunist pope, John Paul II, as an alleged contrast with this leftist gobbledegook. So let us look at John Paul II's discussion of capitalism and communism in his 1987 encyclical, *Sollicitudo Rei Socialis*:

The tension between East and West is an opposition . . . between two concepts of the development of individuals and peoples, both concepts being imperfect and in need of radical correction. . . . This is one of the reasons why the Church's social doctrine adopts a critical attitude towards both liberal capitalism and Marxist collectivism.

My emphasis. The Church has long opposed market capitalism as the core measure of human well-being. Aquinas even taught that interest-bearing loans were inherently unjust in the most influential theological document in Church history. The fundamental reason is that market capitalism measures human life by a materialist rubric. And Jesus radically taught us to give up all our possessions, to renounce everything except our "daily bread," to spend our lives serving the poverty-stricken takers rather than aspiring to be the wealthy and powerful makers. He told the Mark Zuckerberg of his day to give everything away to the poor, if he really wanted to be happy.

Limbaugh has obviously never read the Gospels. He has never read the parables. His ideology is so extreme it even trashes, because it does not begin to understand, the core principles of *capitalism*, as laid out by Adam Smith. Market capitalism is and always has been a regulated construction of government, not some kind of state of nature without it. Indeed, without proper regulation to maintain a proper and fair and transparent market, it is doomed to terrible corruption, inefficiency, injustice, and abuse.

But let us return to Limbaugh's hero, John Paul II, this time in *Centesimus Annus*, written in the wake of Soviet communism's demise:

> *The Marxist solution has failed, but the realities of marginalization and exploita-tion remain in the world, especially the Third World, as does the reality of human alienation, especially in the more advanced countries. Against these phenomena the Church strongly raises her voice. Vast multitudes are still living in conditions of great material and moral poverty. The collapse of the Communist system in so many countries certainly removes an obstacle to facing these problems in an appropriate and realistic way, but it is not enough to bring about their solution.*
>
> *Indeed, there is a risk that a* radical capitalistic ideology *could spread which refuses even to consider these problems, in the* a priori *belief that any attempt to solve them is doomed to failure and which blindly entrusts their solution to the free development of market forces.*

My emphasis again. Could anyone have offered a more potent critique of current Republican ideology than John Paul II? Could anything better illustrate John Paul II's critique of radical capitalist ideology than the GOP's refusal to be concerned in any way about a fundamental question like access to basic health care for millions of citizens in the richest country on Earth?

Sorry, Rush, but if you think this critique of capitalism is something dreamed up by the current pope alone, you know nothing about Catholicism, nothing about John Paul II, and nothing about Christianity. But I guess we knew that already, even though the ditto heads still believe, like that particularly dim bulb Paul Ryan, that Ayn Rand and Jesus Christ are somehow compatible, when they are, in fact, diametrically opposed *in every single respect*.

Notice, however, as I noted yesterday, that the Church in no way disputes the fact that market capitalism is by far the least worst means of raising stan-dards of living and ending poverty and generating wealth that can be used to cure disease, feed the hungry, and protect the vulnerable. What the Church is disputing is that, beyond our daily bread, material well-being is a proper criterion for judging human morality or happiness. On a personal level, the Church teaches, as Jesus unambiguously did, that material goods beyond a certain point are actually pernicious and destructive of human flourishing. I hesitate to think, for example, what Limbaugh would have made of Saint Francis, the pope's namesake. Francis, after all, spurned the inheritance of his father's flourishing business to wash the bodies of lepers, sleep in ditches, refuse all money for labor, and use begging as the only morally acceptable form of receiving any money at all. In the Church of Limbaugh, there is no greater heretic than Saint Francis. Francis even believed in the sanctity of the natural world, regarding animals as reflecting the pied beauty of a mysterious divinity. Sarah Palin, in contrast, sees them solely as dinner.

Which gets to the deeper issue of materialism.

Nothing better demonstrates the antipathy of the current Republican right to Christianity—indeed its constant, relentless war on Christianity—than the following refreshingly candid confession of spiritual barrenness from Limbaugh:

> I want to go back to this quote from the pope again, from his—there's the name for the document. I can't think of it and I don't have it in front of me. "The culture of prosperity deadens us. We are thrilled if the market offers us something new to purchase. In the meantime, all those lives stunted for lack of opportunity seem a mere spectacle. They fail to move us." I'm not even sure what the connection there is.
>
> We are thrilled if the market offers us something new to buy? I guess there's something wrong with that. We're not supposed to be thrilled if there's something new to buy. That's how I interpret it. Now, let me give you a fascinating stat I just learned today. The iPhone 5S, which is the top-of-the-line iPhone, was announced way back in September, and has been in shortage ever since.
>
> They have been unable to meet the demand, for whatever reason. They have just recently caught up, and would you like to know how they did it? They have put one million people on different assembly lines, 600 employees per assembly line at the factory in China at the one factory, where they are making 500,000 iPhones a day, and they still haven't caught up to demand.
>
> That's a lot of people who are thrilled with something new to buy.

Er, yes, Rush. But the pope is not making an empirical observation. Insofar as he is, he agrees with you. What he's saying is that this passion for material things is not what makes us good or happy. That's all. And that's a lot for

Limbaugh to chew on. And if the mania for more and more materialist thrills distracts us from, say, the plight of a working American facing bankruptcy because of cancer, or the child of an illegal immigrant with no secure home, then it is a deeply immoral distraction. There's something almost poignant in Limbaugh's inability even to understand that material goods are not self-evidently the purpose of life and are usually (and in Jesus's stern teachings *always*) paths away from God and our own good and our own happiness.

Limbaugh's only recourse when faced with actual Christianity is to conspiracy theories about translations of the pope's words. Perhaps it's the commies who have perpetrated a massive lie through their control of the media. That was Sarah Palin's response to, when confronted with, you know, Christianity for apparently the first time. But you sense that even Rush is beginning to realize there is something more to this, something that could be very destructive to his sealed, cocooned, materialist ideology of one. *Hang on a minute*, you almost hear him saying to himself. . . .

Yes, Rush, hang on a minute. Christianity is one of the most powerful critiques of radical market triumphalism. And it's now coming—more plainly and unmistakably in our lifetimes—to a church near you.

What Is the Meaning
of Pope Francis?

December 17, 2013 | *THE DISH*

Y ou don't have to be a believer to recognize a moment of grace. By "grace" I mean those precious, rare times when exactly what you were expecting gives way to something utterly different, when patterns of thought and behavior we have grown accustomed to and at times despaired of suddenly cede to something new and marvelous. It may be the moment when a warrior unexpectedly lays down his weapon, when the sternest disciplinarian breaks into a smile, when an ideologue admits error, when a criminal seeks forgiveness, or when an addict hits bottom and finally sees a future. Grace is the proof that hope is not groundless.

How to describe the debut of Pope Francis and not immediately think of grace? For much of this new century, Christianity seemed to be in close-to-terminal crisis. Among the fastest-growing groups in society were the nones—those indifferent to religion entirely. Especially among the young, Christians became increasingly identified with harsh judgments, acrid fundamentalism, the smug bromides of the Prosperity Gospel or, more trivially, neurotic cultural obsessions like the alleged "war on Christmas." Evangelical leaders often came and went in scandal, or intolerance, or both. Obsessed with issues of sexual morality, mainstream evangelicalism and the Catholic hierarchy in America entered into an alliance with one major political party, the GOP, further weakening Christianity's role in transcending politics, let alone partisanship. Christian leaders seemed too often intent on denial of what intelligent people of goodwill saw simply as reality—of evolution, of science, of human diversity, of the actual lives of modern Christians themselves. Christian defensiveness was everywhere, as atheism grew in numbers and confidence and zeal.

To make matters far, far worse, the Catholic hierarchy was exposed these past two decades as, in part, a criminal conspiracy to rape the most innocent and vulnerable and to protect their predators. There is almost nothing as evil as the rape of a child—and yet the institution allegedly representing the love of God on Earth perpetrated it, covered it up, and escaped full accountability for it on a scale that is still hard to fathom. You cannot overstate the brutal toll this rightly took on Catholicism's moral authority. Even once-reflexively Catholic countries—like Ireland and Belgium—collapsed into secularism almost overnight, as ordinary Catholics couldn't begin to comprehend how the successors to Peter could have perpetrated and enabled such evil. And meanwhile, the great argument of the modern, post-1968 papacy—against nonprocreative and nonmarital sex for straights and against all sex for gays— ended in intellectual and practical defeat in almost the entire West, including among most Catholics themselves. American Catholics have long been one of the most supportive religious demographics for marriage equality. And when a debate about contraception and health-care reform emerged in the United States early last year, the Catholic bishops chose to launch a defining crusade against something that countless Catholic women had used at some point in their lives.

And in all this, the papacy was increasingly absent from public debate, focused on building a smaller, purer church in seclusion from what Benedict XVI saw as the moral relativism of modernity. His vision of the Church was securing its ramparts to wait out a new, long age of barbarism (as Saint Benedict had done many centuries before as the Roman Empire crumbled), pulling up the drawbridge in rituals, customs, and doctrines that became almost ends in themselves. This is what some have referred to as the "Benedict Option" for the Church—a term inspired by a powerful jeremiad by the philosopher Alasdair MacIntyre, *After Virtue*, in which he despaired of "the new dark ages already upon us." What we needed, MacIntyre thought, was another Saint Benedict, the man who gave rise to the Church's monastic system—in other words, the kind of small, pure, separate communities that helped Christianity survive after the decline of the Roman Empire. Gone was the sublime, striding confidence of the charismatic anticommunist Pope John Paul II in the first years of his papacy; what remained was what his gregarious, powerful personality had for a while obscured—a pinched, arch-conservative Catholicism, more attuned to early twentieth-century Poland or Bavaria than to the multicultural twenty-first-century generations of an increasingly global world. Three decades after his charismatic appearance on the world stage, we can now clearly see that John Paul II and his successor bequeathed a much stronger papacy in a much weaker church.

And then, out of the blue, two remarkable things: the first modern papal resignation and the whisper of a name emerging from the Sistine Chapel as the conclave of cardinals decided on a successor. The name had always been a sacred one in the long history of Christianity; it was a name no pope had ever dared to claim before, a name that resonated through the centuries with the possibility of starting from scratch, from the street and the gutter, from the leper colonies and the wildernesses.

That name was Francis.

I

There has, of course, been an immediate struggle to co-opt Pope Francis for both "right" and "left" in the exhausted categories of the culture war we seem unable to move beyond in American public life. And perhaps the most important and emphatic thing to be said of Francis so far is that this rubric— especially when drawn from the American political debate—cannot explain or elucidate him. We have to leave those categories behind, because they are a sad and unimaginative disservice to what Francis has so far said and done as the Bishop of Rome. And that's particularly true for those on the American Catholic right who are still insisting, if with ever-greater circumspection, that nothing has changed of any substance at all.

Much of what so many people have been struck by, these traditionalists insist, are merely gestures, surface statements, and acts that are about presentation and public relations, rather than the body of faith itself. Francis has not changed an iota of doctrine, the cold-water throwers insist. He coauthored his first encyclical, *Lumen Fidei*, with his predecessor, Benedict XVI, for whom he has expressed nothing but admiration, affection, and respect. His searing critique of the ideology of unfettered capitalism—though shocking to some with no knowledge of Catholic social thought—is one that both John Paul II and Benedict XVI shared and expressed, at times more passionately. On the social issues that the press fixates on, such as homosexuality, Francis, while starkly different in tone, has not altered the doctrinal substance. Female priests remain a nonstarter. Francis has budged not an inch from the Church's concern for the unborn or for marriage as a heterosexual institution. Move along, they urgently insist. There is nothing new here.

But, of course, there is. There is something quite stupendously new—as Catholics and especially non-Catholics have sensed. No pope emerges and immediately changes teachings that have been integral to decades and centuries of Christian practice and belief. To expect such is to misunderstand the very nature of the Church and its slow, internal means of reflection, renewal, and reform. But without such specific measures, what can we point to? What actually is this newness that cannot quite be summarized by specific, immediate injunctions?

Perhaps the simplest way to understand what's new is to address a first-order question: What is Francis's own understanding of the office he now holds, and how is it different from his predecessors'? Many non-Catholics and some of the most fervent Catholics see the papacy as the defining institution of the Church—even imparting to it an infallibility it has rarely claimed to exercise. The papacy is both the final arbiter of truth or falsehood within the Catholic universe and also a pragmatic institution, designed to bring a vast and often-unruly flock into uniformity. Its power within the Church has waxed and waned over the centuries—vying with local bishops, national bishops' conferences, and more, all the way down to divergent practices from parish to parish—but it became a rallying institution for traditionalists in their fight against the modern world in the nineteenth century—and has remained so ever since. Since it can be the only effective tool for order in the Church, it has long been central to the project of orthodoxy—and it got a new lease of extraordinary life under Pope John Paul II and his successor, Benedict XVI.

Enter Francis. In his immediately famous interview published in English by the Jesuit magazine *America*, the new pope was asked how he would like to describe himself as a way of introduction:

The pope stares at me in silence. I ask him if this is a question that I am allowed to ask. . . . He nods that it is, and he tells me: "I do not know what might be the most fitting description. . . . I am a sinner. This is the most accurate definition. It is not a figure of speech, a literary genre. I am a sinner."

Now this is not doctrinally new. Every pope is a sinner, just as every human being is. But not every pope has immediately and instinctively *defined* himself as such. Not every pope introduces himself by abandoning every trace of inherited, acquired authority that comes with the office itself and begins from scratch, as a human being, as a *sinner*. In fact, from the very beginning of his Pontificate, Francis has consciously abandoned the idea of papal authority as the moral force behind his words and actions. Some of this is in gestures—his refusal to live in the papal palace, for example, preferring to live in the hostel he stayed in while attending the conclave to elect a new pope; his preference for simple vestments in stark contrast to his predecessor's ornate and bedazzled costumes; and his eschewal of the honorifics associated with papal authority in favor of the simple title "Bishop of Rome."

Some of it is in words. I was struck by the first he spoke as pope. On the balcony, before vast crowds, he said, "Brothers and sisters, good evening"—an almost informal, colloquial greeting. Then: "You all know that the duty of the conclave was to give a bishop to Rome. It seems that my brother cardinals have gone almost to the ends of the Earth to get him . . . but here we are. The diocesan community of Rome now has its bishop. Thank you!" Again: he almost goes out of his way to speak to equals, not subjects, and with a touch of humor. And notice again the downplaying of the role of pope: "*a* bishop *to* Rome." He prayed for his predecessor, on traditional lines, but then broke the rules again:

And now I would like to give the blessing, but first—first I ask a favor of you: before the bishop blesses his people, I ask you to pray to the Lord that he will bless me: the prayer of the people asking the blessing for their bishop. Let us make, in silence, this prayer: your prayer over me.

In that simple gesture, he reversed roles with the crowd. He was not there to bless them *until they had prayed for him*—and that was a request, a *favor*, not an instruction. In a vast public spectacle, we stumbled immediately upon intimacy. And that intimacy has continued.

How many popes, for example, have spoken of their internal spiritual experiences in the conclave and after? From the *America* interview:

> *[Francis] tells me that when he began to realize that he might be elected, on Wednesday, March 13, during lunch, he felt a deep and inexplicable peace and interior consolation come over him, along with a great darkness, a deep obscurity about everything else. And those feelings accompanied him until his election later that day.*

Then an insight from when he first realized he had been elected, from a dialogue with Eugenio Scalfari, the atheist founder of *La Repubblica*, who paraphrased Francis's remarks from memory. Francis:

> *Before I accepted I asked if I could spend a few minutes in the room next to the one with the balcony overlooking the square. My head was completely empty and I was seized by a great anxiety. To make it go away and relax I closed my eyes and made every thought disappear, even the thought of refusing to accept the position, as the liturgical procedure allows.*
>
> *I closed my eyes and I no longer had any anxiety or emotion. At a certain point I was filled with a great light. It lasted a moment, but to me it seemed very long. Then the light faded, I got up suddenly and walked into the room where the cardinals were waiting and the table on which was the act of acceptance. I signed it. . . .*

Anyone blessed with a mystical experience will know what he's speaking about. His prayer here is almost Buddhist—making "every thought disappear." But what's more striking than the simpleness of this meditation is how willing he is to open up in public about the deepest moments in his interior life, to divest the papacy of any veiled mystique or authority, and to relate this moment of mysticism not in an encyclical or a papal audience, but to an *atheist* in a *newspaper*.

The importance of this only truly hits home when you consider the project of his two predecessors in the wake of the Second Vatican Council, the Catholic Church's first profound attempt to grapple with the challenges of modernity in a way that was not entirely defensive and afraid. This was the council that gave us the Mass in the vernacular, that recognized the importance of religious freedom, that opened up the avenues of ecumenical dialogue, that attempted to recover the wisdom of the early Church, that brought Scripture back more powerfully into the Catholic conversation, and that finally came to terms with the original sin of the Church: anti-Semitism.

Both John Paul II and Benedict XVI were creatures of this council—with Benedict, then Joseph Ratzinger, known at the time as being sympathetic to reform, even serving as a theological consultant to the council. But in the wake of confusion over the council's implementation, liturgical excesses, theological heresies, and declining church attendance, and as the sexual revolution took ever-firmer root in the West, retrenchment arrived. Pope Paul VI unilaterally doubled down against the pill in 1968 and the young Polish pope who followed in the Reagan-Thatcher era went further still. While never denying the centrality of the moment when Pope John XXIII opened the doors and windows of the Church to the modern world in 1962, both John Paul II and Benedict XVI were intent on correcting what they both viewed as its dangers to orthodoxy. In response to new dialogues about modernity, women, sexuality, and liberation theology, John Paul II and his chief theological enforcer, Ratzinger, rebuilt Catholic doctrine around a newly powerful and authoritative papacy and a rigid, unchangeable set of rules regarding faith and morals. The newly potent papacy, its once-again unquestionable doctrines emanating from Ratzinger's own Congregation for the Doctrine of the Faith, was intent on suppressing heresies of various kinds, monitoring the universities, seminaries, and religious groups for signs of dissent, and reasserting traditional Catholicism against what both men saw as the unraveling of uniformity in the 1960s and 1970s.

They buttressed this increasingly top-down, centralized, thoroughly orthodox governance with the elevation of ultra-conservative trends in the Church, from Opus Dei, with its practices of physical mortification, to the Legionaries of Christ, headed by the notorious child molester Marcial Maciel, and the reactionary Society of Saint Pius X, which included a Holocaust denier among its luminaries. The key to restoring the Church's moral authority and doctrinal orthodoxy was, for both John Paul II and Benedict XVI, a centralized church, where all roads led to the Vatican, and where every bishop was elevated according to his unquestioned dedication to the restorationist project.

And this is the most striking and immediate change since Francis's election. The new pope has not just repudiated that legacy of a supreme pontiff in gestures; he has emphatically reversed it in words and acts, both formal and informal. In his recent Apostolic Exhortation, "The Joy of the Gospel," Francis writes explicitly of the limits of his own influence on the Church:

> Nor do I believe that the papal magisterium should be expected to offer a definitive or complete word on every question which affects the Church and the world. It is not advisable for the Pope to take the place of local Bishops in the discernment of every issue which arises in their territory. In this sense, I am conscious of the need to promote a sound "decentralization."

To repeat: what is said by the papal magisterium is neither definitive nor complete for the whole Church. The voice of the Bishop of Rome is one voice among many. This is a clear and blunt unwinding of a core project for his predecessors, an emphatic return to the themes of the Second Vatican Council. Francis acknowledges that this may mean all sorts of unpredictable ideas, arguments, and practices emerging in the Church again, as the firm papal grip on orthodoxy is relaxed:

> God's word is unpredictable in its power. The Gospel speaks of a seed which, once sown, grows by itself, even as the farmer sleeps. The Church has to accept this unruly freedom of the word, which accomplishes what it wills in ways that surpass our calculations and ways of thinking.

It's worth noting the parable from which the metaphor of the seed comes:

> This is what the kingdom of God is like. A man scatters seed on the ground. Night and day, whether he sleeps or gets up, the seed sprouts and grows, though he does not know how. All by itself the soil produces grain—first the stalk, then the head, then the full kernel in the head.

The papacy cannot control the word or the work of God. It has an "unruly freedom." Few ideas were more anathema to the Church as understood by Joseph Ratzinger. For Ratzinger, "unruly freedom" was the problem, not the solution. But notice also the premise of this parable—in my emphasis. The farmer *does not know* how the seed grows. It is a mystery. And the second great correction of Benedict, after the abrupt removal of the papacy from its authoritarian pedestal, is an epistemology of doubt as the central truth of faith.

Benedict XVI and John Paul II focused on restoring dogmatic certainty as the counterpart to papal authority. Francis is arguing that both, if taken too far, can be sirens leading us *away* from God, not ensuring our orthodoxy but sealing us off in calcified positions and rituals that can come to mean nothing outside themselves. He is not shy about saying this, even though the contrast with his immediate—and still-living—predecessor is close to shocking:

> *In this quest to seek and find God in all things there is still an area of uncertainty. There must be. If a person says that he met God with total certainty and is not touched by a margin of uncertainty, then this is not good. For me, this is an important key. If one has the answers to all the questions—that is the proof that God is not with him. It means that he is a false prophet using religion for himself. The great leaders of the people of God, like Moses, have always left room for doubt. You must leave room for the Lord, not for our certainties; we must be humble.*
>
> *Uncertainty is in every true discernment that is open to finding confirmation in spiritual consolation.*

Or in blunter fashion:

> *If the Christian is a restorationist, a legalist, if he wants everything clear and safe, then he will find nothing. Tradition and memory of the past must help us to have the courage to open up new areas to God.*

Perhaps another way to describe this would be a profound critique of the desiccated promise of fundamentalism. Fundamentalism requires an absolute, unchanging revelation of truth in every particular. It is Truth beyond history, outside of time, revealed definitively and unquestionable in every detail. In its Protestant forms, it can mean a biblical literalism in which every single word in the Bible is to be understood as empirically true. In more recent Catholic formulations, it means that the Truth (and it is always with a capital *T*) is only securely located in an infallible, authoritative vicar of Christ on Earth. Without that total certainty and absolute authority, we are lost in a miasma of our own relativism, mistaking feelings for facts, sins for wishes. Benedict XVI was intimately familiar with this kind of fundamentalism. The apex of his career before the papacy was being the prefect of the Congregation for the Doctrine of the Faith, the Holy Office which was once the Inquisition. In his 1986 disciplining of the theologian Charles Curran, then-prefect Joseph Ratzinger put the rules of his view of the Church this way:

> *The faithful must accept not only the infallible magisterium. They are to give the religious submission of intellect and will to the teaching which the supreme pontiff or the college of bishops enunciate on faith and morals when they exercise the authentic magisterium, even if they do not intend to proclaim it with a definitive act.*

That's an almost totalitarian demand: the religious submission of intellect and will to the "*supreme* pontiff." The totality of that submission rests on Ratzinger's Augustinian notion of divine revelation: it is always a radical gift, it must always be accepted without question, it comes from above to those utterly unworthy below, and we are too flawed, too sinful, too human to question it in even the slightest respect. And if we ever compromise an iota on that absolute, authentic, top-down truth, then we can know nothing as true. We are, in fact, lost forever.

And yet here are the words of the new Bishop of Rome, speaking of relative truths with Rabbi Abraham Skorka of Argentina in 2010:

> *Rabbi, you said one thing, which in part, is certain: we can say what God is not, we can speak of his attributes, but we cannot say what He is. That apophatic dimension, which reveals how I speak about God, is critical to our theology. The English mystics speak a lot about this theme. There is a book by one of them, from the 13th century,* The Cloud of Unknowing, *that attempts again and again to describe God and always finishes pointing to what He is not. . . .*
>
> *I would also classify as arrogant those theologies that not only attempted to define with certainty and exactness God's attributes, but also had the pretense of saying who He was.*

> *The Book of Job is a continuous discussion about the definition of God. There*
> *are four wise men that elaborate this theological search and everything ends with*
> *Job's expression: "By hearsay I had heard of you, but now my eye has seen you."*
> *Job's final image of God is different from his vision of God in the beginning.*
> *The intention of this story is that the notion that the four theologians have is*
> *not true, because God always is being sought and found. We are presented with*
> *this paradox: we seek Him to find Him and because we find Him, we seek Him.*
> *It is a very Augustinian game.*

It is only in living that we achieve hints and guesses—and only hints and guesses—of what the divine truly is. And because the divine is found and lost by humans in time and history, there is no reachable truth for humans outside that time and history. We are part of an unfolding drama in which the Christian, far from clinging to some distant, pristine Truth he cannot fully understand, will seek to understand and discern the "signs of the times" as one clue as to how to live now, in the footsteps of Jesus. Or in the words of T. S. Eliot:

> *There is only the fight to recover what has been lost*
> *And found and lost again and again: and now, under conditions*
> *That seem unpropitious. But perhaps neither gain nor loss.*
> *For us, there is only the trying. The rest is not our business.*

||

How did this deep shift suddenly happen? More to the point, how could it have come from a church hierarchy relentlessly selected and promoted for more than thirty years according to fealty to the Ratzinger project? Where, in other words, did Jorge Bergoglio come from?

The answer is that he was always there. The indispensable English-language biography of the pope, *Pope Francis: Untying the Knots* by Paul Vallely, provides solid evidence that Bergoglio was the runner-up to Ratzinger in the 2005 conclave. Far from being on the margins of the global Church, Bergoglio was at its very center. He was a wunderkind in the Church in the Western Hemisphere, a Jesuit who swiftly soared through the ranks to become the Provincial Superior for the Society of Jesus throughout Argentina at the tender age of thirty-six, just three months after he had taken his final vows as a Jesuit. He remained in that post for the following six years—years in which the Argentine junta initiated its infamous "dirty war" against perceived enemies of the state, a war that would continue with incalculable human cost from 1976 to 1983.

The Argentine context is essential in grappling with who Francis is and how he became the leader he now presents to the world. It helps explain why the American political scene has difficulty placing him on its usual right-left spectrum. And it also gives us an insight into a crisis in his spiritual and moral life, a crucible from which he emerged a changed man.

That crucible was occupying a leading church position in a fascist dictatorship conducting simply horrifying acts of terror, torture, and murder in mass silence and throughout all levels of society. And it is fair to say that during this period, Bergoglio was no hero. He was no outspoken opponent of the regime, no prophet, and no icon of human rights. He was an operator, a leader of an institution whose interests he needed to protect.

One incident clearly impacted him above all others, and it's worth unpacking. The core claim against Bergoglio is that he was complicit in the Argentine Navy's 1976 kidnapping and torture of two Jesuit priests, Orlando Yorio and Francisco Jalics. The two were associated with liberation theology, working with the poor and marginalized—what today we might call organizing them—risking the ire of the junta. Bergoglio told them to cool it, because of both his skepticism of liberation theology at the time and his fear of a wider conflict between the Church and the junta.

While it's difficult to sort through the details and conflicting reports about what happened next, it is clear that when the priests refused to follow his advice he decided he could not embrace their mission or give it the Jesuit imprimatur. While not collaboration with the regime, this did amount to the withdrawal of the Church's protection of these priests, effectively leaving them exposed and vulnerable. It was an act of prudential omission, not commission, and it led to the torture of the priests. It was no real consolation that Bergoglio did not surrender the priests and actually played a part in securing their eventual release. (One of them told the press after Bergoglio's ascension to the papacy that it is "wrong to assert that our capture took place at the initiative of Father Bergoglio . . . the fact is, Orlando Yorio and I were not denounced by Father Bergoglio.") The entire episode understandably came to sting his conscience.

Bergoglio had run the Jesuits with a firm hand, becoming known for crisp decisions and follow-through, if also a certain conservatism and, by his own admission, authoritarianism. He was a very successful and powerful young figure—but his sudden ascent to great authority led to what he clearly came to believe was unwitting complicity in the moral evil of the regime. And this changed him. This passage from the interview with *America* is particularly revealing. Francis was asked how his previous experience in church governance has shaped his vision of the Church:

After a brief pause for reflection, Pope Francis becomes very serious, but also very serene, and he responds:

"In my experience as superior in the Society, to be honest, I have not always behaved in that way—that is, I did not always do the necessary consultation. And this was not a good thing. My style of government as a Jesuit at the beginning had many faults. That was a difficult time for the Society: an entire generation of Jesuits had disappeared. Because of this I found myself provincial when I was still very young. I was only 36 years old. That was crazy. I had to deal with difficult situations, and I made my decisions abruptly and by myself. Yes, but I must add one thing: when I entrust something to someone, I totally trust that person. He or she must make a really big mistake before I rebuke that person. But despite this, eventually people get tired of authoritarianism.

"My authoritarian and quick manner of making decisions led me to have serious problems and to be accused of being ultraconservative. I lived a time of great interior crisis when I was in Cordova. To be sure, I have never been like Blessed Imelda [a goody-goody], but I have never been a right-winger. It was my authoritarian way of making decisions that created problems.

"I say these things from life experience and because I want to make clear what the dangers are. Over time I learned many things. The Lord has allowed this growth in knowledge of government through my faults and my sins. So as Archbishop of Buenos Aires, I had a meeting with the six auxiliary bishops every two weeks, and several times a year with the council of priests. They asked questions and we opened the floor for discussion. This greatly helped me to make the best decisions. But now I hear some people tell me: 'Do not consult too much, and decide by yourself.' Instead, I believe that consultation is very important."

It would be a mistake to believe that Jorge Bergoglio came to question the authoritarian structure of papal supremacy because of some ideological position. He came to doubt it because he saw what it could lead to—*in his own life*. And you can see this in the years following his stint as the Jesuits' leader in Argentina. He became the rector of the Colegio de San José, a position he held for about six years. He traveled to Germany to pursue his doctoral studies, researching the work of Romano Guardini. He taught in Argentina upon his return. And then he was sent to the Jesuit community at Córdoba as an ordinary priest, serving as a confessor and spiritual director, the place where he speaks of his "great interior crisis." These years were a time of exile—he was away from his beloved Buenos Aires. From being one of the youngest and most promising Jesuit leaders, he arrived back at square one. With regrets. And questions. And doubts.

And it was in this period that he became fascinated with a somewhat obscure painting. It's a Baroque painting of the Virgin Mary in a church in Augsburg, Germany, called *Mary, Untier of Knots*. It shows Mary patiently focusing on a long, knotted ribbon, gently untying each knot to leave a white, untangled ribbon behind. Since Francis's introduction of a reproduction of the image in Buenos Aires, it has grown in popularity in South America, with the faithful praying in front of it for Mary to "untie the knots" in their own lives.

What strikes me about it is how undoing knots conveys a way of being in the world. It begins with a recognition that life isn't easy, that a smooth and linear path is rarely given to us, that challenges keep presenting themselves. It is not so much the overcoming of these challenges that defines us, but the manner in which we tackle them.

It's possible to get extremely frustrated by knots, after all, as I remember each time I retrieve a set of iPhone earbuds from the black hole of a coat pocket. Your first thought is just anger: How on Earth did this get so fucking tangled up? Your second impulse is to grab it and shake it or even to pull on it to resolve the issue in one stroke. But that only makes things worse. The knots get even tighter. In the end, you realize your only real option—against almost every fiber in your irate being—is to take each knot in turn, patiently and gently undo it, loosen a little, see what happens, and move on to the next. You will never know exactly when all the knots will resolve themselves—it can happen quite quickly, after a while, or seemingly never. But you do know that patience, and concern with the here and now, is the only way to "solve" the "problem." You don't look forward with a plan; you look down with a practice.

This has a relationship with the concept of "discernment" that is integral to Francis's spiritual life, as it is to any Jesuit's. A Christian life is about patience, about the present, and about trust that God is there for us. It does not seek certainty or finality to life's endless ordeals and puzzles. It seeks through prayer and action in the world to listen to God's plan and follow its always-unfolding intimations. It requires waiting. It requires diligence. Here is how Francis describes it:

> I don't have all the answers; I don't even have all the questions. I always think of new questions, and there are always new questions coming forward. But the answers have to be thought out according to the different situations, and you also have to wait for them. I confess that, because of my disposition, the first answer that comes to me is usually wrong. When I'm facing a situation, the first solution I think of is what not to do. Because of this I have learned not to trust my first reaction. When I'm calmer, after passing through the crucible of solitude, I come closer to understanding what has to be done. . . . You can do a great deal of harm with the decisions you make. One can be very unfair.

It is hard not to see the shadows of the tortured and the disappeared lingering over that epiphany in Bergoglio's life: "You can do a great deal of harm with the decisions you make." And it is hard not to see Mary, the Untier of Knots, as some kind of breakthrough in his understanding of what it requires to do God's will. Even the Mother of God was asked to accept the hardest task of all: to lose her own son for reasons she never fully understood—and simply had to accept—at the time.

III

We may never know why exactly Benedict resigned as he did. But I suspect mere exhaustion of the body and mind was not the whole of it. He had to see, because his remains such a first-rate mind, that his project had failed, that the levers he continued to pull—more and more insistent doctrinal orthodoxy, more political conflict with almost every aspect of the modern world, more fastidious control of liturgy—simply had no impact anymore. You can see how, in the maintenance of order, Benedict had become lost in the rules and categories that Jesus warned against. His great encyclical, *Deus Caritas Est*, reads like an intellectual brilliantly expressing the love of God—but not a pastor who has easily breathed that love into the Church and the world. And so, as Bergoglio had gracefully conceded to him in the 2005 conclave, perhaps one way to see his resignation is as a graceful concession back.

Our relationship with the divine, in Catholic thought, is always a mixture of total unworthiness and yet also essential worthiness. Somehow, we have to understand ourselves as both made by God and yet deeply alienated from God. So how do we live with this tension? For Benedict, the critical posture toward God is vertical—from heaven to Earth, from pontiff to people, and back. This doesn't mean there is no living in the world, no sense of truth in sacramental life, no community, no faith-in-action. But it does emphasize the Augustinian alienation of it all. For Francis, in contrast, the alienation is not so great, and the world more Thomist. The world is good and we live only now, and in it.

And so for Francis, the central posture is clearly horizontal—outward toward others, inclusive, and engaged in constant dialogue. Again, this does not deny the utter grace of divine revelation, but this Christian lives far less stricken in his fallen skin. And so while Benedict offered Mass with his back to the congregation, focused on the divine, Francis, as noted by Paul Vallely, immediately shifted back to facing the people, building a community of equals in the eyes of God. Francis deliberately calls himself the Bishop of Rome, not the Supreme Pontiff, breaking down some of the vertical lines. He is emphatic about decentralization, about a mode of leadership that is closer to community organizing than to unquestioned authority in all things:

> The ministers of the Gospel must be people who can warm the hearts of the people, who walk through the dark night with them, who know how to dialogue and to descend themselves into their people's night, into the darkness, but without getting lost. The people of God want pastors, not clergy acting like bureaucrats or government officials. The bishops, particularly, must be able to support the movements of God among their people with patience, so that no one is left behind. But they must also be able to accompany the flock that has a flair for finding new paths.

The pope must *accompany* those challenging existing ways of doing things! Others may know better than he does. Or, to feminize away the patriarchy:

> *I dream of a church that is a mother and shepherdess. The church's ministers must be merciful, take responsibility for the people, and accompany them like the good Samaritan, who washes, cleans, and raises up his neighbor. This is pure Gospel.*

And, of course, this means an openness to new things, new truths, new understandings. If the central element of fundamentalism is an orientation to a pristine past—an inerrant, literal Scripture which must never be amended; or an apostolic succession descending from the first pope, Peter, to the present day in one, unbreakable chain of unquestionable authority—the key to Francis's expression of faith is an openness to the future, a firm place in the present, and a willingness to entertain doubt, to discern new truths and directions, and to *grow*. Think of Benedict's insistence on submission of intellect and will to the only authentic truth (the pope's), and then read this:

> *Within the Church countless issues are being studied and reflected upon with great freedom. Differing currents of thought in philosophy, theology, and pastoral practice, if open to being reconciled by the Spirit in respect and love, can enable the Church to grow, since all of them help to express more clearly the immense riches of God's word. For those who long for a monolithic body of doctrine guarded by all and leaving no room for nuance, this might appear as undesirable and leading to confusion. But in fact such variety serves to bring out and develop different facets of the inexhaustible riches of the Gospel.*

Underlying all this is a profound shift away from an idea of religion as doctrine and toward an idea of religion as a way of life. Faith is a constantly growing garden, not a permanently finished masterpiece. By this I do not mean to say that doctrine is somehow irrelevant. It isn't. It is still there insofar as we can ever fully understand it. But sometimes, it is appropriate to accept the limitations of what we can understand—and get on with the always deeply simple Christian injunction to love God and to love one another as Jesus loved his friends. We live as temporal, human beings in a finite, fallen world; and faith is, for Francis, a way of life, not a set of propositions. It is a way of life in community with others, lived in the present yet always, deeply, insistently aware of eternity.

Here you feel the profound impact of Saint Ignatius of Loyola's concept of discernment and "contemplation in action." Father Howard Gray, S.J., has put it simply enough:

> Ultimately, Ignatian spirituality trusts the world as a place where God dwells and labors and gathers all to himself in an act of forgiveness where that is needed, and in an act of blessing where that is prayed for.

Life itself provides us with truth beyond that revealed in any text or by any authority. The journey itself changes who we are and that new self, if open to God, is actually our real self. We do not begin in the shadow of a great truth and measure our life by how far we fall shy of it. We live in a world that already contains that truth and we measure our life by our ability to find it. As Michael Oakeshott put it,

> [R]eligion . . . is not, as some would persuade us, an interest attached to life, a subsidiary activity; nor is it a power which governs life from the outside with a, no doubt divine, but certainly incomprehensible, sanction for its authority. It is simply life itself. . . . The man of the world is careless of nothing save himself and his life; but to the religious man, life is too short and uncertain to be hoarded, too valuable to be spent at the pleasure of others, or the past or of the future, too precious to be thrown away on something he is not convinced is his highest good. In this sense, then, we are all, at moments, religious. . . .

This is what Francis captures: the messiness of a Christian faith actually lived. And such a faith has to prioritize — so as not to get caught up in extraneous dogmas or exhausted tropes. Here's a key passage from Francis:

> The dogmatic and moral teachings of the church are not all equivalent. The church's pastoral ministry cannot be obsessed with the transmission of a disjointed multitude of doctrines to be imposed insistently. Proclamation in a missionary style focuses on the essentials, on the necessary things: this is also what fascinates

and attracts more, what makes the heart burn, as it did for the disciples at Emmaus. We have to find a new balance; otherwise even the moral edifice of the church is likely to fall like a house of cards, losing the freshness and fragrance of the Gospel. The proposal of the Gospel must be more simple, profound, radiant. It is from this proposition that the moral consequences then flow.

And so Francis, like Jesus, has had such an impact in such a short period of time simply because of the way he seems to be. His being does not rely on any claims to inherited, ecclesiastical authority; his very way of life is the only moral authority he wants to claim.

IV

Countless tales and aphorisms have been attributed to Saint Francis of Assisi, most of which are apocryphal. But one stands out, along with the lyrics to songs that still ring with strange wonder today. It is his famous injunction: "Preach the Gospel always. If necessary, with words." His preaching was as untraditional as it was effective. He was famous (and not always favorably) for suddenly engaging in wild, interpretive dances on the streets. Legend has him disappearing into flocks of birds to talk and pray with them, and fearlessly approaching a wolf as if there were no real gulf of understanding between species.

In other words, he changed the world not primarily by what he said but by *how he lived*. Giving up an inheritance, he embraced a poverty of almost pathological dimensions. For periods of time, he would have no shelter except the ruins of churches he voluntarily rebuilt or patched up. He refused any money for labor. He hated the exercise of any power even over his own order, preferring to sit on the floor during meetings and if absolutely forced to make a decision, whispering it in another monk's ear. He even refused to ride a horse, because it elevated him above others. In excruciating pain on his deathbed, he reportedly refused a pillow to rest his head on, then succumbed to that small comfort, and then berated a fellow monk who had brought the pillow to him. He lived by standards no one else truly understood, but they didn't need to understand. They merely had to witness.

Much has been made of Francis's gestures since becoming pope. Cynics may regard some of it as public relations—but those cynics, especially by today's standards, are remarkably rare. What some may not have seen is how these actions—of humility, of kindness, of compassion, and of service—are integral to Francis's resuscitation of Christian moral authority. He is telling us that Christianity, before it is anything else, is a way of life, an orientation toward the whole, a living commitment to God through others. And he is telling us that nothing—*nothing*—is more powerful than this.

Could any sustained encyclical ever convey the power of the pope's instinctive embrace of a man in the crowd whose skin was covered with disfiguring tumors? I don't need to tell you about that incident because you all have an image of it instantly in your mind. It is the image that contemporaries must have seen in the life of Saint Francis as well: one of his first acts after his conversion was to wander into a leper colony and embrace its inhabitants, wash their bodies, and tend to their wounds. No words can sum up the power of overcoming visceral human disgust with transcendent love for the person behind that disfiguring mask of disease.

Doctrine is insufficient to convey this truth. And one remembers all too quickly that this was the impact Jesus had. It was not his words alone that transfixed so many around him; it was the manner in which he lived—outside human boundaries, inside the human soul. Jesus gave us no theology. We had to wait for Paul for that. For decades after his crucifixion, it was mainly oral tales of what Jesus had done and the impact he had created that gave us any basis for a theology at all. What Jesus gave us was a mode of living—a mode beyond fear and want and even self-preservation. It wasn't that he died in agony on a cross—thousands and thousands endured similar agonies across the brutal Roman Empire. It was the way he *accepted* that death, and transcended it, that changed human consciousness forever.

And so when Francis talks of Christianity and of the Church, it is not a set of doctrines, let alone a set of politics, that animates him. It is what happens when doctrine cedes to life, and when truth transforms that life. "I have a dogmatic certainty," Francis wryly says. "God is in every person's life. God is in everyone's life. Even if the life of a person has been a disaster, even if it is destroyed by vices, drugs or anything else—God is in this person's life. You can, you must try to seek God in every human life. Although the life of a person is a land full of thorns and weeds, there is always a space in which the good seed can grow. You have to trust God."

When he decided on the Thursday before Easter to wash the feet of several imprisoned juvenile offenders, including two women, it was not the first time he had broken with the tradition of only washing the feet of men. He had done the same thing as Archbishop of Buenos Aires. But it was the first time a pope had simply improvised a ritual formally set down by the Congregation for Divine Worship. And it was not hard to see the message he was sending: that the love of God knows no gender or even denominational boundaries (two of the people whose feet he washed were Muslim). More to the point, simply by doing this—and not explaining it—the act transforms the person doing it. You cannot think your way into this. You have to walk confidently into the adventure of discernment.

And so faith becomes real through living, not thinking. In his dialogue with Scalfari, Francis wrote:

> *I would not speak about, not even for those who believe, an "absolute" truth, in the sense that absolute is something detached, something lacking any relationship. Now, the truth is a relationship! This is so true that each of us sees the truth and expresses it, starting from oneself: from one's history and culture, from the situation in which one lives, etc. This does not mean that the truth is variable and subjective. It means that it is given to us only as a way and a life. Was it not Jesus himself who said: "I am the way, the truth, the life"? In other words, the truth is one with love, it requires humbleness and the willingness to be sought, listened to and expressed.*

The truth "is given to us only as a way and a life." And here is another core aspect of Francis's retelling of Christianity that cannot be emphasized enough: he is an anti-ideological pope. For him, ideology means that something alive and growing has been plucked and pickled. It means that openness to God's unknowable future has been ruled out-of-bounds. And this has a direct meaning for evangelization: "We need to remember that all religious teaching ultimately has to be reflected *in the teacher's way of life*, which awakens the assent of the heart, by its nearness, love and witness." My italics.

And so, yes, "proselytism is solemn nonsense." That phrase—deployed by the pope in dialogue with the Italian atheist Eugenio Scalfari (as reported by Scalfari)—may seem shocking at first. But it is not about denying the revelation of Jesus. It is about *how* that revelation is expressed and lived. Evangelism, for Francis, is emphatically not about informing others about the superiority of your own worldview and converting them to it. That kind of proselytism rests on a form of disrespect for another human being. Something else is needed:

> *Instead of seeming to impose new obligations, Christians should appear as people who wish to share their joy, who point to a horizon of beauty and who invite others to a delicious banquet. It is not by proselytizing that the Church grows, but "by attraction."*

Again, you see the priority of practice over theory, of life over dogma. Evangelization is about sitting down with anyone anywhere and listening and sharing and being together. A Christian need not be afraid of this encounter. Neither should an atheist. We are in this together, in the same journey of life, with the same ultimate mystery beyond us. When we start from that place — of radical humility and radical epistemological doubt — proselytism does indeed seem like nonsense, a form of arrogance and detachment, reaching for power, not freedom. And evangelization is not about getting others to submit their intellect and will to some new set of truths; it is about an infectious joy for a new way of living in the world. All it requires — apart from joy and faith — is patience.

v

Then there is the name.

Francis is arguably the most venerated saint since the time of Jesus. His strangeness and intensity have echoed through the Christian imagination for eight centuries, marking him as a special kind of prophet. A bundle of contradictions to the modern mind, he both remains an advocate of total obedience to church authorities yet is also famous for improvising wildly in their absence; he went to Rome to ensure that his fledgling order might not be deemed heretics for their radically new way of life, and then promptly went on to cast a shadow over much of the decadent Catholicism of that era in dark, decrepit contrast with his simplicity and zeal. Bullheaded, intemperate, paranoid, and mystical, you can see the authorities of the time — secular and religious — treating him gingerly and nervously as some kind of exception to every rule. They knew he was special, but couldn't precisely say why. What they couldn't deny was the profound impact he had on those who encountered him.

Just as you cannot overstate the importance of the name of Benedict that Ratzinger took, so, too, the name of Francis with Bergoglio. But unlike Benedict, no one had ever claimed that sacred name before. Such an act of presumption could not have been made lightly—especially for a Jesuit. But, as Francis has explained, the name came to him in the conclave. What meanings does that name evoke in Christian thought and history? And what signs does it foretell?

You could make an argument that it could signal a new era of Catholic concern for the environment as climate change gathers force. One could also see Saint Francis's famous encounter with the Grand Sultan of Egypt as a harbinger of a papal outreach to Islam. But one overwhelming theme has already emerged in Pope Francis's words and actions that echoes the core obsession of his namesake saint: poverty.

Pope Francis insists—and has insisted throughout his long career in the Church—that poverty is a key to salvation. And in choosing the name Francis, he explained last March in Assisi, this was the central reason why:

> He recalled how, as he was receiving more and more votes in the conclave, the cardinal sitting next to him, Cláudio Hummes of Brazil, comforted him "as the situation became dangerous." After the voting reached the two-thirds majority that elected him, applause broke out. Hummes, 78, then hugged and kissed him and told him "Don't forget the poor," the pope recounted, often gesturing with his hands. "That word entered here," he added, pointing to his head.
>
> While the formal voting continued, the pope recalled: "I thought of wars . . . and Francis (of Assisi) is the man of peace, and that is how the name entered my heart, Francis of Assisi, for me he is the man of poverty, the man of peace, the man who loves and protects others."

The connection between peace and poverty is one made by Saint Francis. His conversion came after he had gone off to war in defense of his hometown, and, after witnessing horrifying carnage, became a prisoner of war. After his release from captivity, his strange, mystical journey began.

What you see in the life of Saint Francis is a turn from extreme violence to extreme poverty, as if only the latter could fully compensate for the reality of the former. This was not merely an injunction to serve the poor. It is the belief that it is only by *being* poor or *becoming* poor that we can come close to God. Saint Francis, it must be said again, was completely pathological about this. His followers were to have no possessions at all. Their shelter had to be rudimentary, if any. They lived peripatetic lives—constantly traveling rather than settling down and achieving even minimal creature comforts. The way of life was so extreme it soon divided Francis's followers between the true mystics and those who wanted some semblance of ordinary life. Saint Francis himself walked and walked through sickness and disease until he died in excruciating pain and blindness at the age of forty-four.

And so when we find ourselves shocked by Pope Francis's denunciations of the ideology of unfettered market capitalism, it seems to me we shouldn't suddenly think of Karl Marx. We should think of a thirteenth-century mystic. There is no law of economics here; there is simply the most basic law of the Franciscan order: "To follow the teachings of our Lord Jesus Christ and to walk in his footsteps." (At the beginning of the order, there was no second law. Why, after all, did they need one?)

And this is where the American left may find it hard to wrestle Pope Francis easily into their worldview, just as the American right has. He is obviously open to the welfare state, to protect the dignity of the vulnerable—and certainly much more supportive of it than the current, dominant Randian faction of the Republican Party. But there is little sense that a political or economic system can somehow end the problem of poverty in Francis's worldview. And there is the discomfiting idea that poverty itself is not an unmitigated evil. There is, indeed, a deep and mysterious view, enunciated by Jesus, and held most tenaciously by Saint Francis, that all wealth, all comfort, and all material goods are suspect and that poverty itself is a kind of holy state to which we should all aspire.

That's why Saint Francis remains such a utopian, mystical figure. There was no weighing in his circle of the merits of a just or an unjust war in a fallen world, as Thomas Aquinas wrestled with. There was simply the urgent imperative to live now without war or possessions. There was the need not for a better doctrine—but *for a way of life*. Saint Francis's inspiration for his new mode of living, according to legend, was a Gospel passage, Matthew 10:9, that he heard one day and immediately followed:

> *Get you no gold, nor silver, nor brass in your purses; no wallet for your journey,*
> *neither two coats, nor shoes, nor staff: for the laborer is worthy of his food.*

Not only was Saint Francis to become homeless and give up his patrimony; he was to travel on foot, wearing nothing but a rough tunic held together with rope.

Whatever else it is, this is not progressivism. It sees no structural, human-devised system as a permanent improver of our material lot. It does not envision a world without poverty, but instead a church of the poor and for the poor. The only material thing it asks of the world, or of God, is daily bread — and only for today, never for tomorrow. If this seems extreme, it's because it is — an unreasonable, radical rebellion against the very nature of our physical selves. It allows for no comfort or security in a bodily sense. It suggests instead that it is only by losing both materially that we have a chance for anything like them spiritually. Of course, the religious association with extreme poverty is not restricted to the Christian tradition. But in Saint Francis, it achieves almost transcendent integrity. Many of his followers, it is worth remembering, were often of his own well-to-do class, just as many early Christians were prosperous traders and businesspeople. It was not so much the experience of poverty that propelled them so much as the renunciation of their own wealth and power. This, observers sensed and recorded, gave them a liberation like no other.

It's only when you absorb this radical — and, frankly, impossible — worldview in its original Franciscan form that you can begin to see what it might say to the world today. Remember that Pope Francis believes we exist in human history and need to discern the signs of the times in our own lives. And Saint Francis is a part of his answer. From this perspective, the idea that a society should be judged by the amount of *things* it can distribute to as many people as possible is anathema. The idea that there is a serious social and political crisis if we cannot keep our wealth growing every year above a certain rate is an absurdity.

To put it mildly, this is a twenty-first-century heresy. Which means, I think, that this pope is already emerging and will likely only further emerge as the most potent critic of the newly empowered global capitalist project. In this, of course, Francis is not new. John Paul II was as aggressively critical of Western capitalism as he was of Eastern communism. But there is an obvious difference between the early 1980s and the 2010s. Back then, communism existed as a rival to capitalism and as a more proximate threat to world peace. Now, the only dominant ideology in the world is the ideology of material gain—through either the relatively free markets of the West or the state-controlled markets of the East. And so the Church's message is now harder to obscure. It stands squarely against the entire dominant ethos of our age. It is the final resistance.

For Francis, history has not come to an end, and capitalism, in as much as it is a global ideology that reduces all of human activity to the cold currency of wealth, is simply another "ism" to be toppled in humankind's unfolding journey toward salvation on Earth.

Doctrinal change—in the sexual or institutional terms that the secular world wants—is not likely to be immediately forthcoming in this papacy (although there is no knowing where the newly invigorated debate Francis has enabled will take us). Doctrine, after all, is not the area where the pope believes the action is, or where he believes our true human ability extends. But a new clarity and passion in the critique of global materialism has emerged already. Francis's criticism of the American-style "golden age" of inequality applies, it should be noted, with even more force to the Chinese model, which does not even allow for religious and political liberty within its planet-destroying plunder. What this pope is clearly doing is pitting a church with renewed moral authority against a market ideology which either denies the unforgivable sin of man-made climate change or celebrates it in a materialist dead end.

But these remain hints and guesses about Francis. And he will surely grow as the Church he accompanies evolves once more. The growth will not come, I suspect, by a total or immediate transformation of the Church's institutional structure (although I wouldn't bet against it in due course), nor by some dramatic concession to secular priorities. Francis will grow as the Church reacts to him; it will be a dynamic, not a dogma, and it will be marked less by the revelation of new things than by the new recognition of old things, in a new language.

It will be, if its propitious beginnings are any sign, a patient untying of our collective, life-denying knots.

Democracies End When They Are Too Democractic

May 1, 2016 | *NEW YORK* magazine

A s this dystopian election campaign has unfolded, my mind keeps being tugged by a passage in Plato's *Republic*. It has unsettled—even surprised— me from the moment I first read it in graduate school. The passage is from the part of the dialogue where Socrates and his friends are talking about the nature of different political systems, how they change over time, and how one can slowly evolve into another. And Socrates seemed pretty clear on one sobering point: that "tyranny is probably established out of no other regime than democracy." What did Plato mean by that? Democracy, for him, I discovered, was a political system of maximal freedom and equality, where every lifestyle is allowed and public offices are filled by a lottery. And the longer a democracy lasted, Plato argued, the more democratic it would become. Its freedoms would multiply, its equality spread. Deference to any sort of authority would wither, tolerance of any kind of inequality would come under intense threat, and multiculturalism and sexual freedom would create a city or a country like "a many-colored cloak decorated in all hues."

This rainbow-flag polity, Plato argues, is, for many people, the fairest of regimes. The freedom in that democracy has to be experienced to be believed— with shame and privilege in particular emerging over time as anathema. But it is inherently unstable. As the authority of elites fades, as Establishment values cede to popular ones, views and identities can become so magnificently diverse as to be mutually uncomprehending. And when all the barriers to equality, formal and informal, have been removed; when everyone is equal, when elites are despised, and full license is established to do "whatever one wants," you arrive at what might be called late-stage democracy. There is no kowtowing to authority here, let alone to political experience or expertise.

The very rich come under attack, as inequality becomes increasingly intolerable. Patriarchy is also dismantled: "We almost forgot to mention the extent of the law of equality and of freedom in the relations of women with men and men with women." Family hierarchies are inverted: "A father habituates himself to be like his child and fear his sons, and a son habituates himself to be like his father and to have no shame before or fear of his parents." In classrooms, "as the teacher . . . is frightened of the pupils and fawns on them, so the students make light of their teachers." Animals are regarded as equal to humans; the rich mingle freely with the poor in the streets and try to blend in. The foreigner is equal to the citizen.

And it is when a democracy has ripened as fully as this, Plato argues, that a would-be tyrant will often seize his moment.

He is usually of the elite but has a nature in tune with the time—given over to random pleasures and whims, feasting on plenty of food and sex, and reveling in the nonjudgment that is democracy's civil religion. He makes his move by "taking over a particularly obedient mob" and attacking his wealthy peers as corrupt. If not stopped quickly, his appetite for attacking the rich on behalf of the people swells further. He is a traitor to his class—and soon his elite enemies, shorn of popular legitimacy, find a way to appease him or are forced to flee. Eventually, he stands alone, promising to cut through the paralysis of democratic incoherence. It's as if he were offering the addled, distracted, and self-indulgent citizens a kind of relief from democracy's endless choices and insecurities. He rides a backlash to excess—"too much freedom seems to change into nothing but too much slavery"—and offers himself as the personified answer to the internal conflicts of the democratic mess. He pledges, above all, to take on the increasingly despised elites. And as the people thrill to him as a kind of solution, a democracy willingly, even impetuously, repeals itself.

And so, as I chitchatted over cocktails at a Washington office Christmas party in December, and saw, looming above our heads, the pulsating, angry televised face of Donald Trump on Fox News, I couldn't help but feel a little nausea permeate my stomach. And as I watched frenzied Trump rallies on C-SPAN in the spring, and saw him lay waste to far more qualified political peers in the debates by simply calling them names, the nausea turned to dread. And when he seemed to condone physical violence as a response to political disagreement, alarm bells started to ring in my head. Plato had planted a gnawing worry in my mind a few decades ago about the intrinsic danger of late-democratic life. It was increasingly hard not to see in Plato's vision a murky reflection of our own hyperdemocratic times and in Trump a demagogic, tyrannical character plucked directly out of one of the first books about politics ever written.

Could it be that the Donald has emerged from the populist circuses of pro wrestling and New York City tabloids, via reality television and Twitter, to prove not just Plato but also James Madison right, that democracies "have ever been spectacles of turbulence and contention . . . and have in general been as short in their lives as they have been violent in their deaths"? Is he testing democracy's singular weakness—its susceptibility to the demagogue—by blasting through the fire walls we once had in place to prevent such a person from seizing power? Or am I overreacting?

Perhaps. The nausea comes and goes, and there have been days when the news algorithm has actually reassured me that "peak Trump" has arrived. But it hasn't gone away, and neither has Trump. In the wake of his most recent primary triumphs, at a time when he is perilously close to winning enough delegates to grab the Republican nomination outright, I think we must confront this dread and be clear about what this election has already revealed about the fragility of our way of life and the threat late-stage democracy is beginning to pose to itself.

Plato, of course, was not clairvoyant. His analysis of how democracy can turn into tyranny is a complex one more keyed toward ancient societies than our own (and contains more wrinkles and eddies than I can summarize here). His disdain for democratic life was fueled in no small part by the fact that a democracy had executed his mentor, Socrates. And he would, I think, have been astonished at how American democracy has been able to thrive with unprecedented stability over the last couple of centuries even as it has brought more and more people into its embrace. It remains, in my view, a miracle of constitutional craftsmanship and cultural resilience. There is no place I would rather live. But it is not immortal, nor should we assume it is immune to the forces that have endangered democracy so many times in human history.

Part of American democracy's stability is owed to the fact that the Founding Fathers had read their Plato. To guard our democracy from the tyranny of the majority and the passions of the mob, they constructed large, hefty barriers between the popular will and the exercise of power. Voting rights were tightly circumscribed. The president and vice president were not to be popularly elected but selected by an Electoral College, whose representatives were selected by the various states, often through state legislatures. The Senate's structure (with two members from every state) was designed to temper the power of the more populous states, and its term of office (six years, compared with two for the House) was designed to cool and restrain temporary populist passions. The Supreme Court, picked by the president and confirmed by the Senate, was the final bulwark against any democratic furies that might percolate up from the House and threaten the Constitution. This separation of powers was designed precisely to create sturdy fire walls against democratic wildfires.

Over the centuries, however, many of these undemocratic rules have been weakened or abolished. The franchise has been extended far beyond propertied white men. The presidency is now effectively elected through popular vote, with the Electoral College almost always reflecting the national democratic will. And these formal democratic advances were accompanied by informal ones, as the culture of democracy slowly took deeper root. For a very long time, only the elites of the political parties came to select their candidates at their quadrennial conventions, with the vote largely restricted to party officials from the various states (and often decided in, yes, smoke-filled rooms in large hotel suites). Beginning in the early 1900s, however, the parties began experimenting with primaries, and after the chaos of the 1968 Democratic convention, today's far more democratic system became the norm.

Direct democracy didn't just elect Congress and the president anymore; it expanded the notion of who might be qualified for public office. Once, candidates built a career through experience in elected or cabinet positions or as military commanders; they were effectively selected by peer review. That elitist sorting mechanism has slowly imploded. In 1940, Wendell Willkie, a businessman with no previous political office, won the Republican nomination for president, pledging to keep America out of war and boasting that his personal wealth inoculated him against corruption: "I will be under obligation to nobody except the people." He lost badly to Franklin D. Roosevelt, but nonetheless, since then, nonpolitical candidates have proliferated, from Ross Perot and Jesse Jackson, to Steve Forbes and Herman Cain, to this year's crop of Ben Carson, Carly Fiorina, and, of course, Donald J. Trump. This further widening of our democracy—our increased openness to being led by anyone; indeed, our accelerating preference for outsiders—is now almost complete.

The barriers to the popular will, especially when it comes to choosing our president, are now almost nonexistent. In 2000, George W. Bush lost the popular vote and won the election thanks to Electoral College math and, more egregiously, to a partisan Supreme Court vote. Al Gore's eventual concession spared the nation a constitutional crisis, but the episode generated widespread unease, not just among Democrats. And this year, the delegate system established by our political parties is also under assault. Trump has argued that the candidate with the most votes should get the Republican nomination, regardless of the rules in place. It now looks as if he won't even need to win that argument—that he'll bank enough delegates to secure the nomination uncontested—but he's won it anyway. Fully half of Americans now believe the traditional nominating system is rigged.

Many contend, of course, that American democracy is actually in retreat, close to being destroyed by the vastly more unequal economy of the last quarter century and the ability of the very rich to purchase political influence. This is Bernie Sanders's core critique. But the past few presidential elections have demonstrated that, in fact, money from the ultrarich has been mostly a dud. Barack Obama, whose 2008 campaign was propelled by small donors and empowered by the internet, blazed the trail of the modern-day insurrectionist, defeating the prohibitive favorite in the Democratic primary and later his Republican opponent (both pillars of their parties' Establishments and backed by moneyed elites). In 2012, the fundraising power behind Mitt Romney—avatar of the 1 percent—failed to dislodge Obama from office. And in this presidential cycle, the breakout candidates of both parties have soared without financial support from the elites. Sanders, who is sustaining his campaign all the way to California on the backs of small donors and large crowds, is, to put it bluntly, a walking refutation of his own argument. Trump, of course, is a largely self-funding billionaire—but like Willkie, he argues that his wealth uniquely enables him to resist the influence of the rich and their lobbyists. Those despairing over the influence of Big Money in American politics must also explain the swift, humiliating demise of Jeb Bush and the struggling Establishment campaign of Hillary Clinton. The evidence suggests that direct democracy, far from being throttled, is actually intensifying its grip on American politics.

None of this is necessarily cause for alarm, even though it would be giving the Founding Fathers palpitations. The emergence of the first black president—unimaginable before our more inclusive democracy—is miraculous, a strengthening, rather than weakening, of the system. The days when party machines just fixed things or rigged elections are mercifully done with. The way in which outsider candidates, from Obama to Trump and Sanders, have brought millions of new people into the electoral process is an unmitigated advance. The inclusion of previously excluded voices helps, rather than impedes, our public deliberation. But it is precisely because of the great accomplishments of our democracy that we should be vigilant about its specific, unique vulnerability: its susceptibility, in stressful times, to the appeal of a shameless demagogue.

What the twenty-first century added to this picture, it's now blindingly obvious, was media democracy—in a truly revolutionary form. If late-stage political democracy has taken two centuries to ripen, the media equivalent took around two decades, swiftly erasing almost any elite moderation or control of our democratic discourse. The process had its origins in partisan talk radio at the end of the past century. The rise of the internet—an event so swift and pervasive its political effect is only now beginning to be understood—further democratized every source of information, dramatically expanded each outlet's readership, and gave everyone a platform. All the old barriers to entry—the cost of print and paper and distribution—crumbled.

So much of this was welcome. I relished it myself in the early aughts, starting a blog and soon reaching as many readers, if not more, as some small magazines do. Fusty old-media institutions, grown fat and lazy, deserved a drubbing. The early independent blogosphere corrected facts, exposed bias, earned scoops. And as the medium matured, and as Facebook and Twitter took hold, everyone became a kind of blogger. In ways no twentieth-century journalist would have believed, we all now have our own virtual newspapers on our Facebook news feeds and Twitter timelines—picking stories from countless sources and creating a peer-to-peer media almost completely free of editing or interference by elites. This was bound to make politics more fluid. Political organizing—calling a meeting, fomenting a rally to advance a cause—used to be extremely laborious. Now you could bring together a virtual mass movement with a single web page. It would take you a few seconds.

The web was also uniquely capable of absorbing other forms of media, conflating genres and categories in ways never seen before. The distinction between politics and entertainment became fuzzier; election coverage became even more modeled on sportscasting; your Pornhub jostled right next to your mother's Facebook page. The web's algorithms all but removed any editorial judgment, and the effect soon had cable news abandoning even the pretense of asking "Is this relevant?" or "Do we really need to cover this live?" in the rush toward ratings bonanzas. In the end, all these categories were reduced to one thing: traffic, measured far more accurately than any other medium had ever done before.

And what mainly fuels this is precisely what the Founders feared about democratic culture: feeling, emotion, and narcissism, rather than reason, empiricism, and public-spiritedness. Online debates become personal, emotional, and irresolvable almost as soon as they begin. Godwin's Law—it's only a matter of time before a comments section brings up Hitler—is a reflection of the collapse of the reasoned deliberation the Founders saw as indispensable to a functioning republic.

Yes, occasional rational points still fly back and forth, but there are dramatically fewer elite arbiters to establish which of those points is actually true or valid or relevant. We have lost authoritative sources for even a common set of facts. And without such common empirical ground, the emotional component of politics becomes inflamed and reason retreats even further. The more emotive the candidate, the more supporters he or she will get.

Politically, we lucked out at first. Obama would never have been nominated for the presidency, let alone elected, if he hadn't harnessed the power of the web and the charisma of his media celebrity. But he was also, paradoxically, a very elite figure, a former state and US senator, a product of Harvard Law School, and, as it turned out, blessed with a preternaturally rational and calm disposition. So he has masked, temporarily, the real risks in the system that his pioneering campaign revealed. Hence many Democrats' frustration with him. Those who saw in his campaign the seeds of revolutionary change, who were drawn to him by their own messianic delusions, came to be bitterly disappointed by his governing moderation and pragmatism.

The climate Obama thrived in, however, was also ripe for far less restrained opportunists. In 2008, Sarah Palin emerged as proof that an ardent Republican, branded as an outsider, tailor-made for reality television, proud of her own ignorance about the world, and reaching an audience directly through online media, could also triumph in this new era. She was, it turned out, a John the Baptist for the true messiah of conservative populism, waiting patiently and strategically for his time to come.

Trump, we now know, had been considering running for president for decades. Those who didn't see him coming—or kept treating him as a joke—had not yet absorbed the precedents of Obama and Palin or the power of the new wide-open system to change the rules of the political game. Trump was as underrated for all of 2015 as Obama was in 2007—and for the same reasons. He intuitively grasped the vanishing authority of American political and media elites, and he had long fashioned a public persona perfectly attuned to blast past them.

Despite his immense wealth and inherited privilege, Trump had always cultivated a common touch. He did not hide his wealth in the late-twentieth century—he flaunted it in a way that connected with the masses. He lived the rich man's life most working men dreamed of—endless glamour and women, for example—without sacrificing a way of talking about the world that would not be out of place on the construction sites he regularly toured. His was a cult of democratic aspiration. His 1987 book, *The Art of the Deal*, promised its readers a path to instant success; his appearances on *The Howard Stern Show* cemented his appeal. His friendship with Vince McMahon offered him an early entrée into the world of professional wrestling, with its fusion of sports and fantasy. He was a macho media superstar.

One of the more amazing episodes in Sarah Palin's early political life, in fact, bears this out. She popped up in the *Anchorage Daily News* as "a commercial fisherman from Wasilla" on April 3, 1996. Palin had told her husband she was going to Costco but had sneaked into JCPenney in Anchorage to see . . . one Ivana Trump, who, in the wake of her divorce, was touting her branded perfume. "We want to see Ivana," Palin told the paper, "because we are so desperate in Alaska for any semblance of glamour and culture."

Trump assiduously cultivated this image and took to reality television as a natural. Each week, for fourteen seasons of *The Apprentice*, he would look someone in the eye and tell them, "You're fired!" The conversation most humane bosses fear to have with an employee was something Trump clearly relished, and the cruelty became entertainment. In retrospect, it is clear he was training—both himself and his viewers. If you want to understand why a figure so widely disliked nonetheless powers toward the election as if he were approaching a reality-TV-show finale, look no further. His TV tactics, as applied to presidential debates, wiped out rivals used to a different game. And all our reality-TV training has conditioned us to hope he'll win—or at least stay in the game till the final round. In such a shame-free media environment, the assholes often win. In the end, you support them because they're assholes.

In Eric Hoffer's classic 1951 tract, *The True Believer*, he sketches the dynamics of a genuine mass movement. He was thinking of the upheavals in Europe in the first half of the century, but the book remains sobering, especially now. Hoffer's core insight was to locate the source of all truly mass movements in a collective sense of acute frustration. Not despair, or revolt, or resignation—but frustration simmering with rage. Mass movements, he notes (as did Tocqueville centuries before him), rarely arise when oppression or misery is at its worst (say, 2009); they tend to appear when the worst is behind us, but the future seems not so much better (say, 2016). It is when a recovery finally gathers speed and some improvement is tangible but not yet widespread that the anger begins to rise. After the suffering of recession or unemployment, and despite hard work with stagnant or dwindling pay, the future stretches ahead with relief just out of reach. When those who helped create the last recession face no consequences but renewed fabulous wealth, the anger reaches a crescendo.

The deeper, long-term reasons for today's rage are not hard to find, although many of us elites have shamefully found ourselves able to ignore them. The jobs available to the working class no longer contain the kind of craftsmanship or satisfaction or meaning that can take the sting out of their low and stagnant wages. The once-familiar avenues for socialization—the church, the union hall, the VFW—have become less vibrant and social isolation more common.

Global economic forces have pummeled blue-collar workers more relentlessly than almost any other segment of society, forcing them to compete against hundreds of millions of equally skilled workers throughout the planet. No one asked them in the 1990s if this was the future they wanted. And the impact has been more brutal than many economists predicted. No wonder suicide and mortality rates among the white working poor are spiking dramatically.

"It is usually those whose poverty is relatively recent, the 'new poor,' who throb with the ferment of frustration," Hoffer argues. Fundamentalist religion long provided some emotional support for those left behind (for one thing, it invites practitioners to defy the elites as unholy), but its influence has waned as modernity has penetrated almost everything and the great culture wars of the 1990s and 2000s have ended in a rout. The result has been a more diverse mainstream culture—but also, simultaneously, a subculture that is even more alienated and despised, and ever more infuriated and bloody-minded.

This is an age in which a woman might succeed a black man as president, but also one in which a member of the white working class has declining options to make a decent living. This is a time when gay people can be married in fifty states, even as working-class families are hanging by a thread. It's a period in which we have become far more aware of the historic injustices that still haunt African Americans and yet we treat the desperate plight of today's white working class as an afterthought. And so late-stage capitalism is creating a righteous, revolutionary anger that late-stage democracy has precious little ability to moderate or constrain—and has actually helped exacerbate.

For the white working class, having had their morals roundly mocked, their religion deemed primitive, and their economic prospects decimated, now find their very gender and race, indeed the very way they talk about reality, described as a kind of problem for the nation to overcome. This is just one aspect of what Trump has masterfully signaled as "political correctness" run amok, or what might be better described as the newly rigid progressive passion for racial and sexual equality of outcome, rather than the liberal aspiration to mere equality of opportunity.

Much of the newly energized left has come to see the white working class not as allies but primarily as bigots, misogynists, racists, and homophobes, thereby condemning those often at the near-bottom rung of the economy to the bottom rung of the culture as well. A struggling white man in the heartland is now told to "check his privilege" by students at Ivy League colleges. Even if you agree that the privilege exists, it's hard not to empathize with the object of this disdain. These working-class communities, already alienated, hear—how can they not?—the glib and easy dismissals of "white straight men" as the ultimate source of all our woes. They smell the condescension and the broad generalizations about them—all of which would be repellent if directed at racial minorities—and see themselves, in Hoffer's words, "disinherited and injured by an unjust order of things."

And so they wait, and they steam, and they lash out. This was part of the emotional force of the Tea Party: not just the advancement of racial minorities, gays, and women but the simultaneous demonization of the white working-class world, its culture and way of life. Obama never intended this, but he became a symbol to many of this cultural marginalization. The Black Lives Matter left stoked the fires still further; so did the gay left, for whom the word "magnanimity" seems unknown, even in the wake of stunning successes. And as the Tea Party swept through Washington in 2010, as its representatives repeatedly held the government budget hostage, threatened the very credit of the United States, and refused to hold hearings on a Supreme Court nominee, the American political and media Establishment mostly chose to interpret such behavior as something other than unprecedented. But Trump saw what others didn't, just as Hoffer noted: "The frustrated individual and the true believer make better prognosticators than those who have reason to want the preservation of the status quo."

Mass movements, Hoffer argues, are distinguished by a "facility for make-believe . . . credulity, a readiness to attempt the impossible." What, one wonders, could be more impossible than suddenly vetting every single visitor to the United States for traces of Islamic belief? What could be more make-believe than a big, beautiful wall stretching across the entire Mexican border, paid for by the Mexican government? What could be more credulous than arguing that we could pay off our national debt through a global trade war? In a conventional political party, and in a rational political discourse, such ideas would be laughed out of contention, their self-evident impossibility disqualifying them from serious consideration. In the emotional fervor of a democratic mass movement, however, these impossibilities become icons of hope, symbols of a new way of conducting politics. Their very impossibility is their appeal.

But the most powerful engine for such a movement—the thing that gets it off the ground, shapes and solidifies and entrenches it—is always the evocation of hatred. It is, as Hoffer put it, "the most accessible and comprehensive of all unifying elements." And so Trump launched his campaign by calling undocumented Mexican immigrants a population largely of rapists and murderers. He moved on to Muslims, both at home and abroad. He has now added to these enemies—with sly brilliance—the Republican Establishment itself. And what makes Trump uniquely dangerous in the history of American politics—with far broader national appeal than, say, Huey Long or George Wallace—is his response to all three enemies. It's the threat of blunt coercion and dominance.

And so after demonizing most undocumented Mexican immigrants, he then vowed to round up and deport all 11 million of them by force. "They have to go" was the typically blunt phrase he used—and somehow people didn't immediately recognize the monstrous historical echoes. The sheer scale of the police and military operation that this policy would entail boggles the mind. Worse, he emphasized, after the mass murder in San Bernardino, that even the Muslim Americans you know intimately may turn around and massacre you at any juncture. "There's something going on," he declaimed ominously, giving legitimacy to the most hysterical and ugly of human impulses.

To call this fascism doesn't do justice to fascism. Fascism had, in some measure, an ideology and occasional coherence that Trump utterly lacks. But his movement is clearly fascistic in its demonization of foreigners, its hyping of a threat by a domestic minority (Muslims and Mexicans are the new Jews), its focus on a single supreme leader of what can only be called a cult, and its deep belief in violence and coercion in a democracy that has heretofore relied on debate and persuasion. This is the Weimar aspect of our current moment. Just as the English Civil War ended with a dictatorship under Oliver Cromwell, and the French Revolution gave us Napoleon Bonaparte, and the unstable chaos of Russian democracy yielded to Vladimir Putin, and the most recent burst of Egyptian democracy set the conditions for General el-Sisi's coup, so our paralyzed, emotional hyperdemocracy leads the stumbling, frustrated, angry voter toward the chimerical panacea of Trump.

His response to his third vaunted enemy, the RNC, is also laced with the threat of violence. There will be riots in Cleveland if he doesn't get his way.

The RNC will have "a rough time" if it doesn't cooperate. "Paul Ryan, I don't know him well, but I'm sure I'm going to get along great with him," Trump has said. "And if I don't? He's gonna have to pay a big price, OK?" The past month has seen delegates to the Cleveland convention receiving death threats; one of Trump's hatchet men, Roger Stone, has already threatened to publish the hotel room numbers of delegates who refuse to vote for Trump.

And what's notable about Trump's supporters is precisely what one would expect from members of a mass movement: their intense loyalty. Trump is their man, however inarticulate they are when explaining why. He's tough, he's real, and they've got his back, especially when he is attacked by all the people they have come to despise: liberal Democrats and traditional Republicans. At rallies, whenever a protester is hauled out, you can almost sense the rising rage of the collective identity venting itself against a lone dissenter and finding a catharsis of sorts in the brute force a mob can inflict on an individual. Trump tells the crowd he'd like to punch a protester in the face or have him carried out on a stretcher. No modern politician who has come this close to the presidency has championed violence in this way. It would be disqualifying if our hyperdemocracy hadn't already abolished disqualifications.

And while a critical element of twentieth-century fascism—its organized street violence—is missing, you can begin to see it in embryonic form. The phalanx of bodyguards around Trump grows daily; plainclothes bouncers in the crowds have emerged as pseudocops to contain the incipient unrest his candidacy will only continue to provoke; supporters have attacked hecklers with sometimes-stunning ferocity. Every time Trump legitimizes potential violence by his supporters by saying it comes from a love of country, he sows the seeds for serious civil unrest.

Trump celebrates torture—the one true love of tyrants everywhere—not because it allegedly produces intelligence but because it has a demonstration effect. At his rallies he has recounted the mythical acts of one General John J. Pershing when confronted with an alleged outbreak of Islamist terrorism in the Philippines. Pershing, in Trump's telling, lines up fifty Muslim prisoners, swishes a series of bullets in the corpses of freshly slaughtered pigs, and orders his men to put those bullets in their rifles and kill forty-nine of the captured Muslim men. He spares one captive solely so he can go back and tell his friends. End of the terrorism problem.

In some ways, this story contains all the elements of Trump's core appeal. The vexing problem of tackling jihadist terror? Torture and murder enough terrorists and they will simply go away. The complicated issue of undocumented workers, drawn by jobs many Americans won't take? Deport every single one of them and build a wall to stop the rest. Fuck political correctness. As one of his supporters told an obtuse reporter at a rally when asked if he supported Trump: "Hell yeah! He's no-bullshit. All balls. Fuck you all balls. That's what I'm about." And therein lies the appeal of tyrants from the beginning of time. Fuck you all balls. Irrationality with muscle.

The racial aspect of this is also unmissable. When the enemy within is Mexican or Muslim, and your ranks are extremely white, you set up a rubric for a racial conflict. And what's truly terrifying about Trump is that he does not seem to shrink from such a prospect; he relishes it.

For, like all tyrants, he is utterly lacking in self-control. Sleeping a handful of hours a night, impulsively tweeting in the early hours, improvising madly on subjects he knows nothing about, Trump rants and raves as he surfs an entirely reactive media landscape. Once again, Plato had his temperament down: A tyrant is a man "not having control of himself [who] attempts to rule others"; a man flooded with fear and love and passion, while having little or no ability to restrain or moderate them; a "real slave to the greatest fawning," a man who "throughout his entire life . . . is full of fear, overflowing with convulsions and pains." Sound familiar? Trump is as mercurial and as unpredictable and as emotional as the daily Twitter stream. And we are contemplating giving him access to the nuclear codes.

Those who believe that Trump's ugly, thuggish populism has no chance of ever making it to the White House seem to me to be missing this dynamic. Neofascist movements do not advance gradually by persuasion; they first transform the terms of the debate, create a new movement based on untrammeled emotion, take over existing institutions, and then ruthlessly exploit events. And so current poll numbers are only reassuring if you ignore the potential impact of sudden, external events—an economic downturn or a terror attack in a major city in the months before November. I have no doubt, for example, that Trump is sincere in his desire to "cut the head off" ISIS, whatever that can possibly mean. But it remains a fact that the interests of ISIS and the Trump campaign are now perfectly aligned. Fear is always the would-be tyrant's greatest ally.

And though Trump's unfavorables are extraordinarily high (around 65 percent), he is already showing signs of changing his tune, pivoting (fitfully) to the more presidential mode he envisages deploying in the general election. I suspect this will, to some fools on the fence, come as a kind of relief, and may open their minds to him once more. Tyrants, like mob bosses, know the value of a smile: precisely because of the fear he's already generated, you desperately want to believe in his new warmth. It's part of the good-cop-bad-cop routine that will be familiar to anyone who has studied the presidency of Vladimir Putin.

With his appeal to his own base locked up, Trump may well also shift to more moderate stances on social issues like abortion (he already wants to amend the GOP platform to a less draconian position) or gay and even transgender rights. He is consistent in his inconsistency, because, for him, winning is what counts. He has had a real case against Ted Cruz—that the senator has no base outside ideological-conservative quarters and is even less likely to win a general election. More potently, Trump has a worryingly strong argument against Clinton herself—or "crooked Hillary," as he now dubs her.

His proposition is a simple one. Remember James Carville's core question in the 1992 election: Change versus more of the same? That sentiment once elected Clinton's husband; it could also elect her opponent this fall. If you like America as it is, vote Clinton. After all, she has been a member of the American political elite for a quarter century. Clinton, moreover, has shown no ability to inspire or rally anyone but her longtime loyalists. She is lost in the new media and has struggled to put away a seventy-four-year-old socialist who is barely a member of her party. Her own unfavorables are only 11 points lower than Trump's (far higher than Obama's, John Kerry's, or Al Gore's were at this point in the race), and the more she campaigns, the higher her unfavorables go (including in her own party). She has a Gore problem. The idea of welcoming her into your living room for the next four years can seem, at times, positively masochistic.

It may be that demographics will save us. America is no longer an overwhelmingly white country, and Trump's signature issue—illegal immigration— is the source of his strength but also of his weakness. Nonetheless, it's worth noting how polling models have consistently misread the breadth of his support, especially in these past few weeks; he will likely bend over backward to include minorities in his fall campaign; and those convinced he cannot bring a whole new swath of white voters back into the political process should remember 2004, when Karl Rove helped engineer anti-gay-marriage state constitutional amendments that increased conservative voter turnout. All Trump needs is a sliver of minority votes inspired by the new energy of his campaign and the alleged dominance of the Obama coalition could crack (especially without Obama). Throughout the West these past few years, from France to Britain and Germany, the polls have kept missing the power of right-wing insurgency.

Were Trump to win the White House, the defenses against him would be weak. He would likely bring a GOP majority in the House, and Republicans in the Senate would be subjected to almighty popular fury if they stood in his way. The 4-4 stalemate in the Supreme Court would break in Trump's favor. (In large part, of course, this would be due to the GOP's unprecedented decision to hold a vacancy open "for the people to decide," another massive hyperdemocratic breach in our constitutional defenses.) And if Trump's policies are checked by other branches of government, how might he react? Just look at his response to the rules of the GOP nomination process. He's not interested in rules. And he barely understands the Constitution. In one revealing moment earlier this year, when asked what he would do if the military refused to obey an illegal order to torture a prisoner, Trump simply insisted that the man would obey: "They won't refuse. They're not going to refuse, believe me." He later amended his remark, but it speaks volumes about his approach to power. Dick Cheney gave illegal orders to torture prisoners and coerced White House lawyers to cook up absurd "legal" defenses. Trump would make Cheney's embrace of the dark side and untrammeled executive power look unambitious.

In his 1935 novel, *It Can't Happen Here,* Sinclair Lewis wrote a counter-factual about what would happen if fascism as it was then spreading across Europe were to triumph in America. It's not a good novel, but it remains a resonant one. The imagined American fascist leader—a senator called Buzz Windrip—is a "Professional Common Man. . . . But he was the Common Man twenty-times-magnified by his oratory, so that while the other Commoners could understand his every purpose, which was exactly the same as their own, they saw him towering among them, and they raised hands to him in worship."

He "was vulgar, almost illiterate, a public liar easily detected, and in his 'ideas' almost idiotic." "'I know the Press only too well,'" Windrip opines at one point. "'Almost all editors hide away in spider-dens, men without thought of Family or Public Interest . . . plotting how they can put over their lies, and advance their own positions and fill their greedy pocketbooks.'"

He is obsessed with the balance of trade and promises instant economic success: "'I shall not be content till this country can produce every single thing we need. . . . We shall have such a balance of trade as will go far to carry out my often-criticized yet completely sound idea of from $3000 to $5000 per year for every single family.'" However fantastical and empty his promises, he nonetheless mesmerizes the party faithful at the nominating convention (held in Cleveland!): "Something in the intensity with which Windrip looked at his audience, looked at all of them, his glance slowly taking them in from the highest-perched seat to the nearest, convinced them that he was talking to each individual, directly and solely; that he wanted to take each of them into his heart; that he was telling them the truths, the imperious and dangerous facts, that had been hidden from them."

And all the elites who stood in his way? Crippled by their own failures, demoralized by their crumbling stature, they first mock and then cave. As one lone journalist laments before the election (he finds himself in a concentration camp afterward): "I've got to keep remembering . . . that Windrip is only the lightest cork on the whirlpool. He didn't plot all this thing. With all the justified discontent there is against the smart politicians and the Plush Horses of Plutocracy—oh, if it hadn't been one Windrip, it'd been another. . . . We had it coming, we Respectables."

And, eighty-one years later, many of us did. An American elite that has presided over massive and increasing public debt, that failed to prevent 9/11, that chose a disastrous war in the Middle East, that allowed financial markets to nearly destroy the global economy, and that is now so bitterly divided the Congress is effectively moot in a constitutional democracy: "we Respectables" deserve a comeuppance. The vital and valid lesson of the Trump phenomenon is that if the elites cannot govern by compromise, someone outside will eventually try to govern by popular passion and brute force.

But elites still matter in a democracy. They matter not because they are democracy's enemy but because they provide the critical ingredient to save democracy from itself. The political Establishment may be battered and demoralized, deferential to the algorithms of the web and to the monosyllables of a gifted demagogue, but this is not the time to give up on America's near-unique and stabilizing blend of democracy and elite responsibility. The country has endured far harsher times than the present without succumbing to rank demagoguery; it avoided the fascism that destroyed Europe; it has channeled extraordinary outpourings of democratic energy into constitutional order. It seems shocking to argue that we need elites in this democratic age—especially with vast inequalities of wealth and elite failures all around us. But we need them precisely to protect this precious democracy from its own destabilizing excesses.

And so those Democrats who are gleefully predicting a Clinton landslide in November need to both check their complacency and understand that the Trump question really isn't a cause for partisan schadenfreude anymore. It's much more dangerous than that. Those still backing the demagogue of the left, Bernie Sanders, might want to reflect that their critique of Clinton's experience and expertise—and their facile conflation of that with corruption—is only playing into Trump's hands. That it will fall to Clinton to temper her party's ambitions will be uncomfortable to watch, since her willingness to compromise and equivocate is precisely what many Americans find so distrustful. And yet she may soon be all we have left to counter the threat. She needs to grasp the lethality of her foe, moderate the kind of identity politics that unwittingly empowers him, make an unapologetic case that experience and moderation are not vices, address much more directly the anxieties of the white working class—and Democrats must listen.

More to the point, those Republicans desperately trying to use the long-standing rules of their own nominating process to thwart this monster deserve our passionate support, not our disdain. This is not the moment to remind them that they partly brought this on themselves. This is a moment to offer solidarity, especially as the odds are increasingly stacked against them. Ted Cruz and John Kasich face their decisive battle in Indiana on May 3. But they need to fight on, with any tactic at hand, all the way to the bitter end. The Republican delegates who are trying to protect their party from the whims of an outsider demagogue are, at this moment, doing what they ought to be doing to prevent civil and racial unrest, an international conflict, and a constitutional crisis. These GOP elites have every right to deploy whatever rules or procedural roadblocks they can muster, and they should refuse to be intimidated.

And if they fail in Indiana or Cleveland, as they likely will, they need, quite simply, to disown their party's candidate. They should resist any temptation to loyally back the nominee or to sit this election out. They must take the fight to Trump at every opportunity, unite with Democrats and Independents against him, and be prepared to sacrifice one election in order to save their party and their country.

For Trump is not just a wacky politician of the far right, or a riveting TV spectacle, or a Twitter phenom and bizarre working-class hero. He is not just another candidate to be parsed and analyzed by TV pundits in the same breath as all the others. In terms of our liberal democracy and constitutional order, Trump is an extinction-level event. It's long past time we started treating him as such.

I Used to Be a Human Being

September 19, 2016 | *NEW YORK* magazine

———————

I was sitting in a large meditation hall in a converted novitiate in central Massachusetts when I reached into my pocket for my iPhone. A woman in the front of the room gamely held a basket in front of her, beaming beneficently, like a priest with a collection plate. I duly surrendered my little device, only to feel a sudden pang of panic on my way back to my seat. If it hadn't been for everyone staring at me, I might have turned around immediately and asked for it back. But I didn't. I knew why I'd come here.

A year before, like many addicts, I had sensed a personal crash coming. For a decade and a half, I'd been a web obsessive, publishing blog posts multiple times a day, seven days a week, and ultimately corralling a team that curated the web every twenty minutes during peak hours. Each morning began with a full immersion in the stream of internet consciousness and news, jumping from site to site, tweet to tweet, breaking news story to hottest take, scanning countless images and videos, catching up with multiple memes. Throughout the day, I'd cough up an insight or an argument or a joke about what had just occurred or what was happening right now. And at times, as events took over, I'd spend weeks manically grabbing every tiny scrap of a developing story in order to fuse them into a narrative in real time. I was in an unending dialogue with readers who were caviling, praising, booing, correcting. My brain had never been so occupied so insistently by so many different subjects and in so public a way for so long.

I was, in other words, a very early adopter of what we might now call living in the web. And as the years went by, I realized I was no longer alone. Facebook soon gave everyone the equivalent of their own blog and their own audience. More and more people got a smartphone—connecting them instantly to a deluge of febrile content, forcing them to cull and absorb and assimilate the online torrent as relentlessly as I had once. Twitter emerged as a form of instant blogging of microthoughts. Users were as addicted to the feedback as I had long been—and even more prolific. Then the apps descended, like the rain, to inundate what was left of our free time. It was ubiquitous now, this virtual living, this never stopping, this always updating. I remember when I decided to raise the ante on my blog in 2007 and update every half hour or so and my editor looked at me as if I were insane. But the insanity was now banality; the once-unimaginable pace of the professional blogger was now the default for everyone.

If the internet killed you, I used to joke, then I would be the first to find out. Years later, the joke was running thin. In the last year of my blogging life, my health began to give out. Four bronchial infections in twelve months had become progressively harder to kick. Vacations, such as they were, had become mere opportunities for sleep. My dreams were filled with the snippets of code I used each day to update the site. My friendships had atrophied as my time away from the web dwindled. My doctor, dispensing one more course of antibiotics, finally laid it on the line: "Did you really survive HIV to die of the web?"

But the rewards were many: an audience of up to one hundred thousand people a day; a new-media business that was actually profitable; a constant stream of things to annoy, enlighten, or infuriate me; a niche in the nerve center of the exploding global conversation; and a way to measure success—in big and beautiful data—that was a constant dopamine bath for the writerly ego. If you had to reinvent yourself as a writer in the internet age, I reassured myself, then I was ahead of the curve. The problem was that I hadn't been able to reinvent myself as a human being.

I tried reading books, but that skill now began to elude me. After a couple of pages, my fingers twitched for a keyboard. I tried meditation, but my mind bucked and bridled as I tried to still it. I got a steady workout routine, and it gave me the only relief I could measure for an hour or so a day. But over time in this pervasive virtual world, the online clamor grew louder and louder. Although I spent hours each day, alone and silent, attached to a laptop, it felt as if I were in a constant cacophonous crowd of words and images, sounds and ideas, emotions and tirades—a wind tunnel of deafening, deadening noise. So much of it was irresistible, as I fully understood. So much of the technology was irreversible, as I also knew. But I'd begun to fear that this new way of living was actually becoming a way of not living.

By the last few months, I realized I had been engaging—like most addicts— in a form of denial. I'd long treated my online life as a supplement to my real life, an add-on, as it were. Yes, I spent many hours communicating with others as a disembodied voice, but my real life and body were still here. But then I began to realize, as my health and happiness deteriorated, that this was not a both-and kind of situation. It was either-or. Every hour I spent online was not spent in the physical world. Every minute I was engrossed in a virtual inter- action I was not involved in a human encounter. Every second absorbed in some trivia was a second less for any form of reflection, or calm, or spirituality. "Multitasking" was a mirage. This was a zero-sum question. Either I lived as a voice online or I lived as a human being in the world that humans had lived in since the beginning of time.

And so I decided, after fifteen years, to live in reality.

Since the invention of the printing press, every new revolution in infor- mation technology has prompted apocalyptic fears. From the panic that easy access to the vernacular English Bible would destroy Christian orthodoxy all the way to the revulsion, in the 1950s, at the barbaric young medium of television, cultural critics have moaned and wailed at every turn. Each shift represented a further fracturing of attention—continuing up to the previously unimaginable kaleidoscope of cable television in the late-twentieth century and the now infinite, infinitely multiplying spaces of the web. And yet society has always managed to adapt and adjust, without obvious damage, and with some more-than-obvious progress. So it's perhaps too easy to view this new era of mass distraction as something newly dystopian.

But it sure does represent a huge leap from even the very recent past. The data bewilder. Every single minute on the planet, YouTube users upload four hundred hours of video and Tinder users swipe profiles over a million times. Each day, there are literally billions of Facebook "likes." Online outlets now publish exponentially more material than they once did, churning out articles at a rapid-fire pace, adding new details to the news every few minutes. Blogs, Facebook feeds, Tumblr accounts, tweets, and propaganda outlets repurpose, borrow, and add top spin to the same output.

We absorb this content (as writing or video or photography is now called) no longer primarily by buying a magazine or paper, by bookmarking our favorite website, or by actively choosing to read or watch. We are instead guided to these info nuggets by myriad little interruptions on social media, all cascading at us with individually tailored relevance and accuracy. Do not flatter yourself in thinking that you have much control over which temptations you click on. Silicon Valley's technologists and their ever-perfecting algorithms have discovered the form of bait that will have you jumping like a witless minnow. No information technology ever had this depth of knowledge of its consumers—or greater capacity to tweak their synapses to keep them engaged.

And the engagement never ends. Not long ago, surfing the web, however addictive, was a stationary activity. At your desk at work, or at home on your laptop, you disappeared down a rabbit hole of links and resurfaced minutes (or hours) later to reencounter the world. But the smartphone then went and made the rabbit hole portable, inviting us to get lost in it anywhere, at any time, whatever else we might be doing. Information soon penetrated every waking moment of our lives.

And it did so with staggering swiftness. We almost forget that ten years ago there were no smartphones and as recently as 2011 only a third of Americans owned one. Now nearly two-thirds do. That figure reaches 85 percent when you're only counting young adults. And 46 percent of Americans told Pew surveyors last year a simple but remarkable thing: they could not live without one. The device went from unknown to indispensable in less than a decade. The handful of spaces where it was once impossible to be connected—the airplane, the subway, the wilderness—are dwindling fast. Even hiker backpacks now come fitted with battery power for smartphones. Perhaps the only "safe space" that still exists is the shower.

Am I exaggerating? A small but detailed 2015 study of young adults found that participants were using their phones five hours a day, at eighty-five separate times. Most of these interactions were for less than thirty seconds, but they add up. Just as revealing: the users weren't fully aware of how addicted they were. They thought they picked up their phones half as much as they actually did. But whether they were aware of it or not, a new technology had seized control of around one-third of these young adults' waking hours.

The interruptions often feel pleasant, of course, because they are usually the work of your friends. Distractions arrive in your brain connected to people you know (or think you know), which is the genius of social, peer-to-peer media. Since our earliest evolution, humans have been unusually passionate about gossip, which some attribute to the need to stay abreast of news among friends and family as our social networks expanded. We were hooked on information as eagerly as sugar. And give us access to gossip the way modernity has given us access to sugar and we have an uncontrollable impulse to binge. A regular teen Snapchat user, as *The Atlantic* recently noted, can have exchanged anywhere between ten thousand and even as many as four hundred thousand snaps with friends. As the snaps accumulate, they generate publicly displayed scores that bestow the allure of popularity and social status. This, evolutionary psychologists will attest, is fatal. When provided a constant source of information and news and gossip about one another—routed through our social networks—we are close to helpless.

Just look around you—at the people crouched over their phones as they walk the streets, or drive their cars, or walk their dogs, or play with their children. Observe yourself in line for coffee, or in a quick work break, or driving, or even just going to the bathroom. Visit an airport and see the sea of craned necks and dead eyes. We have gone from looking up and around to constantly looking down.

If an alien had visited America just five years ago, then returned today, wouldn't this be its immediate observation? That this species has developed an extraordinary new habit—and, everywhere you look, lives constantly in its thrall?

I arrived at the meditation retreat center a few months after I'd quit the web, throwing my life and career up in the air. I figured it would be the ultimate detox. And I wasn't wrong. After a few hours of silence, you tend to expect some kind of disturbance, some flurry to catch your interest. And then it never comes. The quiet deepens into an enveloping default. No one spoke; no one even looked another person in the eye—what some Buddhists call noble silence. The day was scheduled down to the minute, so that almost all our time was spent in silent meditation with our eyes closed, or in slow-walking meditation on the marked trails of the forest, or in communal, unspeaking meals. The only words I heard or read for ten days were in three counseling sessions, two guided meditations, and nightly talks on mindfulness.

I'd spent the previous nine months honing my meditation practice, but, in this crowd I was a novice and a tourist. (Everyone around me was attending six-week or three-month sessions.) The silence, it became apparent, was an integral part of these people's lives—and their simple manner of movement, the way they glided rather than walked, the open expressions on their faces, all fascinated me. What were they experiencing, if not insane levels of boredom?

And how did their calm somehow magnify itself when I was surrounded by them every day? Usually, when you add people to a room, the noise grows; here it was the silence that seemed to compound itself. Attached to my phone, I had been accompanied for so long by verbal and visual noise, by an endless bombardment of words and images, and yet I felt curiously isolated. Among these meditators, I was alone in silence and darkness, yet I felt almost at one with them. My breathing slowed. My brain settled. My body became much more available to me. I could feel it digesting and sniffing, itching and pulsating. It was if my brain were moving away from the abstract and the distant toward the tangible and the near.

Things that usually escaped me began to intrigue me. On a meditative walk through the forest on my second day, I began to notice not just the quality of the autumnal light through the leaves but the splotchy multicolors of the newly fallen, the texture of the lichen on the bark, the way in which tree roots had come to entangle and overcome old stone walls. The immediate impulse—to grab my phone and photograph it—was foiled by an empty pocket. So I simply looked. At one point, I got lost and had to rely on my sense of direction to find my way back. I heard birdsong for the first time in years. Well, of course, I had always heard it, but it had been so long since I listened.

My goal was to keep thought in its place. "Remember," my friend Sam Harris, an atheist meditator, had told me before I left, "if you're suffering, you're thinking." The task was not to silence everything within my addled brain, but to introduce it to quiet, to perspective, to the fallow spaces I had once known where the mind and soul replenish.

Soon enough, the world of "the news," and the raging primary campaign, disappeared from my consciousness. My mind drifted to a trancelike documentary I had watched years before, Philip Gröning's *Into Great Silence*, on an ancient Carthusian monastery and silent monastic order in the Alps. In one scene, a novice monk is tending his plot of garden. As he moves deliberately from one task to the next, he seems almost in another dimension. He is walking from one trench to another, but never appears focused on actually getting anywhere. He seems to float, or mindfully glide, from one place to the next.

He had escaped, it seemed to me, what we moderns understand by *time*. There was no race against it; no fear of wasting it; no avoidance of the tedium that most of us would recoil from. And as I watched my fellow meditators walk around, eyes open yet unavailable to me, I felt the slowing of the ticking clock, the unwinding of the pace that has all of us in modernity on a treadmill till death. I felt a trace of a freedom all humans used to know and that our culture seems intent, pell-mell, on forgetting.

We all understand the joys of our always-wired world—the connections, the validations, the laughs, the porn, the info. I don't want to deny any of them here. But we are only beginning to get our minds around the costs, if we are even prepared to accept that there are costs. For the subtle snare of this new technology is that it lulls us into the belief that there are no downsides. It's all just more of everything. Online life is simply layered on top of offline life. We can meet in person and text beforehand. We can eat together while checking our feeds. We can transform life into what the writer Sherry Turkle refers to as "life-mix."

But of course, as I had discovered in my blogging years, the family that is eating together while simultaneously on their phones is not actually together. They are, in Turkle's formulation, "alone together." You are where your attention is. If you're watching a football game with your son while also texting a friend, you're not fully with your child—and he knows it. Truly being with another person means being experientially with them, picking up countless tiny signals from the eyes and voice and body language and context, and reacting, often unconsciously, to every nuance. These are our deepest social skills, which have been honed through the aeons. They are what make us distinctively human.

By rapidly substituting virtual reality for reality, we are diminishing the scope of this interaction even as we multiply the number of people with whom we interact. We remove or drastically filter all the information we might get by being *with* another person. We reduce them to some outlines—a Facebook "friend," an Instagram photo, a text message—in a controlled and sequestered world that exists largely free of the sudden eruptions or encumbrances of actual human interaction. We become one another's "contacts," efficient shadows of ourselves.

Think of how rarely you now use the phone to speak to someone. A text is far easier, quicker, less burdensome. A phone call could take longer; it could force you to encounter that person's idiosyncrasies or digressions or unexpected emotional needs. Remember when you left voice-mail messages—or actually listened to one? Emojis now suffice. Or take the difference between trying to seduce someone at a bar and flipping through Tinder profiles to find a better match. One is deeply inefficient and requires spending (possibly wasting) considerable time; the other turns dozens and dozens of humans into clothes on an endlessly extending rack.

No wonder we prefer the apps. An entire universe of intimate responses is flattened to a single, distant swipe. We hide our vulnerabilities, airbrushing our flaws and quirks; we project our fantasies onto the images before us. Rejection still stings—but less when a new virtual match beckons on the horizon. We have made sex even safer yet, having sapped it of serendipity and risk and often of physical beings altogether. The amount of time we spend cruising vastly outweighs the time we may ever get to spend with the objects of our desire.

Our oldest human skills atrophy. GPS, for example, is a godsend for finding our way around places we don't know. But, as Nicholas Carr has noted, it has led to our not even seeing, let alone remembering, the details of our environ-ment, to our not developing the accumulated memories that give us a sense of place and control over what we once called ordinary life. The writer Matthew Crawford has examined how automation and online living have sharply eroded the number of people physically making things, using their own hands and eyes and bodies to craft, say, a wooden chair or a piece of clothing or, in one of Crawford's more engrossing case studies, a pipe organ. We became who we are as a species by mastering tools, making them a living, evolving extension of our whole bodies and minds. What first seems tedious and repetitive develops into a skill—and a skill is what gives us humans self-esteem and mutual respect.

Yes, online and automated life is more efficient, it makes more economic sense, it ends monotony and "wasted" time in the achievement of practical goals. But it denies us the deep satisfaction and pride of workmanship that comes with accomplishing daily tasks well, a denial perhaps felt most acutely by those for whom such tasks are also a livelihood—and an identity.

Indeed, the modest mastery of our practical lives is what fulfilled us for tens of thousands of years—until technology and capitalism decided it was entirely dispensable. If we are to figure out why despair has spread so rapidly in so many left-behind communities, the atrophying of the practical vocations of the past—and the meaning they gave to people's lives—seems as useful a place to explore as economic indices.

So are the bonds we used to form in our everyday interactions—the nods and pleasantries of neighbors, the daily facial recognition in the mall or the street. Here, too, the allure of virtual interaction has helped decimate the space for actual community. When we enter a coffee shop in which everyone is engrossed in their private online worlds, we respond by creating one of our own. When someone next to you answers the phone and starts talking loudly as if you didn't exist, you realize that, in her private zone, you don't. And slowly, the whole concept of a public space—where we meet and engage and learn from our fellow citizens—evaporates. Turkle describes one of the many small consequences in an American city: "Kara, in her 50s, feels that life in her hometown of Portland, Maine, has emptied out: 'Sometimes I walk down the street, and I'm the only person not plugged in. . . . No one is where they are. They're talking to someone miles away. I miss them.'"

Has our enslavement to dopamine—to the instant hits of validation that come with a well-crafted tweet or Snapchat streak—made us happier? I suspect it has simply made us less unhappy, or rather less aware of our unhappiness, and that our phones are merely new and powerful antidepressants of a non-pharmaceutical variety. In an essay on contemplation, the Christian writer Alan Jacobs recently commended the comedian Louis C.K. for withholding smartphones from his children. On the Conan O'Brien show, C.K. explained why: "You need to build an ability to just be yourself and not be doing something. That's what the phones are taking away," he said. "Underneath in your life there's that thing . . . that forever empty . . . that knowledge that it's all for nothing and you're alone. . . . That's why we text and drive . . . because we don't want to be alone for a second."

C.K. recalled a moment driving his car when a Bruce Springsteen song came on the radio. It triggered a sudden, unexpected surge of sadness. He instinctively went to pick up his phone and text as many friends as possible. Then he changed his mind, left his phone where it was, and pulled over to the side of the road to weep. He allowed himself for once to be alone with his feelings, to be overwhelmed by them, to experience them with no instant distraction, no digital assist. And then he was able to discover, in a manner now remote from most of us, the relief of crawling out of the hole of misery by himself. For if there is no dark night of the soul anymore that isn't lighted with the flicker of the screen, then there is no morning of hopefulness either. As he said of the distracted modern world we now live in: "You never feel completely sad or completely happy; you just feel . . . kinda satisfied with your products. And then you die. So that's why I don't want to get a phone for my kids."

The early days of the retreat passed by, the novelty slowly ceding to a reckoning that my meditation skills were now being tested more aggressively. Thoughts began to bubble up; memories clouded the present; the silent sessions began to be edged by a little anxiety.

And then, unexpectedly, on the third day, as I was walking through the forest, I became overwhelmed. I'm still not sure what triggered it, but my best guess is that the shady, quiet woodlands, with brooks trickling their way down hillsides and birds flitting through the moist air, summoned memories of my childhood. I was a lonely boy who spent many hours outside in the copses and woodlands of my native Sussex, in England. I had explored this landscape with friends, but also alone — playing imaginary scenarios in my head, creating little nooks where I could hang and sometimes read, learning every little pathway through the woods and marking each flower or weed or fungus that I stumbled on. But I was also escaping a home where my mother had collapsed with bipolar disorder after the birth of my younger brother and had never really recovered. She was in and out of hospitals for much of my youth and adolescence, and her condition made it hard for her to hide her pain and suffering from her sensitive oldest son.

I absorbed a lot of her agony, I came to realize later, hearing her screams of frustration and misery in constant, terrifying fights with my father, and never knowing how to stop it or to help. I remember watching her dissolve in tears in the car picking me up from elementary school at the thought of returning to a home she clearly dreaded, or holding her as she poured her heart out to me, through sobs and whispers, about her dead-end life in a small town where she was utterly dependent on a spouse. She was taken away from me several times in my childhood, starting when I was four, and even now I can recall the corridors and rooms of the institutions she was treated in when we went to visit.

I knew the scar tissue from this formative trauma was still in my soul. I had spent two decades in therapy, untangling and exploring it, learning how it had made intimacy with others so frightening, how it had made my own spasms of adolescent depression even more acute, how living with that kind of pain from the most powerful source of love in my life had made me the profoundly broken vessel I am. But I had never felt it so vividly since the very years it had first engulfed and defined me. It was as if, having slowly and progressively removed every distraction from my life, I was suddenly faced with what I had been distracting myself from. Resting for a moment against the trunk of a tree, I stopped, and suddenly found myself bent over, convulsed with the newly present pain, sobbing.

And this time, even as I eventually made it back to the meditation hall, there was no relief. I couldn't call my husband or a friend and talk it over. I couldn't check my e-mail or refresh my Instagram or text someone who might share the pain. I couldn't ask one of my fellows if they had experienced something similar. I waited for the mood to lift, but it deepened. Hours went by in silence as my heart beat anxiously and my mind reeled.

I decided I would get some distance by trying to describe what I was feeling. The two words "extreme suffering" won the naming contest in my head. And when I had my fifteen-minute counseling session with my assigned counselor a day later, the words just kept tumbling out. After my panicked, anguished confession, he looked at me, one eyebrow raised, with a beatific half smile. "Oh, that's perfectly normal," he deadpanned warmly. "Don't worry. Be patient. It will resolve itself." And in time, it did. Over the next day, the feelings began to ebb, my meditation improved, the sadness shifted into a kind of calm and rest. I felt other things from my childhood—the beauty of the forests, the joy of friends, the support of my sister, the love of my maternal grandmother. Yes, I prayed, and prayed for relief. But this lifting did not feel like divine intervention, let alone a result of effort, but more like a natural process of revisiting and healing and recovering. It felt like an ancient, long-buried gift.

In his survey of how the modern West lost widespread religious practice, *A Secular Age*, the philosopher Charles Taylor used a term to describe the way we think of our societies. He called it a "social imaginary"—a set of interlocking beliefs and practices that can undermine or subtly marginalize other kinds of belief. We didn't go from faith to secularism in one fell swoop, he argues. Certain ideas and practices made others not so much false as less vibrant or relevant. And so modernity slowly weakened spirituality, by design and accident, in favor of commerce; it downplayed silence and mere being in favor of noise and constant action. The reason we live in a culture increasingly without faith is not because science has somehow disproved the unprovable, but because the white noise of secularism has removed the very stillness in which it might endure or be reborn.

The English Reformation began, one recalls, with an assault on the monasteries, and what silence the Protestants didn't banish the philosophers of the Enlightenment mocked. Gibbon and Voltaire defined the Enlightenment's posture toward the monkish: from condescension to outright contempt. The roar and disruption of the Industrial Revolution violated what quiet still remained until modern capitalism made business central to our culture and the ever-more efficient meeting of needs and wants our primary collective goal. We became a civilization of getting things done—with the development of America, in some ways, as its crowning achievement. Silence in modernity became, over the centuries, an anachronism, even a symbol of the useless superstitions we had left behind. The smartphone revolution of the past decade can be seen in some ways simply as the final twist of this ratchet, in which those few remaining redoubts of quiet—the tiny cracks of inactivity in our lives—are being methodically filled with more stimulus and noise.

And yet our need for quiet has never fully gone away, because our practical achievements, however spectacular, never quite fulfill us. They are always giving way to new wants and needs, always requiring updating or repairing, always falling short. The mania of our online lives reveals this: we keep swiping and swiping because we are never fully satisfied. The late British philosopher Michael Oakeshott starkly called this truth "the deadliness of doing." There seems no end to this paradox of practical life, and no way out, just an infinite succession of efforts, all doomed ultimately to fail.

Except, of course, there is the option of a spiritual reconciliation to this futility, an attempt to transcend the unending cycle of impermanent human achievement. There is a recognition that beyond mere doing, there is also being; that at the end of life, there is also the great silence of death with which we must eventually make our peace. From the moment I entered a church in my childhood, I understood that this place was different because it was so quiet. The Mass itself was full of silences—those liturgical pauses that would never do in a theater, those minutes of quiet after Communion when we were encouraged to get lost in prayer, those liturgical spaces that seemed to insist that we are in no hurry here. And this silence demarcated what we once understood as the sacred, marking a space beyond the secular world of noise and business and shopping.

The only place like it was the library, and the silence there also pointed to something beyond it—to the learning that required time and patience, to the pursuit of truth that left practical life behind. Like the moment of silence we sometimes honor in the wake of a tragedy, the act of not speaking signals that we are responding to something deeper than the quotidian, something more profound than words can fully express. I vividly recall when the AIDS Memorial Quilt was first laid out on the Mall in Washington in 1987. A huge crowd had gathered, drifts of hundreds of chattering, animated people walking in waves onto the scene. But the closer they got, and the more they absorbed the landscape of unimaginably raw grief, their voices petered out, and a great emptiness filled the air. This is different, the silence seemed to say. This is not our ordinary life.

Most civilizations, including our own, have understood this in the past. Millennia ago, as the historian Diarmaid MacCulloch has argued, the unnameable, often inscrutably silent God of the Jewish Scriptures intersected with Plato's concept of a divinity so beyond human understanding and imperfection that no words could accurately describe it. The hidden God of the Jewish and Christian Scriptures spoke often by not speaking. And Jesus, like the Buddha, revealed as much by his silences as by his words. He was a preacher who yet wandered for forty days in the desert, a prisoner who refused to defend himself at his trial. At the converted novitiate at the retreat, they had left two stained-glass windows depicting Jesus. In one, he is in the Garden of Gethsemane, sweating blood in terror, alone before his execution. In the other, he is seated at the Last Supper, with the disciple John the Beloved resting his head on Jesus's chest. He is speaking in neither.

That Judeo-Christian tradition recognized a critical distinction—and tension—between noise and silence, between getting through the day and getting a grip on one's whole life. The Sabbath—the Jewish institution co-opted by Christianity—was a collective imposition of relative silence, a moment of calm to reflect on our lives under the light of eternity. It helped define much of Western public life once a week for centuries—only to dissipate, with scarcely a passing regret, into the commercial cacophony of the past couple of decades. It reflected a now-battered belief that a sustained spiritual life is simply unfeasible for most mortals without these refuges from noise and work to buffer us and remind us who we really are. But just as modern street lighting has slowly blotted the stars from the visible skies, so, too, have cars and planes and factories and flickering digital screens combined to rob us of a silence that was previously regarded as integral to the health of the human imagination.

This changes us. It slowly removes—without our even noticing it—the very spaces where we can gain a footing in our minds and souls that is not captive to constant pressures or desires or duties. And the smartphone has all but banished them. Thoreau issued his jeremiad against those pressures more than a century ago: "I went to the woods because I wished to live deliberately, to front only the essential facts of life, and see if I could not learn what it had to teach, and not, when I came to die, discover that I had not lived. I did not wish to live what was not life, living is so dear."

When you enter the temporary Temple at Burning Man, the annual Labor Day retreat for the tech elite in the Nevada desert, there is hardly any speaking. Some hover at the edges; others hold hands and weep; a few pin notes to a wall of remembrances; the rest are kneeling or meditating or simply sitting. The usually ornate and vast wooden structure is rivaled only by the massive tower of a man that will be burned, like the Temple itself, as the festival reaches its climax, and tens of thousands of people watch an inferno.

They come here, these architects of our internet world, to escape the thing they unleashed on the rest of us. They come to a wilderness where no cellular signals penetrate. You leave your phone in your tent, deemed useless for a few ecstatically authentic days. There is a spirit of radical self-reliance (you survive for seven days or so only on what you can bring into the vast temporary city) and an ethic of social equality. You are forced to interact only as a physical human being with other physical human beings—without hierarchy. You dance, and you experiment; you build community in various camps. And for many, this is the high point of their year—a separate world for fantasy and friendship, enhanced by drugs that elevate your sense of compassion or wonder or awe.

Like a medieval carnival, this new form of religion upends the conventions that otherwise rule our lives. Like a safety valve, it releases the pent-up pressures of our wired cacophony. Though easily mockable, it is trying to achieve what our culture once routinely provided, and it reveals, perhaps, that we are not completely helpless in this newly distracted era. We can, one senses, begin to balance it out, to relearn what we have so witlessly discarded, to manage our neuroses so they do not completely overwhelm us.

There are burgeoning signs of this more human correction. In 2012, there were, for example, around 20 million yoga practitioners in the United States, according to a survey conducted by Ipsos Public Affairs. By 2016, the number had almost doubled. Mindfulness, at the same time, has become a corporate catchword for many and a new form of sanity for others. It's also hard to explain, it seems to me, the sudden explosion of interest in and tolerance of cannabis in the past fifteen years without factoring in the intensifying digital climate. Weed is a form of self-medication for an era of mass distraction, providing a quick and easy path to mellowed contemplation in a world where the ample space and time necessary for it are under siege.

If the churches came to understand that the greatest threat to faith today is not hedonism but distraction, perhaps they might begin to appeal anew to a frazzled digital generation. Christian leaders seem to think that they need more distraction to counter the distraction. Their services have degenerated into emotional spasms, their spaces drowned with light and noise and locked shut throughout the day, when their darkness and silence might actually draw those whose minds and souls have grown web weary. But the mysticism of Catholic meditation—of the Rosary, of Benediction, or simple contemplative prayer—is a tradition in search of rediscovery. The monasteries—opened up to more lay visitors—could try to answer to the same needs that the booming yoga movement has increasingly met.

And imagine if more secular places responded in kind: Restaurants where smartphones must be surrendered upon entering, or coffee shops that marketed their non-Wi-Fi safe space? Or, more practical: More meals where we agree to put our gadgets in a box while we talk to one another? Or lunch where the first person to use their phone pays the whole bill? We can, if we want, re-create a digital Sabbath each week—just one day in which we live for twenty-four hours without checking our phones. Or we can simply turn off our notifications. Humans are self-preserving in the long run. For every innovation there is a reaction, and even the starkest of analysts of our new culture, like Sherry Turkle, sees a potential for eventually rebalancing our lives.

And yet I wonder. The ubiquitous temptations of virtual living create a mental climate that is still maddeningly hard to manage. In the days, then weeks, then months after my retreat, my daily meditation sessions began to falter a little. There was an election campaign of such brooding menace it demanded attention, headlined by a walking human Snapchat app of incoherence. For a while, I had limited my news exposure to *The New York Times'* daily briefings; then, slowly, I found myself scanning the clickbait headlines from countless sources that crowded the screen; after a while, I was back in my old rut, absorbing every nugget of campaign news, even as I understood each to be as ephemeral as the last, and even though I no longer needed to absorb them all for work.

Then there were the other snares: the allure of online porn, now blasting through the defenses of every teenager; the ease of replacing every conversation with a texting stream; the escape of living for a while in an online game where all the hazards of real human interaction are banished; the new video features on Instagram, and new friends to follow. It all slowly chipped away at my medi-tative composure. I cut my daily silences from one hour to twenty-five minutes, and then, almost a year later, to every other day. I knew this was fatal—that the key to gaining sustainable composure from meditation was rigorous discipline and practice, every day, whether you felt like it or not, whether it felt as if it were working or not. Like weekly Mass, it is the routine that gradually creates a space that lets your life breathe. But the world I rejoined seemed to conspire to take that space away from me. "I do what I hate," as the oldest son says in Terrence Malick's haunting *Tree of Life*.

I haven't given up, even as, each day, at various moments, I find myself giving in. There are books to be read, landscapes to be walked, friends to be with, life to be fully lived. And I realize that this is, in some ways, just another tale in the vast book of human frailty. But this new epidemic of distraction is our civilization's specific weakness. And its threat is not so much to our minds, even as they shape-shift under the pressure. The threat is to our souls. At this rate, if the noise does not relent, we might even forget we have any.

America and the Abyss

November 3, 2016 | *NEW YORK* magazine

T he most frustrating aspect of the last twelve months has been the notion that we have been in a normal, if truly ugly, election cycle, with one extremely colorful and unpredictable figure leading the Republican Party in an otherwise conventional political struggle over policy. It has been clear for months now, it seems to me, that this is a delusion. A far more accurate account of the past year is that an openly proto-fascist cult leader has emerged to forge a popular movement that has taken over one of the major political parties, eroded central norms of democratic life, undermined American democratic institutions, and now stands on the brink of seizing power in Washington. I made this argument at length in April, when Donald Trump was on the brink of securing the nomination. Everything that has happened since has only made my fears more pressing.

I find myself wondering if I have lost my marbles. It seems far too melodramatic. I am an emotional character—I feared that Obama might have thrown the election away in the first debate in 2012—and there are times in discussions with friends when the catastrophic scenarios we've been airing seem like something out of a dystopian miniseries designed for paranoids. Please, therefore, discount the following as the product of an excitable outlier if you see fit. I sure hope you're right. But as it seems more evident by the day that Donald Trump could very well become the next president of the United States, it is worth simply reiterating the evidence in front of our nose that this republic is in serious danger.

This is what we now know: Donald Trump is the first candidate for president who seems to have little understanding of or reverence for constitutional democracy and presents himself as a future strongman. This begins with his character—if that word could possibly be ascribed to his disturbed, unstable, and uncontrollable psyche. He has revealed himself incapable of treating other people as anything but instruments to his will. He seems to have no close friends, because he can tolerate no equals. He never appears to laugh, because that would cede a recognition to another's fleeting power over him. He treats his wives and his children as mere extensions of his power, and those who have resisted the patriarch have been exiled, humiliated, or bought off.

His relationship to men—from his school days to the primary campaign—is rooted entirely in dominance and mastery, through bullying, intimidation, and, if necessary, humiliation. His relationship to women is entirely a function of his relationship to men: Women are solely a means to demonstrate his superiority in the alpha-male struggle. Women are to be pursued, captured, used, assaulted, or merely displayed to other men as an indication of his superiority. His response to any difficult relationship is to end it, usually by firing or humiliating or ruining someone. His core, motivating idea is the punishment or mockery of the weak and reverence for the strong. He cannot apologize or accept responsibility for failure. He has long treated the truth as entirely instrumental to his momentary personal interests. Setbacks of any kind can only be assuaged by vindictive, manic revenge.

He has no concept of a non-zero-sum engagement, in which a deal can be beneficial for both sides. A win-win scenario is intolerable to him, because mastery of others is the only moment when he is psychically at peace. (This is one reason why he cannot understand the entire idea of free trade or, indeed, NATO, or the separation of powers.) In any conflict, he cannot ever back down; he must continue to up the ante until the danger to everyone around him is so great as to demand their surrender. From his feckless business deals and billion-dollar debts to his utter indifference to the damage he has done to those institutions unfortunate enough to engage him, he has shown no concern for the interests of other human beings. Just ask the countless people he has casually fired, or the political party he has effectively destroyed. He has violated and eroded the core norms that make liberal democracy possible—because such norms were designed precisely to guard against the kind of tyrannical impulses and pathological narcissism he personifies.

Anyone paying attention knew this before he conquered the Republican Party. Look at what has happened since then. He sees the judicial system as entirely subordinate to his political and personal interests, and impugned a federal judge for his ethnicity. He has accused the Justice Department and FBI of a criminal conspiracy to protect Hillary Clinton. He has refused to accept in advance the results of any election in which he loses. He has openly argued for government persecution of newspapers that oppose him—pledging to open up antitrust prosecution against *The Washington Post*, for example. He is the first candidate in American history to subject the press pool to mob hatred—"disgusting, disgusting people"—and anti-Semitic poison from his foulest supporters. He is the first candidate in American history to pledge to imprison his election opponent if he wins power. He has mused about using nuclear weapons in regional wars. He has celebrated police powers that openly deploy racial profiling. His favorite foreign leader is a man who murders journalists, commits war crimes, uses xenophobia and warfare to cement his political standing, and believes in the dismemberment of both NATO and the European Union. Nor has he rejected any of his most odious promises during the primary—from torturing prisoners "even if it doesn't work" to murdering the innocent family members of terror suspects to rounding up several million noncitizens to declaring war on an entire religion, proposing to create a database to monitor its adherents and bar most from entering the country.

We are told we cannot use the term "fascist" to describe this. I'm at a loss to find a more accurate alternative.

The Establishments of both right and left have had many opportunities to stop him and have failed by spectacular displays of cowardice, narrow self-interest, and bewilderment. The right has been spectacularly craven. Trump has no loyalty to the party apparatus that has elevated him to a possible victory next Tuesday—declaring war on the Speaker of the House, attacking the RNC whenever it fails to toady to him, denigrating every single rival Republican candidate, even treating his own vice-presidential nominee as someone he can openly and contemptuously contradict with impunity. And yet that party, like the conservative parties in Weimar Germany, has never seen fit to anathematize him, only seeking to exploit his followers in the vain and foolish delusion that they can control him in the future in ways they have not been able to in the past.

The Republican media complex has enabled and promoted his lies and conspiracy theories and, above all, his hysteria. From the poisonous propaganda of most of Fox News to the internet madness of the alt-right, they have all made a fortune this past decade by describing the world as a hellhole of chaos and disorder and crime for which the only possible solution is a third-world strong-man. The Republicans in Washington complemented this picture of crisis by a policy of calculated obstruction to every single measure a Democratic president has attempted, rendering the Congress so gridlocked that it has been incapable of even passing a budget without constitutional crisis, filling a vacant Supreme Court seat, or reforming a health-care policy in pragmatic fashion. They have risked the nation's very credit rating to vent their rage. They have helped reduce the public support of the central democratic institution in American government, the Congress, to a consistently basement level never seen before—another disturbing analogy to the discredited democratic parlia-ments of the 1930s. The Republicans have thereby become a force bent less on governing than on destroying the very institutions that make democracy and the rule of law possible. They have not been conservative in any sane meaning of that term for many, many years. They are nihilist revolutionaries of the far right in search of a galvanizing revolutionary leader. And they have now found their man.

For their part, the feckless Democrats decided to nominate one of the most mediocre, compromised, and Establishment figures one can imagine in a deeply restless moment of anxiety and discontent. They knew full well that Hillary Clinton is incapable of inspiring, of providing reassurance, or of persuading anyone who isn't already in her corner, and that her self-regard and privilege and moneygrubbing have led her into the petty scandals that have been exploited by the tyrant's massive lies. The staggering decision by FBI director James Comey to violate established protocol and throw the election into chaos to preserve his credibility with the far right has ripped open her greatest vulnerability—her caginess and deviousness—while also epitomizing the endgame of the chaos that the GOP has sought to exploit. Comey made the final days of the election about her. And if this election is a referendum on Clinton, she loses.

Yes, she has shrewdly deployed fear against fear—but she is running against the master of fear. The Democrats, with the exception of Obama, have long been unable to marshal emotion as a political weapon, advancing a bloodless rationalism that has never been a match for the tribal national passions of the right. Clinton's rallies have been pale copies of the bloodthirsty mobs Trump has marshaled and whipped into ever-higher states of frenzy. In every debate, she won on points, but I fear she failed to offer a compelling, simple, and positive reason for her candidacy. Only a party utterly divorced from half the country it seeks to represent could have made such a drastic error of hubris and complacency.

Some—including many who will be voting for Trump—will argue that even if the unstable, sleepless, vindictive tyrant wins on Tuesday, he will be restrained by the system when he seizes power. Let's game this out for a moment. Over the last year, which forces in the GOP have been able to stand up to him? Even his closest aides have been unable to get him to concentrate before a debate. He set up a policy advisory apparatus and then completely ignored it until it was disbanded. His foreign-policy advisers can scarcely be found. He says he knows more than any general, any diplomat, and anyone with actual experience in government. He has declared his chief adviser to be himself. Even the criminal Richard Nixon was eventually restrained and dispatched by a Republican Establishment that still knew how to run the country and had a loyalty to broader American institutions. Such an Establishment no longer exists.

More to the point, if Trump wins, he will almost certainly bring with him the House, the Senate, and the Supreme Court. A President Clinton will be checked and balanced. A President Trump will be pushing through wide-open doors. Who can temper or stop him then? A Speaker who reveals the slightest inclination to resist him will be swiftly dispatched—or subjected to a very credible threat of being primaried. If the military top brass resist his belief in unpredictable or unethical or unlawful warfare, they will surely be fired. As for the administration of justice, he has openly declared his intent to use the power of the government to put his political opponent in jail. As for a free society, he has threatened to do what he can to put his media opponents into receivership.

What is so striking is that this requires no interpretation, no reading of the tea leaves. Trump has told Americans all of this—again and again—in plain English. His own temperamental instability has been displayed daily and in gory detail. From time to time, you can see his poll ratings plummet as revelations that would permanently sink any other candidate have dented his appeal. And then he resiliently and unstoppably moves back up. His bond with his supporters is absolute, total, and personal. It was months ago that he boasted that he could shoot someone on Fifth Avenue and his supporters would still be with him. And he was right. This is not a mark of a democratic leader; it is a mark of an authoritarian cult.

It is also, critically, a function of his platform. Fascism has never been on the ballot in America before. No candidate this close to power has signaled more clearly than Trump that he is a white-nationalist candidate determined to fight back against the browning of America. As mass immigration has changed the demographic identity of the soon-to-be majority-minority country with remarkable speed, and as those made uncomfortable by such drastic change have been dismissed as mere bigots and racists, Trump offers an electrifying hope of revenge and revanchism. The fire he has lighted will not be easily doused. If his policies lead to an economic downswing, he will find others to blame and conspiracies to flush out. If there is Republican resistance to his pledges to roll back free trade, he will call on his base to pressure the leadership to surrender. And if one of his first moves is to abandon the Iran nuclear deal, we will be hurtling rather quickly to a military confrontation, as Iran rushes to build a nuke before Trump can launch military attacks to thwart them. That rush to war would empower him still further.

Yes, he is an incompetent, a dilettante, a man who doesn't know what he doesn't know. Many of his moves will probably lead to a nosedive in support. But Trump cannot admit error and will need to deny it or scapegoat others or divert public attention. Those diversions could well be deeply destabilizing—and galvanized by events. There will doubtless be another incident between police and an unarmed black man under a Trump presidency. Rather than calm the nation, Trump will inflame it. There will be an Islamist terror attack of some kind—and possibly a wave of such attacks in response to his very election. Trump will exploit it with the subtlety of a Giuliani and the brutality of a Putin.

I have long had faith that some version of fascism cannot come to power in America. The events of the past year suggest deep reflection on that conviction. A political hurricane has arrived, as globalization has eroded the economic power of the white working classes, as the cultural left has overplayed its hand on social and racial issues, and as a catastrophic war and a financial crisis have robbed the elites of their credibility. As always in history, you still needed the spark, the unique actor who could deploy demagogic talent to drag an advanced country into violence and barbarism. In Trump, America found one for the ages.

Maybe the worst won't happen on Tuesday. Maybe this catastrophist possible reading of our times is massively overblown. Maybe this short essay will be ridiculed in the future, as either Clinton wins and prevails in power or Trump turns out to be a far different president than he has been a candidate. I sure hope so. But the fact that we may barely avoid a very deep crisis does not mitigate my anxiety. To paraphrase Benjamin Franklin, we live in a republic, if we can keep it. And yet, more than two centuries later, we are openly contemplating throwing it up in the air and seeing where it might land.

Do what you can.

America Wasn't
Built for Humans

September 19, 2017 | *NEW YORK* magazine

From time to time, I've wondered what it must be like to live in a truly tribal society. Watching Iraq or Syria these past few years, you get curious about how the collective mind can come so undone. What's it like to see the contours of someone's face, or hear his accent, or learn the town he's from, and almost reflexively know that he is your foe? How do you live peacefully for years among fellow citizens and then find yourself suddenly engaged in the mass murder of humans who look similar to you, live around you, and believe in the same God, but whose small differences in theology mean they must be killed before they kill you? In the Balkans, a long period of relative peace imposed by communism was shattered by brutal sectarian and ethnic warfare, as previously intermingled citizens split into unreconcilable groups. The same has happened in a developed democratic society—Northern Ireland—and in one of the most successful countries in Africa, Kenya.

Tribal loyalties turned Beirut, Lebanon's beautiful, cosmopolitan capital, into an urban wasteland in the 1970s; they caused close to a million deaths in a few months in Rwanda in the 1990s; they are turning Aung San Suu Kyi, winner of the Nobel Peace Prize, into an enabler of ethnic cleansing right now in Myanmar. British imperialists long knew that the best way to divide and conquer was by creating "countries" riven with tribal differences. Not that they were immune: even in successful modern democracies like Britain and Spain, the tribes of Scots and Catalans still threaten viable nation-states. In all these places, the people involved have been full citizens of their respective nations, but their deepest loyalty is to something else.

But then, we don't really have to wonder what it's like to live in a tribal society anymore, do we? Because we already do. Over the past couple of decades in America, the enduring, complicated divides of ideology, geography, party, class, religion, and race have mutated into something deeper, simpler to map, and therefore much more ominous. I don't just mean the rise of political polarization (although that's how it often expresses itself), nor the rise of political violence (the domestic terrorism of the late 1960s and '70s was far worse), nor even this country's ancient black-white racial conflict (though its potency endures).

I mean a new and compounding combination of all these differences into two coherent tribes, eerily balanced in political power, fighting not just to advance their own side but to provoke, condemn, and defeat the other.

I mean two tribes whose mutual incomprehension and loathing can drown out their love of country, each of whom scans current events almost entirely to see if they advance not so much their country's interests but their own. I mean two tribes where one contains most racial minorities and the other is disproportionately white; where one tribe lives on the coasts and in the cities and the other is scattered across a rural and exurban expanse; where one tribe holds on to traditional faith and the other is increasingly contemptuous of religion altogether; where one is viscerally nationalist and the other's outlook is increasingly global; where each dominates a major political party; and, most dangerously, where both are growing in intensity as they move further apart.

The project of American democracy—to live beyond such tribal identities, to construct a society based on the individual, to see ourselves as citizens of a people's republic, to place religion off-limits, and even in recent years to embrace a multiracial and post-religious society—was always an extremely precarious endeavor. It rested, from the beginning, on an eighteenth-century hope that deep divides can be bridged by a culture of compromise, and that emotion can be defeated by reason. It failed once, spectacularly, in the most brutal civil war any Western democracy has experienced in modern times. And here we are, in an equally tribal era, with a deeply divisive president who is suddenly scrambling Washington's political alignments, about to find out if we can prevent it from failing again.

Tribalism, it's always worth remembering, is not one aspect of human experience. It's the default human experience. It comes more naturally to us than any other way of life. For the overwhelming majority of our time on this planet, the tribe was the only form of human society. We lived for tens of thousands of years in compact, largely egalitarian groups of around fifty people or more, connected to one another by genetics and language, usually unwritten. Most tribes occupied their own familiar territory, with widespread sharing of food and no private property. A tribe had its own leaders and a myth of its own history. It sorted out what we did every day, what we thought every hour.

Tribal cohesion was essential to survival, and our first religions emerged for precisely this purpose. As Dominic Johnson argues in his recent book *God Is Watching You*, almost all indigenous societies had a common concept of the supernatural, and almost all of them saw their worst threats—hunger, disease, natural disasters, a loss in battle—as a consequence of disobeying a god. Religion therefore fused with communal identity and purpose; it was integral to keeping the enterprise afloat, and the idea of people within a tribe believing in different gods was incomprehensible. Such heretics would be killed.

The tribes that best survived (and thereby transmitted their genes to us) were, moreover, those most acutely aware of outsiders and potential foes. A failure to notice incoming strangers could end your life in an instant, and an indifference to the appearances of other human beings could mean defeat at the hands of rivals or the collapse of a tribe altogether. And so we became a deeply cooperative species—but primarily with our own kind. The notion of living alongside people who do not look like us and treating them as our fellows was meaningless for most of human history.

Comparatively few actual tribes exist today, but that doesn't mean that humans are genetically much different. In his book *Tribe*, Sebastian Junger relates a little-known fact about the Americans who pioneered the frontier. In the centuries in which white Europeans lived alongside Native American tribes, many Europeans split off from their fellow colonists, disappeared into the wilderness, and joined Indian society. Almost no natives voluntarily did the reverse. "Thousands of Europeans are Indians, and we have no examples of even one of those Aborigines having from choice become European," wrote one eighteenth-century Frenchman. "There must be in their social bond something singularly captivating and far superior to anything to be boasted of among us." That "something," Junger argues, was being a member of a tribe.

Successful modern democracies do not abolish this feeling; they co-opt it. Healthy tribalism endures in civil society in benign and overlapping ways. We find a sense of belonging, of unconditional pride, in our neighborhood and community, in our ethnic and social identities and their rituals, among our fellow enthusiasts. There are hip-hop and country-music tribes; bros; nerds; Wasps; Dead Heads and Packers fans; Facebook groups. (Yes, technology upends some tribes and enables new ones.) And then, most critically, there is the über-tribe that constitutes the nation-state, a megatribe that unites a country around shared national rituals, symbols, music, history, mythology, and events, that forms the core unit of belonging that makes a national democracy possible.

None of this is a problem. Tribalism only destabilizes a democracy when it calcifies into something bigger and more intense than our smaller, multiple loyalties, when it rivals our attachment to the nation as a whole, and when it turns rival tribes into enemies. And the most significant fact about American tribalism today is that all three of these characteristics now apply to our political parties, corrupting and even threatening our system of government.

If I were to identify one profound flaw in the founding of America, it would be its avoidance of our tribal nature. The Founders were suspicious of political parties altogether—but parties defined by race and religion and class and geography? I doubt they'd believe a republic could survive that, and they couldn't and didn't foresee it. In fact, as they conceived of a new society that would protect the individual rights of all humanity, they explicitly excluded a second tribe among them: African American slaves. Within a century, that moral and political blind spot cleaved the country down the middle and led to the kind of bloody, manic, and brutal tribal warfare we now think of as something that happens somewhere else.

But it did happen here, on a fault line that closely resembles today's tribal boundary. For a century after the Civil War, this divide, while still strong, was nonetheless diluted by myriad other ethnic loyalties, as waves of European immigrants came to America and competed with one another as well as with those already here. Some new tribes, such as Mormons, were accommodated simply by the ever-expanding frontier. And in the first half of the twentieth century, with immigration sharply curtailed after 1924, the World Wars acted as great unifiers and integrators. Our political parties became less polarized by race, as the FDR Democrats managed to attract more black voters as well as ethnic and southern whites. By 1956, nearly 40 percent of black voters still backed the GOP.

But we all know what happened next. The re-racialization of our parties began with Barry Goldwater's presidential campaign in 1964, when the GOP lost almost all of the black vote. It accelerated under Nixon's "southern strategy" in the wake of the civil-rights revolution. By Reagan's reelection, the two parties began to cohere again into the Civil War pattern, and had simply swapped places.

The failed nomination of Robert Bork to the Supreme Court was perhaps the first moment that a hubristic GOP nominated a figure on the far right, and an increasingly vocal left upended previous norms for judicial hearings, using race and gender as political weapons. Mass illegal Latino immigration added to the tribal mix as the GOP, led most notably by Pete Wilson in California, became increasingly defined by white immigration restrictionists and Hispanics moved to the Democrats. Newt Gingrich's revolutionary GOP then upped the ante, treating President Bill Clinton as illegitimate from the start, launching an absurd impeachment crusade, and destroying the comity that once kept Washington from complete partisan dysfunction. Abortion and gay rights further split urban and rural America. By the 2000 election, we were introduced to the red-blue map, though by then we could already recognize the two tribes it identified as they fought to a national draw. Choosing a president under those circumstances caused a constitutional crisis, one the Supreme Court resolved at the expense of losing much of its nonpartisan, nontribal authority.

Then there were other accelerants: the arrival of talk radio in the 1980s, Fox News in the '90s, and internet news and MSNBC in the aughts; the colossal blunder of the Iraq War, which wrecked the brief national unity after 9/11; and the rise of partisan gerrymandering that allowed the GOP to win, in 2016, 49 percent of the vote but 55 percent of House seats. (A recent study found that a full fifth of current districts are more convoluted than the original, contorted district that first gave us the term "gerrymander" in 1812.) The greatest threat to a politician today therefore is less a candidate from the opposing party than a more ideologically extreme primary opponent. The incentives for cross-tribal compromise have been eviscerated, and those for tribal extremism reinforced.

Add to this the great intellectual sorting of America, in which, for generations, mass college education sifted countless gifted young people from the heartland and deposited them in increasingly left-liberal universities and thereafter the major cities, from which they never returned, and then the shifting of our economy to favor the college educated, which only deepened the urban-rural divide. The absence of compulsory military service meant that our wars would be fought disproportionately by one tribe, and the rise of radical Islamic terrorism only inflamed tribal suspicions. Then there's the post-1965 wave of mass immigration, which disorients in ways that cannot be wished or shamed away; the decision among the country's intellectual elite to junk the "melting pot" metaphor as a model for immigration in favor of "multiculturalism"; and the decline of Christianity as a common cultural language for both political parties—which had been critical, for example, to the success of the civil-rights movement.

The myths that helped us unite as a nation began to fray. We once had a widely accepted narrative of our origins, shared icons that defined us, and a common pseudoethnicity—"whiteness"—into which new immigrants were encouraged to assimilate. Our much broader ethnic mix and the truths of history make this much harder today—as, of course, they should. But we should be clear-eyed about the consequence. We can no longer think of the Puritans without acknowledging the genocide that followed them; we cannot celebrate our Founding Fathers without seeing that slavery undergirded the society they constructed; we must tear down our Confederate statues and relitigate our oldest rifts. Even the national anthem now divides those who stand from those who kneel. We dismantled many of our myths, but have not yet formed new ones to replace them.

The result of all this is that a lopsided 69 percent of white Christians now vote Republican, while the Democrats get only 31. In the last decade, the gap in Christian identification between Democrats and Republicans has increased by 50 percent. In 2004, 44 percent of Latinos voted Republican for president; in 2016, 29 percent did. Forty-three percent of Asian Americans voted Republican in 2004; in 2016, 29 percent did. Since 2004, the most populous urban counties have also swung decisively toward the Democrats, in both blue and red states, while rural counties have shifted sharply to the GOP. When three core components of a tribal identity—race, religion, and geography—define your political parties, you're in serious trouble.

Some countries, where tribal cleavages spawned by ethnic and linguistic differences have long existed, understand this and have constructed systems of government designed to ameliorate the consequences. Unlike the United States, they encourage a culture of almost pathological compromise, or build constitutions that, unlike our own, take tribal conflict seriously. They often have a neutral head of state—a constitutional monarch or nonpartisan president—so that the legitimacy of the system is less easily defined by one tribe or the other. They tend to have proportional representation and more than two parties, so it's close to impossible for one party to govern without some sort of coalition. In the toughest cases, they have mandatory inclusion of minority parties in the government.

In Northern Ireland, for example, since the Good Friday Agreement of 1998, there are intricate arrangements in which no regional government for the province can exist without support from at least two parties representing the Catholic minority and the Protestant majority. The first minister and the deputy first minister have to be from different parties, one Catholic and one Protestant. If one or the other drops out, power reverts to Westminster. The Belgian government, to take another example, is required to have both French- and Flemish-speaking parties, representing the two linguistic and cultural tribes that make up the country.

These contrivances are not fail-safe, especially if the divisions are too great— such as Cyprus's experiment in the 1960s. But they can channel tribal conflict constructively and thereby weaken it. The Netherlands is the clearest success story. Its three main tribes (or "pillars," as they became known) were, for many years, Catholic, Protestant, and socialist. Each had its own political culture, media, and unions. But these were divided into five parties (one socialist, one conservative, one Catholic, and two Protestant). In practice, this required tribal cooperation through constant coalition governments that gravitated toward the center. Over time, as secularism took hold, the Netherlands evolved into a much more familiar variety of ideological parties, but its tradition of compromising, coalition governments remains.

The United States is built on a very different set of institutions. There is no neutral presidency here, and so when a rank tribalist wins the office and governs almost entirely in the interests of the hardest core of his base, half the country understandably feels as if it were under siege. Our two-party, winner-take-all system only works when both parties are trying to appeal to the same constituencies on a variety of issues.

Our undemocratic electoral structure exacerbates things. Donald Trump won 46 percent of the vote, attracting 3 million fewer voters than his opponent, but secured 56 percent of the Electoral College. Republicans won 44 percent of the vote in the Senate seats up for reelection last year, but 65 percent of the seats. To have one tribe dominate another is one thing; to have the tribe that gained fewer votes govern the rest—and be the head of state—is testing political stability.

What you end up with is zero-sum politics, which drags the country toward either alternating administrations bent primarily on undoing everything their predecessors accomplished, or the kind of gridlock that has dominated national politics for the past seven years—or both. Slowly our political culture becomes one in which the two parties see themselves not as participating in a process of moving the country forward, sometimes by tilting to the right and sometimes to the left, as circumstances permit, alternating in power, compromising when in opposition, moderating when in government—but one where the goal is always the obliteration of the other party by securing a permanent majority, in an unending process of construction and demolition.

And so by 2017, 41 percent of Republicans and 38 percent of Democrats said they disagreed not just with their opponents' political views but with their values and goals beyond politics as well. Nearly 60 percent of all Americans find it stressful even to talk about Trump with someone who disagrees with them. A Monmouth poll, for good measure, recently found that 61 percent of Trump supporters say there's nothing he could do to make them change their minds about him; 57 percent of his opponents say the same thing. *Nothing* he could do.

One of the great attractions of tribalism is that you don't actually have to think very much. All you need to know on any given subject is which side you're on. You pick up signals from everyone around you, you slowly winnow your acquaintances to those who will reinforce your worldview, a tribal leader calls the shots, and everything slips into place. After a while, your immersion in tribal loyalty makes the activities of another tribe not just alien but close to incomprehensible. It has been noticed, for example, that primitive tribes can sometimes call their members simply people while describing others as

some kind of alien. So the word "Inuit" means "people," but a rival indigenous people, the Ojibwe, call them Eskimos, which, according to lore, means
"eaters of raw meat."

When criticized by a member of a rival tribe, a tribalist will not reflect
on his own actions or assumptions but instantly point to the same flaw in his
enemy. The most powerful tribalist among us, Trump, does this constantly.
When confronted with his own history of sexual assault, for example, he gave
the tiniest of apologies and immediately accused his opponent's husband of
worse, inviting several of Bill Clinton's accusers to a press conference. But in
this, he was only reflecting the now near-ubiquitous trend of "whataboutism,"
as any glance at a comments section or a cable slugfest will reveal. The Soviets perfected this in the Cold War, deflecting from their horrific Gulags by
pointing, for example, to racial strife in the United States. It tells you a lot
about our time that a tactic once honed in a global power struggle between
two nations now occurs within one. What the Soviets used against us we now
use against one another.

In America, the intellectual elites, far from being a key rational bloc resisting this, have succumbed. The intellectual right and the academic left have
long since dispensed with the idea of a mutual exchange of ideas. In a new study
of the voting habits of professors, Democrats outnumber Republicans twelve
to one, and the imbalance is growing. Among professors under thirty-six, the
ratio is almost twenty-three to one. It's not a surprise, then, that once-esoteric
neo-Marxist ideologies—such as critical race and gender theory and postmodernism, the bastard children of Herbert Marcuse and Michel Foucault—have
become the premises of higher education, the orthodoxy of a new and mandatory religion. Their practical implications—such as "safe spaces," speech
regarded as violence, racially segregated graduation ceremonies, the policing
of "microaggressions," the checking of "white privilege"—are now embedded
in the institutions themselves.

Conservative dissent therefore becomes tribal blasphemy. Free speech
can quickly become "hate speech," "hate speech" becomes indistinguishable
from a "hate crime," and a crime needs to be punished. Many members of
the academic elite regard opposing views as threats to others' existences, and
conservative speakers often can only get a hearing on campus under lockdown.
This seeps into the broader culture. It leads directly to a tech entrepreneur like

Brendan Eich being hounded out of a company, Mozilla, he created because he once opposed marriage equality, or a brilliant coder, James Damore, being fired from Google for airing civil, empirical arguments against the left-feminist assumptions behind the company's employment practices.

It's why a young gay freelance writer, Chadwick Moore, could have a record of solid journalism, write a balanced profile of Milo Yiannopoulos for *Out* magazine, and then be subjected to an avalanche of bile from readers and a public denunciation signed by many of his fellow gay journalists. He lost his relationship with the magazine shortly thereafter. Moore is a fascinating case in how tribalism now infects everything. After being ostracized by his own tribe, he flipped, turned into a parody of MAGA conformity, and became an employee of Milo Inc.

There is, of course, an enormous conservative intellectual counter-Establishment, an often-incestuous network of think tanks, foundations, journals, and magazines that exists outside of universities. It, too, has fomented its own orthodoxies, policed dissent, and punished heresy.

Conservatism thrived in America when it was dedicated to criticizing liberalism's failures, engaging with it empirically, and offering practical alternatives to the same problems. It has since withered into an intellectual movement that does little but talk to itself and guard its ideological boundaries. To be a conservative critic of George W. Bush, for example, meant risking not just social ostracism but, for many, loss of livelihood. I recall being applauded by the conservative media—and trashed by the left—when I endorsed Bush in 2000 and used my blog to champion the Iraq War. But when I realized the depth of my mistake, regretted my own tribal rhetoric, and wrote about it, I was immediately transformed into an unmentionable leftist. My writing career survived because I had my own blog and a foot in liberal media. But most others have no such escape routes.

And so, among tribal conservatives, the Iraq War remained a taboo topic when it wasn't still regarded as a smashing success, tax cuts were still the solution to every economic woe, free trade was all benefit and no cost, and so on. Health care was perhaps the most obvious example of this intellectual closure. Republican opposition to the Affordable Care Act was immediate and total. Even though the essential contours of the policy had been honed at the Heritage Foundation, even though a Republican governor had pioneered it in

Massachusetts, and even though that governor became the Republican presidential nominee in 2012, the anathematization of it defined the GOP for seven years. After conservative writer David Frum dared to argue that a moderate, market-oriented reform to the health-care system was not the ideological hill for the GOP to die on, he lost his job at the American Enterprise Institute. When it actually came to undoing the reform earlier this year, the GOP had precious little intellectual capital to fall back on, no alternative way to keep millions insured, no history of explaining to voters outside their own tribe what principles they were even trying to apply.

George Orwell famously defined this mindset as identifying yourself with a movement, "placing it beyond good and evil and recognising no other duty than that of advancing its interests." It's typified, he noted, by self-contradiction and indifference to reality. And so many severe critics of George W. Bush's surveillance policies became oddly muted when Obama adopted most of them; Democrats looked the other way as Obama ramped up deportations to levels higher than Trump's rate so far. Republicans, in turn, were obsessed with the national debt when Obama was in office, despite the deepest recession in decades. But the minute Trump came to power, they couldn't be more enthusiastic about a tax package that could add trillions of dollars to it. No tribe was more federalist when it came to marijuana laws than liberals, and no tribe was less federalist when it came to abortion. Reverse that for conservatives. For the right tribe, everything is genetic except homosexuality; for the left tribe, nothing is genetic except homosexuality. During the Bush years, liberals inveighed ceaselessly against executive overreach; under Obama, they cheered when he used his executive authority to alter immigration laws and impose new environmental regulations by fiat.

As for indifference to reality, today's Republicans cannot accept that human-produced carbon is destroying the planet and today's Democrats must believe that different outcomes for men and women in society are entirely a function of sexism. Even now, Democrats cannot say the words "illegal immigrants" or concede that affirmative action means discriminating against people because of their race. Republicans cannot own the fact that big tax cuts have not trickled down, or that President Bush authorized the brutal torture of prisoners, thereby unequivocally committing war crimes. Orwell again: "There is no crime, absolutely none, that cannot be condoned when 'our' side commits it. Even if one does not deny that the crime has happened, even if one knows that it is exactly the same crime as one has condemned in some other case . . . still one cannot *feel* that it is wrong." That is as good a summary of tribalism as you can get, that it substitutes a feeling—a really satisfying one—for an argument.

When a party leader in a liberal democracy proposes a shift in direction, there is usually an internal debate. It can go on for years. When a tribal leader does so, the tribe immediately jumps on command. And so the Republicans went from free trade to protectionism, and from internationalism to nationalism, almost overnight. For decades, a defining foreign-policy concern for Republicans was suspicion of and hostility to the Soviet Union and Russia. In the 2012 election, Mitt Romney called Moscow the number-one geopolitical enemy of the United States. And yet between 2014 and 2017, a period when Putin engaged in maximal provocation, occupying Crimea and moving troops into Ukraine, Republican approval of the authoritarian thug in the Kremlin leapt from 10 to 32 percent.

And then there is the stance of white evangelicals, a pillar of the red tribe. Among their persistent concerns has long been the decline of traditional marriage, the coarsening of public discourse, and the centrality of personal virtue to the conduct of public office. In the 1990s, they assailed Bill Clinton as the font of decadence; then they lionized George W. Bush, who promised to return what they often called dignity to the Oval Office. And yet when a black Democrat with exemplary personal morality, impeccable public civility, a man devoted to his wife and children and a model for African American fathers, entered the White House, they treated him as a threat to civilization. Even as he gave speeches drenched in Christian allegory and offered a eulogy in Charleston that ended with a cathartic rendition of "Amazing Grace," they retained a suspicion that he was secretly a Muslim. And when they encountered a foulmouthed pagan who bragged of grabbing women by the pussy, used the tabloids to humiliate his wife, married three times, boasted about the hotness of his own daughter, touted the size of his own dick in a presidential debate, and spoke of avoiding STDs as his personal Vietnam, they gave him more monolithic support than any candidate since Reagan, including born-again Bush and squeaky-clean Romney. In 2011, a poll found that only 30 percent of white evangelicals believed that private immorality was irrelevant for public life. This month, the same poll found that the number had skyrocketed to 72 percent.

Total immersion within one's tribe also leads to increasingly extreme ideas. The word "hate," for example, has now become a one-stop replacement for a whole spectrum of varying, milder emotions involved with bias toward others: discomfort, fear, unease, suspicion, ignorance, confusion. And it has even now come to include simply defending traditional Christian, Jewish, and Muslim doctrine on questions such as homosexuality.

Or take the current promiscuous use of the term "white supremacist." We used to know what that meant. It meant advocates and practitioners of slavery, believers in the right of white people to rule over all others, subscribers to a theory of a master race, Jim Crow supporters, George Wallace voters. But it is now routinely used on the left to mean, simply, racism in a multicultural America, in which European Americans are a fast-evaporating ethnic majority. It's a term that implies there is no difference in race relations between America today and America in, say, the 1830s or the 1930s. This rhetoric is not just untrue; it is dangerous. It wins no converts, and when actual white supremacists march in the streets you have no language left to describe them as any different from, say, all Trump supporters, including the 13 percent of black men who voted for him.

Liberals should be able to understand this by reading any conservative online journalism and encountering the term "the left." It represents a large, amorphous blob of malevolent human beings, with no variation among them, no reasonable ideas, nothing identifiably human at all. Start perusing, say, townhall.com, and you will soon stumble onto something like this, written recently by one of my favorite right tribalists, Kurt Schlichter: "They hate you. Leftists don't merely disagree with you. They don't merely feel you are misguided. They don't think you are merely wrong. They hate you. They want you enslaved and obedient, if not dead. Once you get that, everything that is happening now will make sense." And, yes, everything will. How does Schlichter describe the right? "Normals." It's the Inuit and the Eskimos all over again.

This atmosphere can affect even the finest minds. I think of Ta-Nehisi Coates, the essayist and memoirist. Not long ago, he was a subtle, complicated, and beautiful writer. He could push back against his own tribe. He could write critically of the idea that "there never is any black agency—to be

African-American is to be an automaton responding to either white racism or cultural pathology. No way you could actually have free will." He could persuasively push against "nihilism and paranoia" among his own, to champion the idea of being "critical, not just of the larger white narrative, but of the narrative put forth by those around you." He could speak of street culture as someone who lived it and yet knew, as he put it in an essay called "A Culture of Poverty," that " 'I ain't no punk' may shield you from neighborhood violence. But it cannot shield you from algebra, when your teacher tries to correct you. It cannot shield you from losing hours, when your supervisor corrects your work." He could do this while brilliantly conveying the systemic racism that crushes the souls of so many black Americans.

He remains a vital voice but, in more recent years, a somewhat different one. His mood has become much gloomier. He calls the Obama presidency a "tragedy," and describes many Trump supporters as "not so different from those same Americans who grin back at us in lynching photos." He's written about how watching cops and firefighters enter the smoldering World Trade Center instantly reminded him of cops mistreating blacks: they "were not human to me." In his latest essay in *The Atlantic*, analyzing why Donald Trump won the last election, he dismisses any notion that economic distress might have played a role as "empty" and ignores other factors, such as Hillary Clinton's terrible candidacy, the populist revolt against immigration that had become a potent force across the West, and the possibility that the pace of social change might have triggered a backlash among traditionalists. No, there was one meaningful explanation only: white supremacism. And those who accept, as I do, that racism was indeed a big part of the equation but also saw other factors at work were simply luxuriating in our own white privilege because we are never under "racism's boot."

A writer is entitled to shift perspective. What's more salient is his audience. He once had a small but devoted and querulous readership for his often-surprising blog. Today his works are huge best sellers, and it is deemed near blasphemous among liberals to criticize them.

How to unwind this increasingly dangerous dysfunction? It's not easy to be optimistic with Trump as president. And given his malignant narcissism, despotic instincts, absence of empathy, and constant incitement of racial and xenophobic hatred, it's extremely hard not to be tribal in return. There is no divide he doesn't want to deepen, no conflict he doesn't want to start or intensify. How on Earth can we not "resist"?

But we should not delude ourselves that this is all a Trump problem. What Obama could not overcome would have buried Hillary Clinton, who, almost uniquely in public life, carries the scars of our tribal era. Her campaign made no effort to persuade "deplorables," just to condemn them, and her core strategy was not to engage those on the fence but to maximize the turnout of her demographic tribe.

In fact, the person best positioned to get us out of this tribal trap would be . . . well . . . bear with me . . . Trump. The model would be Bill Clinton, the first president to meet our newly configured divide. Clinton leveraged the loyalty of Democrats thrilled to regain the White House in order to triangulate toward centrist compromises with the GOP. You can argue about the merits of the results, but he was able to govern, to move legislation forward, to reform welfare, reduce crime, turn the deficit into a surplus, survive impeachment, and end his term a popular president.

Trump is as much an opportunist as a tribalist; he won the presidency by having an intuitive, instinctive grasp of how to inflame and exploit our tribal divide. His base is therefore more fanatically loyal and his policy views even more, shall we say, flexible than Clinton's. His recent dealings with the Democratic congressional leadership have flummoxed party leaders and disrupted our political storytelling. That's something worth celebrating. His new openness to trade legislating DACA in return for stronger immigration enforcement is especially good news. If Trump is right that he could shoot someone on Fifth Avenue and his followers would still support him, he's surely uniquely capable of cutting deals with the Democrats while keeping much of the Republican base in line (and kneecapping Paul Ryan and Mitch McConnell). Two new polls back this up. Rasmussen found that 72 percent of Republican voters support Trump's working with Democrats; YouGov found that Republicans backed Trump's deal with Schumer and Pelosi by 62 to 18 percent.

The Democrats are now, surprisingly, confronting a choice many thought they would only face in a best-case-scenario midterm election, and their political calculus is suddenly much more complicated than pure resistance. Might the best interest of the country be served by working with Trump? And if they do win the House in 2018, should they seek to destroy Trump's presidency, much like GOP leaders in Congress chose to do with Obama? Should they try to end it through impeachment, as the GOP attempted with Bill Clinton? Or could they try to moderate the tribal divide? Maybe it's no longer a complete fantasy that they might even find a compromise that reforms the Affordable Care Act while allowing Trump to claim he replaced it—and use that as a model for further collaboration. But if Democratic leaders choose to de-escalate our tribal war rather than to destroy their political nemesis, would their base revolt?

Or maybe we can just reassure ourselves that our tribalism is mainly a function of the older generation's racial and cultural panic and we will slowly move through and past it. Maybe Trump's victory is just one last hurrah of an older, whiter American identity that we can outlast without a cathartic crisis or conflict. One trouble with this hopefulness is that "whiteness" is a subjective term. It's possible that more Latinos will identify as white in the future, as other immigrant minorities have over time, thereby maintaining our tribal balance. It's also possible that our ethnic and cultural divide could very much worsen in the meantime, especially as the demise of the old white majority becomes closer to statistical reality. White Christians are panicked and paranoid about religious freedom now. How will they feel when vastly more secular and multiracial generations come to power? And if the Democrats try to impeach a president who has no interest in the stability or integrity of our liberal democracy, and if his base sees it, as they will, as an Establishment attempt at nullifying their vote, are we really prepared to handle the civil unrest and constitutional crisis that would almost certainly follow?

Tribalism is not a static force. It feeds on itself. It appeals on a gut level and evokes emotions that are not easily controlled and usually spiral toward real conflict. And there is no sign that the deeper forces that have accelerated this—globalization, social atomization, secularization, media polarization, ever more multiculturalism—will weaken. The rhetorical extremes have already been pushed further than most of us thought possible only a couple of years ago, and the rival camps are even more hermetically sealed. In 2015, did any of us anticipate that neo-Nazis would be openly parading with torches on a college campus or that antifa activists would be proudly extolling violence as the only serious response to the Trump era?

As utopian as it sounds, I truly believe all of us have to at least try to change the culture from the ground up. There are two ideas that might be of help, it seems to me. The first is individuality. I don't mean individualism. Nothing is more conducive to tribalism than a sea of disconnected, atomized individuals searching for some broader tribe to belong to. I mean valuing the unique human being—distinct from any group identity, quirky, full of character and contradictions, skeptical, rebellious, immune to being labeled or bludgeoned into a broader tribal grouping. This cultural antidote to tribalism, left and right, is still here in America and ready to be rediscovered. That we expanded the space for this to flourish is one of the greatest achievements of the West.

Perhaps I'm biased because I'm an individual by default. I'm gay but Catholic, conservative but independent, a Brit but American, religious but secular. What tribe would ever have me? I may be an extreme case, but we all are nonconformist to some degree. Nurturing your difference or dissent from your own group is difficult; appreciating the individuality of those in other tribes is even harder. It takes effort and imagination, openness to dissent, even an occasional embrace of blasphemy.

And, at some point, we also need mutual forgiveness. It doesn't matter if you believe, as I do, that the right bears the bulk of the historical blame. No tribal conflict has ever been unwound without magnanimity. Yitzhak Rabin had it, but it was not enough. Nelson Mandela had it, and it was. In Colombia earlier this month, as a fragile peace agreement met public opposition, Pope Francis insisted that grudges be left behind: "All of us are necessary to create and form a society. This isn't just done with the 'pure-blooded' ones, but rather with everyone. And here is where the greatness of the country lies, in that there is room for all and all are important." If societies scarred by recent domestic terrorism can aim at this, why should it be so impossible for us?

But this requires, of course, first recognizing our own tribal thinking. So much of our debates are now an easy either-or rather than a complicated both-and. In our tribal certainties, we often distort what we actually believe in the quiet of our hearts, and fail to see what aspects of truth the other tribe may grasp.

Not all resistance to mass immigration or multiculturalism is mere racism or bigotry, and not every complaint about racism and sexism is baseless. Many older white Americans are not so much full of hate as full of fear. Equally, many minorities and women face genuine blocks to their advancement because of subtle and unsubtle bias, and it is not mere victim mongering. We also don't have to deny African American agency in order to account for the historic patterns of injustice that still haunt an entire community. We need to recall that most immigrants are simply seeking a better life, but also that a country that cannot control its borders is not a country at all. We're rightly concerned that religious faith can easily lead to intolerance, but we needn't conclude that having faith is a pathology. We need not renounce our cosmopolitanism to reengage and respect those in rural America, and we don't have to abandon our patriotism to see that the urban mix is also integral to what it means to be an American today. The actual solutions to our problems are to be found in the current no-man's-land that lies between the two tribes. Reentering it with empiricism and moderation to find different compromises for different issues is the only way out of our increasingly dangerous impasse.

All of this runs deeply against the grain. It's counterintuitive. It's emotionally unpleasant. It fights against our very DNA. Compared with bathing in the affirming balm of a tribe, it's deeply unsatisfying. But no one ever claimed that living in a republic was going to be easy—if we really want to keep it.

Kaepernick's Message Is Getting Lost—Along with the Facts on Race and Police Violence

September 29, 2017 | *NEW YORK* magazine

In all the NFL kerfuffle, we've lost sight, it seems to me, of precisely why Colin Kaepernick and now many others have been kneeling. He's not kneeling because he's unpatriotic; he's kneeling because he *is* patriotic, and he wants his country to live up to its ideals. In his words: "I am not going to stand up to show pride in a flag for a country that oppresses black people and people of color. To me, this is bigger than football and it would be selfish on my part to look the other way. There are bodies in the street and people getting paid leave and getting away with murder." His core issue seems to be police interaction with black men, especially shootings. His teammate, Eric Reid, wrote an op-ed on Monday where he elaborated:

> In early 2016, I began paying attention to reports about the incredible number of unarmed black people being killed by the police. The posts on social media deeply disturbed me, but one in particular brought me to tears: the killing of Alton Sterling in my hometown Baton Rouge, La. This could have happened to any of my family members who still live in the area.

Let's unpack Reid's concern at "the incredible number of unarmed black people being killed by the police." My colleague Eric Levitz this week put a number on it: "We live in a country where police gun down 1,000 unarmed, disproportionately black citizens on an annual basis." He gets that number from the recent *Washington Post* attempt to nail down specific data on how common this is. But he falls understandably into the trap that many of us do. Thanks to numerous horrifying videos, and some horrible cases, like those of Philando Castile and Eric Garner, we have come to assume that unarmed black men are being gunned down in large numbers. But the *Washington Post* data do not, in fact, back that idea up.

The Post has indeed found that there's a strikingly consistent number of fatal police shootings each year: close to one thousand people of all races. But that figure includes the armed *and* the unarmed. Fatal police shootings of the unarmed—the issue Kaepernick and Reid cite—are far fewer. In the first six months of this year, for example, *The Post* found a total of twenty-seven fatal shootings of unarmed people, of which black men constituted seven. Yes, you read that right: seven. There are 22 million black men in America. If an African American man is not armed, the chance that he will be killed by the police in any recent year is 0.00006 percent. If a black man is carrying a weapon, the chance is 0.00075. One is too many, but it seems to me important to get the scale of this right. Our perceptions are not reality.

In other policy areas, left-liberals tend to agree with me on this general logic. They usually insist on not confusing an anecdote for solid data. They point out, for example, the infinitesimal chance that you will be killed by a terrorist in order to puncture the compelling and emotional narrative that we are a nation under siege by jihadists. They note that the public's view that crime has been rising is, in fact, a fiction drummed up by Trump—and they cite the kind of data I just provided to prove it. But when it comes to race and police shootings, the data take second place to emotion. This is not bad faith on the part of left-liberals. It's rooted in an admirable concern about a vital topic—the use of violence by the state against citizens. And I have no doubt at all that Kaepernick and Reid are sincere, and I absolutely defend their right to protest in the way they have, and am disgusted by the president's response. But on the deaths of unarmed black men, the left-liberal characterization of the problem just does not match the statistical reality.

How about looking at all such deaths, armed and unarmed, and the context for them? One avenue for understanding what's going on is to ask a national sample of citizens, black and white, about their interactions with police. A Cornell PhD student, Philippe Lemoine, has dug into exactly that: by examining the data from the Police-Public Contact Survey, conducted by the Bureau of Justice Statistics. This is testimony from black people themselves, not the police; it's far less tainted than self-serving police records.

It's a big survey—around 150,000 people, including 16,000 African Americans. And it provides one answer (although not definitive) to some obvious questions. First off, are black men in America disproportionately likely to have contact with the police? Surprisingly, no. In the survey years that Lemoine looked at, 20.7 percent of white men say they interacted at least once with a cop, compared with 17.5 percent of black men. The data also separate out those with multiple encounters. According to Lemoine, black men (1.5 percent) are indeed more likely than whites (1.2 percent) to have more than three contacts with police per year—but it's not a huge difference.

On the key measure of use of force by the cops, however, black men with at least one encounter with cops are more than twice as likely to report the use of force as whites (1 percent versus 0.4 percent). That's the nub of it. "Force," by the way, includes a verbal threat of it, as well as restraining, or subduing. If you restrict it to physical violence, the data are worse: of men who have had at least one encounter with the police in a given year, 0.9 percent of white men reported the use of violence, compared with 3.4 percent of black men. (For force likely to cause physical injury, i.e., extreme force, however, the ratio is actually better: 0.39 percent for white men compared with 0.46 percent of black men.)

What do we make of this data? I think it shows the following: that police violence against black men, very broadly defined, is twice as common as against white men and, narrowly defined as physical force, three times as common, but that there's no racial difference in police violence that might lead to physical harm, and all such violence is rare. (Recall that the 3.4 percent of black men who experience violence at the hands of the police are 3.4 percent of the 17.5 percent of those who have at least one encounter with the cops, i.e., 0.5 percent of all black men.)

Is "rare" a fair judgment? It's certainly a subjective one, and I do not know how I would feel if there were a 0.5 percent chance that any time I encountered a cop I could be subjected to physical violence, as opposed to the 0.2

percent chance that I, as a white man, experience. What makes it worse for black men, of course, is something called history, in which any violence by the state rightly comes with immensely more emotional and political resonance — and geography. Police violence may be rare across the entire country, but it is concentrated in urban pockets, where the atmosphere is therefore more fearful—and there's a natural tendency to extrapolate from that context.

Specific horrifying incidents—like Alton Sterling's death—operate in our psyches the way 9/11 does. It understandably terrified Eric Reid—but also distorted his assessment of the actual risk that one of his family members could suffer the same fate. It's true, too, that the huge racial discrepancy in the prison population affects our judgment. You could also argue that lynching was statistically very rare in the past, but it instilled a real terror that belied this real fact. The problem with this analogy, however, is that we're not talking about extralegal lynchings by civilians, in the context of slavery or segregation or state-imposed discrimination. We're talking about instantaneous decisions by cops, often in contexts where their own lives are at stake as well. Their perspective—and many of these cops are also African American—matters as well.

This is the balance we have to strike. We can and should honor the spirit of the protests. But we cannot allow ourselves to let emotion, however justified, overwhelm reality. To give the impression that police are gunning down black men in America solely because they are black is a dangerous exaggeration that undermines the vital work of the police. It's also a profound indictment of a nation that America, in this respect, simply doesn't deserve.

We All Live on Campus Now

February 9, 2018 | *NEW YORK* magazine

———————

O ver the last year, the most common rebuttal to my intermittent coverage of campus culture has been: Why does it matter? These are students, after all. They'll grow up once they leave their cloistered, neo-Marxist safe spaces. The real world isn't like that. You're exaggerating anyway. And so on. I certainly see the point. In the world beyond campus, few people use the term "microaggressions" without irony or an eye roll; claims of "white supremacy," "rape culture," or "white privilege" can seem like mere rhetorical flourishes; racial and gender segregation hasn't been perpetuated in the workplace yet; the campus Title IX sex tribunals where, under the Obama administration, the "preponderance of evidence" rather than the absence of a "reasonable doubt" could ruin a young man's life and future are just a product of a hothouse environment. And I can sometimes get carried away.

The reason I don't agree with this is because I believe ideas matter. When elite universities shift their entire worldview away from liberal education as we have long known it toward the imperatives of an identity-based "social justice" movement, the broader culture is in danger of drifting away from liberal democracy as well. If elites believe that the core truth of our society is a system of interlocking and oppressive power structures based around immutable characteristics like race or sex or sexual orientation, then sooner rather than later this will be reflected in our culture at large. What matters most of all in these colleges—your membership in a group that is embedded in a hierarchy of oppression—will soon enough be what matters in the society as a whole.

445

And, sure enough, the whole concept of an individual who exists apart from group identity is slipping from the discourse. The idea of individual merit—as opposed to various forms of unearned "privilege"—is increasingly suspect. The Enlightenment principles that formed the bedrock of the American experiment—untrammeled free speech, due process, individual (rather than group) rights—are now routinely understood as mere masks for "white male" power, code words for the oppression of women and nonwhites. Any differences in outcome for various groups must always be a function of "hate," rather than a function of nature or choice or freedom or individual agency. And anyone who questions these assertions is obviously a white supremacist himself.

Polarization has made this worse—because on the left, moderation now seems like a surrender to white nationalism, and because on the right, white identity politics has overwhelmed moderate conservatism. And Trump plays a critical role. His crude, bigoted version of identity politics seems to require an equal and opposite reaction. And I completely understand this impulse. Living in this period is to experience a daily, even hourly, psychological hazing from the bigot-in-chief. And when this white straight man revels in his torment of those unlike him—and does so with utter impunity among his supporters—there's a huge temptation to respond in kind. A president who has long treated women, in his words, "like shit," and bragged about it, is enough to provoke rage in any decent person. But anger is rarely a good frame of mind to pursue the imperatives of reason, let alone to defend the norms of liberal democracy.

And yes, I'm not talking about formal rules—but norms of liberal behavior. One of them is a robust public debate, free from intimidation. Liberals welcome dissent because it's our surest way to avoid error. Cultural Marxists fear dissent because they believe it can do harm to others' feelings and help sustain existing identity-based power structures. Yes, this is not about the First Amendment. The government is not preventing anyone from speaking. But it is about the spirit of the First Amendment. One of the reasons I defended Katie Roiphe against a campaign to preemptively suppress an essay of hers (even to the point of attempting to sabotage an entire issue of *Harper's*) is because of this spirit. She may be wrong, but that does not make her a hobgoblin whose career needs to be ended. And the impulse to intimidate, vilify, ruin, and abuse a writer for her opinions chills open debate. This is a real-world echo of the campus habit of disrupting speakers, no-platforming conservatives, and shouting people down. But now this reflexive hostility to speech is actually endorsed by writers and editors. Journalism itself has become a means of intimidating journalists.

An entirely intended by-product of this kind of bullying—and Roiphe is just the latest victim—is silence. If voicing an "incorrect" opinion can end your career, or mark you for instant social ostracism, you tend to keep quiet. This silence on any controversial social issue is endemic on college campuses, but it's now everywhere. Think of the wonderful *SNL* sketch recently, when three couples at a restaurant stumble onto the subject of Aziz Ansari. No one feels capable of saying anything in public. In the #MeToo debate, the gulf between what Twitter screams and what pops up in your private e-mail in-box is staggering. It's as big a gulf on the left as you find between the public statements and private views of Republicans on Trump. This is compounded by the idea that only a member of a minority group can speak about racism or homophobia, or that only women can discuss sexual harassment. The only reason this should be the case is if we think someone's identity is more important than the argument they might want to make. And that campus orthodoxy is now the culture's as a whole.

Microaggressions? How else do you explain how the glorious defenestration of horrific perpetrators of sexual abuse and harassment so quickly turned into a focus on an unwanted hug or an off-color remark? The whole cultural Marxist idea of a microaggression, after all, is that it's on a spectrum with macro-aggression. Patriarchy and white supremacy—which define our world—come in micro, mini, and macro forms, but it's all connected. A bad date is just one end of a patriarchal curve that ends with rape. And that's why left-feminists are not just interested in exposing workplace abuse or punishing sex crimes, but in policing even consensual sex for any hint of patriarchy's omnipresent threat.

Privacy? Forget about it. Traditionally, liberals have wanted to see politics debated without regard for the private lives of those in the fray—because personal details can distract from the cogency of the argument. But cultural Marxists see no such distinction. In the struggle against patriarchy, a distinction between the public and private makes no sense. In fact, policing private life—the personal is political, remember—is integral to advancing social justice. Ansari is a test case. I have yet to read an article that accounts for the violation of his dignity. There's a reason that totalitarian states will strip prisoners of their clothing. Left-feminists delight in doing this metaphorically to targeted men—effectively exposing them naked to public ridicule and examination because it both traumatizes the object and more importantly sits out there as a warning to others.

Due process? Real life is beginning to mimic college tribunals. When the perpetrator of an anonymous list accusing dozens of men of a whole range of sexual misdeeds is actually celebrated by much of mainstream media (in a fawning *New York Times* profile), you realize that we are living in another age of the Scarlet Letter. Moira Donegan has yet to express misgivings about possibly smearing the innocent—because the cause is far more important than individual fairness. Besides, if they're innocent, they'll be fine! Ezra Klein has openly endorsed campus rules that could frame some innocent men. One of the tweets in response to some of my recent writing on this has stuck in my mind ever since: "[C]an anyone justify why the POSSIBLE innocence of men is so much more important than the DEFINITE safety and comfort of women?" And yet this principle of preferring ten guilty people to go free rather than one innocent person to be found guilty was not so long ago a definition of Western civilization.

Treating people as individuals rather than representatives of designated groups? Almost every corporation now has affirmative action for every victim group in hiring and promotion. Workplace codes today read like campus speech codes of a few years ago. Voice dissent from this worldview and you'll be designated a bigot and fired (see James Damore at Google). The media is out front on this too. Just as campuses have diversity czars, roaming through every department to make sure they are in line, we now have a "gender editor" at *The New York Times*, Jessica Bennett. Her job is to "curate, elevate and expand gender reporting" throughout the newsroom. Among her previous work are forums on male abuse of power. "Our gender content will exist throughout *every section* of the paper and be produced in *every medium*," Bennett explains. And not just gender, of course: "I want everything we do to be intersectional in its approach—and race, class, and gender identity are an important part of that." Does she understand that the very word "intersectional" is a function of neo-Marxist critical race theory? Is this now the guiding philosophy of the paper of record?

Many media organizations now have various private, invitation-only Slack groups among their staffers—and they are often self-segregated into various gender and racial categories along classic campus "safe space" lines. No men are allowed in women's Slack; no non-p-o-c in the people-of-color Slack; and so on. And, of course, there are no such venues for men—in this Orwellian world, some groups are more equal than others. At *The Atlantic*, the identity obsession even requires exhaustive analyses of the identity of sources quoted in stories. Ed Yong, a science writer, keeps "a personal list of women and people of color who work in the beats that I usually cover," so he can make sure that he advances diversity even in his quotes.

Objective truth? Ha! The culture is now saturated with the concept of "your own truth"—based usually on your experience of race and gender. In the culture, it is now highly controversial for individuals in one racial/gender group to write about or portray anyone outside it—because there is no art that isn't rooted in identity. Movies are constantly pummeled by critics not for being bad movies but for being "problematic" on social justice. Books are censored in advance by sensitivity readers to conform with "social justice" protocols. As for objective reality, I was at an event earlier this week—not on a campus—when I made what I thought was the commonplace observation that Jim Crow laws no longer exist. Uncomprehending stares came back at me. What planet was I on? Not only does Jim Crow still exist, but slavery itself never went away! When I questioned this assertion by an African American woman, I was told it was "not my place" to question her reality. After all, I'm white.

Look: I don't doubt the good intentions of the new identity politics—to expand the opportunities for people previously excluded. I favor a politics that never discriminates against someone for immutable characteristics—and tries to make sure that as many people as possible feel they have access to our liberal democracy. But what we have now is far more than the liberal project of integrating minorities. It comes close to an attack on the liberal project itself. Marxism with a patina of liberalism on top is still Marxism—and it's as hostile to the idea of a free society as white nationalism is. So if you wonder why our discourse is now so freighted with fear, why so many choose silence as the path of least resistance, or why the core concepts of a liberal society—the individual's uniqueness, the primacy of reason, the protection of due process, objective truth—are so besieged, this is one of the reasons.

The goal of our culture now is not the emancipation of the individual from the group, but the permanent definition of the individual by the group. We used to call this bigotry. Now we call it being woke. You see: we are all on campus now.

The Poison We Pick

February 20, 2018 | *NEW YORK* magazine

I t is a beautiful, hardy flower, *Papaver somniferum*, a poppy that grows up to four feet in height and arrives in a multitude of colors. It thrives in temperate climates, needs no fertilizer, attracts few pests, and is as tough as many weeds. The blooms last only a few days and then the petals fall, revealing a matte, greenish-gray pod fringed with flutes. The seeds are nutritious and have no psychotropic effects. No one knows when the first curious human learned to crush this bulb-like pod and mix it with water, creating a substance that has an oddly calming and euphoric effect on the human brain. Nor do we know who first found out that if you cut the pod with a small knife, capture its milky sap, and leave that to harden in the air, you'll get a smokable nugget that provides an even more intense experience. We do know, from Neolithic ruins in Europe, that the cultivation of this plant goes back as far as six thousand years, probably further. Homer called it a "wondrous substance." Those who consumed it, he marveled, "did not shed a tear all day long, even if their mother or father had died, even if a brother or beloved son was killed before their own eyes." For millennia, it has salved pain, suspended grief, and seduced humans with its intimations of the divine. It was a medicine before there was such a thing as medicine. Every attempt to banish it, destroy it, or prohibit it has failed.

The poppy's power, in fact, is greater than ever. The molecules derived from it have effectively conquered contemporary America. Opium, heroin, morphine, and a universe of synthetic opioids, including the superpowerful painkiller fentanyl, are its proliferating offspring. More than 2 million Americans are now hooked on some kind of opioid, and drug overdoses—from heroin and fentanyl in particular—claimed more American lives last year than were lost in the entire Vietnam War. Overdose deaths are higher than in the peak year of AIDS and far higher than fatalities from car crashes. The poppy, through its many offshoots, has now been responsible for a decline in life spans in America for two years in a row, a decline that isn't happening in any other developed nation. According to the best estimates, opioids will kill another fifty-two thousand Americans this year alone—and up to half a million in the next decade.

We look at this number and have become almost numb to it. But of all the many social indicators flashing red in contemporary America, this is surely the brightest. Most of the ways we come to terms with this wave of mass death—by casting the pharmaceutical companies as the villains, or doctors as enablers, or blaming the Obama or Trump administrations or our policies of drug prohibition or our own collapse in morality and self-control or the economic stress the country is enduring—miss a deeper American story. It is a story of pain and the search for an end to it. It is a story of how the most ancient painkiller known to humanity has emerged to numb the agonies of the world's most highly evolved liberal democracy. Just as LSD helps explain the 1960s, cocaine the 1980s, and crack the 1990s, so opium defines this new era. I say "era" because this trend will, in all probability, last a very long time. The scale and darkness of this phenomenon is a sign of a civilization in a more acute crisis than we knew, a nation overwhelmed by a warp-speed, postindustrial world, a culture yearning to give up, indifferent to life and death, enraptured by withdrawal and nothingness. America, having pioneered the modern way of life, is now in the midst of trying to escape it.

How does an opioid make you feel? We tend to avoid this subject in discussing recreational drugs, because no one wants to encourage experimentation, let alone addiction. And it's easy to believe that weak people take drugs for inexplicable, reckless, or simply immoral reasons. What few are prepared to acknowledge in public is that drugs alter consciousness in specific and distinct ways that seem to make people at least temporarily happy, even if the consequences can be dire. Fewer still are willing to concede that there is a significant difference between these various forms of drug-induced "happiness"—that the draw of crack, say, is vastly different from that of heroin. But unless you understand what users get out of an illicit substance, it's impossible to understand its appeal, or why an epidemic takes off, or what purpose it is serving in so many people's lives. And it is significant, it seems to me, that the drugs now conquering America are downers: they are not the means to engage in life more vividly but to seek a respite from its ordeals.

The alkaloids that opioids contain have a large effect on the human brain because they tap into our natural "mu-opioid" receptors. The oxytocin we experience from love or friendship or orgasm is chemically replicated by the molecules derived from the poppy plant. It's a shortcut—and an instant intensification—of the happiness we might ordinarily experience in a good and fruitful communal life. It ends not just physical pain but psychological, emotional, even existential pain. And it can easily become a lifelong entanglement for anyone it seduces, a love affair in which the passion is more powerful than even the fear of extinction.

Perhaps the best descriptions of the poppy's appeal come to us from the gifted writers who have embraced and struggled with it. Many of the Romantic luminaries of the early nineteenth century—including the poets Coleridge, Byron, Shelley, Keats, and Baudelaire and the novelist Walter Scott—were as infused with opium as the late Beatles were with LSD. And the earliest and in many ways most poignant account of what opium and its derivatives feel like is provided by the classic memoir *Confessions of an English Opium-Eater*, published in 1821 by the writer Thomas De Quincey.

De Quincey suffered trauma in childhood, losing his sister when he was six and his father a year later. Throughout his life, he experienced bouts of acute stomach pain, as well as obvious depression, and at the age of nineteen he endured twenty consecutive days of what he called "excruciating rheumatic pains of the head and face." As his pain drove him mad, he finally went into an apothecary and bought some opium (which was legal at the time, as it was across the West until the war on drugs began a century ago).

An hour after he took it, his physical pain had vanished. But he was no longer even occupied by such mundane concerns. Instead, he was overwhelmed with what he called the "abyss of divine enjoyment" that overcame him: "What an upheaving from its lowest depths, of the inner spirit! . . . here was the secret of happiness, about which philosophers had disputed for many ages." The sensation from opium was steadier than alcohol, he reported, and calmer. "I stood at a distance, and aloof from the uproar of life," he wrote. "Here were the hopes which blossom in the paths of life, reconciled with the peace which is in the grave." A century later, the French writer Jean Cocteau described the experience in similar ways: "Opium remains unique and the euphoria it induces superior to health. I owe it my perfect hours."

The metaphors used are often of lightness, of floating: "Rising even as it falls, a feather," as William Brewer, America's poet laureate of the opioid crisis, describes it. "And then, within a fog that knows what I'm going to do, before I do—weightlessness." Unlike cannabis, opium does not make you want to share your experience with others, or make you giggly or hungry or paranoid. It seduces you into solitude and serenity and provokes a profound indifference to food. Unlike cocaine or crack or meth, it doesn't rev you up or boost your sex drive. It makes you drowsy—"somniferum" means "sleep inducing"—and lays waste to the libido. Once the high hits, your head begins to nod and your eyelids close.

When we see the addicted stumbling around like drunk ghosts, or collapsed on sidewalks or in restrooms, their faces pale, their skin riddled with infection, their eyes dead to the world, we often see only misery. What we do not see is what they see: in those moments, they feel beyond gravity, entranced away from pain and sadness. In the addict's eyes, it is those who are sober who are asleep. That is why the police and EMS workers who rescue those slipping toward death by administering blasts of naloxone—a powerful antidote, without which death rates would be even higher—are almost never thanked. They are hated. They ruined the high. And some part of being free from all pain makes you indifferent to death itself. Death is, after all, the greatest of existential pains. "Everything one achieves in life, even love, occurs in an express train racing toward death," Cocteau observed. "To smoke opium is to get out of the train while it is still moving. It is to concern oneself with something other than life or death."

This terrifyingly dark side of the poppy reveals itself the moment one tries to break free. The withdrawal from opioids is unlike any other. The waking nightmares, hideous stomach cramps, fevers, and psychic agony last for weeks, until the body chemically cleanses itself. "A silence," Cocteau wrote, "equivalent to the crying of thousands of children whose mothers do not return to give them the breast." Among the symptoms: an involuntary and constant agitation of the legs (whence the term "kicking the habit"). The addict becomes ashamed as his life disintegrates. He wants to quit, but, as De Quincey put it, he lies instead "under the weight of incubus and nightmare . . . he would lay down his life if he might get up and walk; but he is powerless as an infant, and cannot even attempt to rise."

The poppy's paradox is a profoundly human one: If you want to bring heaven to Earth, you must also bring hell. In the words of Lenny Bruce, "I'll die young, but it's like kissing God."

No other developed country is as devoted to the poppy as America. We consume 99 percent of the world's hydrocodone and 81 percent of its oxycodone. We use an estimated thirty times more opioids than is medically necessary for a population our size. And this love affair has been with us from the start. The drug was ubiquitous among both the British and American forces in the War of Independence as an indispensable medicine for the pain of battlefield injuries. Thomas Jefferson planted poppies at Monticello, and they became part of the place's legend (until the DEA raided his garden in 1987 and tore them out of the ground). Benjamin Franklin was reputed to be an addict in later life, as many were at the time. William Wilberforce, the evangelical who abolished the British slave trade, was a daily enthusiast. As Martin Booth explains in his classic history of the drug, *Opium: A History*, poppies proliferated in America, and the use of opioids in over-the-counter drugs was commonplace. A wide range of household remedies were based on the poppy's fruit; among the most popular was an elixir called laudanum—the word literally means "praiseworthy"—which took off in England as early as the seventeenth century.

Mixed with wine or licorice, or anything else to disguise the bitter taste, opiates were for much of the nineteenth century the primary treatment for diarrhea or any physical pain. Mothers gave them to squalling infants as a "soothing syrup." A huge boom was kick-started by the Civil War, when many states cultivated poppies in order to treat not only the excruciating pain of horrific injuries but endemic dysentery. Booth notes that 10 million opium pills and 2 million ounces of opiates in powder or tinctures were distributed by Union forces. Subsequently, vast numbers of veterans became addicted—the condition became known as "Soldier's Disease"—and their high became more intense with the developments of morphine and the hypodermic needle.

They were joined by millions of wives, sisters, and mothers who, consumed by postwar grief, sought refuge in the obliviating joy that opiates offered.

Based on contemporary accounts, it appears that the epidemic of the late 1860s and 1870s was probably more widespread, if far less intense, than today's—a response to the way in which the war tore up settled ways of life, as industrialization transformed the landscape, and as huge social change generated acute emotional distress. This aspect of the epidemic—as a response to mass social and cultural dislocation—was also clear among the working classes in the earlier part of the nineteenth century in Britain. As small armies of human beings were lured from their accustomed rural environments, with traditions and seasons and community, and thrown into vast new industrialized cities, the psychic stress gave opium an allure not even alcohol could match. Some historians estimate that as much as 10 percent of a working family's income in industrializing Britain was spent on opium. By 1870, opium was more available in the United States than tobacco was in 1970. It was as if the shift toward modernity and a wholly different kind of life for humanity necessitated for most working people some kind of relief—some way of getting out of the train while it was still moving.

It is tempting to wonder if, in the future, today's crisis will be seen as generated from the same kind of trauma, this time in reverse.

If industrialization caused an opium epidemic, deindustrialization is no small part of what's fueling our opioid surge. It's telling that the drug has not taken off as intensely among all Americans—especially not among the engaged, multiethnic, urban-dwelling, financially successful inhabitants of the coasts. The poppy has instead found a home in those places left behind—towns and small cities that owed their success to a particular industry, whose civic life was built around a factory or a mine. Unlike in Europe, where cities and towns existed long before industrialization, much of America's heartland has no remaining preindustrial history, given the destruction of Native American societies. The gutting of that industrial backbone—especially as globalization intensified in a country where market forces are least restrained—has been not just an economic fact but a cultural, even spiritual devastation. The pain was exacerbated by the Great Recession and has barely receded in the years since. And to meet that pain, America's uniquely market-driven health-care system was more than ready.

The great dream of the medical profession, which has been fascinated by opioids over the centuries, was to create an experience that captured the drug's miraculous pain relief but somehow managed to eliminate its intoxicating hook. The attempt to refine opium into a pain reliever without addictive properties produced morphine and later heroin—each generated by perfectly legal pharmaceutical and medical specialists for the most enlightened of reasons. (The word "heroin" was coined from the German word *heroisch*, meaning "heroic," by the drug company Bayer.) In the mid-1990s, OxyContin emerged as the latest innovation: a slow-timed release would prevent sudden highs or lows, which, researchers hoped, would remove craving and thereby addiction. Relying on a single study based on a mere thirty-eight subjects, scientists concluded that the vast majority of hospital inpatients who underwent pain treatment with strong opioids did not go on to develop an addiction, spurring the drug to be administered more widely.

This reassuring research coincided with a social and cultural revolution in medicine: in the wake of the AIDS epidemic, patients were becoming much more assertive in managing their own treatment—and those suffering from debilitating pain began to demand the relief that the new opioids promised. The industry moved quickly to cash in on the opportunity: aggressively marketing the new drugs to doctors via sales reps, coupons, and countless luxurious conferences, while waging innovative video campaigns designed to be played in doctors' waiting rooms. As Sam Quinones explains in his indispensable account of the epidemic, *Dreamland,* all this happened at the same time that doctors were being pressured to become much more efficient under the new regime of "managed care." It was a fateful combination: patients began to come into doctors' offices demanding pain relief, and doctors needed to process patients faster. A "pain" diagnosis was often the most difficult and time-consuming to resolve, so it became far easier just to write a quick prescription to abolish the discomfort rather than attempt to isolate its cause. The more expensive and laborious methods for treating pain—physical and psychological therapy—were abandoned almost overnight in favor of the magic pills.

A huge new supply and a burgeoning demand thereby created a massive new population of opioid users. Getting your opioid fix no longer meant a visit to a terrifying shooting alley in a ravaged city; now it just required a legitimate prescription and a bottle of pills that looked as bland as a statin or an

SSRI. But as time went on, doctors and scientists began to realize that they were indeed creating addicts. Much of the initial, hopeful research had been taken from patients who had undergone opioid treatment as inpatients, under strict supervision. No one had examined the addictive potential of opioids for outpatients, handed bottles and bottles of pills, in doses that could be easily abused. Doctors and scientists also missed something only recently revealed about OxyContin itself: its effects actually declined after a few hours, not twelve—thus subjecting most patients to daily highs and lows and the increased craving this created. Patients whose pain hadn't gone away entirely were kept on opioids for longer periods of time and at higher dosages. And OxyContin had not removed the agonies of withdrawal: someone on painkillers for three months would often find, as her prescription ran out, that she started vomiting or was convulsed with fever. The quickest and simplest solution was a return to the doctor.

Add to this the federal government's move in the mid-1980s to replace welfare payments for the poor with disability benefits—which covered opioids for pain—and unscrupulous doctors, often in poorer areas, found a way to make a literal killing from shady pill mills. So did many patients. A Medicaid co-pay of $3 for a bottle of pills, as Quinones discovered, could yield $10,000 on the streets—an economic arbitrage that enticed countless middle-class Americans to become drug dealers. One study has found that 75 percent of those addicted to opioids in the United States began with prescription pain-killers given to them by a friend, family member, or dealer. As a result, the social and cultural profile of opioid users shifted as well: the old stereotype of a heroin junkie—a dropout or a hippie or a Vietnam vet—disappeared in the younger generation, especially in high schools. Football players were given opioids to mask injuries and keep them on the field, they shared them with cheerleaders and other popular peers, and their elevated social status rebranded the addiction. Now opiates came wrapped in the bodies and minds of some of the most promising, physically fit, and capable young men and women of their generation. Courtesy of their doctors and coaches.

It's hard to convey the sheer magnitude of what happened. Between 2007 and 2012, for example, 780 million hydrocodone and oxycodone pills were delivered to West Virginia, a state with a mere 1.8 million residents. In one town, population twenty-nine hundred, more than 20 million opioid prescriptions were processed in the past decade. Nationwide, between 1999 and 2011, oxy-codone prescriptions increased sixfold. National per capita consumption of oxycodone went from around 10 milligrams in 1995 to almost 250 milligrams by 2012.

The quantum leap in opioid use arrived by stealth. Most previous drug epidemics were accompanied by waves of crime and violence, which prompted others, outside the drug circles, to take notice and action. But the opioid scourge was accompanied, during its first decade, by a record drop in both. Drug users were not out on the streets causing mayhem or havoc. They were inside, mostly alone, and deadly quiet. There were no crack houses to raid or gangs to monitor. Overdose deaths began to climb, but they were often obscured by a variety of dry terms used in coroners' reports to hide what was really happening. When the cause of death was inescapable—young corpses discovered in bedrooms or fast-food restrooms—it was also, frequently, too shameful to share. Parents of dead teenagers were unlikely to advertise their agony.

In time, of course, doctors realized the scale of their error. Between 2010 and 2015, opioid prescriptions declined by 18 percent. But if it was a huge, well-intended mistake to create this army of addicts, it was an even bigger one to cut them off from their supply. That is when the addicted were forced to turn to black-market pills and street heroin. Here again, the illegal supply channel broke with previous patterns. It was no longer controlled by the estab-lished cartels in the big cities that had historically been the main source of narcotics. This time, the heroin—particularly cheap, black-tar heroin from Mexico—came from small drug-dealing operations that avoided major urban areas, instead following the trail of methadone clinics and pill mills into the American heartland.

Their innovation, Quinones discovered, was to pay the dealers a flat salary, rather than a cut from the heroin itself. This removed the incentives to weaken the product, by cutting it with baking soda or other additives, and so made the new drug much more predictable in its power and reliable in its dosage. And rather than setting up a central location to sell the drugs—like a conventional shooting gallery or crack house—the new heroin marketers delivered it by car. Outside methadone clinics or pill mills, they handed out cards bearing only a telephone number. Call them and they would arrange to meet you near your house, in a suburban parking lot. They were routinely polite and punctual.

Buying heroin became as easy in the suburbs and rural areas as buying weed in the cities. No violence, low risk, familiar surroundings: an entire system specifically designed to provide a clean-cut, friendly, middle-class high. America was returning to the norm of the nineteenth century, when opiates were a routine medicine, but it was consuming compounds far more potent, addictive, and deadly than any nineteenth-century tincture enthusiast could have imagined. The country resembled someone who had once been accustomed to opium, who had spent a long time in recovery, whose tolerance for the drug had collapsed, and who was then offered a hit of the most powerful new variety.

The iron law of prohibition, as first stipulated by activist Richard Cowan in 1986, is that the more intense the crackdown, "the more potent the drugs will become." In other words, the harder the enforcement, the harder the drugs. The legal risks associated with manufacturing and transporting a drug increase exponentially under prohibition, which pushes the cost of supplying the drug higher, which incentivizes traffickers to minimize the size of the product, which leads to innovations in higher potency. That's why during the prohibition of alcohol much of the production and trafficking was in hard liquor, not beer or wine; why amphetamines evolved into crystal meth; why today's cannabis is much more potent than in the late-twentieth century. Heroin, rather than old-fashioned opium, became the opioid of the streets.

Then came fentanyl, a massively concentrated opioid that delivers up to fifty times the strength of heroin. Developed in 1959, it is now one of the most widely used opioids in global medicine, its miraculous pain relief delivered through transdermal patches, or lozenges, that have revolutionized surgery and recovery and helped save countless lives. But in its raw form, it is one of the most dangerous drugs ever created by human beings. A recent shipment of fentanyl seized in New Jersey fit into the trunk of a single car yet contained enough poison to wipe out the entire population of New Jersey and New York City combined. That's more potential death than a dirty bomb or a small nuke. That's also what makes it a dream for traffickers. A kilo of heroin can yield $500,000; a kilo of fentanyl is worth as much as $1.2 million.

The problem with fentanyl, as it pertains to traffickers, is that it is close to impossible to dose correctly. To be injected at all, fentanyl's microscopic form requires it to be cut with various other substances, and that cutting is playing with fire. Just the equivalent of a few grains of salt can send you into sudden paroxysms of heaven; a few more grains will kill you. It is obviously not in the interests of drug dealers to kill their entire customer base, but keeping most of their clients alive appears beyond their skill. The way heroin kills you is simple: the drug dramatically slows the respiratory system, suffocating users as they drift to sleep. Increase the potency by a factor of fifty and it is no surprise that you can die from ingesting just a half a milligram of the stuff.

Fentanyl comes from labs in China; you can find it, if you try, on the dark web. It's so small in size and so valuable that it's close to impossible to prevent it coming into the country. Last year, 500 million packages of all kinds entered the United States through the regular mail—making them virtually impossible to monitor with the Postal Service's current technology. And so, over the past few years, the impact of opioids has gone from mass intoxication to mass death. In the last heroin epidemic, as Vietnam vets brought the addiction back home, the overdose rate was 1.5 per 10,000 Americans. Now, it's 10.5. Three years ago in New Jersey, 2 percent of all seized heroin contained fentanyl. Today, it's a third. Since 2013, overdose deaths from fentanyl and other synthetic opioids have increased sixfold, outstripping those from every other drug.

If the war on drugs is seen as a century-long game of chess between the law and the drugs, it seems pretty obvious that fentanyl, by massively concentrating the most pleasurable substance ever known to mankind, is checkmate.

Watching as this catastrophe unfolded these past few years, I began to notice how closely it resembles the last epidemic that dramatically reduced life spans in America: AIDS. It took a while for anyone to really notice what was happening there too. AIDS occurred in a population that was often hidden and therefore distant from the cultural elite (or closeted within it). To everyone else, the deaths were abstract, and relatively tolerable, especially as they were associated with an activity most people disapproved of. By the time the epidemic was exposed and understood, so much damage had been done that tens of thousands of deaths were already inevitable.

Today, once more, the cultural and political elites find it possible to ignore the scale of the crisis because it is so often invisible in their—our—own lives.

The polarized nature of our society only makes this worse: a plague that is killing the other tribe is easier to look away from. Occasionally, members of the elite discover their own children with the disease, and it suddenly becomes more urgent. A celebrity death—Rock Hudson in 1985, Prince in 2016—begins to break down some of the denial. Those within the vortex of death get radicalized by the failure of government to tackle the problem. The dying gay men who joined ACT UP in the 1980s share one thing with the opioid-ridden communities who voted for Donald Trump in unexpected numbers: a desperate sense of powerlessness, of living through a plague that others are choosing not to see.

At some point, the sheer numbers of the dead become unmissable. With AIDS, the government, along with pharmaceutical companies, eventually developed a plan of action: prevention, education, and research for a viable treatment and cure. Some of this is happening with opioids. The widespread distribution of Narcan sprays—which contain the antidote naloxone—has already saved countless lives. The use of alternative, less dangerous opioid drugs such as methadone and buprenorphine to wean people off heroin or cushion them through withdrawal has helped. Some harm-reduction centers have established needle-exchange programs. But none of this comes close to stopping the current onslaught. With HIV and AIDS, after all, there was a clear scientific goal: to find drugs that would prevent HIV from replicating. With opioid addiction, there is no such potential cure in the foreseeable future. When we see the toll from opioids exceed that of peak AIDS deaths, it's important to remember that after that peak came a sudden decline. After the latest fentanyl peak, no such decline looks probable. On the contrary, the deaths continue to mount.

Over time, AIDS worked its way through the political system.

More than anything else, it destroyed the closet and massively accelerated our culture's acceptance of the dignity and humanity of homosexuals. But with the opioid crisis, our politics has remained curiously unmoved. The Trump administration, despite overwhelming support from many of the communities most afflicted, hasn't appointed anyone with sufficient clout and expertise to corral the federal government to respond adequately.

The critical Office of National Drug Control Policy has spent a year without a permanent director. Its budget is slated to be slashed by 95 percent, and until a few weeks ago its deputy chief of staff was a twenty-four-year-old former campaign intern. Kellyanne Conway—Trump's "opioid czar"—has no expertise in government, let alone in drug control. Although Trump plans to increase spending on treating addiction, the overall emphasis is on an even more intense form of prohibition, plus an advertising campaign. Attorney General Jeff Sessions even recently opined that he believes marijuana is really the key gateway to heroin—a view so detached from reality it beggars belief. It seems clear that in the future Trump's record on opioids will be as tainted as Reagan's was on AIDS. But the human toll could be even higher.

One of the few proven ways to reduce overdose deaths is to establish supervised injection sites that eventually wean users off the hard stuff while steering them into counseling, safe housing, and job training.

After the first injection site in North America opened in Vancouver, deaths from heroin overdoses plunged by 35 percent. In Switzerland, where such sites operate nationwide, overdose deaths have been cut in half. By treating the addicted as human beings with dignity rather than as losers and criminals who have ostracized themselves, these programs have coaxed many away from the cliff face of extinction toward a more productive life.

But for such success to be replicated in the United States, we would have to contemplate actually providing heroin to addicts in some cases, and we'd have to shift much of the current spending on prohibition, criminalization, and incarceration into a huge program of opioid rehabilitation. We would, in short, have to end the war on drugs. We are nowhere near prepared to do that. And in the meantime, the comparison to ACT UP is exceedingly depressing, as the only politics that opioids appear to generate is nihilistic and self-defeating. The drug itself saps initiative and generates social withdrawal. A few small activist groups have sprung up, but it is hardly a national movement of any heft or urgency.

And so we wait to see what amount of death will be tolerable in America as the price of retaining prohibition. Is it one hundred thousand deaths a year? More? At what point does a medical emergency actually provoke a government response that takes mass death seriously? Imagine a terror attack that killed over forty thousand people. Imagine a new virus that threatened to kill fifty-two thousand Americans this year. Wouldn't any government make it the top priority before any other?

In some ways, the spread of fentanyl—now beginning to infiltrate cocaine, fake Adderall, and meth, which is also seeing a spike in use—might best be thought of as a mass poisoning. It has infected often-nonfatal drugs and turned them into instant killers. Think back to the poison discovered in a handful of tainted Tylenol pills in 1982. Every bottle of Tylenol in America was immediately recalled; in Chicago, police went into neighborhoods with loudspeakers to warn residents of the danger. That was in response to a scare that killed, in total, seven people. In 2016, twenty thousand people died from overdosing on synthetic opioids, a form of poison in the illicit drug market. Some lives, it would appear, are several degrees of magnitude more valuable than others. Some lives are not worth saving at all.

One of the more vivid images that Americans have of drug abuse is of a rat in a cage, tapping a cocaine-infused water bottle again and again until the rodent expires. Years later, as recounted in Johann Hari's epic history of the drug war, *Chasing the Scream*, a curious scientist replicated the experiment. But this time he added a control group. In one cage sat a rat and a water dispenser serving diluted morphine. In another cage, with another rat and an identical dispenser, he added something else: wheels to run in, colored balls to play with, lots of food to eat, and other rats for the junkie rodent to play or have sex with. Call it rat park. And the rats in rat park consumed just one-fifth of the morphine water of the rats in the cage. One reason for pathological addiction, it turns out, is the environment. If you were trapped in solitary confinement, with only morphine to pass the time, you'd die of your addiction pretty swiftly too. Take away the stimulus of community and all the oxytocin it naturally generates and an artificial variety of the substance becomes much more compelling.

One way of thinking of postindustrial America is to imagine it as a former rat park, slowly converting into a rat cage. Market capitalism and revolutionary technology in the past couple of decades have transformed our economic and cultural reality, most intensely for those without college degrees. The dignity that many working-class men retained by providing for their families through physical labor has been greatly reduced by automation. Stable family life has collapsed, and the number of children without two parents in the home has risen among the white working and middle classes. The internet has ravaged local retail stores, flattening the uniqueness of many communities. Smartphones have eviscerated those moments of oxytocin-friendly actual human interaction. Meaning—once effortlessly provided by a more unified and often religious culture shared, at least nominally, by others—is harder to find, and the proportion of Americans who identify as "nones," with no religious affiliation, has risen to record levels. Even as we near peak employment and record-high median household income, a sense of permanent economic insecurity and spiritual emptiness has become widespread. Some of that emptiness was once assuaged by a constantly rising standard of living, generation to generation.

But that has now evaporated for most Americans.

New Hampshire, Ohio, Kentucky, and Pennsylvania have overtaken the big cities in heroin use and abuse, and rural addiction has spread swiftly to the suburbs. Now, in the latest twist, opioids have reemerged in that other, more familiar place without hope: the black inner city, where overdose deaths among African Americans, mostly from fentanyl, are suddenly soaring. To make matters worse, political and cultural tribalism has deeply weakened the glue of a unifying patriotism to give a broader meaning to people's lives—large numbers of whites and blacks both feel like strangers in their own land. Mass immigration has, for many whites, intensified the sense of cultural abandonment. Somewhere increasingly feels like nowhere.

It's been several decades since Daniel Bell wrote *The Cultural Contradictions of Capitalism*, but his insights have proved prescient. Ever-more-powerful market forces actually undermine the foundations of social stability, wreaking havoc on tradition, religion, and robust civil associations, destroying what conservatives value the most. They create a less human world. They make us less happy. They generate pain.

This was always a worry about the American experiment in capitalist liberal democracy. The pace of change, the ethos of individualism, the relentless dehumanization that capitalism abets, the constant moving and disruption, combined with a relatively small government and the absence of official religion, risked the construction of an overly atomized society, where everyone has to create his or her own meaning, and everyone feels alone. The American project always left an empty center of collective meaning, but for a long time Americans filled it with their own extraordinary work ethic, an unprecedented web of associations and clubs and communal or ethnic ties far surpassing

Europe's, and such a plethora of religious options that almost no one was left without a purpose or some kind of easily available meaning to their lives. Tocqueville marveled at this American exceptionalism as the key to democratic success, but he worried that it might not endure forever.

And it hasn't. What has happened in the past few decades is an accelerated waning of all these traditional American supports for a meaningful, collective life, and their replacement with various forms of cheap distraction. Addiction—to work, to food, to phones, to television, to video games, to porn, to news, and to drugs—is all around us. The core habit of bourgeois life—deferred gratification—has lost its grip on the American soul. We seek the instant, easy highs, and it's hard not to see this as the broader context for the opioid wave. This was not originally a conscious choice for most of those caught up in it: most were introduced to the poppy's joys by their own family members and friends, the last link in a chain that included the medical Establishment and began with the pharmaceutical companies. It may be best to think of this wave therefore not as a function of miserable people turning to drugs en masse but of people who didn't realize how miserable they were until they found out what life without misery could be. To return to their previous lives became unthinkable. For so many, it still is.

If Marx posited that religion is the opiate of the people, then we have reached a new, more clarifying moment in the history of the West: opiates are now the religion of the people. A verse by the poet William Brewer sums up this new world:

> Where once was faith,
> there are sirens: red lights spinning
> door to door, a record twenty-four
> in one day, all the bodies
> at the morgue filled with light.

It is easy to dismiss or pity those trapped or dead for whom opiates have filled this emptiness. But it's not quite so easy for the tens of millions of us on antidepressants, or Xanax, or some benzo-drug to keep less acute anxieties at bay. In the same period that opioids have spread like wildfire, so has the use of cannabis—another downer nowhere near as strong as opiates but suddenly popular among many who are the success stories of our times. Is it any wonder that something more powerful is used by the failures? There's a passage in one of Brewer's poems that tears at me all the time. It's about an opioid-addicted father and his son. The father tells us:

> Times my simple son will shake me to,
> syringe still hanging like a feather from my arm.
> What are you always doing, he asks.
> Flying, I say. Show me how, he begs.
> And finally, I do. You'd think
> the sun had gotten lost inside his head,
> the way he smiled.

To see this epidemic as simply a pharmaceutical or chemically addictive problem is to miss something: the despair that currently makes so many want to fly away. Opioids are just one of the ways Americans are trying to cope with an inhuman new world where everything is flat, where communication is virtual, and where those core elements of human happiness—faith, family, community—seem to elude so many. Until we resolve these deeper social, cultural, and psychological problems, until we discover a new meaning or reimagine our old religion or reinvent our way of life, the poppy will flourish.

We have seen this story before—in America and elsewhere.

The allure of opiates' joys is filling a hole in the human heart and soul today as they have since the dawn of civilization. But this time, the drugs are not merely laced with danger and addiction. In a way never experienced by humanity before, the pharmaceutically sophisticated and ever-more-intense bastard children of the sturdy little flower bring mass death in their wake. This time, they are agents of an eternal and enveloping darkness. And there is a long, long path ahead, and many more bodies to count, before we will see any light.

Just Say Yes to Drugs

May 25, 2018 | *NEW YORK* magazine

T he great mystery to me of psychedelic experiences is the centrality of love. I mean, why is it love exactly—overwhelming love—that so many experience under the spell of these molecules? When I first dabbled in the expansion of consciousness, I assumed it was simply some kind of wish fulfill-ment. Maybe as your ego relaxed a little, and your eyes opened for a while, you felt what you always wanted to feel, loved. But that wasn't quite right, because at the same time, I found myself overwhelmed with the feeling of love for *others*, for boundless compassion, sometimes almost painful empathy. I felt more nearly the hurt I had caused others, but instead of being convulsed with guilt, as was usually the case, I experienced only the urge to ask forgiveness and love some more. As I grew more experienced with MDMA (aka Ecstasy), and then psilocybin, and eventually LSD, this sense of love only deepened.

In Michael Pollan's astounding new book, *How to Change Your Mind*, he expresses the same thing: "The flood tide of compassion overflowed its banks . . . a cascading dam break of love . . . 'I don't want to be so stingy with my feelings.' And, 'All this time spent worrying about my heart. What about all the other hearts in my life?'" And yes, this all sounds unbelievably trite. Pollan, who writes seamlessly about his own experiments in psychedelics as well as the exciting discoveries in mental health now opening up before us, puts this perfectly: "*Love is everything.* . . . A platitude is precisely what is left of a truth after it has been drained of all emotion. To desaturate that dried husk with feeling is to see it again for what it is: the loveliest and most deeply rooted of truths, hidden in plain sight."

I have felt this every single time I have ingested a psychedelic. Sometimes it overwhelms me as a metaphysical truth; at others it seems to be incarnated in everything around me, especially when I take what I blasphemously call my annual "Jesus Day" alone in the dunes at the end of Cape Cod, and invite the beauty inside of me. And then there are the moments when this love simply fuses with awe—watching the dawn break over the mountains surrounding the playa at Burning Man; sometimes it comes to me in the form of the Holy Spirit, on the wind and in my oddly opened lungs.

Much of my religious upbringing and strict moral code had informed me that this kind of experience was wicked. I am too young to have experienced the sixties, but old enough to come of age in their aftermath, and to absorb the counterrevolution of the time. This stuff made you crazy; it wrecked an entire generation; it leads to social breakdown; it can lure you into a vortex of addiction—you know the drill by now. Above all: God forbade it. And yet all I can say is that in reality, when I gingerly ventured into the kaleidoscope, this was precisely the *opposite* of what I felt. This, it immediately impressed upon me, was an intimation of godness; it opened my heart to the divine; *this* was a sacrament, a fusing of the material with the ineffable. Pollan tells the story of a woman called Mary who ate two or three spoonfuls of mushrooms one day and, she told him, "had the most profound experience of being with God. I was God and God was me."

The neuroscience of this is fascinating, as Pollan pellucidly explains: psychedelics disarm what's called the Default Mode Network in your brain, the part of it that keeps you alert to danger, performing tasks, scanning the future, remembering the lessons of the past, doing, doing, doing. Some argue that this is the part of the brain we developed later in our evolution, the ego, the engine of natural selection, harnessing our intelligence to order and survival. It edits your experience, stripping out the unnecessary, ordering the whole. It is the governing reason of which the ancients spoke. But behind that DMN is the rest of our consciousness—the being, not the doing. We are much more in touch with this when we're children, when we have not developed the experiences that allow us to predict easily, edit swiftly, and get about our business. The child's wonder, her simple, unfiltered absorption of the world's mystery and awe: this is what a psychedelic experience can mimic in a way. Unless you are like a child, you will not enter the kingdom of heaven.

And so you see things as if for the first time. There were times in my adult life when this happened before, without any assistance: strange, fleeting moments of transcendence. I was walking through a garden in college one day, and noticed a daffodil. The spell lasted less than a minute, but for that time I actually *saw* it. It seemed suspended in time and space, shimmering, communicating, alive. Wordsworth finally made sense! It came again years later in Boston, when a tree rustled in front of me: I can't really explain it, but it filled me with a sense of gratitude and awe. Pollan describes taking a piss in the middle of a psilocybin session: "The bathroom was a riot of sparkling light. The arc of water I sent forth was truly the most beautiful thing I had ever seen, a waterfall of diamonds cascading into a pool, breaking its surface into a billion clattering fractals of light." Imagine that every time you go to the bathroom!

And then there was the vividness of the trees and fallen leaves in the forest surrounding the meditation center I spent ten silent days in a couple of years ago. I realized then that the insights I had gained from psychedelics were indeed available without the drugs. Meditation disarms the ego as well, unpicking the Default Mode Network, bringing you back to your more basic self ("waking up," as Sam Harris would put it) and to the joy of reality. That's why the Buddhists talk of the nonexistence of the self, a doctrine I have had a devil of a time wrapping my DMN around most of my life.

But for me, the psychedelic experience is also deeply Christian. This, it seems to me, is how and who Jesus is and was: the incarnation of the love that these experiences reveal to you—and always suffused with it; not romantic love or friendship, but that universal *agape* that seems abstract to me at times, but that some small mushrooms have sometimes uncovered. My DMN knows, of course, that this is heresy, that there is only one sacrament that you can eat and enter into godness. The rest of me knows that the idea of heresy itself is the DMN's work.

And the word "drug," like "psychedelic," is horribly loaded. Like the miraculous weed, psilocybin comes from the earth. LSD comes from bacteria. They are not addictive; yes, they can be abused, but very few who have had a psychedelic experience want to have it again and again. There is something profound about it that stays with you, for a long time. You see something you cannot unsee. And that space of unity and compassion is always something you can reach back to, a mountaintop you can see from a distance. It helps the most addicted smoker quit, simply because, in the context of awe and love, smoking becomes irrelevant. It reconciles people to death, the way religion used to. It can break depression—by scrambling the furrows and rigid patterns of thought that keep us in a groove of self-orbiting misery. The medical potential is extraordinary.

But it's impossible not to see the social benefits of more widespread use as well—clinically and recreationally. In Sean Illing's conversation with Pollan in Vox, Pollan says something about this moment in America: "The two biggest problems we face are the way we look at nature and the environmental crisis that's resulted, and tribalism." And both, it seems to me, are related to our lack of gratitude—for the Earth and each other. I cannot help but think of these substances as a way to reintroduce people, especially the younger generation, to the great spiritualities of humankind, Christianity and Buddhism particularly.

I think of them also as the real and most powerful antidote to opioids and to the condition the opioids are a misbegotten response to: loneliness, depression, and a lack of meaning. Opioids are one solution to our crisis of meaning, inasmuch as they numb you to sleep. Psychedelics are another: a new unveiling of awe and awakening. In that respect, the sixties got the metaphor wrong. These are not a means to drop out; they are a path to dropping back in.

America's New Religions

December 7, 2018 | *NEW YORK* magazine

———————

E veryone has a religion. It is, in fact, impossible not to have a religion if you are a human being. It's in our genes and has expressed itself in every culture, in every age, including our own secularized husk of a society.

By "religion," I mean something quite specific: a practice, not a theory; a way of life that gives meaning, a meaning that cannot really be defended without recourse to some transcendent value, undying "Truth" or God (or gods).

Which is to say, even today's atheists are expressing an attenuated form of religion. Their denial of any God is as absolute as others' faith in God, and entails just as much a set of values to live by—including, for some, daily rituals like meditation, a form of prayer. (There's a reason, I suspect, that many brilliant atheists, like my friends Bob Wright and Sam Harris, are so influenced by Buddhism and practice Vipassana meditation, and mindfulness. Buddhism's genius is that it is a religion without God.)

In his highly entertaining book *Seven Types of Atheism*, released in October in the United States, philosopher John Gray puts it this way: "Religion is an attempt to find meaning in events, not a theory that tries to explain the universe." It exists because we humans are the only species, so far as we can know, who have evolved to know explicitly that, one day in the future, we will die. And this existential fact requires some way of reconciling us to it while we are alive.

This is why science cannot replace it. Science does not tell you how to live, or what life is about; it can provide hypotheses and tentative explanations, but no ultimate meaning. Art can provide an escape from the deadliness of our daily doing, but, again, appreciating great art or music is ultimately an act of wonder and contemplation, and has almost nothing to say about morality and life.

Ditto history. My late friend, Christopher Hitchens, with a certain glee, gave me a copy of his book *God Is Not Great*, a fabulous grab bag of religious insanity and evil over time, which I enjoyed immensely and agreed with almost entirely. But the fact that religion has been so often abused for nefarious purposes—from burning people at the stake to enabling child rape to crashing airplanes into towers—does not resolve the question of whether the meaning of that religion is true. It is perfectly possible to see and record the absurdities and abuses of man-made institutions and rituals, especially religious ones, while embracing a way of life that these evil or deluded people preached but didn't practice. Fanaticism is not synonymous with faith; it is merely faith at its worst. That's what I told Hitch: great book, made no difference to my understanding of my own faith or anyone else's. Sorry, old bean, but try again.

Seduced by scientism, distracted by materialism, insulated, like no humans before us, from the vicissitudes of sickness and the ubiquity of early death, the post-Christian West believes instead in something we have called progress—a gradual ascent of mankind toward reason, peace, and prosperity—as a substitute in many ways for our previous monotheism. We have constructed a capitalist system that turns individual selfishness into a collective asset and showers us with earthly goods; we have leveraged science for our own health and comfort. Our ability to extend this material bonanza to more and more people is how we define progress, and progress is what we call meaning. In this respect, Steven Pinker is one of the most religious writers I've ever admired. His faith in reason is as complete as any fundamentalist's belief in God.

But none of this material progress beckons humans to a way of life beyond mere satisfaction of our wants and needs. And this matters. We are a meaning-seeking species. Gray recounts the experiences of two extraordinarily brilliant nonbelievers, John Stuart Mill and Bertrand Russell, who grappled with this deep problem. Here's Mill describing the nature of what he called "A Crisis in My Mental History":

> I had what might truly be called an object in life: to be a reformer of the
> world.... This did very well for several years, during which the general improve-
> ment going on in the world and the idea of myself as engaged with others in

struggling to promote it, seemed enough to fill up an interesting and animated existence. But the time came when I awakened from this as from a dream. . . . In this frame of mind it occurred to me to put the question directly to myself: "Suppose that all your objects in life were realized; that all the changes in institutions and opinions that you are looking forward to, could be completely effected at this very instant; would this be a great joy and happiness to you?" And an irrepressible self-consciousness distinctly answered: "No!"

At that point, this architect of our liberal order, this most penetrating of minds, came to the conclusion: "I seemed to have nothing left to live for." It took a while for him to recover.

Russell, for his part, abandoned Christianity at the age of eighteen, for the usual modern reasons, but the question of ultimate meaning still nagged at him. One day, while visiting the sick wife of a colleague, he described what happened: "Suddenly the ground seemed to give away beneath me, and I found myself in quite another region. Within five minutes I went through some such reflections as the following: the loneliness of the human soul is unendurable; nothing can penetrate it except the highest intensity of the sort of love that religious teachers have preached; whatever does not spring from this motive is harmful, or at best useless."

I suspect that most thinking beings end up with this notion of intense love as a form of salvation and solace as a kind of *instinct*. Those whose minds have been opened by psychedelics affirm this truth even further. I saw a bumper sticker the other day. It said: "Loving kindness is my religion." But the salient question is: Why?

Our modern world tries extremely hard to protect us from the sort of existential moments experienced by Mill and Russell. Netflix, air conditioning, sex apps, Alexa, kale, Pilates, Spotify, Twitter . . . they're all designed to create a world in which we rarely get a second to confront ultimate meaning—until a tragedy occurs, a death happens, or a diagnosis strikes. Unlike any humans before us, we take those who are much closer to death than we are and sequester them in nursing homes, where they cannot remind us of our own fate in our daily lives. And if you pressed, say, the liberal elites to explain what they really believe in—and you have to look at what they do most fervently—you discover, in John Gray's mordant view of Mill, that they do, in fact, have "an orthodoxy—the belief in improvement that is the unthinking faith of people who think they have no religion."

But the banality of the god of progress, the idea that the best life is writing explainers for *Vox* in order to make the world a better place, never quite slakes the thirst for something deeper. Liberalism is a set of procedures, with an empty center, not a manifestation of truth, let alone a reconciliation to mortality. But, critically, it has long been complemented and supported in America by a religion distinctly separate from politics, a tamed Christianity that rests, in Jesus's formulation, on a distinction between God and Caesar. And this separation is vital for liberalism, because if your ultimate meaning is derived from religion, you have less need of deriving it from politics or ideology or trusting entirely in a single, secular leader. It's only when your meaning has been secured that you can allow politics to be merely procedural.

So what happens when this religious rampart of the entire system is removed? I think what happens is illiberal politics. The need for meaning hasn't gone away, but without Christianity, this yearning looks to politics for satisfaction. And religious impulses, once anchored in and tamed by Christianity, find expression in various political cults. These political manifestations of religion are new and crude, as all new cults have to be. They haven't been experienced and refined and modeled by millennia of practice and thought. They are evolving in real time. And like almost all new cultish impulses, they demand a total and immediate commitment to save the world.

Now look at our politics. We have the cult of Trump on the right, a demigod who, among his worshipers, can do no wrong. And we have the cult of social justice on the left, a religion whose followers show the same zeal as any born-again evangelical. They are filling the void that Christianity once owned, without any of the wisdom and culture and restraint that Christianity once provided.

For many, especially the young, discovering a new meaning in the midst of the fallen world is thrilling. And social-justice ideology does everything a religion should. It offers an account of the whole: that human life and society and any kind of truth must be seen entirely as a function of social power structures, in which various groups have spent all of human existence oppressing other groups. And it provides a set of practices to resist and reverse this interlocking web of oppression—from regulating the workplace and policing the classroom to checking your own sin and even seeking to control language itself. I think of non-PC gaffes as the equivalent of old swear words. Like the puritans who were agape when someone said "goddamn," the new faithful are scandalized when someone says something "problematic." Another commonality of the zealot then and now: humorlessness.

And so the young adherents of the Great Awokening exhibit the zeal of the Great Awakening. Like early modern Christians, they punish heresy by banishing sinners from society or coercing them to public demonstrations of shame, and provide an avenue for redemption in the form of a thorough public confession of sin. "Social justice" theory requires the admission of white privilege in ways that are strikingly like the admission of original sin. A Christian is born again; an activist gets woke. To the belief in human progress unfolding through history—itself a remnant of Christian eschatology—it adds the Leninist twist of a cadre of heroes who jump-start the revolution.

The same cultish dynamic can be seen on the right. There many profess nominal Christianity and yet demonstrate every day that they have left it far behind. Some exist in a world without meaning altogether, and that fate is never pretty. I saw this most vividly when examining the opioid epidemic. People who have lost religion and are coasting along on materialism find they have few interior resources to keep going when crisis hits. They have no place of refuge, no spiritual safe space from which to gain perspective, no God to turn to. Many have responded to the collapse of meaning in dark times by simply and logically numbing themselves to death, extinguishing existential pain through ever-stronger painkillers that ultimately kill the pain of life itself.

Yes, many evangelicals are among the holiest and most quietly devoted people out there. Some have bravely resisted the cult. But their leaders have turned Christianity into a political and social identity, not a lived faith, and much of their flock—a staggering 81 percent voted for Trump—have signed on. They have tribalized a religion explicitly built by Jesus as anti-tribal. They have turned to idols—including their blasphemous belief in America as God's chosen country. They have embraced wealth and nationalism as core goods, two ideas utterly anathema to Christ. They are indifferent to the destruction of the creation they say they believe God made. And because their faith is unmoored, but their religious impulse is strong, they seek a replacement for religion. This is why they could suddenly rally to a cult called Trump. He may be the least

Christian person in America, but his persona met the religious need their own faiths had ceased to provide. The terrible truth of the last three years is that the fresh appeal of a leader cult has overwhelmed the fading truths of Christianity.

This is why they are so hard to reach or to persuade and why nothing that Trump does or could do changes their minds. You cannot argue logically with a religion—which is why you cannot really argue with social-justice activists either. And what's interesting is how support for Trump is greater among those who do not regularly attend church than among those who do.

And so we're mistaken if we believe that the collapse of Christianity in America has led to a decline in religion. It has merely led to religious impulses being expressed by political cults. Like almost all new cultish impulses, they see no boundary between politics and their religion. And both cults really do minimize the importance of the individual in favor of either the oppressed group or the leader.

And this is how they threaten liberal democracy. They do not believe in the primacy of the individual, they believe the ends justify the means, they do not allow for doubt or reason, and their religious politics can brook no compromise. They demonstrate, to my mind, how profoundly liberal democracy has actually depended on the complement of a tolerant Christianity to sustain itself—as many earlier liberals (Tocqueville, for example) understood.

It is Christianity that came to champion the individual conscience against the collective, which paved the way for individual rights. It is in Christianity that the seeds of Western religious toleration were first sown. Christianity is the only monotheism that seeks no sway over Caesar, that is content with the ultimate truth over the immediate satisfaction of power. It was Christianity that gave us successive social movements, which enabled more people to be included in the liberal project, thus renewing it. It was on these foundations that liberalism was built, and it is by these foundations it has endured. The question we face in contemporary times is whether a political system built upon such a religion can endure when belief in that religion has become a shadow of its former self.

Will the house still stand when its ramparts are taken away? I'm beginning to suspect it can't. And won't.

The Nature of Sex

February 1, 2019 | *NEW YORK* magazine

It might be a sign of the end times, or simply a function of our currently scrambled politics, but earlier this week four feminist activists—three from a self-described radical feminist organization, Women's Liberation Front—appeared on a panel at the Heritage Foundation. Together they argued that sex was fundamentally biological, and not socially constructed, and that there is a difference between women and trans women that needs to be respected. For this, they were given a rousing round of applause by the Trump supporters, religious-right members, natural-law theorists, and conservative intellectuals who comprised much of the crowd. If you think I've just discovered an extremely potent strain of weed and am hallucinating, check out the video of the event.

I've no doubt that many will see these women as anti-trans bigots, or appeasers of homophobes and transphobes, or simply deranged publicity seekers. (The moderator, Ryan Anderson, said they were speaking at Heritage because no similar liberal or leftist institution would give them space or time to make their case.) And it's true that trans-exclusionary radical feminists or TERFs, as they are known, are one minority that is actively *not* tolerated by the LGBTQ Establishment, and often demonized by the gay community. It's also true that they can be inflammatory, offensive, and obsessive. But what interests me is their underlying argument, which deserves to be thought through, regardless of our political allegiances, sexual identities, or tribal attachments. Because it's an argument that seems to me to contain a seed of truth. Hence, I suspect, the intensity of the urge to suppress it.

The title of the Heritage panel conversation—"The Inequality of the Equality Act"—refers to the main legislative goal for the Human Rights Campaign, the largest LGBTQ lobbying group in the United States. The proposed Equality Act—a federal nondiscrimination bill that has been introduced multiple times over the years in various formulations—would add "gender identity" to the Civil Rights Act of 1964, rendering that class protected by antidiscrimination laws, just as sex is. The TERF argument is that viewing "gender identity" as interchangeable with sex, and abolishing clear biological distinctions between men and women, is actually a threat to lesbian identity and even existence—because it calls into question who is actually a woman and includes in that category human beings who have been or are biologically male and remain attracted to women. How can lesbianism be redefined as having sex with someone who has a penis, they argue, without undermining the concept of lesbianism as a whole? "Lesbians are female homosexuals, women who love women," one of the speakers, Julia Beck, wrote last December, "but our spaces, resources and communities are on the verge of extinction."

If this sounds like a massive overreach, consider the fact that the proposed Equality Act—with 201 cosponsors in the last Congress—isn't simply a ban on discriminating against trans people in employment, housing, and public accommodations (an idea with a lot of support in the American public). It includes and rests upon a critical redefinition of what is known as "sex." We usually think of this as simply male or female, on biological grounds (as opposed to a more cultural notion of gender). But the Equality Act would define "sex" as *including* "gender identity," and defines "gender identity" thus: "gender-related identity, appearance, mannerisms, or characteristics, regardless of the individual's designated sex at birth."

What the radical feminists are arguing is that the act doesn't only blur the distinction between men and women (thereby minimizing what they see as the oppression of patriarchy and misogyny), but that its definition of gender identity must rely on stereotypical ideas of what gender expression means. What, after all, is a "gender-related characteristic"? It implies that a tomboy who loves sports is not a girl interested in stereotypically boyish things, but possibly a boy trapped in a female body. And a boy with a penchant for Barbies and Kens is possibly a trans girl—because, according to stereotypes, he's behaving as a girl would. So instead of enlarging our understanding of gender expression—and allowing maximal freedom and variety within both sexes—the concept of "gender identity" actually narrows it, in more traditional and even regressive ways. What does "gender-related mannerisms" mean, if not stereotypes? It's no accident that some of the most homophobic societies, like Iran, for example, are big proponents of sex-reassignment surgery for gender-nonconforming kids and adults (the government even pays for it) while being homosexual warrants the death penalty. Assuming that a nonstereotypical kid is trans rather than gay is, in fact, dangerously close to this worldview. (Some might even see a premature decision to change a child's body from one sex to another as a form of conversion therapy to "fix" his or her gayness. This doesn't mean that trans people shouldn't have the right to reaffirm their gender by changing their bodies, which relieves a huge amount of pressure for many and saves lives. But that process should entail a great deal of caution and discernment.)

The Equality Act also proposes to expand the concept of public accommodations to include "exhibitions, recreation, exercise, amusement, gatherings, or displays"; it bars any religious exceptions invoked under the Religious Freedom Restoration Act of 1993; and it bans single-sex facilities like changing, dressing, or locker rooms, if sex is not redefined to include "gender identity." This could put all single-sex institutions, events, or groups in legal jeopardy. It could deny lesbians their own unique safe space, free from any trace of men. The bill, in other words, "undermines the fundamental legal groundwork for recognizing and combating sex-based oppression and sex discrimination against women and girls."

The core disagreement, it seems to me, is whether a trans woman is right to say that she has always been a woman, was born female, and is indistinguishable from and interchangeable with biological women. That's the current claim reflected in the Equality Act. But is it true that when Caitlyn Jenner was in the 1976 Olympics men's decathlon she was competing as a woman, indistinguishable from any other woman? Contemporary orthodoxy insists that she was indeed competing as a woman, and erases any distinction between a trans woman and a woman. Similarly, public high-school girls track or wrestling teams would have to include female-identifying biological males—even if they keep winning all the trophies, and even if the unfairness is staring you in the face.

Most of us, however, intuitively find this argument hard to swallow entirely. We may accept that Caitlyn Jenner, who came out as a woman in 2015, always understood herself as a woman, and see this psychological conviction as sincere and to be respected. But we also see a difference between someone who lived her life as a man for decades, under the full influence of male chromosomes and testosterone, and who was socially accepted as male and then transitioned . . . and a woman to whom none of those apply. It is highly doubtful that a nontrans woman could have successfully competed against men in athletics in the Olympic decathlon, no less. Whether you look at this biologically (hormones and genitals matter) or socially (Jenner was not subjected to sexism as a man for most of her life), there *is* a difference. If there weren't, would the concept of "trans" even exist?

This is the deeply confusing and incoherent aspect of the entire debate. If you abandon biology in the matter of sex and gender altogether, you may help trans people live fuller, less conflicted lives, but you also undermine the very meaning of homosexuality. If you follow the current ideology of gender as entirely fluid, you actually subvert and undermine core arguments in defense of gay rights. "A gay man loves and desires other men, and a lesbian desires and loves other women," explains Sky Gilbert, a drag queen. "This defines the existential state of being gay. If there is no such thing as 'male' or 'female,' the entire self-definition of gay identity, which we have spent generations seeking to validate and protect from bigots, collapses." Contemporary transgender ideology is not a complement to gay rights; in some ways it is in active opposition to them.

And the truth is that many lesbians and gay men are quite attached to the concept of sex as a natural, biological, material thing. Yes, we are very well aware that sex can be expressed in many different ways. A drag queen and a rugby player are both biologically men, with different expressions of gender. Indeed, a drag queen can also be a rugby player and express his gender identity in a variety of ways, depending on time and place. But he is still a man. And gay men are defined by our attraction to our own biological sex. We are men and attracted to other men. If the concept of a man is deconstructed, so that someone without a penis is a man, then homosexuality itself is deconstructed. Transgender *people* pose no threat to us, and the vast majority of gay men and lesbians wholeheartedly support protections for transgender people. But transgenderist *ideology*—including postmodern conceptions of sex and gender—is indeed a threat to homosexuality, because it is a threat to biological sex as a concept.

And so it is not transphobic for a gay man not to be attracted to a trans man. It is close to definitional. The core of the traditional gay claim is that there is indeed a very big difference between male and female, that the difference matters, and without it homosexuality would make no sense at all. If it's all a free and fluid nonbinary choice of gender and sexual partners, a choice to have sex exclusively with the same sex would not be an expression of our identity, but a form of sexist bigotry, would it not?

There is a solution to this knotted paradox. We can treat different things differently. We can accept that the homosexual experience and the transgender experience are very different, and cannot be easily conflated. We can center the debate not on "gender identity" which insists on no difference between the trans and the cis, the male and the female, and instead focus on the very real experience of "gender dysphoria," which deserves treatment and support and total acceptance for the individuals involved. We can respect the right of certain people to be identified as the gender they believe they are, and to remove any discrimination against them, while also seeing biology as a difference that requires a distinction. We can believe in nature *and* the immense complexity of the human mind and sexuality. We can see a way to accommodate everyone to the extent possible, without denying biological reality. Equality need not mean sameness.

We just have to abandon the faddish notion that sex is socially constructed or entirely in the brain, that sex and gender are unconnected, that biology is irrelevant, and that there is something called an LGBTQ identity, when, in fact, the acronym contains extreme internal tensions and even outright contradictions. And we can allow this conversation to unfold civilly, with nuance and care, in order to maximize human dignity without erasing human difference. That requires a certain amount of courage, and one thing I can safely say about that Heritage panel is that the women who spoke had plenty of it.

Why Joe Biden Might Be the Best Bet to Beat Trump

May 3, 2019 | *NEW YORK* magazine

I f you've been reading the liberal media and Left Twitter the past couple of months, you'd be certain of one thing: Joe Biden is hopelessly out of touch—too old, too white, too male, too handsy, too racist, too misogynist, too unwoke, and far too compromised by his past positions to be the Democratic nominee in 2020. Josh Marshall, while liking Biden, regarded him as "unsuited to the moment in almost every way imaginable." Jamelle Bouie saw him as a repugnant variant of Trumpism: "For decades Biden gave liberal cover to white backlash." My colleague Rebecca Traister recently called him "a comforter of patriarchal impulses toward controlling women's bodies." Ben Smith declared: "His campaign is stumbling toward launch with all the hallmarks of a Jeb!-level catastrophe—a path that leads straight down. . . . Joe Biden isn't going to emerge from the 2020 campaign as the nominee. You already knew that." Michael Tomasky summarized the elite consensus: "Nearly everyone thinks [Biden] can't win the nomination."

"Nearly everyone"—i.e., all my friends and acquaintances in the journalistic and political elite—also thought Hillary Clinton was a shoo-in to win the general election. But Biden has had an extremely good start to his third campaign for president. His announcement video was aimed at those on the left who see Trump as the tip of the spear of white nationalism, and to those swingier voters who simply want to return to normalcy, constitutional order, and, well, decency. That's a message that rallies the base but also appeals to those who may be exhausted by the trauma of Trump. As an opener, perfect. Even, at times, moving.

The polling is just as impressive. In three separate polls released this week, Biden's support is somewhere in the upper 30s, and his nearest competitor is in the mid-teens (or, in one case, low 20s). In a field of twenty candidates, that's a big share, and in Nate Silver's analysis, "Well-known candidates polling in the mid-30s in the early going are about even money to win the nomination, historically." Yes, Biden's riding an announcement bump right now and his numbers may and almost certainly will fade over time. His name recognition is sky-high compared with some others, who could catch up as the campaign progresses. And he might once again gaffe his way into oblivion. But he has a big enough lead to be able to afford a certain amount of erosion.

And his strength is drawn from two contrasting bases: older, moderate whites, and African Americans. Although his share is in the 30s overall, he has a whopping 50 percent share among nonwhite Democrats, according to the latest CNN poll. A Morning Consult poll found him with 43 percent of the black vote, including 47 percent support among African American women. Biden's deep association with Obama gives him a lift in the black vote no other white candidate can achieve. And so it turns out that the base of the Democrats has not been swept into the identity cult of the elite, wealthy, white left. As a brand-new CBS poll finds, Democrats may prefer a hypothetical female nominee over a male (59–41 percent), a black nominee over a white one (60–40 percent), and someone in their forties to someone in their seventies. But that's in the abstract. In reality, Biden seems to scramble these preferences.

He's also been able to reach non-college-educated white men in ways few other candidates could. That's a big fucking deal in Ohio, Pennsylvania, Michigan, and Wisconsin — and if Biden can carry those states, he'll be the next president. He's a union man, and always has been. In what was a brilliant ad lib, Biden began a speech to the International Brotherhood of Electrical Workers by making a joke about the excesses of #MeToo — "I had permission to hug Lonnie," the union leader, he quipped. Later, as he brought some kids onstage, he joked again, as he put his hands on the shoulders of a boy: "He gave me permission to touch him." The crowd's reaction both times was bellows of laughter.

Yes, this might be seen as insensitive, or tone-deaf. It is certainly politically incorrect. But what Biden's joke did was tell the white working class that he has not defected to the woke, white urban elites. This matters. In a recent poll, 80 percent of Americans say "that political correctness is a problem in this country." Hostility to new speech codes from elites was one factor that drove support for Trump in 2016. Americans do not want to abolish all differences between men and women, do not support reparations, and view college campuses as strange, alien pockets of madness. Any Democrat in 2020 has to reach that "exhausted majority" who are sick of all that. Biden has already done it.

Would upping the white working-class vote for the Dems alienate minorities, women, and high-income whites? Maybe. Charles Blow recently argued that these working-class voters are fickle, getting smaller and smaller as a segment of the electorate, and are "hostile to the interests of women and minorities." That is, they're deplorables, unworthy of attention. Clinton tried that strategy. And she lost the presidency because of her thinly veiled contempt for the white working classes in Pennsylvania, Michigan, Wisconsin, and Ohio. The idea that the white working class is incompatible with a multicultural coalition is what two Obama campaigns disproved.

Biden's positive message is a defense of the worker from the excesses of decadent late capitalism. He can effortlessly channel that and compete with Trump in the Rust Belt. Sanders can do this as well—but Bernie, for all his sincerity and authenticity, does not have the heft of a two-term vice president who has long been at the center of his party. For those who simply want to defeat Trump at all costs, Biden, for now, seems the safest bet. He can run on a platform deeply informed by the left's critique of the market, without the baggage of left wokeness or those eager to play into the GOP's hands and explicitly avow "socialism."

That's exactly what the Trump campaign fears. And in the critical head-to-head dynamic against Trump, Biden already seems to have gotten into the president's head. Despite what we have been told is strong internal advice from his mute dauphin-in-law not to engage Biden, Trump couldn't help himself. When Biden got an endorsement from the firefighters union, Trump unleashed a torrent of fifty-eight retweets before 6:30 a.m., all citing firefighters' support for Trump. The president insists that every firefighter, cop, and service member supports him. All of them. And so the president went on to attack the union itself: "I've done more for Firefighters than this dues sucking union will ever do, and I get paid ZERO!" After this sad temper tantrum, Biden was ready for a response: "I'm sick of this President badmouthing unions. Labor built the middle class in this country. Minimum wage, overtime pay, the 40-hour week: they exist for all of us because unions fought for those rights. We need a President who honors them and their work." Biden 1, Trump 0.

In subsequent remarks, Trump revealed his current strategy for reelection: he'll tout a strong economy, fight mass immigration, and run against the threat of "socialism." But he's obviously terrified that Biden won't fit easily into this AOC–Ilhan Omar rubric. He's hoping that the left of the party will kneecap him: "I think Biden would be easier from the standpoint that you will have so much dissension in the party, because it'll make four years ago look like baby stuff. . . . They want the radical left—they want the left movement—and he probably isn't there. And I think you're going to have tremendous dissension [*sic*] just like Hillary did." So the president just told the country that his most potent opponent is no leftist. A "Trump adviser" told *Politico*: "We don't think Biden can make it out of the woke Democrat primary." Boy, are they hoping he doesn't.

The reason Trump is so rattled is that Biden is seven points ahead of him in head-to-head polls right now and, after four years of Trump's assault on this country's constitutional order, Democrats are likely to turn out in high numbers, and back whoever gets nominated. As it becomes clearer that this president regards himself as above the law, and has an attorney general who shares this view and will also target Trump's opponents if told to, opposition could intensify. New data from 2018 show how big Democratic turnout was: 36 percent of young people voted, compared with 20 percent in 2014. Blacks, Hispanics, and Asians all saw their turnout rates soar—up 11, 13, and 13 points, respectively, compared with 2014. When these voters have a chance to get rid of Trump, whoever the nominee is, I have no doubt they'll show up. If Biden could make some inroads with non-college-educated whites and seniors, it could be another big fucking deal. Adding Kamala Harris as his veep could unify the Democratic base behind the ticket.

Two other points: Biden is a Catholic. Anyone who has ever been saturated in American Catholicism can swiftly recognize the figure: old-school but open, a believer in the innate dignity of every human soul, regularly at Mass, deeply comfortable in the world of white ethnic America, surprisingly liberal. Catholics—shockingly, given the depravity of the Republicans—split their vote last time. Move them a few points, as Obama did in 2008, and you have a real shift in our politics. And then there's the fact that Trump's uncanny ability to define someone with a brutal but telling nickname seems to have failed him with Biden. "Sleepy Joe"? I can detect nothing sleepy about this septuagenarian embarking on a third run for president. Biden seems to genuinely flummox Trump. Which is very good news.

There is also, dare I say it, a deeper contrast between the two men. One is decent, kind, generous, funny. The other is indecent, cruel, miserly, and has the callous humor of a bully. There would be a moral gulf between any current Democrat and Trump, of course. But with Biden, we're reminded of the America we thought we knew. Yes, this is partly nostalgia, but no one should underestimate nostalgia in a country as turbulent, afraid, and resentful as America right now. Biden's moment, in my mind, was 2016, but he was prevented from competing by Clinton and Obama. But history takes strange turns. This already feels to me like a two-man race. That may change. It's extremely early, but the odds are with Biden. And the tail winds behind him are intense.

A Plague Is an Apocalypse.
But It Can Bring a New World.

July 21, 2020 | *NEW YORK* magazine

I t's strange that we now see America threatened by a plague. Because without plague, America, as we know it, wouldn't exist.

It may have been the most devastating epidemic in the history of humankind—surpassing in its mortality rates any before or since, including the Black Death in the Europe of the mid-fourteenth century. Smallpox arrived in America with the first Europeans and went on, with several other imported diseases, to wipe out up to 90 percent of the native population in a relatively short amount of time—millions and maybe tens of millions died.

They were horrible, harrowing deaths. The virus *Variola major* incubated for two weeks, followed by an intense few days of fever, before the pustules emerged: first in the mouth, throat, and nasal passages, then all over the body, including around the eyes, where they often caused blindness. A human being would struggle for perhaps ten days, covered in these sores, erupting in bloody and pus-filled bumps—and then, with luck, the illness subsided. The sores healed; the pockmarks, highly visible on the face, remained. The residue from these sores was also terribly infectious and lingered on surfaces or cloth for years—but scholars now consider the vast majority of deaths, just like those from COVID-19, to have been from human-to-human transmission.

Much of the terror of this experience is lost to us moderns because a great deal of the death and suffering occurred before Europeans were even able to witness and record it (though, of course, the trauma for the indigenous reverberated for centuries). But we do know why the toll was so high. Those Native Americans had been the first to discover this continent and, with it, their own sort of American dream—thousands of years before Europeans imagined theirs. They had first arrived, probably over the Bering Land Bridge connecting Alaska and Russia, around fifteen thousand years ago, give or take a few millennia, and they found a whole new world, with no humans at all, packed with huge beasts relatively easy to kill with spears, vast prairies, and natural resources that allowed a vibrant hunter-gatherer population to grow as they conquered a virgin continent. It's not hard to imagine how miraculous this must have felt in the collective memory of these peoples: a long human journey through the bleakest of landscapes into a land of astonishing fecundity—and no human competition.

But because they were often hunter-gatherers, with only a partial reliance on agriculture, they appear to have had little knowledge or experience of plague and no contact with any of the epidemics that had, by then, ravaged Europeans and Eurasians for a few millennia. They domesticated fewer animals and had developed some immunities to many bugs they encountered in their environment.

In this respect, they were blissfully typical of most humans in prehistory. Our species seems never to have experienced epidemic diseases for the vast majority of our time on Earth, encountering them only when we settled down, formed stable, concentrated communities, and started farming and domesticating animals for food. Plagues were usually a function of diseases that jumped from precisely those animals in close proximity and spread through concentrations of the human population in settlements, villages, towns, and cities as civilization began. Humans lived in more intimate relations with animals; their settlements compounded filth, infected water, fleas, and excrement, human and animal. We were unknowingly creating a petri dish and calling it home.

We are wrong, therefore, to think of plague entirely as a threat to civilization. Plague is an *effect* of civilization. The waves of sickness through human history in the past five thousand years (and not before) attest to this, and the outbreaks often became more devastating the bigger the settlements and the greater the agriculture and the more evolved the trade and travel. What made the American plague of the sixteenth century so brutal was that it met a virgin population with no immunity whatever. The nightmare that humans had been dealing with and adapting to in Europe and Asia for millennia came suddenly to this continent all at once, and the population had no defense at all. The New World became a stage on which all the accumulated viral horrors of the Old World converged.

That's why we live in a genocidal graveyard. We always have. But if plague was created by mass urban living, and spread through trade and travel, and made much more likely with every new foray into virgin territory, then this story is far from over because those stories, of course, are far from over as well. As the human population reaches an unprecedented peak, as cities grow, as climate change accelerates environmental disruption, and as globalization connects every human with every other one, we have, in fact, created a near-perfect environment for a novel pathogen-level breakout. COVID-19 is just a reminder of that ineluctable fact and that worse outbreaks are almost certain to come. Compared with past epidemics, this one is, mercifully, relatively mild in its viral impact, even though its cultural and political effects may well be huge. Compared with future ones, against which we may also have no immunity at all, it could serve as a harbinger: we could be the next generation to discover a promised land, only to have it taken brutally and terrifyingly away.

Plagues have often been catalyzing events, entering human history like asteroids hitting a planet. They kill shocking numbers of people and leave many more rudderless, coping with massive loss, incalculable grief, and, often, social collapse. They reorder the natural world, at least for a time, as human cities and towns recede and animal life reemerges and microbes evolve and regroup. They suspend a society in midair and traumatize it, taking it out of its regular patterns and intimating new possible futures. In some cases, a society redefines itself. In others, trauma seems the only consequence.

Imagine, for a moment, what confronted the understandably complacent Romans of the second century CE. Out of the blue, their unparalleled civilization was beset by a disease that they had never known before and that began killing people in staggering numbers. For much of Roman history, they had lived in a near-ideal climate: warm, wet, and relatively stable. Trade was growing, wealth was accumulating, and globalization — via trade across the Indian Ocean and new roads connecting all parts of the empire — was reaching a peak. But in 43 BCE, the first climate shock came, as a volcanic eruption from as far away as Alaska prompted a sudden cold spell, and then, during the second and third centuries, a far more variable and colder climate set in, prompting distant animal species, with their own viruses, to move territory, creating new pathways for pathogens to break out of their familiar habitats.

The disease burden among Romans was already high and getting higher, as Kyle Harper has explored in his groundbreaking book *The Fate of Rome*. Bigger settlements and cities, combined with appalling hygiene (open-cesspool toilets were usually located within the house) and close proximity with domesticated animals, created a network of danger zones. Malaria was a constant, diarrhea ubiquitous; tuberculosis became more common; leprosy arrived and stayed. Some viruses—like *Tatera poxvirus* and a few of its relatives—were carried by only a single species, such as camels or naked-soled gerbils, but they could jump species in certain circumstances, from animals to humans if any were nearby, and then from human to human.

When the inevitable epidemic arrived, in what was likely a form of smallpox, it was one of the deadliest enemies the Romans had ever faced. Its symptoms were, in Harper's words, "fever, a black pustular rash, conjunctival irritation, ulceration deep in the windpipe, and black or bloody stools." The asymptomatic period was about ten days, easily allowing those infected to travel with no one knowing, and death often came within a week or two. By 172 CE, what is now known as the Antonine plague had devastated the Roman military and killed somewhere around one out of every ten people in the Roman Empire. It came and went for at least the better part of a decade, culling the population mercilessly.

Rome staggered on at first, rebuilding and repopulating, and seemed to recover. But as the climate churned, another pathogen wrought havoc, a virus Harper suggests may have been related to Ebola, which caused bloody eyes, a bloody esophagus, and bloody diarrhea. This one hit a society already weakened, and this time Rome struggled to survive. Mercifully, there was an epidemiological reprieve in the following centuries, allowing some population recovery. But then an extraordinary series of volcanic eruptions in the year 536 shifted the odds again. The volcanic activity was greater than at any point in the past three thousand years, spewing a massive amount of debris into the atmosphere, clouding the sun for over a year, destroying crops from China to Ireland, and, once again, producing shifts in microbial and animal behavior. Procopius, a Byzantine historian, noted: "For the sun gave forth its light without brightness, like the moon, during this whole year."

It was likely this sudden weather shift that rebooted human epidemics in the sixth century. Harper notes that volcanic, climate, and weather events affect a whole variety of species. Among them, crucially, are rodents, who may respond by moving out of their accustomed habitat to find warmer or wetter territory, and who naturally carry with them their own viruses and bacteria. A current scholarly hypothesis is that it was probably Chinese marmots, carrying a bacterium called *Yersinia pestis*, that, in these cold years, moved territory and transferred this pathogen to other rodent populations they interacted with, likely by sharing fleas. Among these new carriers were the enterprising and highly mobile black rats, often called ship rats because of their propensity to follow grain and food across the oceans. Scientists have also discovered a mutation in *Y. pestis* in just a single protein-coding gene that emerged, they believe, right before the Roman outbreak in the rat population, making the rodent disease suddenly more transmissible via fleas.

And soon enough, those black rats arrived in the Roman port of Alexandria. They carried with them their own parasite, a flea that lived on the rats' blood and could survive up to six weeks without a host—making it capable of enduring long sea voyages. And as the bacteria spread among the rats, and their population began to collapse, the fleas, desperate for food, sought alternatives. Living very close to the rats, humans were an easy target. Before too long, the bacterium was everywhere, because, once in human blood, it could also be spread via droplets in human breath. For several days after infection, you were asymptomatic; then grotesque black buboes appeared on your body—swollen lymph nodes near where the fleas had bitten. Death often came several days later.

John of Ephesus noted that as people "were looking at each other and talking, they began to totter and fell either in the streets or at home, in harbors, on ships, in churches, and everywhere." As he traveled in what is now Turkey, he was surrounded by death: "Day by day, we too—like everybody—knocked at the gate to the tomb. . . . We saw desolate and groaning villages and corpses spread out on the earth, with no one to take up [and bury] them." The population of Constantinople was probably reduced by between 50 and 60 percent. The first onslaught happened so quickly the streets became blocked by corpses, the dead "trodden upon by feet and trampled like spoiled grapes . . . the corpse which was trampled, sank and was immersed in the pus of those below it," as John put it.

This must have seemed like the end of the world. For most, there was no other explanation. To have the skies go dark for more than a year, and then to see a hideous disease fell half your family and friends, destroying agriculture, city and town life, and religious practices, was an extraordinary trauma. Even the countryside was afflicted, because the rats could scurry and survive anywhere there was food, and, at the same time, the failed harvests following the year of darkness led to widespread malnutrition, weakening immune systems. Imagine living in a city that, only a couple of years previously, had had twice the population: the empty streets, the vacant houses, the silence, and the near madness of the survivors, stricken with PTSD, crippled by grief, desperate for food.

This time, Rome simply could not recover, its armies laid low by disease, its finances depleted, its borders increasingly insecure, its population cut by half. What have sometimes been disparagingly referred to as the Dark Ages were caused, then, by the construction of an advanced, networked, sophisticated civilization and its subsequent destruction by microbes you couldn't even see.

This kind of trauma, the historical record shows, changes us. Reminding humans of our mortality, plagues throw up existential questions that can lead to deep cultural shifts. As the first plagues hit Rome, for example, Christians were often blamed, and the cult of Apollo reemerged. But as the viral and bacterial hits kept coming, these plagues proved to be a tipping point in the move from the old gods to a new one. Christianity showed itself able to assuage the existential angst of constant death in a way the old religions couldn't. Better still, it contained, as Harper notes, a socially useful network "among perfect strangers based on an ethic of sacrificial love." And the Christian willingness to tend to the sick, even in a plague, impressed others. The plague seemed to force Roman society to shake off old patterns, like paganism, and seek new ones, like Christianity.

Centuries later, the Native Americans, similarly, saw smallpox as they saw most terrible events: through the prism of their gods and cosmologies. And as the unimaginable toll mounted, and the invaders seemed spared from the worst, many began to see the disease as some kind of proof of their own iniquity or to believe their gods had forsaken them. Their healing ceremonies and rituals, which sometimes included saunas followed by plunges into icy water, failed again and again. In his masterpiece, *Plagues and Peoples*, William H.

McNeill poignantly notes reports of unprecedented suicides in their ranks and even the abandonment of newborns, as Native Americans lost faith in their own civilization and gods.

And plagues drive people crazy. You might call them mass-disinhibiting events. It's not hard to see why. When the plague returned to a fast-repopulating Europe in the fourteenth century, in the Great Mortality known as the Black Death, up to 60 percent of Europeans perished in an astonishingly short amount of time. When normal life has been completely suspended, and when you don't know if you'll be alive or dead in a week's time, people act out.

A cultish sect, which had first arisen earlier in Italy, emerged in Germany, for example, called the flagellants. These half-naked protesters traveled from town to town on foot in pilgrimages, atoning for the sins they believed had caused the plague, and whipping themselves bloody and raw as penance, in bizarre public rituals that drew big crowds. They rejected the established Church, claimed to have direct access to Jesus and Mary, disrupted Masses, and, as time went by, radicalized still further, becoming increasingly populated by the poor and ever more anti-Semitic. Forbidden to take a bath, shave, or change clothing on their pilgrimages, they also doubtless became unwitting spreaders of the disease as they moved from place to place and masses of panicked penitents greeted them.

Jew hatred, which had been percolating for several centuries, exploded. In the fear and panic of the plague, rumors were started about a Jewish conspiracy to wipe out Christendom. Jews did this by poisoning wells, the slur posited, and in response, pogroms became even more severe than in the past. In Basel, for example, as the writer John Kelly notes in his book *The Great Mortality*, there was a grotesque prefiguring of the twentieth-century Holocaust when a wooden house was built on an island to contain all the Jews in the city, who were then forced into it, locked in, and set aflame as people watched. Jews were bludgeoned to death; they were burned at the stake.

It was as if a plague gave people both an excuse and a license to act out their ugliest impulses. Pope Clement VI issued a bull condemning the violence, making the rather obvious point that "it cannot be true that the Jews . . . are the cause . . . of the plague . . . for [it] afflicts the Jews themselves." But this was not about reason; it was about scapegoating and a sense that anything was permissible as catastrophe struck.

Plagues do not usually unite societies; they often break them apart in this way. Around the turn of the twentieth century, for example, Asian immigrants were blamed for an outbreak of bubonic plague in San Francisco and Honolulu; in 1918, enterprising xenophobes settled on Spain as the source of the new and deadly flu and called it the Spanish Lady, to add a soupçon of misogyny. In the polio outbreaks at the beginning of the past century, immigrants from southern Europe were scapegoated. In general, the wealthy escape from cities in plague times, minorities are blamed, the poor revolt, families are torn apart, and cruelty abounds.

Social class comes to the fore. One estimate of the deaths in 1348–49 found only 27 percent of the fatalities among the wealthy, around 42 to 45 percent among priests, and from 40 to as high as 70 percent among the peasantry. Family members were abandoned in their beds, crime increased, thieves stripped victims of clothes, and people ripped the lead off dead neighbors' roofs. One cleric, Kelly tells us, became known as William the One-Day Priest because he robbed people for six days and celebrated Mass on the seventh.

Some responded to the outbreak by withdrawing from general society in small groups committed to purer, simpler, more abstemious diets to ward off the disease. Others went in the opposite direction. In the words of the Italian writer Giovanni Boccaccio, some "maintained that an infallible way to ward off this appalling evil was to drink heavily, enjoy life to the full . . . gratifying all one's cravings . . . and shrug the whole thing off as one enormous joke." Kelly cites John of Reading, a monk who noted that priests, "forgetful of their profession and rule . . . lusted after things of the world and the flesh."

And with a literally existential event taking place all around them, fourteenth-century Europeans shifted in their spirituality as the Romans had done before them. Just as the sixth-century plague had finished off the old religion of the Roman gods and brought the final triumph of Christianity, so a newly personal and mystical variety of that religion replaced the more institutional one. Sects from the lower classes began to emerge—like the Lollards in England, who rejected key Catholic doctrines and translated the Bible into English. In these rebellious religious subcultures, the seeds of the Reformation were sown.

Paradoxically, the Black Death also reshaped and rebuilt the rural economy to benefit the poor. With half the population suddenly wiped out by bubonic plague, food became plentiful and cheap as soon as the harvests returned, because there were so many fewer mouths to feed, and the price of labor soared because so many workers had perished. Day laborers suddenly had some leverage over the owners of land and exploited it. A manpower shortage also led to innovations. With fewer people on higher wages, for example, the cost of making a book became prohibitive—because it required plenty of scribes and copiers. And so the incentive to invent the printing press was created. Industries like fishing (new methods of curing), shipping (new kinds of ships both bigger and requiring less manpower), and mining (new water pumps) innovated to do more with fewer people. The historian David Herlihy puts it this way: "Plague . . . broke the Malthusian deadlock . . . which threatened to hold Europe in its traditional ways for the indefinite future."

In these two bookends of European plague, in the sixth and then the fourteenth century, you see two ways in which epidemic disease changed society and culture. In one, the disruption and dislocation of mass disease sent the world into a long de-civilizing process; Roman society was gutted and its empire dissolved into various fiefdoms. In the other, a mass-death event triggered a revival, economic and spiritual, in a kind of cleansing process that restarted European society. They were caused by the same disease. In one case, it brought collapse; in the other, rebirth.

Most accounts of the American Revolution focus, understandably, on military and political developments. What most don't account for is the role that smallpox played in almost losing the war for the Americans. The virus had never gone away on this continent since the fifteenth century, had devastated generation after generation of Native Americans, and was a constant threat to the colonies themselves. In the late-eighteenth century, it was still at large—and continued to be spread by troop movements of both the British and the colonists. The British, however, had a clear advantage. Most of their troops had experienced some form of smallpox as children and developed immunity. The Americans—black, native, and colonizers—were in contrast largely vulnerable.

As Elizabeth A. Fenn writes in her recent study *Pox Americana: The Great Smallpox Epidemic of 1775–82*, in 1776, in an early skirmish in the Revolutionary War in Canada, a few thousand American troops were besieged simultaneously by the virus and the British. In a sudden, chaotic retreat, the Americans sought refuge on a swampy island, Île aux Noix, and met a worse enemy. "Oh the groans of the sick," an observer reported. "Scarcely a tent upon this Isle but what contains one or more in distress and continually groaning, & calling for relief, but in vain!" Reported another, having witnessed a barn full of men covered in vermin: "One nay two had large maggots, an inch long, Crawl out of their ears." Still another exclaimed, "My eyes never before beheld such a seen [*sic*] . . . nor do I ever desire to see such another—the Lice and Maggots seem to vie with each other, were creeping in Millions over the Victims; the Doctors themselves sick or out of Medicine." No wonder that in 1776 John Adams was despairing, "The small pox! The small pox! What shall We do with it?"

It was close to impossible for the American troops to gather in large numbers without smallpox running rampant. Quarantining had some impact, but in military retreats or advances it was impractical. George Washington was worried: "Should it spread," he wrote to the Massachusetts House of Representatives in late 1775, smallpox would be "very disastrous & fatal to our army and the Country around it." Washington's brother worried about the effect on recruitment: "I know the dainger [*sic*] of the small pox and camp fever is more alarming to many than the dainger they apprehend from the arms of the enemy." Washington, who had had smallpox as a young man and was immune, eventually decided to oversee an unprecedented campaign to inoculate the entire revolutionary army by inserting small amounts of the virus into the skin to create a much milder illness. After a period of sickness, most recovered and could rejoin the battle with immunity to the plague.

It was arguably the most important military decision Washington ever made, evening the score with the relatively immune British, whose African American allies, never inoculated, suffered terrible losses. Enslaved black people were particularly vulnerable. Jefferson would later guess that of the 30,000 enslaved black Virginians who had joined the British, "about 27,000 died of the small pox and camp fever."

Most Americans today have little, if any, awareness of the role the epidemic played in the war. And this is another curious fact about some plagues but not others: some seem to shift society profoundly, while others, however intense, are almost instantly forgotten. This is especially true when an epidemic coincides with war—as it often does.

If the 1918 flu pandemic were to occur today, one 2013 study found, it would kill between 188,000 and 337,000 Americans. The reason the death toll would be so much lower than the 675,000 Americans who actually died is that medicine has improved. Many of those who died endured bacterial coinfections, which are now far more treatable with antibiotics. Globally, somewhere around 100 million human beings perished.

The flu's symptoms were horrifying. In her book *Pandemic 1918*, Catharine Arnold notes that "victims collapsed in the streets, hemorrhaging from lungs and nose. Their skin turned dark blue with the characteristic 'heliotrope cyanosis' caused by oxygen failure as the lungs filled with pus, and they gasped for breath from 'air-hunger' like landed fish." The nosebleeds were projectile, covering the surroundings with blood. "When their lungs collapsed," one witness recounted, "air was trapped beneath their skin. As we rolled the dead in winding sheets, their bodies crackled—an awful crackling noise which sounded like Rice Crispies [*sic*] when you pour milk over them."

But as the summer of 1918 began in the United States, relief spread. Maybe it was over. And then, in the fall, confident that a vaccine was imminent, several cities, notably Philadelphia, hosted war-bond parades, with large crowds thronging the streets, as with the massive Black Lives Matter marches today (albeit with fewer masks). In the coming weeks, the city morgue was piling bodies on top of bodies, stacked three deep in the corridors, with no ice and no embalming. The stench was rank. City authorities were reduced to asking people to put their dead loved ones out on the street for collection. The second wave of the flu had arrived, brought in large part by troops returning from Europe.

The Army camps were a circle of hell: In Camp Devens, north of Boston, one young doctor arrived to see sixty-three young men die on his first day. The 1918 flu took aim at the younger generation, leaving some older people untouched. "The husky male either made a speedy and rather abrupt recovery or was likely to die," that Camp Devens doctor, helpless in the face of this, reported. The average death toll in the camp was a hundred young men a day, and in the fall morgues were completely overwhelmed. People stole other people's caskets, or gravediggers simply emptied corpses out of them into a pit in order to bury others.

A survivor remembered, "From the moment I got up in the morning to when I went to bed at night, I felt a constant sense of fear. We wore gauze masks. We were afraid to kiss each other, to eat with each other, to have contact of any kind. We had no family life, no school life, no church life, no community life. Fear tore people apart." How on Earth, one wonders, has this been forgotten? The truth is the memory was repressed, but, as after the Black Death, people sublimated the internal stress into the pleasure of the moment. The Roaring Twenties didn't come out of nowhere. In the 1919 Carnival in Rio, the acting out was particularly intense. In her history of the epidemic, *Pale Rider*, Laura Spinney notes how one Rio reveler recalled, "Carnival began and overnight, customs and modesty became old, obsolete, spectral. . . . Folk started to do things, think things, feel unheard-of and even demonic things."

And as in Rome, and in revolutionary America, there was a direct military consequence. In 1918, the flu may have hit the malnourished German troops a little harder than the Allies, stymieing what they thought might be a critical advance in the conflict. A few historians suggest the flu was a factor in Germany's defeat and postwar desolation. President Woodrow Wilson's possible bout of the same flu in Paris forced him to sit out the peace conference for several days. Upon his return, by some accounts, he appeared weakened, and he ultimately failed to prevent the ruinously exorbitant reparations Germany was obliged to pay.

Wilson himself was apparently so intent on winning the war that he never mentioned the influenza in public. Even when he came down with what might have been the illness himself, he kept mum. This is an American pattern. Wilson seemed to ignore the flu entirely; Reagan ignored AIDS in the early years of its devastation; Trump denied that COVID-19 was a threat until he couldn't—and even now he is minimizing it to advance a sputtering economic recovery. But the public was hardly defying them. They, too, preferred denial. Americans focused on victory in Europe and consigned the domestic horror to historical oblivion. Similarly, if you ask young gay men in 2020 about the history of AIDS, a plague that occurred in their own lifetime, you are likely to get platitudes or a blank stare. Some things we simply want to forget.

Katherine Anne Porter, who wrote *Pale Horse, Pale Rider*, a story inspired by her own experience surviving the 1918 flu, said something in an interview once that has stuck with me. The flu poleaxed Porter, then a twenty-eight-year-old chain-smoking journalist for the *Rocky Mountain News*, and after a near-death experience she recovered for the next six months. Her hair turned white, then fell out; hallucinations came and went; she tried to get out of bed and broke her arm; she was told that phlebitis would cripple her for the rest of her life. And yet she lived. And it changed her.

"It just simply divided my life," she wrote, "cut across it like that. So that everything before that was just getting ready, and after that I was in some strange way altered. . . . It was, I think, the fact that I had really participated in death, that I knew what death was, and had almost experienced it. I had what the Christians call the 'beatific vision,' and the Greeks called 'the happy day.' . . . Now if you have had that, and survived it, come back from it, you are no longer like other people, and there's no use deceiving yourself that you are. . . . It took me a long time to realize . . . that I had my own needs, and that I had to live like me."

I feel similarly, as a survivor of the first plague in my lifetime, HIV and AIDS. Within the gay world, AIDS was a plague quite similar in its impact to those in the past that afflicted the general population. Yes, men who have sex with men were not the only victims, but they made up a big majority of US cases in the beginning, and they still do. Around seven hundred thousand Americans have died of AIDS, a toll COVID-19 is unlikely to match, and concentrated in a far smaller population. I saw close friends die, nursed the sick, mourned ex-lovers, watched familiar faces grow old in a few months and lie dead in a few more. For more than a decade, gay men and their families were beset with the helplessness that defines a plague: the knowledge that there is no cure, that there is only prudence, luck, or death. But mainly death.

It changed me—and many others—for good. The liberation of surviving an early brush with death is hard to describe, but like Porter, I learned that I had to live—and live like me. Regardless of the crowd, or accepted opinion, or communal loyalty, I was determined, as the plague changed me to live my life freely, to say what I think, and to do as I pleased. And this is not entirely unusual. Plagues can first depress you, force you to isolate and hunker down. But, in time, they can also prompt a kind of defiance, a very human desire to tell this virus to go to hell and to act in ways that ignore it. Gay men slowly began to try to have sex again and to celebrate the life that sex gave, even as they also always risked, to a greater or lesser extent, illness and death. Over time, as treatments improved and the illness ceased to be a death sentence, condoms, like today's COVID masks, came to be used sporadically, then less and less, until they were largely cast aside.

There lingered, though, the gnawing sense that those of us who survived had to do something to make the staggering number of victims mean something, to honor them and remember them in some way. It was an extraordinary act of collective will that, out of the ashes of a plague, galvanized the many gay men and lesbians who were determined to remake the world in its wake, to insist on formal civic equality and that they be treated with dignity and respect. And within just a couple of decades, we had achieved this—even the right to marry.

It would never have happened so quickly, or at all, without AIDS and how it illuminated the unique stigma homosexuals lived under. In some ways, in fact, the gay-rights movement of the 1990s and 2000s is best understood as a subplot in the narrative of plague. It sounded crazy to talk of marriage equality in 1989, but plagues, as I've noted, make people crazy. The psychological strain, the fear, the anxiety: they build and build until people give themselves permission to scream, to protest, to re-create or reinvent religion, to express themselves fearlessly in public, to reorder the whole.

The extraordinary and near-spontaneous mass gatherings to protest police violence against black people this year, I suspect, are rooted in this same human need. Untethered from normal routines, indeed from work itself, and shut inside with almost no human contact for months, people needed to vent, to transcend the moment and be with one another. The spark, the killing of George Floyd, was not exactly plague related, but, as sometimes in history, disinhibited feelings of very different kinds can still merge into a collective spasm. And in this plague, black people have been disproportionately hit everywhere, in large part the result of the familiar burdens of entrenched poverty and discrimination. It seemed to make some kind of sense, in a world remade by plague, to tackle this injustice more squarely and radically than before.

Plagues, in this way, always present the survivors with a choice. Do we go back to where we were, if that is even possible, or do we somehow reinvent ourselves for a new future? The conflicting desires compete in our minds: to go back to normal or to seize the opportunity to change a society temporarily in flux. We can choose to make a different world, reordering our social compact and our political institutions and our relationship to the natural environment in ways that will protect us against, or at least mitigate the damage from, future plagues. Or we can recognize what was precious in what the plague took from us and seek to restore the status quo ante.

This plague comes, as the Roman plagues did, in a period of great climate change, and of near-peak globalization, which almost certainly means more epidemics are on their way. And it has already set precedents that imply a very different trajectory ahead. In the United States, the federal relief has been extraordinarily generous by American standards, foreshadowing, perhaps, a debt-funded universal basic income and a big redistribution of wealth in the near future. The virus has also proved itself capable of finally cracking the cult of Trump. The president's inability even to fake interest in or competence over the epidemic may well have made his reelection impossible, and his terrible tone in response to massive protests has rattled even his closest allies. The epidemic hasn't ended polarization and may even have intensified it. But it has empowered the opposition in ways previously unimagined. And it may have tilted the balance sufficiently, at least in the short term, that once-inconceivable political change could take place here, in what seemed until just a few months ago an impossibly divided and politically sclerotic country.

In this respect, perhaps, COVID-19 in America may best resemble the bubonic plague outbreak in London in 1665. It devastated the city that summer, prompting an exodus of the wealthy and connected, with perhaps one hundred thousand eventually dying in a city whose population was just under half a million. Worse, it was followed the next year by the Great Fire of London, which effectively razed the heart of the city, ruining many in the merchant class. But this catastrophe was subsequently seen as a chance to rebuild and renew, and many of the greatest landmarks of London were then constructed, as streets were widened, stone replaced wood, and the economy took off again. The pestilence and fire jump-started a revival not just in the economy and public health but also in the sciences and arts.

Do we go back to where we were, or do we somehow reinvent ourselves for a new future?

You can see the potential contours of a similar response today. This plague makes a strong argument for a more aggressive approach to public health, which would mean, at a minimum, extending health insurance to everyone in the country, as well as reform and renewal for the disgraced CDC and WHO. It could unleash a new wave of infrastructure spending to repair the immense damage to the economy. It could, and absolutely should, end the argument over preventing climate change—because it is so deeply connected to new viral outbreaks, as shifts to hotter weather portend a highly dangerous upheaval in the animal and microbial worlds. And while I worry that this plague could well usher in a new era in which traditional liberalism gives way to a freshly invigorated collective leftism, particularly around identity politics, it could also deeply wound the appeal of the populist right in America, which, once in government, failed the core test of preventing an open-ended, lengthy period of infection, sickness, and death.

Some existing trends might also intensify. It's hard to see how a policy of mass immigration or free trade will survive public scrutiny for long in a world where viruses cross borders with such surpassing ease. The US-China relationship, already tense, could deteriorate still further. Living online, with all the isolation and depression and extremism that can generate, is now an even stronger and widespread norm, as we avoid physical interaction even more than we did previously. Same with working from home: atomization of our culture, the already-increasing levels of depression, loneliness, and antisocial behavior, could deepen further. The collapse of small retail has been accelerated, and the power of the giant tech companies is ever greater. And the epidemic has not assuaged the yawning gap between rich and poor. While COVID relief has made a real, temporary impact, the stark social and economic inequality in the country looms as large as ever. Rates of suicide, drug abuse, and overdosing could climb even higher.

And the deeper reasons for our viral vulnerability have not gone away. Just as plague arrived with civilization, so our unprecedented twenty-first-century global civilization has made plague both more likely and more dangerous. We have opened up viral pathways in far more places than the Romans ever dreamed of and created transportation networks of unprecedented speed and dynamism across the entire world. Our unstoppable global economic engine, along with climate change, has prompted mass migration from the Global South to the Global North, the kind of disruption we know makes epidemics more likely. We have penetrated the rain forest and unfrozen the tundra; we are releasing long-buried pathogens whose impact on humans we simply cannot even guess at. We have disturbed the planet in precisely the ways that led to devastating consequences for humans in the past. But more so than ever before. Just in the past few years: Ebola, MERS, SARS, and COVID-19.

And we are not in control. If you are still complacent that human science and technology have removed the potential for the mass extinction of humans, you should wake up. We have lucked out so far. COVID-19 is extremely transmissible but not that fatal to most people, all things considered. But even those countries that are success stories didn't see it coming in the first place and have experienced resilient breakouts. We still have no vaccine—it may be a year or more before we get one, and we do not know how effective it will be. Imagine the next pandemic pathogen as something as devastating as Ebola and as contagious as the flu. We are as defenseless as we have ever been. This relatively mild virus shut the entire world down for a couple of months. What happens when a much worse one shuts it down for longer?

Knowledge of a brutal new virus does not prevent its spread. Only a much more profound reorientation of humankind will lower the odds: moving out of cities, curtailing global travel, ending carbon energy, mask wearing in public as a permanent feature of our lives. We either do this to lower the odds of mass death or let nature do what it does—eventually so winnowing the human stock that we are no longer a threat to the planet we live on.

That's the sobering long view. It is hard to look at the history of plagues without reflecting on the fact that civilizations created them and that our shift from our hunter-gatherer origins into a world of globally connected city-dwelling masses has always had a time bomb attached to it. It has already gone off a few times in the past few thousand years, and we have somehow rebounded, but not without long periods, as in post-Roman Europe, of civilizational collapse. But our civilization is far bigger than Rome's ever was: truly global and, in many ways, too big to fail. And the time bomb is still there—and its future impact could be far greater than in the past. In the strange silence of this plague, if you listen hard, you can still hear it ticking.

The Unbearable Whiteness
of the Classics

February 5, 2021 | *THE WEEKLY DISH*

O ne of the more eye-opening documents you can find online is Martin Luther King Jr.'s handwritten syllabus for a seminar he was teaching at Morehouse College in 1962. It's a glimpse of what King believed an educated black man should know. It's a challenging list: Plato's *Republic*, Aristotle's *Nicomachean Ethics*, Augustine's *City of God*, all the way to Bentham and Mill. There's also a copy of the exam questions he set. Among them: "List and evaluate the radical ideas presented in Plato's *Republic*;" "State and evaluate Aristotle's view of slavery."

What King grasped, it seems to me, is the core meaning of a liberal education, the faith that ideas can transcend space and time and culture and race. There are few things more thrilling than to enter a whole new world from another era—and to see the resilient ideas, texts, and arguments that have lasted (or not) through the millennia. These ideas are bound up, of course, in the specific context and cultures of the past, and it is important to disentangle the two. But to enter the utterly alien world of the past and discover something intimate and contemporary is one of the great joys of intellectual life. MLK wasn't the only classics student among the great civil rights leaders. Malcolm X was too.

My own classical wonderment came from learning Latin. From the age of eleven to eighteen, at my selective high school, I studied, translated, and wrote in Latin. My inner gay-boy nerd marveled at its logic and near-total consistency, the matrix of its grammar, and, over time, even the prose style of its greatest writers. I came to chuckle at Catullus, and at the deadpan irony of Tacitus; I learned how to write sentences by reading Cicero. I shared some of the excitement that so many first experienced when these texts were recovered and engaged again in the Middle Ages and Renaissance.

This strange, ancient, muscular language was also a key to the texts, rituals, and prayers of my church, opening up another dimension of meaning as well. It felt as if, stuck in a small town in England in the dreary 1970s, I had been given the keys to live in another universe. My one regret was not taking Ancient Greek. Imagine if I could read the Gospels in the original!

But I read in *The New York Times* this week, as one does, that, in fact, I was deluding myself. Rather than being liberated, as I felt I was, I was actually being initiated into "white supremacy." And there is now a broadening movement in the academy to abolish or dismantle the classics because of their iniquitous "whiteness."

Racial "whiteness" as a concept would, of course, have been all but meaningless to all the ancient writers I grew to love. It's beyond even an anachronism. How on Earth do you reduce the astonishing variety and depth and breadth of texts from an ancient Mediterranean world to a skin color? How do you read Aristotle and conclude that the most salient quality of his genius was that he was "white"?

You can arrive at this deranged conclusion, it seems, in two contrived ways. One is to view the ancient world as some kind of founding proof of the superiority of the "white race," whatever that means. Imperialists and fascists have always loved this theme; Mussolini was especially fond of it. The very word "fascism" comes from the Roman "fasces," a bound bundle of logs that was used to signify the authority of the state. In the same *New York Times* piece, we are reminded that the "marchers in Charlottesville, Va., carried flags bearing a symbol of the Roman state; online reactionaries adopted classical pseudonyms; the white-supremacist website Stormfront displayed an image of the Parthenon alongside the tagline '*Every* month is white history month.'"

This dreck is not just bigoted; it's ahistorical, anachronistic, and reductionist, and it ignores the vast range of classical thought, in which radicals and liberals have found as much intellectual nourishment as conservatives and reactionaries.

The other way to see the classics as a form of "white supremacy" is to embrace critical race theory. Some now argue that the study of ancient Greece and Rome "forms part of the scaffold of white supremacy" that endures to this day. This is because Western democracies can trace many of their formative ideas back to Greece and Rome—and many of these same democracies went on to practice imperialism and even slavery, thousands of years later. Some even justified their brutality with reference to classical texts. This entwining of the white supremacist assumptions of the Enlightenment with ancient Greece and Rome means the classics are therefore fatally tainted.

I'm sorry, but that's it? That's the argument? An entire, diverse, multifaceted, multicultural civilization that sprawled from Turkey and North Africa to the borders of Scotland—a source of fascination to people of all political persuasions and races over the centuries—cannot be taught because some racists in the past abused its texts? That's like saying that science should no longer exist because some scientists once practiced eugenics.

The man at the center of the *New York Times* profile, one Dan-el Padilla Peralta, is a fascinating case study in all this. He's obviously brilliant and once found liberation in the classics the way I and so many others did. As a black immigrant from the Dominican Republic, he became a prodigy in classical scholarship. As recently as 2015 and late 2016, he was writing things like this: "For a dark-skinned child of the Dominican Diaspora who spent his formative years in Harlem, it was both captivating and empowering to detect the pulse of Greco-Roman antiquity in hip-hop. In the heat of that collision new worlds were born."

And then he was born again. He came to see the white supremacists' co-optation of the classics as inextricable from the classics themselves; and believed their influence had helped not only construct American slavery but the persecution of Haitians by the Dominicans in his native land. He saw these power dynamics working through history, and he suddenly felt complicit in them. This epiphany demanded a wholesale reboot of his intellect—"I had to actively engage in the decolonization of my mind"—and a wholesale dismantling and, if need be, destruction of his entire field of study.

That's quite a leap. The *New York Times* piece attempts to explain Padilla's conflation of the ancients with racism thus: "Classics and whiteness are the bones and sinew of the same body; they grew strong together, and they may have to die together." First: What does that actually mean? Second: How could that claim be falsified? Like all the rest of critical theory, it can't. Or this: race is "a ghostly system of power relations that produces certain gestures, moods, emotions and states of being." It permeates everything everywhere. Like the Holy Ghost?

Perhaps this is the clearest thesis statement: "Enlightenment thinkers created a hierarchy with Greece and Rome, coded as white, on top, and everything else below." I take the point. Yes, Enlightenment figures saw Greece and Rome as civilizational heights—because they *were*. And yes, they linked them to European society, because, after all, much of Europe was occupied by Rome, which was so deeply influenced by the Greeks. They also distinguished white Europeans from the rest of the world's population in troublingly racist ways, from the perspective of the twenty-first century. We should take account of this and note where and when this ugly theme emerges. But that Enlightenment thinkers sometimes misused the classical texts does not invalidate the texts themselves.

And why can't you teach this critique of eighteenth-century racism—*alongside* the classics themselves? Why can you not, for good measure, add great works from other cultures, and expand the idea of classics, rather than rubbish it? Another classicist, Ian Morris, gives this answer in the *New York Times* piece: "Classics is a Euro-American foundation myth. Do we really want that sort of thing?" Well, as a way to understand the roots of our civilization, why shouldn't we?

I've become fascinated by these moments of conversion, of "waking up" to see everything through the prism of race and identity. Padilla did not just become more aware of how the classics had been abused in the Enlightenment, he had a real epiphany. There was no way to reconcile his previous love for the classics from the systemic racism they now represented to him. "Claiming dignity within this system of structural oppression," Padilla says, "requires full buy-in into its logic of valuation." He refuses to "praise the architects of that trauma as having done right by you at the end." So now he teaches classics by getting students to role-play Romans, or as a way to encourage critical theory activism. Everything else must be cleansed.

I'm still stunned by how so many believe this big a leap is the only option; or that these crude binaries—white bad, non-white good—are somehow helpful.

I'm struck by how many intelligent people seem prepared to abandon any consideration of culture, economics, immigration, region, or family structure in understanding racial dynamics in history or today. I'm amazed that racist terms like "whiteness" are now deployed routinely—as if such a thing exists; as if white people, with their vast political, cultural, and personal differences, are somehow interchangeable as a single oppressive mass; as if "white values" is not *on its face* a baldly racist term.

But racial Manichaeism really touches our erogenous zones, as Padilla's newfound zeal shows. To see the world as binary and to choose the side of righteousness makes life much more meaningful. It banishes doubt and complexity. It makes us feel better to be part of a tribe and to have a simple enemy or ally who is clearly visible—just check the color of their skin, as every elite student is now trained to do.

Padilla, it seems to me, was able to resolve some of the huge challenges of modernity and his own psyche and background by surrendering his mind and soul to a purely racial, and thereby tribal, analysis of the world. It is a form of psychological liberation, an epiphany millions also seemed to experience last summer, but it is a dark one. Critical theory, unlike most religions, posits no transcendent escape from its worldly strictures and systems, pinions you to the cross of your various identities, and offers only the promise of permanent struggle as a reward.

I prefer another form of liberation—out of race and identity and into learning, out of one's own identity and into others', out of the present and into the past—another world entirely, waiting to be explored and understood. I believe in the "higher individualism" of "the sovereign human soul that seeks to know itself and the world about it," in the words of W. E. B. Du Bois. There's freedom there, as so many have found in reading the great works of the ancient past. I yearn to be where Du Bois found himself:

> I sit with Shakespeare, and he winces not. Across the color line I move arm and arm with Balzac and Dumas, where smiling men and welcoming women glide in gilded halls. From out of the caves of evening that swing between the strong-limbed Earth and the tracery of stars, I summon Aristotle and Aurelius and what soul I will, and they come all graciously with no scorn nor condescension. So, wed with Truth, I dwell above the veil. Is this the life you grudge

us, O knightly America? Is this the life you long to change into the dull red hideousness of Georgia? Are you so afraid lest peering from this high Pisgah, between Philistine and Amalekite, we sight the Promised Land?

It is a tragic irony of history that while this freedom of the mind was once withheld from generations of African Americans by actual white supremacists, it is now in danger of being withheld once again by neoracists of a different but just as tenacious kind.

Two Sexes. Infinite Genders.

February 26, 2021 | *THE WEEKLY DISH*

Gallup's latest report on the Ls, Gs, Bs, and Ts has raised a few eyebrows. It shows a slow, gradual rise in those identifying as "LGBT" so that it now stands at 5.6 percent of the population—a record.

I know this is a hot topic, but, seriously, I can't see this as a big deal. When I was coming out a hundred years ago, we were constantly told that 10 percent—at least!—of the country was gay. "One in ten" was a common buzz phrase in gay groups, and most gay people believed it. And in what was my first of many heresies as a homosexual, I never bought that. How on Earth did I keep recognizing the same people at march after march and parade after parade if there were over thirty million of us? And why should we care how many of us there are?

When I examine the details of the latest poll, I'm reassured that my intuition was right and all that feel-good propaganda was wrong. It turns out that in 2020, only 1.4 percent of US adults are gay men, and only 0.7 percent are lesbians. So all the gays and lesbians amount to a little over 2 percent of the country's adults. And that seems about right to me.

The surprise, however, is that there are now almost as many people identifying as "trans" as "lesbian." In Generation Z, trans identification (1.8 percent) now beats lesbian ID (1.4 percent) as a proportion of the whole. Over three generations, trans identity has gone from 0.2 percent to 1.8 percent, a staggering 800 percent increase. That may be because anti-trans attitudes are shifting for the better and more people feel able to express themselves; it may also be because of a shift among lesbians to the trans category, as butch dykes increasingly become men; and some of it is probably due to the sheer trendiness of being trans among the young. It's kind of amazing—and wonderful—that trans identity has gone from being freakish to being the coolest thing, among the young. But for some, let's be real here, it may just be identity-slumming when talking to a pollster.

Bisexuals, at 54.6 percent of all "LGBT" identifiers, are now a majority, and in Gen Z, clock in at 72 percent! The qualification to this is that only 3.7 percent of bisexuals live with someone of the same sex while over 30 percent live with someone of the opposite sex. And I have to say I think it's a bit odd that such a big chunk of the "LGBTs" are actually functioning in heterosexual relationships—and that doesn't even count the hetero trans population. If Gallup had added a Q, for "queer," we could include even more fashionable heterosexuals—or maybe, given the absence of that category from the Gallup list—they chose the bisexual category. It's one more reason, I'd argue, that we should disaggregate the "LGBT" construction so actual gay people can be measured more accurately, instead of lumping us in with vague categories that include lots of people in heterosexual relationships.

But does this mean we should panic about increasing gender fluidity in the younger generation? Again, I really don't think so. The sex binary is intrinsic to the survival of our species. That's just biology and human reproductive strategy. Aggregate sex differences—physical, psychological, behavioral—are deeply rooted in our species' DNA. They're not going away because a bunch of Foucault disciples want them to.

But gender is not sex; it's how that sex is expressed and manifested. And if the range of ways to express or describe your sex as man or woman is expanding and evolving, that's a huge win for our culture. It means that many more interpretations of what it is to be a man or a woman are now socially acceptable, liberating people from the expectations of crude gender stereotypes. (This is why I worry that young gay gender-nonconforming kids may be categorized by some as trans, if they exhibit stereotypes of the opposite sex. But gender nonconformity does not mean you're trans. You're more likely to be gay or straight.) So I really don't have much of an objection to the 56 or 112 genders some propose, apart from the fact that some of them are more than a bit silly. I mean: "cavusgender," "ceterofluid," "demifluid," "genderwitched," "quoigender"? You can look them up for yourselves.

I'd argue, in fact, that there are many, many more than 112 ways to express your maleness or femaleness. Just as every person is unique, so is the expression of gender. The combination of a sex and a singular personality is always unique. And what is well worth leaving behind is a crude, binary sense of gender itself. Unlike sex, it really is a spectrum. And it can be crushing for gender-nonconforming kids and adults to live up to stereotypes of their gender; and it can be horribly restrictive for everyone else. There will always be social and cultural group differences in the aggregate, for sure—more men, for example, will, on average, prefer watching sports than women. But a woman who loves football is absolutely no less a woman for it.

As a kid, my otherness didn't have a name. I knew I was a boy—but the day each week that terrorized me the most in my high school was the day I was made to play rugby. I was small, prepubescent at that point, bookish, asthmatic, and physically awkward. Being tackled by a postpubescent boy twice my size and finding my head pushed into knee-deep mud, mixed with my own blood, on a semiregular basis was not exactly my idea of a pleasant afternoon. Neither was being outside in the cold, endless rain, my hands so frozen I couldn't actually unbutton my own rugby shirt afterward, my lungs spasming with another asthma attack.

But the fear of this organized male violence was made much worse because it seemed to impugn my maleness. There were no varying, mixed, or subtle models of masculinity in my childhood and adolescence that I could easily identify with. When in elementary school I was ingenuously asked by a girl "Are you sure you're not a girl?" my response was an immediate no. But I knew what she was getting at. And it ate away at my self-esteem.

Similarly, at my grandparents' one Christmas, my grandmother noticed me in a corner with a book and my younger brother, who was driving a toy truck up and down the carpet, crashing it into the walls. She said to my mother, looking at my brother, and in front of me, "Well at least you now have a real boy." It cut deeply. I remember not pursuing English literature past the age of sixteen, even though I loved it—because studying history was somehow, in my mind, more masculine.

To deepen the self-inflicted wound, my dad was a near model of classic masculinity. He was a superb athlete who had competed for England as a middle-distance runner; he had been captain, first, of his high school rugby team and then of our town's. He was taciturn and bloody-minded, threw his weight around in our house, fished in the North Sea, raised rabbits and chickens, and drove fast. He routinely knocked down parts of our little house whenever he felt bored to add extensions, which he rarely finished. His mates drank lots of beer, and it was clear he was much happier among them than with his own family. He even had a midlife crisis, and bought a racy car and a leather jacket. It was as if he felt the need to act out a near parody of "toxic masculinity."

He wasn't cruel to me, but he never came to any of the school plays I was in, or any of my debating contests. Too girly, I suppose. And of course I felt as if I had let him down. I remember with more than a little poignancy how he once gamely tried to teach me how to kick a soccer ball. And how utterly useless I was.

What he didn't let himself experience to its fullest for a long time was another side of himself. He loved to draw and to paint. After his death a year ago, we found a letter that showed he had once been admitted to the Slade School of Fine Art in London, perhaps the finest such institution in the country, and a great honor. He never told us of this, and I don't know why he turned down the place. Probably his need to earn money, but maybe also the price of gender conformity. But as soon as he retired, and especially after he got divorced, he started painting again—and the results were spectacular. I cannot help but wonder what kind of life he might have had, if he had had the courage of his own, nonconforming desire, what great paintings he might have produced over time.

When I came out to him, he suddenly bent down and sobbed. I was shocked and confused. My dad never cried. I asked him again and again why he was weeping, even as I was relieved he hadn't thrown a punch. And after a while, he looked up and said something I will never forget: "I'm crying because of all you must have gone through growing up, and I never did anything to help you." All that macho bravado dissolved instantly by a father's love.

Later that day, my mother, with her usual blather-mouth, said she thought he was crying because he realized that I had had the nerve to risk my career and future to be who I truly was, and he had never summoned up the courage to do the same. He was, she said, crying for himself. Not that he was gay, but that he loved art. A weight of gender expectations may well have prevented him from realizing his dream.

I have thought of him a lot in the year now since his sudden, unexpected death. We couldn't have a funeral under COVID lockdown. But when we do, we're going to display as many of his paintings as we can.

Acknowledgments

I n over three decades of writing, there is no way I can pay sufficient tribute to so many who have helped, encouraged, or supported me. But my gratitude remains to the many editors who made most of this possible: T. E. Utley and William Deedes, Mike Kinsley, Leon Wieseltier, Dorothy Wickenden, Ann Hulbert, Rick Hertzberg, Adam Moss, Gerry Marzorati, Jim Kelly, Steve Koepp, Martin Ivens, John Witherow, Sarah Baxter, James Bennet, Scott Stossel, Tina Brown, David Haskell, David Wallace-Wells, and Jebediah Reed. I am intensely privileged to have had the guidance of these brilliant, patient, demanding editors.

I'd also like to thank those who took such a risk in supporting me over the years: Marty Peretz, David Bradley, Rupert Murdoch, and the editors and publications who gave me permission to reprint these essays: *The New Republic*, *The New York Times*, *New York* magazine, *The Sunday Times* (of London), *Salon*, *The Advocate*, *The Atlantic*, *Newsweek*, and *The Washington Post*.

In researching this book, and going over millions of words, I owe enormous thanks to several *Dish* interns, colleagues, and researchers: Christopher Van Buren, Matt Sitman, Rahsaan King, Daaim Daanish, and especially Chris Bodenner, who made this happen, and kept on me till it was done. My friend Johann Hari was also a stalwart egger-on; my friend, Chris Grasso, supported me in every decade; and my husband, Aaron Tone, kept me halfway sane throughout. *Dish* readers—aka Dishheads—were unconscripted editors too—constantly criticizing, amending, and finessing my thoughts.

Andrew Wylie and Sarah Chalfant inspired me to go big in this collection, and my editor, Ben Loehnen, brought all of this to fruition.

All errors, misjudgments, and accountability are mine alone.

Index

Abbate, Peter, 13
"Abolition of Torture, The," 225–35
abortion, 40, 113–16, 120, 124, 126, 181–83,
    191, 195, 199, 203, 246, 253, 262–63,
    427, 433
  Roe v. Wade and, 114, 262
  Trump and, 393
Abu Ghraib, 226, 230–34, 238, 239, 254,
    277, 290
ACT UP (AIDS Coalition to Unleash
    Power), 19, 23, 25–29, 45–47,
    83–84, 91, 92, 138, 213, 462, 463
Adams, John, 500
Adderall, 464
Addicts Rehabilitation Center Choir, 20
adoption, 57, 182
Advocate, 168
  "Still Here, So Sorry," 205–7
affirmative action, 160, 198, 433, 448
Affordable Care Act (Obamacare), 328,
    335, 432–33, 438
Afghanistan, 231, 233, 234, 264, 267, 277
African Americans, *see* blacks
After Virtue (MacIntyre), 354
Ahmadinejad, Mahmoud, 245–47
AIDS, xvii, xviii, 15–30, 39, 44, 47, 50,
    75–95, 169, 209, 211–14, 216, 217,
    221, 279–81, 317, 318, 452, 457,
    502–4

ACT UP and, *see* ACT UP
Christianity and, 20–21
in developing world, 190, 194
Diana and, 103, 104
gay marriage and, 3, 4, 257
HIV, *see* HIV
Holocaust analogy and, 81, 82
intravenous drug users and, 16, 25, 80,
    82–83
Memorial Quilt, 35–37, 88, 411
minority men and, 21–25, 82–83, 222
opioid epidemic compared with,
    461–63
as political problem, 81
safe sex and, 18, 19, 23, 213, 317
Treatment Action Group and, 77
treatments for, 15, 26, 26, 53, 76–78,
    86, 87, 206, 213, 317, 462
AIDS Healthcare Foundation, 205
AIDS Project Los Angeles, 217
Albert, Marv, 125
"Alone Again, Naturally," 59–73
Al Qaeda, 227, 233, 234, 247, 265, 267
America, 97–99, 233, 278, 301–3, 410, 477
  blaming of, 123
  Bork on, 121–23
  Civil War in, 303, 424, 426–28, 455–56
  Diana and, 101–4
  Enlightenment principles in, 197, 446

America (*cont.*)
  exceptionalism of, 466
  Founding Fathers of, 228, 248, 337,
    382, 384, 385, 426, 428
  hysterical pessimism about, 121–22
  Native Americans and, 425–26, 456,
    492–93, 496–97, 499
  postindustrial, 456, 464
  smallpox and, 491–93, 496, 499–500
  tribalism in, xvii, 423–40, 465, 472
America, 356, 358, 365
"America and the Abyss," 415–21
American Civil Liberties Union, 123
American Enterprise Institute, 433
American Mercury, 131
American Revolution, 228, 455, 499–500
American Scholar, 31
"America's New Religions," 473–78
"America Wasn't Built for Humans,"
  423–40
amphetamines, 460
Anatomy of Prejudices, The (Young-
  Bruehl), 134–35
Anchorage Daily News, 386
Anderson, Ryan, 479
Ansari, Aziz, 447
"Anti-Semite and Jew" (Sartre), 132
anti-Semitism, 81, 82, 131–34, 137, 138,
    317, 359, 417
  black anti-Semites, 138
  Black Death and, 497
  Holocaust, 81, 82, 92, 133, 136, 141, 497
apartheid, 52, 133
Apprentice, The, 387
Aquinas, Thomas, 67–68, 288, 348, 376
Argentina, 363–64, 366
Aristotle, 63, 288, 509, 510
Army Field Manual, 234
Arnold, Catharine, 501
art, 473–74

Art of the Deal, The (Trump), 386
Aryan Nations, 127
Asian Americans, 428
As Nature Made Him (Colapinto), 149
atheism, 196, 197, 301, 329, 330, 473
Atlantic, xviii, 403, 436, 449
  "Goodbye to All That: Why Obama
    Matters," 261–74
  "Why I Blog," 283–95
Audacity of Hope, The (Obama), 269
Aung San Suu Kyi, 423
Auspitz, Josiah Lee, 31

Baby Boomers, 262–64, 266–69, 272, 275
Bad Religion (Douthat), 329
Bagram detention facility, 233, 277
Balkans, 423
Barozzi, Father, 10
Barr, Bob, 114
Bartlett, Bruce, 309
Barton, Mark, 141
Baudelaire, Charles, 453
Bauer, Jack, 253
Bawer, Bruce, 213
bear culture, xviii, 165–70, 210, 219
Bears on Bears (Suresha), 169
Beck, Julia, 480
Beinart, Peter, 321–23, 325–26
Beirut, 423
Bell, Daniel, 314, 465
Bell Curve, The (Murray and
  Herrnstein), xvii, 318
Benedict, Saint, 354
Benedict XVI, Pope (Joseph Cardinal
  Ratzinger), 64–67, 194, 211, 246,
    269, 354–56, 359–63, 367–69, 375
Bennett, Jessica, 448
Bennett, William, 122
Bensonhurst, 7–14
Berg, Nick, 238

Bergoglio, Jorge, *see* Francis, Pope
Bet Mishpachah, 217
Bible, 199, 248, 401
    Genesis, 71, 148
    Gospels, 246, 249, 329, 348, 369, 371,
        377
    of Jefferson, 327, 330, 331, 333
    Job, 363
    literal interpretation of, 329, 361
Biden, Joe, xvi, 485–89
birth control, *see* contraception
bisexuals, 516
Bismarck, Otto von, 192
Blair, Jayson, 287
Blair, Tony, xvi, 183, 198, 199, 342
Black, Duncan, 293
Black Death, 497–99, 502
Black Leadership Commission on
    AIDS, 22, 23
Black Lives Matter, 389
Black Party, 78–80, 87
Black Power, 163
blacks, 388
    children, 216
    civil rights for, *see* civil rights
        movement, 427, 428
    family and, 23
    gay, 21–24, 82–83, 222
    hatred toward, from other blacks, 139
    police violence toward, 441–44, 504
    racism and, *see* racism
    testosterone levels in, 156–58
    voters, 427, 486
Blade, 218–19
Block, Susan, 112
blogs, blogging, 318, 400, 401
    of Sullivan, xviii, 283–95, 384, 405,
        432; *see also Dish, The*
Blow, Charles, 487
Blum, Deborah, 148

Boccaccio, Giovanni, 498
Bonauto, Mary, 221
Bond, Julian, 272
Booth, Alan, 151
Booth, Martin, 455
Bork, Robert, 121–23, 263, 427
Bosnia, 275
Boston College, 217
Bouie, Jamelle, 485
Boy Meets Boy, 167
Bradley, F. H., 31
brain, Default Mode Network in, 470,
    471
Brewer, William, 454, 466–67
Britain, *see* Great Britain
Broad Channel, Labor Day parade in,
    130–31
Brokeback Mountain, 241–43
Brookhiser, Richard, 175–77
Brooks, David, 117, 309
Brown v. Board of Education, 171, 173
Broyles, Gregory, 22–24
Bruce, Lenny, 455
Bryant, Anita, 212
bubonic plague, 498, 505
    Black Death, 497–99, 502
Buchanan, Patrick, 42, 44, 48, 134, 138
Buddha, Buddhism, 358, 403, 411, 471,
    472, 473
buprenorphine, 462
Bureau of Justice Statistics, 443
Burke, Edmund, xvii, 4, 196, 217
Burning Man, 412, 470
Bush, George H. W., xvi, 37, 110, 190,
    198, 279, 309
Bush, George W., xvi, 173, 189–94, 196,
    198, 199, 202, 242, 254, 263–65, 269,
    270, 274, 277, 281, 297, 303, 309,
    315, 336, 383, 432–34
    abortion and, 183

Bush, George W. (*cont.*)
  conservatism and, 254
  faith of, 246–47
  Iraq War and, 246, 275, 277–78
  9/11 and, 264
  torture and, xviii, 225, 229, 231, 234,
    277, 336, 433
Bush, Jeb, 384
Bush v. Gore, 336
Butenandt, Adolf, 148
Byrd, James, Jr., 127, 130
Byron, George Gordon, Lord, 453

Cain, Herman, 383
Cameron, David, xvi
campus culture, 445–49, 487
Camus, Albert, 36, 86
Canady, Charles T., 114
cannabis, marijuana, 413, 433, 454, 460,
    463, 466–67
capitalism, 347–51, 356, 376–78, 388,
    406, 410, 464, 465, 474
capital punishment, executions, 120, 156,
    228–29
Capote, 241
Card, Andy, 193
Carr, Nicholas, 406
Carson, Ben, 383
Carter, Jimmy, 190, 254
Carville, James, 393
Casey, Robert, Jr., 183
Castile, Philando, 442
Castro, Fidel, 41
Catalans, 423
Cathedral of Hope, 217
Catholic Church, Catholics, 194, 199,
    248, 250, 330, 429, 488–89
  author's faith, xvii, 59–62, 67, 71–73,
    187, 247, 318, 439
  author's grandmother's faith, 250, 332

Biden's faith, 488
  at Boston College, 217
  child molestation and, 187
  contraception and, 329, 354, 359
  fundamentalist, 199, 211, 246, 250,
    361–62
  gay denominations, 217
  homosexuality and, xvii, 23, 43,
    59–73, 138, 187, 222, 246
  Jesuits, 363–67, 375
  meditation and, 413
  in Northern Ireland, 429
  Opus Dei, 183, 186, 359
  Pope Benedict XVI (Joseph Cardinal
    Ratzinger), 64–67, 194, 211, 246,
    269, 354–56, 359–63, 367–69, 375
  Pope Francis, xvii, 347–48, 350–51,
    353–78, 439
  Pope John XXIII, 359
  Pope John Paul II, xvii, 72, 138,
    186–87, 290, 348, 349, 355, 356,
    359, 361, 377–78
  Pope Paul VI, 329, 359
  priesthood, 187, 246
  Second Vatican Council, 186, 358–60
  Thomism and, 42, 44, 63, 72, 368
  Vatican, 63, 211, 269, 359
Catholic Youth Organization (CYO), 11
censorship, 123, 449
census, 299
Chapman, Steve, 309
Character of a Trimmer, The (Halifax), 314
charisma, 102
Chasing the Scream (Hari), 464
Chavez, Cesar, 50
Cheney, Dick, 201, 215, 225, 242, 254,
    277–78, 315, 394
Cherry Jubilee, 79
Chevron, 215
China, 115–16, 239, 322, 506

cholesterol, 148

Christianity, Christians, xvii, 98, 186, 198, 246–50, 317, 318, 327–34, 353–55, 411, 428, 438, 472, 476–78, 503

  AIDS and, 20–21

  Bible and, *see* Bible

  Catholic, *see* Catholic Church, Catholics

  Constitution and, 118

  crisis of, 327–34

  democracy and, 478

  distraction and, 413

  as doctrine vs. way of life, 369–70

  fundamentalist, 199–200, 239, 247, 249, 269, 361, 369

  Gospel and, 246, 249, 329, 348, 369, 371, 377

  homosexuality and, xvii, 21, 435

  Jefferson and, 327–33

  Jesus and, 248–49, 270, 327–31, 333–34, 348, 349, 351, 362, 363, 367, 369, 371–74, 376, 411, 476, 477

  Limbaugh and, 347–51

  and Mary as untier of knots, 366, 367

  and meaning of "secular," 328–29

  Obama's faith, 270–71, 328, 434

  plagues and, 496, 498

  politics and, 332, 428

  poverty and, 375–77

  Protestant, *see* Protestants

  psychedelic experience and, 471

  religious right, xvii, 98, 113, 125, 139, 189–204, 263–64

  Saint Francis and, 330–33, 350, 371, 372, 374–77

  and separation of church and state, 98, 118, 196, 235, 327

  theo-conservatives, 118–19, 125, 196

  torture and, 329

  Trump and, 477–78

"Christianity in Crisis," 327–34

Christianity Today, 123

Christmas, 98

Churchill, Winston, 104, 342

CIA, 225, 227, 228

Citizens United, 336

civil disobedience, 230

Civil Rights Act, 480

civil rights movement, 43, 50, 51, 98, 163–64, 171, 192, 222, 268, 427, 428

  March on Selma, 255

Civil War, 303, 424, 426–28, 455–56

C.K., Louis, 407–8

classics, 509–14

Clement VI, Pope, 497

climate change, 433, 505–6

Clinton, Bill, xvi, 84, 109–14, 116, 119, 120, 122, 125–26, 128, 181, 190, 198, 203, 237, 253, 263, 265, 268, 274, 297, 299, 300, 309, 315, 336, 393, 427, 431, 434, 437

  impeachment of, 112, 114, 125, 263, 427, 437, 438

  Lewinsky and, xviii, 105–7, 110–15, 122–24, 300

  Starr and, xviii, 106, 109–12

Clinton, Hillary, xvi, 190, 261, 264–65, 267–69, 272, 274, 297, 341, 384, 418–19, 437, 485, 487–89

  abortion and, 181–83

  Trump and, 393, 396, 417–19, 421, 436, 437

Clooney, George, 102

Cloud of Unknowing, The, 362

Coalition for Harmony, 12–14

Coates, Ta-Nehisi, 317–19, 435–36

cocaine, 452, 454, 464

  crack, 452–54

Cocteau, Jean, 454–55

Cohen, Leonard, 303

Cohn, Roy, 36, 50

Colapinto, John, 149

Cold War, 233, 275, 431

Coleridge, Samuel Taylor, 453

college campuses, culture of, 445–49, 487

Collier, Peter, 112

Colombia, 439

Columbine High School massacre, 137

Comey, James, 418

Commentary, 114, 120

communism, 186, 190, 197, 349, 378, 423

Confessions of an English Opium-Eater (De Quincey), 453–55

Congregation for Divine Worship, 373

Congregation for the Doctrine of the Faith, 359, 362

Congress, U.S., 418

    House of Representatives, 382, 394, 419, 427, 438

    Senate, 382, 394, 419, 430

conscience, 246

conservatism, conservatives, xvi, xvii, 190–91, 250, 254, 335–37, 418, 439, 465

    America-blaming and, 123

    balance and, 314

    Bork on, 121

    Bush and, 254

    cultural and social, 119

    of doubt, 191, 194–98, 201–4, 314

    economically based, 123–24

    of faith, 191–95, 198–201, 204, 314

    freedom and, 125

    gay marriage and, 1–5, 172–73, 257

    institutions and, 335–37

    intellectuals, 114, 431, 432

    Kain on, 313

    homosexuality and, 113–15

    liberalism and, 120–21, 309, 314, 432

    morality and, 110–26, 191–204

    neoconservatives, 114, 117–18, 314

    Oakeshott and, 33

    Obama and, 253, 254

    paradox of, 124

    in politics of homosexuality, 40–46, 53, 56

    populism and, 386, 506

    religious right, xvii, 98, 113, 125, 139, 189–204, 263–64

    Sullivan's leaving of, 309–11

    theo-conservatives, 118–19, 125, 196

    see also Republican Party, Republicans

Conservative Soul, The (Sullivan), 310

Constitution, U.S., 114, 190, 192, 197, 235, 302, 315, 336, 382, 394

    Christianity and, 118

    torture and, 228

contraception, 113, 115, 182, 183

    Catholic Church and, 329, 354, 359

Conway, Kellyanne, 463

Cornyn, John, 200

cortisol, 149

Coulter, Ann, 262

COVID-19, 491, 493, 502, 503, 505–7

Cowan, Richard, 460

Crain, Chris, 218

Crawford, Matthew, 406

crime, 199, 442

    hate, *see* hate crimes

    murder, *see* murder

    sex differential in, 153–54, 156

    testosterone levels and, 152–54

Crimea, 434

"Crisis of Faith," 189–204

Crisis of Zionism, The (Beinart), 321–23, 325–26

critical race theory, xviii, 448, 511–14

Cromwell, Oliver, 390

Crowley, James, 305–6

Cruise, Tom, 102

Cruising, 214

Cruz, Ted, 393, 396

Cuba, 41

Cultural Contradictions of Capitalism, The (Bell), 465

Cunningham, Michael, 210

Cyprus, 429

Dabbs, James M., 151

Daily Kos, 291

Daily Telegraph, xv–xvi

Damore, James, 432, 448

Davidson, Jo Ann, 183

Dead Right (Frum), 123–24

"Dear Ta-Nehisi," 317–19

Death of Ivan Ilych, The (Tolstoy), 29

Death of Outrage, The (Bennett), 122

Declaration of Independence, 103, 118, 197, 229, 327

"Declaration on Certain Questions concerning Sexual Ethics," 63

Decter, Midge, 118

Deedes, Bill, xv

Default Mode Network (DMN), 470, 471

Defense of Marriage Act, 114, 119, 201

DeGeneres, Ellen, 214, 220

DeLay, Tom, 200, 203, 336

"Democracies End When They Are Too Democratic," 379–97

democracy, 186, 233, 250, 319, 379–97, 416, 418, 424, 446, 465, 478

    Christianity and, 478

    direct, 382, 384

    elites in, 395

    late-stage, 379–81, 388

    media, 384

    Plato on, 379–82

    tribalism and, 426

"Democracy" (Cohen), 303

Democratic Party, Democrats, xvii, 120, 190, 198, 201, 203, 265, 268–69, 328, 386, 418–19, 428, 430, 433, 437, 486–89

    abortion and, 181, 183

    blogs and, 292

    Christian, 428

    immigration and, 427

    professors, 431

    Trump and, 437–38

    see also liberalism

deportation, 433

depression, 146, 150, 160, 472, 506

Depression, Great, 303

De Quincey, Thomas, 453–55

Diana, Princess, xviii, 101–4

Dignity, 217

Dinkins, David, 10, 24

disability benefits, 458

Dish, The, xviii, xix, 343

    "Dear Ta-Nehisi," 317–19

    "The First Elite Conservative to Say Enough," 335–37

    "Leaving the Right," 309–11

    "A Married Man," 257–59

    "Obama, Trimmer," 313–15

    "The Reagan of the Left?," 253–55

    "Rush Limbaugh Knows Nothing about Christianity," 347–51

    "Surprised by Grief," 343–45

    "Thatcher, Liberator," 339–42

    "What Is the Meaning of Pope Francis?," 353–78

    "Why Continue to Build the Settlements?," 321–26

Disraeli, Benjamin, 192

divorce, 120, 124, 125

Dobson, James, 122–23, 201

Dole, Bob, xvi, 120, 309

domestic partnership laws, 1–5, 49, 257
Donegan, Moira, 448
dopamine, 407
Dornan, Robert, 79
Douthat, Ross, 329
drag, 220, 482
Dreamland, 457
Dreams from My Father (Obama), 269,
    273
Drudge, Matt, 287, 291
Drudge Report, 291
drugs, 79–80, 120, 452–53, 459, 506
    AIDS and, 16, 25, 80, 82–83
    cannabis, 413, 433, 454, 460, 463,
        466–67
    cocaine, 452, 454, 464
    crack, 452–54
    fentanyl, 451–52, 460–62, 464, 465
    harm-reduction centers and, 462, 463
    heroin, 451–53, 457–63, 465
    legalization of, xvi–xvii
    LSD, 452, 453, 469, 471
    morphine, 451, 455, 457, 464
    opioids, 451–67, 472, 477
    opium, 451, 453–57, 460
    psychedelic, 469–72, 475
    war on, 460, 463
Du Bois, W. E. B., 513–14
due process, 448
Dugdale, John, 87–88

Ecstasy, 469
education, 193, 268
    classics in, 509–14
    higher, 428, 431, 464
Edwards, John, 253, 265
Egypt, 390
Eich, Brendan, 431–32
Electoral College, 382, 383, 430
Eliot, T. S., 363

Ellison, Ralph, 163
Emerge, 22
"End of Gay Culture, The," 209–23
end-of-life decisions, 191, 194, 199–201,
    246
England
    Civil War in, 390
    London, 505
    Reformation in, 410, 498
    see also Great Britain
Enlightenment, 197, 410, 446, 511, 512
Entine, Jon, 157
Episcopalians, 248
Equality Act, 480–81
Eschaton, 293
Eskimos, 431, 435
estradiol, 148
European Union, 417
evangelicals, 110, 114, 185, 201, 211, 216,
        263–64, 271, 328, 329, 353, 434–35,
        477
executions, capital punishment, 120, 156,
        228–29
Experience and Its Modes (Oakeshott), 31

Fackel, 288
Fairlie, Henry, 97
"Faith Healing" (Larkin), 59
Fama, Joseph, 8, 10, 14
family, 3, 42, 52, 58, 464
    black, 23
    gay marriage and, 172–73, 258
Family Research Council, 134–35
fascism, 394, 396, 510
    Trump and, 390–92, 396, 415–17, 420
Fate of Rome, The (Harper), 494–96
Fayed, Dodi, 103
FBI, 132, 137, 142, 417, 418
Fear of Disclosure, 17
Feliciano, Gina, 14

family values, 3, 4

feminism, xviii, 157, 160, 432, 447–48, 479
    Lewinsky and, 106
    Thatcher and, 339, 341

Fenn, Elizabeth A., 499–500

fentanyl, 451–52, 460–62, 464, 465

Ferraro, Arnaldo, 12–13

Figueroa, Carlos, 306

filibuster, 196, 201, 202, 336

Fiorina, Carly, 383

First Amendment, 446

"First Elite Conservative to Say Enough, The," 335–37

First Things, 117–19

Fischer, David Hackett, 228

Fishback, Ian, 231, 235

Flames Neighborhood Youth Association, 11

Floyd, George, 504

flu pandemic of 1918, 500–503

Focus on the Family, 122

Forbes, James, Jr., 21

Forbes, Steve, 383

Foreign Affairs, 115

foreign policy, 115–16, 189–90, 164, 434

forgiveness, 439

Fortune 50 companies, 215

Fortune 500 companies, 215

Foucault, Michel, 431

Founding Fathers, 228, 248, 337, 382, 384, 385, 426, 428

Fourth of July, 99

Fox Family Channel, 157

Fox News, 202, 380, 418, 427

Francis, Pope, xvii, 347–48, 350–51, 353–78, 439

Francis, Saint, 330–33, 350, 371, 372, 374–77

Francis of Assisi (Thompson), 330

Franco, Paul, 314

Franklin, Benjamin, 421, 455

freedom, 197, 204, 222, 223, 233, 234
    conservatives and, 125
    Declaration of Independence and, 229
    fundamentalism and, 239
    Plato on, 379–80
    religious, 234–35
    and separation of church and state, 235
    torture and, 226, 228, 229, 234, 277

Freedom Rides, 163

free speech, xvii, 123, 431, 446

free trade, 190, 432, 506

French Revolution, 390

Friedersdorf, Conor, 309

Frist, Bill, 201

Frum, David, 111, 123–24, 309, 433

fundamentalism, *see* religious fundamentalism

Furrow, Buford, Jr., 127, 132, 141

Gandhi, Indira, 341

Gandhi, Mahatma, 332

Garner, Eric, 442

Gates, Henry Louis, Jr., 305–7

Gates, Robert, 297

Gaudium et Spes, 63–64

"Gay Cowboys Embraced by Redneck Country," 241–43

gay life, *see* homosexuality and gay life

"Gay Life, Gay Death: The Siege of a Subculture," 15–30

Gay Men's Health Crisis (GMHC), 19, 24–26, 79, 217

gender dysphoria, 483
    transgender individuals, 148, 149, 393, 479–83, 515–16

gender identity and expression, 219, 220, 222, 448, 449, 480–83, 515–19

Geneva, Conventions, 229, 231, 277, 322

genocide, 133

Germany

    Nazi, *see* Nazi Germany

    Weimar, 417

    in World War I, 502

gerrymandering, 427

Gibbon, Edward, 410

Gilbert, Sky, 482

Gingrich, Newt, 336, 427

Giuliani, Rudolph, 128, 202, 253, 264,

    265, 274, 420

Glass, Stephen, 287

Glazer, Nathan, 314

Glendon, Mary Ann, 118

globalization, 420, 438, 456, 505, 506

God, 33, 245–51, 303, 330, 332, 333,

    360–63, 367–70, 372, 373, 376, 377,

    411, 473, 476, 477

God Is Not Great (Hitchens), 474

God Is Watching You (Johnson), 425

gods, 425, 473

Godwin's Law, 385

"Going Down Screaming," 109–26

Goldberg, Jeffrey, 323–25

Goldhagen, Daniel Jonah, 136

Goldwater, Barry, 125, 190, 427

"Goodbye to All That: Why Obama

    Matters," 261–74

Good Friday Agreement, 429

Google, 432, 448

Gore, Al, 190, 263, 277, 383, 393

government

    role in moral issues, 191–204

    size of, 189, 192–93, 313, 315

GPS, 406

grace, 353

Graff, E. J., 221

Graham, Katharine, 104

Graham, Lindsey, 298

gratitude, 472

Gray, Howard, 370

Gray, John, 473–76

Great Britain, 97–99, 195, 198, 199, 233,

    339–42, 423

    Diana and, 101–4

    Northern Ireland, 423, 429

    see also England

Great Depression, 303

Great Fire of London, 505

Great Mortality, The (Kelly), 497, 498

Greece, ancient, 511, 512

Greene, Billy, 176–77

Gregg, Judd, 298–99

Gröning, Philip, 404

Guantánamo Bay detention camp

    (Gitmo), 231, 233–35, 254, 277

Guardini, Romano, 366

Guide to the Classics, A (Oakeshott), 32

Gulf War, xvii, 277

Gyllenhaal, Jake, 242

Haaretz, 321

Halifax, George Savile, Marquis of, 314

Hannity, Sean, 262

happiness, 407, 452, 465, 467

Hari, Johann, 464

Harlem, 20, 128, 131

Harper, Kyle, 494–96

Harper's, 446

Harris, Eric, 137

Harris, Kamala, 488

Harris, Sam, 404, 471, 473

Hart, Jeffrey, 309

Hatch, Richard, 214

hate, 127–44, 446

    and attention given to haters, 144

    hysterical, 134–36

    ignorance and, 134, 143

    love and, 132–33, 135

media obsession with, 144

narcissistic, 134, 135

obsessive, 134, 136

prejudice and, 129, 143

reasonable vs. unreasonable, 133–34

use of word, 435

varieties of, 132–37

within minorities, 139

hate crimes, xviii, 128–30, 132, 137, 139–43, 431

  personal vs. group hate and, 140–42

  criminals as members of hated groups in, 137–40

  involving no violent physical assault, 142

  statistics on, 137, 141–42

Hate Crimes (Jacobs and Potter), 129

hate speech, 138, 431

Hawkins, Yusuf, 8, 11–13

Hayek, Friedrich, 313

health care, 27, 268, 297, 385, 354, 418, 432–33, 456

  Affordable Care Act (Obamacare), 328, 335, 432–33, 438

  COVID-19 and, 505

  managed care, 457

  Medicaid, 193, 458

  Medicare, 189, 192, 336

Hegel, Georg Wilhelm Friedrich, 31, 32

"He Hormone, The," 145–61, 317

Heilemann, John, 194

Helms, Jesse, 279, 281

Helprin, Mark, 85–86, 119–21

Henderson, Russell, 127–28

"Here Comes the Groom," 1–5

Heritage Foundation, 193, 432, 479–80, 483

Herlihy, David, 499

Heroes, Rogues and Lovers (Dabbs), 151

heroin, 451–53, 457–63, 465

Herrnstein, Richard, xvii

heterosexual intercourse, 70–71

  procreation and, 42, 49, 57, 63–64, 66, 70, 258

heterosexual marriage, *see* marriage, heterosexual

Hezbollah, 245

Hilton, Perez, 291

Hispanics and Latinos, 21, 24, 25, 82–83, 216, 222, 299, 427, 428, 438

Hitchens, Christopher, 474

Hitler's Willing Executioners (Goldhagen), 136

HIV, 15, 17–20, 26, 67, 76–78, 86–88, 205–7, 214, 222, 298, 503

  author's positive status and treatment, 78, 92–95, 146, 205–7, 258, 279–80, 344, 400

  immigrants and travelers with, 279–81, 301

  treatments for, 15, 26, 26, 53, 76–78, 86, 87, 206, 213, 317, 462

  see also AIDS

Ho, David, 77

Hobbes, Thomas, 195

Hoffer, Eric, 387–90

Hoffman, Wayne, 169

Holocaust, 81, 82, 92, 133, 136, 141, 497

Homer, 451

homophobia, 19, 21–24, 27, 50–55, 58, 65, 81–82, 133–38, 140, 144, 447, 481

  hysterical hate and, 135

  Rustin and, 164

homosexuality, politics of, xvii, 39–58

  AIDS and, 92

  conservative, 40–46, 53, 56

  liberal, 50–58

  moderate, 48–50, 56

  radical, 44–48, 54, 56

homosexuality and gay life
  AIDS and, *see* AIDS
  alcoholism analogy and, 68–69
  assimilation into mainstream society,
    19, 46, 48, 53–54, 80–83, 213, 221,
    258
  author's sexuality, xvii, 39, 59–62, 67,
    71–73, 93–94, 172, 187, 216, 515,
    517, 518
  bear culture, xviii, 165–70, 210, 219
  black men, 21–24, 82–83, 222
  Catholic Church and, xvii, 23, 43,
    59–73, 138, 187, 222, 246
  children and teens, 47, 214–17, 221
  Christianity and, xvii, 21, 435
  circuit parties, 78–80, 87, 166, 169, 214
  civil society, 217, 219
  club scene, 19–20
  conservatism and, 113–15
  drag, 220, 482
  employee protections and, 215
  end of gay culture, xvii, 209–23
  freedom from responsibility
    associated with, 91
  gay bars, 217–18
  gay rights, 47, 50, 98, 131, 203, 302,
    319, 393, 427, 482, 504
  gender expression changes and, 219
  genetic origins of homosexuality, 42,
    45, 319
  hatred toward homosexuals from
    other homosexuals, 139
  Hispanic men, 21, 24, 25, 82–83
  homosexuality as choice or not,
    42–46, 48, 50, 63–65, 67, 68, 113
  homosexuality as cultural
    construction, 44, 46
  homosexuality as illness, 113, 201–2
  increased visibility of, 215
  lesbians, *see* lesbians

  Lincoln's sexuality, 175–79, 243
  marriage equality, *see* marriage,
    same-sex
  military service and, xviii, 39–41, 44,
    46–51, 55–56, 58, 84, 92
  outing and, xvii, 27, 28, 45
  percentage of gay people in U.S., 515
  political organizations, 218
  press, 218–19
  in Provincetown, 165, 166, 169,
    209–12, 220
  queer identity, 45–48
  religious life and gay denominations,
    217
  separatism and, 19, 47, 48, 83, 172, 221
  sodomy laws and, 41–42, 48–49, 113
  transgender ideology and, 479–83
Hoover, J. Edgar, 50
Hormel, James, 114
House of Representatives, U.S., 382, 394,
  419, 427, 438
Howard Stern Show, The, 386
Howard University, 272
"How Did I Get Iraq Wrong?," 275–78
How to Change Your Mind (Pollan),
  469–71
Hudson, Rock, 462
Huffington, Arianna, 291
Huffington Post, 291
Human Rights Campaign (HRC), 215,
  218, 221
Hummes, Cláudio Cardinal, 375
Hutus, 133, 134
hydrocodone, 455, 458

"I Am Bear; Hear Me Roar," 165–70
identity politics, xvii, 445–46, 448–49,
  506
I. F. Stone's Weekly, 292
Ignatius of Loyola, Saint, 370

Illing, Sean, 472
immigration, immigrants, 134, 141, 389, 390, 392, 420, 426–27, 433, 436, 438, 440
   HIV and, 279–81
   mass, xvii, 427, 428, 439, 465, 506
   Trump and, 389, 390, 392, 393, 420, 437
Immigration and Nationality Act, 279
individualism, 439, 465, 513
individuality, 439
industrialization, 410, 456
   deindustrialization, 456, 464
information technology, 401
Inglis, Bob, 114
Inquisition, 195, 362
Instapundit, 293
"Integration Day," 171–73
International Brotherhood of Electrical Workers, 486
International Committee of the Red Cross, 226
internet, 239, 384–85, 427, 464–65
   blogging on, *see* blogs, blogging
   living online, 399–403, 405–7, 409, 410, 412–14, 506
Intimate World of Abraham Lincoln, The (Tripp), 175–76, 178
Into Great Silence, 404
Inuit, 431, 435
"Invisible Man, The," 163–64
Ipsos Public Affairs, 413
IQ, 317, 319
Iran, 245, 247, 265, 322, 325, 420, 481
Iraq, 423
Iraq War, xvii, 231–35, 245, 246, 254, 262, 264–67, 275–78, 290, 427, 432
   Obama and, 266–67
Ireland, 423, 429
ISIS, 392

Islam, Muslims, 246, 247, 250, 267, 373, 435
   fundamentalism and fanaticism in, 195, 211, 237–39, 245, 269
   Koran and, 199, 234, 246
   terrorism and, *see* terrorism, Islamist
   Trump and, 389, 390
"Islamo-Bullies Get a Free Ride from the West," 237–39
Israel, xvii–xviii, 92, 245, 247, 317, 318
   continued building of settlements in, 321–26
It Can't Happen Here (Lewis), 394–95
"I Used to Be a Human Being," 399–414

Jabotinsky, Vladimir, 323
Jackson, Jesse, 194, 272, 273, 383
Jacobs, Alan, 407
Jacobs, James B., 129
Jalics, Francisco, 364
Japan, 134, 190, 233
Jefferson, Thomas, 248, 455, 500
   Bible of, 327, 330, 331, 333
   Christian faith of, 327–33
Jena, La., 272
Jenner, Caitlyn, 481–82
Jesuits, 363–67, 375
Jesus Christ, 248–49, 270, 327–31, 333–34, 348, 349, 351, 362, 363, 367, 369, 371–74, 376, 411, 476, 477
Jews, 119, 216, 247, 390
   anti-Semitism and, *see* anti-Semitism
   gay, 217
   Israel and, *see* Israel
   Judaism, 246, 411, 435
   Nazi Germany and, *see* Nazi Germany
John XXIII, Pope, 359
John of Ephesus, 495
John of Reading, 498

John Paul II, Pope, xvii, 72, 138, 186–87, 290, 348, 349, 355, 356, 359, 361, 377–78
Johnson, Boris, xvi
Johnson, Charles, 310
Johnson, Dominic, 425
Johnson, James Weldon, 131
Johnson, Ronald, 24
Jones, Paula, 106, 112
Joseph, Stephen, 26
journalism, 284
    blogs, *see* blogs, blogging
    hostility to dissent in, 446–47
Junger, Sebastian, 425–26
Justice Department, 417
"Just Say Yes to Drugs," 469–72
Jyllands-Posten, 237

Kaepernick, Colin, 441, 442
"Kaepernick's Message Is Getting Lost— Along with the Facts on Race and Police Violence," 441–44
Kagan, Robert, 115
Kain, E. D., 313
Karpinski, Janis, 231
Kasich, John, 396
Kaus, Mickey, 241, 291
Keats, John, 453
Kelly, John, 497, 498
Kelly, Ruth, 183
Kennedy, Anthony, 200–201
Kennedy, Edward, 50
Kennedy, John F., 50, 102, 253
Kenya, 423
Kerrey, Bob, 85
Kerry, John, xvi, 182, 190, 202, 264, 280, 309, 393
Keyes, Alan, 215
King, John William, 127
King, Martin Luther, Jr., 50, 163, 272, 303, 332, 509

Kinsey, Alfred, 175
Kinsley, Michael, 285–86
Klebold, Dylan, 137
Klein, Ezra, 448
Knopf, Alfred A., 131
knots, 366–67, 378
Koran, 199, 234, 246
Kosovars, 133–34
Kosovo, 275
Kramer, Larry, 27–28
Kraus, Karl, 288
Krauthammer, Charles, 225, 226, 228–32, 234, 235, 241
Kristol, Irving, 314
Kristol, William, 111–17, 122
Kushner, Tony, 138

Labor Day parade in Broad Channel, 130–31
Labour Party, 183, 198
Landry, Ryan, 220
Larison, Daniel, 309
Larkin, Philip, 59, 222
Latinos and Hispanics, 21, 24, 25, 82–83, 216, 222, 299, 427, 428, 438
laudanum, 455
Law, Bernard Cardinal, 187
"Leaving the Right," 309–11
Lebanon, 423
Ledger, Heath, 242
Lee, Spike, 22
left
    Labour Party, 183, 198
    use of term, 435
    see also Democratic Party, Democrats; liberalism
Legends, 220
Legionaries of Christ, 359
Lemoine, Philippe, 443
Leno, Jay, 105

Lesbian Avengers, 221

lesbians, 5, 209, 210, 214, 216, 515–16
    identities and gender expression
        among, 219, 220
    marriages among, 210, 221
    in Provincetown, 209, 210
    testosterone and, 151
    transgender ideology and, 480–82

Lessing, Gotthold, 250–51

Levitz, Eric, 441–42

Lewinsky, Monica, xviii, 105–7, 110–15,
    122–24, 300

Lewis, Sinclair, 394–95

LGBTQ identity, 479–80, 483, 515–16

liberalism, xvii, 190, 194, 204, 254, 310,
    388, 420–21, 442, 476, 478, 506
    America-blaming and, 123
    Bork on, 121–22
    campus culture and, 445–49
    conservativism and, 120–21, 309, 314,
        432
    Obama and, 253–54, 297
    in universities, 428, 431
    see also Democratic Party, Democrats

libertarians, 110

"Life Lesson," 181–83

Likud Party, 325

Limbaugh, Rush, 298, 347–51

Lincoln, Abraham, 175–79, 243, 303

Lincoln, Mary Todd, 176, 177

Locke, John, 195

"Log Cabin Republican," 175–79

Lollards, 498

London, 505

Long, Huey, 390

Lott, Trent, 113, 114

love, 132, 475
    hate and, 132–33, 135
    psychedelic drugs and, 469, 471, 472

Love Undetectable (Sullivan), 317

Lowry, Rich, 197

LSD, 452, 453, 469, 471

Lugar, Richard, 280

lynching, 127, 131, 436, 449

Maariv, 323–24

MacCulloch, Diarmaid, 411

Maciel, Marcial, 359

MacIntyre, Alasdaire, 354

"Mad, Maddening America, the Wisest
    of All," 301–3

Madison, James, 381

Major, John, xvi

Malcolm X, 164, 509

Malick, Terrence, 414

Malkin, Michelle, 311

Mandela, Nelson, 340, 439

Manzi, Jim, 309

March on Selma, 255

March on Washington, 163

Marcuse, Herbert, 431

Markowitz, Martin, 77

Marlboro Projects, 11–12

marijuana, cannabis, 413, 433, 454, 460,
    463, 466–67

marriage, domestic partnership vs., 1–5,
    49, 257

marriage, heterosexual, 2–4, 56–57, 66,
    201, 434
    Defense of Marriage Act, 114, 119, 201
    divorce and, 120, 124, 125
    gay men and women in, 4, 39
    procreation and, 42, 49, 57, 63–64, 66,
        70, 258
    testosterone levels and, 153

marriage, same-sex, xvi, xvii, xviii, 1–5,
    49, 56–58, 92, 171–73, 196, 199,
    201–2, 210, 211, 215, 216, 219, 221,
    243, 257–58, 263, 302, 388, 394,
    432, 504

marriage, same-sex (*cont.*)
   AIDS and, 3, 4, 257
   of author, 257–59, 302
   civil unions, 190, 201, 257, 263, 302
   conservatives and, 1–5, 172–73, 257
   Defense of Marriage Act and, 114,
      119, 201
   family and, 172–73, 258
   "gay marriage" as misnomer, 172
   lesbian, 210, 221
   partner benefits and, 215
"Married Man, A," 257–59
Marshall, Josh, 291, 485
Marxism, 133, 349, 376, 431, 445–49, 466
Mary, as untier of knots, 366, 367
masculinity, xviii, 219–20, 243
   bear culture, xviii, 165–70, 210, 219
mass movements, 387, 389–90
Mazur, Allan, 151
McCain, John, 128, 202, 231, 253, 265, 298
McCain Amendment, 225
McCall, Nathan, 139
McConnell, Mitch, 336, 437
McGovern, George, 267
McGwire, Mark, 112, 125, 156
McMahon, Vince, 386
McMurtry, Larry, 242
McNeill, William H., 496–97
MDMA, 469
meaning, 465–67, 472, 473–76
Medicaid, 193, 458
Medicare, 189, 192, 336
meditation, 330, 399, 400, 403–5, 408–9,
   413–14, 471, 473
Meir, Golda, 341
Mencken, H. L., 131, 143
methadone, 459, 462
methamphetamine, 454, 460, 464
#MeToo movement, 447, 586
Metropolitan Community Church, 217

Meyerson, Harold, 132
Michael, George, 214
microaggressions, 445, 447
Milk, 302
Milk, Harvey, 212
military, 189–90, 428
   desegregation of, 163
   homosexuals in, xviii, 39–41, 44,
      46–51, 55–56, 58, 84, 92
   Trump and, 394, 419
   women in, 156, 158, 159, 199
Mill, John Stuart, 474–75
Miller, Geoffrey, 231
Million Youth March, 128
mindfulness, 413, 473
minorities, 45, 46, 143, 438
   discrimination against, 50–52, 143
   gender expression among, 222
   Hispanics and Latinos, 21, 24, 25,
      82–83, 216, 222, 299, 427, 428, 438
   HIV/AIDS and, 21–25, 82–83, 222
   Trump and, 393–94
   see also blacks; racism
Minority Task Force on AIDS (MTFA),
   23, 24
Mohammed, Khalid Sheikh, 227, 232
Mondello, Keith, 13, 14
Mondello, Mrs., 13, 14
Montaigne, Michel de, 226, 249, 288–89
Monticello, 455
Moore, Chadwick, 432
Moore, Michael, 190, 262
Mormons, 194, 426
Morning Party, 79
morphine, 451, 455, 457, 464
Morris, Ian, 512
Mould, Bob, 214
Moulitsas, Markos, 291
MoveOn.org, 262
Mozilla, 432

MSNBC, 427

Muhammad, 248

murder, 120, 140, 142

   testosterone levels and, 153, 154

Murdoch, Rupert, 111

Murphy, Eddie, 23

Murray, Charles, xvii

Muslims, *see* Islam, Muslims

Mussolini, Benito, 510

"My America," 97–99

Myanmar, 423

Nader, Ralph, 194

naloxone, 454, 462

Napoleon, 390

Nation, 138, 292

national debt, 190, 298, 389, 433

National Health and Social Life Survey, 215

National Lesbian and Gay Journalists Association, 215

National Museum of American History, 327

National Republican Congressional Committee, 298

National Review, 197, 200, 292

National Survey of Family Growth, 215

Native Americans, 425–26, 456, 492–93, 496–97, 499

NATO, 416, 417

"Nature of Sex, The," 479–83

Nazi Germany, 41, 52, 134, 233

   Jewish Holocaust, 81, 82, 92, 133, 136, 141, 497

Netanyahu, Benjamin "Bibi," 322–25

Netanyahu, Ben-Zion, 323–25

Netherlands, 429

Neuhaus, Richard John, 117–19, 122

New Deal, 192

New Left, 112, 119, 122, 175, 212

New Republic, xvii, xviii, 90, 225, 257, 285, 286, 318

   "The Abolition of Torture," 225–35

   "Alone Again, Naturally," 59–73

   "Crisis of Faith," 189–204

   "The End of Gay Culture," 209–23

   "Gay Life, Gay Death: The Siege of a Subculture," 15–30

   "Here Comes the Groom," 1–5

   "Life Lesson," 181–83

   "The Politics of Homosexuality," 39–58

   "The Princess Bride," 101–4

   "Quilt," 35–37

   "Superstar," 185–87

   "Taken Unseriously," 31–33

   "The Two Faces of Bensonhurst," 7–14

Newsweek, xviii, 292

   "Christianity in Crisis," 327–34

New York, 194

   "America and the Abyss," 415–21

   "America's New Religions," 473–78

   "America Wasn't Built for Humans," 423–40

   "Democracies End When They Are Too Democratic," 379–97

   "I Used to Be a Human Being," 399–414

   "Just Say Yes to Drugs," 469–72

   "Kaepernick's Message Is Getting Lost—Along with the Facts on Race and Police Violence," 441–44

   "The Nature of Sex," 479–83

   "A Plague Is an Apocalypse. But It Can Bring a New World.," 491–507

   "The Poison We Pick," 451–67

   "We All Live on Campus Now," 445–49

   "Why Joe Biden Might Be the Best Bet to Beat Trump," 485–89

New York, xviii

New York, N.Y., 143

    Bensonhurst, 7–14

    Harlem, 20, 128, 131

New Yorker, 242

New York Press, 238

New York Times, xviii, 1, 121, 128, 176, 205,
    287, 329, 414, 448, 510–12

    "Going Down Screaming," 109–26

    "The He Hormone," 145–61, 317

    "Integration Day," 171–73

    "Unsung Heroine," 105–7

    "What's So Bad About Hate?," 127–44

    "When Plagues End: Notes on the
    Twilight of an Epidemic," 75–95,
    317

Nexis, 128

Nietzsche, Friedrich, 44

Nightline, 85

9/11 terrorist attacks, xvii, 193, 229, 238,
    254, 263–65, 277, 315, 427, 436

Nixon, Richard, 190, 264, 265, 419, 427

Nobel Peace Prize, 423

No Child Left Behind Act, 193

Northern Ireland, 423, 429

Novak, Michael, 118

Nunn, Sam, 40, 49

Oakeshott, Michael, xvii, 31–33, 196,
    313–15, 370, 410

Obama, Barack, xvi–xviii, 253–55, 280,
    303, 309, 315, 383–86, 389, 393,
    394, 415, 418, 433, 434, 436–38,
    445, 487, 489

    The Audacity of Hope, 269

    Biden and, 486

    Christian faith of, 270–71, 328, 434

    Dreams from My Father, 269, 273

    Iraq War and, 266–67, 275–76

    Israel and, 322

    moderation of, 315, 386

    race and, 272, 273, 306, 307

    Republican Party and, 297–300

    speeches of, 267, 270–72

    stimulus package and, 297–99

    as trimmer, 313–15

"Obama, Trimmer," 313–15

Obamacare (Affordable Care Act), 328,
    335, 432–33, 438

"Obama's Race Dream Is Swiftly
    Shackled," 305–7

O'Brien, Conan, 407

O'Donnell, Rosie, 214

Office of National Drug Control Policy,
    462–63

Olbermann, Keith, 262

On Human Conduct (Oakeshott), 31–32

opioids, 451–67, 472, 477

opium, 451, 453–57, 460

Opium (Booth), 455

Opus Dei, 183, 186, 359

O'Reilly, Bill, 241, 242, 262

Orwell, George, xvii, 228, 433–34, 449

Out, 168, 432

Outweek, 27

oxycodone (OxyContin), 455, 457–59

oxytocin, 453, 464, 465

Padilla Peralta, Dan-el, 511–13

Paglia, Camille, 167

Pakistan, 265–68

Pale Horse, Pale Rider (Porter), 502

Pale Rider (Spinney), 502

Palestinians, 134, 321–26

Palin, Sarah, xviii, 301, 318–19, 347, 350,
    351, 386–87

Pandemic 1918 (Arnold), 501

pandemics, *see* plagues

Parker, Kathleen, 309

Pascal, Blaise, 288

Pataki, George, 202

patriarchy, 447

Paul, Saint, 66

Paul VI, Pope, 329, 359

Pelosi, Nancy, 437

Pensées (Pascal), 288

People, 102, 103

Perot, Ross, 383

Pershing, John J., 391

Persian Gulf War, xvii, 277

Peter, Saint, 369

"Phobia at the Gates," 279–81

Pinker, Steven, 474

Piss Christ (Serrano), 238

Plague, The (La Peste) (Camus), 36, 86

"Plague Is an Apocalypse. But It Can
    Bring A New World, A," 491–507

plagues, 491–507
    Black Death, 497–99, 502
    bubonic, 498, 505
    Christianity and, 496, 498
    COVID-19, 491, 493, 502, 503, 505–7
    1918 flu, 500–503
    smallpox, 491–93, 396, 499–500

Plagues and Peoples (McNeill), 496–97

Plato, 288, 379–82, 392, 411, 509

"Poison We Pick, The," 451–67

polarization, in politics and society,
    262–65, 274, 424, 446, 462

Police-Public Contact Survey, 443

police violence, 441–44, 504

polio, 498

political correctness, 388, 487

Politico, 488

politics, 159, 328, 426–27, 476
    cults in, 476–78
    of faith, 314
    gerrymandering and, 427
    of homosexuality, *see* homosexuality,
        politics of

illiberal, 476
    organizing in, 385
    polarization in, 262–65, 274, 424, 446
    race and, 427, 428
    religion and, 250, 332, 428
    of skepticism, 314
    tribal identity and, 427, 428, 430
    women in, 159
    zero-sum, 336, 430
    see also Democratic Party,
        Democrats; Republican Party,
        Republicans

"Politics of Homosexuality, The," 39–58

Pollan, Michael, 469–72

Pope Francis (Vallely), 363, 368

poppies, 451–56

Porter, Katherine Anne, 502–3

postmodernism, 431

Potter, Kimberly, 129

poverty, 388
    Christianity and, 375–77

Powell, Colin, 272, 277

power, two types of, 102

Pox Americana (Fenn), 499–500

prejudice
    hate and, 129, 143
    ignorance and, 134
    social purpose in, 143
    see also anti-Semitism; hate;
        homophobia; racism; sexism

President's Emergency Plan for AIDS
    Relief, 280

press
    gay, 218–19
    Islamists and, 237–39
    see also journalism

Prince, 462

"Princess Bride, The," 101–4

prisoners, 120, 444
    testosterone levels of, 152, 153

privacy, 447

procreation, 42, 49, 57, 63–64, 66, 70, 258

progesterone, 149

progress, 474, 477

Prohibition, 192, 460

Protestants, 64, 110, 185, 186, 199, 217,
    246, 269, 328, 329, 361, 410, 429
    Episcopalian, 248
    evangelical, 110, 114, 185, 201, 211, 216,
        263–64, 271, 328, 329, 353, 434–35, 477
    in Northern Ireland, 429
    Reformation, 410, 498

Proulx, Annie, 242

Provincetown, Mass., 165, 166, 169,
    209–12, 220

psychedelics, 469–72, 475
    LSD, 452, 453, 469, 471
    psilocybin mushrooms, 469–71

psychopaths, 132

Puller, Lewis, 85

Puritans, 428

Putin, Vladimir, 390, 393, 417, 420, 434

Queer Eye for the Straight Guy, 167, 168,
    214

queer identity, 45–48

Queer Nation, 19, 45, 47

"Quilt," 35–37

Quinones, Sam, 457–59

Rabin, Yitzhak, 439

race, 424, 449
    critical race theory, xviii, 448, 511–14
    IQ research and, 317
    politics and, 427, 428

racism, 50–52, 54, 133, 135–37, 139, 140, 144,
    254, 303, 435–36, 439–40, 447, 512
    apartheid, 52, 133
    in Bensonhurst, 8–14
    Gates incident and, 305–7

and hatred within minorities, 139

and Labor Day parade in Broad
    Channel, 130–31

lynching, 127, 131, 436, 449

Mencken and, 131, 143

miscegenation, 136, 303

Obama and, 272, 273, 306, 307

police violence and, 441–44, 504

segregation, 134, 163, 164, 171, 173, 192,
    197, 303, 332, 444, 449

slavery, 52, 98, 141, 197, 227, 303, 332,
    426, 428, 435, 444, 449, 500

white supremacy, 127, 420, 426, 435,
    436, 445–47, 449, 510–11, 514

Rand, Ayn, 196, 349, 376

Randolph, A. Philip, 163

rape, sexual assault, 128, 141, 182–83, 447

Rather, Dan, 287

Rationalism in Politics (Oakeshott), 32

Ratzinger, Joseph Cardinal (Pope
    Benedict XVI), 64–67, 194, 211, 246,
    269, 354–56, 359–63, 367–69, 375

Raytheon, 215

Reagan, Ronald, xvi, 37, 98, 101, 102, 110,
    116–17, 124, 189, 190, 192, 193, 198,
    253, 254, 263, 266, 268, 275, 309,
    359, 427, 434, 463, 502

"Reagan of the Left?, The," 253–55

Real World, The, 214

Red Queen, The (Ridley), 152

Reformation, 410, 498

Reid, Eric, 414, 442, 444

Reid, Harry, 183

religion, 247, 269, 303, 425, 465–67, 472,
    473–78, 504
    atheism, 196, 197, 301, 329, 330, 473
    certainty in, 203, 246, 247, 249, 250,
        271, 315
    doubt in, 61, 248, 249, 271
    freedom of, 234–35

fundamentalist, *see* religious
fundamentalism
in gay life, 217
God, 33, 245–51, 303, 330, 332, 333,
360–63, 367–70, 372, 373, 376, 377,
411, 473, 476, 477
Oakeshott on, 370
politics and, 250, 332, 428
spirituality, 330
toleration and, 250, 478
see also Catholic Church, Catholics;
Christianity, Christians; Islam
Religious Freedom Restoration Act, 481
religious fundamentalism, 211, 247–48,
269, 303, 334, 388, 474
Catholic, 199, 211, 246, 250, 361–62
Christian, 199–200, 239, 247, 249, 269,
361, 369
Islamic, 195, 211, 237–39, 245, 269
Repubblica, 358
Republic (Plato), 379–81, 509
Republican Party, Republicans, xvii, 42,
110–11, 117, 126, 215, 265, 269, 335,
376, 418, 428, 430, 433, 434, 437,
438, 488
abortion and, 183
black voters and, 427
blogs and, 292
Christian, 428
foreign policy and, 115
gay vote and, 243
health care and, 432–33
Lincoln's sexuality and, 178–79
Obama and, 297–300
professors, 431
religious right, xvii, 98, 113, 125, 139,
189–204, 263–64
Trump and, 390–91, 394, 396–97, 415,
417–20, 437
see also conservatism, conservatives

"Republican Taliban Declare Jihad on
Obama," 297–300
responsibility, 91, 120, 172
Revolutionary War, 228, 455, 499–500
Reynolds, Glenn, 293
Ridley, Matt, 152, 158, 160
right
Toryism, 125, 309, 340, 341
see also conservatism, conservatives;
Republican Party, Republicans
right to die, 191, 194, 199–201, 246
Riverside Church, 21
Roberts, John, 335–37
Robertson, Pat, 48, 138
Rockefeller, Nelson, 190
Rodman, Dennis, 125
Roemer, Tim, 183
Roe v. Wade, 114, 262
Roiphe, Katie, 106, 446, 447
Roman Catholic Church, *see* Catholic
Church, Catholics
Romans, 493–96, 498, 499, 502, 505, 507,
511, 512
Romney, Mitt, 253, 336, 383, 432–34
Roosevelt, Franklin D., 192, 233, 303,
383, 427
Rove, Karl, 193–94, 203, 263–64, 269, 394
Rumsfeld, Donald, 227, 276–78
"Rush Limbaugh Knows Nothing about
Christianity," 347–51
Russell, Bertrand, 474–75
Russia, 390, 434
Rustin, Bayard, 163–64
Rwanda, 133, 423
Ryan, Paul, 349, 391, 437

Sabbath, 411, 413
Sacred Congregation for the Doctrine of
the Faith, 63
Saddam Hussein, 233, 238, 266, 276

Saint (club), 20

St. Patrick's Cathedral, 28, 138

Salem United Methodist Church, 20–21, 25

Salon, xviii, 132, 291

    "I Am Bear; Hear Me Roar," 165–70

Sanders, Bernie, 383, 384, 396, 487

Santorum, Rick, 183, 215

Sartre, Jean-Paul, 132

Saturday Night Live, 447

Scalfari, Eugenio, 358, 373

Schiavo, Terri, 194, 200–202

Schlafly, Phyllis, 215

Schlichter, Kurt, 435

Schumer, Chuck, 437

Schuyler, George S., 131

Schwarzenegger, Arnold, 202

science, 473, 507, 511

Scissor Sisters, 214

Scoop (Waugh), xv

Scots, 423

Scott, Greg, 89–91

Scott, Walter, 453

"secular," meaning of, 328–29

Secular Age, A (Taylor), 409

secularism, 410

segregation, 134, 163, 164, 171, 173, 192,
    197, 303, 332, 444, 449

    apartheid, 52, 133

Seidman, Susan/Drew, 149

Selleck, Tom, 102

Senate, U.S., 382, 394, 419, 430

September 11 terrorist attacks, xvii, 193,
    229, 238, 254, 263–65, 277, 315, 427,
    436

Serbs, 133–34

Serrano, Andres, 238

Sessions, Jeff, 463

Sessions, Pete, 298

Seven Types of Atheism (Gray), 473–76

sex, 479–83, 516

sexism, 133–37, 143, 144, 317, 433, 439–40

    workplace inequality and, 159–60

Sex on the Brain (Blum), 148

sexual assault, rape, 128, 141, 182–83, 447

sexual harassment, 447–48

Shakespeare, William, 226

Shamir, Yitzhak, 134

Sharpton, Al, 8–14, 272

Shaw, George Bernard, 230

Shelley, Percy Bysshe, 453

Shepard, Matthew, 127–28, 136, 138, 140

Showgirls, 220

Signorile, Michelangelo, 205

silence, 403–4, 409–14

Silicon Valley, 402

Silver, Nate, 486

Singer, Bennett, 164

el-Sisi, Abdel Fattah, 390

Sisters of Perpetual Indulgence, 138

Skorka, Abraham, 362

Slack, 448–49

Slate, 285, 291

    "How Did I Get Iraq Wrong?,"
        275–78

slavery, 52, 98, 141, 197, 227, 303, 332, 426,
    428, 435, 444, 449, 500

Slouching towards Gomorrah (Bork), 121

smallpox, 491–93, 396, 499–500

smartphones, 399, 400, 402–4, 407–8,
    410, 412, 413, 465

Smith, Adam, 348

Smith, Ben (journalist), 485

Smith, Benjamin (shooter), 128, 132

Smith, Gordon, 280

Snapchat, 403

social imaginary, 409

social justice movement, 445, 449,
    476–78

Social Security, 192, 268

Society of Saint Pius X, 359

Socrates, 379, 381

sodomy laws, 41–42, 48–49, 113

Soldier of the Great War, A (Helprin),
　85–86

Sosa, Sammy, 125

South Africa, 133

Southern Voice, 218

South Park, 214

Soviet Union, 110, 116, 277, 341, 349, 434
　Cold War, 233, 275, 431

Sowell, Thomas, 139

Spain, 423

Spectator, 98

Speed, Joshua, 177, 178

Spin, 22

Spinney, Laura, 502

spirituality, 330

sports, 146, 156–57, 159

Stanford University, 148

Starr, Kenneth, xviii, 106, 109–12, 118

State, 272

states' rights, 190, 192

Steele, Shelby, 273

Stein, Gertrude, 138

stem-cell research, 196, 199, 203

Sterling, Alton, 441, 444

steroids, 146

"Still Here, So Sorry," 205–7

stimulus bill, 297–99

Stone, Roger, 391

Studio 54, 20

Sullivan, Andrew
　blogging of, xviii, 283–95, 384, 405,
　　432; *see also Dish, The*
　Catholic faith of, xvii, 59–62, 67,
　　71–73, 187, 247, 318, 439
　conservative movement left by, 309–11
　The Conservative Soul, 310
　dog of, xviii, 343–45
　father of, 517–19

grandmother of, 250, 332, 409, 517
　HIV diagnosis and treatment of, 78,
　　92–95, 146, 205–7, 258, 279–80,
　　344, 400
　homosexuality of, xvii, 39, 59–62, 67,
　　71–73, 93–94, 172, 187, 216, 515,
　　517, 518
　Love Undetectable, 317
　marriage of, 257–59, 302
　meditation practice of, 399, 400,
　　403–5, 408–9, 413–14
　mother of, 408, 517–19
　testosterone supplemented by,
　　145–47, 152, 155, 161, 205
　Virtually Normal, 221

Sunday Times (London), xviii
　"Gay Cowboys Embraced by
　　Redneck Country," 241–43
　"Islamo-Bullies Get a Free Ride from
　　the West," 237–39
　"Mad, Maddening America, the
　　Wisest of All," 301–3
　"My America," 97–99
　"Obama's Race Dream Is Swiftly
　　Shackled," 305–7
　"Republican Taliban Declare Jihad
　　on Obama," 297–300

"Superstar," 185–87

Supreme Court, 41–42, 115, 118, 119, 121,
　201, 382, 383, 389, 394, 418, 419,
　427
　Brown v. Board of Education, 171, 173
　Bush v. Gore, 336
　Citizens United, 336
　Obamacare and, 335
　Roe v. Wade, 114, 262

"Surprised by Grief," 343–45

Survivor, 214

Sweeney, Tim, 24

Syria, 423

Taboo (Entine), 157
"Taken Unseriously," 31–33
Taliban, 266, 298
Talking Points Memo, 291
talk radio, 202, 292, 384, 427
taxes, 196, 198, 199, 268, 432, 433
Taylor, Charles, 409
Tea Party, 389
technology, 401, 406, 464, 507
television, 401
Tempting of America, The (Bork), 121
TERFs (trans-exclusionary radical
        feminists), 479, 480
terrorism, domestic, 424
terrorism, Islamist, 198, 229, 232–34, 247,
        254, 265, 266, 270, 428, 442
    Al Qaeda, 227, 233, 234, 247, 265, 267
    9/11 attacks, xvii, 193, 229, 238, 254,
        263–65, 277, 315, 427, 436
    Trump and, 391–92
terrorism, war on, 119, 230, 233, 235, 266
    torture in, *see* torture
testosterone, 145–61, 167, 317
    author's use of, 145–47, 152, 155, 161, 205
    in black men, 156–58
    crime and, 152–54
    depression and, 146, 150, 160
    women and, 145, 148–52, 154–56, 159,
        160
Texas church shooting, 140
Thanksgiving, 98, 99
"Thatcher, Liberator," 339–42
Thatcher, Margaret, xvi, 198, 199, 275,
        339–42, 359
Thomas, Clarence, 139, 263, 272
Thomas Aquinas, 67–68, 288, 348, 376
Thomism, 42, 44, 63, 72, 368
Thompson, Augustine, 330
Thoreau, Henry David, 412
Thurmond, Strom, 164

Tibet, 322
time, 405
Time, xviii, 292
    "The Invisible Man," 163–64
    "When Not Seeing Is Believing,"
        245–51
Tocqueville, Alexis de, 217, 387, 466, 478
tolerance, 143, 144
toleration, 143
    religious, 250, 478
Tolpuddle Martyrs, xv
Tolstoy, Leo, 29
Tomasky, Michael, 485
Torah, 246
Torch Song Trilogy, 214
torture, xvii, 225–35, 277, 336, 394
    Bush and, xviii, 225, 229, 231, 234, 277,
        336, 433
    Christians and, 329
    "enhanced interrogation techniques,"
        xviii, 317
    freedom and, 226, 228, 229, 234, 277
    religious faith abuse and, 234
    for "slow-fuse" detainees, 232
    spread of, 231–32
    "ticking bomb" scenario and, 229–32
    Trump and, 391–92, 394, 417
    waterboarding, 227
Toryism, 125, 309, 340, 341
totalitarianism, 227, 228, 233, 235, 269,
        277, 332, 447
Toynbee, Polly, 339, 341
toys, 157, 158
Toys "R" Us, 157
Traister, Rebecca, 485
transgender individuals, 148, 149, 393,
        479–83, 515–16
Travolta, John, 101, 102
Treatment Action Group (TAG), 77
Tree of Life, The, 414

tribalism, xvii, 423–40, 465, 472
Tribe (Junger), 425–26
trimmer, 314
  Obama as, 313–15
Tripp, C. A., 175–76, 178
True Believer, The (Hoffer), 387–90
Truman, Harry, 119
Trump, Donald, xvii, xviii, 380–81,
    383–84, 386–97, 415–21, 424, 430,
    431, 433, 434, 436–38, 442, 446,
    462, 476–78, 479, 487
  The Apprentice, 387
  Biden and, 485–89
  Christians and, 477–78
  Clinton and, 393, 396, 417–19, 421,
    436, 437
  COVID-19 and, 502, 508
  Democratic leadership and, 437–38
  as fascist, 390–92, 396, 415–17, 420
  immigration and, 389, 390, 392, 393,
    420, 437
  Islamist terrorism and, 391–92
  Muslims and, 389, 390
  opioid crisis and, 462–63
  Putin and, 393, 417, 420
  Republican Party and, 390–91, 394,
    396–97, 415, 417–20, 437
  sexual assault history of, 431
  torture and, 391–92, 394, 417
Trump, Ivana, 386–87
truth, 449, 473, 476
Turkle, Sherry, 405, 407, 413
Tutsis, 133, 134
"Two Faces of Bensonhurst, The," 7–14
"Two Sexes. Infinite Genders," 515–19
Tylenol, 464
Tyson, Mike, 105

Udry, J. Richard, 151
Ukraine, 434

"Unbearable Whiteness of the Classics,
    The," 509–14
United Nations (UN), 115, 245, 280
United States, *see* America
universities, 428, 431
  campus culture, 445–49
"Unsung Heroine," 105–7
urban-rural divide, 428
Utley, T. E., xv–xvi

Vallely, Paul, 363, 368
Variety, 242
Vatican, 63, 211, 269, 359
  Second Vatican Council, 186,
    358–60
Vico, Giambattista, 32
Vietnam Memorial, 35
Vietnam veterans, 458, 461
Vietnam War, 16, 85–86, 262–65, 267,
    268, 275, 452
Village Voice, 149
Virtually Normal (Sullivan), 221
Voltaire, 410
Vox, 472, 476

Wainwright, Rufus, 214
Wallace, George, 390
Wall Street Journal, 120, 157
Walzer, Michael, 223, 231
Washington, D.C., 301–2
Washington, George, 228, 500
Washington Blade, 218–19
Washington Monthly, 339
Washington Post, 104, 139, 241, 417, 442
  "Phobia at the Gates," 279–81
Washington's Crossing (Fischer), 228
Waters, John, 210
Waugh, Evelyn, xv
"We All Live on Campus Now," 445–49
Weber, Max, 102

Weekly Dish, The, xvi, xviii
    "The Unbearable Whiteness of the
        Classics," 509–14
Weekly Standard, 111–15, 117, 119, 178,
    200, 225
Weigel, George, 118
Weinstein, Michael, 205
welfare, xvii, 92, 119, 120, 124, 125, 192,
    199, 376, 458
whataboutism, 431
"What Is the Meaning of Pope Francis?,"
    353–78
"What's So Bad About Hate?," 127–44
"When Not Seeing Is Believing," 245–51
"When Plagues End: Notes on the
    Twilight of an Epidemic," 75–95,
    317
White, Walter, 131
whiteness, 428, 438, 510, 513
white supremacy, 127, 420, 426, 435, 436,
    445–47, 449, 510–11, 514
white working class, 388–89, 420, 486–87
Whitman, Christie Todd, 202
Whitman, Walt, 243
Whitman-Walker Clinic, 217
"Why Continue to Build the
    Settlements?," 321–26
"Why I Blog," 283–95
"Why Joe Biden Might Be the Best Bet
    to Beat Trump," 485–89
Wilberforce, William, 455
Will & Grace, 214
Willkie, Wendell, 382–83
Williams, Armstrong, 202
Williams, Michelle, 242
Wilson, Pete, 427
Wilson, Woodrow, 502
Winchell, Barry, 136
Winfrey, Oprah, 306
Wingfield, John, 155

Wockner, Rex, 169
wokeness, 449, 477, 487, 488
Wolf, Naomi, 182
Wolfson, Evan, 259
women, 246
    abortion and, *see* abortion
    feminism and, *see* feminism
    in military, 156, 158, 159, 199
    in politics, 159
    rape and other sexual assaults against,
        128, 141, 182–83, 447
    sexism and, *see* sexism
    sexual harassment and, 447–48
    testosterone and, 145, 148–52, 154–56,
        159, 160
    transgender ideology and, 479–83
women, differences between men and,
    145–46, 157–58, 480, 487
    crime and, 153–54, 156
    work and, 156, 158–60
Women's Liberation Front, 479
Woods, Tiger, 273
Woodstock '99, 128
Wordsworth, William, 471
working class, 388–89, 420, 464, 486–87
workmanship, 406
World Church of the Creator, 132
World Pornography Conference, 112
World War I, 92, 426–27, 502
World War II, 92, 233, 426–27
Wright, Bob, 473

Yiannopoulos, Milo, 432
yoga, 330, 413
Yong, Ed, 449
Yorio, Orlando, 364
Young-Bruehl, Elisabeth, 134–35

Zionism, 321–26
Zwickler, Phil, 17

About the Author

ANDREW SULLIVAN is one of today's most provocative social and political commentators. A former editor of *The New Republic*, he was the founding editor of *The Daily Dish*, and has been a regular writer for *The New York Times Magazine*, *The Atlantic*, *Time*, *Newsweek*, *New York* magazine, *The Sunday Times*, and now *The Weekly Dish*. He lives in Washington, D.C., and Provincetown, Massachusetts.